T0344475

IP Multicast Routing Protocols

This book discusses the fundamental concepts that are essential to understanding IP multicast communication. The material covers the well-known IP multicast routing protocols, along with the rationale behind each protocol. The book starts with the basic building blocks of multicast communications and networks, then progresses into the common multicast group management methods used, and finally into the various, well-known multicast routing protocols used in today's networks. IP multicast provides significant benefits to network operators by allowing the delivery of information to multiple receivers simultaneously with less network bandwidth consumption than using unicast transmission. Applications that can benefit greatly from multicast communications and multicast-enabled networks include audio and video conferencing, collaborative computing, online group learning and training, multimedia broadcasting, multi-participant online gaming, and stock market trading.

This book's goal is to present the main concepts and applications, allowing readers to develop a better understanding of IP multicast communication. *IP Multicast Routing Protocols: Concepts and Designs* presents material from a practicing engineer's perspective, linking theory and fundamental concepts to common industry practices and real-world examples.

The discussion is presented in a simple style to make it comprehensible and appealing to undergraduate- and graduate-level students, research and practicing engineers, scientists, IT personnel, and network engineers. It is geared toward readers who want to understand the concepts and theory of IP multicast routing protocols, yet want these to be tied to clearly illustrated and close-to-real-world example systems and networks.

IP Multicast Routing Protocols
Concepts and Designs

James Aweya

CRC Press
Taylor & Francis Group
Boca Raton London New York

CRC Press is an imprint of the
Taylor & Francis Group, an **informa** business

Designed cover image: ©Shutterstock Images

First edition published 2024
by CRC Press
2385 NW Executive Center Drive, Suite 320, Boca Raton FL 33431

and by CRC Press
4 Park Square, Milton Park, Abingdon, Oxon, OX14 4RN

CRC Press is an imprint of Taylor & Francis Group, LLC

© 2024 James Aweya

ISBN: 9781032701943 (hbk)
ISBN: 9781032701929 (pbk)
ISBN: 9781032701967 (ebk)

DOI: 10.1201/9781032701967

Typeset in Times
by codeMantra

Contents

Preface

The three fundamental forms of IP communication are unicast, broadcast, and multicast. A unicast transmission, achieved by placing an IP unicast address in the destination address field of the packet, involves sending a packet to a single destination, typically directed at a single host interface. A broadcast transmission, on the other hand, utilizes an IP broadcast address in the destination address field, disseminating a packet to all hosts within an entire IP subnetwork (subnet) or virtual local area network (VLAN), encompassing all devices within a single broadcast domain. By contrast, a multicast transmission employs an IP multicast address in the destination address field, sending a packet to a set of hosts that have become members of a multicast group. The group is identified by the IP multicast group address, and the member hosts may span different subnets or VLANs within the internetwork.

- **Unicast**: Involves one-to-one transmission, where data flows from one source to a specific destination in any part of the internetwork.
- **Broadcast**: Encompasses one-to-all transmission, where data travels from a single source within a specific network segment (such as an IP subnet or VLAN) to all possible destinations reachable solely within that network segment.
- **Multicast**: Entails one-to-many transmissions, originating from one source to multiple destinations throughout the internetwork. These destinations explicitly express interest in receiving traffic from the source. The collection of hosts receiving identical streams of multicast packets from the same multicast source is called a *multicast group*, and the *multicast group address* serves as the destination address of such packets.

The source address of all IP packets must always be an IP unicast address. The use of an IP multicast address is strictly reserved for the destination address field of a multicast packet and should never be placed in the source address field of an IP packet. IPv4 multicast addresses are characterized by their high-order 4 bits being set to 1110, resulting in the IP address range of 224.0.0.0 to 239.255.255.255, previously designated the IPv4 Class D addresses. An IP multicast address represents a logical grouping of hosts receiving traffic from a common source and not a physical collection of devices. A multicast traffic source employs a multicast address solely to address the multicast data and does not serve specifically to identify the location of the receivers in the network. Every source and receiver in the multicast domain still needs an ordinary IP unicast address when sending data in normal unicast communication.

IP multicast communication is designed to allow individual hosts to join or leave a multicast group at their discretion and at any point during the communication process. This design imposes no restrictions on the number of members in a multicast group or their physical location within the internetwork. Additionally, a host is not required to be a member of multicast group to send data to that group, and a host can be a member of more than one multicast group at any given time.

IP multicast routers employ a group membership protocol to discover which hosts on directly attached networks want to be members of a multicast group. When a host expresses interest in receiving traffic from one or more multicast sources, it transmits a group membership protocol message specifying the desired sources. The directly attached multicast router then initiates the multicast traffic transfer process by adding the host as a receiver on the multicast traffic distribution tree created for that multicast group.

Multicast routers receive and accept multicast packets from a source destined for a multicast group solely on one input interface. They then replicate and send copies of those packets onto one or more output interfaces toward the receivers (sometimes called listeners). Through the use of various protocols, the multicast routers interact and cooperate to establish a multicast distribution tree that links the traffic source and the receiver of the target multicast group. The source serves as the root of the multicast distribution tree and the receivers as the leaves. The multicast routers communicate with each other to establish the multicast distribution tree branches, linking the leaves (receivers) to the root (source). Multicast routers create multicast distribution trees to reach receivers, striving to prevent routing loops and minimize the replication and flow of unwanted packets. Various multicast routing protocols employ their own protocol-specific mechanisms for accomplishing these tasks.

Each IP subnet or VLAN attached to a multicast router with at least one interested receiver constitutes a leaf on the multicast distribution tree. A router can have multiple leaves on different interfaces, which means, the router must send a copy of the multicast packet on each interface with a leaf. When the router adds a new leaf IP subnet or VLAN to the multicast distribution tree (i.e., no copies of the multicast packets were previously sent on the interface to receivers), a new tree branch is created, and replicated packets are forwarded on that interface.

When a router finds that a branch contains no leaves because there are no interested receivers on the interface, the router will prune that branch from the multicast distribution tree, and no multicast packets will be forwarded to that interface. The router replicates and sends multicast packets on multiple interfaces only if those interfaces are on branches of the distribution tree with interested receivers.

Using IP multicast to distribute data to multiple interested hosts in a network other than unicast transmission significantly reduces the overall bandwidth demands on the network. IP multicast provides significant benefits to both the content providers and the network service providers because delivering the same data to multiple receivers simultaneously (using data replication at appropriate points) consumes less network bandwidth than using unicast transmission. Reducing the overall bandwidth demand via IP multicast allows the network to accommodate more end-users and traffic. Applications that can benefit greatly from multicast communications and multicast-enabled networks include audio and video conferencing, collaborative computing, online group learning and training, multimedia broadcasting, multi-participant online gaming, financial trading communications like stock trading, and so on.

Most of the available books on IP multicasting devote a significant portion of their discussions to configuration and troubleshooting examples on a particular vendor's router, which often makes it difficult to discern or grasp the essential concepts of IP multicasting. A majority of existing books tend to be vendor-focused, dealing instead with how a particular vendor's router and the multicast routing protocols running on it are set up and configured, plus other matters related to troubleshooting. This book appeals more to readers who want a detailed discussion of IP multicast routing protocols, yet do not want to be tied down or distracted by the often, lengthy discussions on configuration and troubleshooting instructions and routines, found in a majority of IP multicast routing protocol books.

This book assumes some basic knowledge of Ethernet, IP, and IP unicast routing protocols. The material presented here starts with the basic building blocks of multicast communications and networks, then progresses into the common multicast group management methods used, and then into the various, well-known multicast routing protocols used in today's networks. We focus mainly on multicast routing protocols that fall under the collective name of Protocol Independent Multicast (PIM), PIM Dense Mode (PIM-DM), PIM Sparse Mode (PIM-SM), PIM Source-Specific Multicast (PIM-SSM), and Bidirectional PIM (BIDIR-PIM). We also discuss the main protocols used for multicast end-system discovery such as the Internet Group Management Protocol (IGMP), Multicast Listener Discovery (MLD), and Multicast Source Discovery Protocol (MSDP).

Chapter 1 discusses the basic concepts of packet-based communications and the various mechanisms needed for IP multicast communications. The material presented in this chapter provides the underlying fundamentals for later chapters. Multicast addressing at OSI Layers 1 and 2 provides one of the important mechanisms for one-to-many or many-to-many communication among hosts on a network. This chapter addresses important issues such as how multicast packets are addressed at Layer 2 (Ethernet) and Layer 3 (IP) of the OSI reference model. It delves into the mapping of IP multicast addresses to Ethernet multicast addresses, explores the types of multicast traffic distribution trees used in multicast communications, and discusses IP multicast administrative scoping, a mechanism for limiting the routers and interfaces that can receive and forward a multicast packet. Additionally, it covers the important subject of multicast forwarding and Reverse Path Forwarding (RPF) checks, which play a vital role in preventing multicast routing loop.

Chapter 2 covers the multicast group membership management mechanisms used by multicast receivers and routers to signal or determine which particular receivers are interested in a given multicast traffic flow. IGMP (for IPv4) and MLD (for IPv6) are protocols for discovering multicast group membership in IP networks. This chapter discusses IGMPv1, IGMPv2, and IGMPv3, the three main versions of IGMP, and other important applications of IGMP such as IGMP Snooping and IGMP Proxy. IGMP is a signaling mechanism used by a host to inform its directly attached multicast router that it is interested in receiving traffic destined for particular multicast groups. It is also used by the attached multicast router to discover if there are any hosts on an interface (i.e., the attached network segment) still interested in receiving traffic from any particular multicast groups. IGMPv1 supports the use of an explicit "join" message to a multicast router but uses a timeout mechanism to determine when hosts leave a multicast group. IGMPv2 improves IGMPv1 by adding an explicit leave message to the "join" message, allowing hosts to explicitly signal their intention to leave a multicast group (a feature missing in IGMPv1). IGMPv3 optimizes IGMPv2 by allowing a host to specify the source(s) to include or exclude when requesting multicast traffic for a multicast group.

Chapter 3 outlines the different types of protocol messages used by various multicast routing protocols. We describe the messages that are common to all PIM protocol types, and those that are specific to each PIM protocol type, PIM-DM, PIM-SM and BIDIR-PIM. This chapter illustrates the format of each message type and elucidates how each message is used in the PIM protocol.

Chapter 4 focuses solely on PIM-DM, which is a multicast routing protocol designed for network environments where the receivers for any multicast group are densely distributed throughout the network. PIM-DM operates on a *push model* and assumes that every subnet in the multicast domain has at least one receiver interested in the multicast traffic being sent. In other words, PIM-DM functions based on the assumption that most subnets and hosts in the network will be interested in any given multicast traffic. Consequently, PIM-DM begins by *pushing* or *flooding* multicast traffic to all points in the network; PIM-DM initially sends multicast traffic to all subnets and hosts in the network. Then the PIM-DM routers that do not have any interested receivers will send PIM Prune messages to remove themselves from the multicast distribution tree. PIM-DM is based on an implicit join model, and routers use the *flood-and-prune* method to deliver multicast traffic to all parts of the PIM-DM domain. This approach is employed to determine which parts of the network lack interested receivers. PIM-DM uses source-based multicast distribution trees and maintains a multicast forwarding state in the form (S, G), where S represents the IP address of the multicast source and G is the multicast group address.

Chapter 5 explores PIM-SM, assuming sparse distribution of multicast traffic receivers for any group across the network. PIM-SM employs a *pull model*, with multicast routers and hosts using explicit Joins to request specific multicast traffic. Downstream entities express interest through IGMP Membership Report messages. PIM-SM builds unidirectional multicast shared distribution trees rooted at a Rendezvous Points (RP) for each multicast group, and when required, creates shortest-path trees (SPTs), also called source-rooted trees (SRTs), for each multicast traffic source,. The RP tree (RPT) maintains a multicast forwarding state as (*, G), * representing any source sending to group G. This chapter describes the RP's role and various discovery methods in a PIM-SM domain. For seamless operation, all routers must map a multicast group address (G) to the same RP. Discovery mechanisms, such as Static RP, Embedded-RP, Auto-RP, and Bootstrap Router (BSR), distribute multicast group-to-RP mapping information. This equips PIM-SM routers with the knowledge needed to build the shared tree for requested multicast group traffic.

Chapter 5 also introduces PIM-SSM, delivering multicast packets via (S, G) channels. Hosts, using IGMPv3, directly request specific sources without going through an RP. PIM-SSM forms SPT between hosts and sources for multicast group G. Traffic on (S, G) channels requires a subscription. IGMPv3 enables source selection for multicast subscriptions.

Chapter 6 describes MSDP, which is a protocol that allows receivers located in one PIM-SM domain to learn about active multicast sources in other PIM domains. There is no need to use MSDP if all receivers and sources are located in the same PIM-SM domain. However, MSDP can be used to implement the Anycast-RP mechanism, which allows a network operator to configure multiple RPs (as a fully-meshed MSDP group) in a single PIM-SM domain to provide RP redundancy and load-sharing capabilities. MSDP runs on the same router acting as the RP, and the Anycast-RPs form a peering relationship with each other using MSDP (the RPs form a fully-meshed MSDP peer). MSDP is generally not required if all receivers and sources are located in the same PIM-DM domain. Note that Chapter 5 describes a similar Anycast-RP mechanism for a single PIM-SM domain, but one that does not require the use of MSDP. This mechanism removes the reliance on MSDP when implementing the Anycast-RP mechanism in a PIM-SM domain.

Finally, Chapter 7 discusses BIDIR-PIM, which is a variation of PIM-SM. BIDIR-PIM builds bidirectional multicast shared distribution trees rooted at an RP Address (not necessarily at a physical multicast routing device). BIDIR-PIM routers do not switch to SPTs to receive traffic, as in PIM-SM, and their routes are always wildcard-source, i.e., (*, G) routes. This protocol eliminates the need for routers to maintain (S, G) state, thereby eliminating the need for data-driven protocol events seen in PIM-SM. BIDIR-PIM is simpler than PIM-SM and is most suitable for multicast networks with many dispersed sources and receivers.

In a network that supports IP multicast traffic, such traffic is blocked at routers (i.e., at routed interfaces (or broadcast domain or VLAN boundaries)) unless the network is running a multicast routing protocol like PIM. As mentioned earlier, PIM is a family of routing protocols that construct multicast distribution trees to allow the forwarding of traffic from multicast sources to interested receivers. Hosts within network segments (e.g., IP subnets) use a protocol such as IGMP to signal their desire to receive multicast traffic, while multicast routers use it to determine multicast group membership on their interfaces. PIM relies on the existing unicast routing tables in routers (created by any of several unicast routing protocols such as Routing Information Protocol (RIP), Open Shortest Path First (OSPF), Intermediate System to Intermediate System (IS-IS), and Border Gateway Protocol (BGP)) to identify the best (or least-cost) path back to a multicast source, a process known as RPF. PIM employs this information to set up the multicast distribution tree from the source to receivers for a multicast group. IGMP provides the signaling mechanism between hosts and multicast routers. Both PIM and IGMP must be enabled on each multicast router port that has directly connected hosts with a valid need to join multicast groups.

This book discusses the fundamental concepts that are essential to understanding IP multicast communication. The material covers the well-known IP multicast routing protocols along with the rationale behind each protocol. This book's goal is to present the main concepts and applications, allowing readers to develop a better understanding of IP multicast communication. The material is presented from a practicing engineer's perspective, linking theory and fundamental concepts to common industry practices and real-world examples. The simple and straightforward presentation style adopted in this book makes it appealing to undergraduate- and graduate-level students, research and practicing engineers and scientists, IT personnel, and network engineers.

About the Author

James Aweya, PhD, is a chief research scientist at the Etisalat British Telecom Innovation Center (EBTIC), Khalifa University, Abu Dhabi, UAE. Prior to his current role, he served as a technical lead and senior systems architect with Nortel, Ottawa, Canada, from 1996 to 2009. He was awarded the 2007 Nortel Technology Award of Excellence (TAE) for his pioneering and innovative research on Timing and Synchronization across Packet and TDM Networks. Dr. Aweya has an impressive track record, having been granted 70 US patents and authoring over 54 journal papers, 40 conference papers, and 43 technical reports. He has extensive experience and expertise that spans various aspects of telecom systems design and networking. Additionally, he is the sole author of seven recent engineering books, including this book, focused on telecom systems and networks.

1 IP Multicast Routing Fundamentals

1.1 MODES OF COMMUNICATION

The four main modes of communication in packet networks are *unicast*, *broadcast*, *multicast*, and *anycast*. Strictly speaking, anycast transmission is a form of unicast communication, as the destination address in an anycast transmission is a unicast address. Thus, unicast, broadcast, and multicast are essentially the three fundamental types of communication. These three modes use three fundamentally distinct types of addresses: unicast, broadcast, and multicast. Furthermore, multicast communication may be viewed as a restricted form of broadcast communication, targeting only a specific group of hosts as receivers. Multicast communication in turn may be further categorized as *one-to-many* or *many-to-many* transmission. This section discusses the various forms of communication.

1.1.1 UNICAST COMMUNICATION

Unicast communication refers to transmission from one data source to a single receiver (i.e., a single specific destination point), as illustrated in Figure 1.1. This mode of communication establishes a one-to-one association between a sender and a receiver, with the network delivering a unicast message to a single specific host.

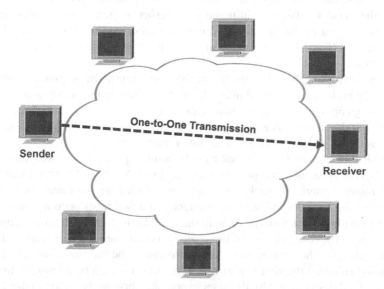

One-to-One Transmission

Sender

Receiver

FIGURE 1.1 Unicast communication – one-to-one transmission.

DOI: 10.1201/9781032701967-1

It is important to note that the source address of all packet types (unicast, broadcast, multicast, anycast) must always be a *unicast address.*

In unicast transmission, the amount of traffic transmitted over the network is proportional to the number of unicast addresses (i.e., destinations) to which traffic is being sent. If a large number of unicast addresses need data from a given source, the data source must send a separate copy of the same data to each of these addresses. Sending many copies of the same data from a source can place tremendous processing and bandwidth demand on the source and the network.

In unicast communication, the destination address field of all transmitted packets contains the unicast address of the target receiving host (i.e., a single target host). Specifically, a unicast address is associated with the address of a single host interface in a network. A host with multiple interfaces will have a unique unicast address for each of those interfaces. Each unicast destination address uniquely identifies a single receiver in the network. This address may have only local significance (on the local network) or may be globally unique. Unicast addresses that have local significance (i.e., are only unique within a specific network) are called private addresses. At Layer 2 of today's networks, the unicast address is mostly an Ethernet Medium Access Control (MAC) address, while at Layer 3, it is a unicast IP address.

The protocols and packet forwarding operations at Layer 2 (Ethernet) are relatively simple and less complex than those at Layer 3 (IP) (see [AWEYARCAP22] [AWEYFCDM22] [AWEYFDVR21] [AWEYLSPV21]). An IP internetwork consists of smaller networks (networks and subnets) that are connected using routers. IP routing is the process by which routers forward IP packets from one network/ subnet to another. Through routing, packets are moved from one part of an IP internetwork to another and eventually to their final destinations. An IP packet contains end-user data intended for the final destination end-system as well as a header that contains routing information (the source and destination IP addresses plus other control data). Traditionally, Ethernet switches (sometimes called bridges) are used for packet forwarding within smaller subnets (called local area networks (LANs)), while IP routers are used for forwarding packets between IP networks and subnets.

IP unicast routing, based on the IP unicast destination address, enables routers to forward IP packets across an IP internetwork from the sending host to a destination host through one or more intermediate routers. A host is any network device (usually an end-user device such as a laptop, workstation, server, or portable mobile device) that runs the TCP/IP protocol and does not perform routing.

An IP router is an IP node that runs IP routing protocols (as well as several other TCP/IP protocols) and performs routing [AWEYFDVR21] [AWEYLSPV21]. An IP router forwards IP packets that are not destined for the router itself, either directly to the final destination (i.e., a directly attached host) or to another router (i.e., the next-hop router) on the route to the final destination. Each router along the path between the data source and the receiver uses the unicast destination address of the packet and the local *routing table* (also called the *routing information base* (RIB)) to determine the next-hop to which the packet should be forwarded for it to get to its final destination. Usually, a more compact form of the routing table called the *forwarding table* (or *forwarding information base* (FIB)) is used for forwarding packets. An IP router extracts the destination IP address of a packet and uses this to perform a lookup in the RIB or FIB to determine the best matching entry that points to the next-hop and outgoing interface (plus other relevant information such as the quality-of-service (QoS) to be provided) for the packet [AWEYFDVR21] [AWEYFCDM22] [AWEYARCAP22].

1.1.2 BROADCAST COMMUNICATION

Broadcast communication is a data transmission mode in which a piece of information is sent from a single source to all other receivers on a particular network or network segment (Figure 1.2). In this mode of communication, there is only one sender, but the information is sent to all receivers within the scope of the broadcast, which in many cases is an entire network segment like an IP subnet or virtual local area network (VLAN). This mode of communication uses a one-to-all association, and the network delivers a sender's message to all nodes in the network segment.

In broadcast communication, the destination address field of all transmitted packets contains a *broadcast address* that represents all hosts on a multiple-access network segment, such as an IP subnet or a VLAN. A packet that is sent to a broadcast address is intended for all hosts attached to that network segment. The network forwards a single packet from a sender to all possibly multiple receivers associated with the broadcast address, but this transmission is limited to the local network segment (IP subnet or VLAN).

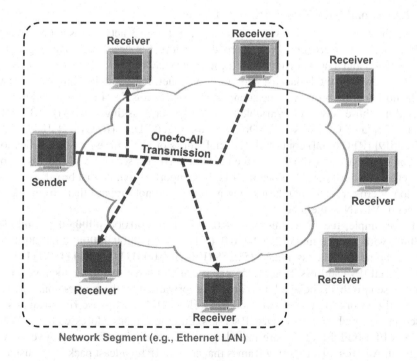

FIGURE 1.2 Broadcast communication – one-to-all transmission in a network segment.

Similar to multicast communication, the network automatically replicates packets as needed so that they reach all the receivers in the network segment. Note that the source address of a packet must never be a broadcast or multicast address (it must always be a unicast address). Routers and hosts understand that packets that contain broadcast destination addresses are addressed to all hosts on the IP subnet or VLAN and, unless specifically configured, routers do not forward such packets. Unless absolutely necessary (for example, as part of some network protocols such as the Address Resolution Protocol (ARP) and Dynamic Host Configuration Protocol (DHCP)), broadcast transmission is disadvantageous when transmitting data to specific hosts in a network because it causes significant waste of network resources.

1.1.2.1 Broadcast Communication at Layer 2

A single source may send broadcast traffic to all possible destinations reachable on a network segment, usually an Ethernet LAN. At Layer 2 (i.e., the Data Link Layer) of networks such as those based on Ethernet, the broadcast address is a specific MAC address. The 48-bit MAC address consisting of all 1s (or FF:FF:FF:FF:FF:FF in hexadecimal notation) is the broadcast address in Ethernet. Layer 2 networks such as those using Ethernet technologies natively support broadcast communication. The ARP mechanism [RFC826] uses Ethernet broadcasts to resolve IP addresses to their corresponding MAC addresses (i.e., the MAC address that is associated with the IP address of an interface).

1.1.2.2 Broadcast Communication at Layer 3

Unlike the Ethernet broadcast MAC address, in Layer 3 networks such as IP networks (i.e., at the Network Layer), a broadcast address is structured as having a network portion and a host portion, with the host port having a specific pattern of all 1s. In IPv4 networks, the broadcast address of a subnet, for example, consists of all 1s in the host address portion of the subnet's address. That is, IPv4 broadcast addresses (including those based on Variable Length Subnet Masking (VLSM) [RFC950] [RFC1878] and Classless Inter-Domain Routing (CIDR) [RFC1517] [RFC1518] [RFC1519] [RFC4632]) contain the special values of all 1s in the host identification portion of the subnet's IP address; the network portion is set to the IP address of the subnet and the host portion is set to all 1s. It is important to note that broadcast packets do not cross router boundaries, that is, routers do not forward them from one IP subnet or VLAN to the other.

For example, the IP address 172.16.0.0/12 (10101100.0001**0000.00000000.000 00000**) with subnet mask 255.240.0.0 (11111111.1111**0000.00000000.00000000**) has the broadcast address 172.31.255.255 (10101100.000**11111.11111111.11111111**). The special IPv4 address 255.255.255.255 is used for broadcast to the local network. Packets sent to this special address are never forwarded by the routers connected to the local network to other networks. DHCP [RFC2131] clients use IP broadcasts to discover and send requests to DHCP servers. Ethernet frames addressed to the MAC address FF:FF:FF:FF:FF:FF are intended to reach every interface on a given LAN segment. Additionally, Ethernet frames that contain IP broadcast packets are usually addressed to this broadcast MAC address.

Using VLSM, network operators can divide an IPv4 address space into subnets with different IP prefix lengths according to the needs of their networks, allowing efficient use of Ipv4 addresses. In CIDR, the network prefix represents the network portion of an IP address and may represent a collection of destinations (i.e., an aggregate or summary address representing an IP supernet).

IPv6 does not support the notion of broadcast as in IPv4 and, as a result, does not define broadcast addresses. Instead, IPv6 uses multicast addressing to the All-Nodes multicast group address FF02:0:0:0:0:0:0:1 (or FF02::1) as a way to reach all nodes within a network scope. The IPv6 address FF02::1 represents all IPv6 nodes within the link-local scope (i.e., all IPv6 nodes in the same topological region as the sender's unicast scope). Currently, no IPv6 protocols are defined to use the All-Nodes address FF02::1. Instead, IP nodes send and receive packets on particular IPv6 link-local multicast addresses, such as FF02::101, which means all Network Time Protocol (NTP) servers on the same link as the sending node. The use of IPv6 link-local multicast addressing (instead of broadcast addresses) results in higher network efficiency because IPv6 nodes simply filter traffic based on multicast address instead of processing all broadcasts or all-hosts multicast traffic.

1.1.3 MULTICAST COMMUNICATION

Multicast communication uses either a *one-to-many* or *many-to-many* association between nodes in the network. These two modes of multicast communication are described in this section. Unlike broadcast packets, multicast packets are replicated and delivered to network segments on which hosts have expressed interest in receiving such packets, that is, to network segments where multicast group members exist (and identified by the *multicast group address*). Note that a multicast address must never appear as the source address in an IP packet and can only be the destination address of a multicast packet. A collection of hosts all receiving the same traffic, usually from the same multicast source, is called *a multicast group*. Multicast routers use a *multicast group membership discovery protocol* to learn about the presence of directly attached group members on their interfaces. Hosts also use the group membership protocol to inform their directly attached multicast routers that they are interested in traffic sent to a multicast group.

IP multicast is a bandwidth-conserving communication method that allows simultaneous delivery of a single data stream to all interested receivers through data replication at branching nodes in the network where paths to receivers diverge. Compared to using unicast or broadcast transmission to serve an arbitrary group of multiple receivers simultaneously, multicast results in minimum consumption of network bandwidth and more efficient delivery of data to the multiple receivers. Multicast transmission lies between the extremes of unicast transmission (one source to one destination) and broadcast transmission (one source to all destinations on a network segment).

1.1.3.1 One-to-Many Multicast Communication

The basic form of multicast communication refers to data transmission in which a piece of information is sent from a single data source to a specific group consisting of two or more receivers that have expressed interest in receiving that information (Figure 1.3). The network delivers replicated copies of a single multicast message to a group of hosts that have expressed interest in receiving the message. These replicated messages in a single transmission are routed simultaneously to many receivers. In the one-to-many mode of communication, there is only one sender transmitting data to be distributed to a specified group of interested receivers. One example of this form of communication is a video server sending a video stream to a group of receivers. In this mode of communication, the source address is always a unicast address, but the destination address (representing a group of receivers) is a *multicast address*.

Without the use of multicasting, delivering high-quality video from even a powerful video server via unicasting to each member of a large group of receivers will task the capability of even a high-bandwidth network. This also presents a major scalability problem for data transfer applications that require simultaneous and sustained high bandwidth. Employing multicasting is one way to significantly scale transmission to larger groups of receivers. Multicasting has become an indispensable tool for delivering data simultaneously to a group of receivers.

Multicasting is advantageous if a network has a group of receivers that require a common set of data at the same time. Where a group of clients have a common need for the same data, multicast transmission provides significant savings in network bandwidth consumption and reduces network load. Ethernet networks support both broadcast and multicast transmissions natively. A network operator can use multicasting to support value-added services, such as real-time audio/video conferencing, distance learning, web radio, telemedicine, web TV, live webcasting, live news broadcast, data warehouse and financial applications (stock quotes), and other bandwidth-critical and time-critical information services.

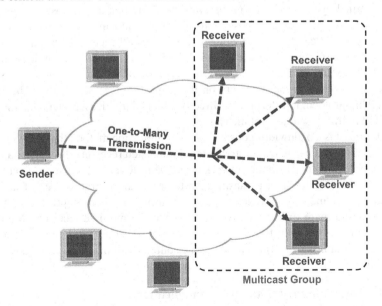

FIGURE 1.3 Unidirectional multicast communication – one-to-many transmission in a multicast group.

Unicast and broadcast transmissions are not suitable for point-to-multipoint data transmissions and do not provide minimum network bandwidth consumption among the three basic modes of communication. A multicast source sends only one copy of data, and that data is forwarded through a *multicast distribution tree* built by one of the various multicast routing protocols. The data is replicated only on nodes where the tree branches to receivers that have expressed interest in the data, reducing redundant traffic.

With the data replication and distribution capabilities of multicast transmission, an increase in the number of receivers does not amplify the load on the multicast source and does not remarkably contribute to the consumption of network resources. Moreover, because the network sends multicast data only to the receivers that require it, it uses relatively less network bandwidth and enhances network security. Additionally, while broadcast transmission is confined to the same IP subnet or VLAN, multicast transmission is not and can cross large geographic boundaries. The group of receivers (i.e., multicast group members) has no physical or geographical boundaries. The receivers can be located anywhere on the internetwork, on different subnets or VLANs, and there are no restrictions on the number of members in a multicast group.

1.1.3.1.1 Multicast Communication at Layer 2

Ethernet frames feature a special bit called the *Individual/Group (I/G)* bit, located as the least-significant bit of the first byte of the destination MAC address. This bit can be set to 1, indicating that the frames should be treated as Ethernet multicast frames and broadcasted on all parts of a LAN. The setting of the I/G bit, also referred to as the *Unicast/Multicast bit*, provides a multicast mechanism at the Data Link Layer. Furthermore, both IPv4 and IPv6 addresses can be mapped to corresponding 48-bit Ethernet multicast MAC addresses, as described in the following section.

1.1.3.1.2 Multicast Communication at Layer 3

An IP multicast group represents a set of multicast receivers identified by an IP multicast address. Hosts must signal their intention to join a multicast group and become members of the group before they can receive the multicast data addressed to that group. It is not necessary for a multicast source to become a member of a multicast group to send data to that particular group. A multicast source can transmit data to multiple multicast groups simultaneously. Additionally, current multicast protocols allow multiple multicast sources to send data to the same multicast group concurrently. Hosts join a multicast group to become members, and the group membership is dynamic, allowing hosts to join or leave a multicast group at any time. Multicast groups are not restricted by geographic boundaries.

A data source uses the multicast address in a multicast packet to address a specific group of hosts in a network that may be interested in receiving the packet. The source designates the multicast group address as the IP destination address in all multicast packets directed to that group. Interested hosts also employ this multicast group address to inform the network, through their directly attached multicast router, that they are interested in receiving multicast packets sent to that group.

IP unicast and multicast packets share the same format, the only difference being the use of a special class of IP destination address (falling within the IPv4 Class D address range from 224.0.0.0 to 239.255.255.255) in the destination address field of multicast packets, representing a specific multicast group. A multicast address cannot serve as a source address, only a unicast address can be carried in the source address field of any packet, including unicast, broadcast, and multicast packets. This book exclusively focuses on IPv4 multicast communication. IPv4 multicast addresses are identified by the binary prefix 1110 (i.e., first or starting 4 bits).

IPv6 multicast addresses utilize the binary prefix 11111111 (or FF00::/8 in hexadecimal notation) [RFC4291]. This prefix is the starting string of every IPv6 multicast address. An IPv6 multicast address serves as an identifier for a group of node interfaces, and an interface may belong to more than one multicast group. A network operator may assign an IPv6 multicast address as a permanent (i.e., well-known or predefined) multicast address or as a transient address [RFC4291]. A multicast address may have an Interface-Local scope, Link-Local scope, Admin-Local scope, Site-Local scope, Organization-Local scope, or Global scope.

1.1.3.1.3 Protocol Requirements for Multicast Communication

This section addresses the basic protocol requirements for implementing multicast communication, encompassing multicast group membership discovery, multicast routing protocols, and optionally, inter-domain multicast source discovery. The discussion in this section seeks to answer the following questions:

- To which address should the multicast source transmit information and how is the information transmitted to the receivers? (Multicast addressing and multicast routing)
- Who are the interested receivers on the network? (Host registration and multicast group membership management)
- How is a receiver in a different multicast domain able to know about active multicast sources in other domains? (Multicast source discovery)

1.1.3.1.3.1 Multicast Group Membership Discovery

A multicast source employs a multicast address to send information to a group of receivers, defining the addressing mechanism. Hosts can join and leave a multicast group dynamically, involving a host registration mechanism. In other words, multicast communication involves the management of group memberships. Hosts on a network utilize a multicast group membership discovery protocol to advertise their interest in receiving multicast traffic for a particular group. A host indicates its interest in becoming a member of a group by using a specific membership discovery protocol to signal its directly connected local multicast router that it wants to join the multicast group. Similarly, the host uses the same protocol to signal its attached router when it wants to leave a multicast group. Additionally, a multicast router also uses that group membership discovery protocol to determine if any multicast group member exists on an interface, enabling it to determine whether to continue forwarding multicast traffic on that interface. The Internet Group Management Protocol (IGMP) for IPv4 ([RFC1112] [RFC2236] [RFC3376] [RFC4604]) and Multicast

Listener Discovery (MLD) for IPv6 ([RFC2710] [RFC3590] [RFC3810]) are the two main multicast group membership discovery protocols in use today.

Unlike broadcast transmission, multicast clients receive multicast packets only if they have previously registered with their directly connected multicast router to do so. Clients join a specific multicast group address using IGMP to send join messages, appropriately called IGMP Membership Report messages, to the connecting multicast router. Similarly, clients can leave a multicast group by sending appropriate IGMP messages, such as IGMPv2 Leave Group messages, to the connected local router. Membership of a group is dynamic, allowing clients to join and leave multicast groups as they wish by sending appropriate IGMP messages, namely IGMP Membership Report and Leave Group messages. Multicast routers also send periodic IGMP Membership Query messages on a network segment (i.e., interface) to determine if there are still active members of multicast groups on the segment.

As mentioned earlier, a multicast group identifies a set of hosts in the multicast domain that indicate interest in a particular multicast data. The group is identified by an IP address allocated from a well-defined range. Traffic directed to a particular multicast address is forwarded to all hosts that are members of the multicast group.

1.1.3.1.3.2 Multicast Routing Protocols

Multicast transmission requires the use of *multicast routing protocols* for facilitating communication between multicast routers. These protocols enable routers to discover nodes that require multicast traffic and build the *multicast distribution tree* for receiving hosts. Protocol Independent Multicast (PIM), which represents a collection of multicast routing protocols (as discussed later), is currently the most relevant protocol set used for multicasting.

The routers in a multicast network employ the multicast routing protocols to determine which networks and subnetworks have active receivers for a particular multicast group. The multicast routers also support various mechanisms to minimize the transmission of packets across parts of the network where there are no active receivers (e.g., PIM Prune messages).

Multicast routers in a multicast domain construct a multicast distribution tree of hosts that have expressed interest in receiving multicast traffic for a particular group. The routers collectively construct a multicast distribution tree for delivering multicast data from a multicast source to receivers. The tree outlines a forwarding path on the network for transmitting multicast data to interested receivers; the tree contains the routes to every host that has joined the multicast group. A source sends a single multicast packet to a designated multicast address, and the multicast routers use the multicast distribution tree to distribute copies of the original packet to the entire group of receivers.

The interface on a multicast router leading toward the multicast traffic source is generally referred to as the *upstream interface*, although it is sometimes loosely called the *incoming* or *inbound interface*. To minimize multicast traffic bandwidth consumption and prevent forwarding loops, it is desirable for only one upstream interface on a multicast router to receive multicast packets. The interfaces on the multicast router leading away from the upstream interface and toward the receivers are *the downstream interfaces*, also sometimes called the *outgoing* or *outbound interfaces.* Generally, the upstream interface is considered to be the interface that holds the best (or lowest-cost) route back to the multicast traffic source (as discussed in a section in the chapter).

The multicast routers between the source and receivers receive packets from upstream nodes, replicate these packets, and forward them on diverging downstream paths, each containing interested receivers. To optimize the use of the network, the multicast routers use the discovered group membership information provided by directly attached routers to determine the downstream nodes to which replicated packets must be sent.

The multicast distribution tree is optimized for the following:

- Multicast routers refrain from sending multicast traffic to network segments without any interested receivers, unless the network is a transit network providing a path to other interested receivers.
- Duplication of multicast packets on branches of the multicast distribution tree is minimized.

The multicast routing protocol is responsible for setting up a multicast distribution tree, ensuring that multicast packets from a multicast data source to a particular multicast group reach all receivers that have joined the group. To send a packet to a particular multicast group, the source host simply sets the destination IP address of the packet to the multicast group address.

The construction of the multicast distribution tree (in most protocols) can be source- or receiver-driven and can be initiated by multicast routers directly attached to the source or receivers. The multicast routers, through the multicast routing protocols, create state information for each multicast distribution tree in the network. A multicast router does not need to learn or be aware of all other multicast distribution trees in use in the network but only needs to know about multicast distribution trees for which it has downstream receivers. This requirement is key to the scalability of multicast services. In contrast, a router operating in unicast mode is required to know how to reach all other unicast addresses in the network, even if it uses a default route to reach such addresses. For this reason, routers use address aggregation or summarization (CIDR) as a key mechanism for scaling unicast routing, especially in network core routers that carry hundreds of thousands of routes. The routing table of core routers can contain routes for the entire Internet.

Any host in the network can become a multicast source and send data to a multicast group. A source is not required to register as a member of a multicast group before it can start sending data to that group, and it does not need to be a member of the group itself. A multicast source is not required to know about the receivers of the group. In some PIM types (as discussed later), only the local connecting multicast router of a source is required to register the source with a Rendezvous Point in the network.

1.1.3.1.3.3 *Inter-Domain Multicast Source Discovery*
In addition to IGMP, which allows hosts to register their interest in particular multicast groups, protocols such as Multicast Source Discovery Protocol (MSDP) ([RFC3618]

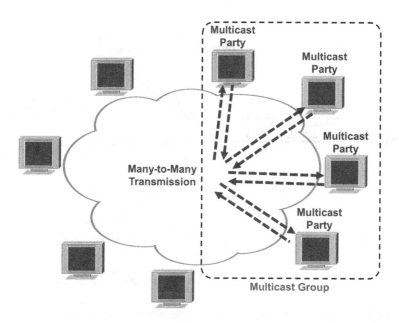

FIGURE 1.4   Bidirectional multicast communication – many-to-many transmission in a multicast group.

[RFC4611] are crucial for inter-domain multicast communication. MSDP enables hosts in one multicast domain to discover active multicast sources in other domains, providing inter-domain access to multicast sources in other domains. The information obtained through MSDP allows a multicast source in one domain to send traffic to hosts in other domains. Intra-domain IP multicasting requires the support of only IGMP and the multicast routing protocols, with assistance from the unicast routing table information.

1.1.3.2   Many-to-Many Multicast Communication

Many-to-many multicasting involves more than one sender and more than one receiver participating in the data transfer (Figure 1.4). In this mode of communication, there are two or more senders that can transmit information to a set of receivers concurrently. For example, in a multi-party voice and/or video conference, each party can send and receive information from the other parties simultaneously (many-to-many voice/video conference).

1.1.4   Anycast Communication

Anycast communication employs a one-to-any association, where a message is routed through a network to any single member of a group of potential receivers, all identified by the same unicast destination address. In anycast communication, a data source sends messages to a single device within a specific group of devices called an anycast group (Figure 1.5). This mode of communication serves not only as an addressing scheme but also as a routing method.

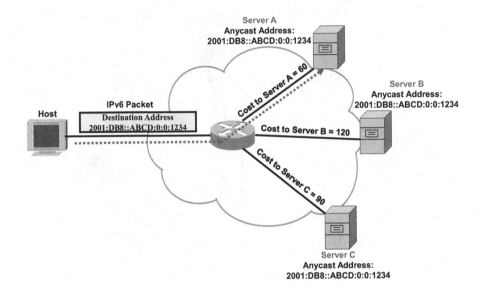

FIGURE 1.5 Anycast communication – one-to-any transmission in an anycast group (IPv6 example).

The network routes a sender's message to any one node out of a group of nodes, typically the one nearest to the sender. An anycast address, which is just a unicast address, is assigned to each member of the anycast group. An anycast group is formed by assigning the same unicast address to multiple devices in a network. There is no exclusive IP (IPv4 and IPv4) address range reserved for anycast addressing.

Anycast addresses are syntactically identical to unicast addresses, differing only in their usage. All of these are unicast addresses and are allocated from the IPv4 or IPv6 unicast address space. When a network operator assigns a unicast address to more than one device interface in a network, thereby turning the address into an anycast address, the operator must explicitly configure the devices to which the address is assigned to be aware that it is using an anycast address.

A message from a source is sent to the topologically nearest device in the anycast group according to the unicast routing protocol metric used. A router that receives a packet directly addressed to an anycast address is routed to the location nearest the sender using the normal unicast routing protocols and metrics, typically based on the lowest number of router hops to be traversed.

1.1.4.1 IPv4 Anycast Communication

In IPv4, anycast communication can be implemented using the Border Gateway Protocol (BGP) [RFC4271]. Multiple hosts, such as web servers usually located in different geographic locations, are assigned the same unicast IP address, known as the anycast address. BGP is used to announce different routes to the anycast address. In this scenario, routers consider the routes announced by BGP as alternative routes to the same destination, even though, in reality, these are routes to different destinations using the same address. Routers use normal routing methods and metrics to select a route to the closest anycast address destination.

1.1.4.2 IPv6 Anycast Communication

IPv6 explicitly supports anycast addressing as described in Section 2.6 of [RFC4291]. This reference provides a detailed description of the IPv6 addressing architecture. Reference [RFC4291] reserves the *Interface Identifier* of $(128-n)$ 0s and the n Subnet Prefix within an IPv6 address as the Subnet-Router Anycast Address.

In addition, [RFC2526] specifies the *IPv6 Reserved Anycast Address* format for the *Unicast Address with EUI-64 Interface Identifier* format and the *Unicast Address with non-EUI-64 Interface Identifier* format. The 128-bit EUI-64 format has a 64-bit Subnet Prefix field, the 57-bit field of all 1s, and a 7-bit Anycast Identifier field. The non-EUI-64 format has an n-bit Subnet Prefix field, $(121-n)$-bit field of all 1s, and a 7-bit Anycast Identifier field. In both formats, the all 1s field and the Anycast Identifier field form the Interface Identifier within the IPv6 address.

Most IPv6 routers that encounter an anycast packet on the path through the network to an anycast address destination cannot distinguish it from any other unicast packet. However, special handling is required at the routers near the anycast address destination, within the scope of the anycast address. These routers are required to route the anycast packet to the "nearest" anycast address interface within that scope, according to the routing metric used (hop count, cost, etc.).

It should be noted, however, that the method of using BGP in IPv4 to advertise multiple routes to multiple hosts assigned the same unicast address (or anycast address) also works in IPv6. This method, which does not depend on anycast-aware routers, can be used to route packets to the closest of several geographically dispersed hosts sharing the same anycast address. This IPv4 approach has the same use cases, problems, and limitations as IPv6 anycast communication.

1.1.4.3 Applications of Anycast Communication

The rapid growth of the Internet and the increasing demand for high-availability network services have spurred network operators to deploy anycast services [RFC4786]. Anycast communication (i.e., anycast addressing and routing) has grown in popularity among network operators and is widely used by content delivery networks hosting web content and Domain Name System (DNS) services. This is done to bring their content closer to end users, for example, to provide efficient content delivery and DNS query resolution. The routing protocol used by the network selects a single receiver from the anycast group based on which is the nearest according to its routing metric (distance or cost measure).

1.1.4.3.1 Anycast Addressing for DNS Services

Multiple DNS servers [RFC1034] [RFC1035] may be configured with anycast addresses to provide a redundant service and improved performance for DNS query processing. For example, all the 13 DNS root servers of the global Internet are implemented as clusters of DNS servers using anycast addressing. The 13 root servers which are placed in multiple locations (11 on different continents) use anycast address announcements to provide decentralized DNS service for the Internet. Authoritative DNS servers also use anycast addressing, as described in [RFC3258]. Today, it is common practice for commercial DNS providers to use anycast addressing to enhance DNS query processing, provide server redundancy, and implement load balancing.

Some anycast services, such as DNS services, preferentially address local nodes on the network as a way to distinguish between local and global nodes and to benefit local users. In this case, BGP routers announce local nodes with the *BGP No-Export Community Attribute* (see Chapter 3 of [AWEYLSPV21]) to prevent peers from announcing these routes to their peers, thereby keeping these announcements in the local area. In an environment that deploys both local and global nodes, BGP route announcements from the global nodes are often prepended with *dummy Autonomous System Numbers* (*ASNs*) (see BGP AS-Path Prepending in Chapter 7 of [AWEYFDVR21]) to make the BGP path longer so that routers will prefer local node announcements over global node ones.

1.1.4.3.2 Anycast Addressing for Content Delivery Networks

Content delivery networks also utilize anycast addressing where content servers are strategically placed in locations closer to the clients' demands. This enables clients in various locations to access the closest content server via anycast communication according to their current location. To provide highly reliable anycast services, service providers typically employ external "heartbeat monitoring" of servers and automatic failover of servers. External heartbeat monitoring of the servers' operations allows routers to withdraw route announcements to a failed server.

In some deployments, the servers are configured to announce the anycast prefix to connecting routers over an Interior Gateway Protocol (IGP) such as OSPF. In this case, if the server fails, the router automatically withdraws route announcements to the failed server. Without server heartbeat monitoring, if the router continues route announcement to a failed server, the server will act as a black hole for client requests.

1.1.4.3.3 Anycast Addressing for Rendezvous Points in Multicast Networks

The concept of Anycast Rendezvous Points (Anycast-RPs) can be used with PIM Sparse-Mode (PIM-SM), as described in Chapter 5, and with Multicast Source Discovery Protocol (MSDP), as described in Chapter 6. The use of Anycast-RPs provides redundancy and load-sharing capabilities for multicast services that depend on the presence of an RP. In a multicast domain with multiple Anycast-RPs, the network automatically selects and routes messages to the topologically closest RP. The Anycast-RPs provide a multicast network with redundancy and fault-tolerance capabilities.

1.2   TYPES OF MULTICAST ROUTING PROTOCOLS

Protocol Independent Multicast (PIM) represents a group of multicast routing protocols, each optimized for a particular network environment. The three main types of PIM protocols are PIM Dense Mode (PIM-DM) [RFC3973], PIM Sparse-Mode (PIM-SM) [RFC7761], and Bidirectional PIM (BIDIR-PIM) [RFC5015]. The name PIM is because these protocols are not dependent on any particular IP unicast routing protocol to function (i.e., they are *routing protocol independent*). PIM uses the same unicast routing table on a router for multicast packet forwarding (i.e., for Reverse Path Forwarding (RPF) check functions) regardless of the unicast routing protocol used to populate the unicast routing table, including static routes. RPF is discussed later in this chapter. PIM employs the routing information that any routing protocol running on the multicast router installs in its Multicast Routing Information Base (MRIB).

Although the PIM protocols are commonly viewed as multicast routing protocols, in reality, they do not exchange routing protocol messages – that is, they do not send or receive multicast routing information to maintain and update multicast routing tables – as older and obsolete multicast routing protocols, such as Distance Vector Multicast Routing Protocol (DVMRP) and Multicast Open Shortest Path (MOSPF), did. PIM uses the same underlying unicast routing protocols and tables to determine the location of nodes in the network, as well as for multicast packet forwarding (based on RPF checks). The protocol messages in PIM are primarily utilized for creating the multicast distribution trees. However, the actual reachability of the nodes in the multicast domain is determined using the underlying unicast routing protocols and their tables. The protocol's routing protocol independence and the lack of multicast routing information exchange and multicast routing tables (unlike in DVMRP and MOSPF) contribute to a significantly lower protocol overhead in PIM, making it more flexible and scalable to implement.

All PIM protocols share a common message header format applicable to all message types. PIM messages are sent directly over IP using Protocol Number 103. These messages are sent either as multicast to the link-local ALL-PIM-ROUTERS multicast group address (224.0.0.13 for IPv4 and FF02::D for IPv6) or as unicast to a specific IP destination address. Some PIM messages, such as the Hello, Join/Prune, and Assert, along with their Options, are common to all PIM protocol types, while others are specific to the PIM protocol type (see Chapter 3).

The Internet Group Management Protocol (IGMP) (IGMPv1 [RFC1112], IGMPv2 [RFC2236], and IGMPv3 [RFC3376] [RFC4604] [RFC4607]) is used for multicast group membership discovery in IPv4 networks. Multicast Listener Discovery (MLD) (i.e., MLDv1 [RFC2710] and MLDv2 [RFC3810]) corresponds to multicast group membership discovery for IPv6 networks. All of these protocols allow hosts to report their multicast group memberships, and multicast routers employ them to determine the group membership on each of their network segments (or interfaces).

All of these multicast group discovery protocols work in concert with various multicast routing protocols to deliver traffic to interested receivers. Although there are certain distinctions involved, protocols such as IGMP and MLD involve host-to-router information communication about group membership interest, while multicast routing protocols involve router-to-router communications about multicast group members (i.e., end-systems interested in particular multicast group traffic). IP hosts use IGMP or MLD to signal their interest in multicast group memberships to any directly attached multicast router, while multicast routers use IGMP to learn, for each of their attached network segments, which multicast groups still have active members.

The Multicast Source Discovery Protocol (MSDP) ([RFC3618] [RFC4611]) is a protocol used between Rendezvous Points (RPs) in PIM-SM domains to allow receivers located in different PIM-SM domains to discover multicast sources in other PIM-SM domains. Routers within a given PIM-SM domain can use various RP discovery mechanisms to learn about which sources and groups are active in the

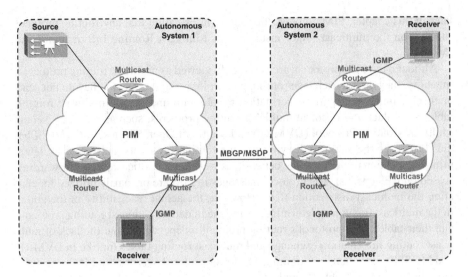

FIGURE 1.6   Use of IP multicast routing protocols.

domain. However, the use of MSDP (between RPs in different PIM-SM domains) enables receivers in one domain to learn about active sources in other PIM-SM domains.

Figure 1.6 illustrates the position of PIM, IGMP, and MSDP in a multicast domain. MSDP is typically used with Multiprotocol Border Gateway Protocol (MBGP) [RFC4760], an extension of BGP [RFC4271] used for exchanging multicast routing (as well as other multiprotocol) information among different autonomous systems. MSDP is employed to propagate multicast source information among different autonomous systems.

1.2.1   PIM-DM

PIM-DM [RFC3973] is a multicast routing protocol designed for network environments where the receivers for any multicast group are densely distributed throughout the network. PIM-DM operates on a *push model* and assumes that every subnet in the multicast domain has at least one receiver interested in the multicast traffic being sent. PIM-DM operates on the assumption that most subnets and hosts in the network will be interested in any given multicast traffic. Therefore, PIM-DM initially *pushes* or *floods* multicast traffic to all points in the network.

Using PIM-DM, multicast traffic is initially sent to all subnets and hosts in the network. Subsequently, PIM-DM routers without any interested receivers send PIM Prune messages to remove (prune) themselves from the multicast distribution tree. PIM-DM operates on an *implicit join model*, and routers employ the *flood-and-prune* method to distribute multicast traffic to all parts of the PIM-DM domain and determine the parts of the network with uninterested receivers.

When a source first starts sending multicast traffic, each PIM-DM router on the source's local network segment (or LAN) receives the traffic and forwards it to all its

PIM-DM neighbors and to all links/interfaces with directly attached hosts that have expressed interest in the traffic. Each router that receives a forwarded packet, in turn, forwards it to downstream nodes, but only after verifying that the packet arrived on its upstream interface (using a mechanism called Reverse Path Forwarding (RPF) check [RFC3704] [RFC8704]). The RPF check (discussed in the subsequent section) ensures that the arriving packet was received on an interface leading back to the multicast traffic source (i.e., the interface is in the router's unicast routing table and corresponds to the packet's source address). If the RPF check fails, the packet is dropped. The RFP checks are implemented to prevent forwarding loops from occurring and circulating multicast packets endlessly in the network. Using PIM-DM, the multicast traffic is initially flooded to all parts of the network.

It is possible that some routers in the network will not be interested in the multicast traffic sent by a source because they do not have directly connected receivers or PIM neighbors interested in the traffic. These routers respond to the receipt of the multicast traffic by sending a PIM Prune message to the upstream router, which, in turn, instantiates a Prune state in its multicast state entries and causes it to stop forwarding the multicast traffic to the downstream neighbor. This may also prompt the upstream router to send a Prune message to its upstream neighbor because it does not need that multicast traffic. This flood-and-prune behavior of PIM-DM eventually results in the multicast traffic sent by a source to a particular group being sent to only those parts of the network that need it.

The Prune state maintained at each router for a multicast group will eventually time out, causing the corresponding multicast traffic to be flooded back into the parts of the network that were previously pruned. This triggers downstream PIM-DM routers not interested in the traffic to send further Prune messages, and the upstream routers to instantiate Prune state once again.

PIM-DM only utilizes source-based multicast distribution trees, also referred to as source-rooted trees (SRT) or shortest-path trees (SPTs). Consequently, it does not employ Rendezvous Points, unlike PIM-SM. This characteristics renders PIM-DM simpler to implement and deploy compared to PIM-SM. PIM-DM proves to be a more efficient multicast protocol when most hosts in the network are interested in the multicast traffic. This efficiency arises from PIM-DM's operational principle, which assumes that any given multicast stream from a source will have at least one downstream receiver. However, its scalability diminishes in larger multicast domains where most hosts are not interested in the multicast traffic.

1.2.2 PIM-SM

PIM-SM [RFC7761] operates on the assumption that multicast traffic receivers for any particular multicast group are sparsely and widely distributed throughout the network, which does not warrant flooding the entire network with periodic multicast traffic as in PIM-DM. In a PIM-SM domain, it is assumed that most subnets and, consequently, attached receivers, in the domain are not necessarily interested in any particular multicast traffic. PIM-SM is designed to limit multicast traffic so that only downstream routers with receivers for a particular group receive traffic for that group. Thus, to receive traffic for a particular multicast group, receivers and their directly connected routers must explicitly inform their upstream neighbors about their interest in particular groups and sources. If a router does not explicitly join the multicast distribution tree for a group, it will not be sent multicast traffic addressed to that group.

Routers in the multicast domain use PIM Join messages to join multicast distribution trees and Prune messages to exit the trees they have joined. Thus, unlike PIM-DM, which employs a *push model*, PIM-SM operates on a *pull model*. In this model, multicast routers and receivers employ an *Explicit Join mechanism* to specifically request multicast traffic to be sent to them. The pull model assumes that downstream routers and hosts do not want multicast traffic unless it is explicitly requested through IGMP Membership Report messages.

By default, PIM-SM works on shared multicast distribution trees, which are multicast distribution trees rooted at some selected router called the Rendezvous Point (RP). PIM-SM uses an *Explicit Join model* in which routers determine the interfaces with the interested receivers and send PIM Join messages upstream to their neighbor leading toward the RP. As these messages travel upstream, a shared multicast distribution tree is built from receivers to the RP. PIM-SM utilizes the RP as the initial source of the multicast group traffic and maintains the multicast state in the form (*, G), as described later. RPs are specific or designated routers in a PIM-SM network that receive notifications of all active multicast sources sending traffic destined to specific multicast address ranges (or, possibly, all multicast addresses). PIM-SM migrates to a source-based tree (SRT) or SPT and maintains a multicast state in the (S, G) if that SPT path is shorter than the path through the RP for a particular multicast group's traffic.

The RP is used by all multicast sources sending traffic to the multicast group. The shared tree is also called the RP tree (RPT). To send traffic to the RP, a multicast source must first forward traffic to its First-Hop Router (FHR), also known as the source's Designated Router (DR) or source-side DR. The DR then registers the source by encapsulating the source's packets in PIM Register messages and sending these through unicast transmission to the RP. The source's DR is a router on the source's local network segment (IP subnet or virtual LAN (VLAN)). On a local network segment with multiple routers, a single DR is elected from all the PIM routers on that segment, preventing multiple and unnecessary PIM Register messages from being sent to the RP. A single attached router is, by default, the DR of the attached host; no DR election is required.

One of the important requirements of PIM-SM is the provision of mechanisms to discover the IP address of an RP using a shared tree for a multicast group. PIM-SM offers various RP discovery mechanisms, such as Static RP configuration, Bootstrap Router (BSR) [RFC5059], Auto-RP, Anycast RP [RFC4610], and Embedded RP.

For a given multicast group G on the shared tree or RPT, PIM-SM routers send PIM (*, G) Join messages to the RP to join the shared tree, where * represents any source. The routers send (*, G) Prune messages to the RP to exit the tree. The shared tree is sometimes called the (*, G) tree.

PIM-SM also supports the use of source-based or source-rooted trees (SRTs). In this mode of operation, a separate multicast distribution tree is built for each multicast source sending traffic to a multicast group. Each SRT is rooted at the source-side DR (the router adjacent to the source), and the source sends traffic directly to the DR (i.e., the root of the SRT). SRTs are created as the shortest-path trees (SPTs) rooted at the source-side DR and are also called SPTs. For a given multicast group G and source S, PIM-SM routers send PIM (S, G) Join messages toward the source-side DR to join the SPT. The routers send (S, G) Prune messages to that DR to leave the SPT. The shared tree is sometimes called the (S, G) tree.

PIM-SM allows the use of SRTs or SPTs under the following circumstances:

- To stop the source-side DR from encapsulating multicast traffic in PIM Register messages and sending them to the RP, the RP may join an SRT.
- To optimize the data path, the Last-Hop Router (LHR), also called the receiver-side DR of a receiving host, may choose to switch from the shared tree to an SPT (a process referred to as the STP switchover). The receiver's DR or receiver-side DR is the local router to which the interested host is directly connected.
- For PIM-SSM (see discussion in the later section), a receiver-side DR will join an SPT from the outset; no shared trees are used.

PIM-SM is a soft-state protocol in which routers timeout all Join states after some time following the reception of the control message that instantiated it. To keep the state alive, routers periodically retransmit all PIM Join messages.

From the preceding discussion, we see the PIM-SM is a multicast routing protocol that blocks traffic unless it is explicitly requested for, while PIM-DM is a protocol that forwards traffic unless requested not to.

1.2.2.1 PIM Source-Specific Multicast (PIM-SSM)

PIM-SSM uses only source-based trees or SRTs and is based on PIM-SM with some modifications ([RFC3569] [RFC4607] [RFC4604] [RFC8313]). PIM-SSM serves as a multicast service model that allows interested hosts to specify (to the receiver-side DR) the multicast source(s) from which they wish to receive traffic, as well as the multicast group to which those sources are sending traffic. The host can specify the particular (S, G) pairs they wish to join. PIM-SSM is a multicast service model that allows hosts to request multicast traffic by specifying both the IP address of the source and the multicast group destination address to receive the traffic. With PIM-SSM, a host identifies a multicast traffic stream with a specified source S and group address G, (S, G), rather than by the group address alone, (*, G), as in PIM-SM.

PIM-SSM provides a Network Layer service called a "channel", identified by a particular source IP address S and an SSM destination IP address (G). A source S sends packets to an SSM destination address G, and any receiver can request these packets by subscribing to the channel (S, G). IGMPv3 for IPv4 and MLDv2 for IPv6 are designed specifically to support PIM-SSM channel subscriptions by hosts. In PIM-SSM, the multicast distribution tree for forwarding multicast traffic is rooted at the source S and is constructed using the PIM-SM capabilities with some small modifications.

1.2.2.2   PIM Sparse-Dense Mode

Typically, a network operator would use either PIM-DM or PIM-SM throughout a multicast domain. However, PIM-DM and PIM-SM may also be used together within a single multicast domain, where PIM-SM is used for some groups and PIM-DM for others. This mixed-mode configuration of PIM is called PIM Sparse-Dense Mode (see discussion in Chapter 5). In this mode of operation, routers in the multicast domain may be configured to use PIM-DM if the RP discovery mechanism fails to find an available RP for a multicast group and to use PIM-SM otherwise.

1.2.3   BIDIR-PIM

BIDIR-PIM [RFC5015] also uses RPs, but it differs from PIM-SM in the method used to transmit multicast traffic from a source to the RP. In PIM-SM, multicast packets are sent by a source's DR to the RP using PIM Register messages that encapsulate the source's packets, or directly to the receiver using an SPT. However, in BIDIR-PIM, the traffic flows to the RP along a shared tree that is bidirectional. This means that traffic flows in both directions along any given branch of the shared tree.

The following are the major differences between BIDIR-PIM and PIM-SM.

- BIDIR-PIM does not use SPTs and routers do not maintain (S, G) state. BIDIR-PIM routers do not switch from a shared tree to an SPT and do not support PIM-SSM. To prevent forwarding loops in BIDIR-PIM, for each RP, a single router on each link is elected as the Designated Forwarder (DF) for the link during RP discovery using the DF Election messages.
- BIDIR-PIM does not use a Designated Router for network segments like PIM-SM.
- BIDIR-PIM does not require PIM Register messages, eliminating the need for encapsulation of multicast packets in PIM Register messages by a source's DR.
- BIDIR-PIM uses simpler multicast data forwarding rules compared to PIM-SM. Unlike PIM-SM, there are no data-driven events in the control plane of BIDIR-PIM.

The main advantage of BIDIR-PIM is that it has better scalability when the network has many sources for each multicast group. However, the absence of SPTs means that multicast traffic is forced to flow only on the relatively inefficient shared tree (rooted at the RP). PIM-SSM and BIDIR-PIM were developed essentially as simpler and scalable variants of PIM, addressing limitations of PIM-DM (see Chapter 4) and PIM-SM (see Chapter 5).

1.2.4   MIXED-MODE PIM CONFIGURATIONS

Typically, a network operator runs PIM-DM, PIM-SM, or BIDIR-PIM alone throughout a multicast domain. However, the operator may use a combination of these three protocols (i.e., mixed-mode PIM configurations) by distributing multicast groups to the different protocols. In such a mixed-mode configuration, each multicast group operates in either PIM-DM, PIM-SM, or BIDIR-PIM mode. In this case, it is not possible to use a single multicast group in more than one PIM mode simultaneously. In such a deployment, the PIM protocols coexist largely independent of one another.

The network operator can implement a mixed-mode network where different protocols coexist because each of these protocols use the same PIM Hello message and protocol. This means that the Hello protocol only needs to run once on each link and the information learned from the Hello message exchange is shared among these three multicast routing protocols. The network operator can manually configure the routers with group ranges for PIM-DM, PIM-SM, and BIDIR-PIM modes.

1.3 MULTICAST GROUP MEMBERSHIP PROTOCOLS

There is a significant difference between the protocols used between hosts and multicast routers, and between the multicast routers themselves.

- A host on a given network segment only needs to inform its directly attached multicast router whether or not it is interested in receiving packets sent to a particular multicast group.
- A host only needs to inform its directly attached multicast router that it is the source of traffic destined for a particular multicast group.

This means a host does not need detailed knowledge of the multicast distribution tree built by the multicast router; it only needs to support a multicast group membership protocol to inform multicast routers of its participation in a multicast group. However, the multicast routing protocols used between adjacent routers must avoid routing loops as they build the multicast distribution tree from the source to any receiver (leaf). To facilitate the host-router communication portion of the multicast transmission, protocols such as IGMP for IPv4 and MLD for IPv6 (see Chapter 2) are used. On the other hand, various PIM protocol types are used for the router-router communication portion of the multicast transmission.

The IGMP and MLD multicast group membership protocols allow multicast routers to detect when a host on a directly connected network segment wants to receive multicast packets for a specific group. Even if more than one host on the network segment has signaled interest in receiving traffic for that multicast group, the directly attached multicast router sends only one copy of each packet for that multicast group on that segment (i.e., interface). On an Ethernet LAN, its inherent broadcast/multicast nature allows multicast packets to reach all interested receivers on it. When IGMP or MLD informs the attached multicast router that there are no interested hosts on the network segment, forwarding of multicast packets ceases, and that leaf is pruned from the multicast distribution tree.

IGMP currently has the following three versions:

- **IGMPv1**: This is the original protocol [RFC1112] that allows a host to send an IGMP Membership Report message (an explicit Join message) to the multicast router to join a multicast group. However, the router can only use a timeout to determine when hosts have left a group.

- **IGMPv2**: Among other features, IGMPv2 [RFC2236] adds an IGMP Leave Group message (an explicit leave message), allowing multicast routers to more easily determine when a multicast group has no interested receivers on an interface.
- **IGMPv3**: Among other features, IGMPv3 [RFC3376] further optimizes group membership management by allowing a host to specify which sources to include or exclude when receiving traffic for a multicast group, which is a key feature of PIM-SSM. It supports source filtering with inclusion and exclusion lists for a multicast group.

The IGMP process can be summarized as follows:

- To join a multicast group, G, a host signals its interests to the attached multicast router through IGMP.
- The multicast router then forwards multicast packets destined for multicast group G to only interfaces on which IGMP Membership Report (i.e., explicit Join) messages have been received.
- In PIM-SM, the host's DR sends periodic PIM Join/Prune messages to the RP responsible for the group. One or more multicast routers are statically or automatically configured as the RP for the group, and all other routers in the domain must explicitly join the group through those RPs.
- Each multicast router along the path toward the RP creates a (*, G) state for the group and sends Join/Prune messages toward the RP. The multicast route entry in the MRIB in the router contains the forwarding state representing part of the multicast distribution tree, including source address S, group address G, the incoming interface from which packets are accepted, the list of outgoing interfaces (to which packets are sent), timers, and flag bits.
  - The incoming interface of the wildcard (*) entry points toward the RP.
  - The outgoing interfaces point to the downstream neighbor routers that have sent Join/Prune messages toward the RP as well as the directly connected hosts that have sent IGMP Membership Report messages to join group G.
- The (*, G) state maintained by the routers creates a shared tree that is rooted at the RP, reaching all members of group G.

For each attached network segment, a multicast router can be either an IGMP Querier or a Non-Querier. The Querier periodically sends general IGMP Query messages on the segment (interface) to solicit multicast group membership information from hosts. The Querier on the network segment allows the attached multicast routers to keep track of group membership on the segment.

Hosts on the network segment that are active members of a multicast group will send IGMP Membership Report messages to the attached router to indicate that status. When a host leaves a multicast group, it will send an IGMP Leave Group message to inform the attached router. A multicast router does not need to know which hosts on an interface are members of a multicast group; it only needs to know that members exist. However, each host keeps track of which multicast groups it is a member of.

1.4 IPv4 MULTICAST ADDRESSES AND MULTICAST SUPPORT AT LAYER 2

This section describes the formats of IPv4 multicast and Ethernet multicast MAC addresses. We also discuss how IPv4 multicast addresses are mapped to corresponding Ethernet MAC addresses when transmitting multicast traffic to hosts on an IP subnet or VLAN. The address ambiguities that may result during IPv4-to-MAC address mapping are also discussed here.

1.4.1 IPv4 MULTICAST ADDRESSES

An *IP multicast address* is a logical identifier for a specific stream of packets that are sent from a multicast traffic source to an arbitrary group of hosts that have expressed interest in the traffic (i.e., by sending IGMP Membership Report messages). The group of recipients of the traffic sent by the multicast source is often referred to as a *multicast group*. It is important to note that the IP multicast address logically identifies both the multicast traffic itself and the group of receivers (i.e., the multicast group). An IP unicast address uniquely identifies only a single endpoint in the network, usually a host interface; each interface on a host has a unique IP unicast address. A multicast source may send traffic before hosts join the multicast group, or may send traffic when one or more hosts subscribe for the traffic. A host may leave a multicast group by sending an IGMP Leave Group message or silently leave without sending such a message.

The now obsolete IP classful addressing scheme reserved the Class D address range for IPv4 multicast addressing. The Class D address space has the binary prefix of 1110 in the first 4 bits of the first byte of the IP address, as illustrated in Figure 1.7. With the elimination of IP classful addressing (Classes A, B, and C) and the adoption of VLSM and CIDR, it is no longer appropriate to refer to IPv4 multicast addresses as Class D addresses, but as IPv4 addresses with the binary prefix 1110 (i.e., simply as IPv4 multicast addresses).

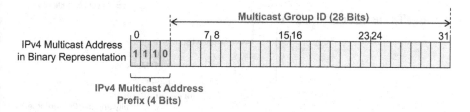

FIGURE 1.7 IPv4 multicast address format.

IPv4 multicast addresses, defined with the binary prefix 1110, span the address range from 224.0.0.0 to 239.255.255.255 in the dotted decimal IP address notation, but still adhere to the old Class D address boundaries. IPv4 multicast addresses have a prefix length of /32 (in CIDR notation), and the IPv4 multicast address range from 232.0.0.0 to 232.255.255.255 can be expressed as 232.0.0.0/8 or 232/8. The reserved address 224.0.0.0 is called the base address and cannot be assigned to any multicast group. The multicast address block of 224.0.0.1 to 224.0.0.255 is reserved for local IP subnet use. Addresses in this range are assigned for various uses on a subnet, such as for routing protocols and local discovery mechanisms.

The multicast address range from 239.0.0.0 to 239.255.255.255 is reserved as IPv4 *administratively scoped addresses* (also called *limited scope addresses*). Multicast packets addressed to administratively scoped multicast addresses do not cross multicast administrative boundaries that have been explicitly configured. Such administratively scoped multicast addresses are locally assigned to be used within the configured boundary and do not need to be unique across administrative boundaries.

1.4.2 ETHERNET MAC ADDRESSES

Each Ethernet interface on a network has a 48-bit MAC address with the format shown in Figures 1.8 and 1.9 (see Appendix A of [AWEYA1BK18]). This address is programmed in the MAC of the network interface; the reason it is called a MAC address. Every network interface card (NIC) or module manufactured is assigned a unique MAC address, as explained below. This prevents any two NICs manufactured from having the same MAC address. Figure 1.9 depicts the structure of the leading byte in the 48-bit Ethernet MAC address format, while Figure 1.10 shows the Ethernet frame format and transmission order (i.e., using Little Endian Bit-Ordering).

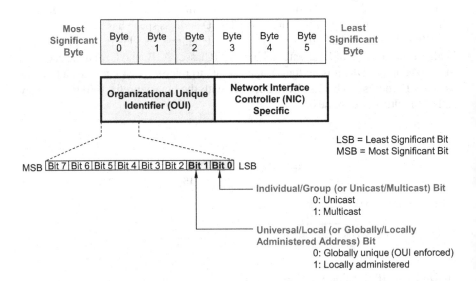

FIGURE 1.8   Ethernet MAC address format.

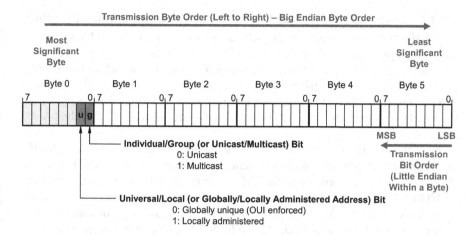

FIGURE 1.9   Leading byte in the 48-bit Ethernet MAC address format.

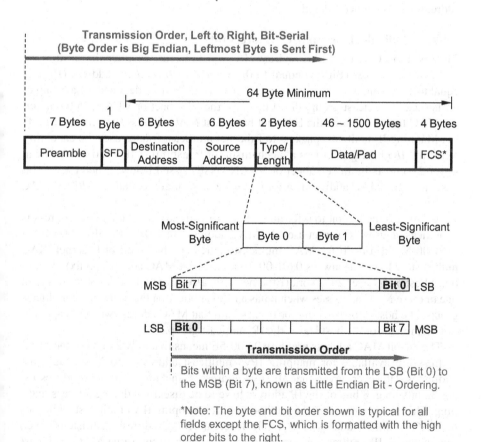

FIGURE 1.10   Ethernet frame format and transmission order – Little Endian Bit-Ordering.

1.4.2.1   Organizational Unique Identifier (OUI) and NIC-Specific Identifier

The OUI is the basic mechanism the IEEE uses to administer MAC addresses globally. It occupies bytes 0–2 of the 6-byte Ethernet MAC address. In the OUI field, bits 0 and 1 of byte 0 are used as the Individual/Group (I/G) bit and the Universally/Locally (U/L) bit, respectively. The IEEE assigns one or more OUIs to each manufacturer of Ethernet network interfaces. Using OUIs, the IEEE has to keep track of fewer (often only one) OUIs per manufacturer instead of individual MAC addresses.

Each manufacturer is responsible for assigning a unique organization-specific identifier for each network interface module manufactured, using the IEEE-assigned OUI. This identifier is known as the NIC-Specific Identifier, and it is a part of the 48-bit MAC address that is assigned to the network interface module by the manufacturer. It occupies bytes 3–5 of the MAC address. The organization (manufacturer) is responsible only for keeping track of the NIC-Specific Identifiers it assigns to manufactured network interface modules. The 24-bit NIC-Specific Identifier field allows a manufacturer to build 16 million network interface modules with unique MAC addresses before it needs another OUI.

1.4.2.2   Individual/Group (I/G) Address Bit

Bit 0 of Byte 0 of the MAC address (I/G bit) indicates whether the destination address is a *unicast* (Bit 0 is equal to 0) or *multicast/broadcast* address (Bit 0 is equal to 1). Setting the I/G bit to 1 means the MAC frame is destined for a group of hosts (i.e., a multicast group) or all hosts on the IP subnet or VLAN. In the latter, the MAC frame contains the Ethernet broadcast MAC address 0xFF.FF.FF.FF.FF. FF. Mapping IP multicast packets to Ethernet multicast frames uses the capability of setting I/G bit equal to 1 as a mechanism for transmitting IP multicast traffic at Layer 2 to hosts in an IP subnet or VLAN, as discussed below. When the I/G bit is set to 1, the MAC address is a *group address*, normally called a *multicast MAC address*.

A host sets the I/G bit to 0 for unicast and to 1 to indicate that a MAC address is a multicast address. Ethernet uses the MAC address range 0x01-00-5E-00-00-00 to 0x01-00-5E-FF-FF-FF for MAC multicast addresses; the prefix of Ethernet MAC multicast addresses is always 0x01-00-5E (i.e., 24-bit MAC address prefix). A multicast host on a Layer 2 network (Ethernet network) listens for Ethernet frames with one of these MAC addresses when it has a local application that joins an IP multicast group. The host stops listening for frames with that MAC address when the application terminates or the host leaves the IP multicast group.

The 24-bit MAC address prefix 0x01-00-5E means that only 24 bits of the MAC address are available for mapping IPv4 multicast addresses to MAC multicast addresses. However, given that all IPv4 addresses, including multicast addresses, are 32 bits long, 8 bits of the IP address have to be discarded during address mapping. This also implies that the method used for mapping IPv4 multicast addresses to MAC multicast addresses is likely to create MAC address "collisions" (i.e., two different IP multicast group addresses mapping to the same MAC multicast address).

1.4.2.3   Universally/Locally (U/L) Administered Address Bit

The second bit of Byte 0 (i.e., bit 1) in the 48-bit Ethernet MAC address is used to indicate if the MAC address is *globally* or *locally* administered. An Ethernet MAC address is *globally* or *universally administered* if the U/L bit is set to 0. If both the I/G and the U/L bits are 0, then the MAC address is unique to a single network interface. The MAC address is universally unique because the address is assigned to the network interface by the manufacturer using a combination of the IEEE-assigned OUI and the organization's NIC-Specific Identifier.

An Ethernet MAC address with the U/L bit set to 1 is a *locally administered MAC address*. Setting this bit to 1 means that someone other than the NIC manufacturer has configured the MAC address. For example, the network administrator of an organization may set the MAC address on a network interface to a value having only local significance, by setting the U/L bit to 1, and then bits 2 through 47 will be set to the locally chosen value. In this case, the organization would have to keep track of the locally administered addresses to make sure that there are no duplicate MAC addresses. However, since all NICs are delivered with universally administered addresses, locally administered addresses are rarely used.

1.4.3   MAPPING IPv4 MULTICAST ADDRESSES TO ETHERNET MULTICAST MAC ADDRESSES

On Layer 2 networks such as those based on Ethernet, IP packets with multicast addresses are conveyed in Ethernet frames with corresponding MAC multicast addresses. The MAC multicast addresses allow the switches in the Ethernet LAN to forward the encapsulated IP multicast packets to all possible receivers of the multicast group. When an Ethernet LAN has receivers for a multicast group, the Last-Hop Router (LHR) attached to that LAN is responsible for encapsulating the IP multicast packet in Ethernet frames and mapping the IP multicast address to a corresponding Ethernet MAC multicast address. The LAN switches use the mapped MAC multicast address to direct the encapsulated IP packets to all host receivers on the LAN.

Each host receiver that is a member of the multicast group will listen at Layer 2 for Ethernet multicast frames carrying the mapped MAC multicast address. This implies that for IP packets to reach the host receivers on the LAN, the IP multicast addresses have to be mapped to the corresponding MAC multicast address, as described in this section. Note that network devices operating at Layer 2 use the Layer 2 (Ethernet) destination addresses for forwarding packets while those operating at Layer 3 use the Layer 3 (IP) destination addresses for forwarding packets.

Note that (for obvious reasons), using Layer 2 broadcast to forward encapsulated IP multicast packets is a highly inefficient and undesirable way of sending multicast packets to receivers on the Layer 2 network. The IP multicast address to MAC address mapping method described here provides a simple yet efficient way for sending multicast packets over an Ethernet LAN.

This section describes how IPv4 multicast addresses are mapped to corresponding Ethernet MAC addresses. The Ethernet address OUI 01:00:5E (consisting of

24 bits), which is owned by the Internet Assigned Numbers Authority (IANA), is used for mapping IPv4 multicast addresses to Ethernet frames. IPv4 multicast packets are mapped to the Ethernet MAC address range 01:00:5E:00:00:00 through 01:00:5E:7F:FF:FF. As illustrated in Figures 1.11 and 1.12, the use of this OUI leaves 23 bits of the MAC address available for mapping the IPv4 multicast group identifier (ID). The first byte (0x01) of the MAC address includes the I/G bit.

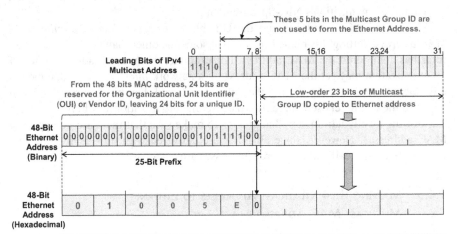

FIGURE 1.11   Mapping of IPv4 multicast address to 48-bit Ethernet MAC address.

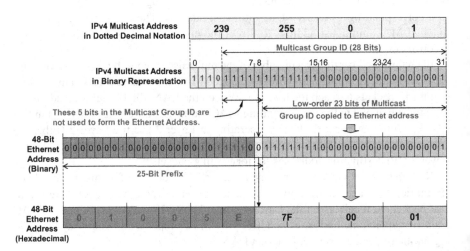

FIGURE 1.12   Example mapping of IPv4 multicast address to 48-bit Ethernet MAC address.

All IP multicast addresses have the first 4 bits set to the multicast prefix 1110, leaving the low-order 28 bits as meaningful address information. When mapping all IP multicast addresses to Ethernet multicast MAC addresses, each MAC address begins with the 24-bit prefix 01:00:5E. This means only half of the 48-bit Ethernet MAC address is available for mapping the IP multicast address.

The steps for converting an IPv4 address to a 48-bit Ethernet MAC address can be summarized as follows:

1. Ignore the first (higher-order) 9 bits of the IPv4 address and copy the remaining 23 bits.
   - **Note**: All IPv4 multicast addresses have the same 4-bit prefix (1110), meaning there are, in reality, only 4 bits in the first or higher-order byte, not 8. The last bits of the IPv4 address must not be dropped because these are almost guaranteed to be host bits, depending on the IP subnet mask used. But the high-order bits of the IPv4 address (i.e., the leftmost bits) are almost always network address bits.
2. Add a 0 as the first bit of the copied 23 bits of the IPv4 address (making 24 bits).
   - **Note**: The first bit of the remaining 24 MAC address bits (after the prefix 01:00:5E) is reserved. Setting this bit to 0 indicates an Internet multicast address, so the 5 bits following the IPv4 address prefix 1110 are dropped.
3. Discard the last (lower-order) 24 bits of the Ethernet MAC address.
4. Copy the 24 bits generated from the IPv4 address above, and use these as the last 24 bits of the Ethernet MAC address.
   - **Note**: The 23 remaining bits of the IPv4 multicast address are mapped, one for one, into the last 23 bits of the MAC multicast address.
5. The Ethernet MAC address now has the 24-bit prefix 01:00:5E, followed by a 0, and then the copied lower-order 23 bits of the IPv4 address.

Given that the next 5 bits following the IP multicast address prefix 1110 are not used in forming the MAC address, as shown in Figures 1.11 and 1.12, this means only the low-order 23 bits of the IP multicast address are placed in the MAC address. Only 23 bits of the MAC address are available for mapping the IP multicast address. Effectively, 28 bits of the IP multicast address map into only 23 bits of the MAC address, which can create address ambiguities in some cases as described below. Note that the address mapping process creates a situation where 32 (2^5) IPv4 multicast addresses could map to the same MAC multicast address.

Once a host determines the MAC multicast address for an IP multicast group, its operating system essentially instructs the network interface card to join or leave the multicast group. Once a multicast group is joined, the host accepts Ethernet multicast frames carrying the mapped MAC multicast address as well as Ethernet frames sent to the host's unicast addresses. The host does so while ignoring (filtering) frames sent to other multicast group addresses. Note that the host can join and receive multicast frames from more than one multicast group at the same time.

1.4.4 ETHERNET MULTICAST MAC ADDRESS AMBIGUITIES

Given that the lower 23 bits of the available 28-bit IPv4 multicast group address are mapped into the 23 bits of the available MAC address space, there is bound to be some ambiguity when mapping multicast addresses and delivering multicast packets, as illustrated in Figure 1.13. Mapping the 28-bit IPv4 multicast group address space to the available 23-bit Ethernet MAC address space means 5 bits of the IPv4 address are lost in the mapping process. These 5 bits result in 2^5 (or 32) address ambiguities, as shown in Figures 1.13 and 1.14. All of these IPv4 multicast addresses map to the same Ethernet multicast MAC address. This also means that each Ethernet

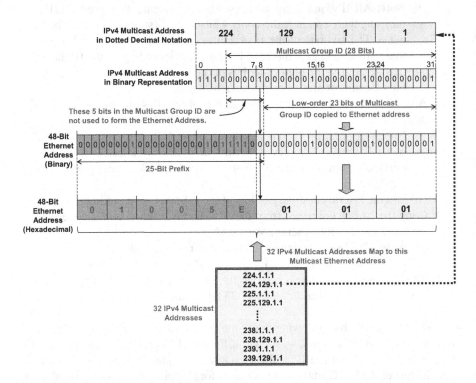

FIGURE 1.13   MAC address ambiguities resulting from IPv4 to MAC address mapping.

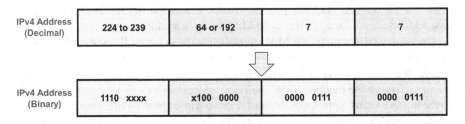

FIGURE 1.14   Examples of IPv4 multicast addresses that can have multicast MAC address overlaps.

multicast MAC address can represent 32 IPv4 multicast addresses, resulting in a 32:1 IPv4 multicast address-to-Ethernet multicast MAC address ambiguity.

This MAC multicast address ambiguity can cause some problems when transmitting IPv4 multicast traffic. For example, if any two hosts on the same IP subnet or VLAN join different multicast groups with IPv4 multicast addresses that differ only in the first 5 bits, Ethernet multicast frames for both multicast groups will be delivered to both hosts, thereby requiring the host network to filter and discard the unwanted packets. Note that if an Ethernet switch is not able to interpret multicast addresses in received packets, then it will flood such packets to all the members of the LAN. In this case, the host software will have to filter all packets sent to multicast groups for which they have not joined.

If host A joins the IP multicast group 225.129.1.1, it will program its Ethernet interface with the multicast MAC address 01:00:5E:01:01:01 to receive traffic sent to this group. However, this Ethernet multicast MAC address may be used by 31 other IP multicast groups. This means that if any of these 31 IP multicast groups is active on the local IP subnet or VLAN of host A, the Ethernet interface of host A will receive each multicast packet sent to any of these 31 IP multicast addresses. The Ethernet interface of host A will have to examine the IP multicast address of each multicast packet to see if the packet is destined for IP multicast group 225.129.1.1, actions which can significantly degrade the processing resources and performance of host A. Continuous filtering of unwanted multicast traffic can degrade the performance of host A. *Furthermore, this multicast MAC address ambiguity makes it difficult to constrain the flooding of multicast traffic in an IP subnet or VLAN based solely on Ethernet multicast MAC addresses since each one can map to 32 different IPv4 multicast addresses.*

1.4.4.1   IPv4 Multicast Addresses to Avoid Using on the Same Network Segment

It is important to avoid using IPv4 multicast addresses within the following ranges on the same network segment: $x.0.0.y$, $x.128.0.y$, $x.0.1.y$, or $x.128.1.y$, where x is from 224 to 239 and y is from 1 to 254 [ALLTELQUSOL]. This is because using these ranges can create MAC address ambiguities.

- When using multicast addresses in the ranges $x.0.0.y$ and $x.128.0.y$, they will map to the same multicast MAC address as addresses in the range $224.0.0.y$.
- Multicast addresses in the address ranges $x.0.1.y$ and $x.128.1.y$, will map to the same multicast MAC address as multicast addresses in the range $224.0.1.y$ will.

It is important to note that most multicast addresses in the ranges $224.0.0.y$ and $224.0.1.y$ are reserved for multicasting messages to all routers on a network segment or for routing protocol messages. Consequently, messages with such destination addresses are always flooded on all interfaces in the relevant IP subnet or VLAN.

This implies that all multicast addresses falling within the ranges of x.0.0.y, x.128.0.y, x.0.1.y, or x.128.1.y will map to multicast MAC addresses that are flooded on every interface in the relevant IP subnet or VLAN. Consequently, using IP

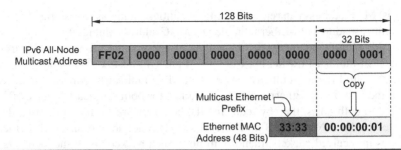

- **IPv6 All-Node Multicast Address**: FF02:0:0:0:0:0:0:1 (All nodes on the local network segment)

- **Ethernet MAC Address (48 Bits)**: 33:33:00:00:00:01

FIGURE 1.15   Mapping IPv6 multicast address to 48-bit Ethernet MAC address: IPv6 All-Nodes Multicast Address example.

multicast addresses in these ranges can result in the generation of Ethernet multicast frames leading to a significant increase in the overall multicast traffic on an Ethernet network. Generally, network administrators try to avoid using IP multicast addresses in these ranges because of the reasons mentioned.

1.4.5   MAPPING IPv6 MULTICAST ADDRESSES TO ETHERNET MAC ADDRESSES

The IPv4 multicast addresses 224.8.7.6 and 229.136.7.6 map to the same Ethernet multicast MAC address, 0x01-00-5E-08-07-06. This mapping process creates a real problem, because a host could be interested in multicast frames sent to only one of those multicast groups, and the host interface software must filter/reject one of them. IPv6 does not have this "collision" problem because of the way IPv6 handles the mapping of multicast group addresses to Ethernet multicast MAC addresses.

The procedure for encapsulating IPv6 multicast packets in Ethernet multicast frames is identical to IPv4, except 0x3333 is used as the destination MAC address prefix (thereby avoiding "collisions") [RFC2464]. To map IPv6 multicast addresses, the lower-order 32 bits of an Ethernet address are the lower-order 32 bits of the multicast IPv6 address. For example, the IPv6 multicast address, ff02::d, maps to the MAC multicast address, 33-33-00-00-00-0D, and the address, ff05::1:3, maps to the MAC multicast address, 33-33-00-01-00-03. Figure 1.15 describes the address mapping process using the IPv6 All-Nodes Multicast Address as an example.

1.5   MULTICAST DISTRIBUTION TREES

Forwarding of multicast traffic in a network is accomplished by multicast-capable routers. Multicast routers in a network create multicast distribution trees along which multicast traffic flows from the source to the receivers. The receivers are an arbitrary group of hosts represented by a multicast group address. A multicast distribution tree allows a single transmission from the data source to a multicast group to branch out at the appropriate multicast routers to the desired receivers. This tree controls the paths that multicast traffic takes through the network to the receivers. The various multicast routing protocols intend to create a spanning tree, preferably, a shortest-path multicast distribution tree, between the multicast source and the receivers.

In a multicast distribution tree, the multicast traffic source, or a designated node in the network, acts as the root while the receivers are the leaves of the tree. Each network segment (IP subnet or VLAN) attached to a router that has at least one interested receiver of a multicast group is a *leaf* on the multicast distribution tree. A multicast router can have leaves on any number of its interfaces and must send a copy of a multicast packet out on each of those interfaces. When a router adds a new leaf network segment to the multicast distribution tree (i.e., no copies of the multicast packets were previously sent on the interface to the network segment), a new branch is built. The leaf is joined to the tree and the router sends replicated packets out on the interface.

When a router determines that a branch contains no leaves because there are no interested receivers on the interface leading to that network segment, it prunes (removes) that branch from the multicast distribution tree and sends no further multicast packets out that interface. The router replicates and sends packets on multiple interfaces only where the multicast distribution tree branches, preventing duplicates.

For each receiver, the multicast routers collectively communicate and coordinate to create, as best as possible, the shortest path on the tree, between the receiver and the multicast source. The multicast distribution tree describes the path that the multicast traffic will take from the source to the receivers. Note that in unicast transmission, the network routes traffic along a single path from the traffic source to the destination address. We describe here source trees (also called source-rooted trees (SRT) or shortest-path trees (SPT)) and shared trees, which are the two basic types of multicast distribution trees.

1.5.1 SOURCE TREES

A source tree is a multicast distribution tree with its root at the multicast traffic source and branches that form a spanning tree through the network to the desired receivers. An SRT is also often called an SPT because it uses the shortest path through the network from the traffic source to any receiver; the forwarding path for multicast traffic is based on the shortest unicast path from any multicast router to the source. The shortest path for each receiver is determined from a unicast routing protocol running on the particular multicast router. Figure 1.16 demonstrates an example of an SPT for a multicast source, Host A, to the multicast group 244.1.1.1, with members being Host B and Host C.

Note that Router A is the Designated Router (DR) for Host A (i.e., the source-side DR), while Routers C and E are the DRs for Hosts B and C, respectively (i.e., receiver-side DRs). The special notation (Source, Group), simplified as (S, G), is used to represent an SPT, where S is the IP address of the multicast traffic source (e.g., 10.1.1.1 for Host A) and G is the multicast group address (e.g., 244.1.1.1 with

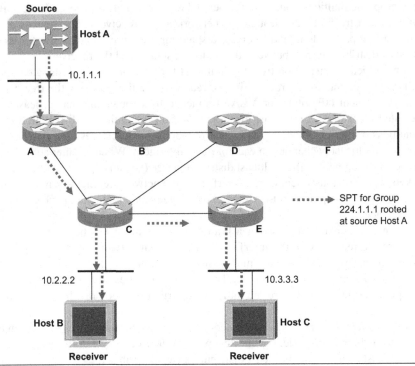

- A source-routed tree (SRT), simply called a source tree, is a multicast distribution tree that is rooted at the multicast traffic source and has branches that form a spanning tree through the network to the traffic receivers. A source tree uses the shortest-path through the network to the receivers and as a result, is also often called the shortest-path tree (SPT).
- Using the (Source, Group) or (S, G) notation, the SPT in the figure is represented as (10.1.1.1, 224.1.1.1).
- A separate SPT is created for each individual source to each multicast group. Another host 10.4.4.4 sending traffic to multicast group 224.1.1.1 will have the SPT (10.4.4.4, 224.1.1.1).

FIGURE 1.16 Source tree example rooted at Host A.

members, Hosts B and C). The SPT in Figure 1.16 is represented as (10.1.1.1, 244.1.1.1). Note that if Host B sends multicast traffic to Host A and Host C, also in multicast group 244.1.1.1, then a separate (S, G) SPT will created, that is, (10.2.2.2, 244.1.1.1).

A separate SPT will be created for each multicast source even if the receivers are in the same multicast group. For every multicast source, a corresponding SPT is constructed that connects the source to all receivers. Once an SPT for a source and its associated group is constructed, all multicast traffic to the members of the group is sent along this SPT. Each router on an SPT has an (S, G) entry with a list of outgoing interfaces.

PIM-DM (see Chapter 4) works on the idea of a source tree structure, where the root of the tree is the multicast traffic source. Using a flood-and-prune approach, PIM-DM routers construct a multicast distribution tree that connects all members of a multicast group.

1.5.2 UNIDIRECTIONAL SHARED TREES

Unlike an SRT (or SPT) in which the root is at the multicast traffic source, the root in a shared tree is placed at a chosen node in the network called a Rendezvous Point (RP), as illustrated in Figure 1.17. There are two types of shared trees: unidirectional and bidirectional shared trees. The multicast distribution tree shown in Figure 1.17 is a unidirectional shared tree.

PIM-SM (see Chapter 5) works based on unidirectional shared tree structures, where the root of the tree is a designated node (the RP) and not necessarily the actual multicast traffic source. In a unidirectional shared tree, multicast data flows only from the RP to the receivers. The RP serves as the meeting place for multicast traffic sources and the receivers of that traffic. This means multicast sources must use some other means to get their traffic to the root (the RP) so that it can be forwarded along the shared tree to the receivers. In a PIM-SM network, multicast sources must first register (via PIM Register messages) with the RP, and then send their traffic to the RP.

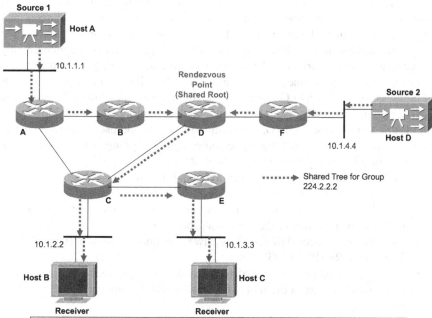

- A shared tree is a multicast distribution tree rooted at a certain point in the network called the Rendezvous Point (RP) in PIM. A shared tree is sometimes called a RP tree (RPT).
- Sources in a shared tree send multicast traffic to the root, the RP, to be forwarded to the receivers. Sources 1 and 2 in the figure send traffic to the RP, Router D, to be forwarded to the receivers Hosts B and C over the shared tree.
- Because all sources use a shared tree rooted at the RP, the Source (S) in the (S, G) notation is represented by the wildcard notation *. Thus, a shared tree is represented by the notation (*, G).
- The shared tree in the figure is represented by (*, 224.2.2.2).

FIGURE 1.17   Unidirectional shared distribution tree example.

This traffic is then forwarded along a shared multicast distribution to the desired receivers in the multicast group.

The RP is the node to which receiver-side DRs of hosts/receivers send PIM Join messages to receive traffic from active multicast sources sending traffic to groups. When an RP is in use, multicast sources transmit their traffic to the RP, which then forwards that traffic to the desired receivers. When receivers join a multicast group on a shared tree, the RP always serves as the root of the tree, and multicast traffic is transmitted from the RP along the tree branches toward the receivers. The root of the shared tree (i.e., the RP) is located somewhere in the core of the multicast network. The shared tree is sometimes called an RP tree (RPT).

PIM-SM assumes that most hosts in the multicast network domain do not want to receive multicast traffic. Thus, it employs a non-flooding multicast distribution model, where multicast sources first register and send traffic directly to the RP. Subsequently, the RP then forwards the traffic to the interfaces and routers where there are receivers of the multicast group. Consequently, the shared tree model sends traffic only to the routers and hosts that specifically request it.

Figure 1.17 illustrates a shared tree rooted at Router D for the multicast group 244.2.2.2 with members, Host B and Host C. In this network, Source 1 and Source 2 send their multicast traffic to the RP, Router D, to be then sent along the shared tree to Host B and Host C. Because the multicast sources use a commonly shared tree in this scenario, the shared tree is represented by the (wildcard notation, G) or (*, G), often pronounced "star comma G". The wildcard notation (*) implies all multicast sources, while G represents the multicast group address. The notation (*, G) represents any multicast traffic source sending to group G. If multiple sources send traffic to multicast group G, the multicast router would use (*, G) to represent the multicast forwarding state for those sources and the group. The shared tree or RPT in Figure 1.17 is represented as (*, 244.2.2.2).

The following are properties of a unidirectional shared tree:

- The RP receives multicast traffic from each source (S) and forwards that traffic to the receivers of the multicast group (G).
- The directly connected router of a receiver is responsible for sending explicit Joins to the RP (PIM (*, G) Joins).
- A single shared tree is created for each multicast group, no matter how many sources exist in the multicast domain and are sending traffic to that group.
- The only routers aware of a multicast group (G) are the ones on the shared tree. Multicast data is sent only to interested receivers.
- Each router on a shared tree has an (*, G) entry with a list of outgoing interfaces.
- Receivers can join the shared tree for a multicast group even if no sources exist yet for that group.
- For a source host other than the RP to send multicast data on the shared tree, its directly connected router must first tunnel the data (via PIM Register messages) to the RP before it can be multicast to the receivers.

- If a receiver is also a source, it cannot use the constructed shared tree on which it is receiving traffic to send its multicast data to the RP (this only applies to PIM-SM, not to BIDIR-PIM). It can only be used to receive multicast data from the RP.
  - An exception occurs when the source (i.e., its directly connected router) is located between the RP and the receivers of the multicast group and is already active on the shared tree. In such cases, the multicast data flows directly from the source (through its directly connected router) to the receivers.
- Multiple RPs can exist in a multicast domain, but there can only be one RP for each multicast group. In other words, there is only one shared tree or RPT per multicast group.

Shared trees can have longer forwarding delays because multicast packets must first be sent to the RP before they can be forwarded to receivers that have explicitly joined the multicast group. However, routers on the shared tree (RPT) have less multicast state to maintain, reducing the amount of memory required.

Although the forwarding path from the RP to a receiver is the shortest path, as determined by the unicast routing protocol, the shortest path from the source to the receiver is not necessarily the same as the path through the RP to the receiver. To address this issue, PIM-SM allows the last-hop router (i.e., the router directly attached to a receiver) to leave the shared tree and join the SPT routed at the source's DR, thereby reducing the length of the forwarding path (a process called SPT switchover).

1.5.3 BIDIRECTIONAL SHARED TREES

In bidirectional shared trees, multicast traffic is allowed to flow in both directions to reach all parties interested in the traffic, as illustrated in Figure 1.18. A unidirectional shared tree only allows traffic to flow from the root (i.e., the RP) toward the receivers, as shown in Figure 1.17. BIDIR-PIM (see Chapter 7) operates based on bidirectional shared tree structures.

BIDIR-PIM constructs bidirectional shared trees that are rooted at an RP address. In this case, the multicast routers do not switch the bidirectional traffic from shared trees to SPTs, as in PIM-SM. This design makes BIDIR-PIM more optimized for smaller multicast routing state sizes rather than for path length. BIDIR-PIM routers maintain multicast routes always as wildcard-source, that is, as (*, G) routes.

A bidirectional (*, G) tree is capable of carrying multicast traffic both from sources located on any branch of the tree toward the RP and from the RP to receivers located on any branch. Consequently, the strict Reverse Path Forwarding (RPF)-based rules normally applied in the other PIM modes do not apply to BIDIR-PIM. Instead, BIDIR-PIM is capable of forwarding traffic from all sources to and from the RP. Any party can receive traffic from the RP, and can also send traffic to RP at any time, as illustrated in Figure 1.18.

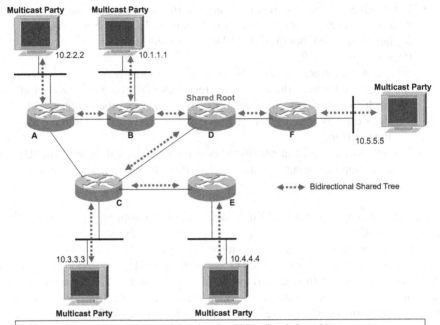

FIGURE 1.18   Bidirectional shared tree example.

Using a bidirectional shared tree, BIDIR-PIM allows multicast routers to minimize the amount of PIM state information they maintain, a feature that is especially
important in networks with many dispersed multicast sources and receivers. In a
BIDIR-PIM network, multicast routers build only multicast group-specific (*, G)
state. Routers require only a single (*, G) state for each multicast group to deliver
traffic to and from all the multicast sources. BIDIR-PIM eliminates the need for multicast routers to maintain (S, G) routes and handle multicast traffic-triggered events
(source or receivers becoming active).

Note that, since BIDIR-PIM does not use the RPF check mechanism for loop prevention, as in the other PIM modes, another mechanism is required for this purpose.
To prevent multicast traffic forwarding loops, BIDIR-PIM allows only one multicast
router on every link in the BIDIR-PIM domain (including multiaccess network links
(e.g., links in an IP subnet) and point-to-point links) to be elected the Designated
Forwarder (DF). The DF is the node on the link that has the best route to the RP
address. The DF is responsible for forwarding multicast traffic from the link toward
the RP address and forwarding multicast traffic onto the link toward the receivers.
BIDIR-PIM relies on a DF election process to select the DF for each interface/link
and each RP address.

1.6 MULTICAST FORWARDING AND REVERSE PATH FORWARDING (RPF) CHECKS

In unicast routing, each router that receives an incoming unicast packet will examine the destination address of the packet and then perform a (unicast) routing table lookup to determine the outgoing interface and the next best router (also called the next-hop router) to which the packet should be forwarded for it to get to its destination. The source address of the incoming packet plays no role in how the packet should be forwarded to reach its destination, other than for detecting and discarding spoofed and maliciously sourced packets. Routers performing unicast forwarding send a packet through the network along a single path from the traffic source to the destination host, having a unicast address in the packet's destination address field; this single path may only change after network routing changes or updates.

1.6.1 RATIONALE BEHIND RPF CHECKS

In multicast routing, a source sends packets to an arbitrary group of receivers represented by a multicast group address carried in the destination address field of the packets. Multicast routers use the source address (which is a unicast address) to determine the direction of the upstream data source. The source of the multicast packet must be an upstream stream data source for the packet to be forwarded to downstream receivers.

The main idea behind multicast packet forwarding is based on where the packets came from (i.e., the IP source address) rather than where they are sent to (i.e., the multicast group address). This distinction makes the mechanisms for forwarding multicast packets quite different from those for forwarding unicast packets. The router first determines if a multicast packet is received on the best interface (path) leading back to the data source before identifying which downstream interfaces have receivers for the multicast group (as indicated by the multicast destination address of the packet). If the packet is received on the correct interface, the router forwards it out to the appropriate downstream interfaces.

The term Reverse Path Forwarding (RPF) [RFC3704] [RFC8704] refers to the process of checking (called RPF checks) if an incoming multicast packet is received on the interface that leads back to the source. This verification allows the packet to be routed away from the source toward the receivers. Figures 1.19 and 1.20 describe, respectively, example scenarios where RPF checks fail and succeed. In contrast to unicast forwarding, the receivers of a multicast packet can appear on any downstream interface of the local forwarding router (often on multiple interfaces). This complexity means the router cannot simply use the destination address, which is a multicast group address, for forwarding multicast packets.

This also means that, in addition to the local router determining if there are active receivers on an interface, it must also ensure that it forwards a packet downstream and away from the multicast traffic source. The RPF checks come in handy for this purpose, ensuring that a received multicast packet arrives on the correct interface leading back to the source (i.e., the best reverse path to the source). This verification allows the packet to be forwarded out to the correct downstream interfaces leading to the receivers.

RPF, which is an incoming interface check, forms the basis of most multicast routing protocols such as PIM-DM, PIM-SM, and PIM-SSM. These protocols typically use the existing unicast routing table to determine the interface on the reverse path leading back to the multicast traffic source. A router uses RPF checks to determine whether to forward or drop an incoming multicast packet. However, BIDIR-PIM which uses bidirectional shared trees, employs a slightly modified process for forwarding packets (as discussed in Chapter 7), as this protocol does not distinguish between incoming and outgoing interfaces. This is because multicast traffic can flow in either direction on the shared tree.

1.6.2 THE RPF CHECK MECHANISM

In Figures 1.19 and 1.20, the router performs an RPF check on an arriving (S, G) packet and forwards the packet if the check is successful, otherwise, the packet is dropped. For each multicast packet arriving on an interface, the router performs the RPF checks as follows:

1. The router performs the longest prefix match (LPM) lookup of the source IP address (S) of the packet in its local unicast routing (or forwarding) table to determine whether the packet has arrived on the lowest-cost reverse-path interface leading back to the multicast traffic source. The router uses the unicast routing table, including *static unicast routes* and multicast routing information obtained via MBGP, for the RPF checks. The routing

RPF Check Fails:

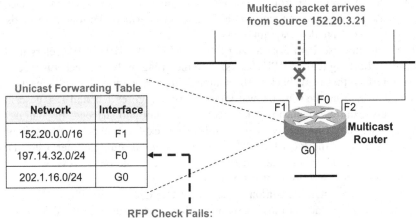

FIGURE 1.19 Reverse Path Forwarding (RPF) check fails.

RPF Check Succeeds:

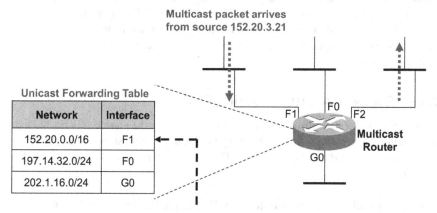

FIGURE 1.20   Reverse Path Forwarding (RPF) check passes.

information to the source may also include *static multicast routes*. The router looks for the interface with the shortest path that leads back to the multicast source.

2. If the packet has arrived on the interface that has the best path leading back to the source, the RPF check is successful, and the packet is forwarded downstream to the receivers.

3. If the packet has arrived on an interface that is not on the reverse path to the source, the RPF check fails, and the packet is discarded.

The incoming or RPF interface is the one that has the lowest-cost path leading back to the multicast traffic source based on both the Administrative Distance (also called the Metric Preference) and Routing Metric values of the possible routes (including static routes) in the unicast routing table to the source. Note that the source may be the actual source (in PIM-DM and PIM-SM) or an RP (in PIM-SM). When multiple interfaces exist with equal least-cost paths back to the source, then the interface with the highest next-hop IP address is selected as the RPF interface for the (S, G) traffic; the router may also use the highest next-hop IP address as the tiebreaker in this case. The use of Administrative Distances and Routing Metrics in unicast routing is discussed in detail in [AWEYFDVR21] and [AWEYFCDM22].

1.6.3   Understanding the Use of Static Multicast Routes

A network administrator may configure *static multicast routes* to override any dynamic route entries in the routing table similar to *static unicast routes*. The difference between these two routes is that the multicast routers do not use static multicast routes for any multicast packet forwarding, while static unicast routes can be used.

Instead, the network administrator uses static multicast routes to statically configure the RPF interface for a source, overriding the RPF interface information indicated in the unicast routing table. An RPF interface or RPF neighbor address is also specified when a static multicast route is configured on a multicast router, just as a static unicast route specifies either an outgoing interface or the IP address of the next-hop neighbor.

1.6.4 ROUTING INFORMATION FOR THE RPF CHECKS

A multicast router determines an optimal route back to the source of a packet using the routing information in the following preference order: static multicast routes, MBGP routes, and then unicast routes. The packet source can mean any one of the following:

- For a packet that arrives on the SPT, the packet source is the multicast source.
- For a packet that arrives on the RPT, the packet source is the RP.
- For a Bootstrap message originated by the BSR of a PIM-SM or BIDIR-PIM domain, the packet source is the elected BSR (see Chapter 5).
- For an MSDP Source-Active message, the message source is the RP in the remote PIM-SM domain that originated the message (MSDP-capable routers perform what is called the MSDP peer-RPF checks, see Chapter 6).

The router selects the optimal route to the packet source as the RPF route as follows:

- If a static multicast route is configured to the source, that route is used as the RPF interface.
- The best MBGP route to the packet source is used as the RPF route.
- If there are multiple unicast routes to the packet source, the route with the highest Metric Preference (also called Administrative Distance) is used as the RPF route.
- If multiple unicast routes with the same Metric Preference exist to the packet source, the route with the lowest Route Metric is used as the RPF route. However, if only a single unicast route exists to the packet source, that route is used as the RPF route.

When searching routes in the MBGP or unicast routing tables, the router uses the longest prefix match principle. That is, the route with the longest prefix becomes the RPF route. If the MBGP or unicast routes have the same prefix length and metrics, the route with the highest next-hop IP address becomes the RPF route.

The RPF route points to an RPF interface and RPF neighbor:

- If the RPF route is a static multicast route, that route specifies an RPF interface and RPF neighbor.
- If the RPF route is an MBGP or unicast route, its outgoing interface is the RPF interface, and the next-hop is the RPF neighbor.

The router checks whether the received packet has arrived on the RPF interface. If yes, the RPF check succeeds, and the packet is forwarded to downstream nodes and directly connected receivers. If no, the RPF check fails, and the packet is discarded.

1.6.4.1 Underlying Assumptions for RPF Checks

The underlying assumptions for using the RPF checks are the following:

- The unicast routing table is currently valid/correct and stable (i.e., the unicast routing protocol must converge for the information to be useful for RPF checks).
- The path used from a multicast source to the local router and the reverse path from the router back to the source are symmetric.

If the first assumption is not true, the RPF check will fail because PIM depends on the unicast routing table for such checks. If the second assumption is not true, the RPF check may accept multicast traffic on a non-optimal path from the source; the path to the source may be the shortest, but the path from the source may not be. In cases where the links on the path are unidirectional, the RPF checks can fail altogether. Because multicast packets can reach the local router via multiple interfaces, the RPF checks are integral to the router's decision to forward packets or not.

1.6.5 RPF Interfaces Types

For multicast traffic arriving on the SPT, the expected incoming interface on a PIM router for a given source and multicast group is the interface leading toward the IP address of the traffic source (usually as determined by the unicast routing table). For traffic arriving on the RPT or shared tree, the expected incoming interface on a PIM router is the interface leading toward the RP. When the unicast routing table points to an ECMP route to the source, PIM must be enabled on all of the constituent paths.

The RPF check may indicate one of two distinct RPF interface types:

1. **Upstream PIM neighbor**: This is the IP address of a valid PIM neighbor from which multicast traffic is accepted for a source. A valid PIM neighbor must exist for the RPF check to succeed and for multicast traffic to be forwarded to downstream nodes. The router sends PIM Join messages toward that next-hop, and multicast data traffic will be forwarded from that upstream interface.
2. **Directly connected multicast source**: This refers to a local PIM-enabled interface on the router to which a multicast source is directly connected. With an entry for this source, the local router will treat the source's multicast traffic flow as directly connected and will forward it if there are any joins from other nodes or other directly connected receivers. Since the RPF interface entry in this case does not point to any specific PIM neighbor on the interface, the local router will not send PIM Join messages toward this directly connected upstream source. Note that this option will work only when the multicast traffic source is directly connected to the router.

An RPF interface override feature allows the network operator to specify a static multicast route to override the normal RPF lookup mechanism using the unicast routing table. In this case, the operator indicates to the router that it may accept multicast traffic on an interface (pointed to by a static multicast route), in addition to the one normally selected by the RPF lookup mechanism. Specifying a static multicast route allows the router to accept multicast traffic from a valid PIM neighbor that is not necessarily on the reverse path toward the source of the multicast traffic (see static multicast routes discussed earlier).

1.6.6   PERIODIC VALIDATION OF THE RPF INTERFACE

When a multicast router receives the *first* multicast packet from a source (S) or RP (*) and addressed to multicast group (G), it will create a corresponding (S, G) or (*, G) entry in its multicast routing (or forwarding) table if the packet arrived on the RPF interface to the source. The router computes the incoming (or RPF) interface for the (S, G) or (*, G) entry by performing an RPF check on that first packet. The RPF interface of a multicast source S is the interface on the PIM router that holds the least-cost path to reach the source S. The next-hop on the RPF interface from the local router is the RPF neighbor.

Typically, multicast routers periodically update the RPF interfaces in the multicast routing tables to account for network changes and to prevent the RPF interface of any (S, G) traffic from appearing in the outgoing interface lists (OILs) of its corresponding (S, G) entry in the multicast routing table. The periodic recomputation of the RPF interfaces also helps in faster multicast routing convergence after network topology changes.

Once an RPF interface is determined for an (S, G) or (*, G) pair and entered the multicast routing table, subsequent packets belonging to that (S. G) or (*, G) pair are RPF checked against the entered RPF interface until it is recomputed. The router periodically determines the RPF interface of an (S, G) or (*, G) pair and updates the multicast routing table.

1.6.7   IMPLEMENTING THE RPF CHECK MECHANISM

Performing the RPF check on each received multicast packet would place a big processing burden on the router. Using the RPF interface of an (S, G) or (*, G) entry in a multicast forwarding table provides a solution to this issue.

Upon receiving an (S, G) or (*, G) multicast packet, the router first searches its multicast forwarding table for a corresponding entry.

1. If the corresponding (S, G) or (*, G) entry does not exist in the multicast forwarding table, the router subjects the packet to an RPF check.
   a. If the receiving interface for the packet is the RPF interface, the RPF check succeeds and the router forwards the packet to all the outgoing interfaces.

b. The router then creates an (S, G) or (*, G) multicast state and installs the entry into its multicast forwarding table, with the RPF interface for the entry set to the receiving interface.

c. If the receiving interface of the packet is not the RPF interface, the RPF check fails and the router discards the packet.

2. If the corresponding (S, G) or (*, G) entry exists in the multicast forwarding table, and the receiving interface for the packet is the RPF interface, the router forwards the packet to all the outgoing interfaces. The router normally does this for packets immediately following a checked packet.

3. If the corresponding (S, G) or (*, G) entry exists in the multicast forwarding table, but the receiving interface for the packet is not the RPF interface in the multicast forwarding table, the router subjects the multicast packet to an RPF check. The router normally does this periodically, especially when routing changes occur and the unicast routing table is updated.

a. If the receiving interface is not the same as the RPF interface in the multicast forwarding table and the RPF interface of the packet has not changed, this implies that the (S, G) or (*, G) entry is still valid/correct but the packet arrived on a wrong path (or interface). The router therefore discards the packet.

b. If the receiving interface is not the same as the RPF interface in the multicast forwarding table and the RPF interface of the packet has changed, this means that the (S, G) or (*, G) entry has expired, and the router updates the RPF interface of the entry to be the receiving interface of the packet. The RPF interface of the (S, G) or (*, G) entry is now new, and the router forwards the packet to all the outgoing interfaces.

1.7 TTL SCOPING AND THRESHOLDS

In the past, most IP multicast implementations used the TTL field in the IP header to achieve some level of scoping for multicast traffic forwarding. Each time a router forwards a multicast packet, it decrements the TTL value in the IP header by one. If the TTL value is decremented to zero, the packet is dropped by the router. Typically, the network operator configures TTL thresholds on multicast packets to confine them to some administratively defined network topological region.

The network operator may configure TTL thresholds on individual multicast router interfaces to prevent multicast packets carrying TTL values less than the TTL thresholds from being forwarded to the interface. The basic forwarding rule for multicast traffic on network interfaces that are configured with TTL thresholds is to not forward a multicast packet across the interface unless its remaining TTL is greater than the interface's configured TTL threshold, as described in Figures 1.21 and 1.22.

Applying TTL thresholds to multicast router interfaces provides an operator with a simple mechanism for preventing the forwarding of multicast traffic beyond the boundary of a network region. Often referred to as *TTL scoping*, this technique simply uses the TTL field in the IP header of the multicast packet. An operator

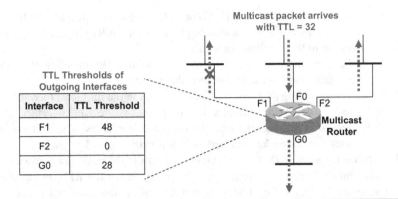

FIGURE 1.21   Applying TTL thresholds to multicast router interfaces.

may want to constrain certain multicast application traffic within a site or region by configuring an initial TTL value so that the multicast traffic would not exceed the TTL thresholds on all multicast router interfaces at the site's or region's perimeter (Figure 1.22).

Network operators used TTL scoping to control the distribution of multicast traffic to lessen the stress on scarce network resources (e.g., bandwidth) or limit the spread of the traffic to provide some form of improved privacy. Note that operators also used the TTL in its traditional role to limit the lifetime of unicast IPv4 packets in networks. Given these often conflicting roles, it was discovered that TTL scoping for multicast traffic is difficult to implement reliably, and the schemes that were used were often complex and difficult to understand.

The use of TTL scoping exposed some serious network problems concerning the interaction of TTL scoping with flood-and-prune protocols such as PIM-DM. It was found that, in many common situations, TTL scoping was able to prevent effective implementation of multicast distribution pruning. For example, when considering the case where a multicast packet arriving at a router has either an expired TTL or failed a TTL threshold, discarding this packet prevents the router from being capable of pruning any upstream sources or being part of the multicast tree of those sources. Thus, this results in the router sinking all multicast traffic, whether or not downstream receivers exist.

It should be noted that while it might be possible for the router to send PIM Prune messages upstream after a packet is discarded, this can result in legitimate multicast traffic being discarded by the router, since subsequent multicast packets may take a different path and arrive at the same router with a larger TTL value. However, the

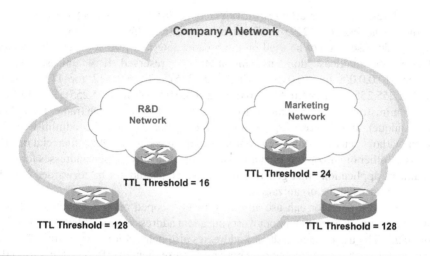

- A company may configure TTL thresholds on router interfaces at the boundary of a specific network to prevent multicast traffic from being forwarded beyond the network boundary.
- Multicast applications appropriately set the initial TTLs of the multicast packets to prevent the TTLs from exceeding the configured TTL thresholds on the boundary router interfaces.
- By setting the initial TTL of multicast packets to 127 or lower, these multicast packets will be constrained to stay within the Company A network.
- By setting the initial TTL of multicast packets originated by multicast applications in the Marketing Network to 23 or lower, these multicast packets will not be forwarded beyond this network.

FIGURE 1.22   TTL scoping: TTL threshold for scoping network boundaries.

use of administratively scoped IP multicast [RFC2365], as described below, provides clearer and simpler semantics for scoping IP multicast traffic.

1.8   ADMINISTRATIVELY SCOPED NETWORK BOUNDARIES

Similar to TTL scoping, a network operator may use *administratively scoped boundaries* to limit the forwarding of multicast traffic beyond a network domain or sub-domain.

1.8.1   WHAT IS AN ADMINISTRATIVELY SCOPED NETWORK BOUNDARY?

Administratively scoped IP multicast has the following two key properties [RFC2365]:

- Packets that are addressed with *administratively scoped IPv4 multicast addresses* (a special range of multicast addresses) do not cross the configured administrative network boundaries.
- Administratively scoped multicast addresses have local significance (i.e., they are locally assigned within a particular network), and therefore, are not required to be unique across administrative boundaries.

The address space for *administratively scoped* (or *limited scope*) IPv4 multicast addresses is defined as 239.0.0.0/8, which means from 239.0.0.0 to 239.255.255.255. These addresses cannot be used on the broader Internet. Instead, they are reserved for private multicast domains similar to the reserved IPv4 unicast address ranges 10.0.0.0/8 (or 10.0.0.0 to10.255.255.255), 172.16.0.0/12 (or 172.16.0.0 to 172.31.255.255), and 192.168.0.0/16 (or 192.168.0.0 to192.168.255.255) [RFC1918].

Administratively scoped multicast addresses are locally unique (rather than globally unique), and different organizations can use them in domains administered by them without causing addressing conflicts. Companies, universities, financial institutions, or other organizations typically use administratively scoped addresses for local multicast applications that generate traffic, which should not be forwarded outside the boundaries of the organization.

A network operator can use administratively scoped multicast addresses freely within a network domain without worrying about address conflicts elsewhere in other domains. The use of such multicast addresses also helps conserve the limited multicast addresses because a network operator can reuse them in different domains in the network without worrying about address conflicts. The only requirement is to configure multicast routers to ensure that administratively scoped multicast addresses do not cross into or pass out of their configured domain.

A router that supports administratively scoped IP multicast (i.e., a boundary router) is configured with scoped IP multicast boundaries per interface. Such a router is configured not to forward administratively scoped multicast packets on an interface when matching boundary address definitions in either direction are met (see Figures 1.23 and 1.24); the router performs bidirectional address checks, thus preventing traffic leakage in both directions when the interface is attached to a multiaccess network. Furthermore, a boundary router always performs pruning of external multicast traffic on the boundary for a PIM-DM network and does not accept external PIM Joins for a PIM-SM network, except for internal traffic in the administratively scoped address range.

An administratively scoped IP multicast network domain is defined by one or more boundary routers with common boundary multicast traffic limiting or filtering capabilities. Such a boundary router is configured to act as a boundary for scoped IP multicast addresses within a defined range (as illustrated in Figures 1.23 and 1.24). Network operators may create a scoped domain in their network if they need to restrict multicast traffic.

The boundary routers typically are configured with filters to prevent multicast traffic in the administratively scoped address from being forwarded outside of the user-defined domain. Within an administratively scoped domain, the administratively scoped address range can be further subdivided to create local multicast boundaries. This subdivision allows the reuse of administratively scoped addresses between the smaller domains.

1.8.2   How Administratively Scoped Network Boundaries Work

As illustrated in Figure 1.23, if a multicast router interface is configured with an administratively scoped boundary, the interface will not allow multicast packets with

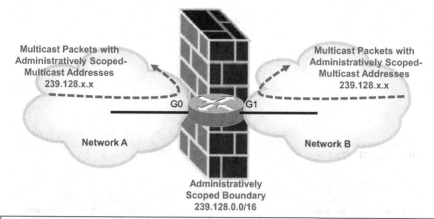

- The boundary router interfaces G0 and G1 are set up with the administratively scoped-multicast addresses 239.128.0.0/16 (i.e., address range 239.128.0.0 through 239.128.255.255) to keep multicast traffic within Network A and Network B, respectively.
- Arriving multicast packets with group addresses that fall in the range of the configured administratively scoped-addresses will not be allowed to enter or exit the interface.
- The router interface provides a firewall for multicast packets carrying the configured administratively scoped addresses.

FIGURE 1.23   Administratively scoped network boundaries.

multicast group addresses that fall in this range to enter or exit the interface, thereby providing firewall capabilities for multicast traffic with group addresses in this range. In Figure 1.23, the network operator configures an administratively scoped boundary for the multicast address range 239.0.0.0–239.255.255.255 on router interface G0. This means multicast packets in this address range cannot cross-interface G0. A firewall for such packets is provided on this interface, preventing them from entering or leaving the interface.

In Figure 1.24, Company A sets up different ranges of administratively scoped addresses on the boundaries of two sub-domains and a bigger domain to prevent multicast traffic from being forwarded outside those specific boundaries. The router interfaces at the network boundaries of both the R&D and Marketing departments are configured with the administratively scoped addresses 239.128.0.0/16 to prevent multicast traffic with addresses in the range of 239.128.0.0–239.128.255.255 from entering or leaving these sub-domains. This also means the address range 239.128.0.0/16 can be used independently in both sub-domains without causing multicast traffic forwarding problems in either sub-domain; administratively scoped addresses can be reused efficiently inside the Company A network. Company A also configures the administratively scoped address 239.0.0.0/8 on the router interfaces at the boundary of the bigger Company A network to prevent multicast traffic with addresses in the range of 239.0.0.0–239.255.255.255 from entering or leaving this network.

It is advisable for organizations that use administratively scoped IP multicast addresses not to rely on them to prevent confidential or sensitive data from being

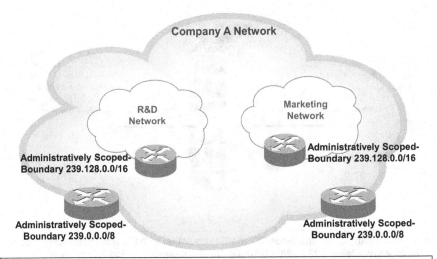

- Company A may configure the administratively scoped-address 239.0.0.0/8 on router interfaces at the network perimeter to prevent multicast traffic from being forwarded beyond the network boundary.
- Multicast packets generated by the R&D Network with group addresses falling within the 239.128.0.0/16 address range will be constrained to stay within the R&D network.
- This set up also allows the administratively scope-address 239.128.0.0/16 to be used independently in the Marketing Network. The multicast operations in the Marketing Network is independent of the R&D Network, allowing more efficient use of multicast addresses within the company.

FIGURE 1.24   Using administratively scoped network boundaries.

forwarded outside the scope region. Where sensitive data is transmitted using administratively scoped IP multicasting, the organization should use some confidentiality mechanism (e.g., encryption) to protect that data. Furthermore, it is important to note that the boundary routers that constrain scoped multicast traffic are not required to have any kind of firewall capability, it is usually sufficient to address scoping only.

1.8.3   PARTITIONING OF PIM-SM AND BIDIR-PIM DOMAINS

Typically, a PIM-SM or BIDIR-PIM domain supports only one BSR, which is responsible for advertising a set of group-to-RP mapping information (called an *RP-Set*) to all routers within the entire domain. The BSR forwards the RP information for all multicast groups within the network scope administered by it. When a single BSR handles the advertising of RP-Set for the entire PIM-SM or BIDIR-PIM domain, this is called a *non-scoped BSR mechanism*. However, to facilitate effective management and not to overwhelm a single BSR, a PIM-SM or BIDIR-PIM domain may be partitioned into one *global-scope zone* and multiple smaller *administratively scoped zones* (simply, called *admin-scope zones*). Administrative scoping involves partitioning the multicast domain into several smaller multicast zones, each with its own BSR mechanism.

Using administrative scoping with local BSR mechanisms effectively eases the processing burden on a single BSR and allows the network operator to provision zone-specific services using private multicast group addresses. Typically, the network operator divides the multicast domain into admin-scope zones that are specific to some multicast groups. *Zone border routers* (*ZBRs*) form the boundary of an admin-scope zone. One BSR is configured for each admin-scope zone, which serves multicast groups within a specific multicast address range.

An admin-scope zone boundary does not allow multicast data and protocol packets, such as PIM Assert messages and Bootstrap messages, for a specific multicast group range, to cross it. The operator may configure multicast group ranges served by different admin-scope zones to overlap. Functioning as a private multicast group address, a multicast group is valid only within its local admin-scope zone. A BSR is configured for the global-scope zone, which serves the multicast groups that do not belong to any configured admin-scope zone.

1.8.4 ADMIN-SCOPE ZONES AND THE GLOBAL-SCOPE ZONE

The *global-scope zone* and each *admin-scope zone* in the multicast domain have their own Candidate-RPs and BSRs. The operation of these devices is limited to only their respective admin-scope zones. Particularly, the election of the active BSR and RP-Set advertisement is performed independently within each admin-scope zone. The ZBRs of each admin-scope zone enforce the boundary of that zone. The ZBRs do not allow multicast information to cross the boundary in either direction as discussed above. Typically, the network operator bases the global-scope zone and admin-scope zones on two factors: *geographical space* and *multicast group address range*.

* **Geographical space**: In this case, the network operator creates admin-scope zones to be logical regions that are specific to particular multicast groups. The multicast packets addressed to these multicast groups are confined within the configured local admin-scope zone and cannot cross the boundary of that zone. For multicast groups in the same address range, the operator creates corresponding admin-scope zones to be geographically separated from one another. This means that a router in one admin-scope zone must not serve other admin-scope zones; each admin-scope zone contains its own routers. However, the global-scope zone covers all routers in the multicast domain. Multicast packets that do not belong to any particular admin-scope zone can be forwarded to the entire multicast (PIM-SM or BIDIR-PIM) domain.
* **Multicast group address range**: In this case, the network operator configures each admin-scope zone to serve specific multicast groups. Usually, the operator configures these addresses to have no overlaps; however, the operator may make them overlap one another. In Figure 1.25, the multicast group address ranges of Admin-Scope Zone 1 and Admin-Scope Zone 2 do not overlap, whereas the multicast group address range of Admin-Scope

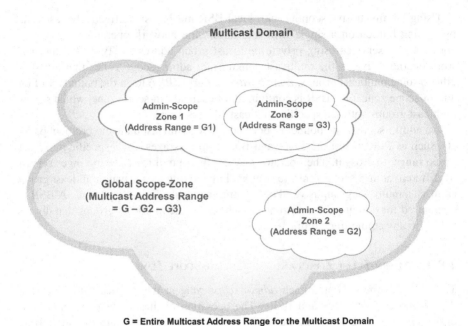

G = Entire Multicast Address Range for the Multicast Domain

FIGURE 1.25   Multicast group address range relationship between admin-scope zones and the global-scope zone.

Zone 3 is a subset of the address range of Admin-Scope Zone 1. The global-scope zone has a multicast group address range that covers all the group addresses except those of all the configured admin-scope zones (i.e., G minus G1 minus G2).

The following describes the relationships between the global-scope zone and the admin-scope zones:

- The global-scope zone and each admin-scope zone support their own BSR and Candidate-RPs that operate only within their respective scope zones. The election of the BSR and RP-Set are confined within each scope zone.
- Each admin-scope zone has ZBRs that enforce its own boundary. The multicast information (such as Candidate-RP-Advertisement messages and Bootstrap messages) is transmitted only within their zones.
- The multicast information in the global-scope zone cannot cross into any admin-scope zone.
- In regards to multicast information propagation, each admin-scope zone is independent of the other zones, as well as independent of the global-scope zone; no propagation of multicast information is allowed between any two admin-scope zones.

1.9 LAYER 2 MULTICAST ROUTING MECHANISMS

The main Layer 2 multicast routing mechanisms include *IGMP Snooping* and *PIM Snooping*, which are used to limit the unnecessary propagation of multicast packets (in IP subnets and VLANs) to Layer 2 switch ports where they are needed. Figure 1.26 illustrates an example use of these Layer 2 multicast mechanisms in a multicast domain. MLD snooping is the counterpart of IGMP Snooping in IPv6 multicast routing, while IPv6 PIM Snooping is the counterpart of IPv4 PIM Snooping.

- **IGMP Snooping (see Chapter 2)**: This is a multicast traffic constraining mechanism that runs on Layer 2 switches. When IGMP Snooping is running on a Layer 2 switch, it manages and controls traffic sent to multicast groups by monitoring and analyzing IGMP messages exchanged between the hosts on the Layer 2 network and the attached multicast routers. IGMP Snooping controls the flooding of multicast packets such that they are constrained to only switch ports that have active multicast group members in the Layer 2 network. By analyzing received IGMP messages, the IGMP Snooping switch establishes mappings between switch ports and multicast groups, and then forwards multicast packets based on these mappings. When IGMP

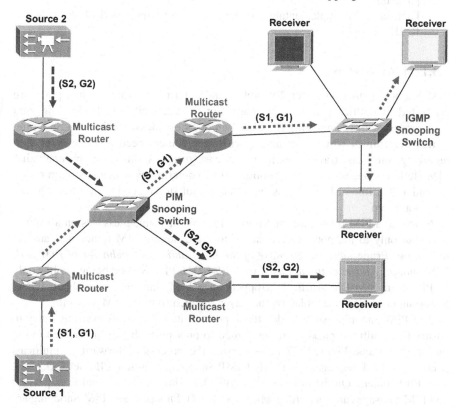

FIGURE 1.26 Layer 2 multicast routing mechanisms.

Snooping is not running on the Layer 2 switch, multicast packets are broadcast on all ports to all devices in the Layer 2 network (except the incoming port). When IGMP Snooping is running on the switch, multicast packets for known multicast groups are forwarded on only switch ports with active group members, rather than broadcast on all ports to all hosts in the Layer 2 network.

• **PIM Snooping (see Chapter 5)**: PIM Snooping, when running on Layer 2 switches, determines which switch ports are interested in multicast packets by analyzing PIM messages received from multicast routers. The Layer 2 switch is then able to add those ports to its multicast forwarding table to ensure that multicast packets can be forwarded to only the ports that are interested in the multicast packets.

The use of IGMP Snooping and PIM Snooping provides the following advantages:

• Reduces broadcast of multicast packets at Layer 2, thus saving network bandwidth.
• Enhances the security of multicast traffic by limiting broadcast of such packets.
• Facilitates the implementation of per-host accounting (particularly, using IGMP Snooping).

1.9.1 PIM Snooping

PIM Snooping runs on Layer 2 switches and determines which switch ports are interested in multicast packets by analyzing the received PIM Hello, Join, and Prune messages. By analyzing the PIM Join or Prune message, the PIM Snooping switch determines which port and downstream routers need to receive (or stop receiving) multicast traffic sent to a multicast group. Additionally, by analyzing PIM Hello messages, the PIM Snooping switch determines which upstream router to send a PIM Join or Prune message to receive (or stop receiving) multicast traffic sent to a group.

Note that a PIM router does not flood PIM Join or Prune messages on all router ports but only to the port corresponding to the upstream PIM router indicated in the Join or Prune message. *Because of the flood-and-prune behavior of PIM-DM, PIM Snooping is generally not used with PIM-DM.* PIM-SM snooping applies only to PIM-SM; PIM-DM traffic is dropped once PIM Snooping is enabled. IGMP Snooping must also be enabled on the Layer 2 switch running PIM Snooping.

The PIM Snooping switch adds those ports to its multicast forwarding entry to ensure that multicast packets are forwarded to only ports that are interested in the multicast packets. Figure 1.27 demonstrates the process of forwarding multicast packets and PIM messages when only IGMP Snooping is used in PIM network along with PIM routers. On the other hand, Figure 1.28 illustrates how multicast packets and PIM messages are forwarded when both IGMP Snooping and PIM Snooping are enabled in the same PIM network [H3CMULTGUID].

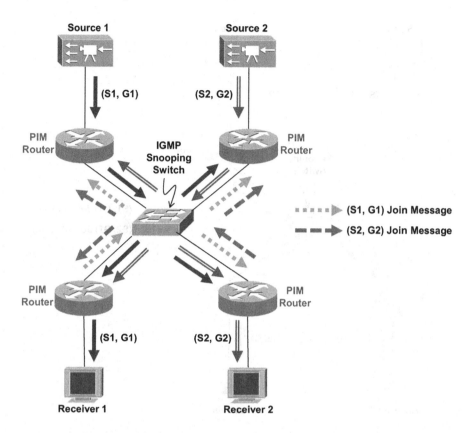

FIGURE 1.27 Multicast packet forwarding with only IGMP Snooping enabled in the network segment.

As shown in these figures, the Layer 2 switch has interfaces connecting to PIM routers in the same IP subnet or VLAN. When using IGMP Snooping without enabling PIM Snooping, the Layer 2 switch discovers and maintains the multicast router ports by listening to PIM Hello messages sent by the PIM routers. The Layer 2 switch broadcasts all types of received PIM messages in the network segment and forwards all multicast packets to all multicast router ports in the network segment. Each PIM router on the network segment, whether interested in the multicast packets or not, will receive all multicast packets and all PIM messages.

When both IGMP Snooping and PIM Snooping are enabled, the Layer 2 switch determines whether the PIM routers are interested in the multicast packets addressed to a multicast group by examining the PIM Join/Prune messages received from them. The Layer 2 switch forwards PIM-SM traffic to a router only when it receives a PIM Join message from the router for downstream receivers. The switch initially blocks all multicast traffic instead of forwarding it because it did not receive a PIM Join message from the downstream router for the group.

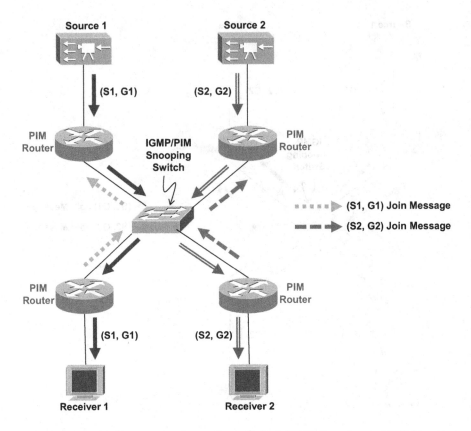

FIGURE 1.28 Multicast packet forwarding with both IGMP Snooping and PIM Snooping enabled in the network segment.

The Layer 2 switch adds only the multicast router ports that are interested in the multicast packets as entries in its multicast forwarding table. The Layer 2 switch then forwards multicast packets to only the PIM routers that are interested in the packets, saving network bandwidth. Typically, a PIM Snooping switch uses the Hold Time seen in the PIM Hello, Join, and Prune messages to time out a multicast router port and neighbor router information. ·

1.10 IP MULTICAST ROUTING ARCHITECTURE

The PIM protocols are designed to be independent of the underlying unicast routing protocols (Routing Information Protocol (RIP), Open Shortest Path First (OSPF), Intermediate System to Intermediate System (IS-IS), Border Gateway Protocol (BGP)). PIM will interact with the configured unicast routing protocol only to the extent needed for it to perform RPF checks. To avoid multicast routing loops, each multicast router in the multicast domain must always know the interface that has the shortest path leading to the source sending traffic to a multicast group. This is an upstream (or incoming) interface called the RPF interface (see the subsequent discussion).

The multicast router must never forward multicast packets back toward a multicast source. All other interfaces on the router are potential downstream (or outgoing) interfaces, leading to directly connecting receivers of the multicast group or to other downstream routers on the multicast distribution tree (i.e., to branches of the tree).

Multicast routers closely monitor the status of the incoming and outgoing interfaces and messages sent by directly connected hosts or routers. The router, through this process, can determine the multicast forwarding state for the interfaces. When the router has a multicast forwarding state for a particular multicast group on an interface, it starts forwarding the corresponding traffic on that interface (i.e., it "turns on" traffic for that multicast group). Interfaces that have a valid forwarding state (i.e., have interested multicast receivers or routers) are added to the router's outgoing interface list (OIL) for that multicast group. These interfaces will receive copies of the group's packets received on the incoming interface. The incoming interface and OIL might be different for different multicast groups.

The multicast forwarding state can be (S, G) for PIM-DM routers, (*, G) and (S, G) for PIM-SM routers, and only (*, G) for BIDIR-PIM routers. Figure 1.29 illustrates a high-level view of the IP multicast routing architecture. This architecture has several multicast routing components and also integrates a suite of unicast IP routing protocols through the Multicast Routing Table Manager. The IP unicast routing protocols include RIP, OSPF, IS-IS, and BGP, which provide the multicast

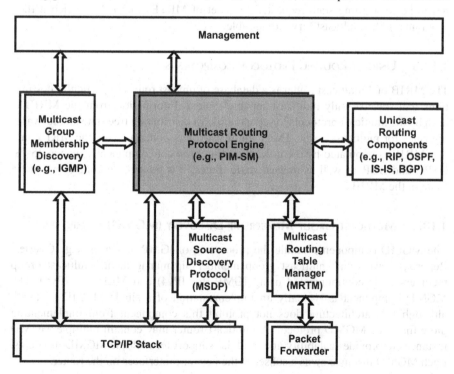

FIGURE 1.29   IP multicast routing architecture.

routing protocols (e.g., PIM-DM, PIM-SM, BIDIR-PIM), the routing information needed to build multicast distribution trees. The components in Figure 1.29 are described here.

1.10.1 MULTICAST ROUTING PROTOCOL ENGINE (MRPE)

This component is a multicast routing protocol stack that implements a single multi-cast routing protocol for a single multicast domain (e.g., PIM-SM). A single multicast router may contain multiple MRPEs to provide redundancy and support for multiple domains, for example, in a multicast border router. Where multiple MRPEs are used to control different multicast domains, these MRPEs communicate their joint for-warding requirements via the multicast border router.

1.10.2 MULTICAST ROUTING TABLE MANAGER (MRTM)

The MRTM is responsible for maintaining the multicast forwarding state in the router's multicast forwarding tables. A single multicast router may contain multi-ple MRTM instances, where each one can receive instructions from one or more MRTEs, on what multicast forwarding state to program. Each instance of MRTM communicates with one or more multicast forwarding tables, which are responsible for forwarding and receiving data packets on a set of interfaces. The MRTM com-bines the forwarding state requested by a set of MRTEs into rules, which it then programs in the multicast forwarding table.

1.10.3 UNICAST ROUTING PROTOCOL COMPONENTS

The MRIB of a multicast router is a database of unicast routes to particular destina-tions that traverse only multicast-capable routers. Information from the MRIB is used by the multicast protocols to set up multicast distribution tree state and forward-ing rules for multicast traffic. Every multicast router contains only one MRIB, and this MRIB is populated by the unicast routing protocol components, such as IS-IS, OSPF, and BGP, as well as unicast static routes; it is possible to configure a static route in the MRIB.

1.10.4 MULTICAST GROUP MEMBERSHIP DISCOVERY (MGMD) COMPONENT

The MGMD components handle the processing of IGMP messages (e.g., Queries, Reports, Leaves) and multicast group membership management. Multicast group membership is communicated using IGMP (for IPv4) and MLD (for IPv6). The MGMD component is typically an implementation of a single MGMD protocol, although this architecture does not prohibit this component from implementing more than one MGMD protocol. A multicast router may contain multiple MGMD instances to provide scalability and modular support for multiple MGMD protocols. Each MGMD instance owns a subset of the network interfaces on the router.

1.10.4.1   IGMP Architecture

IP hosts use IGMP to report their multicast group memberships to their attached multicast routers. Similarly, multicast routers use IGMP to discover which of their directly attached hosts belong to active multicast groups. Most routers now support IGMPv3. IGMP is discussed in detail in Chapter 2. This section describes the main components that form part of the multicast IP routing Architecture in a typical router.

1.10.4.1.1   IGMP Router Component

The IGMP Router component is part of the multicast IP routing architecture. For each of its network interfaces, the IGMP Router component performs the following functions:

- **Periodically sending IGMP Membership Query messages**: A multicast router can be an IGMP Querier or a Non-Querier. Only one Querier is active on a network at any time. Multicast routers monitor Query messages from other multicast routers to determine the status of the Querier. In an IGMPv1 network, one interface must be configured to act as a Querier. In an IGMPv2 or IGMPv3 network, the Querier is the router with the lowest IP address. If the Querier detects an IGMP Query message from a router with a lower IP address, it relinquishes its role to that router.

  Interfaces in IGMPv2 and IGMPv3 modes send two types of group membership Queries to hosts on the network:
  - General Queries to the All-Hosts group address (224.0.0.1)
  - Specific Queries to the appropriate multicast group address

  Interfaces in IGMPv3 mode send the following types of Queries to IGMPv3 hosts:
  - Group-Specific and Source-Specific Queries

  The purpose of an IGMP Membership Query is to discover the multicast groups to which a host belongs. IGMPv2 and IGMPv3 Membership Queries have a Maximum Response Time field. This response time is the maximum time that a host can take to reply to a Query.
- **Receiving IGMP Membership Report messages**: When a multicast router receives an IGMP Membership Report message, it adds the reported group to the membership list for the interface and sets a timer to the *group membership interval*. If this timer expires before the router receives another Membership Report for that group, the router determines that the group has no members left on the interface.
- If the router does not receive any Report messages for a specific multicast group within the *Maximum Response Time*, it assumes that the group has no members on the interface. The router does not forward subsequent multicasts for that group on the interface.
- **Informing the Multicast Routing Protocol Engine that owns the interface of the group membership requirements of the hosts on that interface**: For networks that use only IGMPv1, the interface must be configured

to operate in IGMPv1 mode. However, IGMPv2 and IGMPv3 interfaces can support IGMPv1 hosts. For IGMPv1, an explicit Join (Membership Report) message is sent to the router, but a timeout is used to determine when hosts leave a group. This process wastes processing cycles on the router, especially on older or smaller routers. IGMPv2 adds an explicit leave message to the join (i.e., Leave Group) message so that routers can more easily determine when a group has no interested listeners on an interface. IGMPv3 allows a host to include or exclude a list of source addresses for each multicast group of which the host is a member. Routers merge the source address requirements of different hosts for each group.

Other group membership requirements are determined by configuring IGMP settings for an interface such as the following:

- The method that the router uses to remove hosts from multicast groups (IGMPv2 and IGMPv3 interfaces only).
- The Query Interval the Querier uses to space Query messages when determining multicasts group memberships.
- The time that a Querier waits before sending a new Query message to hosts from which it receives IGMP Leave Group messages.
- The time that a new Querier waits before sending Query messages after it assumes responsibility from another Querier.
- The time that a host can take to reply to a Query message (i.e., the Maximum Response Time).
- The number of times that the router sends each IGMP message from a particular interface.

1.10.4.1.2   IGMP Host Component

The IGMP Host component is another component of the multicast IP routing architecture. Most host systems often provide this functionality as part of the operating system and include the following:

- **Maintaining a list of the multicast groups for which it requires membership**: When a host leaves a group, it sends an IGMP Leave Group message to multicast routers on the network segment (interface). A host generally addresses Leave Group membership messages to the All-Routers multicast group address (224.0.0.2).
- **Responding to IGMP Membership Query messages for the groups in which it is interested**: When a host receives an IGMP Membership Query message, it identifies the multicast groups associated with the Query to determine to which groups it belongs. The host then sets a timer, with a value less than the Maximum Response Time field in the Query message, for each group to which it belongs. When the timer expires, the host multicasts an IGMP Membership Report to that group address.
- **Sending IGMP Membership Report messages when it requires membership of a new multicast group**: IGMPv3 extends IGMPv2 functionality with the ability to include or exclude specific multicast traffic sources

sending traffic to a group. That is, using IGMPv3, hosts signal (S, G) pairs to be included or excluded, as described in Chapter 2.

1.10.4.1.3 IGMP Proxy

A router or a switch may support the IGMP Proxy component that enables it to issue IGMP host messages on behalf of hosts that the router discovered on standard IGMP-enabled interfaces. The router acts as a proxy for its attached IGMP hosts as discussed in Chapter 2. The IGMP Proxy component in the multicast IP routing architecture has the following functionality:

- Learning group membership requirements for each network interface via the Group Membership Interface in Figure 1.29.
- Aggregating these group membership requirements into the Tree Information Base (TIB) Records, and sending them to the Multicast Routing Table Manager.
- Informing the owning IGMP Host component of group membership requirements for the upstream interface when performing IGMP proxying.

1.10.5 MULTICAST SOURCE DISCOVERY PROTOCOL (MSDP) COMPONENT

The MSDP component is a mechanism for connecting multiple PIM-SM domains, allowing multicast sources for a group in one domain to be known to all RPs in different domains. An RP in one PIM-SM domain runs MSDP over TCP to discover multicast sources in other domains. MSDP reduces the complexity of interconnecting multiple PIM-SM domains, by allowing receivers in one PIM-SM domain that are interested in multicast sources in another domain, to use an inter-domain source-based tree (rather than a common shared tree).

REVIEW QUESTIONS

1. Explain the main differences between unicast, broadcast, and multicast transmission.
2. What is anycast transmission? Describe two example use cases of anycast transmission.
3. Explain why the source address of an IP packet cannot be a broadcast or multicast address.
4. What is a multicast group?
5. What is the purpose of a multicast group membership discovery protocol?
6. What is the purpose of a multicast routing protocol?
7. Why are PIM protocols referred to as routing protocol independent?
8. What are the main features of PIM-DM?
9. What are the main features of PIM-SM?
10. What are the main features of PIM-SSM?
11. What are the main features of BIDIR-PIM?
12. What is the purpose of the Multicast Source Discovery Protocol (MSDP)?

13. What is the purpose of the Organizational Unique Identifier (OUI) and NIC-Specific Identifier in an Ethernet MAC address?
14. What is the purpose of the Individual/Group (I/G) bit and the Universally/Locally (U/L) bit in an Ethernet MAC address?
15. Why is there the need to map IPv4 multicast addresses to Ethernet multicast MAC addresses in multicast transmission in Ethernet networks?
16. Explain why mapping IPv4 multicast addresses to Ethernet multicast MAC addresses can result in multicast address ambiguities.
17. Give one example of the type of problems Ethernet MAC multicast address ambiguity can cause in a Layer 2 (Ethernet) network carrying IP multicast traffic.
18. What is a multicast distribution tree?
19. What is a source tree (also called a shortest-path tree (SPT))?
20. What is a unidirectional shared tree?
21. What is a bidirectional shared tree?
22. What is the purpose of the Reverse Path Forwarding (RPF) checks in multicast forwarding?
23. What is the difference between a static unicast route and a static multicast route in PIM multicast forwarding?
24. Explain briefly how TTL scoping is used to constrain the transmission of IP multicast traffic.
25. What are administratively scoped multicast addresses?
26. Explain briefly how administratively scoped IP multicast addresses are used to constrain the transmission of IP multicast traffic.
27. What is the difference between IGMP Snooping and PIM Snooping?

REFERENCES

[ALLTELQUSOL]. Allied Telesis, How to Configure IGMP for Multicasting on Routers and Managed Layer 3 Switches, *AlliedWare(tm) OS How to Note: IGMP*, 2009.

[AWEYA1BK18]. James Aweya, *Switch/Router Architectures: Shared-Bus and Shared-Memory Based Systems*, Wiley-IEEE Press, ISBN 9781119486152, 2018.

[AWEYFDVR21]. James Aweya, *IP Routing Protocols: Fundamentals and Distance-Vector Routing Protocols*, CRC Press, Taylor & Francis Group, ISBN 9780367710415, May 2021.

[AWEYLSPV21]. James Aweya, *IP Routing Protocols: Link-State and Path-Vector Routing Protocols*, CRC Press, Taylor & Francis Group, ISBN 9780367710361, May 2021.

[AWEYFCDM22]. James Aweya, *Designing Switch/Routers: Fundamental Concepts and Design Methods*, CRC Press, Taylor & Francis Group, ISBN 9781032317694, October 2022.

[AWEYARCAP22]. James Aweya, *Designing Switch/Routers: Architectures and Applications*, CRC Press, Taylor & Francis Group, ISBN 9781032317700, October 2022.

[H3CMULTGUID]. H3C, *IP Multicast Configuration Guide, Chapter 3, PIM Snooping Configuration*, H3C Documentation Set.

[RFC826]. David C. Plummer, "An Ethernet Address Resolution Protocol", *IETF RFC 826*, November 1982.

[RFC950]. J. Mogul and J. Postel, "Internet Standard Subnetting Procedure", *IETF RFC 950*, August 1985.

[RFC1034]. P. Mockapetris, "Domain Names – Concepts and Facilities", *IETF RFC 1034*, November 1987.

[RFC1035]. P. Mockapetris, "Domain Names – Implementation and Specification", *IETF RFC 1035*, November 1987.

[RFC1112]. S. Deering, "Host Extensions for IP Multicasting", *IETF RFC 1112*, August 1989.

[RFC1517]. R. Hinden, Ed., "Applicability Statement for the Implementation of Classless Inter-Domain Routing (CIDR)", *IETF RFC 1517*, September 1993.

[RFC1518]. Y. Rekhter and T. Li, "An Architecture for IP Address Allocation with CIDR", *IETF RFC 1518*, September 1993.

[RFC1519]. V. Fuller et al., "Classless Inter-Domain Routing (CIDR): An Address Assignment and Aggregation Strategy", *IETF RFC 1519*, 1993.

[RFC1878]. T. Pummill and B. Manning, "Variable Length Subnet Table for IPv4", *IETF RFC 1878*, December 1995.

[RFC1918]. Y. Rekhter, B. Moskowitz, D. Karrenberg, G. J. de Groot, and E. Lear, "Address Allocation for Private Internets", *IETF RFC 1918*, February 1996.

[RFC2131]. R. Droms, "Dynamic Host Configuration Protocol", *IETF RFC 2131*, March 1997.

[RFC2236]. W. Fenner, "Internet Group Management Protocol, Version 2", *IETF RFC 2236*, November 1997.

[RFC2365]. D. Meyer, "Administratively Scoped IP Multicast", *IETF RFC 2365*, July 1998.

[RFC2464]. M. Crawford, "Transmission of IPv6 Packets over Ethernet Networks", *IETF RFC 2464*, December 1998.

[RFC2526]. D. Johnson and S. Deering, "Reserved IPv6 Subnet Anycast Addresses", *IETF RFC 2526*, March 1999.

[RFC2710]. S. Deering, W. Fenner, and B. Haberman, "Multicast Listener Discovery (MLD) for IPv6", *IETF RFC 2710*, October 1999.

[RFC3258]. T. Hardie, "Distributing Authoritative Name Servers via Shared Unicast Addresses", *IETF RFC 3258*, April 2002.

[RFC3376]. B. Cain, S. Deering, I. Kouvelas, B. Fenner, and A. Thyagarajan, "Internet Group Management Protocol, Version 3", *IETF RFC 3376*, October 2002.

[RFC3569]. S. Bhattacharyya, Ed., "An Overview of Source-Specific Multicast (SSM)", *IETF RFC 3569*, July 2003.

[RFC3590]. B. Haberman, "Source Address Selection for the Multicast Listener Discovery (MLD) Protocol", *IETF RFC 3590*, September 2003.

[RFC3618]. B. Fenner, and D. Meyer, Eds., "Multicast Source Discovery Protocol (MSDP)", *IETF RFC 3618*, October 2003.

[RFC3704]. F. Baker and P. Savola, "Ingress Filtering for Multihomed Networks", *IETF RFC 3704*, March 2004.

[RFC3810]. R. Vida, and L. Costa, Eds., "Multicast Listener Discovery Version 2 (MLDv2) for IPv6", *IETF RFC 3810*, June 2004.

[RFC3973]. A. Adams, J. Nicholas, and W. Siadak, "Protocol Independent Multicast – Dense Mode (PIM-DM): Protocol Specification (Revised)", *IETF RFC 3973*, January 2005.

[RFC4271]. Y. Rekhter, T. Li, and S. Hares, Eds., "A Border Gateway Protocol 4 (BGP-4)", *IETF RFC 4271*, January 2006.

[RFC4291]. R. Hinden and S. Deering, "IP Version 6 Addressing Architecture", *IETF RFC 4291*, February 2006.

[RFC4604]. H. Holbrook, B. Cain, and B. Haberman, "Using Internet Group Management Protocol Version 3 (IGMPv3) and Multicast Listener Discovery Protocol Version 2 (MLDv2) for Source-Specific Multicast", *IETF RFC 4604*, August 2006.

[RFC4607]. H. Holbrook and B. Cain, "Source-Specific Multicast for IP", *IETF RFC 4607*, August 2006

[RFC4610]. D. Farinacci and Y. Cai, "Anycast-RP Using Protocol Independent Multicast (PIM)", *IETF RFC 4610*, August 2006.

[RFC4611]. M. McBride, J. Meylor, and D. Meyer, "Multicast Source Discovery Protocol (MSDP) Deployment Scenarios", *IETF RFC 4611*, August 2006.

[RFC4632]. V. Fuller and T. Li, "Classless Inter-domain Routing (CIDR): The Internet Address Assignment and Aggregation Plan", *IETF RFC 4632*, August 2006.

[RFC4760]. T. Bates, R. Chandra, D. Katz, and Y. Rekhter, "Multiprotocol Extensions for BGP-4", *IETF RFC 4760*, January 2007.

[RFC4786]. J. Abley and K. Lindqvist, "Operation of Anycast Services", *IETF RFC 4786*, December 2006.

[RFC5015]. M. Handley, I. Kouvelas, T. Speakman, and L. Vicisano, "Bidirectional Protocol Independent Multicast (BIDIR-PIM)", *IETF RFC 5015*, October 2007.

[RFC5059]. N. Bhaskar, A. Gall, J. Lingard, and S. Venaas, "Bootstrap Router (BSR) Mechanism for Protocol Independent Multicast (PIM)", *IETF RFC 5059*, January 2008.

[RFC7761]. B. Fenner, M. Handley, H. Holbrook, I. Kouvelas, R. Parekh, Z. Zhang, and L. Zheng, "Protocol Independent Multicast – Sparse Mode (PIM-SM): Protocol Specification (Revised)", *IETF RFC 7761*, March 2016.

[RFC8313]. P. Tarapore, Ed., R. Sayko, G. Shepherd, T. Eckert, Ed., and R. Krishnan, "Use of Multicast across Inter-domain Peering Points", *IETF RFC 8313*, January 2018.

[RFC8704]. K. Sriram, D. Montgomery, and J. Haas, "Enhanced Feasible-Path Unicast Reverse Path Forwarding", *IETF RFC 8704*, February 2020.

2 Multicast Group Membership Management

2.1 INTRODUCTION

The Internet Group Management Protocol (IGMP) for IPv4 and the Multicast Listener Discovery (MLD) for IPv6 are protocols for discovering multicast group membership in IP networks. IGMP has three versions (IGMPv1 [RFC1112], IGMPv2 [RFC2236], and IGMPv3 [RFC3376] [RFC4604]), while MLD has two versions (MLDv1 [RFC2710] and MLDv2 [RFC3810]). IP hosts use IGMP to signal (or report) their desire to join particular multicast groups to immediately attached multicast routers, while multicast routers use IGMP to discover which hosts are members of a multicast group on a directly attached network segment (including IP subnets and point-to-point links).

IGMP and MLD have some very close similarities. The functions supported by MLDv1 are similar and almost equivalent to those supported by IGMPv2, while those supported by MLDv2 are equivalent to IGMPv3. Although IGMPv1 is now obsolete, having been replaced by IGMPv2 and the newer IGMPv3, we include it in our discussions to illustrate how IGMP has evolved and to highlight the features IGMPv1 shares with the newer versions. We explain the workings of IGMPv1 and the features integrated into it to obtain IGMPv2 and IGMPv3.

2.2 BASIC OPERATION

A multicast router uses the information obtained through IGMP to maintain a list of the multicast group memberships on each of its interfaces. The router considers a particular multicast group to be active on an interface if at least one host on that interface has signaled (via IGMP Membership Report message) its desire to receive multicast traffic sent to that group.

The basic operation of IGMP (common to all versions) can be summarized by the following.

- One router called the IGMP Querier, periodically broadcasts IGMP Query messages through its outgoing interfaces to all attached hosts.
- IP hosts respond to the IGMP Query messages by sending IGMP Membership Report messages indicating their multicast group memberships.

DOI: 10.1201/9781032701967-2

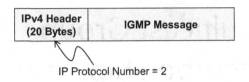

FIGURE 2.1   IGMP message in an IP packet.

- All multicast routers receive the IGMP Membership Report messages and note the multicast group memberships of the active IP hosts on the network segment.
- If a multicast router does not receive a Membership Report message for a particular multicast group for a period of time, it assumes that no more members of the group are on the network segment.

It is important to note that a multicast router itself may be a member of one or more multicast groups, implying that the router will perform both the multicast routing protocol functions (including those required to collect multicast group membership information), and the host multicast group membership functions (to inform itself and other neighboring multicast routers of its multicast group memberships). Thus, a multicast router that is a member of multicast groups is expected to behave as both an IGMP host and a multicast router, which means it may respond to its own transmitted IGMP Query messages.

IGMP messages (all versions) are encapsulated directly in IP packets, with the IP Protocol Number of 2 in the IP packet header (Figure 2.1). Other protocols, such as Internet Control Message Protocol (ICMP) with IP Protocol Number 1, Open Shortest Path First (OSPF) with IP Protocol Number 89, Enhanced Interior Gateway Routing Protocol (EIGRP) with IP Protocol Number 88, and the Stream Control Transmission Protocol (SCTP) with IP Protocol Number 132, are all carried directly in IP packets with their corresponding Protocol Numbers.

Multicast routers send all IGMP messages as raw IP packets with an IP time-to-live (TTL) value of 1, therefore, IGMP messages have local scope and are not forwarded by routers. However, since raw IP transport (by design) is not a reliable transport, some IGMP messages are sent multiple times to provide reliability in message delivery.

2.3 INTERNET GROUP MANAGEMENT PROTOCOL VERSION 1 (IGMPv1)

All IGMPv1 messages have the format depicted in Figure 2.2 [RFC1112]. IGMPv1 contains two types of messages: Membership Query (Type =1) and Membership Report (Type =2). It is important to note that when a multicast router sends an IGMPv1 Membership Query message on a network segment, the Group Address field (as illustrated in Figure 2.2) is zeroed, and this field is ignored when received by any host.

```
0        3      7           15            23           31
┌────────┬──────┬───────────────┬────────────────────────┐
│Version │ Type │   Unused      │       Checksum         │
├────────┴──────┴───────────────┴────────────────────────┤
│                   Group Address                         │
└─────────────────────────────────────────────────────────┘
```

- **Version (4 Bits)**: RFC 1112 specifies version 1 of IGMP.

- **Type (3 Bits)**: Two types of IGMPv1 messages:
  Type Code = 1 (0x1): Membership Query
  Type Code = 2 (0x2): Membership Report

- **Unused (8 Bits)**: This is an unused field. It is set to zero when sent and ignored when received.

- **Checksum (16 Bits)**: This checksum is the 16-bit one's complement of the one's complement sum of the 8-octet IGMP message. To compute the checksum, the Checksum field is set to zero.

- **Group Address (32 Bits)**: In a Host Membership Query message, the Group Address field is set to zero when sent and ignored when received. In a Host Membership Report message, the Group Address field holds the IP host group address of the group being reported.

FIGURE 2.2 IGMPv1 message format.

On the other hand, when a host sends an IGMPv1 Membership Report message, the Group Address field contains the IP address of the multicast group being reported (i.e., the multicast group the host wants to join or is already a member of). The destination address of the IP packet carrying the Report message is also set to the multicast group address being reported. It is important to note that that the source address of the IP packet carrying an IGMPv1 Membership Query or Report message is always set to the IP address of the sending interface.

A multicast router periodically sends IGMPv1 Membership Query messages (sometimes simply called Queries) on a network segment to discover which multicast groups have members. These periodic Query messages are multicast to all hosts and routers on the local network segment. The sending router sets the destination address of the IP packet carrying the Query message to the All-Hosts multicast group address 224.0.0.1 (also called the All-Systems multicast address on the local subnet), and each message carries an IP TTL of 1. Hosts on the network segment respond to a Query message by sending IGMPv1 Membership Report messages (also called Reports), indicating the multicast group to which they belong on the network.

A single Query message applies to all multicast group memberships on the interface (or equivalently, the network segment) on which the Query is sent/received. An IGMPv1 Membership Query message is equivalent to the IGMPv2 General Query message discussed in the subsequent text; both perform the same functions. A Report message applies only to the multicast group membership identified by the Group Address field in the message, and on the interface or network segment on which the Report is sent/received.

Multicast routers transmit Query messages periodically on a network segment as a way of refreshing their knowledge of multicast group memberships on the network. If a router does not receive Report messages for a particular group on a network segment after some number of Query messages have been sent, it assumes that the group has no active members and will stop forwarding remotely originated multicast traffic to that group on the network segment. The routers normally send Query messages infrequently (no more than once a minute according to [RFC1112]) to keep the IGMP transmission overhead on hosts and the network segment very low. However, a multicast router may be configured at startup to transmit several closely-spaced Query messages on a network segment to build up its knowledge of multicast group memberships quickly on the network.

Additionally, anytime a host wants to join a new multicast group on any one of its interfaces, it will immediately send an unsolicited IGMPv1 Membership Report message for that group rather than waiting for a Query message on the interface. Furthermore, to handle the situation where the initial Report message sent may be lost or damaged, a host may send repeated Report messages, once or twice after short delays [RFC1112].

2.3.1   Using IGMPv1 Membership Query and Report Messages

IP hosts on a network segment use two techniques to prevent a sudden surge of concurrent Report messages and to reduce the total number of Reports they transmit:

1. When a host receives a Query message, instead of immediately responding with a Report message, the host starts a countdown *report delay timer* for each of the multicast groups it is a member of on the network interface on which the Query message was received.
   a. The host sets each timer to a different, randomly selected value between 0 and 10 seconds (the default value as per [RFC1112]).
   b. When the *report delay timer* expires, the host generates a Report message for the corresponding multicast group. Using this timer causes Report messages to be spread out over the 10-second report delay interval instead of all occurring at the same time.
2. When a host sends a Report message, it sets the IP destination address of the carrying IP packet equal to the multicast group address reported in the IGMPv1 message's Group Address field, and the IP TTL to 1, enabling other members of the same multicast group on the same network segment to overhear the Report's contents.
   a. If any host on that network sees a Report message for a multicast group to which it belongs, it stops its own timer for that group, and suppresses sending its own Report message for that group (see Section 2.3.3). This is because the attached routers already know that at least one host on the local network segment is interested in the multicast group. This means that under normal circumstances, only the member host whose *report delay timer* expires first will generate a Report message for each group present on the network.

b. It is important to note that all the multicast routers connected to the network segment will receive all Query and Report messages, and therefore, no particular router needs to explicitly address such Report messages. Also, the routers need not know the individual identity of member hosts of a group, but only that at least one host on the network segment belongs to a particular group (i.e., only needs to know if a particular group has any active member).

3. A host may also send an unsolicited IGMP Report message to the address of the multicast group it wants to join, without having to wait for IGMP Query messages from the IGMP Querier.

There are two exceptions to the IGMPv1 Membership Report processing behaviors described earlier:

- First, if a host finds that a *report delay timer* is already running for a particular multicast group when a Query message is received, it does not reset that timer to a new random value but rather will allow it to continue running with its current value.
- Second, a host never sets a *report delay timer* for its membership in the All-Hosts multicast group 224.0.0.1 and never reports that membership.

To be valid, Query and Report messages must have the correct lengths, and correct Checksum field values, as well as carry the correct IP destination address in the IP packet header and the message's Group Address field as discussed previously.

2.3.2   IGMPv1 QUERIER

The main reason for having a single router on a network segment acting as the IGMP Querier when multiple multicast routers exist is to prevent all these routers from sending Query messages and wasting network bandwidth. The IGMP Querier is responsible for sending Query messages, while the Non-Queriers just passively eavesdrop on all Query-Response exchanges.

Unfortunately, [RFC1112], which specifies IGMPv1, does not specify how the IGMPv1 Querier is chosen on a network segment with multiple routers attached. Multicast protocols such as PIM elect a Designated Router (DR) for each network segment when multiple routers exist to perform certain multicast forwarding functions, as discussed in Chapter 5. IGMPv1, therefore, assumes that the DR for the network segment will also perform the Querier functions. Additionally, in IGMPv1, the DR elected by the multicast routing protocol like PIM also performs the IGMP Querier functions. IGMPv2 [RFC2236] clarifies this situation by defining how the Querier is elected on a network segment as discussed later. Chapter 5 describes how the PIM DR is elected for a network segment. By defining the IGMP Querier election process, IGMPv2 keeps the Querier and DR functions separate, meaning a network segment may support two nodes, one dedicated to each function.

2.3.3   IGMP REPORT SUPPRESSION MECHANISM

As discussed earlier, if a member host of a multicast group observes an IGMPv1 Membership Report message for the same group from another host on the same network segment, it cancels its *report delay timer* associated with that group, thereby suppressing the generation of its own Report message for that group. The *IGMP Report Suppression mechanism* has become a useful tool for reducing the amount of IGMP traffic generated on a network segment needed to maintain a multicast group state in routers.

However, because of the Report Suppression mechanism, routers are not able to keep track of the individual hosts on a network segment that are active members of a multicast group on the segment. Multicast routers can only keep track of active multicast groups on a network segment. Also, even if multicast routers were able to keep track of the active members per multicast group, doing so is not desirable for the following reasons:

- This prevents the scalability of IGMP on network segments with a large number of hosts.
- As a multicast router forwards multicast traffic on a multicast group address and interface basis, the router does not need to keep track of the identity of each host member of a multicast group.

2.3.4   IGMPv1 QUERY-RESPONSE PROCESS

IGMP works primarily on a *Query-Response model*, as described in Figure 2.3. It is important to note that this model does not preclude hosts from sending unsolicited IGMPv1 Membership Report messages when they want to join a multicast group. The Query-Response model allows a multicast router to send Query messages on a network segment to determine which multicast groups are active on the segment. An active multicast group is one with at least one host interested in multicast traffic sent to that group.

As a result of the Query-Response message exchange, all multicast routers on the network segment can determine if there are active receivers for multicast groups on the segment. Routers which are Non-Queriers on the network segment passively eavesdrop on the Query-Response exchange to obtain the same information as the current IGMP Querier.

2.3.5   IGMPv1 MULTICAST GROUP JOIN PROCESS

To reduce the time it takes for a new host on a network segment to join a multicast group to receive multicast traffic from the source, the host can immediately send an unsolicited IGMPv1 Membership Report message without having to wait for the next IGMPv1 Membership Query message from the Querier as described in Figure 2.4. Sending unsolicited Report messages significantly reduces the join delays for new hosts on the network interested in receiving traffic from a multicast group.

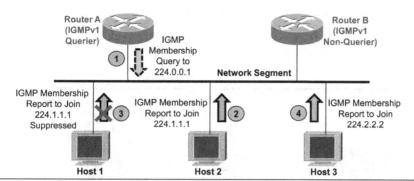

- Router A is assumed to be the IGMPv1 Querier for the network segment and is responsible for sending Query messages.
- Router B is a non-Querier and simply listens on the network segment and records responses from the attached hosts.
- Hosts 1 and 2 each want to join multicast group 244.1.1.1 to receive traffic from the source. Host 3 wants to join multicast group 224.2.2.2.

Processing steps:

1. The IGMPv1 Querier, Router A, periodically sends IGMPv1 Membership Query messages on the network segment with the destination address of the carrying IP packets set to the All-Hosts multicast group address 224.0.0.1. All hosts must listen on this group address to receive Query messages. The Group Address field of the IGMPv1 Query message is set to zero and is ignored when received.
2. All host on the network segment receive the Query message. We assume Host 2 is the first to respond by sending an IGMPv1 Membership Report message with the destination address of the carrying IP packet set to the multicast group address 224.1.1.1. The Group Address field of the IGMPv1 Report message is also set to the group address 224.1.1.1.
3. Because Host 1 is also listening to the multicast group address 224.1.1.1, it also hears the IGMPv1 Report message that was sent by Host 2. Host 1 observes that Host 2 has already informed the routers on the network segment that there is at least one host interested in traffic sent to multicast group 224.1.1.1 and, therefore, suppresses the sending of its Report for group 224.1.1.1. IGMP Report Suppression helps to reduce the amount of traffic on the network segment.
4. Host 3 also receives the IGMPv1 Membership Query message and responds by sending an IGMPv1 Membership Report message with the destination address of the carrying IP packet set to the multicast group address 224.2.2.2. The Group Address field of the IGMPv1 Report message is also set to the group address 224.2.2.2.

This Query-Response exchange allows Router A to be aware of are active members for multicast groups 224.1.1.1 and 224.2.2.2 on the local network segment. Additionally, Router B, which has been eavesdropping on the network segment, also becomes aware of the active members of these multicast groups.

FIGURE 2.3   IGMPv1 Query-Response process.

The destination addresses of the IP packet carrying the Report message and the message's Group Address field are both set to the multicast group address the host wants to join. The IGMPv1 Report message signals to the local multicast router that the host wants to receive traffic from the reported multicast group (in the message's Group Address field). The information in the Report messages allows the multicast routers to maintain appropriate state information about multicast group addresses and their interfaces.

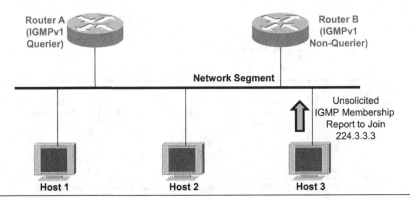

- Let us assume that Host 3 wants to join multicast group 224.3.3.3 to receive traffic from the source.
- Instead of waiting for the IGMPv1 Querier, Router A, to send the next IGMPv1 Membership Query message on the network segment, Host 3 immediately sends an unsolicited IGMPv1 Membership Report message with the destination address of carrying IP packet set to 224.3.3.3. The Group Address field of the IGMPv1 Report message is also set to the group address 224.3.3.3. This Report message informs the routers on the network segment of Host 3's desire to join multicast group 224.3.3.3.

FIGURE 2.4   IGMPv1 multicast group join process.

2.3.6 IGMPv1 Multicast Group Leave Process

Unlike IGMPv2 which defines the Leave Group message, IGMPv1 was designed with simplicity in mind. In IGMPv1, when a host wants to leave a multicast group, it does not send any IGMP message to signal that it simply leaves quietly. IGMPv2 hosts use the Leave Group message to notify the multicast routers that they no longer want to receive traffic from a particular multicast group. In IGMPv1, a leaving host simply stops accepting multicast traffic sent to the multicast group and ceases sending IGMPv1 Membership Report messages in response to Query messages sent by the IGMP Querier to the group.

Therefore, the only way a multicast router using IGMPv1 can confirm that an interface (or network segment) has no longer an active member of a multicast group is when the router stops receiving Report messages for that group. To do this, the IGMPv1 router associates a countdown timer for each multicast group on the interface. When the router receives a Report message for a group on the interface, it resets the timer associated with that group.

The default setting of the IGMPv1 timeout interval is three times the *Query Interval* or 3 minutes. When no Report message is received for the multicast group and the timer expires, the router declares the group as inactive (i.e., no active members on the interface). A 3-minute timeout interval setting means that the router may continue to forward multicast traffic onto the network segment for up to 3 minutes after all members of the multicast group have left. Instead of allowing hosts to leave a multicast group silently, IGMPv2 solves the leave problem by defining the Leave Group message as discussed in the later section.

2.4 INTERNET GROUP MANAGEMENT PROTOCOL VERSION 2 (IGMPv2)

IGMPv2 was developed to address some of the deficiencies of IGMPv1 as discussed previously and to incorporate some features that will provide better multicast group membership management.

2.4.1 KEY IGMPv2 FEATURES

The following are the key features of IGMPv2:

- **IGMPv2 Query messages**: IGMPv2 Query messages (see Figure 2.5) are split into two categories, General Query messages and Group-Specific Query messages.
  - **General Query messages**: A multicast router sends these messages to determine which multicast groups are active on a network segment.

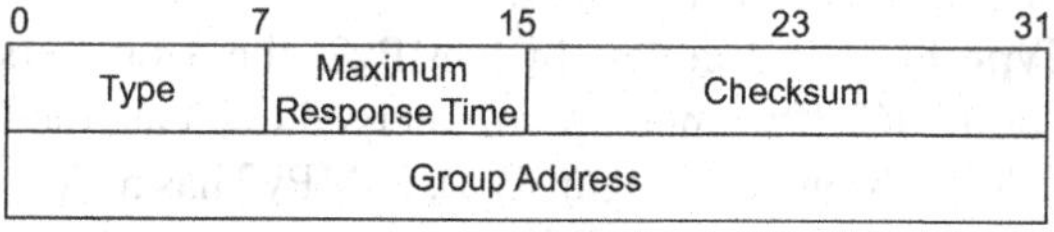

0	7	15	23	31
Type	Maximum Response Time		Checksum	
Group Address				

- **Type (8 Bits)**: RFC 2236 specifies three types of IGMPv2 messages of concern to the host- router interaction:
  - Type Code = 0x11: Membership Query
    There are two sub-types of Membership Query messages:
    - General Query, used to learn which groups have members on an attached network.
    - Group-Specific Query, used to learn if a particular group has any members on an attached network.
  - Type Code = 0x16: Version 2 Membership Report
  - Type Code = 0x17: Leave Group
  An additional type of message, for backwards-compatibility with IGMPv1 is:
  - Type Code = 0x12: Version 1 Membership Report

- **Maximum Response Time (8 Bits)**: This field is meaningful only in Membership Query messages and specifies the maximum allowed time (in units of 1/10 second) a host must wait before sending a responding Report message. In all other messages, this field is set to zero by the sender and ignored by receivers.

- **Checksum (16 Bits)**: The checksum is the 16-bit one's complement of the one's complement sum of the whole IGMP message (the entire IP payload). For computing the checksum, the Checksum field is set to zero. When transmitting packets, the checksum MUST be computed and inserted into this field. When receiving packets, the checksum MUST be verified before processing a packet.

- **Group Address (32 Bits)**: In a Membership Query message, a router sets the Group Address field to zero when sending a General Query and sets it to the group address being queried when sending a Group-Specific Query. In a Membership Report or Leave Group message, a host sets the Group Address field to the IP multicast group address of the group being reported or left.

FIGURE 2.5 IGMPv2 message format.

These messages perform the same function as the IGMPv1 Membership Query messages. A General Query message has its Group Address field set to all zeros when sent (to differentiate it from a Group-Specific Query). The source address of the carrying IP packet is set to the IP address of the sending interface and the destination address is set to the All-Host multicast address 224.0.0.1.

- **Group-Specific Query messages**: These messages allow the IGMP Querier to query specific multicast groups instead of all groups on a network segment. A multicast router sends these messages to determine if a specific multicast group still has any remaining active members; these queries are directed to a single multicast group. For these messages, both the message's Group Address field and the destination address of the carrying IP packet are set to the address of the multicast group being queried. The source address of the IP packet is set to the IP address of the sending interface. It is essential to note that hosts that receive Group-Specific Query messages respond in the same way as when they receive General Query messages.

- **IGMPv2 Type field and codes**: In IGMPv2, the 4-bit Version and 4-bit Type fields of the IGMPv1 message are merged to create the IGMPv2 message Type field, an 8-bit field (Figure 2.5); IGMPv2 has no Version field. The codes assigned to the various IGMPv2 message types have been selected to ensure backward compatibility with IGMPv1. The Type codes enable IGMPv2 routers and hosts to recognize IGMPv1 messages when IGMPv1 routers and hosts also exist on the network.

  - **Type code = 0x11**: IGMPv2 Membership Query (with sub-types, General Query and Group-Specific Query).
    - In the IGMPv1 Membership Query message, the Version field is set to 0x1 and the Type field is set to 0x1. These two values together combine to form the 8-bit value 0x11, which is the same as the Type code for the IGMPv2 Membership Query. The IGMPv2 Type code of 0x11 is chosen to provide compatibility between IGMPv2 and IGMPv1.

  - **Type code = 0x12**: IGMPv1 Membership Report message.
    - In the IGMPv1 Membership Report message, the Version field is set to 0x1 and the Type field is set to 0x2. These two values together combine to form the 8-bit value 0x12, which is the same as the Type code when IGMPv2 carries an IGMPv1 Membership Report. The IGMPv2 Type code of 0x12 is chosen to provide backward compatibility with IGMPv1.

  - **Type code = 0x16**: IGMPv2 Membership Report message.
  - **Type code = 0x17**: IGMPv2 Leave Group message.

- **Query-Response process**: The *IGMPv2 General Query-Response process* is the same as in IGMPv1.

- **Maximum Response Time field**: This field in the IGMPv2 message (previously unused in IGMPv1 messages) allows the IGMP Querier to specify the maximum Query-Response time. This time is used only in IGMP

Membership Query messages and is used to tune the Query-Response process to control the burstiness of host responses and fine-tune host leave latencies.

- **IGMPv2 Leave Group messages**: These messages allow hosts on a network segment to notify attached multicast routers that they wish to leave a multicast group. It is important to note that when a Leave Group or Membership Report message is sent, the message's Group Address field is set to the target multicast group address, and the source address of the carrying IP packet is set to the IP address of the sending interface. For a Report message, the destination address of the carrying IP is the address of the multicast group being reported, while for a Leave Group message, the destination address is the All-Routers multicast group address 224.0.0.2.

- **IGMPv2 Querier election process**: This IGMPv2 allows multicast routers on a network segment to elect the Querier rather than rely on the multicast routing protocol to perform this function.

The destination addresses of the carrying IP packet for IGMPv2 messages are summarized in the following table:

IGMPv2 Message Type	Destination IP Address
General Query	All-Hosts multicast group address (224.0.0.1)
Group-Specific Query	The multicast group being queried
Membership Report	The multicast group being reported
Leave Message	All-Routers multicast group address (224.0.0.2)

2.4.1.1 Purpose of the Maximum Response Time Field

A *Maximum Response Time* can be configured on the IGMP Querier, which then informs (via this field) all hosts on a network segment of the upper limit of the delay they should place on their responses to Query messages. The value in this field specifies the maximum time (in units of 1/10 of a second) that a host on a network segment may wait to send a response to a received Query message.

Hosts on a network segment use the value in this field (default value is 100, meaning 10 seconds) as the upper limit for their *group report-timers*, which are set to random values. The randomly set group report-timers are used by hosts in their Report Suppression process. The Maximum Response Time field value may be tuned to control, either the burstiness of how hosts on a network segment respond to group membership queries or their leave latencies.

Varying the setting of this field allows the network operator (via the IGMPv2 routers) to tune host leave latencies and the burstiness of IGMP traffic on a network segment. The host leave latency is the time between the moment the last host on a network segment leaves a multicast group, and when the multicast routing protocol on attached routers is notified that there are no more members of that group on that segment. This feature is useful when a large number of hosts are active on the network segment (e.g., IP subnet), and there is the need to spread out the responses to Query messages over a long period.

2.4.1.2   Purpose of the IGMPv2 Leave Group Message

IGMPv2 introduced the Leave Group message as a mechanism for improving multicast group membership notification latency. A host on a network segment sends a Leave message to the local multicast router that it wishes to leave a particular multicast group (specified in the Group Address field) and, therefore, is no longer interested in receiving multicast traffic to this group.

Reference [RFC2236] states that a host should send a Leave Group message when it leaves a multicast group for which it was the last host to respond to a Query message, by sending an IGMP Membership Report message. However, given that allowing a host to check if it was the last host to respond to the Query with a Report message will take considerable software code implementation, most IGMPv2 implementations simply allow the host to send a Leave Group message when it leaves a group.

Receiving a Leave group message causes the IGMP Querier to possibly reduce the remaining lifetime of the state information it is maintaining for the group and to send an IGMP Group-Specific Query message to the multicast group. Sending Leave Group messages also optimizes the performance of IGMP Snooping which is used in Ethernet (Layer 2) switches to constrain multicast traffic to only switch ports with active members of a multicast group (see discussion in the subsequent section). If hosts on a LAN do not send Leave Group messages when they leave multicast groups (as in IGMPv1), then the IGMP Snooping switches will have no way to tell when all hosts on a switch port have left a multicast group and, therefore, will continue to forward that multicast traffic out that switch port.

IGMPv2 Group-Specific Query and Leave Group messages enable multicast routers and hosts on a network segment to reduce group leave latencies from minutes to seconds, a problem noticed in IGMPv1. It is important to note that IGMPv3 does not use the Leave Group message because it supports a source address filtering mechanism, offering the same functionality as the IGMPv3 discussed in a later section.

2.4.2   IGMP TIMERS AND DEFAULT VALUES

As discussed previously, multicast routers use IGMP to discover which multicast groups have members on each of the interfaces (or network segments) they are attached to. Each multicast router maintains a list of multicast group memberships for each interface along with a timer for each group membership. A multicast group membership represents simply the router's awareness of the presence of at least one active member of a multicast group on a given interface and not a list of the identities of all the group members on the interface.

IGMPv2 uses several timers, most of which are configurable on IGMPv2 systems (hosts and routers) [RFC2236]. If non-default settings are used, the network operator must ensure that they are consistent among all routers on a single network segment.

- **Robustness Variable**: This variable (default is 2) provides a mechanism for tuning the expected packet loss on a network segment (IP subnet). The network operator may increase the Robustness Variable if a network segment is expected to be lossy. IGMP is designed to be robust to ["Robustness Variable" minus 1] packet losses. This variable must not be 0, and should not be 1.

- **Query Interval**: This is the interval (default is 125 seconds) between General Query messages sent on a network segment by the Querier. The network operator may vary the Query Interval to tune the number of IGMP messages on the network segment; larger values cause the Querier to send IGMP Query messages less often.
- **Query Response Interval**: This specifies the Maximum Response Time (default is 100, meaning 10 seconds) that the Querier inserts into the periodic IGMP General Query messages it sends. The network operator may vary the Query Response Interval to tune the burstiness of IGMP messages on the network segment; using larger values makes the IGMP traffic less bursty, as response messages from hosts are spread out over a larger interval. The number of seconds obtained from the specified Query Response Interval must be less than the Query Interval.
- **Group Membership Interval**: This is the amount of time that must pass before a multicast router declares that a network segment has no more members of a multicast group. This setting of this interval must be the ["Robustness Variable" times the "Query Interval" plus one "Query Response Interval"].
- **Other Querier Present Interval**: This is the length of time that must pass before a multicast router on a network segment decides that there is no longer another multicast router on the segment that should play the role of the Querier. The setting of this interval must be the ["Robustness Variable" times the "Query Interval" plus one half of one "Query Response Interval"].
- **Startup Query Interval**: This is the interval (default is 1/4 of the "Query Interval") between General Query messages that the Querier on a network segment sends at startup.
- **Startup Query Count**: This is the number of Query messages (default is the "Robustness Variable") sent out by a multicast router on a network segment at startup, spaced apart by the "Startup Query Interval".
- **Last Member Query Interval**: This is the Maximum Response Time (default is 10, meaning 1 second) that the Querier on a network segment inserts into Group-Specific Query messages and sends in response to Leave Group messages. It is also the length of the spacing time between Group-Specific Query messages. The network operator may tune this interval to modify the host leave latencies on the network segment. Using a reduced value results in reduced time for multicast routers on a network segment to detect the loss of the last member of a multicast group.
- **Last Member Query Count**: This is the number of Group-Specific Query messages (default is the "Robustness Variable") sent on a network segment before the sending router assumes there are no members of the queried group on the segment.

- **Unsolicited Report Interval**: This is the length of time (default is 10 seconds) a host must wait before repeating the sending of its initial Report of membership for a multicast group.
- **Version 1 Router Present Timeout**: This is the length of time (default is 400 seconds) a host on a network segment must wait after hearing an IGMPv1 Query message before it may send any IGMPv2 messages.

At startup, an IGMP Querier sends IGMP General Query messages at intervals equal to the "Startup Query Interval", which is one-quarter of the IGMP General "Query Interval". The number of Query messages, that is the "Startup Query Count", is configurable. After startup, the IGMP Querier periodically sends IGMP General Query messages at intervals equal to the "Query Interval" to check for multicast group members on the network segment. The network operator can modify the "Query Interval" based on the actual condition of the network.

An IGMPv2 Querier transmits IGMP Group-Specific Query messages at intervals equal to the "Last Member Query Interval" when it receives an IGMP Leave message. The IGMPv3 Querier transmits IGMP Group-and-Source-Specific Query messages at intervals equal to the "Last Member Query Interval" when it receives a multicast group and multicast mapping change Report. The number of Query messages, that is the "Last Member Query Count", has a default setting equal to the "Robustness Variable", which is the maximum number of message retransmissions.

A host starts a *report delay timer* when it receives an IGMP Query message (i.e., General Query, Group-Specific Query, or Group-and-Source-Specific Query) for each multicast group it has joined. The host initializes this timer to a random value in the range of 0 to the Maximum Response Time derived from the IGMP Query message. When the timer expires, that is, decreases to 0, the host sends an IGMP Membership Report message to the corresponding multicast group.

2.4.3 IGMPv2 QUERIER

Only one router on a particular network segment/link (called the IGMP Querier) is responsible for sending IGMP Query messages to the segment. This means a multicast router may assume one of two roles concerning each of its attached network segments: Querier or Non-Querier. Under normal operations, only one Querier must exist per network segment. In IGMPv1, routers depend on the multicast routing protocol to decide which router is to become the IGMP Querier. IGMPv2, on the other hand, introduced an IGMP Querier election mechanism for choosing the Querier on a link (see Figure 2.6), instead of depending on the multicast routing protocol to do so. In IGMPv2, the multicast routers on a network segment use the source IP addresses in the IP packets carrying IGMP General Query messages to elect the IGMP Querier.

The IGMPv2 Querier election process is illustrated in Figure 2.6 and can be summarized as follows:

1. By default, when a multicast router running IGMP first starts up, it assumes the role of the IGMP Querier for the network segment.

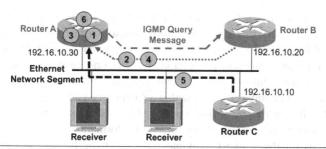

- An IGMP Querier sends IGMP Query messages and receives IGMP Membership Report and Leave messages from hosts on a network segment.
- An IGMP Non-Querier receives only IGMP Membership Report messages from hosts on a network segment.
- For each attached network segment, a multicast router assumes the role of a Querier or Non-Querier for that network. Each network segment has only one Querier at any given time.
- Any multicast router that starts up on an attached network segment starts as a Querier.
- A multicast router on each attached network for which it is the Querier, periodically sends an IGMP General Query message (determined by the "Query Interval Timer") to solicit multicast group membership information.

Processing steps:

1. Router A starts up on the network segment and considers itself the IGMP Querier for the segment. Router A starts sending IGMP General Query messages to other nodes on the network segment.
   - The destination address in the IP packet carrying the General Query message is set to the All-Routers multicast address 224.0.0.1 and the source address set to the IP address of the sending interface. The Group Address field in the IGMPv2 message is zeroed and ignored when received.
2. If Router A hears an IGMP General Query message sent from another router (Router B) with a lower IP address on the network segment, it reverts to the role of a Non-Querier
   - When a router receives a General Query, it compares the source address in the carrying IP packet with its own receiving interface IP address. The router with the lowest IP address assumes the role of the Querier on the network segment.
3. Upon receiving this message, Router A immediately starts the "Other Querier Present Timer", and records Router B as the IGMP Querier of the network segment.
4. If Router A (the Non-Querier) receives another IGMP Query message from Router B (the Querier), it updates the "Other Querier Present Timer".
5. If Router A receives an IGMP General Query message from any other router (Router C) on the network segment with a lower IP address than that of the current Querier, it changes its local Querier setting to Router C and updates the "Other Querier Present Timer".
6. If Router A is still in the Non-Querier state and the "Other Querier Present Timer" expires, it reverts to the role of the Querier.
   - That is, if a multicast router has not heard an IGMP Query message from another router (for a time period equal to the "Other Querier Present Interval"), it assumes the role of Querier.

FIGURE 2.6 IGMPv2 Querier election.

2. If the Querier on the segment receives an IGMP Query message from a router on the same segment with a lower IP address, it stops being the Querier for that segment.

3. If a router has stopped being the Querier for the segment, and has not received an IGMP Query message within a configured period, it assumes the Querier role again.

Each multicast router attached to a network segment starts up as a Querier. If the router receives a Query message from another router on that network segment with a lower IP address, it must revert to a Non-Querier on that network. If the router has not received a Query message from another router on that network segment for a period equal to the "Other Querier Present Interval", it resumes the role of Querier on that network. It is important to note that a router on an attached network segment for which it is the Querier, periodically sends a General Query message every "Query Interval" to solicit multicast group membership information.

All devices on the network segment (excluding the IGMP Querier) start the *query timer*, which is reset whenever an IGMP General Query message is received from the elected IGMP Querier. If no such message is received and the *query timer* expires, it is assumed that the current IGMP Querier has gone down, and the routers on the network segment go through the election process again to elect a new IGMP Querier.

To enable a router to quickly and reliably determine multicast group membership information on startup, it should send General Query messages equal to the "Startup Query Count", and spaced closely but apart by the "Startup Query Interval". It is essential to note that routers send General Query messages addressed to the All-Hosts multicast group address (224.0.0.1), with the Group Address field set to 0, and the Maximum Response Time field set to the value of "Query Response Interval".

Each Non-Querier router on the network segment starts a *querier timer* (i.e., the "Other Querier Present Timer") which is reset each time the router receives a General Query message from the IGMP Querier. The default setting (or duration) of the *querier timer* is two times the Query Timer (i.e., 250 seconds). Any time the querier timer expires, the local router assumes that the IGMP Querier has gone down, and restarts the Querier election process once again to elect a Querier for the network segment.

2.4.4 RESPONDING TO IGMPV2 GROUP MEMBERSHIP QUERIES

IGMPv1 and IGMPv2 both use an *IGMP Membership Report suppression mechanism* to prevent hosts from sending a "storm" of responses when an IGMP Query message is received. When a host on a network segment receives a General Query message, it sets *report delay timers* for each multicast group for which it is a member of that segment on which it received the message (excluding the All-Hosts multicast group). The host sets each timer to a different randomly selected value in the range 0 up to "Maximum Response Time", using the Maximum Response Time field value specified in the Query message.

When a host on a network segment receives a Group-Specific Query for the multicast group being queried and if it is a member of that group, it sets a *report delay timer* to a randomly selected value in the range 0 up to "Maximum Response Time" as above. If a timer for the queried multicast group is already running, the host resets this timer to the random value only if the Maximum Response Time field value in the Query message is less than the remaining value of the running timer.

When the timer associated with a multicast group expires, the host sends an IGMPv2 Membership Report message with the message's Group Address field set to the address of that group, and with the IP packet's TTL set to 1. If the host receives another Report message sent by another host on that network segment while it has an associated timer running for that specified group, it stops this timer but does not send a Report message, to suppress the flooding of duplicate Report messages on the network segment.

The purpose of this IGMP Membership Report suppression mechanism is to ensure that, under most conditions, only one IGMP Report message is sent for each multicast group in response to a single sent IGMP Query message. IGMPv3, on the other hand, eliminated the need for this mechanism, by packing multiple multicast group memberships in a single IGMP Message Report message as a way to reduce the number of messages sent, as discussed in the IGMPv3 section later.

2.4.5 HANDLING IGMP MEMBERSHIP REPORT MESSAGES

As discussed previously, when a host receives an IGMP Query message, it starts a timer with a randomly set expiration time for each group that it is a member of. When this timer expires, the host sends an IGMP Membership Report message addressed to that group. Any other hosts that receive this message and are members of the group, will cancel their timer for the group.

When a router receives a Report message from a host on a network segment, it adds the multicast group address being reported in the message to the list of multicast group memberships for that segment, and sets the timer for that membership to a period equal to the "Group Membership Interval". The router refreshes the timer upon receiving repeated Report messages for that group. If the router does not receive Report messages for a particular multicast group before its timer has expired, the router assumes that the group has no active members on the network segment and that there is no need to forward remotely originated multicast traffic for that group onto the network segment.

When a host on a network segment has the desire to join a multicast group, it should immediately transmit an unsolicited IGMPv2 Membership Report message for that group, in the event it is the first member of that group on that network segment. To handle the situations where the initial Membership Report is lost or damaged, [RFC2236] recommends that the host sends again such messages, once or twice, after short time delays equal to the "Unsolicited Report Interval".

2.4.6 EXPLAINING THE IGMPV2 LEAVE GROUP PROCESS

IGMPv1 has no efficient Leave process for hosts, which means a multicast router will continue forwarding traffic on a network segment for a multicast group for some time (several minutes) even if the last host on that group has left. By adding the Leave Group message, Group-Specific Query message, and the Maximum Response Time field, IGMPv2 can reduce the leave latencies for hosts to a few seconds, which is a significant improvement over IGMPv1.

Figure 2.7 illustrates the IGMPv2 Leave Group process and shows how this process is more efficient than that used in IGMPv1. This example shows that the Leave process in IGMPv2 is more deterministic and significantly reduces host leave latencies.

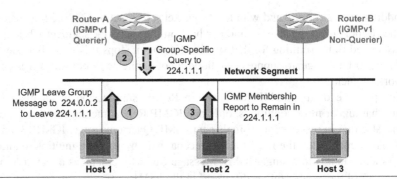

- Hosts 1 and 2 are currently members of multicast group 224.1.1.1, but Host 2 wants to leave the group.

Processing steps when Host 1 leaves the group:

1. Host 1 sends an IGMPv2 Leave Group message on the network segment with the destination address of the carrying IP packet set to the All-Routers multicast address 224.0.0.2. The Group Address field of the Leave Group message is also set to the group address 224.1.1.1. This message informs all routers on the network segment that Host 1 is leaving the group.
2. Router A, the IGMP Querier, notices the Leave Group message from Host 1. However, because a router on the network segment keeps a record of only the active multicast groups on the segment and not the individual host members of those groups. Router A sends an IGMPv2 Group-Specific Query to determine if there are any remaining members of group 224.1.1.1 on the network segment. Router A sends the Group-Specific Query with both of its carrying IP packet's destination address and the IGMPv2 message's Group Address field set to 224.1.1.1. This allows only active members of group 224.1.1.1 to respond to the Group-Specific Query message.
3. Host 2, which is still an active member of group 224.1.1.1, sees the Group-Specific Query and responds with an IGMPv2 Membership Report message to inform the routers on the network segment that there is still an active member of group 224.1.1.1 on the segment. The IGMP Report Suppression mechanism is still used here, allowing other active members of group 224.1.1.1 to suppress sending their Report messages after seeing Host 2's Report message.

Processing steps when Host 2 leaves the group:

4. Host 2 sends an IGMPv2 Leave Group message on the network segment with the destination address of the carrying IP packet set to the All-Routers multicast address 224.0.0.2. The Group Address field of the Leave Group message is also set to the group address 224.1.1.1.
5. Router A sends an IGMPv2 Group-Specific Query to determine if there are any remaining members of group 224.1.1.1 on the network segment. Router A sends the Group-Specific Query with both of its carrying IP packet's destination address and the IGMPv2 message's Group Address field set to 224.1.1.1.
6. Let us assume there are no remaining members of group 224.1.1.1 on the network segment, so no host responds to the Group-Specific Query message from Router A. Thus, Router A receives no response and waits for a time duration equal to the Last Member Query Interval and then sends another Group-Specific Query message to which no host responds. Router A then times out group 224.1.1.1 and stops forwarding multicast traffic to the group on the network segment.

FIGURE 2.7   IGMPv2 Leave Group process.

As discussed in a later section, IGMPv3 does not support the use of Leave Group messages but instead has a source address filtering mechanism that provides the same functionality.

When the Querier of a network segment receives a Leave Group message from a host for a multicast group that still has group members on that interface/segment, it sends the "Last Member Query Count" number of IGMPv2 Group-Specific Query messages spaced apart by the "Last Member Query Interval" to the group being left by the host. The Maximum Response Time field of these Group-Specific Query messages is also set to the "Last Member Query Interval". If the router does not receive Report messages after the response time of the last query expires, it assumes that the queried multicast group has no members on the network segment, as discussed previously. During this time, any router transition from Querier to Non-Querier is ignored, and the sending router keeps transmitting the Group-Specific Query messages.

Multicast routers that are Non-Queriers on a network segment must ignore Leave Group messages, and the Querier on the segment should ignore Leave Group messages sent to groups for which there are no group members on the interface. When a Non-Querier receives a Group-Specific Query message on a network segment, and if the *group membership timer* associated with that queried group is greater than the "Last Member Query Count" times the Maximum Response Time field value specified in the message, the Non-Querier sets the *group membership timer* to that resulting value.

2.5 INTERNET GROUP MANAGEMENT PROTOCOL VERSION 3 (IGMPv3)

IGMPv3 introduced the idea of "source filtering", which is a mechanism for a system to signal its interest in receiving multicast traffic sent to a particular multicast group address, but only from specific IP source addresses, or from all source addresses but excluding specific source addresses. Multicast protocols may use that information to avoid delivering multicast traffic from specific sources to network segments where there are no interested receivers. It is important to note that IGMPv3 Membership Query messages are not subjected to source filtering and these messages must always be processed by hosts and multicast routers.

The IGMPv3 Membership Report message was introduced to allow a host to include or exclude the list of source addresses for each multicast group of which it is a member or wants membership. Multicast routers receive IGMPv3 Report messages and can merge the IP source address requirements of different hosts for each multicast group. The IGMPv3 Membership Report feature (source filtering), in particular, is required to support PIM-Source-Specific Multicast (PIM-SSM) which is discussed in the PIM-SM chapter (Chapter 5). MLDv2, which works with IPv6, implements similar functionality as IGMPv3.

The two messages that are relevant to IGMPv3 are as follows:

- **Type code = 0x11**: IGMP Membership Query (for all versions)
- **Type code = 0x22**: IGMPv3 Membership Report

To support interoperation with previous versions of IGMP, IGMPv3 must also support the following three message types:

- **Type code = 0x12**: IGMPv1 Membership Report
- **Type code = 0x16**: IGMPv2 Membership Report
- **Type code = 0x17**: IGMPv2 Leave Group

Hosts and routers that receive unrecognized message types must silently ignore them. IGMPv3 is designed to be backward compatible with previous versions of IGMP. To remain backward compatible with IGMPv1 and IGMPv2 systems, an IGMPv3 multicast router must also implement IGMPv1 and IGMPv2.

2.5.1 IGMPv3 MEMBERSHIP QUERY MESSAGE

The IGMPv3 Membership Query message *maintains the same type code* (0x11) as the IGMPv2 Membership Query message but has slightly a different format with additional fields as shown in Figure 2.8. A multicast router sends IGMPv3 Membership Query messages on an interface to query the multicast reception state of interfaces on the same network segment as the sending interface.

The IGMP Querier sets the Group Address field to zero when sending a General Query message. The Querier sets this field to the multicast group address being queried when sending a Group-Specific Query or the newer IGMPv3 Group-and-Source-Specific Query message.

2.5.1.1 IGMPv3 Query Variants

IGMPv3 supports the following three variants of the Query message:

- **General Query message**: A multicast router sends this message to learn the *complete* multicast reception state of the interfaces on the same network segment on which the message is transmitted. In this message, the router sets both the Group Address field and the Number of Sources (N) field to zero.
- **Group-Specific Query message**: A multicast router sends this message to learn the reception state of the interfaces on the same network segment on which the message is transmitted, concerning a *single* multicast group address. In this message, the router sets the Group Address field to the multicast group address of interest and sets the Number of Sources (N) field to zero.
- **Group-and-Source-Specific Query message**: A multicast router sends this message to learn if any interface on the network segment on which the message was transmitted wants to receive packets sent to a specified multicast group address, from any of a specified list of sources. In this message, the router sets the Group Address field to the multicast group address of interest and sets the Source Address [i] fields to the source address(es) of interest.

In IGMPv3, routers send General Query messages with the IP destination address of the carrying IP packet set to 224.0.0.1, which is the All-Hosts (or All-Systems)

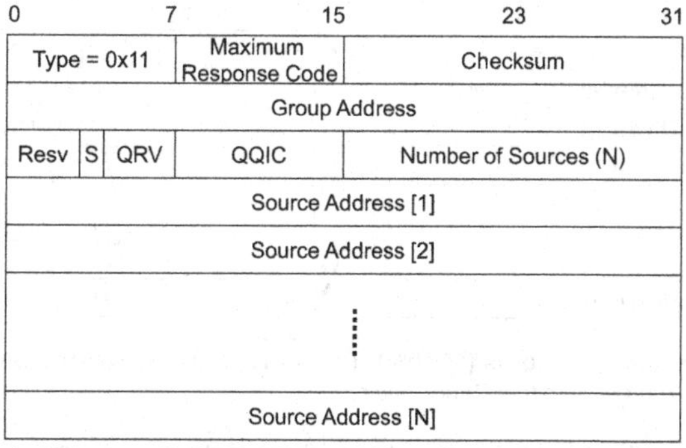

```
0           7          15          23          31
┌──────────────┬──────────────┬──────────────────────────┐
│ Type = 0x11  │   Maximum    │        Checksum          │
│              │Response Code │                          │
├──────────────┴──────────────┴──────────────────────────┤
│                   Group Address                         │
├────────┬─┬──────┬──────────┬──────────────────────────┤
│ Resv   │S│ QRV  │   QQIC   │  Number of Sources (N)    │
├────────┴─┴──────┴──────────┴──────────────────────────┤
│                 Source Address [1]                      │
├─────────────────────────────────────────────────────────┤
│                 Source Address [2]                      │
├─────────────────────────────────────────────────────────┤
│                                                         │
│                        ⋮                                │
│                                                         │
├─────────────────────────────────────────────────────────┤
│                 Source Address [N]                      │
└─────────────────────────────────────────────────────────┘
```

QRV = Querier Robustness Variable; QQIC = Querier's Query Interval Code; Resv = Reserved

- **Group Address (32 Bits):** The Group Address field is set to zero when sending a General Query message and set to the multicast group address being queried when sending a Group - Specific Query or Group-and-Source-Specific Query message.

- **Resv (4 Bits):** This field is set to zero on transmission and ignored on reception.

- **S Flag (1 Bit):** This bit is called the Suppress Router-Side Processing bit. When set to 1, the S Flag indicates to any receiving multicast routers that they are to suppress the normal timer updates they perform upon hearing a Query message. It does not, however, suppress the querier election or the normal "host-side" processing of a Query message that a router may be required to perform as a consequence of itself being a multicast group member.

- **QRV (3 Bits):** If non-zero, the QRV field contains the "Robustness Variable" value used by the querier, i.e., the sender of the Query message. If the querier's "Robustness Variable" exceeds 7, the maximum value of the QRV field, the QRV is set to zero. Routers adopt the QRV value from the most recently received Query message as their own "Robustness Variable" value, unless that most recently received QRV was zero, in which case the receivers use the default "Robustness Variable" value specified in RFC 3376 Section 8.1 or a statically configured value.

- **QQIC (8 Bits):** This field specifies the "Query Interval" used by the querier. The actual interval, called the Querier's Query Interval (QQI), is represented in units of seconds and is derived from the Querier's Query Interval Code as described in RFC 3376 Section 4.1.7.

- **Number of Sources (16 Bits):** The Number of Sources (N) field specifies how many source addresses are present in the Query message. This number is zero in a General Query or a Group-Specific Query message, and non-zero in a Group-and-Source-Specific Query message. This number is limited by the MTU of the network over which the Query is transmitted. For example, on an Ethernet with an MTU of 1500 bytes, the IP header including the Router Alert Option consumes 24 bytes, and the IGMP fields up to including the Number of Sources (N) field consume 12 bytes, leaving 1464 bytes for source addresses, which limits the number of source addresses to 366 (1464/4).

- **Source Address [i] (32 Bits):** These fields are a vector of N IP unicast addresses, where N is the value in the Number of Sources (N) field.

FIGURE 2.8 IGMPv3 Query message format.

multicast address. Routers send Group-Specific and Group-and-Source-Specific Query messages with the IP destination address of the carrying IP packet set equal to the multicast group address of interest. However, systems on the network segment on which such messages are sent must accept and process any Query message whose IP

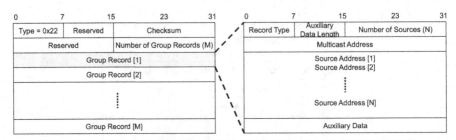

• **Number of Group Records (16 Bits)**: This field specifies how many Group Records are present in this Report message.
• **Group Record (32 Bits)**: This is a block of fields containing information pertaining to the sender's membership in a single multicast group on the interface from which the Report message is sent.
• **Record Type (8 Bits)**: This specifies the type of Group Record that is included in the Report message.
• **Auxiliary Data Length (8 Bits)**: This field contains the length of the Auxiliary Data field in this Group Record, in units of 32-bit words. It may contain zero, to indicate the absence of any auxiliary data.
• **Number of Sources (16 Bits)**: This field specifies the number of source addresses that are present in this Group Record.
• **Multicast Address (32 Bits)**: This field contains the IP multicast address to which this Group Record pertains.
• **Source Address [i] (32 Bits)**: This field is a vector of N IP unicast addresses, where N is the value in this record's Number of Sources (N) field.
• **Auxiliary Data**: This field, if present, contains additional information pertaining to this Group Record. RFC 3376 (for IGMPv3) does not define any auxiliary data. Therefore, implementations of IGMPv3 MUST NOT include any auxiliary data (i.e., MUST set the Auxiliary Data Length field to zero) in any transmitted Group Record, and MUST ignore any auxiliary data present in any received Group Record. The semantics and internal encoding of the Auxiliary Data field are to be defined by any future version or extension of IGMP that uses this field.

FIGURE 2.9   IGMPv3 Report message format.

Destination Address field contains any of the unicast or multicast addresses assigned to the interface on which the Query message arrived.

2.5.2 IGMPv3 Membership Report Message

An IP system sends IGMPv3 Membership Report messages on an interface to report to or inform routers on the network segment on which the message was transmitted, the current multicast reception state of the interface, or changes in the interface's multicast reception state. IGMPv3 Membership Report messages have the format depicted in Figure 2.9.

2.5.2.1   Conceptual IP System Service Interface for Requesting IP Multicast Traffic

To better understand the key functions and workings of IGMPv3, it is important to first review, at a high level, the service interface used for receiving multicast traffic in IP systems. Reference [RFC3376] considers conceptually, the service interface within an IP system, as the interface used by upper-layer protocols and application programs to request the lower IP Layer to enable or disable the reception of multicast traffic sent to specific multicast group addresses. A system's IP service interface that takes full advantage of IGMPv3's capabilities must support the following operation:

IPMulticastListen (socket, interface, multicast_address, filter_mode, source_list) where

- *socket* is an implementation-specific parameter used by the system to distinguish among different entities (e.g., processes or programs) that are requesting services within the system (e.g., the socket parameter used in Unix system calls).
- *interface* is a local parameter that uniquely identifies the network interface on which reception of multicast traffic sent to the specified multicast group address is to be enabled or disabled. An interface may be physical (e.g., an Ethernet interface) or logical/virtual (e.g., sub-interface or switched virtual interface (SVI) on a physical interface).
- *multicast_address* is the multicast group address to which the requested multicast traffic is sent.
- *filter_mode* is a parameter that can be either INCLUDE or EXCLUDE. When set to INCLUDE, multicast traffic sent to the specified multicast address must come from only those source addresses listed in the *source_list* parameter. When set to EXCLUDE, multicast traffic sent to the specified multicast address must come from all source addresses except those listed in the *source_list* parameter.
- *source_list* is an unordered list of zero or more source addresses from which multicast traffic to a given multicast group address is desired or not desired, depending on the setting of the *filter_mode* parameter.

IGMPv1 and IGMPv2 did not support source filtering as in IGMPv3 and had simpler service interfaces consisting of *Join operations* to enable reception of multicast traffic sent to a given multicast address from *all sources on a given interface* and *Leave operations* to disable reception of multicast traffic sent to a given multicast address from *all sources on a given interface*. The equivalent operations in the IGMPv3 IP system service interface are as follows:

- The IGMPv1/v2 Join operation in IGMPv3 is equivalent to:
  IPMulticastListen (socket, interface, multicast_address, EXCLUDE, {}) where {} is an empty source_list.
- The IGMPv2 Leave operation in IGMPv3 is equivalent to:
  IPMulticastListen (socket, interface, multicast_address, INCLUDE, {})

2.5.2.2 Multicast State Maintained by a Receiving System

- **Socket State**: The system creates a multicast reception state (consisting of a set of records) for each socket on which the IPMulticastListen operation has been invoked of the following conceptual form:

  (interface, multicast_address, filter_mode, source_list)

  IGMPv3 introduced the new feature of filtering multicast packets based on the multicast reception state of a socket (which is a parameter of the IGMPv3 service interface). IGMPv1 and IGMPv2 did not support filtering based on multicast join state, instead, when a Join operation is performed on a socket, this simply causes the host to join a multicast group on the given interface, and multicast packets sent to that multicast group could be passed on to all sockets whether or not they had joined that group.

- **Interface State**: The system also creates a multicast reception state (consisting of a set of records) for each of its interfaces of the following conceptual form in addition to the per-socket multicast reception state:

  (multicast_address, filter_mode, source_list)

  Not more than one set of records can exist per multicast address for a given interface.

2.5.2.3 IGMPv3 Group Record Types

IGMPv3 supports the following types of *Group Records* that systems may include in a Report message:

- **Current-State Record**: A system (i.e., host) sends this Record in response to a Query message received on an interface. This Record reports the current reception state of the system interface on which the message is received, concerning *a single multicast group address*. The Current-State Record in turn has the following two Record Types:

Report Type Value and Name	Meaning
1 = MODE_IS_ INCLUDE	This Record indicates that the interface on which the Query message is received has a filter mode of INCLUDE for the specified multicast group address. The Source Address [i] fields in this Group Record contain the interface's source list for the specified multicast group address if it is non-empty.
2 = MODE_IS_ EXCLUDE	This Record indicates that the interface on which the Query message is received has a filter mode of EXCLUDE for the specified multicast group address. The Source Address [i] fields in this Group Record contain the interface's source list for the specified multicast group address if it is non-empty.

- **Filter-Mode-Change Record**: A system sends this Record on an interface whenever the invocation of the *IPMulticastListen* operation locally causes a change of the filter mode (i.e., a change from INCLUDE to EXCLUDE, or from EXCLUDE to INCLUDE) associated with the interface-level state entry for a particular multicast group address. The system includes this Record in a Report message sent from the interface on which the filter mode change occurred. The Filter-Mode-Change Record in turn has the following two Record Types:

Report Type Value and Name	Meaning
3 = CHANGE_TO_ INCLUDE_MODE	This Record indicates that the interface has changed to the filter mode INCLUDE for the specified multicast group address. The Source Address [i] fields in this Group Record contain the interface's new source list for the specified multicast group address if it is non-empty.
4 = CHANGE_TO_ EXCLUDE_MODE	This Record indicates that the interface has changed to the filter mode EXCLUDE for the specified multicast group address. The Source Address [i] fields in this Group Record contain the interface's new source list for the specified multicast group address if it is non-empty.

- **Source-List-Change Record**: A system sends this Record whenever the invocation of *IPMulticastListen* operation locally causes a change of source list for the interface-level state entry associated with a particular multicast group address (which does not happen together with a change of filter mode). The system includes this Record in a Report sent from the interface on which the change of source list occurred. The Source-List-Change Record in turn has the following two Record Types:

Report Type Value and Name	Meaning
5 = ALLOW_NEW_ SOURCES	This Record indicates that the system wishes to receive packets from a list of additional sources sent to the specified multicast address as specified by the Source Address [i] fields in this Group Record. If the change indicates an INCLUDE source list, then these are the source addresses that were added to the list; if the change indicates an EXCLUDE source list, then these are the source addresses that were deleted from the list.
6 = BLOCK_OLD_ SOURCES	This Record indicates that the system no longer wishes to receive packets from a list of the sources sent to the specified multicast address as specified by the Source Address [i] fields in this Group Record. If the change indicates an INCLUDE source list, then these are the source addresses that were deleted from the list; if the change indicates an EXCLUDE source list, then these are the source addresses that were added to the list.

If a change of source list results in both a system desiring packets from new sources and blocking packets from old sources, then it will send two Group Records for the same multicast group address, one Record

Type set to ALLOW_NEW_SOURCES and one Record Type set to BLOCK_OLD_SOURCES.

A system sends an IGMP Report message with the carrying IP packet having a valid IP source address for the sending interface. However, Reference [RFC3376] specifies that routers MUST accept a Report message carried in an IP packet with a source address of 0.0.0.0. *Systems send IGMPv3 Report messages with the IP destination address of the carrying IP packet set to 224.0.0.22, which is the multicast address on which all IGMPv3-capable multicast routers listen.*

An IGMPv3-capable system that is operating in IGMPv1 or IGMPv2 compatibility modes sends IGMPv1 or IGMPv2 Report messages to the multicast group specified in the Group Address field of the Report message. In addition, a system must accept and process any IGMPv1 or IGMPv2 Report messages carried in IP packets with an IP Destination Address field containing any of the unicast or multicast addresses assigned to the interface on which the Report message arrives.

The size of a message a system can send out on an interface is determined by the maximum transmission unit (MTU) of the network on which it will be sent. Thus, if a system is to send a Report message and finds that the set of Group Records required does not fit within the size limit of a single Report message, then the system will send the required Group Records in separate Report messages as needed to report the entire set.

If the system finds that a single Group Record contains many source addresses such that the Record does not fit within the size limit of a single Report message, and if the Group Record Type *is not* MODE_IS_EXCLUDE or CHANGE_TO_EXCLUDE_MODE, then the system will split the Record into multiple smaller Group Records. In this case, each subset contains a different set of source addresses and each is sent in a separate Report message.

If the Record Type *is* MODE_IS_EXCLUDE or CHANGE_TO_EXCLUDE_MODE, then the system will send a single Group Record containing as many source addresses as would fit within the Record, and the remaining source addresses will not be reported. In this case, the choice of which source addresses to report is arbitrary; however, it is preferable to report the same set of sources in each subsequent Report message, rather than reporting different source addresses each time.

2.5.2.3.1   IGMPv3 (S, G) Join/Leave Process

As discussed earlier, IGMPv3 does not support explicit Leave Group messages as in IGMPv2. Instead, it uses the source filtering mechanism based on the Group Record Types described already for leaving multicast groups. Figure 2.10 describes how a host can use the Group Record Types to join and leave certain sources sending traffic to a particular multicast group. IGMPv3 enhances the IGMPv2 leave process by introducing the capability in IGMPv3 Membership Report message for a host to signal to its directly attached router that it does not want to receive traffic from a particular group, source, or channel by *including* or *excluding* sources, groups, or channels in the Membership Report message.

IGMPv3 extends IGMPv2's Join/Leave multicast group mechanism to allow hosts on a network segment to join and leave specific source/group pairs by issuing specific

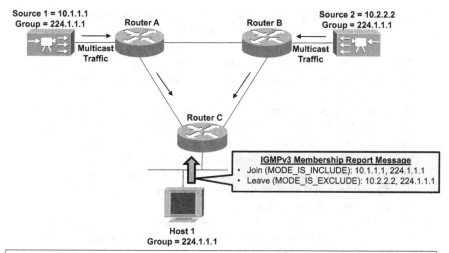

- Two sources, Source 1 (10.1.1.1) and Source 2 (10.2.2.2) send multicast traffic to group 224.1.1.1.
- Host wants to receive multicast traffic sent to group 224.1.1.1 from Source 1 but not from Source 2.
- So, Host 1 sends an IGMPv3 Membership Report message to its Designated Router (DR), Router C, containing a list of (S, G) that it wishes to join (i.e., Group Record type = MODE_IS_INCLUDE) and a list of (S, G) that it wishes to leave (i.e., Group Record type = MODE_IS_EXCLUDE).
- The DR, Router C, receives the IGMPv3 Membership Report message and uses the information in it to allow traffic from Source 1 to flow to Host 1 but prunes traffic from Source 2.

FIGURE 2.10   IGMPv3 (S, G) Join/Leave process.

Group Records contained in IGMPv3 Membership Report messages as already discussed. The Designated Router (DR) of a network segment receives Group Records from hosts and decides which sources and groups are permitted to send traffic on the segment and which ones are to be pruned as described in Figure 2.10.

2.5.3   IGMPv3 Timers, Counters and Default Values

IGMPv3 supports all the timers, counters, and default values in IGMPv2 except for the following differences:

- **Query Response Interval**: This is the Maximum Response Time (default is 100, meaning 10 seconds) that the router uses to compute the Maximum Response Code field value that it inserts into periodic General Query messages.
- **Last Member Query Interval**: This is the Maximum Response Time (default is 10, meaning 1 second) that the router uses to compute the Maximum Response Code field value that it inserts into Group-Specific Query messages sent in response to Leave Group messages. It is also the Maximum Response Time used in computing the Maximum Response Code field value inserted into Group-and-Source-Specific Query messages.

- **Last Member Query Count**: This is the number of Group-Specific Query messages (default is Robustness Variable) the router sent on the network segment before it assumes that there are no group members on that segment. This is also the number of Group-and-Source-Specific Query messages the router sent before it assumes the network segment has no listeners for a particular source.
- **Older Version Querier Interval**: This is the timeout a host uses for transitioning back to IGMPv3 mode once it hears an older IGMP version Query message. When a host receives an older version Query message, it will set its "Older Version Querier Present Timer" equal to "Older Version Querier Interval". The host must set this value to the "Robustness Variable" times the "Query Interval" seen in the last Query message received by the host plus one "Query Response Interval".
- **Older Host Present Interval**: This is the timeout a multicast router uses for transitioning a multicast group back to IGMPv3 mode once it receives an older IGMP version Membership Report sent for that group. When the router receives an older IGMP version Report message, it will set its "Older Host Present Timer" equal to "Older Host Present Interval". The router must set this value to the "Robustness Variable" times the "Query Interval" plus one "Query Response Interval".

2.5.4 IGMPv3 Actions Performed by Multicast Group Members

IGMP (all versions) is an asymmetric protocol and specifies separate behaviors for multicast routers and for multicast group members (which can be hosts or multicast routers themselves that are interested in receiving multicast packets). We describe in this section the IGMPv3 functions that apply to all multicast group members [RFC3376]. The IGMPv3 functions that apply to multicast routers are described in the next section. It is important to note that a multicast router that is also a member of a multicast group performs both IGMPv3 functions, receiving and responding to IGMP message transmissions of its neighbors, as well as transmissions of its own IGMP messages.

A system performs the IGMPv3 functions described in this section on all its interfaces on which multicast traffic reception is enabled, even if more than one of these interfaces is connected to the same network (for example, when Layer 2 link aggregation or bundling feature is used on multiple interfaces). The All-Hosts (or Systems) multicast address, 224.0.0.1, is handled as a special case of multicast transmission. On all hosts, including multicast routers, all interfaces on which multicast reception is supported are permanently enabled for the reception of packets sent to the All-Hosts multicast address from all sources

IGMPv3 actions on an interface are triggered by the following two types of events:

- A change in the reception state of the interface, caused by the invocation of the *IPMulticastListen* operation locally.
- Reception of a Query message.

In the discussions following, we use the term "State-Change Record" as a representative term to refer to either a Filter-Mode-Change Record or a Source-List-Change Record. We also describe the contents of a Group Record associated with a particular multicast group address using the following notation:

Notation	Meaning
IS_IN (x)	Record Type MODE_IS_INCLUDE, source addresses x
IS_EX (x)	Record Type MODE_IS_EXCLUDE, source addresses x
TO_IN (x)	Record Type CHANGE_TO_INCLUDE_MODE, source addresses x
TO_EX (x)	Record Type CHANGE_TO_EXCLUDE_MODE, source addresses x
ALLOW (x)	Record Type ALLOW_NEW_SOURCES, source addresses x
BLOCK (x)	Record Type BLOCK_OLD_SOURCES, source addresses x

where x is either:

- a capital letter (e.g., "A"), representing the set of source addresses, or
- a set expression (e.g., "A+B"), where "A+B" denotes the union of two sets A and B, "A*B" denotes the intersection of two sets A and B, and "A−B" denotes the removal of all elements of set B from set A.

2.5.4.1 Action Triggered by Change of Interface State

When the *IPMulticastListen* operation is invoked locally on a system, this may cause the multicast reception state of an interface to change as discussed previously. The per-interface entry for a single multicast group address is affected by each of such changes. Upon detecting a change in the interface state, the system will immediately transmit a "State-Change Report" out of that interface. To determine the type and contents of the Group Record(s) in that Report, the system compares the filter mode and source list for the affected multicast group address before and after the change, according to the following rules:

Old State	New State	"State-Change Record" Sent
INCLUDE (A)	INCLUDE (B)	ALLOW (B−A), BLOCK (A−B)
EXCLUDE (A)	EXCLUDE (B)	ALLOW (A−B), BLOCK (B−A)
INCLUDE (A)	EXCLUDE (B)	TO_EX (B)
EXCLUDE (A)	INCLUDE (B)	TO_IN (B)

If the source list that the system computes for either an ALLOW or a BLOCK "State-Change Record" is empty, then that Group Record will be omitted from the Report message. To handle the situation where the State-Change Report sent may be missed by one or more multicast routers, the system will retransmit that Report ["Robustness Variable"−1] more times, with the Reports spaced apart by intervals chosen at random in the range 0 to "Unsolicited Report Interval".

If the system detects that more changes to the same interface state entry have occurred before it has completed all the retransmissions of the "State-Change Report" for the first change, each of such additional changes will cause the system to immediately transmit a new "State-Change Report". The system computes the contents of the newly transmitted Report as follows:

- Similar to the processing of the first Report, the system compares the interface state for the affected multicast group before and after the latest change.
- The system builds the difference Group Records for the Report according to the rules described earlier.
- However, the system does not transmit these Records in a Report message, but instead merges them with the contents of the pending Report, that is, to create the new "State-Change Report".

The rules that the system uses for merging the difference Group Records resulting from the interface state change and the pending Report are described in a later section. As soon as the system transmits the merged "State-Change Report", this terminates the retransmissions of the earlier "State-Change Reports" for the same multicast group address. This transmission also becomes the first of the ["Robustness Variable"−1] transmissions of the "State-Change Reports" used to handle missed Reports by multicast routers as discussed previously.

Each time the system includes a source in the difference Group Records computed previously, it maintains a retransmission state for that source until ["Robustness Variable"−1] "State-Change Reports" have been sent. The system does this to ensure that a series of successive interface state changes do not break IGMPv3's robustness.

If the system detects that the interface reception-state change that triggered the new Report is a filter-mode change, then it will include a Filter-Mode-Change Record in the next ["Robustness Variable"−1] "State-Change Reports". This applies even if the system experiences any number of source-list changes in that period. The system must maintain a retransmission state for the multicast group until the ["Robustness Variable"−1] "State-Change Reports" have been transmitted. After transmitting the ["Robustness Variable"−1] "State-Change Reports" with the Filter-Mode-Change Records after the last filter-mode change, and if the system has scheduled additional Reports caused by source-list changes to the interface reception, then it will include the Source-List-Change Records in the next "State-Change Report".

Each time the system transmits a "State-Change Report", it determines the contents of the Report as follows:

- If the system determines that the Report should contain a Filter-Mode-Change Record, and if the current filter mode of the interface is INCLUDE, the system will include a TO_IN Record in the Report, otherwise it will include a TO_EX Record.
- If instead, the system determines that the Report should contain Source-List-Change Records, it will include an ALLOW and a BLOCK Record, the contents of which are built according to the following rules:

Record	Sources Included
TO_IN	All in the current interface state that must be forwarded
TO_EX	All in the current interface state that must be blocked
ALLOW	All with retransmission state that must be forwarded
BLOCK	All with retransmission state that must be blocked

2.5.4.2   Action on Reception of a Query Message

Each time a system receives a Query message, it does not send a response immediately, instead, it delays the response by a randomly selected length of time, bounded by the Maximum Response Time value derived from the Maximum Response Code field in the received Query message. A system may receive several Query messages on different interfaces and of different types (e.g., General Query, Group-Specific Query, and Group-and-Source-Specific Query messages), each of which may require its own randomly selected delayed response.

Before sending a response to a received Query message, the system must first examine pending responses that it had previously scheduled, and try to send a combined response that captures the contents of all of these responses. This means, the system must be able to maintain the following state:

- A per-interface timer that can be used for scheduling responses to General Query messages.
- A per-group and interface timer that can be used for scheduling responses to Group-Specific and Group-and-Source-Specific Query messages.
- A per-group and interface list of sources that it will report in the response to a Group-and-Source-Specific Query message.

When a system receives a new Query message on an interface with the Router-Alert Option [RFC2113] [RFC6398], and provided the system has a state to report, it will select a random delay for a response in the range 0 to Maximum Response Time, where the Maximum Response Time is derived from Maximum Response Code in the received Query message. The purpose of placing the Router-Alert Option in an IP packet is to inform transit routers receiving the packet to examine the contents of the packet more closely (i.e., contents that require relatively complex processing in routers along the packet's path). The system uses the following rules to determine if a Report (of a particular type) needs to be scheduled. The system considers the rules in the order given and only the first matching rule is applied:

1. If the system finds that there is a pending response to a previous General Query message that is scheduled sooner than the selected random delay, it does not need to schedule an additional response.
2. If the system detects that the received Query is a General Query message, then it uses the interface timer to schedule a response to that General Query message after the selected random delay. It will then cancel any previously pending response to a General Query message.
3. If the system detects that the received Query is a Group-Specific Query or a Group-and-Source-Specific Query message and no pending response to a previous Query for the queried multicast group exists, then it will use the *Group Timer* to schedule a Report. If the system detects that the received Query is a Group-and-Source-Specific Query message, it will record the list of queried sources (in a Group Record) to be used when generating a response.

4. If the system determines that it already has a pending response to a previous Query scheduled for the queried multicast group and that either the new Query is a Group-Specific Query message or the recorded source list associated with the group is empty, then it will clear the group source-list and schedule a single response using the Group Timer. The system will schedule the new response to be sent at the earliest of the remaining time for the pending Report and the selected random delay.
5. If the system determines that the received Query is a Group-and-Source-Specific Query message and it has a pending response for the queried multicast group with a non-empty source list, then it will augment the group source list to contain the list of sources in the new Query and schedule a single response using the Group Timer. The system will schedule the new response to be sent at the earliest of the remaining time for the pending Report and the selected random delay.

When the system detects that the timer for a pending response Record has expired, it will transmit on the corresponding interface, one or more Report messages containing one or more Current-State Records as follows:

1. If the system detects that the expired timer is the interface timer (i.e., a timer that is associated with a pending response to a General Query message), then it will send one Current-State Record for each multicast group address for which the specified interface has reception state (*multicast_address, filter_mode, source_list*) as described earlier. This Current-State Record for the interface contains the multicast address and its corresponding filter mode (MODE_IS_INCLUDE or MODE_IS_EXCLUDE) and source list. The system packs multiple Current-State Records into individual Report messages, within the allowed message size limits.
2. If the system detects that the expired timer is a Group Timer and the list of recorded sources for that multicast group is empty (i.e., a timer that is associated with a pending response to a Group-Specific Query message), then it will send a single Current-State Record for that group address, if and only if the interface has reception state for that group address. This Current-State Record contains the multicast group address and its corresponding filter mode (MODE_IS_INCLUDE or MODE_IS_EXCLUDE) and source list.
3. If the system detects that the expired timer is a Group Timer and the list of recorded sources for that multicast group is not empty (i.e., a timer that is associated with a pending response to a Group-and-Source-Specific Query message), then it will determine the contents of the responding Current-State Record from the interface state and the pending response Record, if and only if the interface has reception state for that group address. The determination is done according to the following:

Interface State	Set of Sources in the Pending Response Record	Current-State Record
INCLUDE (A)	B	IS_IN (A*B)
EXCLUDE (A)	B	IS_IN (B−A)

If the system finds that the resulting Current-State Record has an empty set of source addresses, then it will not send a response. Finally, after generating any required Report messages, the system will clear the source lists associated with any reported groups.

2.5.5 IGMPv3 Actions Performed by Multicast Routers

As discussed earlier, a multicast router uses IGMP to learn on each of its directly attached network segments, which multicast group addresses are of interest to the systems (or hosts) attached to those segments. IGMPv3 further introduces the capability for a multicast router to learn which sources (sending multicast traffic to a particular multicast address), are of interest to the systems on the network segments. The information obtained by the multicast routers via IGMP is passed to the multicast routing protocol running in the router, allowing it to deliver the multicast traffic to all network segments where there are interested receivers.

This section describes the IGMPv3 functions that are performed by multicast routers. It is important to note that a multicast router may also become a member of multicast groups, and therefore, also performs the group member functions of IGMPv3 as described earlier. A multicast router performs the IGMPv3 multicast router-related functions described in this section on each of its directly attached network segments. In the case where a multicast router has more than one interface directly attached to the same network (i.e. when link aggregation is used), then it only needs to operate IGMPv3 over one of those interfaces. On each router interface on which IGMPv3 is running, the router must enable the reception of IGMPv3 (Report) messages sent to the multicast address 224.0.0.22, which is the multicast address on which all IGMPv3-capable multicast routers listen on. The multicast router must also perform the group member functions of IGMPv3 for that multicast address on that interface.

A multicast router only needs to know that at least one group member on an attached network segment is interested in multicast traffic sent to a particular multicast group address from a particular source. A multicast router is not required to keep track of which individual group member (system) is interested in any particular multicast group traffic or source.

2.5.5.1 Conditions for Sending IGMPv3 Query Messages

Multicast routers send General Query messages periodically on their attached network segments to learn group membership information on those networks. The routers use the responses from the Query messages to build and refresh the multicast group membership state of systems on those attached network segments. Systems on each network segment respond to these Query messages by sending Current-State Group Records in IGMPv3 Membership Report messages that indicate their group membership state, and the set of sources they wish to receive multicast traffic from.

A system that is a member of a particular multicast group may report interest in receiving or not receiving traffic from particular sources. When the desired reception state of the system changes, it will report these changes by sending Report messages carrying Filter-Mode-Change Records or Source-List-Change Records. The system sends these Records to indicate an explicit state change in a multicast group in either the source list or filter mode of the Group Record. When a system on a network segment terminates membership of a group, or no longer desires traffic from a particular source, the attached multicast router must send a Query message to other members of the group or listeners of the source on the network segment, before deleting the group (or source) and pruning the associated traffic.

Multicast routers also send specific Query messages to enable all systems on a network segment to respond to changes in group membership. A multicast router sends a Group-Specific Query message to check if there are systems on the segment that desire the reception of traffic from a specified group, or to refresh the desired reception state for a particular multicast group. A router sends a Group-Specific Query message when it receives a State-Change record indicating a system is leaving a particular multicast group.

The router uses the Group-and-Source Specific Query message to verify if there are systems on a network segment that desire to receive multicast traffic from a set of sources. Group-and-Source-Specific Query messages on a network segment contain a list of sources for a particular multicast group which systems on that segment have expressed their desire to no longer receive traffic from. A multicast router sends this query to learn if any systems on the network segment have the desire to receive multicast traffic sent to the specified group address from the specified source addresses. It is important to note that multicast routers send Group-and-Source-Specific Query messages only in response to State-Change Records and NOT in response to Current-State Records.

2.5.5.2 IGMPv3 State Maintained by Multicast Routers

Multicast routers that run IGMPv3 maintain state for each multicast group and each attached network segment (i.e., interface). The group state consists of a filter mode, a list of sources, and various IGMPv3-related timers. For each attached network segment running IGMPv3, the multicast router records the desired multicast reception state for that segment. The router maintains a state which conceptually consists of a set of records of the form:

(multicast address, group timer, filter mode, (source records))

Each source record in the group state is of the form:

(source address, source timer)

If systems on a network segment desire all sources within a given multicast group, the router keeps an empty source record list with filter mode set to EXCLUDE. This means systems on that network segment desire traffic from all sources sent to this group to be forwarded to them. This IGMPv3 feature is equivalent to a multicast group join in IGMPv1 or IGMPv2.

2.5.5.2.1 Definition of Multicast Router Filter Mode

To keep the internal state to a minimum, IGMPv3 routers maintain a filter mode for each multicast group on each attached network segment (i.e., interface). A multicast router uses this filter mode to compact and reduce the total desired reception state of a multicast group into a smaller set, but at the same time satisfy the group memberships of all systems on the segment/interface. The filter mode may change when the router receives particular types of Group Records from systems on the network segment, or when certain timer conditions occur. In the following sections, the term "router filter mode" refers to the filter mode of a particular multicast group on a particular network segment attached to a router. We describe in the Section 2.5.5.4, the changes that can occur on a router filter mode when a Group Record is received.

Conceptually, when a router receives a Group Record, it will update the router filter mode for that multicast group to cover all the sources that systems on the network segment have requested using the least amount of internal state. As a rule, once the router receives a Group Record with a filter mode of EXCLUDE, it will set the router filter mode for that multicast group to EXCLUDE.

When the router filter mode for a multicast group on a network segment is EXCLUDE, the source record list in the Group Record contains the following two types of sources:

- The set of sources that represents conflicts in the desired multicast reception state of the router interface. This set of sources must be forwarded by some router on the network.
- The set of sources which systems on the network segment have requested to not receive traffic from. Section 2.5.5.2.1.1 describes the reasons for keeping this second set of sources when the router filter mode is in EXCLUDE mode.

When a router filter mode for a multicast group on a network segment is INCLUDE, the source record list in the Group Record represents the list of sources for that group those systems on the segment desire traffic from. This represents the total set of sources for that group, and multicast traffic from each source in the list must be forwarded by some router on the network.

Because a Group Record in a Membership Report received on an interface with a filter mode of EXCLUDE will cause the router to transition the interface's filter mode for that group to EXCLUDE, the router needs a mechanism for transitioning the filter mode back to INCLUDE. If all systems on an interface (i.e., network segment) with a Group Record in EXCLUDE filter mode stop reporting, it is desirable to transition the router filter mode for that group back to INCLUDE mode. The transition to INCLUDE mode occurs when the Group Timer expires as explained in the subsequent sections.

2.5.5.2.1.1   The Need for State-Change Messages

IGMPv3 specifies two types of Membership Reports: Current-State Reports and "State-Change Reports". This section describes why IGMPv3 needs both types of Reports. Multicast routers need to be able to tell the difference between Membership Reports that are sent by systems on a network segment in response to Query messages from those that are sent by systems because of a change in interface state:

- The multicast router uses the Membership Reports that are sent in response to Membership Query messages mainly to refresh its existing state; these Reports typically do not cause transitions in state at the router.

- Membership Reports sent by systems on a network segment in response to changes in interface state require the receiving router to take some action when such Reports are received (see discussion in a later section).

If a router is not able to distinguish between these two types of Reports, then the router would end up treating all Membership Reports as potential changes in interface state, possibly, resulting in increased processing load at the router as well as an increase in IGMP traffic on the network.

2.5.5.2.1.2 Elimination of Host Report Suppression

In IGMPv1 and IGMPv2, a system on a network segment would cancel its transmission of a pending Membership Report if it observes a similar Report from another group member on that network segment. However, IGMPv3 does not support the suppression of host Membership Reports as in previous IGMP versions. The elimination of the Report Suppression feature in IGMPv3 has the following benefits:

- Multicast routers may want to track group membership status per host on an interface. This allows the routers to track multicast group membership status for, possibly, accounting purposes and to implement fast system leaves.
- Membership Report suppression does not help LAN switches that implement IGMP Snooping. Such switches depend on Membership Report messages from hosts on a LAN segment to be able to discover active multicast receivers and to constrain multicast traffic to only switch ports that have multicast group members.
- Eliminating Membership Report suppression means hosts will have fewer IGMP messages sensing and processing, leading to a simpler host IGMP state machine implementation.
- In IGMPv3, a single Membership Report from a host combines multiple multicast Group Records, thereby, decreasing the number of Report messages sent. In comparison, IGMPv1 and IGMPv2 require a host to report each multicast group in a separate Report message.

2.5.5.2.1.3 Switching Router Filter Modes from EXCLUDE to INCLUDE

If there exist hosts on an interface that causes the router filter mode to be in both EXCLUDE and INCLUDE modes for a single multicast group, the router must set the router filter mode to be in EXCLUDE mode (see the subsequent section). In EXCLUDE mode, the router forwards multicast traffic from all sources except those sources that are in the exclusion source list. If all hosts on an interface that cause the router filter mode to be in EXCLUDE mode cease to exist, the router should switch the router filter mode of the interface back to INCLUDE mode, an action that must be done seamlessly without interrupting the multicast traffic flow to existing receivers.

One way of accomplishing this is to allow the router to keep track of all sources that are in INCLUDE mode and which host on the interface desired traffic from those sources even though the router filter-state of the interface itself is in EXCLUDE mode. If the Group Timer associated with the multicast group expires while the router filter mode of the interface is in EXCLUDE mode, this implies that no hosts in

EXCLUDE mode exist on the interface (otherwise a host on the interface would have sent a Membership Report to refresh the Group Timer). When this timer expires, the router can then switch the router filter mode of the interface back to INCLUDE mode seamlessly, while still forwarding multicast traffic on the interface from the list of sources currently in its source list.

2.5.5.2.2 Definition of Multicast Group Timers

The Group Timer is only used when a received Group Record for a multicast group causes the router to place the router filter mode for the interface in EXCLUDE mode. This timer indicates the time it takes for the router filter mode of the multicast group on the interface to expire, thereby, requiring a switch to the INCLUDE mode. A Group Timer, which is maintained for each group on each attached network segment, is a timer that is decremented and with a lower bound of zero. A router updates Group Timers according to the types of Group Records received.

When a Group Timer expires and when a router filter mode for a multicast group on an interface is EXCLUDE, this means that there are no systems in EXCLUDE mode on the attached network segment. When this happens, the router will transition the router filter mode to INCLUDE. The actions taken by the router when a Group Timer expires while in EXCLUDE mode are described in Section 2.5.5.5.

The role of the Group Timer in the multicast router is summarized as shown in Table 2.1.

2.5.5.2.3 Definition of Source Timers

The multicast router maintains a *Source Timer* for each source record and this timer is decremented with a lower bound of zero. The router updates the Source Timers according to the type and router filter mode of the multicast Group Record received. The router always updates Source Timers (for a particular group) whenever a received Record for that group contains the source. Section 2.5.5.4 describes the setting of Source Timers for each type of Group Record received by the router.

When a router has a source record with a running timer associated with a router filter mode for a multicast group on an interface that is in INCLUDE mode, this implies

TABLE 2.1

Role of the Group Timer in Multicast Router

Group Filter Mode	Group Timer Value	Actions/Comments
INCLUDE	Timer >= 0	All members in INCLUDE mode
EXCLUDE	Timer > 0	At least one member is in EXCLUDE mode.
EXCLUDE	Timer == 0	No more systems interested in traffic to the group.
		1. If all Source Timers have expired, then delete Group Record.
		2. If there are still source record timers running, then switch router filter mode to INCLUDE using those source records with running timers as the INCLUDE source record state.

that the interface has currently one or more systems (in INCLUDE filter mode) interested in receiving traffic from that source. If the router detects that a Source Timer has expired with the router filter mode for the multicast group in INCLUDE mode, it will conclude that systems on that interface no longer desire traffic from that particular source, and will delete the associated source record.

The router treats Source Timers differently when the router filter mode for a multicast group is in EXCLUDE mode. If a source record has a running timer associated with a router filter mode for a multicast group on an interface that is in EXCLUDE mode, this means that there is at least one system on the interface that is interested in traffic from the source, and the router should therefore forward that traffic on the interface. Sections 2.5.5.2.1.1 and 2.5.5.2.1.3 describe the reasons why it is desirable for a multicast router to keep state for sources on a particular multicast group while the interface is in EXCLUDE mode and there are still systems requesting traffic from those sources.

If the router detects that a Source Timer has expired with the router filter mode for the multicast group in EXCLUDE mode, it will inform the running routing protocol that the associated interface is no longer systems interested in traffic from the affected source. When the router filter mode for the group is EXCLUDE, the router only deletes source records when the Group Timer expires. We describe in the next section the actions that a multicast router takes depending on the value of a Source Timer.

2.5.5.3   IGMPv3 Source-Specific Forwarding Rules

When a multicast router receives a multicast packet from a source sent to a particular multicast group, it must decide whether to forward the packet onto an attached network segment or not. The router makes this decision using the information obtained from the running multicast routing protocol and information from IGMPv3, to ensure that traffic from all sources and groups that are desired on a network segment are forwarded. The information obtained from IGMPv3 does not override the multicast routing information, for example, if the router sees that the router filter mode for a multicast group G on an interface is EXCLUDE, it may still forward multicast packets for sources in the exclusion list to a transit network segment.

Table 2.2 summarizes the forwarding suggestions made by IGMPv3 to the routing protocol running in the router for traffic sent from a source to a multicast group. The actions taken by the multicast router for different Source Timer states and router filter modes of the multicast group are also summarized.

2.5.5.4   Multicast Router Action on Reception of IGMPv3 Report Messages

This section describes the actions taken by a multicast router when it receives IGMPv3 Membership Report messages from systems on a network segment.

2.5.5.4.1   Reception of Current-State Records

When a router receives Current-State Records, it will update both its group and Source Timers. In some circumstances, when the router receives a certain type of Group Record, this may cause the router filter mode for that multicast group on the

TABLE 2.2

IGMPv3 Source-Specific Forwarding Rules

Group Filter Mode	Source Timer Value	Action
INCLUDE	TIMER > 0	Suggest forwarding traffic from the source
INCLUDE	TIMER == 0	Suggest stopping forwarding traffic from the source and removing the source record. If there are no more source records for the group, delete the Group Record
INCLUDE	No Source Elements	Suggest not to forward traffic from the source
EXCLUDE	TIMER > 0	Suggest forwarding traffic from the source
EXCLUDE	TIMER == 0	Suggest not to forward traffic from the source (DO NOT remove Group Record)
EXCLUDE	No Source Elements	Suggest forwarding traffic from the source

interface to change. Table 2.3 describes the actions a multicast router will take (concerning state and timers) upon receiving Current-State Records.

2.5.5.4.2 Reception of Filter-Mode-Change and Source-List-Change Records

When a system detects a change in the global state of a multicast group, it will send either a Filter-Mode-Change Record or a Source-List-Change Record for that group. Similar to Current-State Records, a multicast router must take certain actions upon receiving these Records, and possibly change its own state to reflect the new membership state desired by the sending systems.

A multicast router must send Query messages to systems on a network segment that have requested to no longer receive traffic from certain sources sending traffic to a multicast group. When a multicast router sends a Query message or receives a Query message for a specific set of sources, it will lower its Source Timer interval for those sources to a small interval equal to "Last Member Query Time" seconds. If the router receives Group Records in response to the Query messages from systems expressing interest in receiving traffic from the queried sources, it will update the corresponding timers.

Similarly, when a router sends Query messages to a specific multicast group, it will lower its Group Timer interval for that group to a small interval equal to "Last Member Query Time" seconds. If the router receives any Group Records from systems on an interface indicating EXCLUDE mode interest in the multicast group within that interval, it will update the Group Timer for the multicast group and continue (without any interruption) indicating to the multicast routing protocol to forward traffic to the group.

During a "Last Member Query Time" query period, the router's IGMPv3 component will continue to suggest to the multicast routing protocol to forward traffic on the interface from the multicast groups or sources that it is querying. If the "Last Member Query Time" seconds have elapsed and the router has not received a Record from systems on the interface expressing interest in the queried group or sources, it may prune the group or sources from the interface.

TABLE 2.3

Multicast Router Actions upon Reception of Current-State Records

Router State	Report Received	New Router State	Actions
INCLUDE (A)	IS_IN (B)	INCLUDE (A+B)	(B) = GMI
INCLUDE (A)	IS_EX (B)	EXCLUDE (A*B, B−A)	(B−A) = 0
			Delete (A−B)
			Group Timer = GMI
EXCLUDE (X, Y)	IS_IN (A)	EXCLUDE (X+A, Y−A)	(A) = GMI
EXCLUDE (X, Y)	IS_EX (A)	EXCLUDE (A−Y, Y*A)	(A−X−Y) = GMI
			Delete (X−A)
			Delete (Y−A)
			Group Timer = GMI

RFC 3376 uses the following notation to describe the updating of Source Timers. The notation (A, B) represents the total number of sources for a particular multicast group, where:

- A = set of source records whose Source Timers > 0 (Sources that at least one system on the network segment has requested traffic from)
- B = set of source records whose Source Timers = 0 (Sources that IGMPv3 will suggest to the routing protocol to not forward traffic from)

It is important to note that there will only be two sets when the router filter mode for a multicast group on an interface is EXCLUDE. When the router filter mode for a group on an interface is INCLUDE, a single set is used to describe the set of sources requested to be forwarded (e.g., simply (A)).

- GMI (Group Membership Interval) is the time in which group memberships will time out.
- LMQT (Last Member Query Time) is the total time spent after the Last Member Query Count retransmissions. LMQT represents the "leave latency", or the difference between the transmission of a membership change and the change in the information given to the routing protocol.

Within the "Actions" column:

- "A=J", means the set A of source records that should have their Source Timers set to value J.
- "Delete A" means that the set A of source records that should be deleted.
- "Group Timer=J" means that the Group Timer for the group that should be set to value J.

Table 2.4 describes the changes in group state and the action(s) taken by a multicast router when it receives either Filter-Mode-Change or Source-List-Change Records. This table also describes the Query messages that the Querier on a network segment sends when it receives a particular Report message. To maintain the robustness of IGMPv3, the Querier will transmit Query messages triggered by actions in the table, "Last Member Query Count" times, and every "Last Member Query Interval".

While scheduling the transmission of new Query messages, if the Querier detects that there are already pending Queries to be retransmitted for the same multicast group, it will merge the new and pending Queries. In addition, Reports received from systems on an interface for a multicast group that has pending Queries may affect the

TABLE 2.4

Query Messages That the Querier on a Network Segment Sends When It Receives a Particular Report Message

Router State	Report Received	New Router State	Actions
INCLUDE (A)	ALLOW (B)	INCLUDE (A+B)	(B) = GMI
INCLUDE (A)	BLOCK (B)	INCLUDE (A)	Send Q(G, A*B)
INCLUDE (A)	TO_EX (B)	EXCLUDE (A*B, B−A)	(B−A) = 0
			Delete (A−B)
			Send Q(G, A*B)
			Group Timer = GMI
INCLUDE (A)	TO_IN (B)	INCLUDE (A+B)	(B) = GMI
			Send Q(G, A−B)
EXCLUDE (X, Y)	ALLOW (A)	EXCLUDE (X+A, Y−A)	(A) = GMI
EXCLUDE (X, Y)	BLOCK (A)	EXCLUDE (X+(A−Y), Y)	(A−X−Y) = Group Timer
			Send Q(G, A−Y)
EXCLUDE (X, Y)	TO_EX (A)	EXCLUDE (A−Y, Y*A)	(A−X−Y) = Group Timer
			Delete (X−A)
			Delete (Y−A)
			Send Q(G, A−Y)
			Group Timer = GMI
EXCLUDE (X, Y)	TO_IN (A)	EXCLUDE (X+A, Y−A)	(A) = GMI
			Send Q(G, X−A)
			Send Q(G)

RFC 3376 uses the following notation for describing the Query messages sent:

- "Q(G)" describes a Group-Specific Query Message to G.
- "Q(G, A)" describes a Group-and-Source Specific Query message to G with source-list A. If source-list A is null due to the action (e.g., A*B), then no query is sent as a result of the operation.

contents of those Queries. Section 2.5.5.6.3 describes the process by which routers build and maintain the state of pending Queries.

2.5.5.5 Switching Multicast Router Filter Modes

A multicast router uses the Group Timer for transitioning the router filter mode on an interface from the EXCLUDE to INCLUDE mode. When the router detects that a Group Timer has expired with a router filter mode in EXCLUDE, it assumes that the attached network segment has no systems with a filter mode of EXCLUDE on it. When the router detects that the router filter mode for a multicast group on an interface is EXCLUDE and the Group Timer has expired, it will transition the filter mode for that group to INCLUDE.

When a router switches the filter mode of a multicast group on an interface to INCLUDE, it uses the source records with their running Source Timers as its state. If the router detects that there are any source records with Source Timers greater than zero (i.e., systems on the interface have requested for multicast traffic to be forwarded from such source), it will switch the filter mode to INCLUDE using those source records. The router will delete source records (from the previous filter mode of EXCLUDE mode) whose timers are zero.

For example, if the router filter mode state for a multicast group on an interface is EXCLUDE (X, Y) and the Group Timer for that group expires, the router will switch to the filter mode of INCLUDE with state INCLUDE (X). Recall that the notation (X, Y) represents the total number of sources for a particular multicast group, where:

- X = set of source records whose Source Timers > 0 (Sources that, at least one system on the network segment, has requested traffic from)
- Y = set of source records whose Source Timers = 0 (Sources that IGMPv3 will suggest to the routing protocol to not forward traffic from)

2.5.5.6 Action on Reception of Query Messages

This section describes the actions taken by systems on a network segment when they receive Query messages.

2.5.5.6.1 Timer Updates

When a multicast router sends or receives a Query message with the Suppress Router-Side Processing flag set to zero, it must update the local timers to reflect the correct timeout values for the sources or multicast group being queried. The timer actions taken by the router when sending or receiving a Group-Specific or Group-and-Source-Specific Query message with the Suppress Router-Side Processing flag set to zero are described as follows:

Query	Action
Q(G, A)	Source Timer for sources in A is lowered to LMQT
Q(G)	Group Timer is lowered to LMQT

When the router sends or receives a Query message with the Suppress Router-Side Processing flag set to 1, it will not update its timers.

2.5.5.6.2 Querier Election

IGMPv3 uses the same Querier election mechanism in IGMPv2 to elect a single Querier for each network segment. When a multicast router receives a Query message with a lower IP address in the source IP address field of the carrying IP packet, it will set the "Other-Querier-Present" timer equal to "Other Querier Present Interval", and then stop sending Query messages on the network segment if it was the previously elected Querier. After the router's "Other-Querier Present" timer expires, it will begin sending General Query messages on the network segment.

2.5.5.6.3 Building and Sending Specific Query Messages

This section describes how a multicast router constructs and sends Specific Query messages to systems on a network segment.

2.5.5.6.3.1 Building and Sending Group-Specific Query Messages

When the multicast router encounters an action "Send Q(G)" in Table 2.4, it must lower the Group Timer to "Last Member Query Time" (LMQT). The router must then immediately transmit a Group-Specific Query message on the network segment and also, schedule the retransmissions of ["Last Member Query Count"−1] number of Query messages to be transmitted every "Last Member Query Interval" over an interval equal to "Last Member Query Time".

When the router is transmitting a Group-Specific Query message, and detects that the Group Timer is larger than LMQT, it will set the "Suppress Router-Side Processing" bit to 1 in the Query message.

2.5.5.6.3.2 Building and Sending Group- and-Source-Specific Query Messages

When the Querier router encounters an action "Send Q(G, X)" in Table 2.4, it must perform the following actions for each of the sources in X of multicast group G on the associated interface, with Source Timer greater than LMQT:

- Set the number of retransmissions of Query messages for each source to "Last Member Query Count".
- Lower the Source Timer to LMQT.

The router must then immediately transmit a Group-and-Source-Specific Query message on the network segment, and also schedule the retransmission of ["Last Member Query Count"−1] several Query messages to be transmitted every "Last Member Query Interval" over an interval equal to "Last Member Query Time". The router calculates the contents of these Query messages as follows:

- When constructing a Group-and-Source-Specific Query message for a multicast group G on a network segment, the router sends two separate Query messages for that group:
  - The first Query message sent has the "Suppress Router-Side Processing" bit set to 1 and contains all the sources that have retransmission state and timers greater than LMQT.
  - The second Query message sent has the "Suppress Router-Side Processing" bit set to zero and contains all the sources that have retransmission state and timers less than or equal to LMQT.
- If either of the two Query messages constructed by the router does not contain any sources, then the router will suppress the transmission of the message.

It is important to note that if the multicast router has scheduled a Group-Specific Query message to be transmitted at the same time as a Group-and-Source-Specific Query message for the same multicast group on an interface, then it may suppress the transmission of the Group-and-Source-Specific Query message with the "Suppress Router-Side Processing" bit set to 1.

2.5.5.7 Summary of IGMPv3 Features

Other than the main feature of source filtering, IGMPv3 supports the following additional features over IGMPv2:

- State in an IGMPv3 router is maintained as Group plus List-of-Sources, rather than simply as Group as in IGMPv2.
- IGMPv3 defines interoperability with IGMPv1 and IGMPv2 systems as operations on the state.
- IGMPv3 introduced an IP Service Interface that allows the specification of source lists.
- The IGMPv3 Querier includes its Robustness Variable and Query Interval in Query messages it sends, to allow synchronization of these variables on multicast routers on a network segment that are Non-Queriers.
- The Maximum Response Time that the Querier sends in Query messages has an exponential range, and IGMPv3 changes the maximum from 25.5 seconds to about 53 minutes, allowing IGMPv3 to be used on links with huge numbers of systems.
- IGMPv3 allows hosts on a network segment to retransmit state-change messages, providing increased robustness for the protocol.
- IGMPv3 defines additional data sections, allowing future extensions of the protocol.
- Systems send IGMPv3 Membership Report messages to the multicast address 224.0.0.22, which assists IGMP Snooping switches to better constrain multicast traffic to only switch ports that have active multicast group members.
- IGMPv3 Membership Report messages can contain multiple Group Records, allowing systems on a network segment to report the full current state using fewer messages.
- IGMPv3 systems no longer perform Membership Report Suppression, simplifying host implementations and allowing the use of explicit group membership tracking.
- IGMPv3 introduced a new Suppress Router-Side Processing (S) flag in Query messages, which fixes robustness issues when using IGMPv2.

Table 2.5 compares the features of IGMPv1, IGMPv2, and IGMPv3.

2.6 IGMP SNOOPING

IGMP Snooping is a mechanism that can be configured on each broadcast domain (IP subnet or VLAN) to reduce unnecessary propagation of multicast traffic within the domain. This section discusses why multicast traffic constraining mechanisms like IGMP Snooping are needed in Layer 2 networks and how they work. Our focus here is on Layer 2 networks based on Ethernet and those that use IEEE 802.1D transparent bridging [IEEE802.1D2004]. Reference [AWEYFCDM22] describes in greater detail, the design of Ethernet switches, the IEEE 802.1D bridging algorithm, and how broadcast and multicast frames are handled in Ethernet networks.

TABLE 2.5

Comparing the Features of IGMPv1, IGMPv2, and IGMPv3

Feature	IGMPv1	IGMPv2	IGMPv3
IETF specification	RFC 1112	RFC 2236	RFC 3376
First byte value for Query message	0x11	0x11	0x11
Group address in General Query message	0.0.0.0	0.0.0.0	0.0.0.0
IPv4 destination address for General Query message	224.0.0.1	224.0.0.1	224.0.0.1
Default Query Interval	60 seconds	125 seconds	125 seconds
First byte value for Report message	0x12	0x16	0x22
Group address in Report message	Multicast group address being joined	Multicast group address being joined	Multicast group address being joined
IPv4 destination address for Report message	Multicast group address being joined	Multicast group address being joined	224.0.0.22
IGMP Report Suppression mechanism available?	Yes	Yes	No
Can Maximum Response Time be configured?	No, fixed at 10 seconds	Yes, 0–25.5 seconds	Yes, 0–53 minutes
Can a host send a message to leave a group?	No, does not support explicit leave message	Yes. Type code for IGMPv2 Leave Group message is 0x17	Yes
IPv4 destination address for Leave Group message	No, does not support Leave Group message; host silently leaves	224.0.0.2	No, does not support specific leave message; instead, uses Report message to leave a group and source
Can a router send a Group-Specific Query message?	No, does not support Group-Specific Query message	Yes, indicates the group address for which the device is querying	Yes, indicates the group address for which the device is querying
Can a router send a Group-and-Source-Specific Query message?	No, doesnotsupportGroup-and-Source-Specific Query message	No, doesnotsupportGroup-and-Source-Specific Query message	Yes, indicates the group and source addresses for which the device is querying
Can a host send source and group-specific Report messages?	No	No	Yes, such IGMPv3 Membership Reports are sent to the address 224.0.0.22
Rule for Electing a Querier?	None, depends on multicast routing protocol running	Yes, router with the lowest IP address on the network segment	Yes, router with the lowest IP address on the network segment
Compatible with other Versions of IGMP?	Not applicable	Yes, with IGMPv1	Yes, with both IGMPv1 and IGMPv2

2.6.1   Why We Need Multicast Traffic Constraining Mechanisms in Layer 2 Networks

An Ethernet switch running the IEEE 802.1D transparent algorithm forwards an incoming Ethernet frame by looking up the destination MAC address of the frame in a MAC address table (i.e., a Layer 2 forwarding table) to determine the outgoing port or ports on which to forward the frame. The switch also learns the MAC address-to-port mappings to populate the MAC address table. The switch examines the source MAC address of each incoming frame to learn the port on which the sending station resides, and then enters the MAC address and the port number in the MAC address table if that information does not already exist.

If the switch receives an Ethernet frame and there is no matching entry for its destination MAC address in the MAC address table, the switch floods the frame on all ports except the port on which the frame was received. The switch floods an Ethernet frame when it has not yet learned the port on which the destination MAC address resides (i.e., unknown destination MAC address), and when the destination MAC address is a broadcast or multicast MAC address. For an unknown destination MAC address, the switch has no choice but to flood the frame on all switch ports. When the switch eventually sees a frame with such a destination MAC address, it enters that address and receives the port number in the MAC address table, and from then on, frames with that address will be correctly forwarded.

Ethernet frames with a broadcast MAC address (i.e., FF.FF.FF.FF.FF.FF, in hexadecimal) are meant to be flooded, and the switch always floods such frames. Frames with multicast MAC addresses are also flooded similarly as those with a broadcast MAC address. This is because the switch has no way of knowing which of its ports hold multicast group members (which are generally dynamic in nature and membership can occur on any port and at any given time). For this reason, the switch simply floods multicast frames as if they were broadcast frames. Flooding of multicast packets leads to inefficient use of network bandwidth, particularly when the packets are targeted to only a small number of receivers on the Ethernet LAN. Multicast packets are flooded onto segments of the Ethernet LAN even where no host has expressed interest in receiving the packets.

Thus, given that broadcast and multicast frames can propagate in the Ethernet LAN, leading to unnecessary consumption of network bandwidth and resources, it is desirable to employ multicast traffic-limiting mechanisms such as IGMP Snooping. Broadcast frames must not be similarly constrained since they are meant to be flooded, and also, because several protocols such as DHCP (Dynamic Host Configuration Protocol) and ARP (Address Resolution Protocol) rely on broadcasts to function well as described in Chapter 5 of [AWEYFCDM22]. DHCP and its broadcast-based behavior are described in Reference [AWEYARCAP22].

2.6.2   What is IGMP Snooping?

In an IP subnet or VLAN without IGMP Snooping (see Figure 2.11), each switch simply floods all the multicast traffic that it receives on all ports in that broadcast domain (except the port on which the traffic was received). In networks where IP multicast

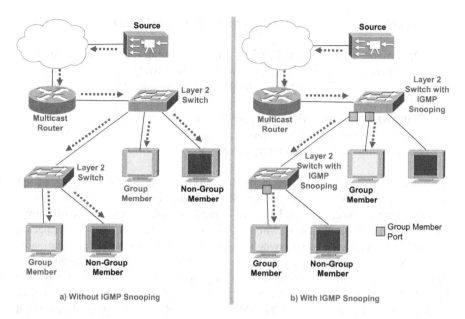

a) Without IGMP Snooping   b) With IGMP Snooping

FIGURE 2.11   IGMP Snooping.

traffic is significantly high, this process can result in significant and unnecessary bandwidth usage. IGMP Snooping provides the benefit of constraining multicast traffic to those segments of the LAN (i.e., broadcast domain) where hosts have expressed interest in receiving multicast packets addressed to a group address, thereby conserving network bandwidth.

Using IGMP Snooping allows the switches to detect IGMP Membership Query and Report messages, and to manage multicast traffic propagation throughout the broadcast domain. The process by which the switches listen to the IGMP messages is called IGMP Snooping. IGMP Snooping allows the switches to direct the multicast traffic to only switch ports with active multicast group members. MLD snooping is the counterpart of IGMP Snooping used to reduce the flooding of IPv6 multicast packets.

IGMP Snooping on the broadcast domain serves as a multicast constraining mechanism, improving multicast forwarding efficiency in the domain. Layer 2 (Ethernet) switches may be configured to listen to IGMP messages and maintain state information in their forwarding tables about which hosts have subscribed to a given multicast group. An IGMP Snooping switch creates Layer 2 multicast forwarding entries by listening to IGMP messages that are exchanged between the hosts and the attached multicast router(s) of the Layer 2 network. The switches then use the learned IGMP state information to forward multicast traffic that is destined to a given multicast group to only a limited set of ports and hosts, instead of forwarding the traffic to all ports regardless of IGMP joins and leaves. IGMP Snooping provides bandwidth conservation on those segments of the broadcast domain where no host has expressed interest in receiving the traffic addressed to a multicast group address.

The benefits of IGMP Snooping can be summarized as follows:

- **Optimized bandwidth utilization**: IGMP Snooping reduces the flooding of multicast packets on the LAN. The switch selectively forwards multicast packets to only ports that have group members instead of flooding them to all ports in a LAN.
- **Improved security**: IGMP Snooping helps prevent denial-of-service attacks when unknown sources send multicast packets that otherwise would have been continuously flooded on the LAN.

There are no firm rules or requirements for implementing IGMP Snooping except the recommendations provided in [RFC4541]. Actual implementation depends on the processing resources and architecture of the host switch. In some architectures, enabling IGMP Snooping on a switch would seriously degrade the overall packet forwarding performance of the switch. In many cases, efficient implementation of IGMP Snooping requires the use of hardware forwarding engines, or special hardware assist modules in the switch, because the processing load and state information the IGMP Snooping switch maintains is generally higher than what is expected of the traditional Ethernet switch. The additional load IGMP Snooping places on an Ethernet switch design without IGMP Snooping in mind (i.e., one that lacks special Layer 3 assist hardware) may lead to significant performance degradation and loss of both unicast and multicast packets.

2.6.3 How IGMP Snooping Works

The actions an IGMP Snooping switch will perform depend on the IGMP message type: Query, Report (IGMP "Join"), and Leave Group. Simply, when an IGMP Snooping switch receives an IGMP Report message on a port from a host signaling a desire to join a multicast group, it will add that port and possibly, group to its forwarding table. When the switch receives the last IGMP Leave Group message on a port from a host indicating a desire to leave a particular multicast group, it will remove that port and possibly, a group from the forwarding table.

2.6.3.1 IGMP Snooping and Forwarding Interfaces

To determine how to forward multicast traffic, the IGMP Snooping switch first determines the type of interfaces it supports and then maintains information about those interfaces in its multicast forwarding table:

- **Multicast router interfaces**: These are local interfaces/ports that lead toward multicast routers or IGMP Queriers. The IGMP Snooping switch registers all of these ports in its *multicast router port list*. The Snooping switch typically determines these ports by listening to PIM Hello and IGMP Query messages sent by multicast routers. Router ports are of the following types:
  - **Dynamic router port**: When the Snooping switch receives an IGMP General Query message on a port whose source IP address is not 0.0.0.0

or receives a PIM Hello message, it adds that port to its *dynamic router port list*. At the same time, the switch starts an *aging timer* for that port. If the switch receives either of these messages before the timer expires, it resets the timer. If the switch does not receive either of these messages when the timer expires, it deletes the port from the dynamic router port list.

- **Static router port**: When the network administrator configures a port statically as a router port, the Snooping switch adds that port to its *static router port list*. The Snooping switch does not age out a static router port; it can only be deleted manually.
- **Multicast group member interfaces**: These are local interfaces that lead toward hosts that are members of one or more multicast groups. The IGMP Snooping switch registers all these ports in its forwarding table. The switch determines these ports by listening to IGMP Membership Report messages sent by hosts. Member ports are of the following types:
  - **Dynamic member port**: When the Snooping switch receives an IGMP Membership Report message on a port, it adds that port to its *dynamic member port list* as an outgoing member interface. At the same time, the switch starts an aging timer for the port. If the switch receives an IGMP Report message before the timer expires, it resets the timer. If the switch does not receive an IGMP Report message when the timer expires, it deletes the port from the associated dynamic member list.
  - **Static member port**: When the network administrator statically configures a port as a member port, the Snooping switch adds that port to the associated *static member port list* as an outgoing member interface. The Snooping switch does not age out a static member port; it can only be deleted manually.

By monitoring IGMP traffic, the IGMP Snooping switch learns about these interfaces. If IGMP Query messages or PIM updates are received on an interface, the IGMP Snooping switch adds that interface to its multicast forwarding table and marks it as a *multicast router interface or port*. If IGMP Membership Report messages are received on an interface for a multicast group, the IGMP Snooping switch adds that interface to its multicast forwarding table and marks it as a *multicast group member interface or port*.

Typically, the IGMP Snooping switch ages out learned interface entries in its multicast forwarding table after a period. For example, if the switch does not receive IGMP Query or PIM Hello messages on a learned multicast router interface within a certain interval, it will remove the entry for that interface from its multicast forwarding table. For the IGMP Snooping to learn which interfaces are multicast router interfaces and group member interfaces, the Layer 2 network must support an IGMP Querier.

2.6.3.1.1 Constraining Multicast Traffic to Well-Known IP Multicast Addresses

Some networks may have routers that have no interest in IGMP traffic and multicast traffic sent to hosts on a network segment, but still generate their own multicast messages, for example, when running routing protocols like OSPF. When a Snooping switch receives multicast packets from such a router, it adds the port leading to that router to its *All-Groups port list*. This means IGMP and multicast traffic is unnecessarily sent to that router. Using IGMP features (as described in [ALLTELQUSOL]) to prevent that router from receiving unwanted traffic is, particularly, helpful when the network administrator cannot or does not want to control the traffic at the router. The network administrator can use this IGMP feature to prevent such traffic, by limiting the ports that the Snooping switch adds to the All-Groups list, or by stopping particular types of traffic from causing the switch to add ports to the All-Groups list.

The Snooping switch adds a port to its All-Groups list when it determines that the port has a router attached to it. When the Snooping switch receives a multicast packet on a port, it compares the destination IP address of the packet with a list of well-known multicast group addresses (see Table 2.6). If there is a match, the switch considers the multicast packet to be from a "router", and adds the attached port to the All-Groups list.

2.6.3.1.2 Static Ports

A network administrator can also configure an interface on the switch as a *static multicast router interface/port* or a *static group member interface* in the multicast forwarding table (a configuration feature called *Static IGMP*). The switch adds a *static interface* (an unlearned interface) to its multicast forwarding table permanently and does not subject that entry to aging. The switch can have a mix of *dynamically learned* and *statically configured* interfaces.

If all hosts attached to a port of the Snooping switch are interested in multicast packets addressed to a particular multicast group, or multicast packets that a particular multicast source sends to a particular group, that port can be configured as a *static group member port* of the specified multicast group or the specified source and

TABLE 2.6
Some Well-Known Router Multicast Group Addresses

Address Name	Address
IGMPv1/v2/v3 Queries multicast group address (the All-Hosts multicast group address, all hosts on the same network segment)	224.0.0.1
IGMPv3 Reports multicast group address	224.0.0.22
All routers on this subnet (the All-Routers multicast group address, all routers on the same network segment)	224.0.0.2
All OSPF Routers on a network segment address	224.0.0.5
OSPF Designated Routers on a network segment address	224.0.0.6
RIP2 Routers on a network segment address	224.0.0.9
All PIM Routers on a network segment address	224.0.0.13
All EIGRP Routers on a network segment address	224.0.0.10
VRRP multicast group address	224.0.0.18

multicast group. A port can also be configured as a static router port, through which the Snooping switch can forward all the multicast traffic that it receives.

The Snooping switch does not respond to Query messages from the IGMP Querier for static group member ports. When a port is configured as a static group member port or the configuration on the port is canceled, the Snooping switch does not send an unsolicited IGMP Report or an IGMP Leave Group message [H3CMULTGUID].

The network administrator may configure Static IGMP on a Layer 2 switch with specified multicast group-to-interface or group-to-port mappings, for any of the following reasons [ALLTELQUSOL]:

- A switch port includes hosts that cannot send IGMP Membership Report messages
- To guarantee that a specific multicast stream is immediately available on a switch port without any delay if any host has joined the multicast group on the port.

A typical use of Static IGMP is when protocols like Service Location Protocol (SLP or srvloc) [RFC2608] are run in the network. SLP is a protocol for service discovery that allows computing devices to discover services in a LAN without prior configuration. SLP uses extensively multicasting, especially devices that first join a network use multicasting to find other devices. SLP hosts transmit multicast messages that need to be forwarded to designated switch ports. SLP Request messages are sent via multicast to the reserved administratively scoped SLP multicast address, 239.255.255.253. The network operator may want switches to forward SLP messages to ports that have servers that need to respond to these messages. Static IGMP allows the network administrator to specify the switch ports that have hosts that will respond to messages for this multicast group or are interested in these messages. When an IGMP static entry is created on a switch, it immediately appears in the switch's IGMP Snooping table and IGMP table.

2.6.3.1.3   Aging Timers for Dynamic Ports

Typically, an IGMP Snooping switch maintains several *aging timers* for dynamic ports as described in Table 2.7 [H3CMULTGUID]. The IGMP Snooping switch applies the port aging mechanism to only dynamic ports; static ports are never aged out.

2.6.3.2   Handling IGMP Membership Query Messages

An IGMP Query message is one sent by the IGMP Querier (which can be a multicast router or a Layer 2 switch configured for such functions) requesting a response from an interface if any host exists on it that is a member of a multicast group. If there is no multicast router on a network segment acting as the IGMP Querier, then a Layer 2 switch on the segment must play this role to elicit multicast group membership information from the hosts on the network.

TABLE 2.7

Aging Timers for Dynamic Ports in the IGMP Snooping Switch

Timer	Description	Message Types before Timer Expiry	Action after Timer Expiry
Dynamic multicast router port aging timer	For each dynamic multicast router port, the switch sets a timer initialized to a *dynamic router port aging time.*	Non-receipt of an IGMP Query message of which the source IP address is not 0.0.0.0 or PIM Hello message	The switch deletes this port from its multicast router port list.
Dynamic group member port aging timer	When a host on a port dynamically joins a multicast group, the switch sets a timer for the port, which is initialized to a *dynamic member port aging time.*	Non-receipt of an IGMP Membership Report message.	The switch deletes this port from the IGMP Snooping forwarding table.

The IGMP Querier periodically sends IGMP General Query messages to all systems (hosts and routers) on an interface to determine if any multicast group members exist on it. Upon receiving an IGMP General Query message, the IGMP Snooping switch forwards that message to all of its ports on that broadcast domain (IP subnet or VLAN) except the port on which the message was received. The switch also performs the following actions:

- If the port on which the message is received is a dynamic router port in the switch's multicast router port list, the switch resets the aging timer of this dynamic router port.
- If the port on which the message is received is not a dynamic router port in the switch's multicast router port list, the switch adds this port to the multicast router port list and sets an aging timer for this dynamic router port.

2.6.3.3 Handling IGMP Membership Report Messages

An IGMP Membership Report message is one sent by a host to the IGMP Querier and other multicast routers (including IGMP Snooping switches) on the network segment to indicate that it is a member of (or one that desires to be a member of) the multicast group indicated in the message. A host sends an IGMP Report message to signal an interest in a multicast group membership or as a response to Query messages if it is still a multicast group member.

Upon receiving an IGMP Report message from a host on a switch port, the IGMP Snooping switch forwards that message to all its other ports leading to routed interfaces in the broadcast domain (IP subnet or VLAN). A routed interface is a physical router port (not a Layer 2 interface) that can receive and route IP packets to other devices. A routed interface, here, means a neighboring multicast router interface including those of the IGMP Querier. *Note that until the switch knows which outgoing ports lead to routed interfaces, it will forward the Report message to all other ports* (Figure 2.12). It also performs a look-up in its forwarding table for a matching entry as follows (Figure 2.12):

- If no matching entry is found in the forwarding table, the IGMP Snooping switch adds a new forwarding entry with the receiving port as a dynamic group member port; the port added to the outgoing port list (also called the outgoing interface list (OIL)). The switch also starts a *group membership expiry timer* for the receiving port to track the amount of time that elapses before it decides that the port has no more members of a multicast group.
- If a matching entry is found in the forwarding table but that matching entry does not contain the port on which the message was received, the IGMP Snooping switch adds the receiving port to the forwarding table's OIL. The switch also starts a group membership expiry timer for that port.
- If a matching entry is found in the forwarding table and that matching entry contains the port on which the message was received (the port is already a dynamic member port), the Snooping switch restarts the group membership expiry timer for the port.

Figure 2.12 also describes how the IGMP Snooping switch determines which of its ports leads to routed interfaces. The switch may be manually configured to know which ports lead to routed interfaces. If the Snooping switch knows which ports lead to routed interfaces, it can efficiently forward Report messages on only those ports to conserve network bandwidth usage. Configuring the IGMP Snooping switch to automatically detect which ports lead to routed interfaces enables it to efficiently use IGMP Snooping. Indiscriminately forwarding Report messages on all switch ports defeats the purpose of IGMP Snooping in the first place, except at the start of system operation when the switch is yet to discover routed interfaces.

The IGMP Snooping switch does not forward a Report message on non-router ports (i.e., on multicast group member ports) because doing so will cause all the attached hosts that are monitoring the reported multicast address to suppress sending their own Report messages after receiving this Report message according to the IGMP Report Suppression mechanism discussed earlier. Forwarding Report messages on group member ports prevents the Snooping switch from determining whether the reported multicast group still has active multicast group members attached to those ports.

2.6.3.4 Detection of Routed Interfaces on a Network Segment

For efficient operation of IGMP Snooping, a Snooping switch must be able to detect which of its ports connect (directly or indirectly) to multicast routers to avoid flooding multicast packets indiscriminately on all ports. Generally, devices on a network segment can detect the presence of routers by listening to special protocol messages sent by routers such as OSPF Hello messages, IS-IS Hello messages, PIM Hello messages, IGMP Membership Query messages, VRRP messages, and so on.

Other than IGMP Query messages, an IGMP Snooping switch, in particular, can detect the presence of multicast routers on the network segment by listening

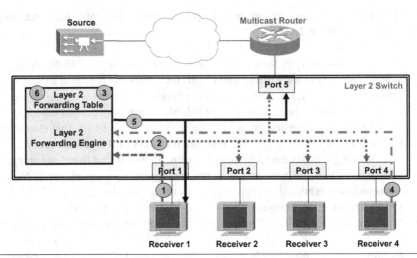

Processing steps:
1. Receiver 1 signals its desire to join multicast group 224.1.2.3 by multicasting an unsolicited IGMP Membership Report to the group with a Ethernet multicast MAC destination address 01:00:5E:01:02:03.
2. Assuming that initially the Layer 2 forwarding table has no entries for this multicast MAC address, the Layer 2 forwarding engine floods the IGMP Membership Report on all ports including the router port, Port 5 (see note).
3. The forwarding engine also enters the port on which the IGMP Membership Report message was received (Port 1) and the router port (Port 5) into the forwarding table.
   - As a result of this entry, the forwarding engine will forward any future Ethernet multicast frames addressed to the multicast MAC address 01:00:5E:01:02:03 to only these ports (Ports 1 and 5) and not to the other ports.
   - The forwarding engine also continues to look out for other IGMP messages addressed to this multicast MAC address.
4. Receiver 4 also signals its desire to join multicast group 224.1.2.3 by multicasting an unsolicited IGMP Membership Report to the group with an Ethernet multicast MAC destination address 01:00:5E:01:02:03.
5. Examining the forwarding table, the forwarding engine forwards the new Membership Report to only Ports 1 and 5.
6. The forwarding engine then adds the port (Port 4) on which the second Membership Report (with multicast MAC destination address 01:00:5E:01:02:03) was received to the forwarding table. The forwarding table now has Ports 1, 4, and 5 associated with the multicast MAC destination address 01:00:5E:01:02:03.
   - At this point, the forwarding engine will constrain any multicast traffic sent to multicast MAC destination address 01:00:5E:01:02:03 to only Ports 1, 4, and 5.

Note: IGMP Snooping switches detect router ports (i.e., ports that are connected to routers) by listening to IGMP Query messages, PIM Hello messages, OSPF Hello messages, Virtual Router Redundancy Protocol (VRRP) messages and other special routing protocol messages sent periodically by routers. A snooping switch listens on each port and infers from such messages that a router is connected to a particular port.

FIGURE 2.12   Joining a multicast group on a Layer 2 switch running IGMP Snooping.

to PIM Hello messages, Multicast Router Discovery (MRD) messages [RFC4286], and VRRP messages (in the case where multiple multicast routers are used to provide routing redundancy). Listening solely to Query messages is not reliable since an active Querier may not be the Designated Router (DR) for the network segment which is responsible for forwarding multicast packets onto and from the segment if multiple routers exist. It is important to note that the DR is also elected and might be the active Querier for the segment. The DR, surely, will periodically transmit multicast-related messages (PIM Join/Prune messages) on the network segment which can be detected by the IGMP Snooping switch.

An IGMP Snooping switch must maintain a list of multicast routers and the ports on which they are connected which can be done using any combination of the following methods [RFC4541]:

- The Snooping switch can send Multicast Router Solicitation messages [RFC4286]. It may also listen to (i.e., snoop) Multicast Router Advertisement messages sent by multicast routers to other nodes. A device on a network segment sends Multicast Router Solicitation messages to solicit Multicast Router Advertisement messages from multicast routers attached to the network segment. A router sends Multicast Router Advertisement messages to announce that IP multicast forwarding is enabled on the advertising interface. A router sends a Multicast Router Termination message when it stops IP multicast routing functions on the sending interface. A multicast router sends unsolicited Multicast Router Advertisement messages periodically on all interfaces on which multicast forwarding is enabled or sends Multicast Router Advertisement messages in response to Multicast Router Solicitation messages.
- The Snooping switch can listen to IGMP Membership Query messages and note the arrival port and the message's source IP address as long as it is not 0.0.0.0.
- Some ports of the Snooping switch may be explicitly configured by management to forward IGMP Membership Report messages to router ports, in addition to, or instead of any of the earlier methods.

2.6.3.5   Handling IGMP Leave Group Messages

An IGMP Leave Group message is one sent by a host to the multicast routers on the network segment to indicate that it has ceased being a member of a specific multicast group. The IGMP Snooping switch performs the following actions when a host ceases to be a member of a multicast group:

- IGMPv1 hosts do not send any Leave Group messages when they leave a multicast group. This means the IGMP Snooping switch is not able to immediately update the status of a port that connects to an IGMPv1 receiver host even if it leaves. In this case, the Snooping switch does not remove that port from the OIL in the associated forwarding entry until the group membership timer expires.
- IGMPv2 hosts send IGMP Leave Group messages, while IGMPv3 hosts send appropriate (and equivalent) "source filtering" messages when they leave a multicast group. Upon receiving such leave messages, the

Snooping switch forwards them to all routed ports in the broadcast domain (IP subnet or VLAN). The active IGMP Querier of the network segment (upon receiving this message) then sends an IGMP Group-Specific Query message to the multicast group to determine if the group still has active receivers attached to the interface on which the leave message was received.

- Upon receiving the IGMP Group-Specific Query from the Querier, the Snooping switch forwards that message to all its other ports to determine if a multicast group member exists in the broadcast domain (IP subnet or VLAN). The switch then waits for any IGMP Report messages sent in response from the directly connected hosts. If the switch does not receive any IGMP Report message on the port on which the leave message was received and the group membership timer expires, it removes that port from the forwarding entry for the multicast group.

- When the switch sees an IGMP Leave Group message on a dynamic group member port, it first checks whether a forwarding table entry for that group exists, and, if one exists, whether its OIL contains that dynamic port.

  - If a forwarding table entry does not exist or its OIL does not contain the dynamic port, the Snooping switch discards the IGMP Leave Group message instead of forwarding it on any switch port.

  - If the forwarding table entry exists and its OIL contains the dynamic port, the Snooping switch forwards the IGMP Leave Group message to all router ports in the network segment. Because the switch does not know whether any other hosts attached to the port are still listening to that multicast group address, it does not immediately delete the port from the OIL of the forwarding table entry for that group. Instead, it resets the aging timer for the dynamic port.

  - If the Snooping switch receives any IGMP Report message on a dynamic member port in response to the IGMP Group-Specific Query message before its aging timer expires, this indicates that a host attached to the port is expecting to receive or is receiving multicast packets for that multicast group. The switch therefore resets the aging timer of that port.

  - If the Snooping switch receives no IGMP Report message in response to the IGMP Group-Specific Query message on the port before its aging timer expires, this indicates that no hosts attached to the port are still listening to that group address. The switch then deletes the port from the OIL associated with the entry in the forwarding table for that multicast group when the aging timer expires.

It is important to note *that in Figure 2.13, the IGMP Snooping switch also performs the functions of the IGMP Querier for the network segment (or broadcast domain), that is, it is also an IGMP Snooping Querier* (see Section 2.6.5). In an IP multicast network that runs IGMP, one multicast router, the IGMP Querier, is responsible for sending IGMP Query messages, so that all multicast devices can establish and maintain multicast forwarding entries for active multicast groups.

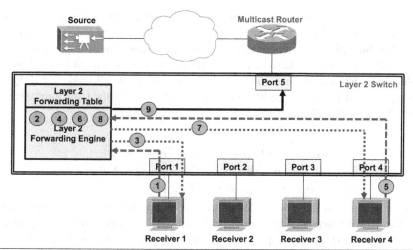

- Let us assume Receivers 1 and 4 are already members of multicast group 224.1.2.3 with corresponding multicast MAC address 01:00:5E:01:02:03.

Processing steps:
1. Receiver 1 signals its desire to leave the group by multicasting an IGMP Leave Group message to 224.0.0.2 (which is the All Routers Multicast Group Address or All Routers on this Subnet) with corresponding multicast MAC address 01:00:5E:00:00:02.
   - Note that unlike IGMP Membership Report messages (which are transmitted to a target multicast group address), Leave Group messages are sent to the All Routers Multicast Group Address (224.0.0.2).
2. The forwarding engine intercepts the Leave Group message and does not forward it to any other ports.
3. The forwarding engine responds to the Leave Group message by sending an IGMP General Query message back on Port 1 to check if there are any other receivers that are members of multicast group 224.1.2.3.
   - Note that multiple receivers of this group may be connected to this port via downstream switches.
4. If the forwarding engine receives another IGMP Report message from another receiver on Port 1, it will quietly discard the Leave Group message previously received from Receiver 1. This case means there are other group members on Port 1 other than Receiver 1.
   - If, on the other hand, the forwarding engine does not receive a Report message on Port 1, it will delete Port 1 from the forwarding table (we assume this is the case in this example). Because another non-router port (Port 4) is still in the forwarding table, the forwarding engine does not send an IGMP message to the multicast router.
5. Receiver 4 signals its desire to leave the group by multicasting an IGMP Leave Group message to the All Routers Multicast Group Address.
6. Once again, the forwarding engine intercepts this Leave Group message and does not forward it to any other ports.
7. The forwarding engine responds to the Leave Group message from Receiver 4 by sending an IGMP General Query message back on Port 4 to check if there are any other receivers that are members of multicast group 224.1.2.3.
8. We assume in this case there are no other receivers of this multicast group on Port 4, and no Report message is received on this port. So, the forwarding engine deletes Port 4 from the forwarding table.
9. Because Port 4 is the last non-router port in the forwarding table for multicast group 224.1.2.3 with corresponding multicast MAC address 01:00:5E:01:02:03, the forwarding engine deletes this entry and then forwards an IGMP Leave Group message to the multicast router for normal processing.

FIGURE 2.13   Leaving a multicast group on a Layer 2 switch running IGMP Snooping.

However, an ordinary Layer 2 switch (that is capable of broadcast and multicast) does not support IGMP, and therefore cannot send IGMP Query messages. However, an IGMP Snooping Querier function can be implemented on a Layer 2 switch in an IP subnet or VLAN where multicast traffic is forwarded only at Layer 2 and no multicast routers are present. In this case, this Layer 2 switch sends IGMP Query messages, so that multicast forwarding entries can be established and maintained at Layer 2 (see Section 2.6.5).

2.6.3.5.1   How Hosts Leave Multicast Groups on an IGMP Snooping Switch That Does NOT Support IGMP Querier Functions: Queries and Timers

When a host on a switch port leaves a multicast group, the IGMP Snooping switches and the IGMP Querier check which ports still have members that belong to that group. These devices will stop forwarding the traffic to the multicast group on any ports that have no active members. This section summarizes the leave process and the timers used. We assume here that the network *supports an IGMP Querier that is separate from the IGMP Snooping switches*; the Snooping switches do not support IGMP Querier functions. The IGMP Querier in this case may also be the sole multicast router responsible for sending multicast onto the attached Layer 2 network segment.

The basic process when a host leaves a multicast group on a dynamic member port can be summarized as follows [ALLTELQUSOL]:

1. The host sends an IGMP Leave Group message to indicate that it no longer needs to receive that multicast group traffic.
2. The IGMP Snooping switch receives the Leave Group message and forwards it toward the Querier and other attached multicast routers.
3. For all switch ports that belong to the multicast group being left, the IGMP Querier changes its internal group membership timer to a short value (e.g., 2 seconds).
4. The IGMP Querier sends an IGMP Group-Specific Query message to determine which other hosts on the network still belong to that multicast group.
5. The IGMP Snooping receives the Group-Specific Query message. For all switch ports that belong to that multicast group, the Snooping switch changes its internal group membership timer to a short value (e.g., 2 seconds) unless the timer is already short. The switch forwards the Query message on all its ports.
6. The IGMP Querier waits for the Last Member Query Interval time (1 second by default), and then sends a second Group-Specific Query message.
7. The Snooping switch snoops this second Group-Specific Query message and uses it to set the internal group membership timer for each port unless the timer is already short (which will be the case if the Snooping switch received the first Group-Specific Query message). The switch forwards the Group-Specific Query message on all its ports.

8. If the Snooping switch receives an IGMP Membership Report message on a switch port, it sets the port timer to the default Timeout Interval value and continues to forward the multicast stream on that port. Otherwise, the timers for that port expire and the Snooping switch stops forwarding the multicast stream on that port.

When the IGMP Querier sends a Group-Specific Query message for a multicast group in response to a Leave Group message, it updates a timer for ports that forward traffic for that group. The timer value is obtained by multiplying the following two values together [ALLTELQUSOL]:

- **Last Member Query Count (LMQC):** This is the number of Group-Specific Query messages that the Querier sends (default is 2).
- **Last Member Query Interval (LMQI):** This is the time interval between the Group-Specific Query messages (default is 1 second).

The default LMQC and LMQI values, already cited, give a timeout of 2 seconds for a timer for ports that forward traffic for the multicast group. Therefore, in this case, by default, the IGMP Querier must see the response from a host within 2 seconds of sending the first IGMP Group-Specific Query message.

When the IGMP Snooping switch receives a Group-Specific Query message from the Querier, it may update a timer for switch ports that forward traffic to that multicast group. In Reference [ALLTELQUSOL], the Snooping switch calculates the timer value by taking the LMQI value that it receives from the Querier and multiplying it by the Snooping switch's own LMQC. The Snooping switch only reduces the timer if it receives an IGMP Leave Group message followed by a Group-Specific Query message, one of these messages is not enough. The Querier and Snooping switch port-specific Group Timers have the same default value, 2 seconds. This is because both devices have the same LMQC value.

The IGMP Querier and the Snooping switches keep multicast group membership timeout values for each port [ALLTELQUSOL]. During general multicast traffic forwarding, these timeouts are set to 260 seconds (by default). When a host leaves a multicast group, any of these devices reduce these timeouts to make multicast forwarding stop quickly after the last host leaves. The devices use the LMQC and LMQI to determine the value of the timeout during this group leave process (2 seconds with the default LMQC and LMQI according to [ALLTELQUSOL]):

- On the IGMP Querier, the timeout during the leave process $= LMQC \times LMQI$
- On the Snooping switches, the timeout during the leave process $= LMQI$ from Querier $\times$ LMQC from Snooping switch

Reference [ALLTELQUSOL] describes potential problems with changing the values of these counters and timers and other IGMP counters and timers. The network administrator must be aware of the likely effect on the network when these values are changed as explained in [ALLTELQUSOL].

2.6.3.5.2   How Hosts Leave Multicast Groups on an IGMP Snooping Switch That ALSO Supports IGMP Querier Functions

When the IGMP Snooping switch (which also functions as the IGMP Querier) receives an IGMP Leave Group message on a dynamic member port, it first checks whether it has a forwarding entry that matches the multicast group address in the message. The leave process on the Snooping switch can be summarized as follows:

1. If the Snooping switch does not find a match for the multicast group, it discards the IGMP Leave Group message.
2. If the Snooping switch finds a match but the receiving port is not an outgoing interface listed in the forwarding entry for the multicast group, it discards the IGMP Leave Group message.
3. If the Snooping switch finds a match and the receiving port is not the only outgoing interface in the forwarding entry for the multicast group, it performs the following actions:
   a. Discards the IGMP Leave Group message.
   b. Sends an IGMP Group-Specific Query to determine whether the multicast group still has active receivers attached to the receiving port.
   c. Sets the aging timer for the receiving port to two times the IGMP Last Member Query Interval.
4. If the Snooping switch finds a match and the receiving port is the only outgoing interface in the forwarding entry for the multicast group, it performs the following actions:
   a. Forwards the IGMP Leave Group message to all router ports in the network segment (IP subnet or VLAN).
   b. Sends an IGMP Group-Specific Query message to determine whether the multicast group still has active receivers attached to the receiving port.
   c. Sets the aging timer for the receiving port to two times the IGMP Last Member Query Interval.

After receiving the IGMP Leave Group message on a port, the IGMP Querier function in the Snooping switch resolves the multicast group address in the message. Then, it sends an IGMP Group-Specific Query message through the receiving port to the multicast group. A normal IGMP Querier in a network will send the IGMP Group-Specific Query message through all its router ports to all members of the multicast group. The Snooping switch then waits for the responding IGMP Membership Report messages from the directly connected hosts. For the dynamic member port that received the IGMP Leave Group message, the Snooping switch also performs one of the following actions:

- If the switch receives an IGMP Report message on the port before the aging timer expires, it resets the aging timer.
- If the switch does not receive an IGMP Report message when the aging timer expires, it deletes the port from the forwarding entry for the multicast group.

2.6.3.6 Maintaining a Multicast Group on a Layer
2 Switch Running IGMP Snooping

An IGMP Snooping switch (just like a multicast router) cannot always count on receiving a Leave Group message (or its IGMPv3 equivalent) for a multicast group from hosts on an interface to determine if there are still any active members of that group left on that interface. Recall that IGMPv1 does not even support Leave Group messages, meaning that the host can simply leave a multicast group without indicating such actions to the multicast router. Furthermore, Leave Group messages that are sent may not even get to the intended targets (IGMP Snooping switch and multicast router) because of network traffic overload or congestion.

For these reasons, the IGMP Snooping switch (just like the multicast router) must rely on the IGMP Query-Response mechanism to maintain a multicast group membership state for each port. The IGMP Snooping switch uses the Query-Response mechanism to determine when a host has left a multicast group on one of its ports. In Figure 2.14, the multicast router (which we assume is also the IGMP Querier) on Port 5 of the IGMP Snooping switch periodically transmits an IGMP General Query message on that port to solicit IGMP Membership Report messages from hosts still interested in receiving multicast traffic. The IGMP Snooping switch intercepts the Query message and retransmit it on all its other ports.

Any host that is still a multicast group member on any one of these ports will respond with a Report message. These Report messages signal to the IGMP Snooping switch which ports still have active multicast group members, allowing the switch to keep a state about group membership per port even in the absence of Leave Group message reception on the ports. The Snooping switch needs to transmit only one of these Report messages it receives to the multicast router in response to the received General Query message.

2.6.3.7 Handling Send-Only Multicast Hosts on a Layer
2 Switch Running IGMP Snooping

A multicast source S that sends packets to multicast group G is not required to join that group to be able to send data, it only sends packets to the network to be forwarded to any interested receiver that has joined group G. Thus, a multicast source does not send IGMP Membership Report messages for the group it is sending to (unless the source itself wants to be a member of another multicast group). In this case, the IGMP Snooping switch, being a Layer 2 switch, would have to flood all multicast packets throughout the network segment similar to broadcast packets. This means a send-only multicast host sending packets in the network segment appears to the IGMP Snooping switch as an unconstrained traffic source (see Figure 2.15), thereby creating the need for a way to constrain such traffic in Snooping switch.

Allowing the IGMP Snooping switch to simply flood the packets from the multicast source (a send-only host) can lead to performance degradation and network overload depending on the nature of the traffic sent. If no host on the switch ports sends a Report message for the traffic sent by the multicast source, then the IGMP Snooping switch can direct that traffic to only the multicast router (via Port 5 in Figure 2.15) rather than continuously flooding the packets from this send-only host (i.e., the multicast source)

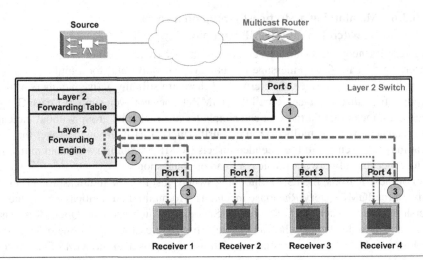

• An IGMP Snooping switch cannot always count on receiving an IGMP Leave Group message when a receiver of a multicast group leaves the group.
• Also, a receiver running IGMPv1 does not support the use of Leave Group messages and will leave a group quietly.
• A Leave Group message sent by a receiver may also be lost due to network congestion.
• For these reasons, IGMP Snooping switches use the IGMP General Query/Report mechanism for group/port state maintenance.
• Let us assume Receivers 1 and 4 are already members of multicast group 224.1.2.3 with corresponding multicast MAC address 01:00:5E:01:02:03.

Processing steps:
1. The multicast router periodically multicasts an IGMP General Query message to 224.0.0.1 (which is the All Hosts Multicast Group Address or All Systems on this Subnet) with corresponding multicast MAC address 01:00:5E:00:00:01.
2. The forwarding engine intercepts this General Query message and retransmits it out all ports.
3. Each receiver that is a member of the multicast group (i.e., Receivers 1 and 4) sends an IGMP Report message in response to the General Query message.
    • Because the forwarding engine intercepts all IGMP messages, the receivers do not hear each other's IGMP Report messages, which effectively forces each receiver to send an IGMP Report message.
    • The above action is necessary for the forwarding engine to receive an IGMP Report message on every port on which a group member is located as well as allow the forwarding engine to maintain those ports in the port list of the forwarding table.
4. In order to keep the IGMP Group Membership alive in the multicast router, the forwarding engine must forward at least one of the received IGMP Report messages for the multicast group to the multicast router.

FIGURE 2.14 Maintaining a multicast group on a Layer 2 switch running IGMP Snooping.

through all its ports [CISCPRWILL03]. So, as long as no Report messages are received from any switch port, it is more desirable for the Snooping switch to forward all of these packets to the multicast router. Here again, the Snooping switch must detect which of its ports are connected to routed interfaces as discussed earlier.

2.6.4 RECOMMENDATIONS FOR IGMP SNOOPING

Reference [RFC4541] provides several recommendations based on industry best practices for implementing IGMP Snooping. These findings are summarized

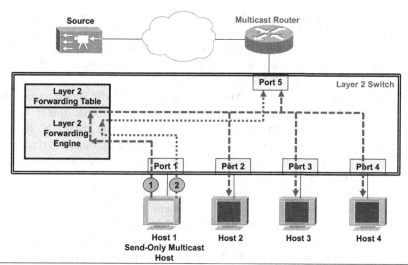

FIGURE 2.15   Handling send-only multicast hosts on a Layer 2 switch running IGMP Snooping.

in this section. The functionality of an IGMP Snooping switch can be separated into control actions (i.e., IGMP message forwarding) and data forwarding actions (i.e., multicast packet forwarding).

2.6.4.1   IGMP Message Forwarding

The control actions performed by an IGMP Snooping switch are as follows:

- **Forwarding IGMP Membership Report messages**: When IGMP Membership Report messages are received by a Snooping switch, these messages should be forwarded only to those ports leading to routed interfaces (i.e., ports where multicast routers are attached). Report messages should not be forwarded to ports on which only hosts are attached since this negates the benefits of IGMP Snooping. When IGMPv1 and IGMPv2 are used, sending Report messages to other hosts on other switch ports can unintentionally result in hosts being prevented from joining a specific multicast group (because of the IGMP Membership Report Suppression feature which is a requirement for IGMPv1 and IGMPv2 hosts as described earlier). Also, if the Snooping switch does not receive a Report message from any host on a port, it will not forward multicast traffic on that port. An IGMPv3-only network does not experience this problem since IGMPv3 does not support IGMP Membership Report Suppression.

- **Forwarding IGMP Query Messages**: When the IGMP Snooping switch receives IGMP General Query messages on a multicast router interface, it should forward them to all other interfaces in the LAN. IGMP Group-Specific Query messages received on a multicast router interface are forwarded on only those interfaces in the LAN that have members of the multicast group.

- **Handling IGMP Proxy Devices**: An IGMP network may also contain IGMP Proxy devices that implement proxy reporting of IGMP Membership Report messages. An IGMP Proxy device receives Report messages from downstream hosts, summarizes those Reports, and uses the information provided to build internal multicast group membership states. A proxy-reporting device may use the all-zeros (0.0.0.0) as its source IP address when forwarding any summarized Report messages upstream. For this reason, when a Snooping switch receives IGMP Membership Report messages with the source IP address set to 0.0.0.0, it must not reject such messages.

- **Handling unrecognized IGMP messages**: All unrecognized IGMP messages that are received by an IGMP Snooping switch must be flooded to all other ports and the switch must not attempt to use any information contained beyond the end of the IP header.

- **Link Layer topology awareness**: An IGMP Snooping switch should be aware of any changes in the Link Layer (Ethernet) topology caused by the Spanning Tree Protocol (STP) operation, including any STP variant such as Rapid Spanning Tree Protocol (RSTP) and Multiple Spanning Tree Protocol (MSTP). When the Snooping switch detects that a port is enabled or disabled by STP, it may send (i.e., spoof) an IGMP General Query message (i.e., assuming the Snooping switch is also capable of performing Querier processing functions) on all active ports that connect to non-router nodes to reduce network convergence time. Non-Querier Snooping switches in the network segment should be aware of whether the "Snooping switch Querier" is operating in IGMPv3 mode. If this is the case, the Snooping switch should not send (spoof) any General Query messages unless it can send an IGMPv3 Query message that conforms to the most recent information sent by the network segment's true Querier. The Snooping switch should under no circumstance send a spoofed IGMPv2 Query message onto an IGMPv3 network since this may create excessive network disruption.

   If the Snooping switch is not the true Querier of the network segment, it should use the all-zeros address (0.0.0.0) as the source IP Address in these proxy Query messages (even though some hosts that receive Query messages with 0.0.0.0 as the source IP address may elect to not process them).

When multicast routers receive such proxy Query messages, they must not include them in the (true) Querier election process.

- **Handling IGMP and IP header errors**: An IGMP Snooping switch must not use information in IGMP messages with header checksum or integrity errors or carried in IP packets with such errors. Such messages should not be flooded by the Snooping switch but, if it does, it should also log such error events (i.e., increment an error log counter).
- **Handling host leaves and deleting forwarding table entries**: An IGMP Snooping switch must not rely exclusively on the reception of IGMP Leave Group messages to determine when receivers on switch ports have left multicast groups, allowing corresponding entries should be removed from the forwarding table. The Snooping switch should implement a configurable membership timeout mechanism for deleting group entries in the forwarding table such as the router-side functionality of the IGMP discussed earlier.

2.6.4.2   Multicast Packet Forwarding

The multicast forwarding actions performed by an IGMP Snooping switch are as follows:

- **Handling non-IGMP packets outside 224.0.0.X range**: Packets that are received by the Snooping switch with destination IP address outside the 224.0.0.X range, which are not IGMP messages, should be forwarded according to the group-based port membership entries in its forwarding table; they must also be forwarded on routed interfaces.
- **Handling non-IGMP packets within the 224.0.0.X range**: Packets received by the Snooping switch with a destination IP address in the 224.0.0.X range and are not IGMP messages must be forwarded on all other ports. Addresses in the 224.0.0.X address range are defined as link-local (and are not to be routed), making it unnecessary for the Snooping switch to keep state for each address in this range. Also, some protocols use addresses in the 224.0.0.X address range for their operations without issuing IGMP join messages (see Table 2.6). Thus, these protocols would fail if the Snooping switch were to prune such messages due to not receiving a join group message from routers issuing messages with addresses in the 224.0.0.X address range.
- **Handling unregistered IPv4 multicast packets**: An unregistered IPv4 multicast packet is one that is received with a destination IP address that does not match any of the multicast group addresses announced in earlier IGMP Membership Report messages. These are multicast packets destined for a multicast group that has no current members. If a Snooping switch receives such a packet, it must forward it to all ports connected to the routed interface (i.e., to all multicast router interfaces).
- **Handling registered IPv4 multicast packets**: When the Snooping switch receives registered multicast packets, it should forward them to those host interfaces in the LAN that have members of the multicast group, as well as to all multicast router interfaces in the LAN.

- **Handling IPv4 non-multicast packets**: The Snooping switch should always flood all IPv4 non-multicast packets on all other ports in the forwarding state as per normal IEEE 802.1 bridging operations.
- **Forwarding tables**: An IGMP Snooping switch may maintain forwarding tables based on either IP addresses or MAC addresses. If both types of forwarding tables are supported by an IGMP Snooping switch, Reference [RFC4541] recommends the default behavior to be the use of IP address-based forwarding. IP address-based forwarding is preferred because mapping IP multicast addresses to corresponding Ethernet multicast MAC addresses can create MAC address ambiguities as described in Chapter 1 (32 IP addresses can map to 1 Ethernet multicast MAC address).
- **IP header checksum errors**: A Snooping switch that relies on information in the IP header should verify that the IP header checksum is correct. If a checksum error happens, the Snooping switch must not incorporate the information contained in the packet into the forwarding table, the packet should be discarded.
- **Handling IGMPv3 Membership Report messages**: When a Snooping switch receives IGMPv3 Membership Report messages with "INCLUDE source" and "EXCLUDE source" Group Records on a shared LAN segment, it needs to forward the superset of all those Group Records onto that shared segment. The Snooping switch must forward traffic from a particular source S to a group G if at least one host on the shared LAN segment sends an IGMPv3 Membership Report with Group Record type INCLUDE (Source_list1, G) or EXCLUDE (Source_list2, G), where S is an element of Source_list1 and not an element of Source_list2.

2.6.5 WHAT IS AN IGMP SNOOPING QUERIER?

As discussed earlier, one out of several routers in a network may be configured to act as an IGMP Querier for a network. However, in networks where no node is present to act as a multicast router and Querier, a LAN switch may be configured as an IGMP Snooping Querier to generate the needed IGMP messages that end hosts use to subscribe to multicast traffic. The Layer 2 IGMP Snooping Querier performs the functions of the multicast router Querier when the network does not have a multicast router (i.e., PIM and IGMP are not configured).

2.6.5.1 When Do We Need an IGMP Snooping Querier?

In a network that supports IP multicast routing, one multicast router is elected as the IGMP Querier. However, if multicast traffic in an IP subnet or VLAN only needs to be forwarded at Layer 2, a multicast router is not required. However, without a multicast router on the Layer 2 network segment, another switch on the network must be configured as the IGMP Querier, so that it can send out IGMP Query messages to local hosts.

Also, to enable an IGMP Snooping switch to learn which of its local interfaces are multicast router interfaces and group member interfaces, the LAN must support an

IGMP Querier. The Querier is often in a multicast router attached to the LAN, but
if there is no multicast router on the LAN, the IGMP Snooping switch itself can be
configured as an IGMP Querier (see Figure 2.16).

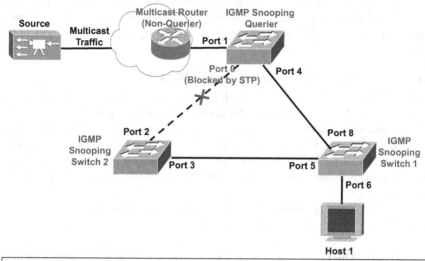

When a host joins a multicast group:
1. IGMP Snooping Querier starts receiving multicast traffic for multicast group G from the
   source S. The Snooping Querier has no interested receivers yet and so does not forward
   multicast traffic.
2. The Snooping Querier sends an IGMP General Query message to find out if there are any
   interested receivers on the network. IGMP Snooping Switch 1 receives the General Query
   message on Port 8, snoops the Query message, and creates an All Groups entry in its
   forwarding table for Port 8.
3. Snooping Switch 1 forwards the General Query message out all ports. We assume no
   receivers exist, so no receiver replies to the General Query message.
4. Host 1 joins group G by sending an IGMP Membership Report to the group address.
5. Snooping Switch 1 receives the Membership Report message on Port 6, snoops the
   message, and adds a group entry for Port 6. Snooping Switch 1 forwards the Report
   message out its All Groups port.
6. The Snooping Querier receives the Report message on Port 4 and adds a group entry for
   port 4. The Snooping Querier starts forwarding multicast traffic out Port 4.
7. Snooping Switch 1 receives the multicast traffic and forwards it out Port 6.
8. The Snooping Querier continues to send General Query messages periodically. These
   messages keep the All Groups entries alive on the Snooping Switches.
When a host leaves a multicast group:
1. When a host wants to stop receiving multicast traffic from a group, it sends an IGMP Leave
   message with a destination address of the group.
2. The Snooping Switch forwards the Leave message out its All Groups port, and the
   message arrives at the IGMP Snooping Querier.
3. At this point, the IGMP Snooping Querier sends a series of Group-Specific Query
   messages (e.g., 2 messages) to check if any other host is still listening to this group.
4. If the Snooping Switch receives a response to the Group-Specific Query, it forwards the
   response to the Snooping Querier and continues to forward the multicast traffic to the ports
   that want to receive it.
   • If the Snooping Switch does not receive a response to the Group-Specific Query
     messages, it stops forwarding the multicast traffic.

FIGURE 2.16 IGMP Snooping Querier example.

Similar to the ordinary IGMP Snooping switch, the IGMP Snooping Querier monitors IGMP traffic on the LAN and uses the port information learned to forward multicast traffic to only the downstream interfaces that lead to interested receivers of multicast groups. The IGMP Snooping Querier conserves bandwidth by sending multicast traffic only to interfaces connected to the host that are members of multicast groups, instead of flooding the traffic to all the downstream interfaces in the LAN.

2.6.5.2 How the IGMP Snooping Querier Works

The IGMP Snooping Querier monitors IGMP messages exchanged between receivers and multicast routers and uses the information gleaned from the messages to build a multicast forwarding table, a database of multicast groups and local interfaces that lead to members of the multicast groups. When the IGMP Snooping Querier receives multicast packets, it uses the multicast forwarding table to selectively forward the packets to only the local interfaces that lead to members of the appropriate multicast groups.

The IGMP Snooping Querier (like any ordinary Querier) sends out the following types of Query messages to hosts on the LAN:

- **General Query**: To check whether any host on the LAN is interested in traffic to any multicast group.
- **Group-Specific Query (IGMPv2 and IGMPv3 only)**: To check whether any host on the LAN is interested in traffic to a specific multicast group. The Querier sends this Query in response to a host leaving a multicast group, allowing an attached multicast router to quickly determine if any remaining hosts are interested in traffic to the multicast group.
- **Group-and-Source-Specific Query (IGMPv3 only)**: To check whether any host on the LAN is interested in multicast traffic from a specific source to a multicast group. The Querier sends this Query in response to a host indicating that it is no longer interested in receiving traffic destined for a multicast group from a multicast source, allowing an attached multicast router to quickly determine if any remaining hosts are interested in receiving multicast traffic from that source.

The IGMP Snooping Querier sends periodic IGMP General Query messages to all the devices in the LAN, ensuring that the Snooping switches update group membership tables, thereby preventing multicast traffic loss.

If multiple switches in the LAN are configured to be IGMP Snooping Queriers, the switch with the lowest IP source address takes precedence and becomes the active Snooping Querier. When the Layer 2 networks contain multiple Snooping Queriers, one is elected as the Querier, based on the device's IP address. The switches with higher IP source addresses stop sending IGMP Query messages unless they do not receive IGMP Query messages for a configured period. If the Snooping switch with a higher IP source address does not receive any IGMP Query messages during that period, it starts sending Query messages again, as already described in the IGMP Querier election process.

It is important to note that the hosts on the LAN that are multicast listeners send IGMP Membership Report messages to indicate that they want to join a particular multicast group or are still group members, and IGMP Leave Group messages (IGMPv2 and IGMPv3 only) to indicate that they want to leave a particular multicast group.

A host can join multicast groups by sending an unsolicited IGMP Membership Report message to a multicast router that specifies the multicast group it wants to join, or by sending a Report message in response to a General Query from a Querier. In Figure 2.16, the IGMP Snooping Querier continues to forward multicast traffic to the LAN provided that at least one host on it responds to the periodic IGMP General Query messages. A host must continue to respond to the periodic IGMP General Query messages for it to remain a member of a multicast group. When the IGMP Snooping Switch receives IGMP Membership Report messages on a host interface, it should forward it to the multicast router interfaces in the same LAN but not to the other host interfaces in the LAN.

A host can leave a multicast group by not responding to periodic Query messages, a process generally called a "silent leave." This is the only method for IGMPv1 hosts to leave a multicast group. A host can also send an IGMP Leave Group message to inform the multicast router that it is leaving a multicast group. This is the method used by IGMPv2 hosts to leave a multicast group. Unlike IGMPv2, IGMPv3 does not support explicit Leave Group messages. Instead, it uses the source filtering mechanism based on the Group Record Types (i.e., the EXCLUDE mode as described earlier) for leaving one or more multicast groups.

When an IGMPv3 host sends an IGMPv3 Membership Report message in INCLUDE mode, it is interested in traffic to a multicast group only from those sources in the message's source address list. If the host sends a Membership Report message in EXCLUDE mode, it is interested in traffic to a multicast group from any source except the sources in the message's source address list.

2.7   IGMP PROXY

The multicast routing concept discussed here is limited only to tree topologies with roots at an access node and branches reaching out into the access network to the end hosts. One typical example of such a tree topology is an access aggregation node with only one connection to the core network and many connections to the end hosts. We assume that the root of the tree (i.e., the access node) is connected to the wider Internet multicast infrastructure.

In such a tree topology, which is typical in many access networks, running a multicast routing protocol is not necessary. It is sufficient for the access node to act as a proxy to learn multicast group membership information in the access network, and simply forward multicast packets to end hosts based upon that information. The access device, acting as an *IGMP Proxy* [RFC4605], listens to IGMP messages from attached host devices to learn multicast group memberships and replicates multicast traffic from the upstream multicast infrastructure to only branches that have group members. Two access nodes can be used in an active-active redundancy configuration to achieve higher reliability. An IGMP Proxy is sometimes called an *IGMP Snooping Proxy*.

2.7.1 Deploying IGMP Proxy Devices

A large-scale network that supports multicast routing may have many leaf networks. A leaf network refers to an end node of a multicast distribution tree. A leaf network is an IP subnet or VLAN on which only multicast host receivers are attached. It is often a very tedious task to configure and manage all these many leaf networks. Thus, the network operator can reduce the task of configuring and managing the leaf networks without affecting the distribution of multicast traffic to them, by enabling IGMP Proxying on devices on those leaf networks. This example shows how important IGMP Proxy devices have become to enterprise and service provider networks. The IGMP Proxy devices in the leaf networks act as hosts to the exterior multicast network. They receive multicast traffic for a group only when some of the hosts directly connected to them become multicast group members.

Each IGMP Proxy device in the tree topology (i.e., leaf network) must be manually configured to have an upstream interface and several downstream interfaces [RFC4605]. Also, if several devices exist within the tree topology that can act as an IGMP Querier, the IP addressing scheme applied to the tree topology should be configured to ensure that the IGMP Proxy device wins the IGMP Querier election so that it can adequately perform the proxying function and to forward multicast traffic. The IGMP Querier election rule requires that a node must have the lowest IP address to win the Querier election process. The tree topology has no other multicast routers except the IGMP Proxy devices within, and the root of the tree is connected to the wider multicast infrastructure. PIM and IGMP are configured only on the interfaces of the routers that are upstream of the IGMP Proxy device.

The IGMP-based forwarding discussed here is limited to a single administrative domain and only works in a simple tree topology. In access networks with more complex architectures than a simple tree topology, and where a more robust failover mechanism is desired than using simple dual active-active access nodes, or where more than one administrative domain is involved, the use of a multicast routing protocol within the access network is the better approach. Figures 2.17 and 2.18 present high-level descriptions of the use of IGMP Proxy devices in a tree topology.

2.7.1.1 Terminology

The discussion about IGMP Proxy requires the following definitions [RFC4605]:

- **Upstream Interface**: This is an interface on an IGMP Proxy device (also called the *Host Interface*) in the direction of the root of the tree. The Upstream Interface is the interface on which IGMP Proxying is configured and acts as a host that is running IGMP; the reason it is called the *Host Interface*. It is also called the *Proxy Interface*.
- **Downstream Interface**: This is an interface on an IGMP Proxy device (also called the *Router Interface*) that is not in the direction of the root of the tree. This interface acts as a router that is running IGMP; the reason it is called the Router Interface.
- **Group Mode**: An interface is in IGMPv1 mode if an IGMPv1 Membership Report message for a multicast group is received (by the IGMP Proxy).

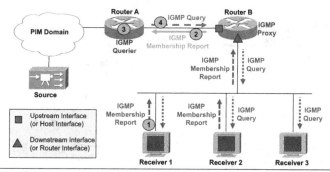

- The IGMP Proxy device acts as follows:
  - As a host for the upstream IGMP Querier (e.g., forwards IGMP Membership Report/Leave messages to the upstream router).
  - As an IGMP Querier for the downstream receiver hosts (e.g., forwards IGMP Query messages from the Querier to the hosts).

Example processing steps for IGMP Membership Reports, Queries and Leaves:

1. Receiver 1 signals its desire to join a multicast group (to which none of its other hosts have joined) by sending a new IGMP Membership Report message to Router B (the IGMP Proxy).
2. The IGMP Proxy receives the IGMP Membership Report message and in turn sends a new unsolicited IGMP Membership Report message to Router A (the IGMP Querier).
3. The IGMP Querier receives the IGMP Membership Report message from the IGMP Proxy and creates a (S,G) state entry in its multicast routing table (MRT).
   - We assume multicast traffic is now forwarded from the IGMP Querier to the IGMP Proxy and downstream to the receivers.
4. Every time the IGMP Querier sends a Query message to the IGMP Proxy, the Proxy will intercept that message and in turn send another IGMP Query message on the downstream interfaces.
   - When the IGMP Proxy receives an IGMP Query message from the Querier, it may respond with a Report message to the Querier according to the state entries in its multicast forwarding table (MFT).

Notes:

- The IGMP Proxy generates entries for its MFT according to IGMP Report/Leave messages received on downstream interfaces. It receives multicast traffic from the upstream router and forwards it to downstream interfaces according to the matching MFT entries.
- When the IGMP Proxy receives an IGMP Membership Report message from a host for a multicast group, it searches the MFT for the group:
  - If the multicast group is not found in the MFT, the IGMP Proxy sends an unsolicited IGMP Membership Report message for the group to the IGMP Querier and adds the group to the MFT.
  - If the group is found in the MFT, the IGMP Proxy does not send a Report message to the IGMP Querier.
- When the IGMP Proxy receives an IGMP Leave Group message for a group from a host, it sends an IGMP Group-Specific Query message through the downstream interface on which the Leave message was received to check whether this group has other members attached to the interface:
  - If no other members of this group are on the interface, the IGMP proxy deletes the interface from the forwarding entry of the group in the MFT.
  - The IGMP Proxy also checks whether there are group members on other interfaces. If members exist, the IGMP Proxy does not send an IGMP Leave Group message for this group to the Querier. If no members exist, the IGMP Proxy sends an unsolicited IGMP Leave Group message for this group to the Querier and deletes the group entry from the MFT.
  - If there are group members on the interface, the IGMP Proxy continues forwarding multicast traffic to the interface.

FIGURE 2.17 IGMP Proxy Example 1.

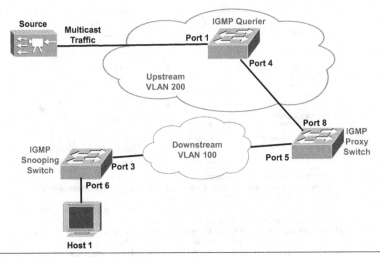

When a host joins a multicast group:
1. The multicast source sends traffic for group 224.12.13.14 to the IGMP Querier through Port 1.
2. The IGMP Snooping switch detects the multicast traffic stream.
3. Host 1 (attached to the Snooping switch) sends an IGMP Membership Report message for the group 224.12.13.14.
4. The Snooping switch forwards the Report message in an unmodified state through its All Groups ports, specifically Port 3 in this case
5. The IGMP Proxy receives the Report message on its downstream interface on VLAN 100. The IGMP Proxy then creates a new IGMP Membership Report with itself as the sender and sends this message upstream to the IGMP Querier 1through VLAN 200.
6. The Querier receives the proxied Report message from the IGMP Proxy and notes that Proxy is interested in traffic for the group 224.12.13.14. The Querier sends the multicast traffic for the group to the IGMP Proxy on Port 4.

When a host leaves a multicast group:
1. When Host 1 on the Snooping switch wants to stop receiving the multicast traffic to group 224.12.13.14, it sends an IGMP Leave Group message.
2. The Proxy sends an IGMP Leave Group message via its upstream interface only when the last interface on the Proxy leaves the group.
3. The Proxy does not respond to IGMP Join or Leave Group messages received via its upstream interface, but only to those received via downstream interfaces.
4. The Proxy does respond to IGMP Query messages received via its upstream interface.
5. When the Proxy sends a Leave Group message upstream, the upstream IGMP Querier sends an IGMP Membership Query. The Proxy takes that Query and proxies it to the downstream interface, VLAN 100, with its own IP address as the source address. This means any other interested hosts on the Snooping switch can declare their interest in continuing to receive the multicast traffic.

FIGURE 2.18   IGMP Proxy Example 2.

An interface is in IGMPv2 mode if an IGMPv2 Membership Report message is received but no IGMPv1 Report message is seen. An interface is in IGMPv3 mode if an IGMPv3 Membership Report message is received but no IGMPv1 or IGMPv2 Report message is seen.

- **Subscription**: When an interface is in IGMPv1 or IGMPv2 mode, the subscription of the interface is a multicast group membership (G). When an interface is in IGMPv3 mode, the subscription of the interface is an

IGMPv3 state entry with the tuple (*multicast address, group timer, filter mode, source-element list*).

- **Membership Database**: An IGMP Proxy device maintains this database and merges or combines the multicast group membership information of each of its downstream interfaces into it. This database holds a set of multicast group membership records of the form:

(multicast_address, filter_mode, source_list)

An IGMP Proxy provides a means for a node in a tree topology to receive any or all multicast traffic from an upstream multicast router if it is not able to run PIM but runs only IGMP. IGMP Proxy cannot be used on the same interface on which PIM-DM or PIM-SM is enabled. In a simple tree topology that requires multicast traffic, it is not necessary to run multicast routing protocols such as PIM-DM or PIM-SM on edge devices. Instead, IGMP Proxying can be configured on these devices as already described. The edge device acts as an IGMP Proxy when IGMP Proxying is configured:

- The IGMP Proxy device acts as a host for the upstream IGMP Querier.
- The IGMP Proxy device acts as an IGMP Querier for the downstream receiver hosts.

An IGMP Proxy sends IGMP Membership Report and Leave Group messages to an upstream network segment on behalf of downstream devices and also sends IGMP Query messages to downstream devices. The IGMP Proxy acts like an IGMP Querier to the downstream network segment and as a host to the upstream network segment. It is important to note that an IGMP Proxy can only have one configured upstream network segment (IP subnet or VLAN) and only works in networks with tree-like topologies.

2.7.2 IGMP PROXY REQUIREMENTS AND BEHAVIORS

An IGMP Proxy device has a single upstream interface connected to the wider multicast infrastructure and one or more downstream interfaces leading to end hosts. Interfaces designated as upstream and downstream are explicitly configured without the use of any protocol (i.e., no protocol is used to determine the interface type each interface assumes). An IGMP Proxy performs the host portion of IGMP on its upstream interface and the router portion of IGMP on its downstream interfaces. It is important to note that the router portion of IGMP must not be performed on the upstream interface of an IGMP Proxy device.

2.7.2.1 IGMP Proxy Multicast Group Membership Database and Behaviors

An IGMP Proxy device maintains a *multicast group membership database* (sometimes called the multicast forwarding table), in which it stores the group membership information of all the downstream interfaces. Each entry of this database consists of the multicast group address, filter mode, and source list. Each entry represents a collection (or consolidation) of the group members in the same multicast group on each downstream interface.

The Proxy performs host functions on the upstream interface using the multicast group membership database. It responds to IGMP Query messages according to the information in the database or sends IGMP Membership Report (join) and Leave messages when the database changes. The Proxy performs router functions on the downstream interface by participating in the IGMP Querier election, sending Query messages, and maintaining group memberships based on the received IGMP Membership Report messages.

The group membership database on the IGMP Proxy device holds the merger of all subscriptions on any downstream interface. The IGMP Proxy device sends IGMP Membership Report messages on the upstream interface when it receives Query messages and sends unsolicited Membership Report or Leave Group messages (on that interface) when the membership database changes. It is important to note that IGMP is not symmetric on routers and hosts; the IGMP functions are not similar on these devices.

2.7.2.1.1 Host (or Upstream) Interface Behavior

An IGMP Proxy issues IGMP host messages on behalf of hosts that it has discovered on its interfaces. The Proxy device acts as a proxy for downstream attached hosts and performs the host portion of the IGMP on the upstream interface. When the IGMP Proxy device's upstream interface receives an IGMP Query message, it responds with an IGMP Membership Report message on the same interface according to the entries in its group membership database. When the membership database changes, it sends Report/Leave messages on the upstream interface to the access device. The IGMP Proxy device has the following host behaviors:

- When it receives an IGMP Query message from the upstream device, it responds with IGMP Membership Report messages on the same interface according to entries in its group membership database; for the active multicast groups, it has learned on downstream interfaces.
- When a host joins a multicast address group for which none of its other hosts belong, it sends an unsolicited IGMP Membership Report for that group on the upstream interface.
- When the last host in a particular multicast group leaves the group, it sends an unsolicited IGMP Leave Group for that group on the upstream interface (addressed to the multicast IP address 224.0.0.2).

2.7.2.1.2 Router (or Downstream) Interface Behavior

The IGMP Proxy device generates entries for its group membership database according to the IGMP Membership Report and Leave messages received on downstream interfaces. It receives multicast traffic from the upstream access device and forwards it to downstream interfaces that are specified in the matching entries of the group membership database. The IGMP Proxy device has behaviors similar to an IGMP router. The IGMP Proxy device has the following router behaviors:

- When the Proxy device receives an IGMP Membership Report message on a downstream interface for a group, it searches its group membership database for the group.

- If the group is not found in the group membership database, it sends an unsolicited IGMP Report message for the group to the upstream access device and adds the group to the group membership database.
- If the group is found in the group membership database, it does not send an IGMP Report message to the upstream access device.
- When the Proxy device receives an IGMP Leave Group message for a group, it sends an IGMP Group-Specific Query message through the downstream interface on which the Leave message was received, to check whether the group still has other members attached to the interface.
    - If the interface has no other members of the group, the Proxy device deletes the interface from the forwarding entry of the group in the group membership database. The Proxy device then checks whether the group has members on any of its other interfaces. If members exist, the Proxy device does not send an IGMP Leave Group message for the group to the upstream access device. If no members exist, the Proxy device sends a Leave Group message for the group to the upstream access device.
    - If the group still has other members attached to the receiving interface, the Proxy device continues forwarding multicast traffic on the interface.

Table 2.8 summarizes how an IGMP Proxy processes IGMP messages [H3CMULTGUID].

When an IGMP Proxy device receives a multicast packet that is destined for a particular group (or channel in PIM-SSM)), it forwards the packet using a list consisting of the upstream interface and any downstream interface (on which it is the IGMP Querier) that has a subscription pertaining to the multicast group. The IGMP Proxy may build the list dynamically or from cached information. The Proxy excludes the interface on which the multicast packet was received from the list and forwards the packet on the remaining interfaces.

2.7.2.2   IGMP Proxying and IGMP Versions

An IGMP Proxy device performs on each of its downstream interfaces, the router portion of IGMP. An IGMP Proxy generally can support IGMPv1, IGMPv2, and IGMPv3. Each downstream interface is explicitly configured with the version of IGMP used, and the default is the highest version supported by the system. The IGMP Proxy develops and maintains a set of subscriptions separately for each downstream interface. The Proxy also merges or consolidates the subscriptions on each downstream interface into the group membership database. The set of membership records in the membership database is of the form (*multicast_address*, *filter_mode*, *source_list*).

Each membership record created by the IGMP Proxy is the result of the consolidation of all subscriptions for that record's *multicast_address* on the downstream interfaces. If the Proxy determines that some subscriptions are IGMPv1 or IGMPv2 subscriptions, it will convert these subscriptions to IGMPv3 subscriptions. The Proxy will first preprocess the IGMPv3 subscriptions and the converted subscriptions to remove the subscriptions with expired timers and, if the filter mode is EXCLUDE, remove every source whose Source Timer is greater than 0.

TABLE 2.8

Processing IGMP Messages on an IGMP Proxy

IGMP Message	Action
IGMP General Query	When this messaged is received, the Proxy forwards it to all ports but the receiving port. In addition, the Proxy generates a Report message according to the multicast group memberships it maintains and sends that Report on all multicast router ports.
IGMP Group-Specific Query	In response to such a Query message for a certain multicast group, the Proxy sends a Report message for the group on all multicast router ports if the forwarding entry for the group still contains a group member port.
IGMP Membership Report	When this message is received for a multicast group, the Proxy looks up the entry in the multicast forwarding table for the multicast group. If the Proxy finds a forwarding entry with the receiving port as a dynamic group member port in the OIL, it resets the aging timer for the entry. If the Proxy finds the forwarding entry but the OIL does not include the receiving port, it adds the port to the OIL as a dynamic group member port and starts an aging timer for it. If no forwarding entry is found, the Proxy creates the entry, adds the receiving port to the OIL as a dynamic group member port, and starts an aging timer for the port. Then, it sends a Report message to the group on all router ports.
IGMP Leave Group	In response to such a message for a multicast group, the Proxy sends an IGMP Group-Specific Query message on the receiving port. After making sure that no group member port is in the forwarding entry for the multicast group, the Proxy sends an IGMP Leave message to the group on all router ports.

Then the IGMP Proxy will merge the preprocessed subscriptions using the merging rules (for multiple multicast group memberships on a single interface) to create the membership record (as specified in Section 3.2 of [RFC3376], the IGMPv3 specification). For example, let us assume that there are two downstream interfaces, Interface_1 and Interfcae_2, that have subscriptions for multicast group address G. Interfcae_1 has an IGMPv2 subscription that is (G). Interface_2 has an IGMPv3 subscription that has multicast group membership information (G, INCLUDE, (S1, S2)). The IGMP Proxy converts Interface_1's subscription to an IGMPv3 subscription that has multicast group membership information (G, EXCLUDE, NULL). The IGMP Proxy then preprocesses and merges the subscriptions, giving the final membership record (G, EXCLUDE, NULL).

The IGMP Proxy device performs on the upstream interface, the host portion of IGMP. If an IGMPv1 or IGMPv2 Querier exists on the upstream interface of the proxy, then it will perform IGMPv1 or IGMPv2 functions on the upstream interface accordingly as described in Figures 2.17 and 2.18. Otherwise, the proxy will perform IGMPv3 functions on the upstream interface.

If the IGMP Proxy device performs IGMPv3 functions on the upstream interface, then any time the composition of the membership database changes, it will report those database changes (via Membership Report messages) on the upstream interface as if it were a host performing the action. If the Proxy device performs

IGMPv1 or IGMPv2 functions on the upstream interface, then any time it creates or deletes membership records, it will report those changes on the upstream interface. It will ignore all other changes. When the Proxy device sends Membership Report messages using IGMPv1 or IGMPv2, it uses only the multicast address field in the membership record.

- Each time the IGMP Proxy device receives multicast packets on its upstream interface, it will forward them to each downstream interface based on the subscriptions of the downstream interfaces, whether or not it is the IGMP Querier on each interface.
- The Proxy device forwards packets received on any downstream interface to the upstream interface, and to each downstream interface (other than the interface on which the packets arrived) based upon the interface's subscriptions, whether or not it is the IGMP Querier on each interface.
- The Proxy device may use a packet forwarding cache to avoid making the same forwarding decision for each packet. The proxy updates the forwarding cache any time any of the information used to build it changes.

2.7.2.3 IGMP Proxying and PIM-SSM

The IGMP Proxy device should be compliant with the IGMPv3 requirements for PIM-SSM to support PIM-SSM [RFC4604] (see discussion in Chapter 5). It is important to note that the Proxy device should be compliant with both the IGMP Host and Router requirements for PIM-SSM since it performs IGMP Host functions on the upstream interface, and IGMP Router functions on each downstream interface.

An interface on the IGMP Proxy can be configured to perform the IGMPv1 or IGMPv2 function, in which case, the Proxy will not maintain the PIM-SSM semantic for that interface. However, an IGMP Proxy device should ignore IGMPv1 or IGMPv2 subscriptions sent to SSM addresses. More importantly, the IGMP Proxy should not forward packets with SSM addresses to interfaces with IGMPv2 or IGMPv1 subscriptions for these addresses.

2.8 IGMP QUERY SOLICITATION

IGMP Query Solicitation is an IGMP feature developed for Allied Telesis switches [ALLTELQUSOL]. It is included here to show one example of proprietary IGMP features that are added to Layer 2 switches other the well-known and industry-accepted features such as IGMP Snooping and IGMP Proxying. An Allied Telesis switch sends an *IGMP Query Solicit message* when it detects a Layer 2 network topology change triggered by the Spanning Tree Protocol (STP), Rapid Spanning Tree Protocol (RSTP), Multiple Spanning Tree Protocol (MSTP), or the Telesis's Ethernet Protection Switched Ring (EPSR) protocol [ALLTELEPSR]. The IGMP Querier of the network upon seeing the Query Solicit message, responds by sending an IGMP General Query message immediately without waiting for the multicast group to time out. Doing this allows the network to remap the multicast group to the new Layer 2 topology as quickly as possible.

Ethernet switches run STP or its newer variants RSTP to prevent forwarding loops in Ethernet networks, and to ensure that backup paths are available when links fail. Both protocols have slow responses to network failures, like 30 seconds or more. EPRS and similar protocols provide protection and loop prevention within Ethernet ring-based topologies with performance that is better than either STP or RSTP. EPSR was designed to offer rapid detection of link failures with failover recovery rates of less than 50 milliseconds, a rate that is equivalent to that provided by legacy time division multiplexing (TDM) equipment like SONET/SDH devices.

The goal of IGMP Query Solicitation is to minimize the loss of multicast data after a topology change in a Layer 2 network that is running STP, RSTP, MSTP, or EPSR for loop protection [ALLTELQUSOL]. Without Query Solicitation, when changes in the underlying Link Layer topology of a network occur, multicast data flow to receivers can stop for some time (e.g., up to several minutes), depending on which switch port goes down and how much of the multicast group timeout period is left. The goal of IGMP Query Solicitation is to greatly reduce this disruption.

IGMP Query Solicitation monitors STP, RSTP, MSTP, and EPSR messages for topology changes. When a switch in the Layer 2 network (i.e., Ethernet network) detects a topology change (see Figure 2.19), it generates a Query Solicit message, which is a special IGMP Leave message developed by Allied Telesis [ALLTELQUSOL]. The switch upon detecting the change, transmits the IGMP Query Solicit message on all its ports, and the message is then flooded on all ports in the Layer 2 network

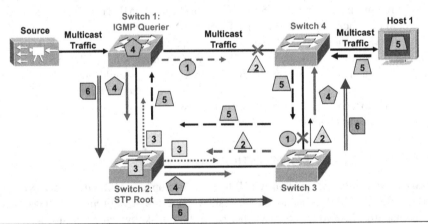

1. Initial state: Port on Switch 3 is in the blocking state. Multicast traffic from the source to Host 1 flows via Switches 1 and 4.
2. The link from Switch 1 to Switch 4 goes down. Switch 3 ceases being in the blocking state and sends topology change information.
3. Switch 2 receives the topology change information and sends a Query Solicit message.
4. Switch 1 receives the Query Solicit message and then sends an IGMP General Query message.
5. Host 1 receives the IGMP General Query message and responds with an IGMP Membership Report message.
6. Final state: Multicast traffic flows from the source to Host 1 via Switches 1, 2, 3, and 4.

FIGURE 2.19 IGMP Query Solicitation example.

on which the Query Solicitation feature is enabled. When the IGMP Querier of the network receives the Query Solicit message, it sends out an IGMP General Query on all of its ports in the network and waits for multicast receivers to respond with IGMP Membership Report messages. These IGMP Membership Report messages allow all IGMP Snooping switches throughout the network (which has just gone through a topology change) to update their snooping information to reflect the network topology change [ALLTELQUSOL]. IGMP Query Solicit messages are sent with the multicast group address set to 0.0.0.0.

IGMP Query Solicitation works on the root bridge of a Layer 2 network running STP, RSTP, or MSTP, and on the master node in a Layer 2 network running EPSR. By default, the root bridge (for STP, RSTP, or MSTP instance) or master node (for an EPSR instance) always sends an IGMP Query Solicit message when any of the following events occur in the network:

- When an STP Bridge Protocol Data Unit (BPDU) packet with the Topology Change (TC) flag set arrives at the root bridge.
- When an STP port on a switch in the Layer 2 network changes from the Discarding state to the Forwarding state.
- When the Layer 2 forwarding database of a switch gets flushed by EPSR.

If necessary, the network administrator can configure a multicast receiver in the Layer 2 network to respond more quickly to the IGMP General Query message from the Querier by tuning the IGMP timers, especially the IGMP Query Response Interval. Figure 2.19 shows how IGMP Query Solicitation works when a switch port goes down in the Layer 2 network.

On Layer 2 networks running STP, RSTP, MSTP, or EPSR, IGMP Query Solicitation is not normally required on the Layer 2 switches other than the STP root bridge or EPSR master node. Therefore, this feature is only enabled on the STP root bridge and the EPSR master node. However, some Layer 2 may need to run IGMP Query Solicitation on all switches, for example, if the root bridge does not support IGMP Query Solicitation. In this case, the STP root bridge is a switch that does not support IGMP Query Solicitation and does not send Query Solicit messages. Every switch that runs IGMP Query Solicitation will send a Query Solicit message when it detects a network topology change.

2.9 WHAT IS IGMPv2 FAST LEAVE?

Ordinarily, when an IGMP Snooping switch or IGMP-enabled multicast router sees an IGMP Leave Group message, it waits for an IGMP Membership Query or Group-Specific Query message before setting the multicast group entry timeout to 2 seconds. IGMP Fast Leave allows the IGMP Snooping switch to remove the interface from the forwarding table entry without first sending out an IGMP Group-Specific Query message on the interface. With Fast Leave, the IGMP Snooping switch removes the multicast group entry from the switch port as soon as the Leave Group message is seen unless a multicast router was learned on the port. For this reason, IGMP Fast Leave should only be configured on switch ports that have only one host per port.

IGMP Fast Leave allows the network administrator to enhance control over router or switch bandwidth. Enabling Fast Leave enables the IGMP Snooping switch to stop transmitting multicast traffic to a group on a port as soon as it receives an IGMP Leave Group message from a host on that port; no timeouts are observed by the switch.

When a host sends an IGMP Leave Group message, the IGMP Querier responds with an IGMP Membership Query message and waits for a configured time for a response. The benefits of IGMP Fast Leave are as follows:

- Without Fast Leave, the IGMP Snooping waits the same length of time as the IGMP Querier then expires the multicast group entry in its snooping table if it receives no response.
    - When the IGMP Snooping sees an IGMP Membership Query message from the Querier, it accordingly sets its expiry time for the multicast group to match that of the Querier. If the Snooping switch receives no IGMP Membership Report message by the time the counters go to zero, then the host's entry is removed from both the IGMP Querier and Snooper.
- With Fast Leave, the IGMP Snooping switch expires the multicast group entry as soon as it sees an IGMP Leave Group message from the host. So, by the time the Querier sends an IGMP Membership Query message, the Snooping switch would have already expired the multicast group entry in its snooping table and, therefore, stopped sending the multicast traffic to the host.
    - With Fast Leave, the Snooping switch removes that port from the multicast group in the snooping table as soon as receives the Leave Group message from the host.

It is not useful to enable Fast Leave on a switch port when it has more than one host, since there may be other hosts attached to the port still interested in the multicast traffic when one host of the group leaves. In such as case, if Fast Leave is enabled on a switch port, one Leave Group message from a host on the port would lead to the switch dropping the multicast stream for every host on that port.

Some IGMP Snooping switches have a Fast Leave feature with *multiple host modes* [ALLTELQUSOL]. In the multiple host mode, the Snooping switch tracks which host on a given port are joined to a given multicast group. In this case, the Snoop switch shuts off traffic to the multicast group on that port as soon as the last host leaves the group on the port.

In the *single host mode*, as soon as the Snooping switch receives an IGMP Leave Group message for a multicast group on a port, it shuts off completely multicast traffic to the group on that port. This mode assumes that there are no other hosts on the switch port that are still interested in receiving the multicast traffic, and therefore, is suitable only for cases where a single host is directly attached to a Snooping switch port.

2.10 IGMPv3 EXPLICIT-HOST TRACKING AND FAST LEAVE

IGMPv3 supports a source-based filtering that allows a host and router to specify the particular multicast source addresses that should be allowed or blocked for a particular multicast group. When using IGMPv3 snooping, the Snooping switch maintains IGMPv3 states based on the IGMPv3 messages it receives for a particular multicast group in a particular IP subnet or VLAN. The switch either allows or blocks multicast traffic based on the following information in these IGMPv3 messages [CISCIGMPSNO]:

- Source lists
- Filtering options: Allow (INCLUDE) or block (EXCLUDE)

The states that the IGMPv3 Snooping switch maintains can be used for *IGMPv3 explicit-host tracking* and statistics collection. The Snooping switch typically deletes source-only entries periodically (e.g., every 5 minutes), and relearns the information to ensure that they are still valid.

A network may use IGMPv3 for *explicit tracking* of multicast membership information on any IGMPv3-enabled port. The network administrator may use the resulting *IGMPv3 explicit-tracking database* for proxy reporting, statistics collection, and Fast Leave processing for IGMPv3 hosts. When explicit tracking is enabled on an IGMP Snooping switch port, it processes the IGMPv3 Membership Report message it receives from a host on the port, and builds an IGMPv3 explicit-tracking database that contains the following information:

- The port on which the host is connected
- The multicast source channels reported by the host
- The list of sources for each multicast group reported by the hosts
- The filter mode for each multicast group reported by the host
- The router filter mode of each multicast group
- The list of hosts requesting traffic from a source for each multicast group

It is important to note that IGMPv3 explicit-host tracking has to be enabled for IGMPv3 Fast Leave processing and proxy reporting to work.

IGMPv3 Snooping switch implements Fast Leave processing by maintaining source-group-based membership information. When Fast Leave processing is enabled on a port, a host sends an IGMPv3 Group Record message with BLOCK_OLD_SOURCES for a specific multicast group when it no longer wants to receive traffic from particular sources. When the Snooping switch receives such a message from a host, it parses the list of sources in the message or the given multicast group. If this source list is the same as the source list subscribed to by the host (received in the host's IGMPv3 Report message), the switch removes the host from the interface and stops forwarding the related multicast group traffic to the host. If the source lists do not match, the Snooping switch does not remove the host from the port until the host is no longer interested in receiving multicast traffic from any source.

REVIEW QUESTIONS

1. What is the purpose of the IGMP Membership Query message? Include in your answer the differences between an IGMP General Query, Group-Specific Query, and Group-and-Source-Specific Query.
2. What is the purpose of the IGMP Membership Report message? Include in your answer the differences between an IGMPv1/v2 Membership Report and an IGMPv3 Membership Report.
3. Explain why IGMPv2 introduced the Leave Group message.
4. What is the purpose of the IGMP Report Suppression mechanism?
5. What is the role of the IGMP Querier in a multicast network?
6. What is the main criterion for choosing the IGMPv2 or IGMPv3 Querier of a network?
7. How is the IGMPv1 Querier determined in a network?
8. Explain why IGMPv3 does not support an explicit leave message and how hosts leave in IGMPv3.
9. Explain briefly what IGMP Snooping is and its main benefits.
10. What is the difference between a multicast router port and a group member port on an IGMP Snooping switch?
11. How does an IGMP Snooping switch determine which of its ports lead to routers, including multicast routers?
12. How is an IGMP Snooping Querier different from an ordinary IGMP Snooping switch? Include in your answer why an IGMP Snooping Querier may be needed in a network.
13. What is an IGMP Proxy? Include in your answer the roles of the Upstream (or Host) Interface and the Downstream (or Router) Interface on the IGMP Proxy device.
14. What is the purpose of the multicast group membership database in an IGMP Proxy device?
15. What is the purpose of the IGMP Query Solicitation feature in Allied Telesis switches?
16. What is IGMP Fast Leave and when is it not recommended for use on IGMP Snooping switches?

REFERENCES

[ALLTELEPSR]. Allied Telisis, EPSRing(tm) (Ethernet Protection Switched Ring), *White Paper*, 2016.

[ALLTELQUSOL]. Allied Telesis, How to Configure IGMP for Multicasting on Routers and Managed Layer 3 Switches, *AlliedWare(tm) OS How to Note: IGMP*, 2009.

[AWEYFCDM22]. James Aweya, *Designing Switch/Routers: Fundamental Concepts and Design Methods*, CRC Press, Taylor & Francis Group, ISBN 9781032317694, October 2022.

[AWEYARCAP22]. James Aweya, *Designing Switch/Routers: Architectures and Applications*, CRC Press, Taylor & Francis Group, ISBN 9781032317700, October 2022.

[CISCIGMPSNO]. Cisco Systems, *Cisco IOS Software Configuration Guide, Release12.2(33) SXH and Later Releases*, Chapter 32, Configuring IGMP Snooping and MVR for IPv4 Multicast Traffic.

[CISCPRWILL03]. B. Williamson, *Developing IP Multicast Networks*, Vol. 1, Cisco Press, 2003.

[H3CMULTGUID]. H3C, *IP Multicast Configuration Guide, Chapter 8, MSDP Configuration*, H3C SR8800 Documentation Set.

[IEEE802.1D2004]. IEEE Std. *802.1D-2004 IEEE Standard for Local and Metropolitan Area Networks: Media Access Control (MAC) Bridges*, June 2004.

[RFC1112]. S. Deering, "Host Extensions for IP Multicasting", *IETF RFC 1112*, August 1989.

[RFC2113]. D. Katz, "IP Router Alert Option", *IETF RFC 2113*, February 1997.

[RFC2236]. W. Fenner, "Internet Group Management Protocol, Version 2", *IETF RFC 2236*, November 1997.

[RFC2608]. E. Guttman, C. Perkins, J. Veizades, and M. Day, "Service Location Protocol, Version 2", *IETF RFC 2608*, June 1999.

[RFC2710]. S. Deering, W. Fenner, and B. Haberman, "Multicast Listener Discovery (MLD) for IPv6", *IETF RFC 2710*, October 1999.

[RFC3376]. B. Cain, S. Deering, I. Kouvelas, B. Fenner, and A. Thyagarajan, "Internet Group Management Protocol, Version 3", *IETF RFC 3376*, October 2002.

[RFC3810]. R. Vida and L. Costa, "Multicast Listener Discovery Version 2 (MLDv2) for IPv6", *IETF RFC 3810*, June 2004.

[RFC4286]. B. Haberman and J. Martin, "Multicast Router Discovery", *IETF RFC 4286*, December 2005.

[RFC4541]. M. Christensen, K. Kimball, and F. Solensky, "Considerations for Internet Group Management Protocol (IGMP) and Multicast Listener Discovery (MLD) Snooping Switches", *IETF RFC 4541*, May 2006.

[RFC4604]. H. Holbrook, B. Cain, and B. Haberman, "Using Internet Group Management Protocol Version 3 (IGMPv3) and Multicast Listener Discovery Protocol Version 2 (MLDv2) for Source-Specific Multicast", *IETF RFC 4604*, August 2006.

[RFC4605]. B. Fenner, H. He, B. Haberman, and H. Sandick, "Internet Group Management Protocol (IGMP)/Multicast Listener Discovery (MLD)-Based Multicast Forwarding ("IGMP/MLD Proxying")", *IETF RFC 4605*, August 2006.

[RFC6398]. F. Le Faucheur, Ed., "IP Router Alert Considerations and Usage", *IETF RFC 6398*, October 2011.

3 Protocol Independent Multicast (PIM) Message Types

3.1 INTRODUCTION

All PIM protocol messages are carried directly in IPv4 packets with the IP Protocol Number 103 (see Figure 3.1). PIM messages are transmitted either through unicast (e.g., Graft, Graft-Ack, Registers, and Register-Stop messages) or as multicast with the IP TTL set to 1 and addressed to the IPv4 ALL-PIM-ROUTERS multicast group address, 224.0.0.13 (e.g., Hello, Join, Prune, and Asserts messages). The corresponding IPv6 ALL-PIM-ROUTERS' multicast group address is ff02::d. Table 3.1 lists the messages used by the various PIM protocols and the type of destination addresses used. The IP header TTL for the unicast PIM messages is the system's normal unicast IP TTL.

The source address in the PIM unicast protocol messages is a domain-wide reachable address, while the source address in PIM multicast protocol messages can be the link-local address of the PIM router interface on which the message is being transmitted. This chapter describes the message formats used in the different PIM protocols: PIM-DM, PIM-SM, and BIDIR-PIM.

3.2 MESSAGES USED BY ALL PIM PROTOCOL CATEGORIES

As shown in Table 3.1, message types such as Hello, Join, Prune, and Assert are common to all PIM protocols, while the others are PIM protocol-specific. The messages common to all PIM categories are sent as multicast messages and addressed to the ALL-PIM-ROUTERS multicast group address (224.0.0.13). Messages sent to the reserved multicast address 224.0.0.13 are forwarded on a hop-by-hop basis to all PIM routers in the multicast domain (i.e., flooded to all routers in the PIM domain). Although the common PIM messages have the same format across all the

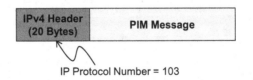

FIGURE 3.1 PIM message in an IP packet.

DOI: 10.1201/9781032701967-3

TABLE 3.1

PIM Message Types

Messages Common to All PIM Categories	
Hello	Multicast to ALL-PIM-ROUTERS (224.0.0.13)
Join	Multicast to ALL-PIM-ROUTERS
Prune	Multicast to ALL-PIM-ROUTERS
Assert	Multicast to ALL-PIM-ROUTERS
PIM-DM Specific Messages	
Graft	Unicast on RPF interface to multicast source
Graft-Ack	Unicast to source of Graft message
State-Refresh	Multicast to ALL-PIM-ROUTERS
PIM-SM Specific Messages	
Register	Unicast to Rendezvous Point (RP)
Register-Stop	Unicast to source of Register message
Bootstrap	Multicast to ALL-PIM-ROUTERS
Candidate RP Advertisement	Unicast to Domain's Bootstrap Router (BSR)
BIDIR-PIM Specific Messages	
Designated Forwarder (DF) Election Offer	Multicast to ALL-PIM-ROUTERS
DF Election Winner	Multicast to ALL-PIM-ROUTERS
DF Election Backoff	Multicast to ALL-PIM-ROUTERS
DF Election Pass	Multicast to ALL-PIM-ROUTERS

PIM protocols, the way each protocol uses these messages may differ in some ways because of the differences in the operational structure of each PIM protocol.

3.2.1 PIM HEADER COMMON TO ALL PIM MESSAGES

Although the PIM protocols used protocol-specific messages, all the PIM messages use a common PIM header as shown in Figure 3.2. If a PIM router receives a PIM message with an unrecognized PIM Version or Type field, or if the destination address of the message does not correspond to those in Table 3.1, the router must discard the message and should log an error message to the network operator in a rate-limited manner.

The PIM Checksum field value is computed similar to the standard IPv4 header checksum computation. In other words, the PIM router computes it as the 16-bit one's complement of the one's complement sum of the entire PIM protocol message. For PIM Register messages, the router does not include the encapsulated "Multicast data packet" section of the Register message when computing the PIM Checksum field value. Before computing the Checksum, the router zeros the Checksum field. If the length of the PIM message is not an integral number of 16-bit words, the router will pad the message with a trailing byte of zero before computing the Checksum field value.

```
0    3      7           15            23          31
   PIM
   Version  Type   Reserved          Checksum
```

- **PIM Version (4 Bits)**: Version is 2

- **Type (3 Bits))**: The following PIM message types have been defined;

  Message Type   Destination
  ----
  0 = Hello   Multicast to ALL-PIM-ROUTERS
                                                  (i.e., Multicast Address 224.0.0.13)
  1 = Register (PIM-SM only)   Unicast to Rendezvous Point (RP)
  2 = Register-Stop (PIM-SM only)   Unicast to source of Register packet
  3 = Join/Prune   Multicast to ALL-PIM-ROUTERS
  4 = Bootstrap (PIM-SM only)   Multicast to ALL-PIM-ROUTERS
  5 = Assert   Multicast to ALL-PIM-ROUTERS
  6 = Graft (PIM-DM only)   Unicast to RPF'(S)
  7 = Graft-Ack (PIM-DM only)   Unicast to source of Graft packet
  8 = Candidate-RP-Advertisement (PIM-SM only)   Unicast to Domain's Bootstrap Router (BSR)
  9 = State-Refresh (PIM-DM only)   Multicast to ALL-PIM-ROUTERS
  10 = DF Election   Multicast to ALL-PIM-ROUTERS
  11 = ECMP Redirect   Multicast to ALL-PIM-ROUTERS
  12 = PIM Flooding Mechanism   Multicast to ALL-PIM-ROUTERS

- **Reserved (8 Bits)**: This field is set to zero on message transmission and ignored upon receipt.

- **Checksum (16 Bits)**: This is a standard IP checksum (i.e., the 16-bit one's complement of the one's complement sum of the entire PIM message) excluding the "Multicast data packet" section of the Register message. To compute the checksum, the checksum field is first zeroed. If the packet's length is not an integral number of 16-bit words, the packet is padded with a trailing byte consisting of 0s before computing the checksum.
```

**FIGURE 3.2**   PIM header common to all PIM messages.

When computing the PIM Checksum for an IPv6 packet, the fields used in checksum computation also include the IPv6 "pseudo-header", as specified in Section 8.1 of RFC 8200 [RFC8200]. The router prepends the IPv6 "pseudo-header" to the PIM header for the purpose of computing the PIM Checksum. The PIM router sets the "Upper-Layer Packet Length" in the IPv6 pseudo-header to the length of the PIM message, except when computing the PIM Checksum in Register messages, where the router sets it to the length of the PIM Register message header (which is 8 bytes). The IPv6 Next Header value used in the IPv6 pseudo-header is 103.

### 3.2.2   REDEFINITION OF THE 8-BIT RESERVED FIELD IN THE PIM COMMON HEADER

References [RFC3973] and [RFC7761] specify 8 bits in the PIM common header as "Reserved", as shown in Figure 3.2. While all PIM message types use this common header, [RFC3973] and [RFC7761] specify these bits as unused in the PIM protocol specification.

- Reference [RFC8736] renames the 8 reserved bits in the common PIM header as "PIM message type Flag Bits" (or simply, "Flag Bits") and describes how they are to be used on a per-PIM message type basis, as depicted in Figure 3.3.
```

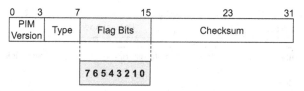

- RFC 8736 updates the definition of the Reserved field in RFC 7761 and refers to this field as the "PIM message type Flag Bits" or, simply, "Flag Bits".
- Unless otherwise specified, all the flag bits for each PIM type are Reserved (as initially defined in RFC 7761) MUST be set to zero on transmission and ignored upon receipt.
- The specification of a new PIM type MUST indicate whether the bits should be treated differently.
- **Flag Bits for Type 4 (Bootstrap Message)**: PIM message type 4 (Bootstrap), defined in RFC 5059, defines flag bit 7 as the No-Forward (N) bit. The usage of bit 7 is defined in RFC 5059, and the remaining 7 flag bits are reserved.
- **Flag Bits for Type 10 (DF Election Message)**: PIM message type 10 (DF Election), defined in RFC 5015, specifies that the four most significant flag bits (bits 4-7) are to be used as a subtype. The usage of those bits is defined in RFC 5015 and the remaining flag bits are reserved.
- **Flag Bits for Type 12 (PFM Message)**: PIM message type 12 (PIM Flooding Mechanism), defined in RFC 8364, defines flag bit 7 as the No-Forward bit. The usage of the bit is defined in RFC 8364, and the remaining flag bits are reserved.

0 3	7		15	23 31	
PIM Version	Type = 4	N	Reserved	Checksum	PIM Header in Bootstrap Message

0 3	7		15	23 31	
PIM Version	Type = 10	Subtype	Resv	Checksum	PIM Header in DF Election Message

0 3	7		15	23 31	
PIM Version	Type	Subtype	FB	Checksum	PIM Header in Message Types 13, 14, and 15

- The Flag Bits for PIM message types 13, 14, and 15 are used as Type Space Extension bits as defined in RFC 8736.
- RFC 8736 defines a new Subtype field using the four most significant flag bits (bits 4-7). The notation type.subtype is used to reference these new extended types.
- The remaining four flag bits (bits 0-3) are reserved to be used by each extended type (abbreviated as FB).

FIGURE 3.3   Flag bits in PIM header.

- Reference [RFC5059] redefines bit 7 in the Flag bits in the PIM header of the Bootstrap message as the "No-Forward (N)" bit and the remaining bits as "Reserved".
- The four most significant bits (bits 4–7) are redefined as a "Subtype" field in the PIM header of the DF Election message in [RFC5051] (and the remaining bits as "Reserved").
- Bit 7 is redefined as the "No-Forward" bit in the PIM header of the PIM Flooding Mechanism message in [RFC8364], and the remaining bits as "Reserved".
- Reference [RFC8736] redefine bits 4–7 as a new "Subtype" field and bits 0–3 as "Reserved" in PIM message types 13, 14, and 15. In addition, Reference [RFC8736] creates a registry containing the usage of the Flag bits for each PIM message type.

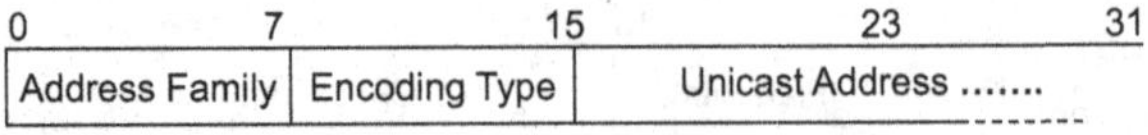

```
0          7         15        23        31
 ┌─────────────────┬──────────────┬──────────────────────┐
 │ Address Family  │ Encoding Type│  Unicast Address ......│
 └─────────────────┴──────────────┴──────────────────────┘
```

- **Address Family (8 Bits)**: The PIM address family of the 'Unicast Address' field of this address.

    0 = Reserved
    1 = IPv4
    2 = IPv6

- **Encoding Type (8 Bits)**: This specifies the type of encoding used within a specific Address Family. The value '0' is reserved for this field and represents the native encoding of the Address Family.

- **Unicast Address**: This specifies the unicast address as represented by the given Address Family and Encoding Type (e.g., 32-bit IPv4 or 126-bit IPv6 address).

FIGURE 3.4 Encoded unicast address format.

- In addition to the definition of the Flag bits for the PIM message types discussed in Reference [RFC8736] and shown in Figure 3.3 (i.e., for PIM message types 4, 10, 12, 13, 14, and 15), all the Flag bits for other PIM message types are specified as "Reserved", as described in the PIM protocol specification in [RFC3973] and [RFC7761].

3.2.3 ENCODED ADDRESS FORMATS

The address formats for encoding unicast, multicast group, and source addresses in PIM messages are illustrated in Figures 3.4, 3.5, and 3.6, respectively. An Address Family Identifier (AFI) identifies an individual network addressing scheme or numbering plan to avoid ambiguities in the use of individual addresses where they may otherwise be ambiguous (e.g., IPv4 has AFI = 1 and IPv6 has AFI = 2). The list of AFIs is maintained by the Internet Assigned Numbers Authority (IANA). The Address Family field holds the AFI of the address in the Unicast Address, Multicast Group Address, or Source Address fields.

The Encoding Type field value represents the type of encoding (i.e., the native encoding) used within the specific AFI placed in the Address Family field. References [RFC3973] and [RFC7761] reserved the value '0' for the Encoding Type field. The 8-bit Mask Length field in Figure 3.5, and Figure 3.6 contains a value that is used as a mask and represents the number of contiguous '1' bit that are left-justified.

When this mask is combined with the multicast group address, it describes a range of multicast groups. The mask is less than or equal to the address length (in bits) for the specified AFI and Encoding Type. If the router sends a PIM message for a single multicast group address, then it must set the Mask Length equal to the address length (in bits) for the specified AFI and Encoding Type. For example, the Mask Length is equal to 32 for IPv4 native encoding and 128 for IPv6 native encoding.

When the mask is combined with the source address, it describes the IP subnet to which the source is attached. The PIM router ignores any PIM message received with any other mask length. The flag bits in the encoded address formats are described in Figures 3.5 and 3.6.

0	7	15				23	31
Address Family	Encoding Type	B	Reserved	Z	Mask Length		
Multicast Group Address							

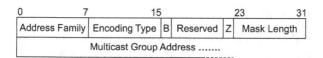

- **B (1 Bit)**: This indicates that the group range uses Bidirectional PIM (BIDIR-PIM). For PIM-SM and PIM-DM, this bit MUST be set to zero.
- **Reserved (14 Bits):** This field is set to zero on message transmission and ignored upon receipt.
- **Z (1 Bit)**: This indicates that the group range is an administrative scope zone and is used in the Bootstrap Router Mechanism only. For all other purposes, this bit is set to zero and ignored on receipt.
- **Mask Length (8 Bits)**: The value in this field is the number of contiguous one bits that are left-justified and used as an address mask. When combined with the group address, it describes a range of groups. It is less than or equal to the address length in bits for the given Address Family and Encoding Type. If the message is sent for a single group, then the Mask Length must equal the address length in bits for the given Address Family and Encoding Type (e.g., 32 for IPv4 native encoding and 128 for IPv6 native encoding).
- **Group Multicast Address**: This field contains the group address (e.g., 32-bit IPv4 multicast group address).

FIGURE 3.5 Encoded multicast group address format.

0	7	15				23	31
Address Family	Encoding Type	Reserved	S	W	R	Mask Length	
Source Address							

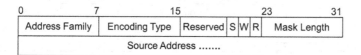

- **S (1 Bit)**: This is called the Sparse bit and is set to 1 for PIM-SM. It is used for PIM Version 1 compatibility.
- **W (1 Bit)**: This is called the WildCard (or WC) bit and is for use with PIM Join/Prune messages. The WC-bit = 1 indicates that the address being joined is an RP address rather than a multicast source address.
- **R (1 Bit)**: This is called the Rendezvous Point Tree(or RPT or) bit and is for use with PIM Join/Prune messages. If the WC bit is 1, the RPT bit MUST be set to 1. The RPT-bit = 1 indicates that the message is propagated along a shared tree to the RP.
- **Mask Length (8 Bits)**: When combined with the source address, it describes a source subnet. The Mask Length MUST be equal to the mask length in bits for the given Address Family and Encoding Type (32 for IPv4 native and 128 for IPv6 native). A router SHOULD ignore any messages received with any other mask length.
- **Source Address**: This field contains the source address (e.g., 32-bit IPv4 address).

FIGURE 3.6 Encoded source address format.

3.2.4   PIM Hello Message Format

PIM routers (all PIM versions) send Hello messages (see Figure 3.7) to detect neighboring PIM routers [RFC3973] [RFC7761]. A PIM router sends Hello messages periodically on each of its PIM-enabled interfaces, and these messages are addressed to the ALL-PIM-ROUTERS multicast group address 224.0.0.13. PIM routers must send Hello messages on all PIM-enabled interfaces, even on point-to-point interfaces. A Hello message carries several Options [RFC3973] [RFC5015] [RFC7761], as described in Figure 3.8.

One of the most important Option types is the Hold Time. A router sends a Hold Time value to inform the receiver to declare the neighbor adjacency with the sender as expired when it does not receive further Hello messages (after waiting a period greater than the Hold Time). PIM routers that receive unknown Options in Hello messages must ignore them, and such Options should not prevent the router from forming a neighbor relationship.

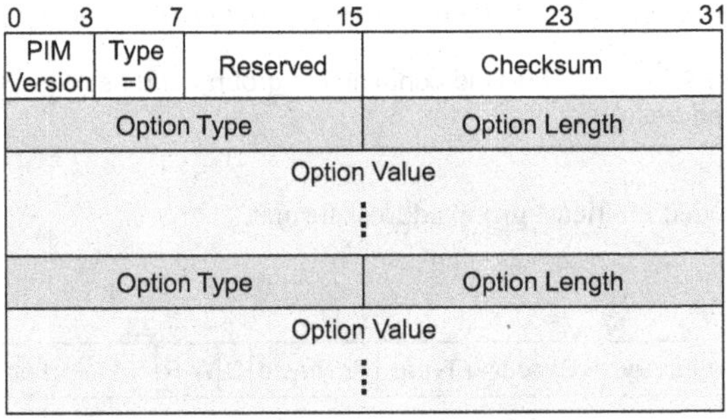

0   3   7   15   23   31
PIM Version / Type = 0 / Reserved / Checksum
Option Type / Option Length
Option Value ⋮
Option Type / Option Length
Option Value ⋮

- **Option Type (16 Bits)**: This specifies the type of the option given in the following Option Value field.

Option Type	Description
0	Reserved
1	Hello Hold Time
2	LAN Prune Delay
3 - 16	Reserved
17	To be assigned by IANA
18	Deprecated and SHOULD NOT be used
19	DR Priority (PIM-SM Only)
20	Generation ID
21	State-Refresh Capable
22	Bidirectional Capable
24	Address List
25 - 65000	To be assigned by IANA
65001 - 65535	Reserved for Private Use

- **Option Length (16 Bits)**: This specifies the length of the Option Value field in bytes.

- **Option Value**: This is a variable-length field that carries the value of the option.

FIGURE 3.7   Hello message format.

a) Option Type 1: Hold Time

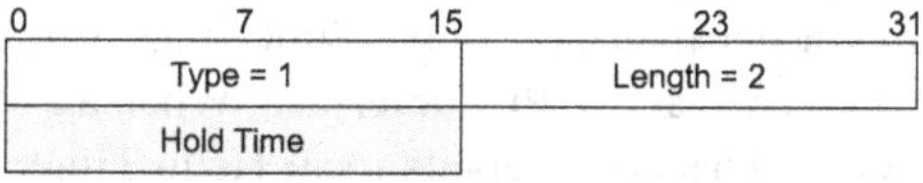

0	7	15	23	31
Type = 1			Length = 2	
Hold Time				

- **Hold Time (16 Bits)**: Hold Time (in seconds) is the amount of time a receiver must keep the neighbor reachable.

b) Option Type 2: LAN Prune Delay

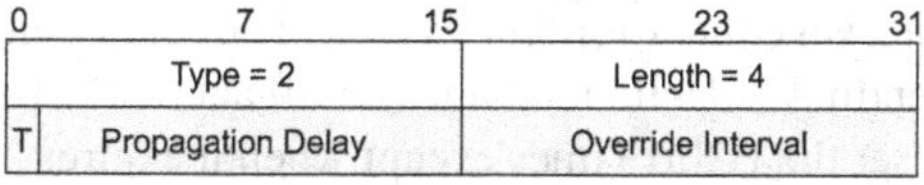

0	7	15	23	31
Type = 2			Length = 4	
T	Propagation Delay		Override Interval	

- **T (1 Bit)**: This bit specifies the ability of the sending router to disable Join suppression. This bit is used by PIM-SM and SHOULD be set to 0 by PIM-DM routers and ignored upon receipt.
- **Propagation Delay (7 Bits)**: This delay value is inserted by a router to express the expected message propagation delay on the link. It is used by upstream routers to figure out how long they should wait for a Join Override message before pruning an interface.
- **Override Interval (8 Bits)**: To avoid synchronization of Override messages when multiple downstream routers share a multi-access link, the sending of such messages is delayed by a small random amount of time. Each router expresses its view of the amount of randomization necessary in this field.

c) Option Type 19: DR Priority

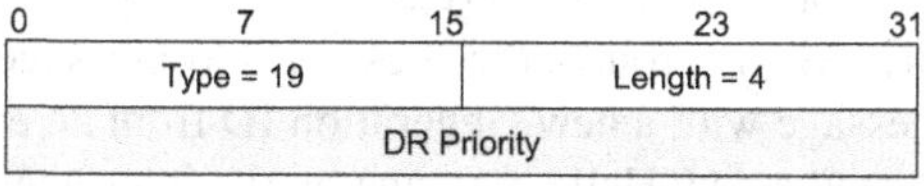

0	7	15	23	31
Type = 19			Length = 4	
DR Priority				

DR Priority (32 Bits): This field contains an unsigned number that is used in the designated router (DR) election.

d) Option Type 20: Generation ID

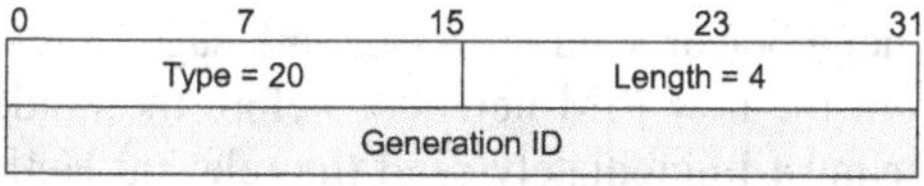

0	7	15	23	31
Type = 20			Length = 4	
Generation ID				

- **Generation ID (32 Bits)**: This is a random 32-bit value for the interface on which the Hello message is sent. The Generation ID is regenerated whenever PIM forwarding is started or restarted on the interface.

e) Option Type 24: Address List

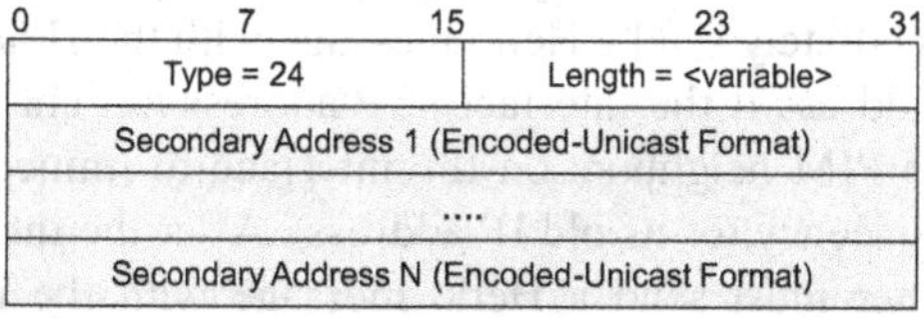

0	7	15	23	31
Type = 24			Length = <variable>	
Secondary Address 1 (Encoded-Unicast Format)				
		....		
Secondary Address N (Encoded-Unicast Format)				

- **Secondary Address**: A router communicates its interface's secondary addresses to its PIM neighbors to provide them with a mechanism for mapping next-hop information obtained through their multicast routing information base (MRIB) to a primary address that can be used as a destination for Join/Prune messages. All addresses within a single Address List must belong to the same address family.

FIGURE 3.8 PIM Option types.

3.2.4.1   Sending Hello Messages

A PIM router maintains a per-interface Hello Timer that is used to trigger when Hello messages are sent on each active PIM interface. When a PIM router first starts or has enabled PIM on an interface, it sets its local Hello Timer to a random value between 0 and *Triggered_Hello_Delay*. Randomly setting the timer value prevents the synchronization of Hello messages if multiple routers on a network segment start simultaneously. After sending the initial Hello message, the PIM router sends a Hello message every time interval equal to *Hello_Period*. The router may set a single Hello Timer to trigger the sending of Hello messages on all active PIM-enabled interfaces. The router does not reset the Hello Timer except when it expires.

It is important to note that a PIM router will not accept PIM Join, Prune, or Assert messages from a neighbor router unless it has first received a Hello message from that neighbor. Thus, if a PIM router intends to send a Join, Prune, or Assert message on an interface on which no Hello message has yet been received (with the currently configured interface's IP address), then the router must immediately send a Hello message on that interface without having to wait for the Hello Timer to expire. The router can then send the intended Join, Prune, or Assert message after sending the Hello message.

To allow a new PIM router that has started or one that has rebooted to discover PIM neighbors quickly, when a router receives a Hello message from a new PIM neighbor or a Hello message with a new Generation ID from an existing PIM neighbor, the router should send a new Hello message on the interface on which the message is received after waiting a random delay between 0 and *Triggered_Hello_Delay*. Sending this new Hello message should not change the timing of the periodically scheduled Hello messages. In the event a PIM router has to send a Join or Prune message to the new PIM neighbor or send an Assert message in response to receiving an Assert message from the new PIM neighbor before the randomly chosen delay has expired, the router must immediately send the relevant Hello message without waiting for the Hello Timer to expire, followed by the planned Join, Prune, or Assert message. Failing to do this will cause the new PIM neighbor to discard the Join, Prune, or Assert message.

Before an interface on a PIM router goes down or changes its primary IP address, the router should immediately send a Hello message with the Hold Time set to zero, but using the old IP address if the interface's IP address has changed. Sending this Hello message causes PIM neighbors on the interface to immediately remove the sending neighbor's adjacency (or its old IP address). After the interface's IP address has changed, the router must send a Hello message with the interface's new IP address. If one of the secondary IP addresses on an interface changes, the router should send a Hello message with an updated Address List Option and a non-zero Hold Time value. Sending this Hello message immediately causes the PIM neighbors to update the sender's list of secondary addresses.

3.2.4.2   Receiving Hello Messages

When a PIM router receives a Hello message, it records the interface on which the message was received, the sender of the message, and any information contained in any recognized Option type in the Hello message (see Figure 3.8). The router retains this information for some time (several seconds) equal to the value in the Hold Time field of the received Hello message. If the router receives a new Hello message from a particular neighbor N on interface I, it resets the Neighbor Liveness Timer (N, I) to the Hold Time of the newly received Hello message [RFC3973] [RFC7761]. If the router receives a Hello message from a new neighbor, it sends its own Hello message after waiting for a delay randomly selected from the interval 0 to *Triggered_Hello_Delay*.

3.2.4.3 Hold Time Option (Option Type 1)

The value in the Hold Time field is the number of seconds the receiver of the PIM Hello message must keep the neighbor adjacency as reachable if no new Hello message is received on the adjacency. All PIM routers must always include the Hold Time Option in the Hello messages they send. It is recommended that a PIM router should set the Hold Time in the Hello Message to a value that is reasonable enough for the receiver to keep the neighbor adjacency associated with the sender active until it receives a new Hello message. References [RFC3973] and [RFC7761] recommend that the Hello time be set to 3.5 times the value of *Hello_Period* for most links.

If the sending router sets the Hold Time to 0xffff (in hexadecimal notation), the receiver must not time out that neighbor adjacency. This feature is useful for on-demand links as a way to prevent the adjacent routers from sending periodic Hello messages to keep the link up. If a PIM router receives a Hello message with the Hold Time set to 0, then it will immediately expire the corresponding neighbor state.

When a PIM router brings down an interface or changes its IP address, it should immediately send a Hello message with the Hold Time set to 0 (using the old IP address if the IP address was changed) to cause any neighboring PIM routers to immediately delete the old information. Hello, messages with a Hold Time field value set to 0 are effectively goodbye messages, and PIM routers that receive such messages should immediately time out the PIM information about that neighbor adjacency.

3.2.4.4 LAN Prune Delay Option (Option Type 2)

PIM routers on multiaccess LANs (such as those based on Ethernet) include the LAN Prune Delay Option [RFC3973] [RFC7761] in Hello messages to allow for the tuning of the prune propagation delay on that LAN. The T bit in this Option specifies the ability of the router originating the Option to disable Join suppression; this is used by routers in a PIM-SM domain. PIM-DM routers should set this bit to 0 and ignore it upon receipt. The Propagation Delay (also referred to as the LAN Prune Delay) and Override Interval fields contain time interval values that are expressed in units of milliseconds.

Although References [RFC3973] and [RFC7761] do not specify mechanisms, it is possible for upstream PIM routers to explicitly track the individual downstream routers that have sent Join messages if Join suppression is disabled (i.e., if the routers can send Join messages). Using the T bit in the LAN Prune Delay Option, a PIM router can advertise its desire to disable Join suppression. Unless all PIM routers on a LAN negotiate the Join suppression capability, it is not possible to explicitly track and disable the Join suppression mechanism.

The value in the Propagation Delay field expresses a router's view of the expected message propagation delay on the link and is a value that is configurable by the system administrator. Upstream PIM routers use this value to determine how long it takes for a Join override message to reach them before pruning the corresponding interface. The administrator should enforce a lower bound on the permitted Propagation Delay values to account for scheduling and processing delays within the PIM router. Such internal delays within the router (if unaccounted for) may cause the router to process received messages later or send messages later than intended.

Setting the Propagation Delay field to a very low value may result in temporary outages in multicast packet forwarding because a downstream PIM router will not be able to send a Join message to override a Prune message from a neighbor before the upstream PIM neighbor stops forwarding multicast packets. When all PIM routers on a LAN can negotiate a Propagation Delay value that is different from the default ones, the routers choose the largest value from those advertised on the LAN by each PIM neighbor.

The PIM router that originates a LAN Prune Delay Option on interface I sets the Propagation Delay field to the *Propagation_Delay*(I) value configured on the interface, and the Override Interval field value to the configured *Override_Interval*(I) value. A router that receives these Option field values will use them to tune the value of the *Effective_Override_Interval*(I) and the timer values derived from it. Chapters 4 and 5 describe how these Option values affect the behavior of a PIM router.

PIM routers on multiaccess LANs should include the LAN Prune Delay Option in all Hello messages they send. A router includes this Option to advertise its capability of using values other than the Propagation Delay and Override Interval default values, which affect the setting of the Prune-Pending, Upstream Join, and Override Timers. It is important to note that routers on the LAN will not use the information provided in the LAN Prune Delay Option unless all PIM neighbors on the LAN advertise the Option (similar to the DR Priority Option).

3.2.4.5 Designated Router (DR) Priority Option (Option Type 19)

The 32-bit DR Priority field value in this Option [RFC7761] is an unsigned number (the default priority is 1) used in the DR election process, as described in Chapter 5. PIM routers on a network segment (i.e., both multiaccess LAN and on point-to-point interfaces) receive Hello messages with this Option, and the router with the numerically larger DR Priority field value is always preferred as the DR for the network segment. A network administrator, through the DR Priority Option, can assign a numerically larger DR Priority value to a particular PIM router to give preference to it in the DR election process.

A PIM router should include the DR Priority Option in every Hello message it sends on an interface, even if that interface is not explicitly configured with a DR Priority. It is required to include the DR Priority Option because the DR election process (which is priority-based) is only activated on a PIM router interface when all PIM neighbors on that interface signal their capability of using the Hello message's DR Priority Option.

When a PIM router receives a Hello message on an interface, its view of the current DR can change, for example, when the adjacency with a PIM neighbor times out, or when the router's own DR Priority changes. If the receiving PIM router assumes the DR role or ceases to be the DR on that interface, this causes the DR Register state machine (see Chapter 5) on the interface to change state, and the subsequent actions taken by the router are determined by that interface's state machine.

3.2.4.6 Generation ID Option (Option Type 20)

The 32-bit Generation ID field value in this Option [RFC3973] [RFC7761] is a randomly generated value for the PIM router interface on which the Hello message is sent. The PIM router regenerates the Generation ID whenever it starts or restarts PIM forwarding on the interface. PIM uses the Generation ID to detect PIM router reboots. PIM routers should always include the Generation ID Option in all Hello messages they send.

When a PIM router receives a Hello message from a neighbor with a new Generation ID, it should discard any old Hello information about that neighbor and replace that with the information taken from the new Hello message. Receiving a new Generation ID on an interface may cause a new DR to be elected on that interface.

3.2.4.7 State-Refresh Capable Option (Option Type 21)

A PIM-DM router that is the First-Hop Router (FHR) attached to a multicast source, periodically sends (S, G) State-Refresh messages along the SPT to prevent the pruned state on interfaces from timing out. Only State-Refresh Capable PIM-DM routers use the State-Refresh Capable Option. PIM-DM routers send the State-Refresh Option in Hello messages to inform neighbors that they are capable of performing the State-Refresh functions, as described in Chapter 4. The Interval field in the State-Refresh Option [RFC3973] is the State-Refresh Interval (in seconds) configured on the router interface (see State-Refresh Option format in Section 3.3). PIM-DM routers set the Reserved field to zero and ignore this field upon receipt.

3.2.4.8 Bidirectional Capable Option (Option Type 22)

The Bidirectional Capable Option is included in Hello messages to advertise a PIM router's ability to participate in the BIDIR-PIM protocol [RFC5015]. Only BIDIR-PIM capable routers use the Bidirectional Capable Option. The format of this Option is described in Section 3.5.

3.2.4.9 Address List Option (Option Type 24)

A PIM router originates a Hello message with the Address List Option [RFC7761] on an interface to advertise all the secondary IP addresses associated with that interface. A router must include this Option in all Hello messages if it has secondary IP addresses associated with the interface and may omit it if no secondary addresses are configured on the interface.

The primary IP address of a PIM neighbor is the IP address that the neighbor uses as the source IP address in the PIM Hello messages that it sends. Note that the IP address of a PIM neighbor may not be unique within the neighbor's database due to multicast traffic scoping. However, the IP address must be unique when considering the IP addresses of all the PIM neighbors on a specific PIM router interface.

A router must communicate its interface secondary IP addresses to PIM neighbors to provide them with a mechanism for mapping the next-hop information obtained through their multicast routing information base (MRIB) to a primary address that can be used as the destination address for sending PIM Join/Prune messages. A router can obtain the primary address of a PIM neighbor's interface from the source IP address field in the IP packets carrying PIM Hello messages. PIM routers use the Address List Option in the Hello message to advertise their secondary addresses. A PIM router must not list the primary address of the source interface within the Address List Option.

When a PIM router processes a Hello message received with an Address List Option, it will completely replace any previously associated secondary addresses for that neighbor with the list of secondary addresses in the Option. If a PIM Hello message is received and does not contain an Address List Option, then the router must delete all secondary addresses associated with the neighbor. If the router receives a Hello with an Address List Option that includes the primary address of the sending router in the list of secondary addresses, then the router uses the addresses listed in the Option to update the associated secondary addresses for that neighbor, excluding the primary address.

A PIM router that receives secondary addresses in the Address List Option on an interface must check all these advertised addresses against the previously advertised secondary addresses by all PIM neighbors on that interface. If the router detects an address conflict, and that a received secondary address was previously advertised by another PIM neighbor, then the router must maintain only the most recently received secondary address and should log an error message to the network administrator in a rate-limited manner.

All the secondary addresses carried in an Address List Option must be of the same address family (i.e., have the same AFI). Routers are not permitted to mix IPv4 and IPv6 secondary addresses within the same Address List Option. Furthermore, the address family of the secondary addresses in the Address List Option in the Hello message should be the same as the IP source and destination addresses of the IP packet carrying the Hello message.

3.2.5   PIM Join/Prune Message Format

PIM routers send Join or Prune messages [RFC3973] [RFC7761] toward upstream sources (in PIM-DM and PIM-SM) and RPs (in PIM-SM only). PIM-DM and PIM-SM routers send Join messages toward the actual multicast source to build source-rooted trees (SRTs), also called shortest-path trees (SPTs), while PIM-SM routers send Join messages toward the RP to build shared trees (also called RP trees (RPTs)). Routers send Prune messages to prune an SRT or shared tree branch when all multicast group members leave that branch. PIM applies the same message format for both Joins and Prunes, as shown in Figure 3.9. As illustrated in this figure, Join/Prune messages contain one or more multicast group sets, with each group set possibly containing two source lists, Joined Sources, and Pruned Sources (either of which may be empty in a given message, depending on the information being communicated to routers on the multicast distribution tree).

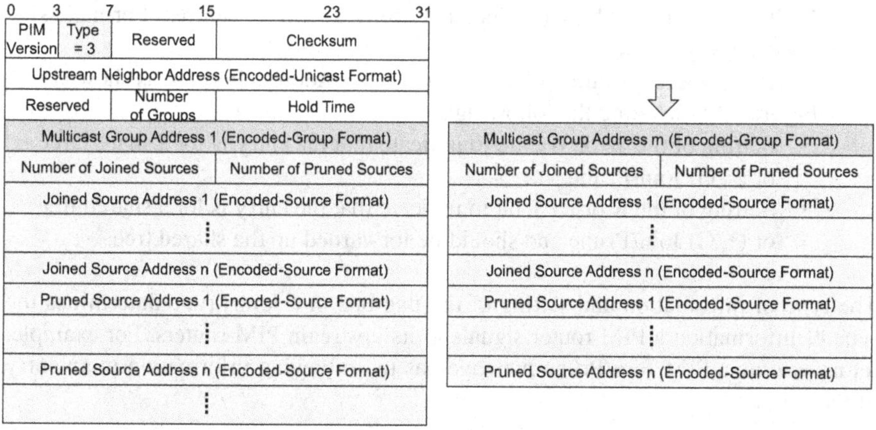

0 3	7	15	23	31
PIM Version	Type = 3	Reserved	Checksum	
Upstream Neighbor Address (Encoded-Unicast Format)				
Reserved		Number of Groups	Hold Time	
Multicast Group Address 1 (Encoded-Group Format)				
Number of Joined Sources		Number of Pruned Sources		
Joined Source Address 1 (Encoded-Source Format)				
⋮				
Joined Source Address n (Encoded-Source Format)				
Pruned Source Address 1 (Encoded-Source Format)				
⋮				
Pruned Source Address n (Encoded-Source Format)				
⋮				

Multicast Group Address m (Encoded-Group Format)
Number of Joined Sources | Number of Pruned Sources
Joined Source Address 1 (Encoded-Source Format)
⋮
Joined Source Address n (Encoded-Source Format)
Pruned Source Address 1 (Encoded-Source Format)
⋮
Pruned Source Address n (Encoded-Source Format)

- **Unicast Upstream Neighbor Address**: This is the primary address of the upstream neighbor that is the target of the message. PIM-DM routers MUST set this field to the RPF next hop.

- **Reserved (8 Bits)**: This is transmitted as zero and ignored on receipt.

- **Number of Groups (8 Bits)**: This is the number of multicast group sets contained in the message.

- **Hold Time (16 Bits)**: This is the amount of time (in seconds) the receiving router MUST keep the Join/Prune state alive. If the Hold Time is set to '0xFFFF', the receiver SHOULD hold the state until canceled by the appropriate canceling Join/Prune message, or timed out according to local policy.

- **Multicast Group Address**: This has format as in Encoded Group Address Format figure.

- **Number of Joined Sources (16 Bits)**: This is the number of Join source addresses listed for a given group.

- **Number of Pruned Sources (16 Bits)**: This is the number of Prune source addresses listed for a group.

- **Join Source Address 1 .. n**: This list contains the sources from which the sending router wishes to continue to receive multicast messages for the given group on the interface on which the message is sent.

- **Prune Source Address 1 .. n**: This list contains the sources from which the sending router does not wish to receive multicast messages for the given group on the interface on which the message is sent.

FIGURE 3.9   Join/Prune message format.

It is important to note that although we use "Join message" and "Prune messages" as if they are distinct PIM messages, these are actually different portions of a single PIM message type, as shown in Figure 3.9. We adopt these terms only to help the reader to fully appreciate the distinct use of these portions of the PIM Join/ Prune message.

As shown in Figures 3.4–3.6 and 3.9, the entries of the Join list and Prune list of the PIM Join/Prune message share a common format and contain the following information (among others):

- Multicast Group Address (in Encoded Multicast Group Address Format, as shown in Figure 3.5).
- Multicast Source Address (in Encoded Source Address Format, as shown in Figure 3.6) including the following:
  - Setting of the W or WC bit to indicate that the entry is for a shared tree or (*, G) Join/Prune.
  - Setting of the R or RPT bit to indicate that the entry is for a shared tree or (*, G) Join/Prune and should be forwarded up the shared tree.

The type of information and setting of the flag bits in a Join/Prune determines the type of information a PIM router signals to its upstream PIM routers. For example, let us assume a PIM Join/Prune message has the following information in an entry of the Join list:

- **Multicast Source Address**: 192.10.10.10
- **Multicast Group Address**: 224.10.10.10
- **Setting of W and R bits**: ON (i.e., set to 1)

This indicates that the entry is a (*, G) Join for the multicast group 224.10.10.10, with RP set to 192.16.20.20. Let us consider a PIM Join/Prune message with the following information in the Prune list entry:

- **Multicast Source Address**: 192.20.20.20
- **Multicast Group Address**: 224.20.20.20
- **Setting of W and R bits**: OFF (i.e., set to 0)

This indicates that the entry is an (S, G) Prune for the multicast group 224.20.20.20, with the source being 192.20.20.20 (i.e., the actual address of the multicast source).

When creating a single PIM Join/Prune message, the PIM router must ensure that all the Multicast Group addresses, Joined Source addresses, and Pruned Source addresses in the message have the same address family. The router is not allowed to mix IPv4 and IPv6 addresses within the same message. Furthermore, the router must ensure that the address family of the fields in the message matches those in the IP source and destination addresses of the IP packet carrying the message. This alignment allows maximum flexibility in the implementation of dual-stack IPv4/IPv6 routers. If a PIM router receives a Join/Prune message that has mixed address families, only those addresses in the message that belong to the same address family as the unicast PIM upstream neighbor address should be processed.

A PIM router sends (S, G) Prune messages toward the upstream neighbor (i.e., RPF neighbor as determined by the unicast routing table) for multicast source S to indicate that it does not want traffic from S addressed to multicast group G. Let us consider a scenario where we have two downstream routers, Routers A and B, and where Router A wishes to continue receiving multicast packets from the upstream, but Router B does not. In this case, Router A will send a PIM (S, G) Join message to the upstream neighbor in response to the (S, G) Prune message sent by Router B to override the (S, G) Prune message. *This is the only situation where a Join message is used in PIM-DM.* Sending PIM Prune messages prevents future multicast packets from propagating to routers and network segments that do not have active multicast group members.

3.2.5.1 Use of the Join/Prune Message in PIM-DM

PIM-DM operates on a *push principle* and utilizes only SRTs to deliver (S, G) multicast traffic to interested receivers. PIM-DM pushes or floods (S, G) multicast traffic to all nodes in the network under the assumption that all subnets in the multicast domain have at least one interested receiver of the (S, G) traffic. However, to minimize the unnecessary consumption of precious network resources such as router processing power and bandwidth, PIM-DM routers send Prune messages up the SRT (toward the source) to turn off unwanted multicast traffic. Sending such messages allows routers on SRT branches with no receivers to prune such branches from the SRT, leaving only branches with interested receivers. For this reason, PIM-DM is sometimes referred to as a *flood-and-prune* multicast protocol.

Each Prune message has a timeout (i.e., the Hold Time) associated with it. When the message (or Prune) times out, the receiving router places the pruned interface in the forwarding state and starts forwarding multicast traffic out of the interface again. The router maintains the interface in the Prune state for the duration of the Hold Time unless the router receives a Join or Graft message that removes or overrides the Prune. If the downstream router still does not want to receive the (S, G) multicast traffic, it will send another Prune message to turn off that traffic.

In the case where a router sends an (S, G) Prune message on a multiaccess network with several other routers (e.g., an IP subnet) to turn off multicast traffic from a source, any of the other routers, by overhearing this (S, G) Prune message, can override it by sending a PIM (S, G) Join message on the multiaccess network if it has active receivers for the (S, G) traffic. This mechanism is referred to as PIM *Prune Override* since any downstream neighbor on the network can send *overriding PIM Join messages.*

3.2.5.2 Use of the Join/Prune Message in PIM-SM

PIM-SM operates based on a *pull model* in which routers and hosts deploy an *Explicit Join mechanism* to request multicast traffic to be sent to them. Routers use PIM Join messages to request multicast traffic while hosts use IGMP Membership Report messages. Routers also employ PIM Prune messages to tear down multicast distribution tree branches (shared trees and SPTs) when they are no longer needed. IGMPv2 hosts, for example, send Leave Group messages to leave a multicast group.

3.2.5.2.1   Shared Tree Joins/Prunes

In the default mode of operation, PIM-SM adopts a shared tree to send traffic from the RP (i.e., the root) to the receivers. The shared tree is sometimes called an RP tree (RPT). To construct the shared tree for multicast group G, a router sends a (*, G) Join message toward the root of the tree (i.e., the RP). The wildcard symbol denotes the RP of the shared tree. It is important to note that the RP Address is carried in the Encoded Source Address Format (see Figure 3.6), and the W and R bits are set to 1, indicating that the corresponding Joined or Pruned Source field contains an RP

Address, not the address of the actual multicast source. The (*, G) Join message is forwarded router by router (i.e., hop by hop) toward the RP, constructing a branch of the shared tree as it travels toward the RP. A router that does not already have directly connected receivers will send a (*, G) Join message towards the RP as soon as it receives an IGMP Membership Report message from a new receiver.

A leaf router can send a (*, G) Prune message up the shared tree toward the RP when it no longer needs traffic sent to multicast group G (created through explicit Join messages). This happens when a router no longer has directly connected receivers or downstream multicast routers for multicast group G. Host receivers can silently leave a group or send a corresponding IGMP Leave Group message to their DRs (see IGMP discussion in Chapter 2). Allowing leaf routers to send Prune messages greatly improves the leave time in the network, instead of relying solely on the shared tree branches to time out. On SPTs, routers send (S, G) Prune messages, as discussed in the subsequent text.

3.2.5.2.2   Shortest-Path Tree Joins/Prunes

In some cases, the receiver-side DR of a receiver may join an SRT (or SPT) to receive multicast traffic from the source directly instead of through the RP. In this case, the DR sends a (S, G) Join message in the direction of the source to construct the SPT to the receivers. Constructing the SPT allows routers with directly connected receivers (i.e., DRs) to use direct paths to the source, bypassing the root (or RP) and enabling receivers to receive multicast traffic via more direct paths. A DR with any interested receivers (detected through IGMP Membership messages) sends an (S, G) Join message toward the source S, and as the message travels hop by hop to the source, the SPT is built. It is important to note that the SPT is constructed up to the source-side DR and not to the source itself, that is, from the receiver-side DR to the source-side DR.

It is important to note that branches of a multicast distribution tree (shared tree or SPT) must be refreshed periodically to prevent them from timing out and being deleted, thereby stopping the flow of multicast traffic to the receivers. To prevent branches from timing out, routers send periodic Join messages up the distribution tree branches as a way of periodically refreshing the branches. Essentially, this periodic Join refresh mechanism maintains the tree and prevents the branches from timing out.

Routers can send (S, G) Prune messages to prune SPT branches, just as (*, G) Prunes are used to prune shared tree branches. If a router (i.e., receiver-side DR) no longer has directly connected receivers for (S, G) multicast traffic, it can send a (S, G) Prune message toward source S, that is, to its RPF (or upstream) neighbor.

It is important to note that routers on a multiaccess network that are part of a shared or SPT can also send PIM Join messages to override a Prune message if they still have active receivers of the multicast traffic to be pruned. Overriding Joins can be applied to shared trees or SPTs.

3.2.5.2.3   Requesting Multicast Traffic in PIM-SM

This section summarizes the main steps involved in requesting multicast traffic from an RP or directly from the multicast source. Some parts of the discussion here also apply to PIM-DM. A PIM-SM router receives requests for multicast traffic to a group in one of two ways; in the form of IGMP Membership Report messages from directly connected hosts or in the form of PIM Join messages from downstream routers. The leaf router, that is, the First-Hop Router (FHR) directly connected to a requesting host, is the router that receives the IGMP Membership Report messages. A PIM-SM router processes these requests in the same way as follows:

- If the PIM-SM router receives a new request for a multicast group G that it is already forwarding traffic to on one or more of its interfaces, then it will simply add that downstream interface (on which the request arrived) as a new entry in the list of outgoing interfaces. The router does not need to signal any upstream router for the traffic or send an acknowledgment to the requestor; it simply starts forwarding the multicast traffic out of the interface on which the request arrived.
- If the router was not already forwarding the multicast traffic requested, then the router handles the request as follows:
  - Unless preconfigured with information, the router does not know the multicast source (if any) that might be transmitting the requested traffic, so it cannot simply send a request toward that source to ask for a copy of the traffic. Instead, the router has to rely on an RP in the multicast domain to provide the traffic. By searching its multicast group-to-RP mapping information (received from an RP discovery mechanism such as the Bootstrap Router (BSR), as discussed in Chapter 5), the router learns the address of the RP that is responsible for providing the requested multicast traffic.
  - The router sends a PIM (*, G) Join message as a way of requesting the traffic toward the RP. This message is not unicast to the RP; instead, it is sent via multicast toward the neighbor that is the next-hop on the path toward the RP. This upstream neighbor, in turn, will forward the message to its next-hop neighbor on the path toward the RP. The message is forwarded hop by hop until either it arrives at a router that is already receiving the requested traffic or it reaches the RP.
  - If the PIM (*, G) messages reach a router that is already receiving the multicast traffic requested (on its way to the RP), then this router will start sending the traffic down the path on which the Join message arrived; the router will not forward the Join message any further upstream toward the RP.
  - If the PIM (*, G) message ends up reaching the RP, then the RP will start forwarding the multicast traffic down on the path on which the Join message arrived (i.e., along the shared tree or RPT). If the RP has never received the requested traffic, then it will simply ignore the Join message; PIM has no mechanism for signaling to a node that a particular multicast traffic does not exist.

Once the router that sent the PIM (*, G) message (i.e., the LHR) receives the requested multicast traffic, it will see the IP address (S) of the actual multicast source. At that point, the LHR can take the opportunity to send a PIM (S, G) Join message directly towards the source (S), requesting the traffic, instead of having to receive the traffic via the RP. As soon as the multicast traffic starts arriving along a direct path from the source to the LHR, it prunes itself from the traffic arriving from the RP. At that point, the LHR continues to receive the traffic directly from the source (i.e., via the SPT).

3.2.6 PIM ASSERT MESSAGE FORMAT

A multiaccess network segment (e.g., Ethernet LAN) may have multiple routers, and as a result, multiple paths to either a multicast source or the RP may exist. This can lead to the routers attached to the network segment receiving duplicate multi-cast packets from those multiple paths. PIM deploys the Assert message [RFC3973] [RFC7761] to resolve which router on a multiaccess network segment should be the multicast packet *forwarder* when multiple routers exist on the network segment to the multicast source or RP.

A PIM router sends an Assert message when it receives a multicast packet from another router on the outgoing interface for that packet (i.e., on an outgoing inter-face on which the router itself would normally have forwarded that packet). A PIM router may also send Assert messages in response to an Assert message received from another router on the network segment. Figure 3.10 demonstrates the format of the PIM Assert message.

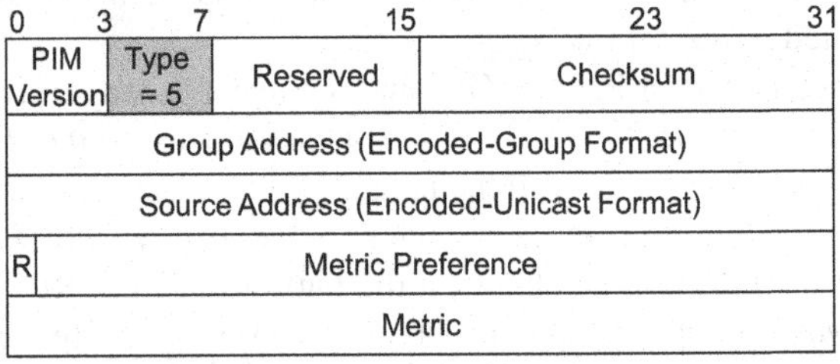

0 3   7   15   23   31
PIM Version / Type = 5 / Reserved / Checksum
Group Address (Encoded-Group Format)
Source Address (Encoded-Unicast Format)
R / Metric Preference
Metric

- **Group Address**: This is the group address for which the router wishes to resolve the forwarding conflict.

- **Source Address**: This is the source address for which the router wishes to resolve the forwarding conflict. The source address MAY be set to zero for (*, G) Asserts.

- **R (1 Bit)**: This is called the RPT bit and is set to 1 for Assert (*, G) messages, and 0 for Assert (S, G) messages.

- **Metric Preference (31 Bits)**: This is the preference value assigned to the unicast routing protocol that provided the route to the multicast source or Rendezvous Point.

- **Metric (32 Bits)**: This is the unicast routing table metric associated with the route used to reach the multicast source or Rendezvous Point. The metric is in units applicable to the unicast routing protocol used.

FIGURE 3.10 Assert message format.

PIM routers can send Assert messages to resolve a forwarding conflict for all multicast traffic sent to a given multicast group G (i.e., (*, G) traffic) or for multicast traffic sent by a specific source S to a multicast group G (i.e., (S, G) traffic):

- **Assert (S, G) message**: PIM routers send source-specific Assert messages when they need to forward multicast packets from a specific source on the SPT (i.e., SPTbit is TRUE) and must contend with other routers on the network segment to be the *forwarder*. PIM Assert (S, G) messages have the Group Address field set to the multicast group address G and the Source Address field set to the multicast source address S. For this message, the router sets the RPT (or R) bit to 0, the Metric Preference (sometimes called the Administrative Distance) to MRIB.pref (S), and the Routing Metric to MRIB.metric (S).
- **Assert (*, G) message**: PIM routers send group-specific Assert messages when they need to forward multicast packets sent by any source on the shared tree (or RPT) to a multicast group and must contend with other routers on the network segment to be the forwarder. Assert (*, G) messages have the Group Address field set to the multicast group G. For data-triggered Assert messages, the IP source address of the data packet that triggered the Assert may be used as the Source Address field of the Assert (*, G) message, otherwise, this field is set to zero. The router sets the RPT bit (or R) to 1, the Metric Preference to MRIB.pref (RP(G)), and the Routing Metric to MRIB. metric (RP(G)).

3.2.6.1 PIM AssertCancel Messages

An Assert message for (S, G) that carries an *infinite metric* (in both the Metric Preference and Routing Metric fields) is referred to as an *AssertCancel (S, G) message*. It is to be noted that an infinite metric (or *infinity metric*) value is specific to each routing protocol; different routing protocols use different values as infinite metrics. The routing protocol RIP uses 16 as the infinity metric. The Cisco Administrative Distance measure (which is equivalent to the Metric Preference) uses 255 as "Unknown" or "route is invalid", which is equivalent to an infinite metric in this metric.

The Assert Winner on a multiaccess network segment sends an (S, G) (or (*, G)) AssertCancel message when it deletes the (S, G) (or (*, G)) multicast forwarding state that had caused the Assert process to occur. Other PIM routers on the multiaccess network segment with (S, G) (or (*, G)) forwarding state that see an Assert message with the infinite metric (i.e., an AssertCancel message) will send their own (S, G) (or (*, G)) Assert messages and take over multicast packet forwarding, thereby generating duplicate multicast traffic, which in turn causes the routers to elect a new forwarder for the network segment.

For example, a PIM-DM router that is the Assert Winner sends an AssertCancel (S, G) message when it changes its upstream interface to the current interface. Other PIM-DM routers with forwarding state on the network segment that see this message with infinite Assert metric, will be forced to send their own Assert messages so that an Assert Winner can be reestablished. The Assert process is described in detail in Chapter 4 for PIM-DM and Chapter 5 for PIM-SM.

AssertCancel messages serve simply as an optimization mechanism for the PIM Assert process. Although the original Assert timeout mechanism (i.e., the Assert Timer (S, G)) will eventually allow the network segment (to which the PIM router is attached) to become consistent, sending AssertCancel (S, G) messages simply promotes faster network convergence. Routers do not require special processing for an AssertCancel (S, G) message since it is simply an Assert (S, G) message from the current Assert Winner.

3.3 PIM-DM SPECIFIC MESSAGES

This section describes additional messages that are specific to PIM-DM: Graft, Graft-Ack, and State-Refresh messages [RFC3973].

3.3.1 GRAFT MESSAGE AND GRAFT-ACK MESSAGE FORMAT

A PIM-DM router sends a Graft message [RFC3973] to the upstream neighbor to rejoin a multicast distribution tree branch that was previously pruned to receive multicast packets. PIM-DM enables a router to quickly graft a previously pruned branch back onto the SRT. This happens, for example, when a new receiver on an SRT branch that was previously pruned joins the multicast group. In this case, the receiver-side Designated Router (DR) detects the new receiver (via a received IGMP Membership Report message for (S, G) multicast traffic, sometimes called an "IGMP Join" message), and immediately sends a PIM Graft message up the SRT (toward the source). As soon as the upstream router receives the Graft message, it immediately places the interface on which the message is received in the forwarding state and starts sending (S, G) multicast traffic toward the receiver if its upstream or incoming link was not previously pruned.

The PIM Graft message has the same format as the Join/Prune message, as depicted in Figure 3.9, except the following:

- The Type field is set to 6.
- The source address(es) is placed in the Join section of the message.
- The Hold Time field is zero and is ignored when the Graft is received.

If a router in a PIM-DM domain sends a Graft message and does not receive a Graft-Acknowledgment (Graft-Ack) message from the upstream router within a specified period, it keeps sending new Graft messages at a rate that is determined by a configurable interval, known as the Graft_Retry_Period, until it receives a Graft-Ack message from the upstream router. The sending router utilizes the Graft Retry Timer for this purpose. The Graft_Retry_Period (with a default value of 3 seconds) of this timer is the length of time, in the absence of the receipt of a Graft-Ack message, that the router must wait before retransmitting a Graft message to the upstream neighbor. In PIM-DM, the Graft message is the only message type that uses an acknowledgment mechanism.

The PIM Graft-Ack message format [RFC3973] is identical to the received Graft message, except for the following:

- The Type field is set to 7.
- The Upstream Neighbor Address field in the message is set to the source address of the Graft message and is ignored upon receipt.

3.3.2 State-Refresh Capability Option and State-Refresh Message Formats

In a PIM-DM network, pruned interfaces (i.e., interfaces in the pruned state) can resume forwarding multicast packets when their prune timers expire, even when downstream nodes do not need the multicast packets. To address this issue, the PIM-DM router directly connected to a multicast source, known as the First-Hop Router (FHR) of the SRT, sends periodic State-Refresh messages [RFC3973] to refresh (S, G) state entries in PIM-DM routers on the SRT. The FHR sends a State-Refresh message, which is propagated hop by hop to all downstream nodes in the entire PIM-DM network, resetting the prune timers on all the PIM router interfaces. Upon receiving State-Refresh messages, interfaces that do not need to forward multicast packets remain in the prune state.

The PIM-DM State-Refresh feature greatly reduces the periodic flood-and-prune of multicast packets to PIM-DM network areas with no active members of a multicast group. Figure 3.11 depicts the format of the State-Refresh Capability Option carried in PIM Hello messages, while Figure 3.12 illustrates the format of the State-Refresh message sent by the FHR of a multicast traffic source [RFC3973].

State-Refresh messages are sent with the IP destination address set to the IPv4 multicast address 224.0.0.13 (i.e., the ALL-PIM-ROUTERS address), the PIM Version set to 2, and an IP header TTL of 1. As with all PIM message types, the State-Refresh message is sent with the IP header protocol number 103. The State-Refresh message has a type value of 9. The IP source address of the IP packet carrying the State-Refresh message is set to the IP address of the interface on which the message is sent, and *the IP source address is rewritten hop by hop when a PIM-DM router propagates the message; the router rewrites its sending interface address as the source address of the propagated message.*

The State-Refresh message, as shown in Figure 3.12, contains the Multicast Group Address, Multicast Source Address, Originator (i.e., FHR) Address (used for debugging purposes), routing information (i.e., Metric Preference and Routing Metric) required by the LAN Assert mechanism, State-Refresh message TTL value for scope control (which is different from the IP header TTL), and several flags, as

0	7	15	23	31
Type = 21			Length = 4	
Version = 1	Interval		Reserved	

- **Interval (8 Bits)**: The value in this field is the router's configured State-Refresh Interval in seconds. The State-Refresh Capable Option MUST be used by State-Refresh capable PIM-DM routers.

- **Reserved (16 Bits)**: This field is set to zero and ignored upon receipt.

FIGURE 3.11   State-Refresh Capability Option format.

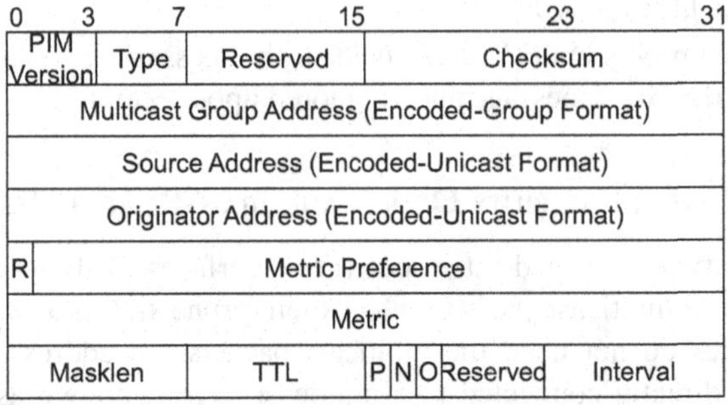

0 3	7	15	23	31
PIM Version	Type	Reserved	Checksum	
Multicast Group Address (Encoded-Group Format)				
Source Address (Encoded-Unicast Format)				
Originator Address (Encoded-Unicast Format)				
R	Metric Preference			
Metric				
Masklen	TTL	P N O Reserved	Interval	

- **Multicast Group Address**: This is the multicast group address in the Encoded Multicast Address format.

- **Source Address**: This is the address of the data source in the Encoded Unicast Address format.

- **Originator Address**: This is the address of the first hop router in the Encoded Unicast address format.

- **R (1 Bit)**: This is called the Rendezvous Point Tree bit and is set to 0 for PIM-DM and Ignored upon receipt.

- **Metric Preference (31 Bits)**: This is the preference value assigned to the unicast routing protocol that provided the route to the source.

- **Metric (32 Bits)**: This is the cost metric of the unicast route to the source. The metric is in units applicable to the unicast routing protocol used.

- **Masklen (8 Bits)**: This is the length of the address mask of the unicast route to the source.

- **TTL (8 Bits)**: This is the Time To Live of the State-Refresh message. It is decremented each time the message is forwarded. Note that this is different from the IP Header TTL, which is always set to 1.

- **P (1 Bit)**: This is the Prune indicator flag and MUST be set to 1 if the State-Refresh is to be sent on a Pruned interface. Otherwise, it MUST be set to 0.

- **N (1 Bit)**: This is the Prune Now flag and SHOULD be set to 1 by the State-Refresh originator on every third State-Refresh message and SHOULD be ignored upon receipt. This is for compatibility with earlier versions of State-Refresh.

- **O (1 Bit)**: This is the Assert Override flag and SHOULD be set to 1 by upstream routers on a LAN if the Assert Timer (S,G) is not running and SHOULD be ignored upon receipt. This is for compatibility with earlier versions of State-Refresh.

- **Reserved (6 Bits)**: This field is set to zero and ignored upon receipt.

- **Interval (8 Bits)**: This field is set by the originating router to the interval (in seconds) between consecutive State-Refresh messages for this (S,G) pair.

FIGURE 3.12   State-Refresh message format.

described in Figure 3.12. The routing information, State-Refresh message TTL, and flags can be rewritten by each hop that forwards the message.

The originating router (i.e., FHR) initializes the State-Refresh message TTL value to either a locally configured value or to the largest TTL observed in multicast packets from the source seen so far. Each downstream router decrements this TTL value by 1 before forwarding the State-Refresh message to downstream nodes. A router will only forward the State-Refresh message if its TTL value is greater than 0 and larger than the configured local TTL threshold. This prevents State-Refresh messages from propagating to PIM-DM areas where routers have not created (S, G) state.

The flags in the State-Refresh message consist of the Prune Indicator flag, Prune Now flag, and Assert Override flag. A PIM-DM router clears the Prune Indicator flag when the State-Refresh message is transmitted on an outgoing interface in the Forwarding state and sets it when the State-Refresh message is transmitted on an interface in the Pruned state. In other words, if the Prune (S, G) Downstream state machine (see Chapter 4) on interface I is in the Pruned state, then the PIM-DM router must set the Prune Indicator bit to 1 in the State-Refresh message being sent over I. Otherwise, the router must set the Prune Indicator bit to 0.

3.4 PIM-SM SPECIFIC MESSAGES

This section describes additional messages that are specific to PIM-SM: Register, Register-Stop, Bootstrap Message, and Candidate-RP-Advertisement messages [RFC5059] [RFC7761].

3.4.1 REGISTER MESSAGE FORMAT

PIM-SM routers that act as source-side DRs (or First-Hop Routers (FHRs)) send PIM Register messages [RFC7761] to RPs when they receive multicast packets from sources that need to be transmitted on the RP tree (i.e., the shared tree). The FHR sets the source IP address of the IP packet carrying the PIM Register message to the IP address of the sending interface and the destination IP address to the unicast IP address of the RP. The IP header TTL of the IP packet carrying the Register message is the system's normal unicast IP TTL. Figure 3.13 illustrates the format of the PIM Register message.

It is important to note that to reduce the overhead incurred when encapsulating the PIM Register message in an IP packet, the FHR computes the checksum for the Register message only on the first 8 bytes of the message, including the common PIM header and the next 4 bytes, but excluding the portion containing the multicast data packet. For interoperability reasons, an RP should accept a PIM Register message carrying a checksum that is computed over the entire PIM Register message. When calculating the checksum, the FHR sets the "Upper-Layer Packet Length" of the IPv6 pseudo-header to 8.

The multicast data packet (portion of the Register message) sent by the source must be of the same address family (i.e., with the same AFI) as the PIM packet encapsulating it; in other words, an IPv4 data packet must be encapsulated in an IPv4 PIM message. Note that the FHR decrements the IP header TTL of the original IP packet before encapsulation, just like any other IP packet that is forwarded. Furthermore, the RP decrements the IP header TTL of the original IP packet after decapsulating it, before forwarding the IP packet along the shared tree.

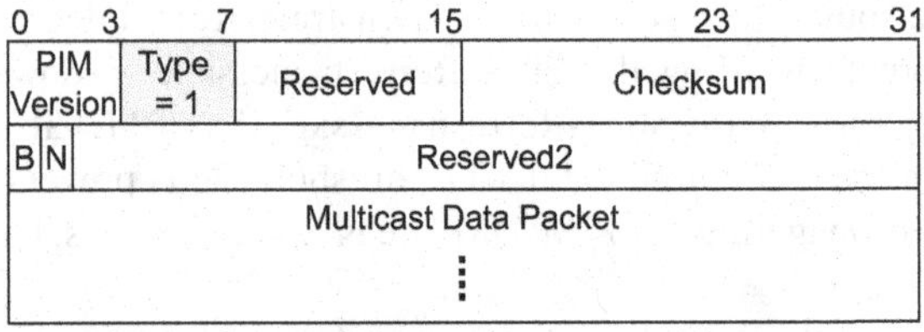

```
 0     3     7           15              23          31
┌───────┬──────┬────────────────┬──────────────────────┐
│ PIM   │ Type │   Reserved     │      Checksum        │
│Version│ = 1  │                │                      │
├─┬─┬───┴──────┴────────────────┴──────────────────────┤
│B│N│                  Reserved2                        │
├─┴─┴───────────────────────────────────────────────────┤
│              Multicast Data Packet                    │
│                       ⋮                               │
└───────────────────────────────────────────────────────┘
```

- **B (1 Bit)**: This is called the Border bit and is deprecated in RFC 7761. A router MUST set the B bit to 0 on transmission and MUST ignore it on reception.

- **N (1 Bit)**: This is called the Null-Register bit and is set to 1 by a DR that is probing the RP before expiring its local Register-Suppression Timer. This bit is set to 0, otherwise.

- **Reserved2 (30 Bits)**: This is transmitted as zero and ignored on receipt.

- **Multicast Data Packet**: This is the original packet sent by the source. The original packet must be of the same Address Family as the encapsulating PIM packet, e.g., an IPv6 data packet must be encapsulated in an IPv6 PIM packet.

FIGURE 3.13   Register message format.

The FHR sets the Null-Register (N) bit to 1 when it is probing the RP before the local Register-Suppression Timer expires and sets it to 0, otherwise. The FHR (i.e., source-side DR) sends Null-Register messages to the RP to signal the presence of multicast sources attached to it as part of the PIM Register-Suppression mechanism. The PIM Null-Register messages (which carry information about a single multicast source and group) are sent periodically from the FHR to the RP during the *Register_ Probe_Time* to keep the multicast state alive at the RP as long as the attached source is active.

When an RP stops serving receivers of multicast group receivers or when it formally starts receiving multicast data from the multicast source via its source-side DR, it sends a PIM Register-Stop message to the DR. Upon receiving the Register-Stop message, the source-side DR stops sending PIM Register messages with encapsulated multicast data packets and starts a Register-Stop Timer. When this timer expires, the source-side DR sends a PIM Null-Register message (which is simply a PIM Register message with no encapsulated multicast data packets) to the RP. If the source-side DR receives a PIM Register-Stop message from the RP during the Register_Probe_Time, it will reset its Register-Suppression Timer; otherwise, it will start sending PIM Register messages containing multicast data packets again to the RP when the Register-Suppression Timer expires. Chapter 5 describes in detail the use of the PIM Null-Register message.

For an (S, G) Null-Register message, the multicast data packet portion of the Register message contains a dummy IP header with S as the source IP address, and the multicast group address G as the destination IP address. When the FHR generates an IPv4 Null-Register message, it fills the fields in the dummy IPv4 header according to Table 3.2. The FHR may fill other IPv4 header fields with any value that is valid for that field.

TABLE 3.2

Information for Creating the (S, G) Null-Register Message for IPv4

Field	Value
IP Version	4
Header Length	5
Checksum	Header checksum
Fragmentation Offset	0
More Fragments	0
Total Length	20
IP Protocol	103 (PIM)

TABLE 3.3

Information for Creating the (S, G) Null-Register Message for IPv6

Field	Value
IP Version	6
Next Header	103 (PIM)
Length	4
PIM Version	0
PIM Type	0
PIM Reserved	0
PIM Checksum	PIM checksum, including IPv6 pseudo-header

Upon receiving (S, G) Null-Register messages and if the Header Checksum field is non-zero, the RP will verify the checksum and discard Null-Register messages that have a bad checksum. The RP should not check the value of any individual fields in the Null-Register message; a correct checksum in the IP header is sufficient. The RP must not check the checksum if the Header Checksum field is zero.

For IPv6, the FHR generates a dummy IP header followed by a dummy PIM header with values according to Table 3.3, in addition to using S as the source IP address, and the multicast group address G as the destination IP address. The FHR may fill other IPv6 header fields with any value that is valid for that field.

Upon receiving IPv6 (S, G) Null-Register messages and if the dummy PIM header is present, the RP should check the checksum and discard Null-Register messages with bad checksums.

3.4.2 REGISTER-STOP MESSAGE FORMAT

An RP sends, via unicast, a PIM Register-Stop message [RFC7761] to the sender (i.e., FHR) of the PIM Register message. The IP source address of the IP packet

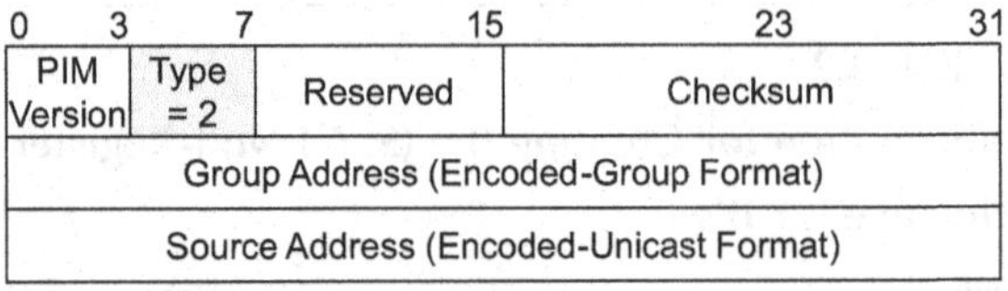

0 3	7	15	23	31
PIM Version	Type = 2	Reserved	Checksum	
Group Address (Encoded-Group Format)				
Source Address (Encoded-Unicast Format)				

- **Group Address**: This is the group address written in the destination address field of the Multicast Data Packet carried in the Register message.

- **Source Address**: This is the host address written in the source address field of the Multicast Data Packet carried in the Register message. A special wildcard value consisting of an address field of all zeros can be used to indicate any source.

FIGURE 3.14   Register-Stop message format.

carrying the PIM Register-Stop message is the destination address used in the Register message's IP packet. The IP destination address of the IP packet carrying the Register-Stop message is the source address used in the Register message's IP packet. Figure 3.14 displays the format of the PIM Register-Stop message.

The Group Address field in the Register-Stop message is the multicast group address written in the destination address field of the multicast data packet encapsulated in the PIM Register message. Note that for PIM Register-Stop messages, the Mask Length field (in the Encoded Multicast Group Address format, as illustrated in Figure 3.5) contains the full IP address length times 8 (e.g., 32 for IPv4 native encoding) if the Register-Stop message is sent for a single multicast group.

The Source Address in the PIM Register-Stop message is the IP address written in the source address field of the multicast data packet encapsulated in the PIM Register message. The format of this address is the encoded unicast address format, as depicted in Figure 3.4. An address field consisting of all zeros is a special wildcard value that can be used to indicate any source.

3.4.3   Bootstrap Message Format

PIM-SM (see Chapter 5) adopts the concept of a Rendezvous Point (RP), which enables receivers in a PIM-SM domain to discover and receive traffic from sources that send to a particular multicast group. The Bootstrap Router (BSR) [RFC5059] is a mechanism that allows multicast routers in a PIM-SM domain to learn the set of multicast group-to-RP mappings required for them to receive and forward multicast packets to interested receivers. Bootstrap messages are sent via multicast to the ALL-PIM-ROUTERS multicast group address (224.0.0.13) and with the IP TTL set to 1. In some cases (as described in [RFC5059]), Bootstrap messages may be sent via unicast to a specific PIM-SM neighbor.

To use the BSR mechanism, some of the routers within a PIM-SM domain are configured as Candidate-RPs, that is, as potential RPs for the domain. The PIM-SM domain will eventually use a subset of the Candidate-RPs as the actual RPs for the domain. In addition, some of the routers in the PIM-SM domain are configured as Candidate-BSRs. The Candidate-BSRs participate in a BSR election process, and one of them is elected the BSR for the PIM-SM domain.

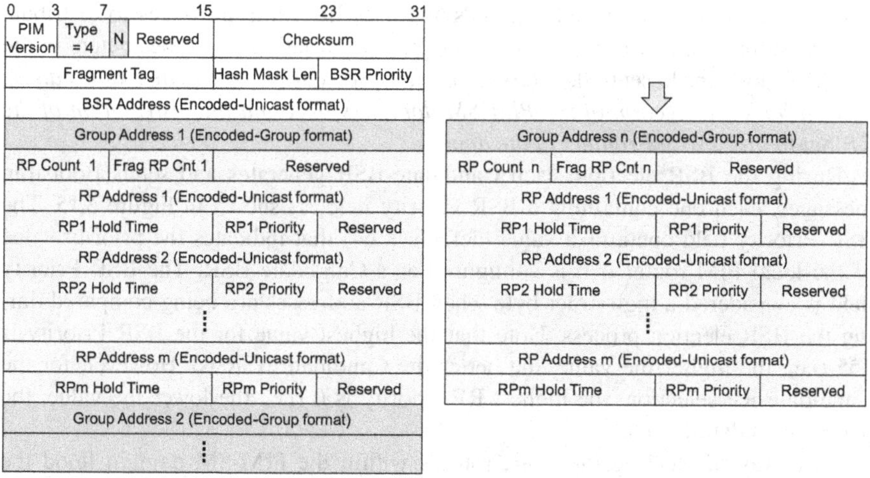

0	3	7		15		23		31
PIM Version	Type = 4	N	Reserved		Checksum			
Fragment Tag				Hash Mask Len		BSR Priority		
BSR Address (Encoded-Unicast format)								

Group Address 1 (Encoded-Group format)				Group Address n (Encoded-Group format)		
RP Count 1	Frag RP Cnt 1	Reserved		RP Count n	Frag RP Cnt n	Reserved
RP Address 1 (Encoded-Unicast format)				RP Address 1 (Encoded-Unicast format)		
RP1 Hold Time	RP1 Priority	Reserved		RP1 Hold Time	RP1 Priority	Reserved
RP Address 2 (Encoded-Unicast format)				RP Address 2 (Encoded-Unicast format)		
RP2 Hold Time	RP2 Priority	Reserved		RP2 Hold Time	RP2 Priority	Reserved
⋮				⋮		
RP Address m (Encoded-Unicast format)				RP Address m (Encoded-Unicast format)		
RPm Hold Time	RPm Priority	Reserved		RPm Hold Time	RPm Priority	Reserved
Group Address 2 (Encoded-Group format)						
⋮						

- **Type (3 Bits)**: This is the PIM Message Type. Value is 4 for a Bootstrap message.

- **N (1 Bit)**: This is called the No-Forward bit and when set, it means the Bootstrap message fragment is not to be forwarded.

- **Fragment Tag (16 Bits)**: This is a randomly generated number which is used to distinguish the fragments belonging to different Bootstrap messages; fragments belonging to same Bootstrap message carry the same 'Fragment Tag'.

- **Hash Mask Len (8 Bits)**: This is the length (in bits) of the mask to use in the hash function. For IPv4, RFC 5059 recommends a value of 30 and a value of 126 for IPv6.

- **BSR Priority (8 Bits)**: This contains the BSR priority value of the included BSR.

- **BSR Address**: This is the address of the bootstrap router for the domain.

- **Group Address 1....n**: This is the group ranges (address and mask) with which the Candidate-RPs are associated.

- **RP Count 1....n (8-Bit fields)**: This is the number of Candidate-RP addresses included in the whole Bootstrap message for the corresponding group range.

- **Frag RP Cnt 1..m (8-Bit Fields)**: This is the number of Candidate-RP addresses included in this fragment of the Bootstrap message, for the corresponding group range. This field facilitates parsing of the RP-Set for a given group range, when carried over more than one fragment.

- **RP address 1....m**: This is the address of the Candidate-RPs, for the corresponding group range.

- **RP1....m Hold Time (16-Bit Fields)**: This is the Hold Time (in seconds) for the corresponding RP. This field is copied from the 'Hold Time' field of the associated RP stored at the BSR.

- **RP1..m Priority (8-Bit Fields)**: This is the 'Priority' of the corresponding RP and Encoded-Group Address. This field is copied from the 'Priority' field stored at the BSR when receiving a C-RP-Advertisement message. The highest priority is '0' (i.e., unlike BSR priority, the lower the value of the 'Priority' field, the better). Note that the priority is per RP and per Group Address.

FIGURE 3.15 Bootstrap message format.

All the routers in the PIM-SM domain learn the result of the BSR election through Bootstrap messages (see Figure 3.15). The Candidate-RPs then report their candidacy to the Candidate-BSR that is elected the BSR for the PIM-SM domain, which selects a subset of these Candidate-RPs and uses Bootstrap messages to distribute corresponding multicast group-to-RP mapping information to all the routers in the PIM-SM domain. Essentially, *Bootstrap messages carry information that can be used in both the election of the PIM-SM domain's BSR and the distribution of the RP-Set to all PIM-SM routers in the domain.*

During the BSR election, each Candidate-BSR generates and sends Bootstrap messages, each one containing a BSR Priority field, as shown in Figure 3.15. The BSR Priority field contains a value (default is 64) that indicates the priority value of the local PIM router if it is configured as a Candidate-BSR. The BSR Priority field is considered a high-order byte when BSR addresses are being compared during the BSR election process. Note that the highest value for the BSR Priority is 255 (i.e., the higher the value, the better the Candidate-BSR is). However, for the Candidate-RP selection, the highest RP Priority is 0 (i.e., the lower the value, the better Candidate-RP is).

As a way of electing the BSR, routers within the PIM-SM domain flood the Bootstrap messages throughout the domain, and a Candidate-BSR that receives a message with a higher-priority Candidate-BSR than itself will suppress sending further Bootstrap messages for some time. The single Candidate-BSR remaining becomes the elected BSR for the PIM-SM domain, and its Bootstrap messages will inform all the other PIM-SM routers in the domain that it is the elected BSR.

When a router in the PIM-SM receives a Bootstrap message, it will extract the multicast group-to-RP mappings contained in the message and add that information to its local pool of group-to-RP mappings obtained from other sources such as via static RP configuration. The router then proceeds to calculate the final group-to-RP mappings from this pool according to specific rules configured for the particular multicast routing protocol running in the router (PIM-SM or BIDIR-PIM). The router uses the group-to-RP mappings and PIM Join/Prune information to construct multicast distribution trees.

A PIM-SM router may divide a Bootstrap message into "semantic fragments" if it determines that the resulting IP packet would not fit into the maximum allowed IP packet size of an interface. A router can send a single Bootstrap message as multiple semantic fragments (each fragment carried in a separate IP packet), as long as the router tags each fragment of the semantic fragments as belonging to the same Bootstrap message. The format of a single non-fragmented Bootstrap message is the same as the format of each *Bootstrap semantic fragment*.

Each Group Address field in the Bootstrap message contains the multicast group address ranges (i.e., group address and mask) the listed Candidate-RPs are associated with. If a Bootstrap semantic fragment contains administratively-scoped address ranges, the group address range in the first Group Address field of the fragment must satisfy the following conditions:

- It must have the "Z- bit" (i.e., Administrative Scope Zone bit) in the Encoded Multicast Group Address format (see Figure 3.5) set to 1.
- For IPv4, it must be the multicast group address range for the entire administratively-scoped address range. This is required even if the RP-Set has no RPs for the entire administratively-scoped address range; in this case,

the sub-ranges for the RP-Set are specified in other Group Address fields in the fragment along with the associated RPs.
- For IPv6, the Mask Length must be a minimum of 16 and have the scope ID of the administratively-scoped address range.

Each RP Count field in the Bootstrap message contains the total number of Candidate-RP Addresses included in the message for the corresponding Group Address field. A PIM-SM router will not replace its old RP-Set for a given multicast group address range (in the Group Address field) until or unless it has received RP Addresses equal to "RP Count" for that group address range. This is because the RP Addresses could be carried over several Bootstrap semantic fragments. If the router receives only part of the RP-Set for a given group address range, it will discard the RP-Set without updating the RP-Set for that specific group address range.

The BSR Address, all Group Addresses, and all RP Addresses within a single Bootstrap message must be of the same address family. Additionally, the address family of the address fields in the Bootstrap message must be of the same address family as the IP source and destination addresses of the IP packet carrying the message. This allows maximum flexibility in the implementation of dual-stack IPv4/IPv6 routers.

3.4.4 CANDIDATE-RP-ADVERTISEMENT MESSAGE FORMAT

After the BSR election, each Candidate-RP in the PIM-SM domain transmits Candidate-RP-Advertisement messages [RFC5059] periodically to the elected BSR. A Candidate-RP-Advertisement message contains a Priority field that indicates the priority of the advertising Candidate-RP, as well as a list of multicast group addresses for which the candidacy is advertised (see Figure 3.16). This enables the BSR to learn about possible RPs in the PIM-SM domain that are currently operating and reachable. Candidate-RP-Advertisement messages are sent via *unicast* to the elected BSR of the domain.

After receiving Candidate-RP-Advertisement messages from the Candidate-RPs, the BSR will select a subset of them to form the RP-Set (RP-Set formation process). In general, the BSR does this while ensuring that the RP-Set is neither too large that all the PIM-SM routers in the domain cannot be informed (i.e., learn) about the RP-Set, nor too small that the multicast traffic load is excessively concentrated on some RPs. The BSR should also aim to create an RP-Set that does not change frequently.

When the BSR sends subsequent Bootstrap messages, it includes the RP-Set it has created. The BSR floods Bootstrap messages throughout the PIM-SM domain (RP-Set flooding process), ensuring that the RP-Set will quickly spread out and reach all the PIM-SM routers in the domain. The BSR periodically originates Bootstrap messages to ensure RP-Set information consistency after device and/or network failure restoration.

The RP Address and all Group Addresses within a Candidate-RP-Advertisement message must be of the same address family. Additionally, the address family of the address fields in the message must be of the same address family as the IP source and destination addresses of the IP packet carrying the message. This provision provides a high degree of flexibility for implementing dual-stack IPv4/IPv6 routers.

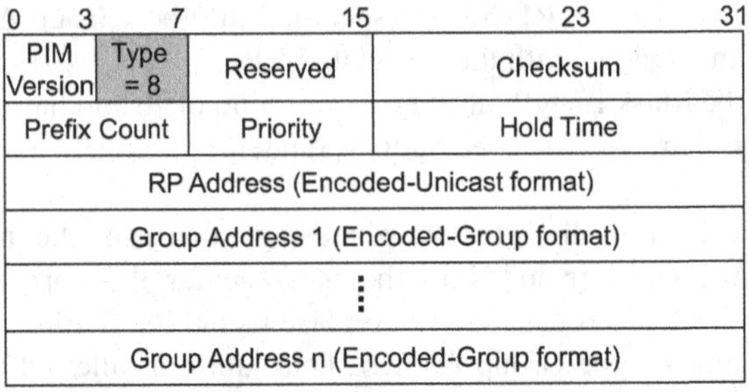

0 3	7		15	23	31
PIM Version	Type = 8	Reserved		Checksum	
Prefix Count		Priority		Hold Time	
RP Address (Encoded-Unicast format)					
Group Address 1 (Encoded-Group format)					
⋮					
Group Address n (Encoded-Group format)					

- **Type (3 Bits)**: This is the PIM Message Type. Value is 8 for a Candidate-RP-Advertisement message.

- **Prefix Count (8 Bits)**: This is the number of Encoded-Group Addresses included in the message, indicating the group range for which the Candidate-RP is advertising. Candidate-RPs MUST NOT send Candidate-RP-Advertisement messages with a Prefix Count of '0'.

- **Priority (8 Bits)**: This is the 'Priority' of the included RP for the corresponding Encoded-Group Address (if any). The highest priority is '0' (i.e., the lower the value of the 'Priority' field, the higher the priority). This field is stored at the BSR upon receipt along with the RP address and corresponding Encoded-Group Address.

- **Hold Time (16 Bits)**: This is the amount of time (in seconds) the advertisement is valid. This field allows advertisements to be aged out. This field should be set to 2.5 times C_RP_Adv_Period.

- **RP Address**: This is the IP address of the interface the router uses to advertise itself as a Candidate-RP. This IP address is usually the router's loopback interface address.

- **Group Address-1....n**: This is the group ranges for which the Candidate-RP is advertising.

FIGURE 3.16   Candidate-RP-Advertisement message format.

3.5   BIDIR-PIM SPECIFIC MESSAGES

BIDIR-PIM, PIM-DM, and PIM-SM share several control messages (i.e., the Hello and Join/Prune messages) as well as the Encoded Unicast address format shown in Figure 3.4. This section describes additional messages that are specific to BIDIR-PIM: Bidirectional Capable PIM Hello Option, DF Election Offer, DF Election Winner, DF Election Backoff, and DF Election Pass messages [RFC5015].

3.5.1   BIDIRECTIONAL CAPABLE PIM HELLO OPTION FORMAT

A PIM router sends Hello messages with the Bidirectional Capable Option (Hello Option Type = 22) to advertise its ability to participate in the BIDIR-PIM protocol. Figure 3.17 depicts the format of the Bidirectional Capable Option [RFC5015].

0 3 7 15 23 31
Type = 22	Length = 0

FIGURE 3.17 Bidirectional Capable PIM Hello Option format.

If a BIDIR-PIM router receives a PIM Hello message from a neighbor that does not contain the Bidirectional Capable Option, the router must log an error to the network administrator in a rate-limited manner.

3.5.2 Designated Forwarder Election Message Format

DF Election messages have four subtypes (1 = Offer, 2 = Winner, 3 = Backoff, 4 = Pass) and are used in the election of the DF of a link in a BIDIR-PIM domain [RFC5015]. All of the DF Election messages share a common header, as shown in Figure 3.18. Unlike Offer and Winner messages, which support only the fields described in Figure 3.18, Backoff and Pass messages have extra fields, as shown in Figures 3.19 and 3.20, respectively.

In BIDIR-PIM, the *Rendezvous Point (RP) Address* is a routable address (i.e., reachable from all routers in the BIDIR-PIM domain) used as the root of the shared multicast distribution tree for a range of multicast groups. The RP Address does not necessarily have to correspond to the IP address of a real router interface in the BIDIR-PIM domain. Routers in the BIDIR-PIM domain send Join messages for a BIDIR-PIM group that propagates hop by hop toward the RP Address.

In BIDIR-PIM, a single elected router (i.e., the DF) exists on every link, including both multiaccess and point-to-point links, within the BIDIR-PIM domain for each RP Address. *The router on the link with the best route to the RP Address (determined by comparing the metrics in the MRIB) becomes the link's DF.* The DF for a given RP Address is responsible for forwarding traffic flowing downstream onto its link and forwarding traffic flowing upstream from its link toward the RP Link. The DR does this downstream/upstream traffic forwarding for all the bidirectional multicast groups that map to the RP Address. Another responsibility of the DF on a link is receiving and processing Join messages from downstream routers on the link, as well as forwarding multicast packets to interested local receivers (discovered via IGMP Membership Report messages).

The *RP Link* for a particular RP Address is the physical link to which the RP Address is assigned (i.e., configured). In BIDIR-PIM, all multicast traffic sent to multicast groups that map to a specific RP Address is forwarded on the RP Link of that RP Address. Within a BIDIR-PIM domain, the RP Link is the only link on which a DF election does not take place.

For the election of the DF for a particular RP Address, BIDIR-PIM routers on a link use Offer, Winner, Backoff, and Pass messages to exchange their own unicast routing metric information for reaching the RP Address. A router calculates its advertised metric using the RPF Interface and the MRIB-provided metric to reach the RP Address.

0 3 7			15	23 31
PIM Version	Type = 10	Subtype	Resv	Checksum
RP Address (Encoded-Unicast Format)				
Sender Metric Preference				
Sender Metric				

Resv = Reserved

- **PIM Version (4 Bits)**: The PIM Version number is 2.

- **Type (4 Bits)**: All DF-Election PIM control messages share the PIM message Type of 10.

- **Subtype (4 Bits)**: DF Election messages have the following Subtypes:
  1 = Offer
  2 = Winner
  3 = Backoff
  4 = Pass

- **Rsvd (4 Bits)**: This field is set to zero on transmission and ignored on receipt.

- **Checksum (16 Bits)**: This field contains the standard IP checksum that is used, that is, the 16-bit one's complement of the one's complement sum of the entire PIM message. For computing the checksum, the checksum field is zeroed.

- **RP Address**: This is the bidirectional RP Address for which the election occurs. The address format is described in RFC 7761, Section 4.9.1.

- **Sender Metric Preference (32 Bits)**: This is the preference value assigned to the unicast routing protocol that the message sender uses to obtain the route to the RP Address.

- **Sender Metric (32 Bits)**: This is the unicast routing table metric used by the message sender to reach the RP Address. The metric is in units, applicable to the unicast routing protocol used.

FIGURE 3.18   Designated Forwarder Election message format.

3.5.3   OFFER MESSAGE

A BIDIR-PIM router on a given link sends an Offer message (Offer {*OfferingID*, *Metric*}) when it believes that it has a better metric to the RP Address than the metrics that have been seen on Offer messages so far. Initially, when a DF has not been elected on a link, BIDIR-PIM routers trying to discover a new RP Address will start participating in the DF election process by transmitting Offer messages. The Offer messages that a router sends include the router's metric to reach the RP Address. Routers periodically retransmit Offer messages with a period equal to *Offer_Interval*. Chapter 7 describes details of the DF election process and how Offer messages are used.

3.5.4   WINNER MESSAGE

A BIDIR-PIM router sends a Winner message (Winner {*DF-ID, DF-Metric*}) when it assumes the role of the DF on a link or when it reasserts being the DF upon receiving

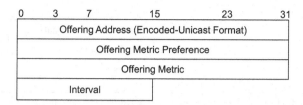

In addition to the fields defined for the DF Election message (i.e., the common election message format), the Backoff message has the following fields.

- **Offering Address**: The address of the router that made the last (best) Offer.

- **Offering Metric Preference (32 Bits)**: This is the preference value assigned to the unicast routing protocol that the offering router uses to obtain the route to the RP Address.

- **Offering Metric (32 Bits)**: This is the unicast routing table metric used by the offering router to reach the RP Address. The metric is in units applicable to the unicast routing protocol used.

- **Interval (16 Bits)**: This is the backoff interval in milliseconds to be used by routers with worse metrics than the offering router.

FIGURE 3.19 Backoff message format.

Offer messages with worse metrics. When the DF of a link receives an Offer message with a metric that is worse than its current metric, it responds with a Winner message to other BIDIR-PIM routers on the link, declaring its DF status and advertising its better metric. When the originator of the Offer message receives the Winner message (from the DF), it records the identity of the DF and abort its DF election process. Details of the DF election process and how Winner messages are used are presented in Chapter 7.

3.5.5 Backoff Message

The DF of a link sends a Backoff message (Backoff {*DF-ID*, *DF-Metric*, *OfferingID*, *OfferMetric*, *BackoffInterval*}) to acknowledge better metrics in the Offer messages it has received. The Backoff message instructs other routers on the link with equal or worse metrics in their Offer messages to wait until the DF passes responsibility to the router that sent the best metric.

When the DF of a link receives an Offer message with a metric that is better than its current metric, it records the identity and metrics of the router originating the message and responds with a Backoff message (see extra fields in Figure 3.19). The Backoff message instructs the sender of the Offer message to hold off for a short period (*Backoff_Period*), while the unicast routing stabilizes, and other BIDIR-PIM routers on the link have the chance to send their metrics via Offer messages.

The Backoff message from the DF includes the new metric and address of the router that sent the Offer message. All BIDIR-PIM routers on the link that have

0	3	7	15	23	31
New Winner Address (Encoded-Unicast Format)					
New Winner Metric Preference					
New Winner Metric					

In addition to the fields defined for the DF Election message (i.e., the common election message format), the Pass message has the following fields.

- **New Winner Address**: This is the address of the router that made the last (best) Offer.

- **New Winner Metric Preference (32 Bits)**: This is the preference value assigned to the unicast routing protocol that the offering router uses to obtain the route to the RP Address.

- **New Winner Metric (32 Bit)**: This is the unicast routing table metric used by the offering router to reach the RP Address. The metric is in units applicable to the unicast routing protocol used.

FIGURE 3.20   Pass message format.

pending Offer messages with metrics worse than the metric in the Backoff message (including the router that sent the original Offer message), will hold on to any further Offer messages for a period specified in the Backoff message.

If another BIDIR-PIM router sends an Offer message with a better metric during the *Backoff_Period*, the DF repeats the Backoff message for this new Offer message and restarts the *Backoff_Period*. Chapter 7 describes details of the DF election process and how Backoff messages are used.

3.5.6 Pass Message

A BIDIR-PIM router, that is currently acting as the DF on a link during the *Backoff_Period* (Old DF), sends a Pass message (Pass {*Old-DF-ID*, *Old-DF-Metric*, *New-DF-ID*, *New-DF-Metric*}) when it wants to pass forwarding responsibility to a router that previously sent an Offer message with the best metric. The *Old-DF-Metric* is the current metric of the acting DF at the time it sends the Pass message.

Before the *Backoff_Period* expires, the currently acting DF on the link will nominate the BIDIR-PIM router that sent the Offer message with the best metric as the new DF for the link using a Pass message (see extra fields in Figure 3.20). The Pass message includes the identities and metrics of both the acting and nominated DFs. The acting DF then stops performing the DF tasks after transmitting the Pass message. The nominated DF, as soon as it receives the Pass message, assumes the role of the link's DF. All other BIDIR-PIM routers on the link recognize and record the new DF and its metric. Chapter 7 describes details of the DF election process and how Pass messages are used.

REVIEW QUESTIONS

1. What is the purpose of the PIM Hello message?
2. Explain briefly the use of the various PIM Options carried in Hello messages: Hold Time Option (Option Type 1), LAN Prune Delay Option (Option Type 2), Designated Router (DR) Priority Option (Option Type 19), Generation ID Option (Option Type 20), State-Refresh Capable Option (Option Type 21), Bidirectional Capable Option (Option Type 22), and Address List Option (Option Type 24).
3. What is the purpose of the PIM Join/Prune message? Explain the difference between an (S, G) Join/Prune message and a (*, G) Join/Prune message.
4. What is the purpose of the PIM Assert message?
5. What is a PIM AssertCancel message?
6. Explain briefly the use of the PIM Graft and Graft-Ack messages in a PIM-DM domain.
7. What is the purpose of the PIM State-Refresh message?
8. Explain briefly the use of the PIM Register and Register-Stop messages in a PIM-SM domain.
9. What is a PIM Null-Register message and its purpose in PIM-SM?
10. What is the purpose of the PIM Bootstrap message?
11. What is the purpose of the PIM Candidate-RP-Advertisement message?
12. Explain briefly the purpose of the DF election messages subtypes: Offer, Winner, Backoff, and Pass messages.

REFERENCES

[RFC3973]. A. Adams, J. Nicholas, and W. Siadak, "Protocol Independent Multicast – Dense Mode (PIM-DM): Protocol Specification (Revised)", *IETF RFC 3973*, January 2005.

[RFC5015]. M. Handley, I. Kouvelas, T. Speakman, and L. Vicisano, "Bidirectional Protocol Independent Multicast (BIDIR-PIM)", *IETF RFC 5015*, October 2007.

[RFC5059]. N. Bhaskar, A. Gall, J. Lingard, and S. Venaas, "Bootstrap Router (BSR) Mechanism for Protocol Independent Multicast (PIM)", *IETF RFC 5059*, January 2008.

[RFC7761]. B. Fenner, M. Handley, H. Holbrook, I. Kouvelas, R. Parekh, Z. Zhang, and L. Zheng, "Protocol Independent Multicast – Sparse Mode (PIM-SM): Protocol Specification (Revised)", *IETF RFC 7761*, March 2016.

[RFC8200]. S. Deering and R. Hinden, "Internet Protocol, Version 6 (IPv6) Specification", *IETF RFC 8200*, July 2017.

[RFC8364]. IJ. Wijnands, S. Venaas, M. Brig, and A. Jonasson, "PIM Flooding Mechanism (PFM) and Source Discovery (SD)", *IETF RFC 8364*, March 2018.

[RFC8736]. S. Venaas and A. Retana, "PIM Message Type Space Extension and Reserved Bits", *IETF RFC 8736*, February 2020.

4 PIM Dense Mode (PIM-DM)

4.1 INTRODUCTION

PIM-DM is a multicast routing protocol that is most suitable for small-sized networks with multicast group members that are densely distributed across the network [RFC3973]. Similar to PIM-SM [RFC7761], PIM-DM utilizes the underlying unicast routing information to flood multicast packets to all routers in the multicast domain. All the PIM protocols do not support a topology discovery mechanism, unlike unicast routing protocols such as OSPF and IS-IS. PIM-DM employs mostly the same packet formats as PIM-SM.

PIM-DM utilizes the *push model* for multicast forwarding and operates under the assumption that nearly all possible segments of the multicast domain (e.g., IP subnets or VLANs) have at least one receiver interested in receiving the multicast traffic sent by a source to a multicast group. Consequently, the multicast traffic is flooded to all conceivable parts of the network, i.e., to all branches of the multicast tree. PIM-DM routers subsequently prune back, i.e., "turn off" tree branches that do not have receivers for the flooded multicast traffic, either explicitly (by sending Prune messages) or implicitly (through multicast state timeouts when no PIM Join messages from routers are received).

Multicast packets to a group are flooded to all segments of the network, and then the PIM-DM routers prune off tree branches without interested multicast receivers, leaving only those branches that contain receivers. This *flood-and-prune* process takes place periodically. Pruned branches are allowed to resume multicast packets forwarding when the Prune state maintained by PIM-DM routers times out. Multicast packets are then reflooded down those branches and pruned once again when necessary. When a new receiver joins a multicast group on a previously pruned branch, to reduce the join latency, PIM-DM uses a *Graft mechanism*. This mechanism allows routers on the previously pruned branch to quickly resume multicast packet forwarding without waiting for the next flooding period.

The design of PIM-DM is simple and is not built with a specific network topology discovery mechanism or protocol in mind. However, this simplicity means that PIM-DM incurs more network overhead due to its flood-and-prune behavior in the multicast domain, which could have been avoided if it was supplied with sufficient topology information. Providing PIM with topology information could have helped multicast routers decide whether an interface leads to any downstream members of a particular multicast group.

However, PIM-DM chooses a simplified and flexible design with additional network overhead over one that depends on a specific topology discovery protocol with network overhead. The simplicity and benefits of PIM-DM are most evidently seen

DOI: 10.1201/9781032701967-4

when used in a network with a large number of multicast receivers in most segments of the network. PIM-DM is most suitable for networks in which the bandwidth consumed because of periodic flooding of multicast traffic is not a major issue.

PIM-DM utilizes the five PIM message types previously outlined in Chapter 3: Hello, Join/Prune, Graft, Graft-Ack, Assert, and State-Refresh. This chapter elaborates on the principal characteristics of PIM-DM, its flood-and-prune behavior, which encompasses the Prune Override feature, the PIM Assert mechanism, the PIM-DM Grafting process, and the PIM-DM State-Refresh feature.

4.2 PIM-DM OVERVIEW

To better understand multicast routing protocols, we define the following terminology:

- **Multicast Routing Information Base (MRIB):** This is a database that holds multicast topology information, typically derived from the unicast routing table of protocols such as OSPF or IS-IS. The MRIB may also be derived from routing protocols such as Multiprotocol BGP (MBGP) [RFC4760], a protocol that can carry multicast-specific topology information. PIM-DM typically uses the unicast routing table to determine the RPF interfaces for arriving multicast packets but may also use the MRIB for the same purpose. In PIM-SM, routers may use the MRIB to determine the interface and next-hop to which PIM Join/Prune messages are to be sent. A PIM router may use the MRIB to determine the routing metrics to a destination address when the PIM Assert process is invoked; these routing metrics are used when PIM routers on a network segment send and process PIM Assert messages (see Chapter 3).
- **Tree Information Base (TIB):** This represents the collection of states that a PIM router maintains. The router creates the information in the TIB through the reception of PIM Join/Prune messages, PIM Assert messages, and IGMP information from local hosts (collected via IGMP Membership Report, Query, and Leave messages [RFC2236] [RFC3376]). The TIB essentially stores the state of all multicast distribution trees at a PIM router.
- **Multicast Forwarding Information Base (MFIB):** Although the TIB contains all the states needed for a PIM router to forward multicast packets, its structure is not efficient for fast packet forwarding. Forwarding multicast packets using the TIB can be very inefficient. In practice, multicast routers normally construct a smaller, more compact, and efficient forwarding table from the TIB state, called the MFIB, which is used for actual multicast packet forwarding. The MFIB contains the most relevant multicast forwarding information that is distilled from the TIB.
- **Reverse Path Forwarding (RPF):** This is a multicast forwarding mode that ensures a multicast packet received by a router is forwarded to other interfaces only if it is received on an interface with the best (i.e., least-cost) unicast path leading back to the data source. In other words, the interface is the one the router would normally use to reach the source in unicast transmission mode.

- **Upstream Interface**: This is an interface (also known as the RPF interface) that leads toward the source of the multicast packet (the actual data source or the RP). This interface points toward the root of the multicast distribution tree, either a source or the RP.
- **Downstream Interface**: This is an interface that leads away from the root of the multicast distribution tree. Downstream interfaces consist of all interfaces leading to multicast receivers, including local interfaces terminating on the router itself.
- **(S, G) Pair**: This represents the source (S) and multicast group address (destination) G associated with a multicast packet.

The RPF interface is the local PIM interface that has the least-cost path leading back to the multicast traffic source. If multiple least-cost paths exist, the interface with the highest IP address to the source is used as the RPF interface. The router recomputes the RPF interface periodically to account for network topology changes that may cause it to change. Doing this periodically also allows multicast routing to converge faster after a network topology change.

The PIM protocols provide multicast forwarding by leveraging unicast static routes and unicast dynamic routes generated by any unicast routing protocol running on the router (RIP, OSPF, IS-IS, BGP), including routes provided by MBGP if enabled on the device. Multicast routing can be implemented on the device independent of the particular unicast routing protocols running on the device, as long as the corresponding multicast routing entries are created through the supplied routes.

The multicast distribution tree used by PIM-DM is a source-rooted tree (SRT), also known as a source-based tree (SBT) or shortest-path tree (SPT). This is a multicast distribution tree with its root at the source, and the multicast group members serve as its "leaves". It is referred to as an SPT because it offers the shortest path from the multicast source to the receivers.

All PIM protocols use the RPF mechanism for implementing multicast forwarding. Any multicast packet arriving on an interface of a PIM router is subject to an RPF check. If the RPF check succeeds, the router creates the corresponding multicast routing entry (mainly for the first packet, as discussed in Chapter 1), and then forwards the packet. If the RPF check fails, the router simply discards the packet.

PIM-DM assumes that when a source in the multicast domain starts transmitting multicast packets, all downstream systems are interested in receiving those packets. Initially, PIM-DM floods multicast packets to all areas of the network. PIM-DM uses RPF to prevent multicast packets from looping while they are being flooded. If some segments (i.e., multicast distribution tree branches) of the multicast domain do not have multicast group members, PIM-DM prunes off those tree branches by instantiating Prune state (associated with the (S, G) traffic).

PIM-DM routers send a Prune message (see Chapter 3) to initiate the pruning of unwanted tree branches. A Prune state has a finite lifetime defined by the PIM header Hold Time field value. When that lifetime expires, a PIM-DM router will once again forward multicast packets on the previously pruned tree branches. When a host joins as a new member for a multicast group G in a pruned area, the Last-Hop Router (LHR) attached to the host (also generally referred to as the host's receiver-side Designated Router (DR)), upon seeing the host's IGMP Membership

Report message, will send a PIM-DM Graft message (see Chapter 3) toward the source S for the multicast group as a way of turning the pruned branch back into a multicast traffic forwarding branch.

A PIM-DM domain undergoes flood-and-prune cycles, involving periods of multicast packets flooding followed by pruning of unwanted branches. A PIM-DM router resumes multicast forwarding on pruned interfaces when the Prune state times out. To prevent this occurrence, the router directly connected to the multicast source periodically transmits an (S, G) State-Refresh message. This message is forwarded hop by hop along the initial multicast flooding path of the PIM-DM domain. Its purpose is to refresh the prune timer state of all the PIM-DM routers on the path. PIM-DM routers send State-Refresh messages to minimize repeated flooding and pruning of multicast packets associated with a particular (S, G) traffic (see Chapter 3). The router(s) directly connected to the multicast traffic source send a State-Refresh message that propagates throughout the PIM-DM domain. When a router receives a State-Refresh message on its RPF interface, this causes an existing Prune state to be refreshed.

PIM-DM differs from PIM-SM (see Chapter 5) in the following two main ways:

- PIM-DM does not send periodic Join messages, as PIM-SM does; instead, it only transmits (explicitly) Prune and Graft messages when necessary.
- PIM-DM does not use Rendezvous Points (RPs) as in PIM-SM since it is based on network-wide flooding and pruning of multicast packets. In PIM-SM, an RP serves as the root of the shared multicast distribution tree. PIM-DM employs only source-rooted trees (SRTs), as discussed in Chapter 1.

4.3   PIM-DM PROTOCOL STATE

This section describes the protocol states (also called the TIB) that a multicast router should maintain for PIM-DM to function correctly. The TIB contains the state of all the multicast distribution trees that a multicast router maintains, and the router uses this state to build its multicast forwarding table. The router updates the multicast forwarding table anytime the relevant state in the TIB changes.

PIM-DM creates an (S, G) state in every router in the multicast domain when a source, S, sends traffic to a multicast group, G. However, a PIM-DM router, unlike PIM-SM, does not maintain a Keepalive Timer (in its TIB) for each (S, G) route. A PIM-DM router maintains an (S, G) route entry and its associated state information in the TIB as long as there is an active timer associated with that entry. The various PIM-DM timers are described in the subsequent section. The PIM-DM router deletes all information pertaining to that (S, G) route in the TIB when no active timer is associated with the entry.

On the other hand, a PIM-SM updates the (S, G) Keepalive Timer whenever it forwards a multicast packet using the (S, G) forwarding state (see PIM-SM timers in Chapter 5). The PIM-SM router uses the Keepalive Timer to maintain the (S, G) state in the TIB, ensuring its persistence in the absence of explicit (S, G) Join messages.

As stated in [RFC3973], the protocol state described here is an abstract view of what a PIM-DM router maintains and does not necessarily mean that an actual implementation of PIM-DM should maintain protocol state in this form. This abstract definition is needed to specify the behavior of the PIM-DM router. A developer is free to implement PIM-DM to maintain whatever internal protocol state as needed, as long as the implementation provides the same externally visible protocol behavior and can interoperate with other PIM-DM implementations.

All the PIM-DM timers in [RFC3973] are assumed to be countdown timers (because they are easier to implement than count-up timers). A countdown timer is initialized to a value and then counts down to zero, at which point it typically triggers an action. However, this does not prevent a timer from being implemented as a count-up timer, where the timer stores the absolute expiry time and compares each count-up value against a real-time clock.

Note that the PIM-DM timers, including the Hello Timer, Neighbor Liveness Timer, (S, G) Assert Timer, (S, G) Prune Timer, (S, G) **Prune-Pending Timer**, (S, G) Graft Retry Timer, (S, G) Upstream Override Timer, (S, G) Prune Limit Timer, (S, G) Source Active Timer, and (S, G) State-Refresh Timer, are all Global Timers. When a timer is initialized or reinitialized with a value, it is set to the default PIM-DM value (or appropriate values as configured by the network operator).

Note that PIM protocol events or system configuration changes may cause the default value of a timer to change on a specific interface. A PIM router may set some of the timers, such as the Prune-Pending and Upstream Override Timers, to values that depend on the settings of the *Propagation_Delay* and *Override_Interval* values on the corresponding interface.

4.3.1 GENERAL PURPOSE PIM-DM PROTOCOL STATE

A PIM-DM router maintains the following non-group-specific state in its TIB.

4.3.1.1 Interface State for Each PIM-DM Interface

The router maintains the following state for each PIM-DM-enabled interface:

- **Hello Timer**: The *Hello_Period* of this timer (with a default value of 30 seconds) is the periodic interval for sending PIM Hello messages. The *Triggered_Hello_Delay* (with a default value of 5 seconds) of this timer is the random interval a router has to wait before sending the initial Hello message when it boots up or sending a triggered Hello message to a PIM neighbor that is rebooting.
- **State-Refresh Capable**: This indicates whether the local interface is enabled for State-Refresh functions.
- **LAN Delay Enabled**: This indicates whether the local interface is enabled to send and receive Hello messages with the LAN Prune Delay Option.
- **Effective_Propagation_Delay**: The *Propagation_delay_default* of this parameter (with default value of 0.5 seconds) represents the Propagation Delay over the link (or LAN) connected to the interface.
- **Effective_Override_Interval**: The *t_override_default* of this parameter (with default value of 2.5 seconds) represents the delay interval over which the PIM router selects a random delay (or waiting time) when scheduling a delayed PIM Join message.

A PIM router sends Hello messages on every PIM-enabled interface once every *Hello_Period* seconds. When the router powers up, it initializes the Hello Timer to a random interval from 0 to *Triggered_Hello_Delay* to prevent synchronization of Hello messages. When the router detects a new or rebooting neighbor, it sends a responding Hello message within an interval selected randomly from 0 to *Triggered_Hello_Delay*.

4.3.1.2 Neighbor State for Each PIM-DM Neighbor

The router maintains the following state for each PIM-DM neighbor. This includes information obtained from the neighbor's Hello message:

- **Neighbor's Generation ID**: This is the Generation ID field value in the Hello message's Generation ID Option sent by the PIM neighbor.
- **Neighbor's LAN Prune Delay (i.e., Propagation Delay field value)**: This is the Propagation Delay field value in the Hello message's LAN Prune Delay Option sent by the PIM neighbor.
- **Neighbor's Override Interval**: This is the Override Interval field value in the Hello message's LAN Prune Delay Option sent by the PIM neighbor.
- **Neighbor's State-Refresh Capability**: This is set to show that the PIM neighbor has sent a State-Refresh Capability Option in a Hello message, indicating that it can support the State-Refresh functions.
- **Neighbor Liveness Timer**: The *Default_Hello_Holdtime* of this timer (with a default value of 3.5 times the *Hello_Period*) is the default Hold Time a PIM router uses to keep a Neighbor State alive. The *Hello_Holdtime* is the Hold Time value taken from the Hold Time Option contained in a neighbor's Hello message. A router should set the Hold Time value in a Hello message to 3.5 times the *Hello_Period*. Note that a PIM router sends a Hello message every time interval equal to *Hello_Period*.

4.3.2 (S, G) STATE

A PIM-DM router maintains the following state for each (S, G) pair in the TIB.

4.3.2.1 State for Each PIM-DM Interface

The router maintains the following state:

- **Local Membership State**: One of the following is stored:
  - NoInfo" or "Include"
- **PIM (S, G) Prune State**: The following information is stored:
  - **One of the following is stored**: "NoInfo", "Pruned", or "PrunePending".
  - **(S, G) Prune-Pending Timer**: The *J/P_Override_Interval* of this timer is the short period a PIM router must wait after receiving a Prune message to allow other routers on the LAN to override the Prune message. The router sets the *J/P_Override_Interval* to the sum of the *Effective_ Override_Interval* and *Effective_Propagation_Delay* of the interface. If all routers on a LAN send Hello messages with the LAN Prune Delay

Option, then the router must set both parameters to the largest value on the LAN. Otherwise, the router must set the interface's *Effective_ Override_Interval* to 2.5 seconds, and the *Effective_Propagation_ Delay* to 0.5 seconds. Note that both *Effective_Propagation_Delay* and *Effective_Override_Interval* are values that are interface-specific and may change when the router receives Hello messages.

- **(S, G) Prune Timer**: The *Prune_Holdtime* of this timer is the Hold Time field value read from the received Prune message. The Hold Time field value in a Prune message (see Chapter 3) is the amount of time (in seconds) the router must maintain the Prune state of the receiving interface alive upon receiving the message.
- **(S, G) Assert Winner State**: The following information is stored:
  - **One of the following is stored**: "NoInfo", "I lost Assert", or "I won Assert".
  - **(S, G) Assert Timer**: The *Assert_Override_Interval* of this timer (with a default value of 3 seconds) is the short time interval the Assert Winner must wait to resend an Assert message before an Assert times out. The *Assert_Time* (with a default of 180 seconds) of this timer is the period the PIM router must wait after the last Assert before timing out the Assert state.
  - **Assert Winner's IP Address**: This is the IP address of the corresponding interface of the Assert Winner.
  - **Assert Winner's Assert Metric**: This is the Metric of the corresponding interface of the Assert Winner.

    Note that, for historical reasons, the PIM Assert message does not contain a Hold Time field. Thus, it is not recommended to change the *Assert_Time* from its default value. If all PIM routers on a LAN indicate (via the State-Refresh Option of the Hello message) that they are capable of performing State-Refresh functions, then the *Assert_Time* is three times the Interval (S, G) received in the State-Refresh message (see message format in Chapter 3).

4.3.2.2   Upstream Interface-Specific State

A PIM-DM router maintains the following state for the Upstream interface:

- **Graft/Prune State**: The following information is stored:
  - **One of the following is stored**: "NoInfo", "Pruned", "Forwarding", or "AckPending".
  - **(S, G) Graft Retry Timer**: The *Graft_Retry_Period* of this timer (with a default value of 3 seconds) is the time a PIM router must wait before retransmitting a Graft message when it has not received a Graft-Ack message.
  - **(S, G) Upstream Override Timer**: The *t_override* of this timer is a randomly selected delay between 0 and the interface's *Override_Interval*. It is a short period a PIM router must wait before sending a PIM Join message to override another router's Prune message. This random delay

is used to prevent PIM Join message implosion on the network segment. If all routers on a LAN send the LAN Prune Delay Option in their Hello messages, then the PIM router must set the *Override_Interval* on the interface to the largest value received on the LAN. Otherwise, the router must set the *Override_Interval* on the interface to 2.5 seconds.

- **(S, G) Prune Limit Timer**: The *t_limit* of this timer (with a default of 210 seconds) is used to prevent Prune message storms on a LAN.
- **Originator State**: The following information is stored:
  - **(S, G) Source Active Timer**: The *SourceLifetime* of this timer (with a default value of 210 seconds) is the period a PIM router must wait after receiving a multicast packet from a directly attached source before continuing to send State-Refresh messages.
  - **(S, G) State-Refresh Timer**: The *StateRefreshInterval* of this timer (with a default value of 60 seconds) is the time interval a PIM router must wait before sending the next State-Refresh message (i.e., the interval between messages).

4.4 PIM-DM NEIGHBOR DISCOVERY AND HELLO MESSAGES

As discussed in Chapter 3 and above, PIM routers use a neighbor discovery mechanism, consisting of exchanging PIM Hello messages, to establish adjacencies with PIM neighbors. PIM routers discover PIM neighbors and maintain relationships with those PIM neighbors by periodically multicasting PIM Hello messages to all PIM routers on the local network segment. A PIM router sends Hello messages periodically on every PIM-enabled interface, allowing it to learn the PIM neighboring information pertinent to each interface. A PIM router sends a Hello message on each of its PIM-enabled interfaces every *Hello_Period* (with a default value of 30 seconds) and addresses it to the ALL-PIM-ROUTERS multicast group address, 224.0.0.13.

A Hello message carries the Hold Time Option, which contains a value that informs the receiving PIM neighbor how long to wait before expiring the adjacency with the message sender if no further Hello messages are received. PIM routers need to keep track of PIM adjacencies to be able to build and maintain correct multicast distribution trees. PIM works on ensuring correct multicast distribution trees.

4.4.1 HANDLING PIM-DM ROUTER FAILURES

If a router receives a PIM Hello message from an active neighbor containing a different Generation ID (see Section 3.2.4.6 in Chapter 3), then this likely indicates that the neighbor has restarted and may not have the correct (S, G) state. In this scenario, the message receiver will send a Hello message after waiting a random delay between 0 and *Triggered_Hello_Delay* before sending any other Hello messages. If the neighbor router is downstream of the message receiver, the receiver may resend the last State-Refresh message for any (S, G) pairs in its MRIB for which it is the Assert Winner, indicating its Prune and Assert status to the downstream neighbor. The receiver should send these State-Refresh messages immediately after the Hello message (see Hello and State-Refresh messages in Sections 3.2.4 and 3.3.2, respectively, of Chapter 3). If the neighbor is an upstream neighbor router for an (S, G) entry in its MRIB, the receiver may cancel its Prune Limit Timer to allow a Prune message to be sent and a Prune state in the upstream neighbor to be reestablished.

Upon startup, a PIM-DM router may utilize any State-Refresh messages it has received (within the *Hello_Period* after sending its first or initial Hello message on an interface) to establish multicast state information. The source interface of the State-Refresh message will be the RPF interface of the multicast source (S), and the router will set the Prune status for all interfaces according to the setting of the Prune Indicator bit in the State-Refresh message. If the router detects that the Prune Indicator is set (to 1), it should set the Prune Limit Timer to *Prune_Holdtime* and set the Prune Timer on all downstream interfaces to the State-Refresh message's Interval field value times two. The PIM-DM router should then propagate the received State-Refresh message.

4.5   DESIGNATED ROUTER IN PIM-DM

Other than for establishing adjacencies with PIM neighbors, PIM routers use the 32-bit DR Priority field value in the DR Priority Option of Hello messages for electing the Designated Router (DR) for multiaccess networks (e.g., Ethernet LANs). The router with the highest DR Priority field value becomes the DR. However, if all of these values are equal, then the router with the highest IP address is elected the DR (the IP address in the source address field of the Hello message is used as the tie-breaker). When routers receive a Hello message without the DR Priority Option or if the DR Priority value is equal to zero, then they know that the message sender does not support the DR Priority Option and will, therefore, use the source IP address of the message for the DR election.

The DR Priority Option of Hello messages is described in Chapter 3. However, note that the DR has less meaning or significance in PIM-DM than in PIM-SM due to the design and operation of PIM-DM. The DR plays a more significant role in PIM-SM than in PIM-DM. The role of the DR in PIM-SM and the DR election processes are discussed in detail in Chapter 5.

Recall from Chapter 2 that IGMPv1 does not support an IGMP Querier election mechanism, as in IGMPv2 and IGMPv3. This means PIM-DM routers may use the DR Priority field value carried in the Hello message's DR Priority Option described in Chapter 3 to elect an IGMP v1 Querier for a network segment. When a PIM-DM router has IGMPv1 enabled on an interface, the DR may also function as the IGMPv1 Querier since IGMPv1 does not have a Querier election mechanism. Other than this, the role of the DR in PIM-DM is less significant. Thus, the only time that a DR has any meaning in PIM-DM is when IGMPv1 is used on a PIM-DM router interface. In this case, the DR also functions as the IGMPv1 Querier since IGMPv1 does not support a Querier election mechanism.

In PIM-SM, on the multicast source side, the DR is responsible for receiving multicast packets from a source and encapsulating them in PIM Register messages for transmission to the domain's RP. The source-side DR (also called the FHR) is also responsible for responding to PIM Register-Stop messages sent by the RP and for sending PIM Null-Register messages to the RP when required. The receiver-side DR (also called the LHR) is responsible for receiving IGMP Membership Report messages from attached hosts and sending PIM (*, G) Join messages toward the domain's RP. The receiver-side DR is also responsible for detecting when all receivers of a multicast group leave and sending (*, G) Prune messages to the RP.

Note that the receiver-side DR in PIM-SM, when constructing and maintaining SPTs, is responsible for sending (S, G) Join and (S, G) Prune messages toward the FHR when necessary. Also, note that the DR on a multiaccess network may or may not be the Assert Winner on that network. The Assert Winner on a multiaccess network is primarily responsible for forwarding multicast packets from the source onto the network toward the downstream nodes, while the receiver-side DR is responsible for sending PIM Join/Prune messages to its upstream PIM neighbor toward the multicast traffic source (real source or RP). The role of the DR in PIM-DM and PIM-SM can be easily discerned from this discussion.

Note that the IGMPv2/v3 Querier election on a multiaccess network is based on the router with the lowest IP address, as discussed in Chapter 2. This is done to ensure that the DR on a multiaccess network is less likely to be the IGMP Querier for the same network, thereby avoiding burdening a single router with both DR and Querier responsibilities.

4.6 PIM-DM DATA PACKET FORWARDING RULES

In PIM-DM, when a router receives the *first* multicast packet from source S and is destined for group G, it will create an (S, G) entry in the TIB for the corresponding traffic. The incoming (or RPF) interface for the (S, G) entry is computed by the router performing an RPF check on the packet. Recall from Chapter 1 that if a PIM-DM router receives an (S, G) multicast packet, it will first perform an RPF check to determine whether the packet should be accepted based on the interface on which the packet arrived and the TIB state. The router discards the packet if it fails the RPF check; that is, the packet is not forwarded to any downstream interface. Packets for which the router cannot find a route to the source are discarded.

If the received packet passes the RPF check, the router constructs an outgoing interface list (OIL) for the packet. If this OIL is not empty, the router will forward the packet to all interfaces listed in it. If the receiving interface is the RPF interface for the packet's source (S) and it is not in the Prune state (i.e., UpstreamPState (S, G)!= Pruned in [RFC3973]), the router forwards the packet on all interfaces in OIL. If the OIL is empty, the router will perform a prune process for the (S, G) pair associated with the packet. Note that the incoming (or RPF) interface of an (S, G) traffic must never be in the OIL of that (S, G) traffic to avoid traffic looping.

Note also that a PIM-DM router will always forward received (S, G) multicast packets to neighboring multicast group members on an interface in all cases except when that interface is in an Assert Loser state (when the interface is pruned, as described below). Additionally, receiving a PIM Prune message should not prevent the delivery of multicast packets on an interface with group members because that Prune can be overridden by a Join message received from a downstream neighbor.

Although a network operator may set up multicast group scope boundaries to be identical to the multicast routing area boundaries, the operator may partition a (smaller) multicast routing area for a particular multicast group. In such a case, the PIM-DM routers must NOT send any multicast packets addressed to a particular group across the scope boundary created for that group.

4.7   PIM-DM PRUNE, JOIN, AND GRAFT MESSAGES

From our discussion in Chapter 3, the following can be said about PIM Prune, Join, and Graft messages:

- A router sends PIM Prune messages toward the upstream neighbor to indicate which source(s) and their associated multicast group(s) it does not want to receive traffic from.
- A downstream Router A that wishes to continue receiving multicast packets will send a PIM Join message to the upstream router to override a Prune message sent by another downstream Router B (on the same network segment). PIM-DM uses the PIM Join message only in such situations.
- A router sends a PIM Graft message to the upstream router to rejoin an SPT branch that was previously pruned to receive multicast packets.

Note that all PIM Join, Prune, and Graft messages used in PIM-DM are sent concerning a specific source and group.

4.7.1   Upstream PIM-DM Prune, Join, and Graft Messages

The Upstream (S, G) state machine on a PIM-DM router for sending PIM Prune, Graft, and Join messages has the following three states (Figure 4.1):

- **Forwarding**: The Upstream (S, G) state machine starts in this state (i.e., its initial state). The state machine also transitions to this state if the router's OIL (S, G)!= NULL.
- **Pruned**: In this state, the OIL (S, G) is empty (i.e., OIL (S, G) == NULL). In this state, the router will not forward multicast packets from source S to multicast group G.
- **AckPending**: The router transitions from the Pruned to the AckPending state because a transition has occurred in the Downstream (S, G) state machine for one of the interfaces in the OIL (S, G), indicating that the router should again forward traffic from source S to multicast group G. The state machine is in this state if the router sent a PIM Graft message to the RPF interface of S but has not yet received a Graft-Ack message.

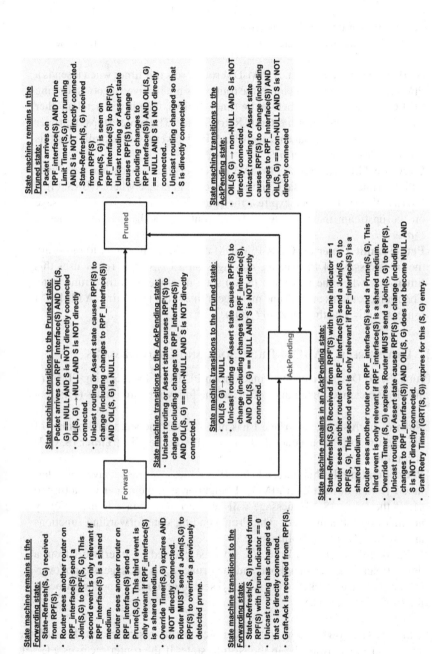

FIGURE 4.1 Upstream (S, G) Interface state machine.

If the router receives a PIM Graft-Ack message for the (S, G) entry, and the message's destination address does not match the IP address of interface I, then these state machine state transitions must not occur.

Also, the Upstream (S, G) state machine supports the following three timers:

- **Graft Retry Timer (S, G)**: A PIM-DM router sets this timer when it sends a PIM Graft message upstream. If the router has not received a corresponding PIM Graft-Ack message before the timer expires, then it will send another Graft message and reset the Graft Retry Timer. The router stops the timer when a Graft-Ack message is received. A PIM-DM router normally sets this timer to *Graft_Retry_Period*.
- **Override Timer (S, G)**: A PIM-DM router sets this timer when it receives a PIM Prune (S, G) message on the upstream interface where OIL(S, G)!= NULL. When the timer expires, the router sends a Join (S, G) message on the upstream interface. A PIM-DM router typically sets this timer to *t_override*.
- **Prune Limit Timer (S, G)**: A PIM-DM router uses this timer to rate-limit the transmission of PIM Prune messages on a LAN. The router uses this timer only when the Upstream (S, G) state machine is in the Prune state. The router cannot send a Prune message if this timer is running. A PIM-DM router usually sets this timer to *t_limit*.

4.7.2 DOWNSTREAM PIM-DM PRUNE, JOIN, AND GRAFT MESSAGES

The Prune (S, G) Downstream state machine in PIM-DM for receiving PIM Prune, Join, and Graft messages on an interface I has the following three states (Figure 4.2):

- **NoInfo**: In this state, interface I has no (S, G) Prune state, and neither of the two timers (Prune Timer (S, G, I)) nor **Prune-Pending Timer** (S, G, I) is running.
- **PrunePending**: In this state, a Prune (S, G) message was received on interface I from a downstream PIM-DM neighbor, and the router is waiting to see if the Prune (S, G) message will be overridden (via a Join (S, G)) by another downstream router. The PrunePending state forwarding functions are the same as in the NoInfo state.
- **Pruned**: In this state, a Prune (S, G) was received on interface I from a downstream PIM-DM neighbor, and the Prune (S, G) message was not overridden. Multicast packets from source S sent to group G are no longer being forwarded on interface I.

The Prune (S, G) Downstream state machine on the upstream interface of the PIM-DM router must always be in the NoInfo state. If the router receives a Graft, Prune, or Join message on interface I, and the IP address contained in the message's Upstream Neighbor Address field does not match the IP address of interface I, then these state machine state transitions must not occur (see message format in Chapter 3).

State machine remains in the Pruned state:
- Router receives a Prune(S, G) on the interface I with the upstream neighbor field set to the IP address of I.
- Router sends State-Refresh(S, G) out interface I. The router has refreshed the Prune(S, G) state on interface I. The router MUST reset the Prune Timer(S, G, I) to the Holdtime from an active Prune received on interface I.

State machine transitions to the NoInfo state:
- Router receives a Join(S, G) on the interface I with the upstream neighbor field set to the IP address of I.
- Router receives a Graft(S, G) on interface I with the upstream neighbor field set to the IP address of I. Router sends a GraftAck-back to the Graft originator and cancels the Prune Timer(S, G, I).
- The Prune Timer (S, G, I) expires, indicating that it is again time to flood packets from S addressed to group G onto interface I.
- RPF_Interface(S) becomes interface I (i.e., the upstream interface for S has changed). The PruneTimer (PT(S,G,I)) MUST be cancelled.

State machine transitions to the Pruned state:
- The Prune-Pending Timer(S, G, I) expires, indicating that no neighbors have overridden the previous Prune(S, G) message.

State machine transitions to the PrunePending state:
- Router receives a Prune(S, G) on interface I with the upstream neighbor field set to the IP address of I.

State machine remains in an NoInfo state:
- Router receives a Graft(S, G) on the interface I with the upstream neighbor field set to the IP address of I. Router MUST unicast a GraftAck-(S, G) to the originator of the Graft(S, G) message.

State machine transitions to the NoInfo state:
- Router receives a Join(S, G) on interface I with the upstream neighbor field set to the IP address of I.
- Router receives a Graft(S, G) on interface I with the upstream neighbor field set to the IP address of I. Router MUST unicast a Graft Ack-message to the Graft originator.
- RPF_Interface(S) becomes interface I (i.e., the upstream interface for S has changed).

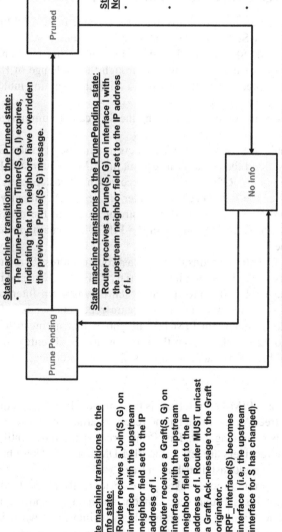

FIGURE 4.2   Prune (S, G) Downstream Interface state machine.

Also, the Prune (S, G) Downstream state machine supports the following two timers:

- **Prune-Pending Timer (S, G, I)**: The router sets this timer when it receives a valid Prune (S, G) message. When the **Prune-Pending Timer** (S, G, I) expires, it causes interface I to transition to the Pruned state.
- **Prune Timer (S, G, I)**: The router sets this timer when the **Prune-Pending Timer** (S, G, I) expires. When the Prune Timer (S, G, I) expires, it causes interface I to transition to the NoInfo state, thereby allowing the router to forward multicast packets from S to group G on the interface.

4.8   INITIAL FLOODING AND PRUNING IN THE PIM-DM

As noted above, multicast traffic distribution to receivers in PIM-DM is solely based on SRTs (also called SPTs). As soon as a multicast source starts sending traffic, PIM-DM routers build SPTs on the fly using a flood-and-prune mechanism. PIM-DM uses the neighbor information discovered through the exchange of Hello messages and the RPF check mechanism to construct a minimal spanning multicast distribution tree, that is, the SRT or SPT.

The flood-and-prune process of building the SPT can be summarized as follows:

- When a multicast source S sends packets to a multicast group G, PIM-DM routers first flood the packets throughout the PIM-DM domain. Each router first performs an RPF check on a received multicast packet, and if the packet passes the RPF check, the router creates an (S, G) entry in its TIB and forwards the packet to all downstream nodes in the network. In the flooding process, all the routers in the PIM-DM domain create an (S, G) entry in the TIB.
  - An (S, G) entry contains the multicast source address S, multicast group address G, the incoming interface (i.e., RPF interface), and its OIL.
- Then, each PIM-DM router prunes each downstream interface without receivers. A router with no downstream receivers sends a PIM Prune message to its upstream PIM-DM neighbor, instructing it to delete the corresponding interface from the OIL for the (S, G) entry, and stop forwarding subsequent packets addressed to that multicast group on that interface.

A prune process on a PIM-DM interface is first initiated by a leaf router on the multicast distribution tree. A router that has no receivers attached to it sends a PIM Prune message to its upstream neighbor. This Prune process continues until only branches with downstream receivers are left in the PIM-DM domain. These branches constitute the SPTs of the multicast distribution tree.

The flood-and-prune process takes place periodically in the PIM-DM domain. Each router maintains a Prune state timeout mechanism, and the router restarts multicast packet forwarding on a pruned branch (interface) when its Prune state times out. The branch/interface is pruned again when it no longer has any multicast receivers.

4.8.1 To Flood or Not to Flood?

When a multicast source begins transmitting traffic, PIM-DM initially considers all routers in the multicast domain to be on the SPT. Each router regards the incoming interface of the source traffic as the interface in the direction of the source, i.e., the least-cost path to the source determined by the unicast routing protocol. The outgoing interfaces are considered as those leading to downstream nodes, i.e., away from the source. *It is important to note that a PIM-DM router only floods traffic on interfaces where at least one PIM-DM neighbor has been detected through Hello messages or at least one directly connected receiver has been identified through IGMP Membership Report messages. Multicast packets are not forwarded on interfaces indiscriminately.*

4.8.2 RPF Checks and Determining the Incoming Interface

When a PIM-DM initially receives a multicast packet, it performs an RPF check using its unicast routing table to ensure that it arrives on the correct interface with the least-cost path leading back to the source. The router takes the source IP address of the packet and performs the longest prefix matching (LPM) search in the unicast routing table to determine if the packet was received on the interface with the least-cost path back to the source.

This least-cost path interface becomes the incoming interface for the (S, G) traffic. If multiple equal least-cost paths (interfaces) exist in the unicast routing table leading back to the multicast source, the router will select only one interface, usually the interface associated with the highest next-hop IP address, as the incoming interface. This means a PIM router (all PIM protocols) can have only one incoming interface for each (S, G) traffic. This incoming interface is often called the RPF interface for the (S, G) traffic. The RPF interface becomes unambiguous when multiple unequal paths exist in the unicast routing table.

4.8.3 Flooding and Pruning

Figures 4.3 and 4.4 describe the initial multicast traffic flooding process, the sending of Prune messages where necessary, and the sending of Join messages as a way of overriding Prune messages. In Figure 4.3, Routers A and B initiate the traffic flooding process, which may result in duplicate traffic arriving at certain points of the multicast distribution tree. The interconnectivity of the routers will most often result in redundant paths and duplicate traffic at various points in the PIM-DM domain. Thus, the PIM-DM routers interact (via Prune and Join messages) to trim down the initial multicast distribution tree to a minimal spanning distribution tree, the SPT.

When a PIM-DM receives multicast packets from an upstream neighbor for source S and addressed to multicast group G (i.e., (S, G) traffic), it will send a Prune message (see Chapter 3) to the upstream neighbor if it does not wish to receive that (S, G) traffic. In Figure 4.3, Router J has no active receivers for the (S, G) multicast traffic and, therefore, signals its desire to not receive this traffic by sending an (S, G) Prune message to Router E. When Router E receives the Prune message for the (S, G) traffic on an outgoing interface, it places that interface in the Prune state and

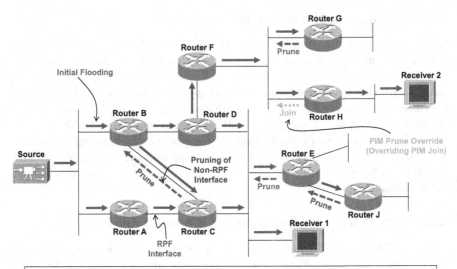

PIM-DM Multicast Distribution Tree Initial Flooding:
- All routers in the PIM-DM network participate in forwarding multicast traffic on all of their outgoing interfaces regardless of if there are active downstream PIM neighbors or receivers.
- This is the initial flooding (even on redundant paths) before any pruning takes place to create a minimal spanning tree of all PIM-DM routers.

PIM-DM Pruning of Non-RPF Interface:
- Router C sends a Prune message to Router B because it sees that multicast traffic is arriving on a non-RPF interface to the multicast source.
- We assume that the routing protocol metric to the source from Router C is better via the link between Routers A and C than via the link between Routers B and C.
- Router B responds to the Prune message by pruning its outgoing link to Router C.

PIM-DM Pruning:
- Router J, being a leaf router without any directly connected receivers, sends a Prune message to Router E, which responds by pruning its link to Router J.
- Because Router E has no directly connected receivers and all downstream links have been pruned, Router E also sends a Prune message to Routers C and D.
- Although Router E sends a Prune message for this source to Routers C and D, this message is ignored because Receiver 1 is directly connected to the common network shared by Routers C, D, and E.
- Router E continues to send Prune messages (albeit ignored) as long as the source continues to send multicast traffic.

PIM-DM Prune Override:
- A PIM-DM router still expects to receive PIM Join messages from downstream PIM neighbors that want to continue receiving multicast traffic even on an interface on which a Prune message was previously received.
- Router G being a leaf router without any directly connected receivers, sends a Prune message on the shared network to Router F.
- However, because Prune messages are sent as multicast to the IP address 224.0.0.13 (i.e., the All-PIM-Router group address), Router H also receives the Prune message sent by Router G to Router F.
- As Router H has a directly connected receiver (Receiver 2), it sends a PIM Join message to override the Prune message sent by Router G to Router F.

FIGURE 4.3   Initial flooding and pruning in the PIM-DM distribution tree.

stops forwarding the (S, G) traffic on that interface. If Router E's outgoing interface is connected to a multiaccess network (e.g., IP subnet), then we assume that no other downstream routers and directly connected receivers on the network want to receive this (S, G) traffic.

A Prune message has a timeout associated with it (carried in the Hold Time field of the message, as described in Chapter 3). When the receiving router (Router E) receives the (S, G) Prune message and it eventually times out (i.e., the Prune times out), the router places the outgoing interface in the forwarding state and starts forwarding (S, G) multicast traffic on it again. The outgoing interface remains in the Prune state for the duration of the Hold Time unless the Prune is removed or overridden by a Join or Graft message (as discussed in the subsequent section). If the downstream router, Router J, still does not need the (S, G) multicast traffic, it will send another (S, G) Prune message to turn off that traffic. The outgoing interface may go through periodic flood-and-prune processes depending on the receiver dynamics on the interface.

4.8.4 WHEN TO SEND PRUNE MESSAGES

This section summarizes the conditions under which PIM-DM sends Prune messages:

- **When a router receives multicast traffic from a PIM-DM neighbor on a non-RPF point-to-point link**: For example, in Figure 4.3, Router C sends a Prune message to Router B because it has received multicast traffic on a non-RPF interface. We assume in this case that the interface from Router C to Router A has the least-cost path to the multicast traffic source. The same idea is illustrated in Figure 4.4.
- **A router is a leaf router on the multicast distribution tree with no directly connected receivers**: Router J in Figure 4.3 has no interested receivers for the (S, G) traffic and, so, sends a Prune message to Router E to turn off the (S, G) traffic.
- **A router is a non-leaf router on the multicast distribution with no directly connected receivers and receives a Prune message from a downstream PIM-DM neighbor on a point-to-point link**: Router E in Figure 4.3 has no directly connected receivers for the (S, G) traffic and also receives a Prune message from Router J. In this case, Router E sends a Prune message upstream to turn off the (S, G) traffic.
- **A router is a non-leaf router on the multicast distribution with no directly connected receivers and receives a Prune message from a downstream PIM-DM neighbor on a multiaccess network that is NOT overridden by a Join message sent by another neighbor on the same network**: If Router F in Figure 4.3, with no directly connected receivers, receives a Prune message from Router G, and this message is not overridden by a Join message from Router H (because it has not receivers), then Router F will send a Prune message upstream to Router D to turn of the (S, G) traffic.

As discussed above, a PIM-DM router must first determine which interfaces are non-RPF interfaces so that it can send Prune messages on those interfaces in case multicast traffic is received on them. Only one RPF interface (i.e., the least-cost interface to the multicast source according the unicast routing table) must exist at any

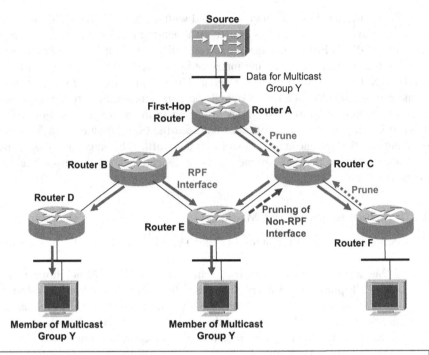

- PIM-DM uses RPF and a flood-and-prune mechanism.
- PIM-DM uses a source-rooted tree (SRT) algorithm that establishes a tree that connects each source in a multicast group to the members of the group. All traffic for the multicast group passes along this SRT.
- When a source sends a multicast packet to a First-Hop Router (FHR) to be sent to hosts belonging to multicast group Y, the FHR multicasts that packet to its neighbor PIM routers. The PIM neighbors, in turn, forward the packet to their PIM neighbors and the hosts that belong to the multicast group Y.
- If a PIM neighbor has no hosts that belong to the multicast group Y and has no other PIM neighbors, it returns a Prune message to the FHR. The FHR does not multicast subsequent packets for that group to PIM neighbors who respond with Prune messages.
- If a host on a branch that was previously pruned requests to join multicast group Y, it sends an IGMP message to its FHR. The FHR then sends a Graft message upstream.
- PIM routers send Join messages on multiaccess interfaces to override Prune messages.
- If a PIM router sent a Prune message to indicate that it has no hosts for a multicast group, and one of its hosts subsequently requests to send a packet to that group, the router sends a Join message to the FHR.

FIGURE 4.4   PIM-DM operation.

given time, with all other interfaces marked as non-RPF interfaces. In Figure 4.4, we assume that the link between Router E and Router B provides the least-cost path to the multicast source.

4.8.5   PIM-DM PRUNE OVERRIDE

Let's consider the case of the downstream routers, Routers G and H, on the multiaccess network in Figure 4.3. Router H wishes to continue receiving multicast packets from the upstream neighbor, Router F, but Router G does not. In this case, Router H will send a PIM Join in response to Router G's Prune message to override it. *This is the only situation where PIM-DM uses Join messages.*

A PIM-DM router that receives a Prune message from a downstream neighbor on a multiaccess network expects to receive a Join message from any neighbor on that network that wishes to continue receiving the multicast traffic. This is *because PIM-DM does not keep track of its neighbors on an interface. The PIM-DM router may be aware of the presence of a neighbor on an interface (via Hello messages), but it still expects a Join message from an interested neighbor anytime a Prune message is received on that interface.*

PIM Prune messages are sent via multicast to the ALL-PIM-ROUTERS multicast group address (224.0.0.13), enabling all routers on the multiaccess network to hear them. Those still interested in the (S, G) traffic will promptly respond with a Join (S, G) message to override the Prune (S, G) message.

4.8.6 REDUCING PIM PRUNE MESSAGE PROPAGATION DELAY ON LANS

The *J/P_Override_Interval* of the (S, G) Prune-Pending Timer is the short period during which a PIM router must wait after receiving a Prune message to allow other neighbors on the multiaccess network to send Join messages and override the Prune message. To ensure efficient pruning, the *J/P_Override_Interval* is set to the sum of the *Effective_Override_Interval* and *Effective_Propagation_Delay* of the interface, as discussed above. A router initiates the Prune-Pending Timer immediately upon receiving a Prune message from a neighbor on a multiaccess network. If the router does not receive an overriding Join message to cancel this timer, it will implement the prune on the multiaccess interface when the timer expires.

If all PIM-DM routers on a network segment (LAN) support the LAN Prune Delay Option (for Hello messages as described in Chapter 3), then those routers will use the received Propagation Delay (also referred to as LAN Prune Delay) and Override Interval field values carried in the LAN Prune Delay Option to adjust their *J/P_Override_Interval* on the LAN interface (and that interface becomes LAN Delay enabled). To prevent synchronization of Prune Override messages (which are essentially PIM Join messages) when multiple downstream PIM-DM routers share a multiaccess network (i.e., have interfaces to the same IP subnet), the routers on this network will delay the sending of these messages by a small random amount of time. The period of sending these messages (which can be randomized by small delays) is configurable, with a default value of 3 seconds.

Each PIM-DM router on the LAN indicates its view of the amount of added small random delay necessary in the Override Interval field of the Hello message's LAN Prune Delay Option. When all PIM-DM routers on a LAN opt to use the LAN Prune Delay Option, then those routers must set their *Override_Interval* to the largest Override Interval field value sent on the LAN.

The Propagation Delay field value inserted by a PIM-DM router in the LAN Prune Delay Option (which is configurable by the network administrator) expresses the expected message propagation delay on the LAN. When all PIM-DM routers on the LAN choose to use the LAN Prune Delay Option, these routers must set their *Propagation_Delay* to the largest Propagation Delay field value sent on the LAN.

It is beneficial for PIM-DM implementers to enforce a lower bound on the permitted Propagation Delay values to allow for internal scheduling and processing delays within the PIM-DM router. Incorrect setting of the Propagation Delay values may cause received PIM Prune Override (i.e., Join) messages to be processed later and trigger these messages to be sent later than intended. Setting the Propagation Delay to a very low value on the LAN may result in temporary outages in multicast packet forwarding because a downstream router will not be able to send a PIM Join message to override a PIM Prune message sent by a neighbor on the same LAN before the upstream neighbor router stops forwarding multicast packets.

4.9   PIM-DM ASSERT MECHANISM

If multiple multicast routers connect to a multiaccess network segment, such as an Ethernet LAN, duplicate multicast packets may flow to that network segment. To stop duplicate multicast packet flows, the PIM Assert mechanism is used to elect a single multicast forwarder on the multiaccess network.

4.9.1   TURNING OFF DUPLICATE MULTICAST PACKET FORWARDING ON MULTIACCESS NETWORK SEGMENTS

Figures 4.3 and 4.5 illustrate situations in which duplicate multicast traffic can be delivered on a network segment to downstream nodes. PIM uses the Assert mechanism to elect an effective multicast traffic forwarder for the network segment. This is done to turn off all but one flow of the multicast traffic on the network segment. *It is important to note that the PIM Assert mechanism does not prevent the duplication of multicast packets on the multiaccess network segment; instead, it uses the presence of duplicate multicast packets as a trigger to activate the election of a single forwarder for the multicast traffic, thereby preventing further duplication of the traffic.*

In Figure 4.5, both Router A and Router B receive an (S, G) multicast packet from the upstream PIM neighbor and forward the packet via their local interface F0 onto the local multiaccess network segment. As a result, the downstream router receives two identical multicast packets from Router A and Router B. Additionally, Router A and Router B receive duplicate multicast packets forwarded by the other router on their respective local interface F0. Upon detecting this condition, both routers send a PIM Assert message on the local multiaccess network segment through the interface on which the duplicate multicast packet was received.

To trigger the PIM Assert mechanism, when a router receives a multicast packet on an interface that is expected to be an outgoing interface for that packet (i.e., the interface is in the OIL for that multicast source), it sends an Assert message (see Chapter 3) through that interface. This action enables all routers on that interface to determine the forwarder for the multicast traffic. Assert messages are addressed to the ALL-PIM-ROUTERS multicast group address, 224.0.0.13.

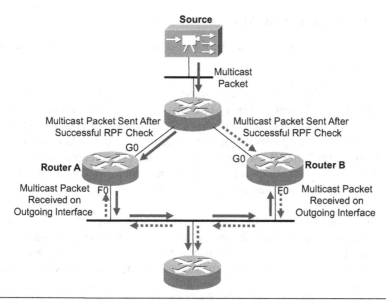

- If there exists parallel paths to a multicast source (particularly, on multiaccess networks with multiple PIM routers), duplicate packets can travel downstream through different PIM routers in the network. If a forwarding PIM router receives a multicast packet on its outgoing interface, that router identifies that packet as a duplicate multicast packet and notifies the PIM router responsible for the duplicate packet using the PIM Assert mechanism.
- The PIM routers responsible for the multicast packet duplication send Assert messages to each other to determine which router becomes the forwarder for the network segment. Downstream PIM routers listen for the Assert messages to discover which router becomes the forwarder.
- The PIM Assert mechanism is applicable to all PIM types when parallel paths exist to an upstream PIM router or source.

FIGURE 4.5 Detecting multicast packet duplication.

Each Assert message contains the multicast source address (S), the multicast group address (G), the Metric Preference (also called the Administrative Distance), and the Routing Metric associated with the unicast routing protocol that provided the route to the multicast traffic source from the perspective of the sender (see details in Chapter 3). All the routers on the network segment receive each Assert message and examine the metrics contained within to determine which router has the best metric (i.e., least-cost path) to the multicast source. The router with the best metric is elected as the forwarder of the multicast traffic sent by the source to the network segment. The router with the best metric continues to forward traffic on the network segment from the source uninterrupted, while the others cease further traffic forwarding. In the event there is a tie in the metric values, the router with the highest source IP address wins the Assert process and becomes the forwarder.

4.9.2 (S, G) ASSERT STATE MACHINE

The PIM (S, G) Assert state machine for interface I has the following three states (see Figure 4.6):

- **NoInfo**: In this state, interface I of the router has no (S, G) Assert state.
- **I am Assert Winner (Winner State)**: In this state, the router is the winner of the (S, G) Assert process on interface I. The router is now responsible for forwarding multicast packets from source S addressed to group G via interface I.
- **I am Assert Loser (Loser State)**: In this state, the router has lost the (S, G) Assert process on interface I. The router must not forward multicast packets from source S addressed to group G via interface I.

In addition, the PIM router also maintains an Assert Timer (S, G, I) for the PIM (S, G) Assert state machine. This timer is used by Assert Losers to determine when to time out the (S, G) Assert state and by the Assert Winner to know when to resend (S, G) Assert messages. The main features of the (S, G) Assert process are as follows:

- The winner of the Assert process for (S, G) acts as the local forwarder for (S, G) traffic on behalf of all downstream routers and multicast group members.
- When an Assert Loser receives a Prune (S, G), Join (S, G), or Graft (S, G) message sent to it, it will initiate a new Assert process so that the PIM routers on the network segment can renegotiate an Assert Winner, and for the downstream router to correct its RPF interface for source S.
- The Assert Winner for (S, G) sends an (S, G) AssertCancel message, allowing it to cancel the Assert (it won), when it is about to stop forwarding (S, G) multicast packets. This may happen, for example, when the winner router is being taken down (and when the router is required to send a canceling Assert message).

4.9.3 PIM ASSERT MECHANISM

The PIM Assert mechanism can be described as follows:

1. When a PIM-DM router compares the Assert metrics for (S, G) on a given interface, it will first compare the Metric Preference values, and if necessary, the Routing Metric as described in Figure 4.7 (the router with the first lower value wins the PIM-DM Assert).
   a. The router with the higher Metric Preference to the multicast source wins the Assert process.
   b. If both routers have the same Metric Preference to the multicast source, the router with a smaller Routing Metric to the multicast source wins the Assert process.
2. If these metric values are equal, then the router with the highest IP address (derived from the source IP address of the IP packet carrying the Assert message) wins the Assert process.

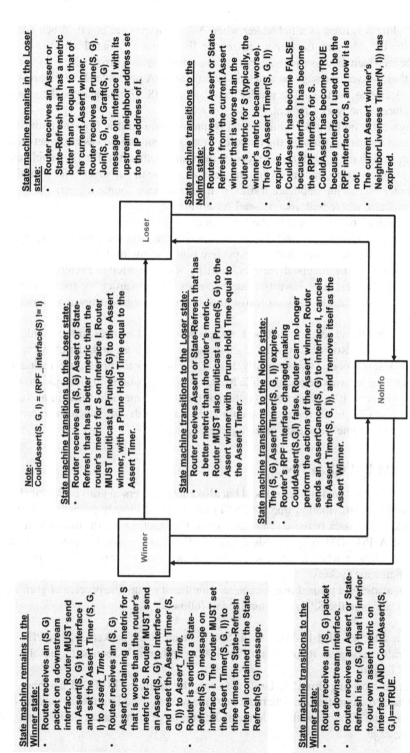

FIGURE 4.6 (S, G) Assert state machine.

The IP address is used as a tiebreaker when Assert metrics are equal. When comparing the IP addresses, the router utilizes the IP address associated with the local interface on which the Assert messages from the other neighbor are received. By comparing these Assert message parameters, either Router A or Router B in Figure 4.5 will be elected as the unique forwarder for subsequent (S, G) multicast packets onto the multiaccess network segment.

In Figure 4.8, both Router C and Router D start receiving traffic from the multicast source and forward it through the outgoing interface onto the downstream network segment. Additionally, each router receives the same multicast traffic (i.e., duplicate traffic) on its outgoing interface from the network segment, namely, traffic from the other router. Receiving duplicate traffic from the multicast source triggers the PIM Assert process, where both routers send Assert messages onto the network segment to resolve which router should be the forwarder.

Router C and Router D send Assert messages containing the Metric Preference and Routing Metric values of their respective routes to the multicast source. Both routers compare the received metrics, starting with the Metric Preference. The router with the best (i.e., lowest) value becomes the forwarder for the multicast source and continues to forward traffic to the network segment toward Router E and Receiver 1.

In Figure 4.8, we assume that both routers have equal metrics to the multicast source. However, Router C has the highest source IP address and, therefore, wins the PIM Assert process. Consequently, Router C continues to forward the multicast traffic onto the network segment, while Router D prunes its outgoing interface to the network segment. It is important to note that the Hold Time field value in a Prune message (see Chapter 3) represents the duration (in seconds) for which the receiver must keep the Prune state upon receiving the message.

4.10 PIM-DM GRAFTING

PIM-DM is a flood-and-prune protocol but also allows routers to graft back branches of the multicast distribution tree (i.e., SPT) that were previously pruned. PIM-DM can quickly graft back branches and start forwarding multicast traffic to downstream receivers. A PIM-DM router sends a PIM Graft message (see Chapter 3) to the upstream neighbor when it wants to rejoin a branch that was previously pruned to receive multicast packets.

When a host on a pruned interface joins a multicast group, the process of grafting that interface onto the SPT is summarized as follows:

- The attached PIM-DM that needs to receive multicast packets sends a PIM Graft message to its upstream PIM-DM neighbor, as a request to join the SPT again.
- Upon receiving this PIM Graft message, the upstream PIM-DM neighbor places the interface on which the message was received into the forwarding state and responds with a PIM Graft-Ack message to the sender of the Graft message.

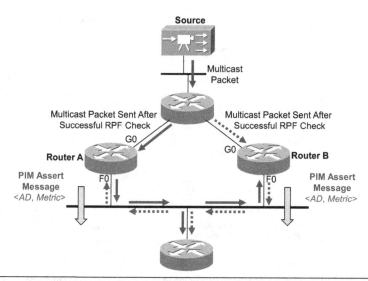

- Routers A and B receive multicast traffic from the source through their G0 interface and forward it via their F0 interface onto a shared Ethernet network.
- As a result, each router receives a multicast packet from the source via its F0, that is, in its outgoing interface list.
- This triggers Routers A and B to send PIM Assert messages to resolve which router should be the forwarder.
- The Metric Preference is similar to the Administrative Distance (AD) or Route Preference, which indicates the trustworthiness or believability of the unicast routing information source when multiple routing sources provide routes to the same destination. The lower the Administrative Distance, the more believable the routing information source.
- Routers A and B send and receive PIM Assert messages that contain the unicast routing protocol Metric Preference and Metric for the multicast source.
- The Metric Preference is in the higher-order portion of the compared value while the Metric is in the lower-order portion of the value.
- Routers A and B compare the values in the PIM Assert messages. The router with the lowest value (i.e., the best metric to the multicast source when both Metric Preferences (i.e., Administrative Distances) and Metrics are considered) are the winner of the PIM Assert process:
  1. The router with the best Metric Preference (i.e., lowest AD) becomes the winner.
  2. If the routers have the same Metric Preference, the router with the lowest Metric becomes the winner.
  3. If both routers have the same Metric, the router with the highest IP address becomes the winner.
- The loser (or losers when more than two routers are involved in the PIM Assert process) stops sending multicast traffic on its outgoing interface onto the shared Ethernet network by pruning its interface for this multicast traffic source.

FIGURE 4.7 PIM Assert mechanism.

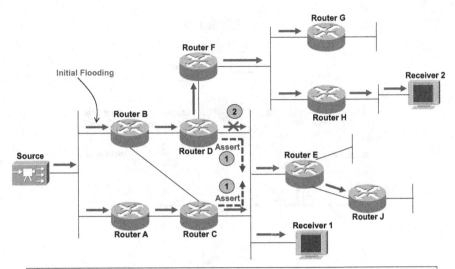

- Routers C and D send PIM Assert messages in response to receiving multicast traffic from the source via their outgoing interface connected to the common network connected to Router E.
- In the figure, we assume Router C and D have the same routing protocol metric and Router C has the highest IP address.
  - Router C wins the PIM Assert process and continues to forward multicast traffic from the source onto the shared network with Router E.
  - Router D prunes its outgoing interface and stops sending traffic onto the shared network.

FIGURE 4.8   PIM-DM Assert example.

- If the sender of the Graft message does not receive a PIM Graft-Ack message from its upstream PIM-DM neighbor, it will continue sending Graft messages at a configurable interval until it receives a Graft-Ack message from its upstream neighbor.

Figure 4.9 describes how the PIM-DM grafting process works. We assume that Router J had previously pruned its link to Router E because it had no directly connect receivers for the (S, G) multicast traffic. Receiver 3 then newly joins the multicast group by sending an (S, G) IGMP Membership Report message to its designated router, Router J.

When Router J receives the IGMP Membership Report (or join) message from Receiver 3, it already has the (S, G) state in its forwarding entries, even though the interface to Router E was pruned. Router J, upon receiving the join message from Receiver 3, therefore, knows that it has to send a PIM Graft message to Router E to restart the flow of the (S, G) multicast traffic. Router E receives the Graft message from Router J and responds with a PIM Graft-Ack message. *Note that pruning an interface as a result of receiving an (S, G) Prune message does not cause the router to delete the interface from the OIL of the (S, G) entry. Instead, the router only marks the interface as pruned (Prune State) and then starts the Prune Timer.* The interface is returned to the forwarding state if this timer expires.

Note that Router E previously sent a PIM Prune message to Router C to prune the (S, G) traffic, although it was ignored because Router C still has a directly connected receiver on the network, Receiver 1. Router E continues to send a PIM Graft to Router C, which immediately responds with a PIM Graft-Ack message. The (S, G) multicast traffic then starts flowing through Router E and Router J to Receiver 3. *By using a PIM Graft message, Router J avoids having to wait for the previously sent (S, G) Prune to time out, thereby reducing the delay Receiver 3 would have experienced in receiving the (S, G) multicast traffic.*

4.11 PIM-DM STATE-REFRESH

As discussed above, PIM-DM builds SRTs that operate on a flood-and-prune principle. PIM-DM floods (S, G) multicast packets from a source to all areas of a multicast domain, and PIM-DM routers that receive the (S, G) multicast packets and

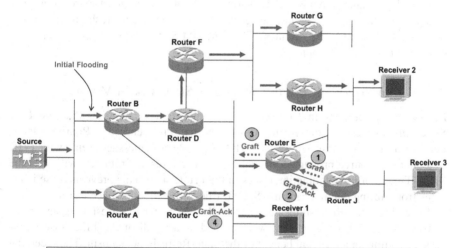

- The PIM-DM Graft mechanism allows a PIM-DM network to graft back branches of the multicast distribution tree that are previously pruned. This allows PIM -DM to restart the flow of multicast traffic with minimum delay.
- In the figure, Receiver 3 joined the multicast group via Router J, requiring PIM-DM to graft back Router J.
- Router J receives IGMP Membership Report from Receiver 3 and then sends a PIM Graft message to Router E to restart the flow of multicast traffic to Receiver 3.
- Note that Router J still maintains the multicast state of the source even thought it was pruned for this source, allowing it to send Graft messages when a receiver or PIM neighbor joins.
- Router E receives the Graft message from Router J and responds with a Graft-Ack message.
- Router E also sends a Graft message to Router C which immediately responds with a Graft-Ack message.
- Multicast traffic then begins to flow through Routers E and J to Receiver 3.

FIGURE 4.9 PIM-DM Grafting.

have no directly connected multicast group G members or PIM-DM neighbors will send an (S, G) Prune message back on the SPT tree toward the multicast source. As a result, PIM-DM does not flood subsequent multicast packets to pruned branches of the SPT. However, the Prune state in PIM-DM routers times out approximately every 3 minutes, and PIM-DM will have to reflood the entire PIM-DM domain with multicast packets, triggering once again the resending of (S, G) Prune messages. This reflooding of unwanted multicast packets throughout the PIM-DM domain consumes network bandwidth and node processing resources.

The PIM-DM State-Refresh feature allows the PIM-DM routers to keep the Prune state from timing out by enabling the First-Hop Router (FHR) attached to the multicast source to periodically send (S, G) State-Refresh messages along the SRT (see Figure 4.10). These control messages refresh the Prune state on the outgoing interfaces of each PIM-DM router in the SPT. Upon receiving State-Refresh messages, PIM-DM routers keep their Prune states from timing out, saving network bandwidth because the reflooding of unwanted multicast traffic to pruned branches of the SRT is greatly reduced. The State-Refresh feature also enables PIM-DM routers to recognize topology changes in the PIM-DM domain (i.e., a new multicast source joining or an existing source leaving a multicast group) before the State-Refresh timeout period (with a default setting of 3 minutes). The PIM-DM State-Refresh message format is described in detail in Chapter 3.

4.11.1 PURPOSE OF THE ROUTING METRICS IN STATE-REFRESH MESSAGES

Noting our discussion in Chapter 3, it is important to mention that the PIM State-Refresh message format includes the Metric Preference and Routing Metric fields (similar to the Assert message). When State-Refresh messages sent by the FHR of a multicast source propagate through the SRT and reach a router, it will reset the Prune Timers of its outgoing interfaces in the Prune state. This prevents these interfaces from timing out and causing (S, G) traffic to be reflooded once again.

Receiving State-Refresh messages also allows a router to refresh outgoing interfaces to a network segment that were pruned as a result of the PIM Assert process, providing an additional benefit of the State-Refresh mechanism. The receiving router can accomplish this because the State-Refresh message also contains the same basic routing metrics used in the Assert message for the Assert process. Sending State-Refresh messages further reduces the protocol overhead in PIM-DM because it eliminates the need for routers attached to a network segment to rerun the Assert process to prune outgoing interfaces (i.e., redundant paths) that produce duplicate multicast packets, as discussed above.

4.11.2 ORIGINATION (S, G) STATE MACHINE

This section describes how a PIM-DM originates PIM State-Refresh messages. The PIM-DM router directly connected to a multicast source generates these messages periodically. The router maintains one Origination (S, G) state machine for each (S, G) entry in its TIB. This state machine has the following two states (see Figure 4.11):

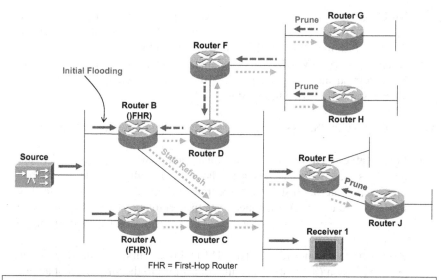

FHR = First-Hop Router

- PIM-DM constructs a source-based multicast distribution trees that operate on a flood and prune principle. Multicast packets from a source are flooded to all areas of the PIM-DM network.
- PIM routers that receive multicast packets and have no directly connected multicast group members or PIM neighbors send a Prune message back on the distribution tree toward the source of the packets.
  - As a result, subsequent multicast packets are not flooded to pruned branches of the distribution tree.
- However, the pruned state in PIM-DM routers times out approximately every 3 minutes and the entire PIM-DM network is reflooded with multicast packets and Prune messages.
  - This reflooding of unwanted traffic throughout the PIM-DM network consumes network bandwidth.
- The PIM-DM State-Refresh mechanism keeps the pruned state in PIM-DM routers from timing out by allowing the FHRs to periodically send State-Refresh messages on the source-based distribution tree. These control messages refresh the prune state on the outgoing interfaces of each router in the distribution tree.
- To achieve State-Refresh, the FHRs send (S, G) State-Refresh messages in the PIM-DM network whose (S, G) distribution tree has been pruned by Prune and Assert mechanisms.
  - In the figure, we assume Receiver 1 is the only active member of Group G and is receiving packets from the Source S.
  - To refresh the state of the tree to prevent the pruned interfaces from timing out, the FHRs A and B periodically send (S, G) State-Refresh messages.
  - When these messages reach the PIM-DM routers along the original (S, G) distribution tree, these routers reset the Prune timers in their (S, G) outgoing interfaces lists, thereby, preventing the interfaces from timing out and causing (S, G) traffic to be again flooded throughout the PIM-DM network.

FIGURE 4.10 PIM-DM State-Refresh.

- **NotOriginator**: The Origination (S, G) state machine starts in this state (i.e., its starting state). A PIM-DM router in this state will not originate State-Refresh messages for the source S sending to group G.
- **Originator**: A PIM-DM router in this state will periodically originate State-Refresh messages. Only a PIM-DM router directly connected to a source S may transition to this state.

Also, the Origination (S, G) state machine supports the following two timers:

- **State-Refresh Timer (S, G)**: This timer controls when the PIM-DM router generates State-Refresh messages. The router initially sets the timer when the Origination (S, G) state machine transitions to the Originator state. The PIM-DM router cancels the timer when the Origination (S, G) state machine transitions to the NotOriginator state. The router normally sets the timer to *StateRefreshInterval*.
- **Source Active Timer (S, G)**: The PIM-DM router first sets this timer when the Origination (S, G) state machine transitions to the Originator state and resets it upon receipt of each multicast packet from source S addressed to multicast group G. The Origination (S, G) state machine transitions to the NotOriginator state when this timer expires. The router normally sets this timer to *SourceLifetime*.

If a multicast source is directly connected to a PIM-DM router interface (i.e., the router is the First-Hop Router (FHR)) and the router creates an (S, G) entry, the router will initiate the State-Refresh Timer (S, G). This timer controls the periodic transmission of PIM State-Refresh messages, which are propagated hop by hop down the (S, G) multicast distribution tree. A State-Refresh message received by a PIM-DM router on the RPF interface causes existing (S, G) Prune state to be refreshed.

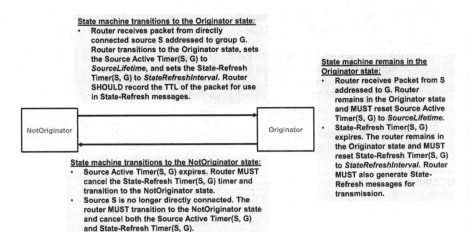

FIGURE 4.11   Origination (S, G) State-Refresh state machine.

4.11.3 ORIGINATING STATE-REFRESH MESSAGES

The introduction of PIM-DM State-Refresh message, which serves as a heartbeat message, prevents the periodic timeout of (S, G) Prune state in PIM-DM routers, greatly reducing the reflooding of multicast packets on the pruned branches of the SPT that expire periodically (see Figure 4.10). Furthermore, sending these messages causes multicast tree topology changes to be realized faster than the traditional 3-minute timeout.

For each (S, G) entry that a PIM-DM FHR creates for a source that is directly connected to it, the router will originate State-Refresh messages upon expiry of the (S, G) State-Refresh Timer on all PIM-DM interfaces with active PIM-DM neighbors, except the interface connected to the source (i.e., the RPF interface). In addition, when the State-Refresh Timer (S, G) expires, the router will restart the State-Refresh Timer (S, G) with its default value and refresh all (S, G) pruned interface timers.

The FHR will no longer originate (S, G) State-Refresh messages when the corresponding (S, G) entry in its TIB times out. The router updates the (S, G) entry timer only if it receives a multicast packet from the source S and not upon expiry of the State-Refresh Timer (S, G). All other PIM-DM routers in the PIM-DM domain will forward State-Refresh messages only when received from a PIM-DM neighbor.

4.11.4 RECEIVING STATE-REFRESH MESSAGES

A PIM-DM router floods State-Refresh messages away from the RPF interface and down the (S, G) tree using the address of the multicast traffic source included in the message; the source address is used to determine the RPF interface. When a PIM-DM router receives a State-Refresh message for a given (S, G) pair, it will perform the following:

- Whenever a PIM-DM receives an (S, G) State-Refresh message on the RPF interface for S and has no existing (S, G) entry, it will create an (S, G) entry. If the Prune Indicator flag in the State-Refresh message is set by the sender to indicate a forwarding branch, then the router will set all outgoing interfaces (i.e., all non-incoming interfaces) with PIM-DM neighbors to the Forwarding state in the new (S, G) entry. Otherwise, the router will create the new (S, G) entry with the Prune state on all outgoing interfaces.
- If the PIM-DM router receives an (S, G) State-Refresh message on an interface other than the RPF interface of S and has no existing (S, G) entry, then the message will be ignored. If the interface on which the message was received corresponds to a LAN, then the router may still process the message according to the normal PIM Assert rules described earlier.
- If the PIM-DM receives an (S, G) State-Refresh message on an (S, G) downstream interface, then it will ignore the message. If the interface on which the message was received corresponds to a LAN, the router may still process the message according to the normal PIM Assert rules described earlier.

- If the PIM-DM router receives an (S, G) State-Refresh on an (S, G) incoming interface from a PIM-DM router other than the upstream neighbor toward the source (i.e., the RPF neighbor or Assert Winner), then the router will ignore State-Refresh message. However, the router may still process the message according to the normal PIM Assert rules described earlier.
- If the PIM-DM router receives an (S, G) State-Refresh message on an (S, G) incoming interface from the upstream neighbor (i.e., RPF neighbor or Assert Winner), then the router will refresh all (S, G) pruned interface timers. Furthermore, if the router detects that the (S, G) pair is a negative cache entry, then it will also refresh the entry timer to its default value. A negative cache entry is found to not exist for some reason (i.e., indicates that information about the requested (S, G) pair does not exist).
- If the PIM-DM router receives an (S, G) State-Refresh message on an (S, G) incoming interface from the upstream neighbor (i.e., RPF neighbor or Assert Winner) and the message's Prune Indicator flag is set (indicating that the sender forwarded the message down a pruned branch), but the local (S, G) entry in the PIM-DM router is not a negative cache entry, then the router will clear the Prune Indicator flag in the message and send a Graft message upstream. To avoid duplicate Graft message generation due to different downstream routers responding to the same State-Refresh message, the router delays sending the Graft message by a random interval smaller than 3 seconds and will cancel any scheduled Graft message if one is received from another router on the LAN.

  Let us consider a scenario where there are multiple downstream PIM-DM routers on a LAN, some routers with forwarding cache entries and some with negative cache entries. In this case, the routers with the negative caches will send a (S, G) Prune message upon receiving each (S, G) State-Refresh message, while the routers with the forwarding cache entries will have to send (S, G) Join messages to override the (S, G) Prune messages. To reduce the amount of control traffic created on the LAN due to this behavior, a router with negative cache entry must respond with a (S, G) Prune message to an (S, G) State-Refresh message with the Prune Indicator flag cleared if the Prune Now flag is set in the State-Refresh message. This Prune Now flag will be set by the originator of the State-Refresh message in one out of three State-Refresh messages transmitted. Downstream PIM-DM routers may also respond with an (S, G) Prune message upon receiving (S, G) State-Refresh messages with the Prune Now flag cleared.
- If the PIM-DM router receives an (S, G) State-Refresh message on an (S, G) incoming interface from the upstream neighbor (i.e., RPF neighbor or Assert Winner), then the router will retransmit the State-Refresh message on all PIM-DM interfaces other than the (S, G) interface on which the message was received, provided that the State-Refresh message TTL is greater than 0 and larger than the configured TTL threshold for the interface, and that multicast boundary addresses have not been configured on the interface for

the multicast group specified in the message. The IP header of the IP packet carrying the retransmitted State-Refresh message specifies the outgoing interface address as the source IP address of the IP packet, and the sending router rewrites the State-Refresh message with its local Metric Preference, Routing Metric, and Mask Length (Masklen), which indicates routing information for reaching the multicast source S. If the router detects that the (S, G) entry has Prune state for the interface on which the State-Refresh message is being transmitted, the router will set the Prune Indicator flag in the message to indicate a pruned branch. The router decrements the TTL field of the forwarded State-Refresh message by one (i.e., to be one less than that of the received message).

4.11.5   PROCESSING STATE-REFRESH MESSAGES ON LANS

On multiaccess LANs with multiple PIM-DM routers, PIM State-Refresh messages also serve as PIM Assert messages. PIM-DM routers on the LAN use the routing metric information (Metric Preference and Routing Metric as described in Chapter 3) in the State-Refresh messages to decide which router is the Assert Winner. In most ways, the processing of such State-Refresh messages by routers on the LAN is identical to the PIM Assert processing rules described earlier.

The PIM-DM Assert rules described rely on the periodic timeout of the Prune state in PIM-DM routers attached to the LAN to recover from situations where the Assert Winner on a LAN ceases to exist. Sending State-Refresh messages prevents this situation from happening. On a leaf LAN of the (S, G) tree with multiple forwarding PIM-DM routers, there are no downstream PIM-DM routers to timeout nor join toward the new forwarding router if the Assert Winner ceases to exist. The remaining forwarding router on the LAN that continuously receives periodic State-Refresh messages will be able to refresh the prune timers of their outgoing interfaces, and will not time out and start forwarding multicast packets.

Downstream PIM-DM routers on a LAN that receive an (S, G) State-Refresh message with the Assert Override flag set will discard the stored Metric Preference and Routing Metric values for the Assert Winner and use the sender of the State-Refresh message as their new PIM-DM RPF neighbor.

4.11.6   HANDLING PIM-DM ROUTER FAILURES

A PIM Hello message may contain the Generation ID Option (see Chapter 3). When a router receives a PIM Hello message from an existing PIM neighbor and the Generation ID differs from the previously seen Generation ID, this means the PIM neighbor has restarted and may not contain the (S, G) state. To allow the recreation of the missing (S, G) state, for each (S, G), all routers that are upstream of the failed router can send a new (S, G) State-Refresh message on the interface on which the Hello message was received.

To avoid a burst of State-Refresh messages arriving at the recovering router, the router should randomly space the transmission of State-Refresh messages for different (S, G) entries over a period of time. The length of this transmission period can be configured locally on the router with a recommended default value of 3 seconds. The router should set the Prune Indicator flag in the State-Refresh message to indicate if the recovering router is on a forwarding or pruned branch of the (S, G) tree.

4.12   PIM-DM/PIM-SM INTERACTIONS

PIM-DM was not designed to be used directly with PIM-SM, even though both share a common PIM header format and use the same Hello, Join/Prune and Assert message formats. It is particularly important to note that a PIM-DM router cannot tell if a neighbor is a PIM-SM router based on the Hello messages it receives.

If a PIM-DM router and a PIM-SM router become neighbors in the multicast routing domain, a simplex adjacency will be effectively formed between the two routers, with the PIM-DM router able to send all multicast packets to the PIM-SM router, while the PIM-SM router will not be able to send multicast packets to the PIM-DM router because the PIM-DM router cannot join (i.e., has no means of joining) the PIM-SM shared tree (or RP tree) rooted at the RP. *PIM-DM has no mechanism that allows a PIM-DM router to join a shared tree (i.e., join an RP), which means, a PIM-DM router cannot receive traffic from an RP. Additionally, PIM-DM routers do not send PIM (*, G) Join messages, which are meant for routers on the shared tree including the RP.*

However, the common PIM header and the other message formats they share permits the implementation of a hybrid or mix PIM-SM/DM network that uses PIM-SM when an RP is known in the network, and PIM-DM when one is not (see Auto-RP discussion in Chapter 5).

REVIEW QUESTIONS

1. Explain why PIM-DM is referred to as a flood-and-prune multicast protocol. Include in your explanation why PIM-DM uses a push model for multicast traffic distribution.
2. Explain the difference between the MRIB, TIB, and MFIB in a PIM router.
3. What is Reverse Path Forwarding (RPF) in PIM?
4. What do the incoming interface and outgoing interface specifically mean on a PIM router during multicast packet forwarding?
5. How do PIM routers discover each other in a PIM domain?
6. What is the role of the Designated Router (DR) in PIM-DM?
7. How does a PIM-DM router know during the flooding process that received multicast traffic may or may not be flooded on a particular interface?
8. What is the purpose of the PIM Prune message in PIM-DM?
9. How is the PIM Join message used in PIM-DM (i.e., under what circumstances is this message used)?
10. What is the purpose of the PIM Assert mechanism?
11. How are the PIM Graft and Graft-Ack messages used in PIM-DM?
12. What is the purpose of the PIM State-Refresh message and mechanism?

13. What is the purpose of the routing metrics (Metric Preference and Routing Metric) in State-Refresh messages?
14. Explain the reason why when a PIM-DM router and a PIM-SM router become neighbors in a multicast routing domain, the PIM-DM router can send multicast packets to the PIM-SM router, but the PIM-SM router is not able to send multicast packets to the PIM-DM router.

REFERENCES

[**RFC2236**]. W. Fenner, "Internet Group Management Protocol, Version 2", *IETF RFC 2236*, November 1997.
[**RFC3376**]. B. Cain, S. Deering, I. Kouvelas, B. Fenner, and A. Thyagarajan, "Internet Group Management Protocol, Version 3", *IETF RFC 3376*, October 2002.
[**RFC3973**]. A. Adams, J. Nicholas, and W. Siadak, "Protocol Independent Multicast – Dense Mode (PIM-DM): Protocol Specification (Revised)", *IETF RFC 3973*, January 2005.
[**RFC4760**]. T. Bates, R. Chandra, D. Katz, and Y. Rekhter, "Multiprotocol Extensions for BGP-4", *IETF RFC 4760*, January 2007.
[**RFC7761**]. B. Fenner, M. Handley, H. Holbrook, I. Kouvelas, R. Parekh, Z. Zhang, and L. Zheng, "Protocol Independent Multicast – Sparse Mode (PIM-SM): Protocol Specification (Revised)", *IETF RFC 7761*, March 2016.

5 PIM Sparse Mode (PIM-SM)

5.1 INTRODUCTION

This chapter describes the design of the Protocol Independent Multicast-Sparse Mode (PIM-SM) [RFC7761] and how it distributes multicast traffic originating from sources to multicast groups. PIM-SM, similar to PIM-DM and BIDIR-PIM, serves as a multicast routing protocol that utilizes the underlying unicast routing table (created by routing protocols such as RIP, OSPF, IS-IS, and BGP), any configured unicast static routes, as well as any multicast routing information provided by a protocol such as Multiprotocol BGP (MBGP) [RFC4760] for network topology discovery. MBGP was designed for interdomain (IPv4/IPv6 unicast and multicast) network topology discovery, particularly, for advertising routes between autonomous systems. PIM-SM builds unidirectional multicast shared distribution trees rooted at a Rendezvous Point (RP) for each multicast group (see Figure 5.1). When required, it creates shortest-path trees (SPTs), also called source-rooted trees (SRTs), for each multicast traffic source (see Figure 5.2). The PIM-SM shared tree is sometimes called the RP tree (RPT). The SRT (or SPT) is also occasionally referred to as the source-specific tree (SST) or source-based tree (SBT).

PIM-SM operates under the assumption that receivers interested in multicast traffic from each source in the multicast domain are sparsely and widely distributed. Therefore, the network only needs to send multicast packets on branches that have at least one interested receiver (signaled through hosts IGMP Membership Report messages). Unlike PIM-DM, which employs a *push model*, PIM-SM uses *a pull model* in which routers and receivers use an *Explicit Join mechanism* to request multicast traffic to be sent specifically to them. The pull model assumes that downstream routers and hosts do not want multicast traffic unless it is explicitly requested via PIM Join messages (from routers) and IGMP Membership Report messages (from host receivers).

PIM-SM employs an *Explicit Join* model in which routers determine which interfaces have the interested receivers and then send PIM Join messages toward their upstream neighbors on the path to the RP. As these messages travel upstream to the RP, the shared multicast distribution tree is built from receivers to the RP. Due to the Explicit Join model, PIM-SM can constrain multicast traffic to only areas of the multicast domain that need it. This model prevents PIM-SM from having the inefficiencies seen in PIM-DM's flood-and-prune behavior, where multicast traffic is initially flooded indiscriminately to all parts of the network, and then interfaces without receivers are pruned off.

PIM-SM uses the RP as the initial source of multicast group traffic and maintains a multicast state in the form (*, G), as described in the later section. PIM-SM

DOI: 10.1201/9781032701967-5

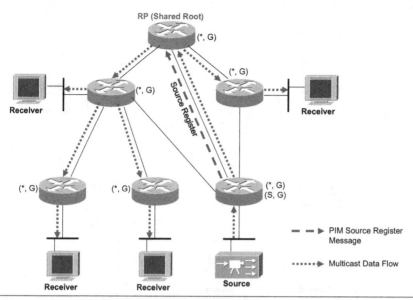

- The operation of PIM-SM centers around a unidirectional shared tree whose root is the RP. This shared tree is sometimes called an RP tree (RPT) because it is rooted at the RP.
- A unidirectional shared tree only permits multicast traffic to flow from the root (the RP) along the shared tree toward the receivers. This means a multicast source must use some method to get the traffic to the RP to be forwarded to the receivers.
- One method is to allow the RP to join a source tree (i.e., SPT) rooted at the multicast source, allowing it to pull traffic from the source for distribution along the shared tree to the receivers.
  - Sources must register with the RP to get the multicast traffic they generate to flow along the shared tree via the RP.
  - The source registration process with the RP triggers an SPT Join (also called an SRT) by the RP toward the source when there are active receivers for the multicast group in the network.
- The router that is directly connected to the receiver of a multicast group (i.e. the Last-Hop Router (LHR)) joins the shared tree. The LHR prunes itself from the shared tree when it no longer has directly connected receivers for the multicast group.

FIGURE 5.1 Unidirectional shared tree from the Rendezvous Point (RP).

migrates to an SRT or SPT and maintains a multicast state in the form (S, G) if that SPT path is shorter than the path through the RP for a particular multicast group's traffic. This means that PIM-SM is a *receiver-initiated multicast protocol*, supporting both shared trees and SPTs, and is not dependent on any specific unicast routing protocol.

Unlike PIM-DM, which uses a *flood-and-prune* approach for distributing multicast traffic, PIM-SM efficiently distributes multicast traffic to multicast groups that may span wide area networks. The flood-and-prune behavior of PIM-DM makes it unsuitable for large- and medium-sized multicast networks. The pull model of PIM-SM makes it suitable for medium- and large-sized multicast networks with multicast group members that are sparsely and widely distributed. Although PIM-SM may use the underlying unicast routing table (and any configured unicast static routes) to provide Reverse Path Forwarding (RPF) information for building the multicast

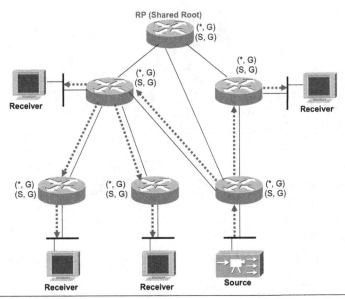

- PIM-SM allows receivers to receive multicast traffic via a shared tree or via an SPT (i.e., SRT).
- PIM-SM supports an Explicit Join mechanism for receivers to join the shared tree in addition to a mechanism for receivers to join an SPT whose root is a particular source.
- By allowing receivers to join the (S, G) SPT, multicast traffic is routed directedly along the SPT to the receivers without having to go through the RP.
    - This reduces data transfer latency and possibly congestion at the shared RP.
    - However, routers along the (S, G) SPT must create and maintain (S, G) state entries in their multicast routing tables (MRTs) which requires a little more router resources.
    - PIM-SM builds the SPT using (S, G) Joins and Prunes.
- PIM-SM uses the shared tree (rooted at the RP) to deliver the first few multicast packets from a source and also as a way to allow receivers to know that a source is active since each source in a PIM-SM must first register with the RP (via its First-Hop Router (FHR)).

FIGURE 5.2 Unidirectional source tree.

distribution tree (i.e., the RPT or SPT), it is not dependent on any particular unicast routing protocol, just like PIM-DM and BIDIR-PIM.

PIM-SM uses the PIM messages already described in Chapter 3, including Hello, Join/Prune, Assert, Register, Register-Stop, Bootstrap, and Candidate-RP-Advertisement.

The Graft and Graft-Ack messages are specific to PIM-DM only, while the Register, Register-Stop, Bootstrap, and Candidate-RP-Advertisement messages are unique to PIM-SM. Both protocols employ the Hello, Join/Prune, and Assert messages.

5.2 PIM-SM OVERVIEW

Before delving into the details of PIM-SM, let's define the following terms, which should be considered in addition to those defined in Chapter 4 for PIM-DM: Each multicast group needs to be associated with the IP address of designated RP in the multicast domain.

- **Rendezvous Point (RP)**: This is a router in a PIM-SM domain configured to serve as the root of a multicast distribution tree and to relay traffic from a multicast traffic source to a multicast group. Routers with directly connected receivers for a multicast group send PIM Join messages towards the RP, and traffic from multicast sources is sent to the RP to be forwarded to interested receivers of the multicast group. The RP address is used as the root of a group-specific shared tree with branches extending to all routers in the PIM domain that are interested in traffic sent to the group. The RP registers multicast sources that want to announce themselves and send data to multicast group members. The RP also joins receivers that want to receive data for a multicast group to the shared tree. Multicast routers send packets on the shared tree in such a way that they reach all interested receivers.
- **Designated Router (DR)**: On a shared multiaccess network (such as an Ethernet LAN), there may be multiple PIM-SM routers connected to it. One of these routers on this network is elected as the DR to act on behalf of directly connected hosts concerning the sending of multicast packets from a source to the RP (i.e., the router is called a source-side DR or First-Hop Router (FHR)), or sending PIM Join messages to the RP when directly connected hosts request traffic from a source and addressed to a multicast group (i.e., router is called a receiver-side DR or Last-Hop Router (LHR)). A single DR is elected for each multiaccess network using a simple DR election process.
- **RPF Neighbor**: The RPF Neighbor of a PIM router, usually concerning a multicast source address or RP address, is the PIM neighbor that the unicast routing table or MRIB indicates as the next-hop on the best or least-cost path leading to that address. In PIM-SM, the RPF neighbor is the PIM router that a PIM Join message for a multicast group should be sent to when a modifying Assert state is absent.
  - RPF_interface (S) is the interface that the MRIB on the PIM router indicates as the least-cost interface to the multicast traffic source S.
  - RPF_interface (RP) is the interface that the MRIB on the PIM router indicates as the least-cost interface to the RP for multicast group G. The exception is that, at the RP itself, it is the interface on which multicast data packets carried in PIM Register messages are received and decapsulated (i.e., it is the "virtual" interface on which PIM Register messages containing encapsulated multicast packets are received).

PIM-SM assumes that the multicast domain does not necessarily have hosts that need to receive multicast data when a source is active. Instead, routers with interested receivers of a particular multicast group must specifically request for the multicast data to be forwarded to them before the request is honored. Therefore, the core task of PIM-SM is to implement multicast forwarding by building and maintaining RPTs. Each RPT is rooted at a particular router in the PIM-SM domain (i.e., the RP), and through it, the multicast data travels along the RPT to the leaf routers and the host receivers. There is a single RPT for each multicast group in the PIM-SM domain, regardless of the number of multicast sources.

When a host receiver is interested in multicast traffic addressed to a specific multicast group, the leaf router directly connected to it sends a PIM Join message to the RP corresponding to that multicast group. The path along which the PIM Join message travels hop by hop until it reaches the RP forms a branch of the RPT.

When a multicast source first sends multicast packets addressed to a multicast group, its directly connected PIM router, the FHR or source-side Designated Router (DR), first registers the source with the RP responsible for the group. The source-side DR unicasts a PIM Register message encapsulating the first multicast packets to the RP. Upon receiving the PIM Register message, the RP triggers the establishment of a more efficient SPT rooted at the source-side DR. The SPT allows the multicast source to send subsequent multicast packets along the SPT to the RP. Upon receiving the multicast packets over the SPT, the RP then replicates and delivers those multicast packets to the receivers along its RPT. It is important to note that multicast packets are replicated only where the distribution tree branches, and this process of replication automatically repeats until the multicast packets reach the receivers.

All PIM protocol types (PIM-DM, PIM-SM, BIDIR-PIM) rely on an underlying network topology discovery protocol to populate the MRIB. The routes in MRIB may be supplied directly by a unicast routing protocol (RIP, OSPF, IS-IS, BGP) or by a multiprotocol routing protocol such as MBGP. Regardless of how the MRIB is created, its primary purpose in a PIM router is to provide the next-hop router that lies on an RPF path to a multicast source or RP.

The PIM router employs the MRIB to determine the next-hop PIM neighbor to which it will send a PIM Join/Prune message. Multicast traffic (from a source or RP) flows along the reverse direction of the path created by the PIM Join messages. Thus, unlike the unicast RIB, which specifies the next-hop router that a unicast packet would take to get to its destination, the MRIB provides the reverse-path information to the source or RP and also indicates the path that a multicast packet would take from its originator (source or RP) to the router that has the MRIB.

The following functions (some already discussed in Chapter 4 for PIM-DM) are common to both PIM-DM and PIM-SM:

- PIM Neighbor Discovery using PIM Hello messages.
- Recalculation of the RPF interface on a PIM router when its unicast routing table changes.
- Election of a DR on multiaccess network segments like IP subnets or VLANs (although the role of the DR is less significant in PIM-DM as discussed in Chapter 4).
- Use of PIM Assert messages to elect a Designated Forwarder on multiaccess network segments.
- Use of PIM Prune Overrides (i.e., a PIM Join message to override a Prune message) on multiaccess network segments.

In PIM-SM, the RPF interface is the local PIM interface that has the least-cost path leading back to the multicast traffic source for (S, G) traffic, or the RP for (*, G) traffic. If multiple least-cost paths exist, then the interface with the highest IP address to the source (or RP) is normally used as the RPF interface. The RPF interface is recomputed periodically to account for network topology changes that may cause it to change. Periodic recomputation of the RPF interface is necessary to allow the multicast routing to converge quickly after a network topology change.

The next sub-sections provide an overview of PIM-SM. The goal here is to provide an introduction to how PIM-SM works before delving into the details of the protocol. The operation of PIM-SM can be split into three phases, although, all these three phases may occur simultaneously.

5.2.1 PIM-SM Operational Phases

This section describes the three phases of PIM-SM operations; creating the RPT, sending and processing PIM Register-Stop messages, and switching to the SPT.

For PIM-SM to operate, the PIM-SM domain must support the following important elements:

- An underlying unicast routing protocol (e.g., OSPF, IS-IS) for the routers to provide routing table information to PIM-SM.
- RPs to become the root of the shared tree for multicast groups (and to register multicast sources, accept joins from receivers, and forward data to the group).
- RP discovery mechanism such as the Bootstrap Router (BSR) mechanism to send RP information to all routers to enable them to learn multicast group-to-RP mappings.

5.2.1.1 Phase One: Creating the Rendezvous Point (RP) Tree

Two types of operations can occur in phase one, receiver-side and source-side operations.

5.2.1.1.1 Receiver-Side Operations

A host sends an IGMP Membership Report message [RFC2236] [RFC3376] to express its interest in receiving traffic sent to a multicast group G. The elected DR for the host's network segment (e.g., IP subnet), also called the receiver-side DR or LHR, upon receiving the IGMP Membership Report message, sends a PIM (*, G) Join message toward the RP for that multicast group. The PIM (*, G) Join message is forwarded hop by hop toward the RP for group G, and each PIM-SM router that receives it instantiates a multicast distribution tree state for group G.

The forwarded PIM (*, G) Join message eventually either reaches the RP for group G or a PIM-SM router that already has a (*, G) Join state created for group G. When many hosts join group G in the PIM-SM domain, their (*, G) Join messages converge on the RP for group G and form a multicast distribution tree for that group that is rooted at that RP. This shared tree anchored at the RP is known as the RPT because it is shared by all multicast sources sending traffic to group G.

PIM-SM routers resend/refresh PIM Join messages periodically as long as the receiver remains in the group. When all receivers attached to the DR (i.e., on a leaf-network) leave multicast group G, the DR will send a PIM (*, G) Prune message toward the RP for group G. However, if the DR does not send a PIM (*, G) Prune message for some reason, the (*, G) state in the DR (and on routers on the leaf-network with no interested receivers) will eventually time out.

5.2.1.1.2 Source-Side Operations

When a multicast data source first starts sending packets destined for a multicast group G, its DR, also called the source-side DR or FHR, takes those multicast data packets, encapsulates them in PIM Register messages (which, in turn, are carried in IP packets), and sends them via unicast directly to the RP. These IP packets have a destination address set to the IP address of an interface of the RP, a destination address that must be an IP unicast address. The primary purpose of the PIM Register message is to inform the RP of a new multicast source within the PIM-SM domain. The source-side DR sends PIM Register messages to the RP for its directly connected sources.

Upon receiving the unicast PIM Register messages with the encapsulated multicast data packets, the RP decapsulates them to extract the original multicast packets and forwards these multicast packets onto the RPT. The multicast packets then follow the RPT downstream to receivers that have joined group G. PIM-SM routers, along the RPT with (*, G) multicast state, will replicate packets wherever the RPT branches with receivers, and the multicast packets will eventually reach all the receivers for that multicast group. The process by which the source-side DR encapsulates data packets from the source and sends them to the RP is called *Registering*, and the unicast packets in which the multicast data packets are encapsulated are called PIM Register messages.

At the end of phase one, IP unicast packets encapsulating multicast packets are flowing to the RP, which then decapsulates these packets and forwards them natively over the RPT to the multicast receivers.

5.2.1.2 Phase Two: Sending and Processing PIM Register-Stop Messages

Encapsulation of multicast data packets from a source in PIM Register messages and sending them via unicast to the RP is inefficient for two reasons:

- Encapsulation (at the source-DR) and decapsulation (at the RP) may involve relatively expensive processing for a PIM-SM router to perform, operations which depend heavily on the router architecture and whether the router has appropriate hardware for these tasks.
- Sending multicast packets to the RP and then forwarding them from the RP along the RPT downstream to receivers may result in these packets traveling a relatively long distance to reach receivers that may be close to the multicast source (i.e., source-side DR). For many real-time applications (such as streaming voice and video, gaming, and real-time time transactions), this increased latency may degrade application performance, or the bandwidth consumption may be undesirable.

Although a PIM-SM implementation may send multicast data packets from a source to the RP via PIM Register indefinitely, for the reasons cited earlier, practical PIM-SM implementations allow the RP to normally switch to native multicast data packet forwarding. In such PIM-SM implementations, when the RP receives a PIMM Register message encapsulating multicast data packet from source S to group G, it will normally initiate the creation of a shorter and less-processing intensive multicast traffic path to the source by sending a source-specific PIM (S, G) Join message toward the multicast source S (actually to the source-side DR of source S).

This PIM (S, G) Join message travels hop by hop toward the multicast source S, while at the same time instantiating (S, G) multicast state in the PIM-SM routers along the path. The PIM-SM routers use only the (S, G) multicast state to forward multicast packets for group G if those packets are sent by source S.

The PIM (S, G) Join message sent by the RP eventually reaches the DR of source S or a router that has already created an (S, G) multicast state. In the former case, the source-side DR then starts sending natively, multicast packets from source S, which flow through the routers with (S, G) state toward the RP. These multicast data packets may also reach PIM-SM routers along the path toward the RP with (*, G) multicast state, and these routers can take a shortcut to receive multicast packets directly from the source S rather than through the RPT.

While the RP is in the process of creating the source-specific (S, G) path to source S, it will continue to receive multicast data packets from S but encapsulated in PIM Register messages. When multicast packets from S (via the source-side DR) also start to arrive natively through the (S, G) path at the RP, the RP will receive duplicate copies of each of these multicast packets. When this happens, the RP will start to discard the PIM Register messages encapsulating copies of these multicast packets and will send a PIM Register-Stop message back to the source-side DR of source S to prevent the DR from unnecessarily encapsulating further multicast data packets.

At the end of phase two, multicast packets from source S will flow natively along the source-specific (S, G) path to the RP, and from there, along the RPT to the receivers. Where the (S, G) path and RPT path intersect, the PIM-SM router may draw multicast traffic from source S from the source-specific (S, G) path (instead of from the RPT), thus, avoiding getting traffic from the longer detour path going through the RP.

It is importantto note that a source S may start sending multicast traffic before or after a receiver joins the multicast group G. In other words, phase two may happen before the RPT to the receiver is constructed.

5.2.1.3   Phase Three: Switching to the Shortest-Path Tree (SPT)

Although an RP can send a PIM (S, G) Join message toward the source to create a native multicast path that removes the encapsulation overhead in PIM Register messages, doing so does not necessarily result in optimized multicast forwarding paths to the receivers. For many receivers, the multicast paths that go through the RP may involve traffic taking significantly longer paths when compared with paths that bypass the RP and go directly from the source to the receivers.

To create multicast forwarding paths that have lower latencies or more efficient bandwidth utilization, PIM-SM allows the receiver-side DR (or LHR) of a receiver of a multicast group G, to optionally initiate the transfer of multicast traffic from a source S to group G from the shared tree (RPT) to a source-specific SPT. To do this, the receiver-side DR issues a PIM (S, G) Join message toward source S. This message travels hop by hop while instantiating (S, G) state in the routers along the path to source S. Eventually, this PIM (S, G) Join message either reaches the source-side DR of source S or reaches a router that already has the (S, G) state. When the message reaches either of these endpoints, multicast data packets from source S start flowing along the paths and through the routers with the (S, G) state until they reach the receiver.

As soon as the (S, G) path is created to the source, the receiver-side DR (or a router upstream of the DR) will receive two copies of the multicast data packets: One from the RPT and the other from the newly established SPT. When the receiver-DR or upstream router starts receiving the first packets from the SPT, it will start dropping the packets for group G from source S that arrive via the RPT. When this happens, the DR or upstream router sends a PIM (S, G) Prune message toward the RP, a message known as an *(S, G, rpt) Prune message*. This Prune message travels hop by hop, instantiating (S, G, rpt) Prune state in the routers along the path toward the RP, which also indicates that multicast traffic from source S to group G should NOT be forwarded on this path. The (S, G, rpt) Prune message is propagated until it reaches the RP or a router on the path that still needs multicast traffic from source S for other receivers.

After the (S, G, rpt) Prune state is created, the receiver-side DR will receive multicast traffic from source S along the SPT created between the receiver and S. Furthermore, the RP receives multicast traffic from source S, but this traffic is no longer sent to the receiver-side DR along the RPT. At this point and as far as the receiver-side DR (or LHR) is concerned, the SPT is the final multicast distribution tree to source S for group G traffic.

5.2.2 SOURCE-SPECIFIC JOINS AND PRUNES

Unlike IGMPv1 and IGMPv2, IGMPv3 allows a host receiver to join a group G and specify that it only wants to receive multicast traffic destined to this group from a particular source S. If a receiver expresses this desire, and no other receiver on its network requires all the traffic for group G, then the receiver-side DR may omit sending a (*, G) Join to the RP to set up the RPT and instead issue a source-specific (S, G) Join only to the source-side DR of the desired source S.

The multicast addresses range, 232.0.0.0 to 232.255.255.255, is currently reserved for source-specific multicast (SSM) in IPv4 (see discussion on PIM-SSM in Section **5.18**). For multicast group addresses in this range, receivers are required to only issue source-specific IGMPv3 (S, G) joins (using IGMPv3 Membership Report messages as described in Chapter 2). If a PIM router receives a non-source-specific join for a multicast group in this SSM address range, it will ignore this request.

IGMPv3 allows a host receiver to join a multicast group and to specify that it only wishes to receive traffic sent to multicast group G if that traffic does not come from a particular source or set of sources. In this case, the receiver-side DR will send a (*, G) Join request as normal but may combine this request with an (S, G, rpt) Prune that excludes each of the sources that the receiver does not wish to receive traffic from.

5.2.3 MULTIACCESS TRANSIT LANs

The PIM-SM discussion so far assumes that the PIM-SM has point-to-point transit links. However, in real-world networks, the use of multiaccess network segments (i.e., LANs) such as those based on Ethernet for transit is not uncommon. The use of multiaccess network segments can cause some complications in the use of PIM-SM for the following three reasons:

- **Issuing PIM (*, G) Join messages to different upstream routers**: Two or more routers on the multiaccess network segment may transmit PIM (*, G) Join messages to different upstream PIM-SM routers on the segment because they have MRIB entries that are in conflict regarding how to reach the RP. This causes PIM-SM to set up at least two paths on the RPT, resulting in duplicate copies of all the shared tree multicast traffic to be sent to the multiaccess network segment and the joining routers.
- **Issuing PIM (S, G) Join messages to different upstream routers**: Two or more routers on the multiaccess network segment may transmit PIM (S, G) Join messages to different upstream PIM-SM routers on the segment because they have MRIB entries that are in conflict regarding how to reach multicast source S. This causes PIM-SM to set up at least two paths on the source-specific tree, resulting in duplicate copies of all the multicast traffic to be sent from source S to the multiaccess network segment and the joining routers.
- **Issuing a PIM (*, G) Join and (S, G) Join messages to different upstream routers**: A router on the multiaccess network segment may transmit a PIM (*, G) Join message to one upstream PIM-SM router on the segment, and another router on the segment may transmit a PIM (S, G) Join message to a different upstream PIM-SM router on the same segment. When this happens, multicast packets from source S may reach the network segment over both the RPT and the SPT. If a receiving node downstream of the joining (*, G) router does not issue an (S, G, rpt) Prune, then multicast packets will flow via both the RPT and SPTs to the multiaccess network segment.

In all of the above cases, duplicate multicast traffic is being sent to the multiaccess network segment because more than one PIM-SM upstream router will end up having PIM-SM (*, G) or (S, G) join state. PIM-SM does not prevent duplicate (*, G) and/or (S, G) joins from flowing onto the multiaccess network segment, instead, when duplicate multicast traffic reaches the network segment from different upstream PIM-SM routers, these routers will notice this duplicate traffic, causing them to elect a single *forwarder* for forwarding the traffic downstream onto the network segment. The routers elect the *forwarder* using PIM Assert messages (see Chapter 3), which resolve the problem as follows (i.e., the *PIM Assert process*):

- The election is done in favor of the upstream PIM-SM router that has (S, G) state or, if none of these routers or both routers have (S, G) state, then the election is done in favor of the router with the best metric to the RP in the case of RPTs, or the best metric to the multicast traffic source in the case of SPTs.

Note that the downstream PIM-SM routers on the multiaccess network segment also
receive these PIM Assert messages, causing subsequent PIM Join messages to be
sent to the upstream PIM-SM router that won the PIM Assert process. In this case,
the Assert Winner becomes the RPF neighbor for any downstream PIM-SM router
that has a PIM Join/Prune message to be sent upstream toward the source (see PIM
Assert process discussion in the appropriate section later). This is the RPF neighbor
as modified by the Assert process.

It is important to note that PIM-SM adopts the PIM Assert mechanism, which is
similar to that of PIM-DM.

5.2.4   RP DISCOVERY

Since the RP is a core component of PIM-SM, routers in a PIM-SM domain that
wish to join an (*, G) RPT or have a PIM (*, G) state, need to know the IP address of
the RP for the group G. The PIM-SM routers obtain the RP address through static
(i.e., manual) configuration or automatically through an Embedded-RP or a bootstrap mechanism.

The *Bootstrap Router (BSR) mechanism* [RFC5059] is one way for routers in
a PIM-SM domain to dynamically learn the presence and addresses of RPs in the
domain. This mechanism provides a way for routers to learn the identities of the
RPs in the network. Using a simple election process (as described in a later section), one router in each PIM domain is elected as the active *BSR*. Several of the
other routers in the PIM-SM domain are configured as *Candidate-RPs*, which periodically announce their RP candidacy status via unicast transmission to the BSR.
The BSR then selects from the Candidate-RPs, a set of qualifying *Candidate-RPs*
(simply called an *RP-Set*) and uses Bootstrap messages to periodically announce
this set to the routers in the PIM-SM domain. The PIM-SM domain floods the
Bootstrap messages hop by hop throughout the domain until all routers in the
domain learn the RP-Set.

Every router that receives the RP-Set uses a hash function to hash the multicast
group address G into the RP-Set to map the group G to an RP (which becomes
the active RP for group G). Each router performs this mapping while using an
order-preserving hash function (i.e., a hash function that minimizes changes in the
group-to-RP mapping if the RP-Set changes). The router uses the resulting RP as the
RP for multicast group G. As every router in the domain receives *the same RP-Set*
and runs the same hashing algorithm on the received RP-Set, all routers will select
an identical RP for a given multicast group address or address group range. In the
event the current RP fails for some reason, all routers will quickly apply the common
hashing algorithm on the RP-Set to select a new RP for the group or group range.

5.2.5   RPF CHECKS ON RPT AND SPT

A receiver sends an IGMP Membership Report message to signal its desire to join
a multicast group. PIM-SM routers then forward multicast packets on all interfaces,

leading to receivers that have *explicitly joined* a multicast group. Each router performs an RPF check before forwarding a received multicast packet. The type of RPF check performed by a router depends on whether the multicast distribution tree is an RPT or an SPT.

- If the tree is an RPT, the router performs the RPF check using the IP address of the RP.
  - The router has a (*, G) entry rather than an (S, G) entry. The source sends multicast packets to the RP rather than directly to the LHRs of the multicast group, and the RP forwards them over the RPT to the receivers. In this case, before sending a packet, the router checks its unicast routing table (or MRIB) to see if the packet arrives from the RP on the correct interface.
- If the tree is an SPT, the router performs the RPF check using the IP address of the actual multicast source.
  - The router has an (S, G) entry for the source. The source uses the SPT to send multicast packets to the receivers. In this case, the router performs the RPF check, by looking up the IP address of the multicast source in its unicast routing table (or MRIB) to see if the packet arrives from the source on the correct interface.

If multicast packets arrive on the correct interface, the router forwards them on all interfaces in its outgoing interface list (OIL) that lead to downstream receivers if any one of the following conditions is true:

- The router has received a PIM (*, G) or (S, G) Join message from a downstream PIM-SM router on the interface.
- The router has a directly attached receiver on an interface that has explicitly joined the multicast group G (by sending an IGMP Membership Report message).
- The router interface has been manually configured to join the multicast group G.

Note that in PIM-SM, each (*, G) state entry in a router's MRIB is typically created as a result of an *Explicit Join operation* (i.e., *created on demand*), and this is caused by the receipt of either a PIM (*, G) Join from a downstream PIM neighbor, or an IGMP Membership Report message from a directly connected host that wants to join multicast group G.

The router maintains an OIL for each (*, G) or (S, G) entry. Each entry specifies an incoming interface and one or more outgoing interfaces. The OIL of a (*, G) or (S, G) state must never contain the incoming interface of the associated multicast traffic, otherwise, traffic looping will occur. Because the source of a (*, G) entry is different from that of an (S, G) entry, PIM-SM computes the incoming interfaces for these entries differently, using the IP address of the RP as the RPF address for the (*, G) entry and the IP address of the actual source as the RPF address for the (S, G) entry.

The incoming interface of the (*, G) entry always points to the RP, while that of the (S, G) always points to the actual multicast source S.

5.3   PIM PROTOCOL STATE

We describe in this section all the protocol states that PIM-SM routers should maintain for multicast traffic routing in a PIM-SM domain to function correctly. The PIM-SM protocol state is maintained in the TIB as described earlier. The TIB holds the protocol state of all the multicast distribution trees at a PIM-SM router. Although the PIM-SM specification [RFC7761] defines the PIM-SM mechanisms and operations in terms of the TIB, actually PIM-SM implementations use the PIM-SM protocol state in the TIB to build a multicast forwarding table (i.e., MFIB), which is then used for packet forwarding operations. The MFIB is updated any time the relevant protocol state in the TIB changes

The PIM-SM specification only provides a precise abstract protocol state definition (to specify the PIM-SM router's behavior) and does not suggest that actual PIM-SM implementations need to maintain the protocol state in this form. PIM-SM implementations can maintain any internal state they require, as long as they are conformant with the PIM-SM specification and provide the same externally visible PIM-SM protocol behavior.

The protocol state in the TIB can be divided into the following three sections:

- **(*, G) state**: This is a protocol state that maintains the shared tree (i.e., RPT) for multicast group G; G is the destination IP address of the multicast packet (i.e., multicast group address).
- **(S, G) state**: This is the protocol state that maintains an SRT (or SPT) for multicast traffic source S and group G. Note that the SRT (or SPT) is occasionally called the source-specific tree; S is the source IP address of the multicast packet.
- **(S, G, rpt) state**: This is a protocol state that maintains source-specific information about multicast traffic source S on the RPT for multicast group G. For example, if a node is receiving multicast traffic from source S on the SPT, this node will normally have pruned off this traffic on the RPT. The Prune state that the node maintains is the (S, G, rpt) state. The parameter rpt is the IP address of the RP for multicast group G.

We describe in detail the various protocol states that should be maintained by a PIM-SM router in the subsequent section. It is to be noted that a PIM-SM router will only maintain protocol state when it is relevant for multicast data packet forwarding operations. For example, the "NoInfo" state in a PIM-SM implementation (i.e., router) might be assumed in the absence of other PIM-SM protocol state information rather than being maintained explicitly.

5.3.1   GENERAL-PURPOSE STATE

A PIM-SM router maintains the following non-group-specific state.

5.3.1.1 Interface State for Each PIM-SM Interface

The router maintains the following state for each PIM-SM-enabled interface:

- **Hello Timer**: The *Hello_Period* of this timer (with a default value of 30 seconds) is the periodic time interval for sending PIM Hello messages. The *Triggered_Hello_Delay* of this timer (with a default value of 5 seconds) is the random interval a router has to wait before sending the initial Hello message when it boots up, or before sending a triggered Hello message to a PIM neighbor that is rebooting.
- **Effective_Propagation_Delay**: The *Propagation_delay_default* of this parameter (with a default value of 0.5 seconds) is the Propagation delay over the link (or LAN) connected to the interface.
- **Effective_Override_Interval**: The *t_override_default* of this parameter (with a default value of 2.5 seconds) is the delay interval over which the PIM router selects the random delay (or waiting time) when scheduling a delayed PIM Join message.
- **Suppression State**: One of the following is stored {"Enable", "Disable"}.

5.3.1.2 Neighbor State for Each PIM-SM Neighbor

The router maintains the following state for each PIM-SM neighbor. This includes information obtained from the neighbor's PIM Hello message:

- **Neighbor's Generation ID**: This is the Generation ID field value in the Hello message's Generation ID Option from the PIM neighbor.
- **Neighbor's LAN Prune Delay (i.e., Propagation Delay field value)**: This is the Propagation Delay field value in the Hello message's LAN Prune Delay Option from the PIM neighbor.
- **Neighbor's Override Interval**: This is the Override Interval field value in the Hello message's LAN Prune Delay Option from the PIM neighbor.
- **Neighbor Liveness Timer**: The *Default_Hello_Holdtime* for this timer, set by a default value of 3.5 times the *Hello_Period*, functions as the default Hold Time a PIM router uses to keep a Neighbor State alive. The *Hello_Holdtime* is the Hold Time value taken from the Hold Time Option contained in a neighbor's Hello message. It is recommended that a router configures the Hold Time value in a Hello message to be 3.5 times the *Hello_Period*. It is important to note that a PIM router sends a Hello message every time interval equal to *Hello_Period*.

5.3.1.3 Designated Router (DR) State

The router maintains the following state for each interface connected to a multi-access network segment:

- **Designated Router's IP Address**: This is the IP address of the current elected DR of the network segment.
- **DR's DR Priority**: This is the DR Priority field value contained in the Hello message's DR Priority Option sent by the current DR of the network segment.

5.3.2   (*, G) State

The PIM-SM router maintains the following state for each multicast group G.

5.3.2.1   (*, G) State for Each Interface

- **Local Membership State**: One of the following is stored {"NoInfo", "Include"}
- **PIM (*, G) Join/Prune State**: The PIM-SM router creates this state as a result of receiving PIM (*, G) Join/Prune messages on the interface. The router uses this state to calculate the outgoing interface list (OIL) for multicast group G, and to decide whether it should send a PIM Join (*, G) message upstream.
  - **One of the following states is stored**: {"NoInfo", "Join", "Prune-Pending"}
  - **(*, G) Prune-Pending Timer**: The router sets this timer when it receives a valid PIM Prune (*, G) message. When this timer expires, the Interface State reverts to "NoInfo" for multicast group G.
  - **(*, G) Join/Prune Expiry Timer (or (*, G) Expiry Timer)**: The router restarts this timer when it receives a valid PIM Join (*, G) message. When this timer expires, the Interface State reverts to "NoInfo" for the multicast group G. The *J/P_HoldTime* of this timer is taken from the PIM (*, G) Join/Prune message and is the Hold Time field value in the message. The Hold Time field value is the amount of time (in seconds) the receiving router must keep the Join/Prune state alive. The Hold Time field value is ignored in Prune messages.
- **(*, G) Assert Winner State**: The PIM-SM router creates this state as a result of receiving or sending PIM (*, G) Assert messages on the interface.
  - **One of the following states is stored**:{"NoInfo", "I lost Assert", "I won Assert"}
  - **(*, G) Assert Timer**: (*, G) Assert Losers use this timer to time out (*, G) Asserts, while the (*, G) Assert Winner uses it to resend (*, G) Asserts.
  - **(*, G) Assert Winner's IP Address (AssertWinner)**: This is the IP address of the router that won the PIM (*, G) Assert process.
  - **(*, G) Assert Winner's Assert Metric (AssertWinnerMetric)**: This is the metric of the best route to the RP from the (*, G) Assert Winner's perspective.

A PIM-SM router applies a host group management protocol such as IGMP (or MLD for IPv6) running on the interface to determine the local membership state of the interface. The router does not need to keep the local membership state if it is not the DR on that interface unless it won a (*, G) Assert on the interface for multicast group G. However, a non-DR may optionally maintain a local membership state in case it becomes the DR or Assert Winner. Reference [RFC7761] recommends storing this information, if possible, as doing so reduces the time it takes to converge to stable operating conditions after a network failure that causes a change of DR on the interface.

5.3.2.2 Non-interface-Specific (*, G) State

- **Upstream (*, G) Join/Prune State**: One of the following states is stored {"NotJoined (*, G)", "Joined (*, G)"}. This state reflects the state of the Upstream (*, G) state machine described in the subsequent section.
- **Upstream (*, G) Join/Prune Timer**: The PIM-SM router uses this timer to determine when to send out periodic PIM Join (*, G) messages and to override Prune (*, G) messages sent by PIM-SM peers on an upstream interface connected to a multiaccess network segment (LAN).
- **Last RP Used**: This is the last RP used for multicast group G. The PIM-SM router must store the last RP used for group G because if the RP changes, it must tear down the state and rebuild them for groups whose RP has changed.
- **Last RPF Neighbor toward RP That Was Used**: This is the last PIM-SM neighbor that provides the best route to the RP for multicast group G. The PIM-SM router must store the last RPF neighbor toward the RP because, if changes occur in the MRIB, then its RPF PIM-SM neighbor leading to the RP may change. If the RPF neighbor changes, then the router needs to send a new PIM Join (*, G) message to the new upstream PIM-SM neighbor and a Prune (*, G) message to the old upstream PIM-SM neighbor. Similarly, if the PIM-SM router detects that the upstream RPF neighbor leading to the RP has restarted or rebooted (by receiving a changed Generation ID in a PIM Hello message, as discussed in Chapter 3), then it should re-instantiate the state by transmitting a PIM Join (*, G) to the neighbor.

5.3.3 (S, G) STATE

The PIM-SM router maintains the following state for each source/group pair (S, G).

5.3.3.1 (S, G) State for Each Interface

- **Local Membership State**: One of the following states is stored {"NoInfo", "Include"}
- **PIM (S, G) Join/Prune State**: The PIM-SM router creates this state as a result of receiving PIM (S, G) Join/Prune messages on the interface. It uses this state to calculate the OIL and to decide whether to send a PIM Join (S, G) message upstream.
  - **One of the following states is stored**: {"NoInfo", "Join", "Prune-Pending"}
  - **(S, G) Prune-Pending Timer**: The PIM-SM router sets this timer when it receives a valid PIM Prune (S, G) message. When this timer expires, the per-interface state machine for receiving PIM (S, G) Join/Prune messages reverts to the "NoInfo" state.
  - **(S, G) Join/Prune Expiry Timer (or (S, G) Expiry Timer)**: The PIM-SM router sets this timer when it receives a valid PIM Join (S, G) message. When this timer expires, the state machine reverts to the "NoInfo" state.

- **(S, G) Assert Winner State**: The PIM-SM router creates this state as a result of receiving or sending PIM (S, G) Assert messages on the interface.
  - **One of the following states is stored**: {"NoInfo", "I lost Assert", "I won Assert"}
  - **(S, G) Assert Timer**: Assert Losers use this timer to time out (S, G) Asserts, while the (S, G) Assert Winner uses it to resend (S, G) Asserts.
  - **(S, G) Assert Winner's IP Address (AssertWinner)**: This is the IP address of the router that won the PIM (S, G) Assert process.
  - **Assert Winner's Assert Metric (AssertWinnerMetric)**: This is the metric of the best route to the RP from the (S, G) Assert Winner's perspective.

A PIM-SM router uses a local source-specific membership management protocol such as IGMPv3 running on the interface to determine the local membership state of the interface and to specify that a particular source should be included. The router stores this state after resolving any IGMPv3 inconsistencies between group members on the LAN. The router does need to keep this state if it is not the DR on the interface unless it won a (*, G) Assert on the interface for multicast group G. However, [RFC7761] recommends storing this information (on non-DRs), if possible, since doing so reduces the time it takes to converge to stable operating conditions after a network failure that causes a change of DR on the interface.

5.3.3.2   Non-interface-Specific (S, G) State

- **Upstream (S, G) Join/Prune State**: This state reflects the state of the Upstream (S, G) state machine as described in the subsequent section below.
  - **One of the following States Is Stored**: {"NotJoined (S, G)", "Joined (S, G)"}
  - **Upstream (S, G) Join/Prune Timer**: The PIM-SM router uses this timer to determine when to send out periodic PIM Join (S, G) messages and to override PIM Prune (S, G) messages sent by PIM-SM peers on an upstream interface connected to a LAN.
  - **Last RPF Neighbor toward S That Was Used**: The PIM-SM router stores the last RPF neighbor leading to the multicast traffic source S because if changes occur in the MRIB, then the RPF PIM-SM neighbor leading to the source S may change. If the RPF neighbor changes, then the router needs to send a new PIM Join (S, G) message to the new upstream PIM-SM neighbor and a Prune (S, G) message to the old upstream PIM-SM neighbor. Similarly, if the router detects that the upstream PIM-SM neighbor leading to source S has rebooted (by receiving a changed Generation ID in a PIM Hello message), then it should re-instantiate the state by transmitting a PIM Join (S, G) message.
  - **SPTbit (Indicates (S, G) State Is Active)**: The PIM-SM router uses the SPTbit to indicate whether multicast packet forwarding is taking place on the SPT (i.e., (S, G) tree), or the RPT (i.e., (*, G) tree). A PIM-SM router can create an (S, G) state and still forward multicast traffic on

the (*, G) state during the period when the SPT is being constructed. When SPTbit is FALSE, the PIM-SM router uses only the (*, G) state to forward multicast packets from source S to group G. When SPTbit is TRUE, the router uses both the (*, G) and (S, G) state for packet forwarding.

- **(S, G) Keepalive Timer**: This timer is updated anytime the PIM-SM router forwards multicast data packets using the (S, G) state. The router uses this timer to maintain the (S, G) state alive when explicit PIM (S, G) Join messages are not received. Among other uses, using this timer is necessary, for example, when the RP sends PIM (S, G) Join messages to stop the source-side DR from encapsulating further multicast packets in PIM Register messages, and then PIM (S, G) Prune messages to the source-DR to prevent multicast traffic from needlessly reaching the RP.

The *Keepalive_Period* of the (S, G) Keepalive Timer (which has a default value of 200 seconds) is the time interval after the last (S, G) multicast data packet was sent during which the PIM-SM router will maintain the (S, G) Join state even in the absence of PIM (S, G) Join messages. The *RP_Keepalive_Period* of the Keepalive Timer is used as the *Keepalive_Period* at the RP when a PIM Register-Stop message is sent to source S for multicast group G. The default value of the *RP_Keepalive_Period* is $(3 \times Register\_Suppression\_Time + Register\_Probe\_Time)$. At the RP, the *Keepalive_Period* must be at least the *Register_Suppression_Time*, if not the (S, G) state may be timed out by the RP before the next PIM-SM Null-Register message arrives. Thus, the RP sets the (S, G) Keepalive Timer to max (*Keepalive_Period*, *RP_Keepalive_Period*) when a PIM Register-Stop message is sent. The use of the PIM Register and Register-Stop messages and their related timers is discussed in detail in the subsequent section.

- **Additional (S, G) State at the DR:**
  - **(S, G) Register State**: One of the following states is stored {"Join", "Prune", "Join-Pending", "NoInfo"}. A source-side DR uses the (S, G) Register State to keep track of whether to encapsulate multicast data in PIM Register messages to be sent to the RP on the Register Tunnel.
  - **(S, G) Register-Stop Timer**: The source-side DR uses the (S, G) Register-Stop Timer to track how long to wait before encapsulating again, multicast data packets in PIM Register messages for a given (S, G) pair.

5.3.4 (S, G, RPT) STATE

For each (S, G) pair for which a PIM-SM router also has a (*, G) state, the router also maintains the following state.

5.3.4.1 (S, G, rpt) State for Each Interface

- **Local Membership State**: One of the following states is stored {"NoInfo", "Exclude"}

- **PIM (S, G, rpt) Join/Prune State**: The PIM-SM router creates this state when it receives PIM (S, G, rpt) Join/Prune messages on the interface. The router uses this state for calculating the OIL for multicast group G and adding Prune (S, G, rpt) messages to Join (*, G) messages.
  - **One of the Following State Is Stored**: {"NoInfo", "Pruned", "Prune-Pending"}
  - **(S, G, rpt) Prune-Pending Timer**: The PIM-SM router sets this timer when it receives a valid Prune (S, G, rpt) message. When this timer expires, the Per-Interface state machine for receiving (S, G, rpt) Join/ Prune messages moves to the Prune state.
  - **(S, G, rpt) Join/Prune Expiry Timer**: The PIM-SM router sets this timer when it receives a valid Prune (S, G, rpt) message. When this timer expires, the state machine reverts to the NoInfo state.

A PIM-SM router uses a local source-specific membership management protocol such as IGMPv3 running on the interface to determine the local membership state of the interface and to specify that, although the (*, G) Include state is also maintained, a particular source should be excluded. The PIM-SM router stores this state after resolving any IGMPv3 inconsistencies between group members on the LAN. The PIM-SM router does not need to keep this state if it is not the DR on the interface unless it won a (*, G) Assert on the interface for multicast group G. However, [RFC7761] recommends storing this information (on non-DRs) if possible, since doing so reduces the time it takes to converge to stable operating conditions after a network failure that causes a change of DR on the interface.

5.3.4.2   Non-interface-Specific State

- **Upstream (S, G, rpt) Join/Prune State:**
  - **One of the Following States Is Stored**: {"RPTNotJoined (G)", "NotPruned (S, G, rpt)", "Pruned (S, G, rpt)"}
  - **(S, G, rpt) Override Timer**: The PIM-SM uses this timer to delay sending (S, G, rpt) Join messages to prevent implosions of transmitted (S, G, rpt) Join messages.

A PIM-SM router uses the Upstream (S, G, rpt) Join/Prune state along with the (S, G, rpt) Override Timer to send the correct override (S, G, rpt) Join messages in response to (S, G, rpt) Join/Prune messages sent by upstream peers on a LAN.

5.4   PIM TIMERS

PIM-SM maintains the timers listed in Table 5.1. The timers are implemented as countdown timers as these are easier to implement and use. A countdown timer is set to a value and counts down to zero, at which point, it typically triggers an action. These timers can also be implemented as count-up timers, where the router stores a timer's absolute expiry time and compares it against a real-time clock.

When a PIM router starts or restarts timers, it sets them to the default values in [RFC7761]. Note that the default value of a timer on a specific interface may

TABLE 5.1

PIM Timers

PIM Entity		Timer
Global Timers	Per interface	• Hello Timer
		• Per PIM neighbor:
		• Neighbor Liveness Timer
		• Per Multicast Group (G):
		• (*, G) Join Expiry Timer
		• (*, G) Prune-Pending Timer
		• (*, G) Assert Timer
		• Per Source (S):
		• (S, G) Join Expiry Timer
		• (S, G) Prune-Pending Timer
		• (S, G) Assert Timer
		• (S, G, rpt) Prune Expiry Timer
		• (S, G, rpt) Prune-Pending Timer
	Per Group (G)	• (*, G) Upstream Join Timer
		• Per Source (S):
		• (S, G) Upstream Join Timer
		• (S, G) Keepalive Timer
		• (S, G, rpt) Upstream Override Timer
	At the DRs or relevant Assert	• Per Source, Group pair (S, G):
	Winners only	• Register-Stop Timer

change due to protocol events or configuration. A PIM router sets some of the timers (e.g., Prune-Pending, Upstream Join, Upstream Override) to values that depend on the settings of the *Propagation_Delay* and *Override_Interval* of the corresponding interface.

5.5 PIM-SM PACKET FORWARDING RULES

The PIM-SM packet forwarding rules can be summarized as follows:

- First, the PIM-SM router will restart (or start) the (S, G) Keepalive Timer if the multicast traffic source is on a directly connected network segment (LAN).
- Second, the PIM-SM router checks if it should set the SPTbit because it is switching from the RPT to the SPT.
- Next, the router checks whether a received multicast packet should be accepted based on the TIB state and the interface on which the packet arrived.
- If the router determines that the multicast packet should be forwarded using the (S, G) state, then it will build an OIL for the packet. If the OIL is not empty, then the router will restart the (S, G) state Keepalive Timer.

- If the router determines that the multicast packet should be forwarded using the (*, G) state, then it will just build an OIL for the packet. The router also checks if it should initiate a switchover from the RPT to start receiving multicast traffic from source S on an SPT.
- Finally, the router removes the incoming interface (of the multicast packets from source S to group G) from the OIL it has just created, and if the resulting OIL is not empty, the router will forward the packet out of the interfaces in the OIL.

5.5.1 LAST-HOP ROUTER SWITCHOVER FROM RPT TO SPT

PIM-SM allows the LHR (i.e., receiver-side DR) to join the RP to receive multicast traffic from source S sent to group G over the shared tree. Once multicast traffic from source S to group G arrives at an LHR, this router has the option of switching from the RPT to receive the traffic on an SPT. The policy decision for the LHR to switch to the SPT is implementation-dependent and may be a "switch on first multicast packet" policy, where the LHR switches to the SPT upon receiving a single multicast packet on the SPT for the source S and group G. The switchover policy may be based on receiving a few multicast packets (e.g., 3 packets) on the SPT.

5.5.2 SETTING AND CLEARING THE (S, G) SPTBIT

PIM-SM routers use the (S, G) SPT-bit to distinguish whether multicast packet forwarding is being done on the (*, G) or the (S, G) state. When a PIM-SM router is switching from the RPT to the SPT, there is a transitional period during which multicast packets will be arriving at the router on the RPT (due to upstream (*, G) state), while the router is establishing the upstream (S, G) state (i.e., the SPT to the source). During this transitional period, the router should continue to receive and forward multicast packets through (only) the (*, G) state.

Continuing to receive multicast on the upstream (*, G) state prevents temporary multicast packet forwarding "black holes" that could have been created if the router sent a Prune (S, G, rpt) to the RP before the upstream (S, G) state has been fully established. The PIM-SM router sets the (S, G) SPTbit if it has created the appropriate (S, G) join state, if a multicast packet arrived on the correct upstream interface for the multicast traffic source S, and if one or more of the following conditions apply:

- The source S is directly connected to the PIM-SM router.
- The RPF interface to the multicast source S is different from the RPF interface to the RP. Also, a multicast packet arrived from the source S on the RPF_interface(S), meaning, the SPT must have been established.
- No other router has expressed interest in multicast packets on the RPT.
- RPF (S, G) as modified by the Assert process is the same as RPF (*, G), as modified by the Assert process, in which case, the router will not be able to know if the SPT has been established, meaning, the router should just switch to the SPT immediately. The router sets the (S, G) SPTbit only if the RPF neighbor toward source S is valid.

5.6 THE DESIGNATED ROUTER IN PIM-SM

A multiaccess network segment (e.g., an Ethernet LAN) may have multiple PIM-SM routers connected to it. A single router on this network is elected the DR, to act on behalf of the other routers and the directly connected hosts concerning the PIM-SM protocol. The PIM router elected DR serves as the only multicast forwarder on the multiaccess network segment. A multiaccess network must always have an elected DR no matter whether the network connects to multicast sources or receivers.

- The DR at the multicast source side (called the source-side DR or FHR) sends PIM Register messages to the RP to register the source. The source-side DR also responds to PIM Register-Stop messages sent by the RP and sends Null-Register messages to the RP when required.
- The DR at the receiver side (called the receiver-side DR or LHR) performs the following functions:
  - Sends PIM (*, G) Join messages to the RP when an attached host receiver sends an IGMP Membership Report message requesting to join multicast group G.
  - Sends a PIM (*, G) Prune message to the RP when all attached receivers leave multicast group G.
  - Sends a PIM (S, G) Join message to the source-side DR of source S to initiate the construction of an (S, G) SPT, allowing it to switch from the (*, G) RPT to the more efficient (S, G) SPT.
- Note that IGMP must be enabled on the PIM router that acts as the receiver-side DR before receivers attached to it can join multicast groups through IGMP Membership Report messages.

Furthermore, the PIM-SM specification makes no distinction between multiaccess LANs and point-to-point interfaces, thus, DR election takes place on all interfaces, LAN and point-to-point. DR election is done using the information contained in PIM Hello messages. PIM routers also use Hello messages to negotiate PIM Options, allowing routers to enable additional functionality or parameters, as discussed in Chapter 3.

5.6.1 DESIGNATED ROUTER AND SENDING PIM HELLO MESSAGES

PIM routers send Hello messages periodically on each PIM-enabled interface. Such messages allow a PIM router to discover the PIM neighbor routers on each interface. Sending PIM Hello messages allows the routers to elect a DR for a network segment and negotiate additional PIM capabilities, as discussed earlier. Each PIM router records the information contained in Hello received from each PIM neighbor.

PIM routers send Hello messages on all active PIM interfaces, including physical point-to-point links, and these messages are sent via multicast to the ALL-PIM-ROUTERS multicast group address (224.0.0.13 for IPv4 and ff02::d for IPv6). Sending messages to the reserved multicast address 224.0.0.13 means they are forwarded on a hop-by-hop basis until they reach all PIM routers in the multicast domain (i.e., essentially flooded to all PIM routers in the PIM multicast domain).

The following are important actions that relate to sending PIM Hello messages:

- **The Hello Timer**: A PIM router uses a per-interface Hello Timer to determine when to send Hello messages on each active PIM interface. When a PIM router enables a PIM interface or first powers it up, it sets the Hello Timer of that interface to a random value that lies between 0 and *Triggered_Hello_Delay*. Sending randomly delayed Hello messages prevents the synchronization of Hello messages if multiple PIM routers on the same network segment are powered on simultaneously. After the PIM router sends the initial randomly delayed Hello message, subsequent messages must be sent every *Hello_Period* seconds. The router should not reset the Hello Timer except when it expires.

- **Accepting Join/Prune or Assert Messages**: A PIM router will not accept a PIM Join/Prune or Assert message from a PIM neighbor unless it has first received a Hello message from that neighbor. Thus, if a neighbor needs to send a Join/Prune or Assert message to a PIM router to which it has not yet sent a Hello message with its currently configured IP address, then it must immediately transmit a Hello message to the router without waiting for the Hello Timer to expire, and then transmit the relevant Join/Prune or Assert message it intended to send.

- **The DR Priority Option**: A network administrator can assign a preference level to a particular PIM router to be used in the DR election process. A PIM router interface can be given a numerically larger DR Priority value (the default priority is 1) and the router can use the DR Priority Option in Hello messages to announce this priority to other PIM routers on the network segment (see Chapter 3). PIM routers should include the DR Priority Option in every Hello message they send, even if a DR Priority is not explicitly configured on that interface. Including this Option in every Hello message is necessary because the DR election process, which is priority-based, is only enabled on a PIM interface when all PIM neighbors on that interface advertise that they can use the DR Priority Option.

- **The Generation ID Option**: PIM router should include the Generation ID Option in all Hello messages they send (see Chapter 3). A PIM router regenerates a random 32-bit value each time it starts or restarts PIM forwarding on an interface (including when the router itself restarts) and includes this value in the Generation ID Option. When a PIM router receives a Hello message with a new Generation ID from a neighbor, it will discard any old Hello message information about that neighbor and replace that with the information in the new Hello message. Receiving a new Generation ID may cause a new DR to be elected on that interface.

- **The LAN Prune Delay Option**: PIM router should include the LAN Prune Delay Option in all Hello messages they send on multiaccess LANs. A PIM router sends this Option to advertise its capability to use values other than the default values for the *Propagation_Delay* and *Override_Interval*. These two parameters affect the setting of the Prune-Pending Timer, Upstream Join Timer, and Override Timer.

- **The Address List Option**: A PIM router includes the Address List Option in Hello messages to advertise all the secondary IP addresses associated with the interface on which the message is sent. A PIM router must include this Option in all Hello messages if it has secondary IP addresses associated with the sending interface and may omit this Option if there are no secondary IP addresses on the interface.

- **Triggered Hello Messages**: To allow a PIM router that has newly powered up or one that has rebooted to learn about PIM neighbors quickly, when a PIM router receives a Hello message from such a new neighbor or receives a Hello message with a new Generation ID from an existing PIM neighbor, it should immediately send a new Hello message on the receiving interface after a randomly selected delay between 0 and *Triggered_Hello_Delay*. Sending this *triggered Hello message* should not change the timing of the router's scheduled *periodic Hello message*. If a PIM router needs to transmit a PIM Join/Prune message to the new PIM neighbor or transmit a PIM Assert message in response to an Assert message sent by the new neighbor before the randomly selected Hello message delay has expired, then it must immediately transmit the relevant Hello message without waiting for the Hello Timer to expire, and then follow this with the transmission of the Join/Prune or Assert message. If the router fails to send the triggered Hello message, then the new PIM neighbor will discard the PIM Join/Prune or Assert message.

- **Hello Messages with a Zero Hold Time**: Before a PIM router takes down an interface or changes its primary IP address, it should send a Hello message immediately with a zero Hold Time value (with the interface's old IP address if the IP address is being changed). Sending such a Hello message will cause the PIM neighbors to immediately delete this neighbor (or its old interface's IP address). After changing the IP address of an interface, the router must transmit a Hello message with the new IP address. If the router changes one of the secondary IP addresses of an interface, it should immediately send a Hello message with an updated Address List Option and a non-zero Hold Time. Sending such a Hello message will cause the PIM neighbors to immediately update the sender's list of secondary IP addresses.

5.6.2 Designated Router Election

When a PIM router receives a PIM Hello message on interface I, it will record the following information about the sending PIM neighbor:

- **Neighbor.interface**: This is the router interface on which the Hello message was received.
- **Neighbor.primary_IP_address**: This is the IP address that the PIM neighbor used in the source IP address field of the Hello message.
- **Neighbor.Generation_ID**: This is the Generation ID of the PIM neighbor.
- **Neighbor.DR_Priority**: This is the DR Priority field value of the PIM neighbor if present in the neighbor's Hello message.

- **Neighbor.DR_Priority_present**: This is a flag that indicates if the DR Priority field was present in the neighbor's Hello message.
- **Neighbor.timeout**: This is a timer (also known as the Neighbor Liveness Timer) value that the router uses to time out the Neighbor State when it becomes stale. The PIM router resets the Neighbor Liveness Timer to *Hello_Holdtime* (obtained from the Hello message's Hold Time Option) whenever it receives a Hello message containing a Hold Time Option or to *Default_Hello_Holdtime* if the Hello message does not contain the Hold Time Option. The PIM router deletes the Neighbor state when the *neighbor. timeout* expires.

PIM routers determine the DR on interface I as follows (see Figure 5.3). Routers on the interface send PIM Hello messages to one another:

- The PIM router with the highest DR Priority field value becomes the DR.
- If all of the DR Priority field values are equal, then the PIM router with the highest IP address is elected as the DR (i.e., the source IP address of the PIM Hello message is used as the tiebreaker).

When a PIM router receives a PIM Hello message without the DR Priority Option, or if the DR Priority value is equal to zero, then the router knows that the message sender does not support the DR Priority Option and will, therefore, use the source IP address of the PIM Hello message for the DR election. When the elected DR fails, the timeout in received PIM Hello messages triggers a new DR election process among the remaining routers.

As discussed in Chapter 3, it is important to note that the DR Priority value which should be carried in every PIM Hello message, is a 32-bit unsigned number, and the PIM routers always prefer the numerically larger priority value in the DR election process. A PIM router's view of the current DR on an interface may change when it receives PIM Hello messages from neighbors when a PIM neighbor times out, or when there has been a change in the router's own DR Priority value. If a PIM router assumes the role of the DR or ceases to be the DR on an interface, this will normally cause a change in state in the DR Register state machine. The subsequent actions taken by the PIM router are determined by the DR Register state machine. Recall that all active PIM-SM interfaces must take part in the DR election process including point-to-point interfaces.

Figure 5.4 summarizes the PIM-SM operations around the RP.

5.6.3 Reducing Prune Propagation Delay on LANs

Other than the information a PIM router records for the DR election process, the router also maintains the following per-PIM neighbor information, which is obtained from the LAN Prune Delay Option carried in Hello messages:

- **Neighbor.LAN_Prune_delay_present**: This is a flag that indicates if the Hello message from the PIM neighbor contains the LAN Prune Delay Option.

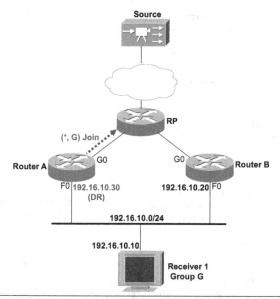

- There are two types of DRs In a PIM-SM domain:
  - The receiver-side DR which sends PIM Join and PIM Prune messages from the receiver's network toward the RP. This DR is the Last-Hop Router (LHR) for a multicast transmission from a specific source.
  - The source-side DR which sends PIM Register messages from the multicast traffic source network to the RP. This router is the First-Hop Router (FHR) for a multicast transmission from a specific source.
- Using PIM Hello messages, PIM elects a DR on each multiaccess network (such as a shared Ethernet network).
  - The reason for a DR on such networks is that, because PIM-SM uses the Explicit Join model, only the DR (i.e., Router A) should send PIM (*, G) Join messages to the RP for the shared tree to be constructed for multicast group G.
  - If both Router A and Router B are allowed to send (*, G) Join messages to the RP, parallel paths will be created and duplicate multicast traffic would be delivered to Receiver 1.
  - Also, if Receiver 1 happens to be the source of multicast traffic to group G, Router A being the DR, will be responsible for sending PIM Register messages to the RP.
    - Here too, without a DR, if Router A and Router B were permitted to send PIM Register messages to the RP, the RP would receive duplicate multicast traffic.

The DR election process is as follows:

1. The PIM routers on the multiaccess network send Hello messages to one another. The Hello messages contain the DR Priority (i.e., PIM Option 19) for the DR election. The router with the highest DR Priority value is elected as the DR.
2. The PIM router with the highest IP address is elected the DR under one of following conditions:
   - All the PIM routers have the same DR Priority.
   - A PIM router does not support carrying the DR Priority Option in PIM Hello messages.

If the elected DR fails, its PIM neighbor lifetime (also known as the Neighbor Liveness Timer) expires and the other routers will initiate the election of a new DR.

FIGURE 5.3 PIM Designated Router and election process.

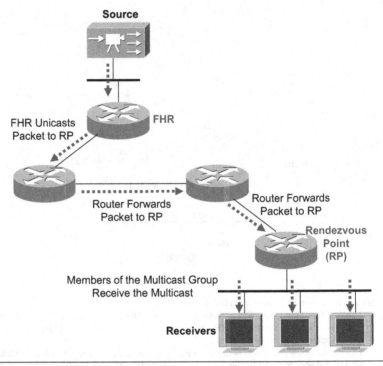

- PIM-SM uses shared trees. In a shared tree, a source forwards multicast packets destined to a multicast group to a directly connected router called the First-Hop Router (FHR). On a multiaccess network with multiple PIM routers, one router is selected as the designated router (DR) and plays the role of the FHR.
- The FHR encapsulates the source's multicast packets in PIM Register messages and unicasts them to an assigned RP router, which then forwards the packets to members of the multicast group.
- In PIM-SM, the RP announces a source and provides shared tree paths from the source to members of a multicast group before any multicast packets are sent natively to group members.
- The LHR transmits Join messages to the RP to become part of the shared tree that enables distribution of packets to the multicast group members.
- A host's LHR sends Join messages to the RP when the host wants to join a group.
- When a host wants to leave a group, it communicates with its LHR through IGMP. When the LHR no longer has any hosts that belong to a particular group, it sends a Prune message to the RP.
- If a PIM-SM router does not receive information from a PIM neighbor or host within a specific time (i.e., the Hold Time), it removes the associated information from its multicast routing tables.

FIGURE 5.4   PIM-SM operation.

- **Neighbor.tracking_support**: This is a flag that stores the value of the T bit in the LAN Prune Delay Option if it is included in the PIM neighbor's Hello message. This flag indicates if the PIM neighbor can disable PIM Join message suppression (see T bit in Chapter 3).
- **Neighbor.propagation_delay**: This stores the Propagation Delay field value in the LAN Prune Delay Option if included in the PIM neighbor's Hello message. The value inserted by a PIM router in the Propagation Delay field of the LAN Prune Delay Option indicates the expected message propagation delay on the interface. This value should be configurable by the network administrator. Upstream PIM routers use this to determine how long to wait before receiving a PIM Join override message before pruning an interface. A PIM implementation should allow the network administrator to enforce a lower bound on the permitted values for the Propagation delay to account for scheduling and processing delays within the PIM router. Failure to account for such delays may cause a PIM router to process received messages later as well as send triggered messages later than intended. Setting the Propagation Delay too small may cause temporary outages in multicast packet forwarding because a downstream PIM router will not be able to send a PIM Join message to override a Prune message sent by a PIM neighbor before the upstream PIM neighbor stops multicast packet forwarding. When all PIM routers on an interface are capable of negotiating a Propagation Delay value different from the default value, they should choose the largest value among those advertised by each PIM neighbor.
- **Neighbor.override_interval**: This stores the Override_Interval field value in the LAN Prune Delay Option if included in the PIM neighbor's Hello message. To prevent synchronization of override Join messages when multiple downstream PIM routers exist on a multiaccess network segment like an Ethernet LAN, each router delays the sending of such messages by a small randomly selected delay. The length of the small random delay should reflect the total number of PIM routers on the interface. Each PIM router on the interface indicates its view of the amount of random delay necessary on the network segment in the Override Interval field of the Hello message's LAN Prune Delay Option. When all PIM routers on an interface are capable of negotiating an Override Interval that is different from the default value, they should choose the largest value among those advertised by each PIM neighbor.

The PIM router deletes this additional state along with the DR neighbor state when the PIM *neighbor.timeout* expires. Similar to the DR Priority Option, the PIM router does not use the information provided in the LAN Prune Delay Option unless all PIM neighbors on an interface (i.e., network segment) advertise this Option.

Although not specified in the PIM-SM specification, it is possible for a PIM-SM implementation to include mechanisms that would allow upstream PIM routers to explicitly track the join membership of individual downstream PIM routers if they are allowed to send Join messages (i.e., Join suppression is disabled). A PIM router uses the T bit of the LAN Prune Delay Option in Hello messages to advertise its desire to disable Join suppression. Unless all PIM routers on an interface negotiate this capability, it is not possible to explicitly track and disable the Join suppression mechanism.

5.6.4 MAINTAINING SECONDARY IP ADDRESS LISTS

As discussed in Chapter 3, a PIM router must communicate the secondary IP addresses of its interfaces to PIM neighbors. This is to provide them with a mechanism for mapping the next-hop information in their MRIBs to a primary IP address that can then be used as the destination IP address of PIM Join/Prune messages. A PIM router obtains the primary IP address of a neighbor from the source IP address used in the neighbor's PIM Hello messages. The router obtains the secondary IP addresses from the Address List Option of the Hello message. The router must not include the primary IP address of the sending interface within the Hello message's Address List Option, only secondary addresses can be listed.

In addition to the information a PIM router maintains for the DR election process, it records the following per-PIM neighbor information taken from the neighbor's Hello message Address List Option:

- **Neighbor.secondary_address_list**: This is a list of secondary IP addresses advertised by the PIM neighbor on the PIM interface where the Hello message was transmitted.

5.7 PIM REGISTER MESSAGES

The DR of a multicast traffic source (i.e., source-side DR) sends a PIM Register message containing multicast data packets to the RP when multicast data packets need to be transmitted on the RPT. The DR sets the IP source address of the PIM Register message to the address of the DR's sending interface and the destination address to the RP's address. The IP TTL of the IP packet carrying the PIM Register message is the system's normal unicast IP TTL.

The source-side DR on a multiaccess network segment or point-to-point link is responsible for encapsulating multicast packets from local sources for the relevant multicast groups and unicasting them in PIM Register messages to the RP, unless the DR has recently received a PIM Register-Stop message for that (S, G) or (*, G) from the RP. When the source-side DR or FHR receives a PIM Register-Stop message from the RP, it starts an (S, G) Register-Stop Timer which it uses to maintain this state. Right before the expiry of the (S, G) Register-Stop Timer, the DR sends a PIM (S, G) Null-Register message to the RP which causes it to refresh the Register-Stop information it has maintained about the DR for the (S, G) pair. However, if the (S, G) Register-Stop Timer running at the DR expires, the DR will resume encapsulating multicast packets from the source into PIM Register messages and unicasting them to the RP.

5.7.1 Sending PIM Register Messages from the DR

Every PIM-SM router, whether on a multiaccess LAN or point-to-point links, has the capability of being elected as a DR for that network segment. PIM-SM routers use the state machine described in Figure 5.5 for implementing the PIM Register functionality. The PIM-SM specification [RFC7761] represents the mechanism for encapsulating multicast packets in Register messages to be sent to the RP as a Register-Tunnel interface, which the source-side DR adds to or removes from the OIL of the (S, G) state.

If the source-side DR maintains a Register state, it does so only for directly connected multicast sources, and this state is per-(S, G). The source-side DR maintains the following four states in the Per-(S, G) Register state machine:

- **Join**: In this state, the Register-Tunnel has "joined" the RP (i.e., linked the RP to the source-side DR). The "join" action is implicit, but one can view this action as the RP joining the DR on the Register-Tunnel interface.
- **Prune**: In this state, the source-side DR has "pruned" the Register-Tunnel, which occurs when the DR has received a PIM Register-Stop message from the RP.
- **Join-Pending**: In this state, the source-side DR has pruned the Register-Tunnel but is contemplating adding it back.
- **NoInfo (No information)**: This is the initial state of the Per-(S, G) Register state machine, and when the PIM router has not been elected the DR.

In addition to the above, the DR maintains an (S, G) Register-Stop Timer if the Register state machine is not in the NoInfo state. The *Register_Suppression_Time* of the (S, G) Register-Stop Timer (with a default value of 60 seconds) is the time interval during which the DR *stops* sending PIM Register messages containing (S, G) multicast packets to the RP after receiving a PIM Register-Stop message from the RP. The *Register_Probe_Time* of the (S, G) Register-Stop Timer (with a default value of 5 seconds) is the period before the (S, G) Register-Stop Timer expires, when the source-side DR may send a PIM (S, G) Null- Register message to the RP to cause it to possibly resend a PIM (S, G) Register-Stop message.

Note that upon receiving a multicast packet from a directly connected source, the source-side DR needs to set the Keepalive Timer (S, G) according to the packet forwarding rules before computing CouldRegister (S, G) in the (S, G) Register state machine. Otherwise, the first multicast packet from the source would not be registered (i.e., sent via a PIM Register message).

The source-side DR decrements the IP time-to-live (TTL) of a multicast packet from a source before encapsulating it in a PIM Register message to be forwarded on the Register-Tunnel. The encapsulating PIM Register message uses the normal TTL that the source-side DR would use for any locally generated IP packet. The DR should copy the IP Explicit Congestion Notification (ECN) bits from the original multicast packet to the IP header of the encapsulating Register message. The DR should not independently set the ECN bits in the PIM Register message. Furthermore, the DR should copy the Diffserv Code Point (DSCP) from the original multicast packet to the IP header of the encapsulating PIM Register message. The DR may independently set the DSCP based on static configuration or traffic classification.

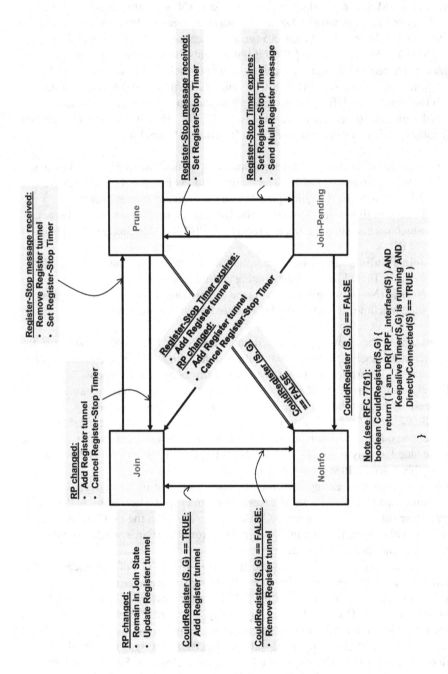

FIGURE 5.5   Per-(S, G) Register state machine at a Designated Router.

5.7.2 RECEIVING REGISTER MESSAGES AT THE RP

The RP restarts the Keepalive Timer (S, G) when multicast packets from the source-side DR arrive on the proper Register-Tunnel interface, and the RP wants to switch to the (S, G) SPT, or the SPTbit is already set. This may cause the Upstream (S, G) state machine (see the subsequent discussion) to send a PIM (S, G) Join to the DR if the inherited_olist (S, G) is not NULL. The inherited_olist (S, G) is the OIL that a PIM router uses for multicast packet forwarding from source S to group G using both source-specific and group-specific states [RFC7761].

The RP should preserve the (S, G) state that it created upon receiving a PIM Register message from the source-side DR for a time period of at least ($3 \times Register\_Suppression\_Time$). Otherwise, the RP may stop sending a PIM (S, G) Join before the source-side DR for the (S, G) pair has restarted sending PIM Register messages. Multicast traffic from source S to group G would then be interrupted until the (S, G) Register-Stop Timer at the DR expires. Thus, the RP should restart the Keepalive Timer (S, G) to ($3 \times Register\_Suppression\_Time + Register\_Probe\_Time$).

When the RP forwards multicast packets received from the Register-Tunnel, it decrements the TTL of the original multicast data packet after it is decapsulated from the PIM Register message. The RP copies the IP ECN bits from the IP header of the PIM Register message to the decapsulated multicast packet. Additionally, the RP should copy the DSCP from the IP header of the PIM Register message to the decapsulated multicast packet. The DSCP of the inner multicast packet may be retained by the RP, or the RP may re-classify the packet and apply a different DSCP.

5.8 PROCESSING PIM JOIN/PRUNE MESSAGES

A PIM router sends a PIM Join message toward upstream sources to build source trees (SPT) and toward RPs to build shared trees (RPTs). The router sends a PIM Prune message to upstream sources to prune SPTs when receivers leave multicast groups as well as when sources stop using the RPT to send multicast packets.

As described in Chapter 3, the contents of a PIM Join/Prune message include a list of multicast groups as well as a list of *Joined* and *Pruned* multicast sources for each group. When a PIM router processes a received PIM Join/Prune message, it considers each Joined or Pruned source for a listed group as effectively individual entries, and each of such sources (for a group) applies to one or more of the following state machines:

- When the router is processing a received PIM Join/Prune message with the Upstream Neighbor Address field containing the router's own address, then the (*, G) Joins and Prunes can affect both the (*, G) and (S, G, rpt) Downstream state machines in the router, while the (S, G) and (S, G, rpt) Joins and Prunes can only affect in the router itself, their respective Downstream state machines.
- When the router is processing a received PIM Join/Prune message with the Upstream Neighbor Address field containing the address of another PIM router, a majority of the Join or Prune messages could affect each Upstream state machine in the router itself.

In general, a PIM router should only accept a PIM Join/Prune message for processing if it is received from a known PIM neighbor. Recall that a PIM router discovers PIM neighbors through PIM Hello messages. If a PIM router receives a PIM Join/Prune message from another router with a particular IP source address and the router has not received a PIM Hello message associated with that IP source address, then the router should discard that PIM Join/Prune message without further processing. In addition, if the router receives a PIM Hello message from a PIM neighbor that was authenticated, then the router must authenticate all PIM Join/Prune messages from that neighbor.

5.8.1 Multicast Group Set Source List Rules for PIM Join/Prune Messages

As discussed in Chapter 3, a PIM Join/Prune message may contain one or more multicast group sets, each set containing two multicast traffic source lists, the *Joined Sources list,* and the *Pruned Sources list*. The different types of multicast *Group Sets* and Source List entries that can be carried in a PIM Join/Prune message are described in this section. PIM specifies only one valid Group Set type, the *Group-Specific Set.*

5.8.1.1 Group-Specific Set

A PIM router creates a *Group-Specific Set* by writing a valid IP multicast address in the Multicast Group Address field of the PIM Join/Prune message, and the mask length of the IP multicast address in the Mask Length field of the encoded Multicast Group Address (see Figure 3.5: Encoded multicast group address format in Chapter 3). Each PIM Join/Prune message that a PIM router builds should not carry more than one Group-Specific Set for the same IP multicast address. Each Group-Specific Set in a PIM Join/Prune message being constructed may contain (*, G), (S, G, rpt), and (S, G) Source List entries in the Joined Sources list or the Pruned Sources list portion of the message (see Figure 3.9: Join/Prune message format in Chapter 3).

- **(*, G) Source List Entry**: A PIM router adds this entry to a PIM Join/Prune message when it sends the message towards the RP for the specified multicast group (G) to express its interest (or lack thereof) in receiving multicast packets destined for multicast group G through the RPT. Only one *(*, G) Source List entry* must be carried in both the Joined Sources and Pruned Sources list portions of a Group-Specific Set.

  Each (*, G) Source List entry has its Source Address field set to the IP address of the RP for multicast group G, the Mask Length field of the encoded Source Address (see Figure 3.6: Encoded source address format in Chapter 3) set to the full length of the IP multicast address G, and both the W (i.e., WildCard) bit and the R (i.e., RPT) bit of the Encoded Source Address set (to 1).

- **(S, G, rpt) Source List Entry**: A PIM router adds this entry to a PIM Join/Prune message when it sends the message towards the RP for the specified group (G) to express its interest (or lack thereof) in receiving multicast packets through the RPT sent by the specified source S to group G. For each IP source address, the *(S, G, rpt) Source List entry* must be carried in only one of the Joined Sources lists and Pruned Sources list portions of a Group-Specific Set, not both.

Each (S, G, rpt) Source List entry has its Source Address field set to the IP address of the multicast traffic source S, the Mask Length field of the encoded Source Address set to the full length of the IP source address S, and the WC bit cleared (i.e., set to 0) and the RPT bit set (to 1) in the Encoded Source Address.

- **(S, G) Source List Entry**: A PIM router adds this entry to a PIM Join/Prune message when it sends the message towards the specified source (S) to express its interest (or lack thereof) in receiving multicast packets through the SPT destined for the source S to the specified group G. For each IP source address, the *(S, G) Source List entry* must be carried in only one of the Joined Sources lists and Pruned source lists of a Group-Specific Set, not both.
- Each (S, G) Source List entry has its Source Address field set to the IP address of the multicast traffic source S, the Mask Length field of the encoded Source Address set to the full length of the IP source address S, and both the WC and RPT bits of the Encoded Source Address cleared (i.e., set to 0).

The above rules are sufficient to prevent a PIM router from combining invalid Source List entries in Group-Specific Sets. However, PIM allows several combinations that have a valid interpretation [RFC7761]:

- Combining a (*, G) Join entry and an (S, G, rpt) Join entry in the same Join/Prune message is redundant because the (*, G) entry already provides the information supplied by the (S, G, rpt) entry. The same applies to a (*, G) Prune entry and an (S, G, rpt) Prune entry.
- A PIM router also does not generate a combination of a (*, G) Prune entry and an (S, G, rpt) Join entry in the same PIM Join/Prune message. A PIM router only sends (S, G, rpt) Joins when it is receiving all traffic for a multicast group on the RPT and wishes to indicate a change for the particular source. Since sending a (*, G) Prune indicates that the router no longer wishes to receive traffic from the RPT, sending the (S, G, rpt) Join would be meaningless.
- As the PIM Join/Prune message a PIM router sends is targeted to a single PIM neighbor, including both an (S, G) Join entry and an (S, G, rpt) Prune entry in the same message is usually redundant. The router uses the (S, G) Join to inform the neighbor that it wishes to receive traffic from the particular source on the SPT. It is, therefore, unnecessary for the router to send an (S, G, rpt) Prune to indicate that it no longer wishes to receive that traffic on the RPT. However, a valid interpretation exists for this combination of (S, G) Join entry and (S, G, rpt) Prune entries in the same message. A downstream PIM router may need to inform its upstream PIM neighbor only to start forwarding multicast traffic from a specific source once the neighbor has started receiving traffic from that source on the SPT.
- A PIM router could use the combination of an (S, G) Prune entry and an (S, G, rpt) Join entry in the same message to switch from receiving multicast traffic from a particular source on the SPT back to receiving that traffic on the RPT (provided that the RPF neighbor for the SPT and RPT is the same). However, the PIM-SM specification [RFC7761] does not specify a mechanism for explicitly switching back to the RPT.

5.8.2 MULTICAST GROUP SET FRAGMENTATION IN PIM JOIN/PRUNE MESSAGES

When a PIM router is in the process of building a PIM Join/Prune to be sent to a particular PIM neighbor, it should try to include as much of the information it needs to be sent to the PIM neighbor in the message. This implies that the router should add one Group Set for each multicast group with pending information to be transmitted to the neighbor and include within each Group Set all relevant Source List entries.

If the PIM router has a large amount of multicast state, the number of entries that it must include may result in the PIM Join/Prune message being larger than the maximum allowed IP packet size. In most such cases, the router may split the entries and place them in multiple PIM Join/Prune messages.

However, there is an exception when the router is dealing with Group Sets that contain a (*, G) Joined Source List entry. The router sends this Group Set with (*, G) entry to express its interest in receiving all traffic on the RPT destined for the specified group, and the Group Set must include an (S, G, rpt) Pruned Source List entry for every multicast source that the router does not wish to receive traffic from. The router must not split this list of (S, G, rpt) Pruned Source List entries into multiple PIM Join/Prune messages.

If the PIM router determines that only N (S, G, rpt) Prune entries will fit into a maximum-sized PIM Join/Prune message, but it has more than N (S, G, rpt) Prune entries to add to the message, then it must include the first N IP addresses (numerically smallest in network byte order) and ignore the rest of the entries (i.e., not included them in the message).

5.8.3 RECEIVING (*, G) JOIN/PRUNE MESSAGES

When a PIM router receives a PIM Join (*, G) message, it must first verify if the RP in the message matches the router's idea of which RP is associated with group G, that is, RP(G). If the router detects that the RP in the message does not match RP(G), then it should silently discard the PIM Join (*, G). However, the router should still process other source list entries in the message, such as (S, G, rpt) or (S, G) in the same Group-Specific Set. If no RP information for group G is available in the router (e.g., the router has not recently received a BSR message), then the router may elect to accept the PIM Join (*, G) message and treat the RP in the message as RP(G). The router processes received PIM Prune (*, G) messages even if the RP in the message does not match RP(G).

The PIM router maintains the Downstream Per-Interface (*, G) state machine for receiving PIM (*, G) Join/Prune messages, as shown in Figure 5.6. The following three states are maintained for the state machine for a PIM interface:

- **NoInfo**: In this state, the interface has no (*, G) Join state and has no timers running.
- **Join**: In this state, the interface has (*, G) Join state, causing the router to forward multicast packets addressed to group G on the interface, except if the interface also has (S, G, rpt) Prune information, or the router lost a PIM Assert process on the interface.
- **Prune-Pending**: In this state, the router has received a PIM Prune (*, G) message on the interface from a downstream PIM neighbor and is waiting to see whether the (*, G) Prune message will be overridden by a (*, G) Join message sent by another downstream PIM router. In regards to multicast packet forwarding, the Prune-Pending state and the Join state function the same way.

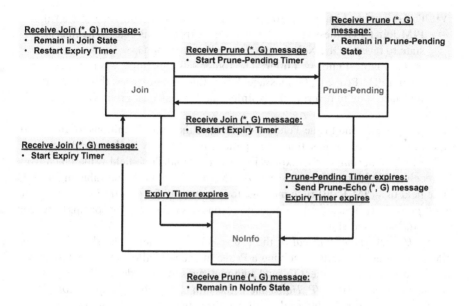

FIGURE 5.6 Downstream Per-Interface (*, G) state machine.

In the state machine in Figure 5.6, the transition events, "Receive Join (*, G) message" and "Receive Prune (*, G) message", imply PIM Join and Prune (*, G) messages are received on an interface with the Upstream Neighbor Address fields of the messages set to the router's primary IP address on the interface. If the Upstream Neighbor Address field contains an incorrect address, then the state transitions associated with receiving these messages in this state machine must not occur, although receiving such messages may cause state transitions in other state machines in the router.

For an unnumbered IP interface on a point-to-point link, the router's IP address should be the same as the source IP address that the router uses in the source address field of PIM Hello messages sent over that unnumbered interface. However, to allow for backward compatibility (with the old PIM-SM specification) on point-to-point links, it is recommended that the PIM router also accepts PIM Join/Prune messages with an Upstream Neighbor Address field of all zeros.

The "Send PruneEcho (*, G) message" action in the state machine, as illustrated in Figure 5.6, is triggered when the PIM router stops multicast data packet forwarding on an interface because of receiving a PIM Prune (*, G) message on that interface. A PruneEcho (*, G) represents a PIM Prune (*, G) message that an upstream PIM router sends on a multiaccess network segment (LAN) with its own IP address in the message's Upstream Neighbor Address field. The purpose of a PruneEcho (*, G) message is to provide additional reliability so that, in the event a PIM Prune (*, G) message, which should have been overridden by another PIM router (through a Join (*, G)), is lost locally on the multiaccess network segment, then the PruneEcho (*, G) message may be received and cause the Prune (*, G) override to happen. A PIM router does not need to send a PruneEcho (*, G) message on an interface that has only a single PIM neighbor during the time the Per-Interface (*, G) state machine is in the Prune-Pending state.

In addition, the router maintains two timers for the state machine:

- **(*, G) Expiry Timer**: The router restarts this timer when it receives a valid PIM Join (*, G) message. When this timer expires, this causes the interface state to revert to the NoInfo state for multicast group G.
- **(*, G) Prune-Pending Timer**: The router sets this timer when it receives a valid PIM Prune (*, G) message. When this timer expires, this causes the interface state to revert to the NoInfo state for multicast group G.

The Expiry Timer and Prune-Pending Timer have the same definitions for the (*, G), (S, G), and (S, G, rpt) states, thus, their parameters will only be described here.

The *J/P_HoldTime* of the Expiry Timer is the Hold Time field value taken from the received PIM Join/Prune message. A PIM router should set the value in the Hold Time field in a PIM Join/Prune message to be sent to ($3.5 \times t\_periodic$). The parameter *t_periodic* (with a default value of 60 seconds) is the period (or spacing) between PIM Join/Prune messages.

The *J/P_Override_Interval* of the Prune-Pending Timer is the short period the PIM router must wait after receiving a Prune message to allow other routers on the multiaccess network segment to send Join messages to override the Prune message. The default value of the *J/P_HoldTime* is the sum of *Effective_Propagation_Delay* and *Effective_Override_Interval*. Note that these two parameters are interface-specific values that may change when the PIM router receives Hello messages.

5.8.4 Receiving (S, G) Join/Prune Messages

A PIM-SM router also maintains a Downstream Per-Interface (S, G) state machine for receiving PIM (S, G) Join/Prune messages on an interface, as illustrated in Figure 5.7. This state machine is almost identical to the Downstream Per-Interface (*, G)

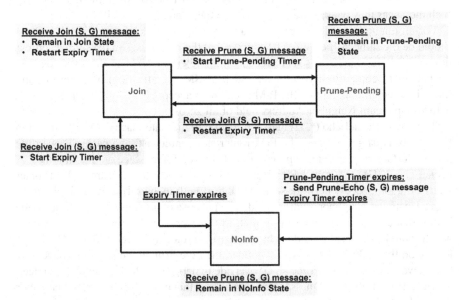

FIGURE 5.7   Downstream Per-Interface (S, G) state machine.

state machine for receiving (*, G) Join/Prune messages as discussed above. This state machine has the following three states:

- **NoInfo**: In this state, the interface has no (S, G) Join state and has no timers running as well.
- **Join**: In this state, the interface has (S, G) Join state, causing the router to forward multicast packets from source S to group G on the interface if the (S, G) state is active (the SPTbit is set), except if the router lost a PIM Assert process on the interface.
- **Prune-Pending**: In this state, the router has received a PIM Prune (S, G) message on the interface from a downstream PIM neighbor and is waiting to see whether the (S, G) Prune message will be overridden by a (S, G) Join message sent by another downstream PIM router. In regards to multicast packet forwarding, the Prune-Pending state and the Join state function the same way.

In addition, the router maintains two timers for the state machine:

- **(S, G) Expiry Timer**: The router sets this timer when it receives a valid PIM Join (S, G) message. When this timer expires, this causes the state machine to revert to the NoInfo state for the (S, G) pair.
- **(S, G) Prune-Pending Timer**: The router sets this timer when it receives a valid PIM Prune (S, G) message. When this timer expires, this causes the state machine to revert to the NoInfo state for the (S, G) pair.

The preceding discussion about the Downstream Per-Interface (*, G) state machine, which covers receiving Join and Prune (S, G) messages on an interface with the Upstream Neighbor Address fields of the messages set to the router's primary IP address on the interface, unnumbered IP interfaces on point-to-point links, the "Send PruneEcho (S, G)" action in the state machine, and the parameters of the two state machine timers, also applies here and will not be repeated.

5.8.5   RECEIVING (S, G, RPT) JOIN/PRUNE MESSAGES

The PIM-SM router maintains a Downstream Per-Interface (S, G, rpt) state machine for receiving (S, G, rpt) Join/Prune messages on an interface, as shown in Figure 5.8. This state machine has the following five states:

- **NoInfo**: In this state, the interface has no (S, G, rpt) Prune state and has no (S, G, rpt) timers running.
- **Prune**: In this state, the interface has (S, G, rpt) Prune state, causing the router not to forward multicast packets from source S addressed to group G on the interface even though the interface has an active (*, G) Join state.
- **Prune-Pending**: In this state, the router has received a Prune (S, G, rpt) message on the interface from a downstream PIM neighbor and is waiting to see whether another downstream PIM router will send a Join (S, G, rpt) message to override the Prune (S, G, rpt) message. In regards to multicast packet forwarding, the Prune-Pending state and the NoInfo state function the same way.

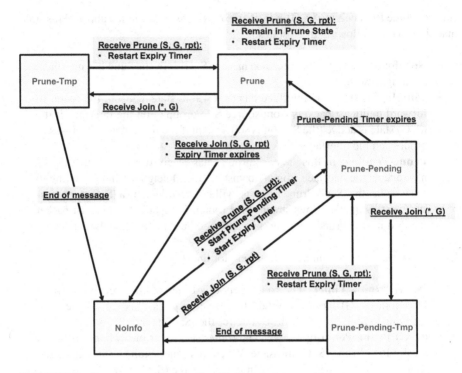

FIGURE 5.8 Downstream Per-Interface (S, G, rpt) state machine.

- **PruneTmp**: This is a transient state that, in regards to multicast packet forwarding purposes, behaves exactly like the Prune state. In this state, the router has received a PIM (*, G) Join message, which may cancel, that is, override the (S, G, rpt) Prune message. As the router parses the PIM Join/Prune message from top to bottom, it first enters the PruneTmp state if the message contains a (*, G) Join entry. As the router continues to parse the message, it will normally encounter an (S, G, rpt) Prune entry, which will cause it to reinstate the Prune state. However, if the router reaches the end of the message without encountering such an (S, G, rpt) Prune entry, it will revert to the NoInfo state in the state machine. As the state machine does not spend time in this state, no timers can expire.
- **Prune-Pending-Tmp**: This is also a transient state that is identical to the PruneTmp state except that it is associated with the Prune-Pending state rather than the Prune state. For multicast packet forwarding purposes, the Prune-Pending-Tmp state behaves exactly like the Prune-Pending state.

In addition, the router maintains two timers for this state machine:

- **(S, G, rpt) Expiry Timer**: The router sets this timer when it receives a valid Prune (S, G, rpt) message. When this timer expires, this causes the state machine to revert to the NoInfo state.

- **(S, G, rpt) Prune-Pending Timer**: The router sets this timer when it receives a valid Prune (S, G, rpt) message. When this timer expires, this causes the state machine to move to the Prune state.

The transition event "End of Message" in the state machine, means the end of the compound Join/Prune message has been reached. The transition events, "Receive Join (S, G, rpt)", "Receive Prune (S, G, rpt)", and "Receive Join (*, G)", imply that PIM Join or Prune messages are received on an interface with the Upstream Neighbor Address fields of the messages set to the router's primary IP address on the interface. If the Upstream Neighbor Address field contains an incorrect address, then the state transitions associated with receiving these messages in this state machine must not occur, although receiving such messages may cause state transitions in other state machines in the router.

The preceding discussion about the Downstream Per-Interface (*, G) state machine, which covers about unnumbered IP interfaces on point-to-point links, and the parameters of the two state machine timers, also applies here and will not be repeated.

5.8.6 Sending (*, G) Join/Prune Messages

The Downstream per-interface (*, G) state machines (discussed earlier) on a PIM router hold (*, G) Join state from downstream PIM routers. The router uses this Join state to determine whether it needs to propagate a received PIM Join (*, G) message upstream toward the RP.

If a PIM router on a multiaccess network segment needs to propagate a PIM Join (*, G) message upstream, it must also look out for messages from other routers on its upstream interface on that network segment, and these messages may modify the router's behavior.

- If the router notices a PIM Join (*, G) message also sent to the correct upstream PIM neighbor, it should suppress sending its own Join (*, G) message.
- If the router observes a PIM Prune (*, G) message also sent to the correct upstream PIM neighbor, it should be ready to override that Prune message by sending a Join (*, G) message quickly.
- If the router notices that the Generation ID of the correct upstream PIM neighbor has changed, then this indicates that the upstream neighbor has lost state, and the router should be ready to refresh the state by sending a PIM Join (*, G) message almost immediately.
- If a PIM (*, G) Assert process takes place on the router's upstream interface, and this changes the router's view of the upstream PIM neighbor, the router should be ready to inform the Assert Winner of downstream PIM routers by sending a PIM Join (*, G) message almost immediately.
- Furthermore, if the router's MRIB changes to indicate that the next-hop PIM router toward the RP has changed, and either the upstream interface toward the RP has changed or there is no Assert Winner on the upstream interface, the router should switch from the old next-hop router and use the new next-hop to join toward the RP.

A PIM router maintains an Upstream (*, G) state machine that contains the following two states (see Figure 5.9):

- **NotJoined**: This state indicates that the PIM router does not need to send a PIM (*, G) Join toward the RP for multicast group G (i.e., should not join the RPT).
- **Joined**: This state indicates that the PIM router should send a PIM (*, G) Join toward the RP for group G (i.e., should join the RPT).

In Figure 5.9, RPF (*, G) is the RPF neighbor as modified by the PIM Assert process. The router also maintains a single timer, the (*, G) Upstream Join Timer, that it uses to trigger the sending of PIM Join (*, G) messages to the upstream next-hop toward the RP (i.e., the RPF (*, G) as modified by the Assert process). The *t_periodic* of this timer (with a default value of 60 seconds) is the time interval between PIM Join/Prune messages.

The *t_suppressed* of this timer is the period the router must suppress sending a PIM Join message to see if another PIM router will send a Join/Prune message. The parameter *t_suppressed* depends on the upstream interface's Suppression State ("Enable", "Disable") and is zero when suppression is disabled on the interface. The default value

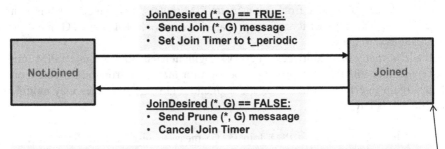

JoinDesired (*, G) == TRUE:
- **Send Join (*, G) message**
- **Set Join Timer to t_periodic**

NotJoined   Joined

JoinDesired (*, G) == FALSE:
- **Send Prune (*, G) messaage**
- **Cancel Join Timer**

Note:
- **JoinDesired (*, G) is TRUE when the router has a forwarding state that would cause it to forward traffic for group G using the shared tree state.**
- **Note that although JoinDesired is TRUE, the router may suppress sending a Join (*, G) message because another router has sent a Join (*, G) onto the upstream interface.**

The following transitions occur within the Joined state:
- **Timer expires: Send Join (*, G) message; Set Join Timer to t_periodic**
- **See Join (*, G) message to RPF (*, G): Increase Join Timer to t_joinsuppress**
- **See Prune (*, G) message to RPF (*, G): Decrease Join Timer to t_override**
- **RPF (*, G) interface changes due to an Assert: Decrease Join Timer to t_override**
- **RPF (*, G) interface changes not due to an Assert: Send Join (*, G) message to new next-hop; Send Prune (*, G) message to old next-hop; Set Join Timer to t_periodic**
- **RPF (*, G) Generation ID changes: Decrease Join Timer to t_override**

FIGURE 5.9   Upstream (*, G) state machine.

of *t_suppressed* is a random value between $(1.1 \times t\_periodic)$ and $(1.4 \times t\_periodic)$ when suppression is enabled on the interface, otherwise, the value is 0.

The *t_override* of the (*, G) Upstream Join Timer is the random delay a PIM router must wait before sending a PIM Join message to prevent response implosion when multiple routers on the multiaccess network segment send Join messages to override a Prune message. The default value of this parameter is a random value between 0 and *Effective_Override_Interval*. The *t_override* on an interface depends on the Effective Override Interval indicated by the upstream interface, which is communicated in the LAN Prune Delay Option in PIM Hello messages (as discussed in Chapter 3). The *t_override* on an interface may change when Hello messages are received.

5.8.7 SENDING (S, G) JOIN/PRUNE MESSAGES

The PIM router also maintains Upstream per-interface (S, G) state machines that hold the Join state from downstream PIM routers. The router uses this Join state to determine whether it needs to propagate a Join (S, G) upstream toward the multicast traffic source S for group G. The PIM requirements for this state machine are similar to those for the Upstream Per-Interface (S*, G) state machine discussed earlier and so will not be repeated here.

A PIM router maintains an Upstream (S, G) state machine that contains the following two states (see Figure 5.10):

* **NotJoined**: In this state, the Downstream state machines of the router and its local host membership information (obtained via IGMP Membership Report messages) do not indicate that the router needs to join the SPT for the (S, G) pair.
* **Joined**: In this state, the Downstream state machines of the router and its local host membership information indicate that the router should join the SPT for the (S, G) pair.

In the figure, RPF (S, G) is the RPF neighbor as modified by the PIM Assert process. In addition, the router maintains one timer, the (S, G) Upstream Join Timer, that it uses to trigger the sending of PIM Join (S, G) messages to the upstream next-hop toward the multicast source S, (i.e., RPF (S, G) as modified by the PIM Assert process). The parameters of this timer are similar to those defined for the (*, G) Upstream Join Timer, and, thus, they will not be repeated here (*t_periodic*, *t_suppressed*, and *t_override*).

5.8.8 (S, G, RPT) PERIODIC MESSAGES

The (S, G, rpt) Join and Prune messages that a PIM router sends are simply (S, G) Join or Prune messages sent on the RPT with the RPT bit set, either to modify the results of PIM (*, G) Joins that were already sent on the RPT or to override the behavior of other upstream PIM peers on the multiaccess network segment.

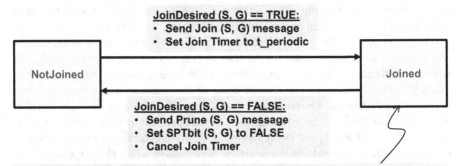

The following transitions occur within the Joined state:
- **Timer expires**: Send Join (S, G) message; Set Join Timer to t_periodic
- **See Join (S, G) message to RPF (S, G)**: Increase Join Timer to t_joinsuppress
- **See Prune (S, G) message to RPF (S, G)**: Decrease Join Timer to t_override
- **See Prune (S, G, rpt) message to RPF (S, G)**: Decrease Join Timer to t_override
- **See Prune (*, G) message to RPF (S, G)**: Decrease Join Timer to t_override
- **RPF (S, G) interface changes due to an Assert**: Decrease Join Timer to t_override
- **RPF (S, G) interface changes not due to an Assert**: Send Join (S, G) message to new next-hop; Send Prune (S, G) message to old next-hop; Set Join Timer to t_periodic
- **RPF (S, G) Generation ID changes**: Decrease Join Timer to t_override

Note:
- JoinDesired (S, G) is TRUE when the router has a forwarding state, causing it to forward traffic for group G using the source tree state.
- The source tree state can be as a result of either active source-specific Join state or the (S, G) Keepalive Timer and active non -source-specific state.
- Note that although JoinDesired is TRUE, the router may suppress sending a Join (S, G) message because another router has sent a Join (S, G) onto the upstream interface.

FIGURE 5.10   Upstream (S, G) state machine.

Section 4.5.6 of [RFC7761] describes the rules that a PIM router uses to include a Prune (S, G, rpt) message in a Join (*, G) message. When a PIM router is about to send a PIM Join (*, G) message toward the RP, it applies the rules described in pseudocode in [RFC7761], for each (S, G) pair for which it has a state, to determine whether to include a Prune (S, G, rpt) entry in the compound Join/Prune message to be sent.

It should be noted that a Join (S, G, rpt) message is not normally sent as a periodic message but only as an (S, G, rpt) triggered message.

5.8.9 State Machine for (S, G, rpt) Triggered Messages

The next section describes the rules that a PIM router applies for sending (S, G, rpt) triggered messages. A PIM router maintains an Upstream state machine for (S, G, rpt) triggered messages and for each (S, G) pair, when it has created a (*, G) Join state and the router itself or any of its upstream peers on the multiaccess LAN wishes to prune the multicast source S off the RPT.

This state machine has three states, one of which is when the router has no (*, G) Join state. If the router has (*, G) Join state, then the state machine must be in one of the other two states. The three states are as follows (Figure 5.11):

- **Pruned (S, G, rpt)**: This state indicates that the router has (*, G) Join state, but (S, G, rpt) HAS been pruned.
- **NotPruned (S, G, rpt)**: This state indicates that the router has (*, G) Join state, and (S, G, rpt) has NOT been pruned.
- **RPTNotJoined (G)**: This state indicates that the router has NO (*, G) Join state.

In the figure, RPF (*, G), RFP (S, G), and RPF (S, G, rpt) each imply the RPF neighbor as modified by the PIM Assert process. In addition, the PIM router maintains an (S, G, rpt) Upstream Override Timer, which is used to delay the sending of triggered Join (S, G, rpt) messages to prevent triggered messages implosions on a multiaccess network segment. The router uses this timer only to set the *t_override* value already described above.

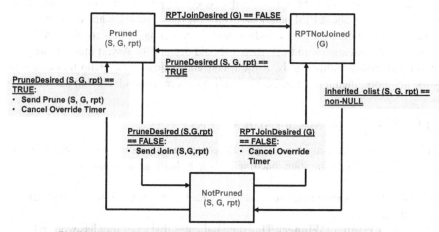

FIGURE 5.11   Upstream (S, G, rpt) state machine for triggered messages.

5.9 PROCESSING PIM ASSERT MESSAGES

In the case where multiple PIM routers peer over a multiaccess network segment like an Ethernet LAN, more than one upstream PIM router could have a valid multicast forwarding state for a packet, leading to packet duplication on the LAN. The PIM protocol does not provide mechanisms for specifically preventing duplicate packets from appearing on the LAN.

Instead, PIM upstream routers detect the presence of duplicate packets on the LAN and then elect a single *forwarder* among them for the LAN to prevent further multicast packet duplication on the LAN. The routers elect the *forwarder* using PIM Assert messages, as described in Chapter 3. PIM employs Assert messages to resolve forwarder conflicts between routers on a multiaccess LAN. A PIM router sends an Assert message when it receives a multicast data packet on the interface it would normally use to forward that packet.

The router may also send a PIM Assert message in response to an Assert message sent by another router on the LAN. The Assert messages that are exchanged on the LAN are also received by downstream routers on the LAN, and the receipt of this message causes the downstream routers to send subsequent Join/Prune messages to the upstream router that won the Assert process (i.e., the Assert Winner); the Assert Winner becomes the correct upstream PIM neighbor for such messages.

In general, a PIM router should only accept an Assert message for processing if it is sent by a known PIM router. As discussed earlier, the PIM router uses Hello messages to learn about PIM neighbors. If a PIM router receives an Assert message containing a particular IP source address and the router has not received a PIM Hello message from that source address, then it should discard the Assert message without further processing. Additionally, if the router authenticated the Hello message sent by the neighbor, then it must authenticate all Assert messages from that neighbor.

5.9.1 (S, G) ASSERT MESSAGE STATE MACHINE

The (S, G) Assert state machine that a PIM router maintains for an interface is illustrated in Figure 5.12. The state machine has the following three states:

- **NoInfo**: This state indicates that the router has no (S, G) Assert state on the interface.
- **Assert Winner (Winner)**: This state indicates that the router has won an (S, G) Assert on the interface. The router is now the elected *forwarder* responsible for forwarding multicast packets from source S destined for group G out of the interface. *Regardless of whether another PIM router is the current DR on the interface, while it is the Assert Winner, it is also responsible for forwarding multicast packets onto the interface (LAN) on behalf of local hosts on the interface that have sent IGMP Membership Reports that specifically request traffic from source S (and group G).*
- **Assert Loser (Loser)**: This state indicates that the router has lost an (S, G) Assert on the interface. The router must not forward multicast packets from source S destined for group G onto the interface. *If the router is the current DR on the interface, it is no longer responsible for forwarding*

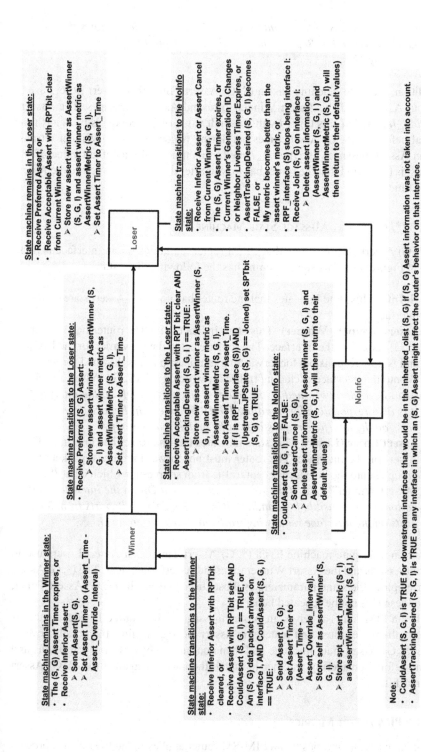

State machine remains in the Winner state:
- The (S, G) Assert Timer expires, or
- Receive Inferior Assert:
  - ➤ Send Assert(S, G).
  - ➤ Set Assert Timer to (Assert_Time - Assert_Override_Interval)

State machine transitions to the Winner state:
- Receive Inferior Assert with RPTbit cleared, or
- Receive Assert with RPTbit set AND CouldAssert (S, G, I) == TRUE, or
- An (S, G) data packet arrives on interface I, AND CouldAssert (S, G, I) == TRUE:
  - ➤ Send Assert (S, G).
  - ➤ Set Assert Timer to (Assert_Time - Assert_Override_Interval).
  - ➤ Store self as AssertWinner (S, I).
  - ➤ Store spt_assert_metric (S, I) as AssertWinnerMetric (S, G, I).

State machine remains in the Loser state:
- Receive Preferred Assert, or
- Receive Acceptable Assert with RPTbit clear from Current Winner:
  - ➤ Store new assert winner as AssertWinner (S, G, I) and assert winner metric as AssertWinnerMetric (S, G, I).
  - ➤ Set Assert Timer to Assert_Time

State machine transitions to the Loser state:
- Receive Preferred (S, G) Assert:
  - ➤ Store new assert winner as AssertWinner (S, G, I) and assert winner metric as AssertWinnerMetric (S, G, I).
  - ➤ Set Assert Timer to Assert_Time

State machine transitions to the Loser state:
- Receive Acceptable Assert with RPT bit clear AND AssertTrackingDesired (S, G, I) == TRUE:
  - ➤ Store new assert winner as AssertWinner (S, G, I) and assert winner metric as AssertWinnerMetric (S, G, I).
  - ➤ Set Assert Timer to Assert_Time.
  - ➤ If (I is RPF_interface (S)) AND (UpstreamJPState (S, G) == Joined) set SPTbit (S, G) to TRUE.

State machine transitions to the NoInfo state:
- CouldAssert (S, G, I) == FALSE:
  - ➤ Send AssertCancel (S, G).
  - ➤ Delete assert information (AssertWinner (S, G, I) and AssertWinnerMetric (S, G, I) will then return to their default values)

State machine transitions to the NoInfo state:
- Receive Inferior Assert or Assert Cancel from Current Winner, or
- The (S, G) Assert Timer expires, or
- Current Winner's Generation ID Changes or Neighbor Liveness Timer Expires, or
- AssertTrackingDesired (S, G, I) becomes FALSE, or
- My metric becomes better than the assert winner's metric, or
- RPF_interface (S) stops being interface I:
- Receive Join (S, G) on Interface I:
  - ➤ Delete assert information (AssertWinner (S, G, I) and AssertWinnerMetric (S, G, I) will then return to their default values)

Note:
- CouldAssert (S, G, I) is TRUE for downstream interfaces that would be in the inherited_olist (S, G) if (S, G) Assert information was not taken into account.
- AssertTrackingDesired (S, G, I) is TRUE on any interface in which an (S, G) Assert might affect the router's behavior on that interface.

FIGURE 5.12 Per-Interface (S, G) Assert state machine.

multicast packets onto the interface (LAN) to satisfy local hosts that sent IGMP Membership Reports that specifically request traffic from source S and group G.

In addition, the state machine has an (S, G) Assert Timer that Assert Losers use to time out Asserts and the Assert Winner to resend Asserts messages. The *Assert_Override_Interval* of this timer (with a default value of 3 seconds) is the short time interval before an (S, G) Assert times out during which the Assert Winner retransmits an Assert message. The *Assert_Time* of this timer (with a default value of 180 seconds) is the period that the router has to wait after the last Assert before the Assert state is timed out.

5.9.2   (*, G) Assert Message State Machine

The (*, G) Assert state machine that a PIM router maintains for an interface is illustrated in Figure 5.13. The state machine has the following three states:

- **NoInfo**: This state indicates that the router has no (*, G) Assert state on the interface.
- **Assert Winner (Winner)**: This state indicates that the router has won an (*, G) Assert on the interface. The router elected the forwarder for the LAN and is now responsible for forwarding multicast packets destined for group G onto the interface excluding traffic for which it has (S, G) "Assert Loser" state. *Regardless of whether the router is the current DR on the interface, it is also responsible for handling IGMP Membership Reports from local hosts on the interface requesting traffic addressed to group G.*
- **Assert Loser (Loser)**: This state indicates that the router has lost an (*, G) Assert on the interface. The router must not forward multicast packets for group G onto the interface except traffic from sources for which it has (S, G) "Assert Winner" state. *If the router is the current DR on the interface, it is no longer responsible for handling IGMP Membership Reports from local hosts on the interface requesting traffic destined for group G.*

In addition, this state machine has a (*, G) Assert Timer that Assert Losers use to time out Asserts and the Assert Winner to resend Asserts messages. The (*, G) Assert Timer employs the same parameters as those discussed for the (S, G) Assert Timer, and so these will not be repeated here.

When a PIM router receives an Assert message with a source IP address that is not zero, the router must first match the Assert message against the possible events in the (S, G) Assert state machine and then continue to process any transitions and actions before considering whether to match the message against the (*, G) Assert state machine.

5.9.3   PIM Assert Metrics

The parameters and metrics that a PIM-SM router applies in the PIM Assert process are the RPTbit flag, Metric Preference, Routing Metric, and the source IP address

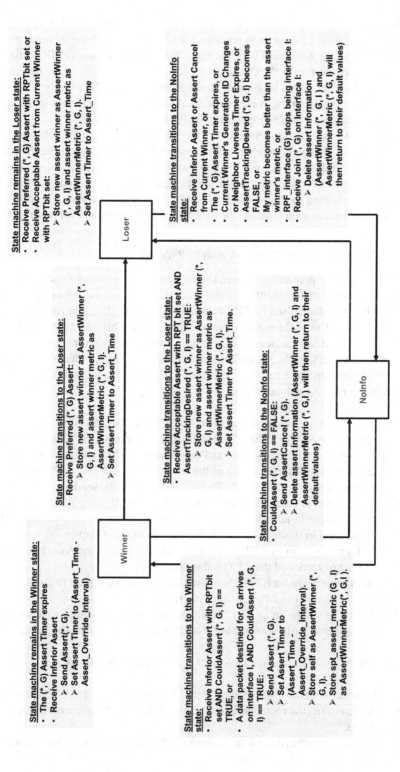

FIGURE 5.13 Per-Interface (*, G) Assert state machine.

of the received message. These parameters and metrics are carried in appropriate fields in a PIM Assert message, as described in Chapter 3. The Metric Preference and Routing Metric are associated with the route to a particular (unicast) IP destination (a multicast source for an (S, G) Assert or RP for a (*, G) Assert), as determined by the MRIB. The source IP address is simply the primary IP address of the PIM router that sent the Assert message on the local interface; this address is in the source address field of the IP packet containing the PIM Assert message.

When a PIM router compares these metrics, it compares them in the following order, the RPTbit flag, Metric Preference, and Routing Metric fields, where the first lower value wins the PIM Assert process. If all the values in the fields are equal, the primary IP address of the PIM router that originated the Assert message is used as a tiebreaker, with the router having the highest IP source address winning the Assert process. Note that PIM-DM routers do not include the RPT bit (or RPT-bit) in the PIM Assert process.

5.9.4 SUMMARY OF THE PIM-SM ASSERT PROCESS

As discussed in the preceding section, two or more routers on a multiaccess network segment may have different information about how to reach the RP or the multicast source. They could each send a PIM Join message to two different routers closer to the RP for an RPT or to the multicast source for an SPT. This could potentially cause duplicate copies of the multicast traffic to flow toward the receiver.

When the routers on the network segment notice duplicate multicast data packets on the segment, they elect a single router (i.e., a forwarder) to forward the packets, by each sending PIM Assert messages.

1. If one of the upstream routers is on an SPT (i.e., has (S, G) state) and the other is on an RPT (i.e., has (*, G) state), the router on the SPT has the shortest path to the multicast source and therefore wins the Assert election. Note that the Source Address field and the setting of the RPTbit flag in the PIM Assert message identify the (S, G) or (*, G) state of the sender.
   - If a router is on an SPT, the Source Address field of the Assert message is set to the IP address of the multicast source, and the RPTbit flag (or R bit) is set to 0 (see PIM Assert message format in Chapter 3).
   - If a router is on an RPT, the Source Address field of the Assert message is set to zero, and the RPTbit flag is set to 1.
2. If both routers are on RPTs, the router with the shortest path to the RP (the lowest Metric to the RP) wins the Assert.
3. If both routers are on an SPT, then the router with the shortest path to the multicast source (the lowest Metric to the source's DR) wins the Assert.

In either Step (2) or (3), the Assert Winner is determined as follows:

- The router with the lower unicast Metric Preference wins the Assert process.
- If there is a tie, the router with lower unicast Routing Metric wins the Assert process.
- If there is a tie, the router with the highest IP address wins the Assert process.

The result of an Assert election times out after the *Assert_Time*. As long as the condition that caused the duplication of multicast packets on the network segment remains unchanged, the Assert Winner sends a PIM Assert message at the *Assert_Override_Interval* interval, before the last Assert messages time out. When the last downstream router leaves the SPT, the Assert Winner sends an AssertCancel message (see the subsequent discussion) to indicate that it is about to stop forwarding multicast data packets on the SPT. Upon seeing this message, any RPT downstream routers then switch back to the RPT.

5.9.5 UNDERSTANDING THE ROLE OF THE DESIGNATED ROUTER AND ASSERT WINNER IN PIM-SM

The router that wins the PIM Assert election forwards the multicast data packets from the source onto the multiaccess network, and MAY in some cases also act as the local DR for any IGMP host members on the multiaccess network segment depending on its architecture. Note that the DR election process on the multiaccess network is independent of the Assert process on the same network. The role of the DR and the Assert Winner in PIM-SM can be explained as follows:

- The source-side DR is responsible for receiving multicast packets from a source and encapsulating them in PIM Register messages for transmission to the domain's RP. It is also responsible for responding to PIM Register-Stop messages sent by the RP.
- The receiver-side DR is responsible for receiving IGMP Membership Report messages from attached hosts and sending PIM (*, G) Join messages toward the domain's RP. It is also responsible for detecting when all receivers of a multicast group leave and sending (*, G) Prune messages to the RP. In the case of building the SPT, it is responsible for sending (S, G) Join and (S, G) Prune messages toward the FHR of a multicast source when necessary. All routers attached to the network segment will hear IGMP Membership Report messages transmitted on the network, but only the DR will send Join messages for those Report messages.
- The Assert Winner on the multiaccess network is mainly responsible for forwarding multicast packets from the source onto the network toward the downstream nodes and to local attached hosts. Although the DR will send Join messages when it receives IGMP Reports from attached hosts, it is the Assert Winner that will forward data from the multicast source to those hosts.

    However, from the PIM Assert process preceding discussion, regardless of which router is the elected DR on the network segment, it is the Assert Winner that will handle all IGMP requests and sends PIM Join/Prune messages on behalf of attached hosts and downstream PIM routers. The elected DR will also be aware of the results of the Assert process and the Assert Winner and will know when to cease acting as the DR to allow the Assert Winner to perform its functions. Note also that, unlike the Assert process, the DR election process does not use routing metrics, meaning, the Assert process produces the router (i.e., Assert Winner) that has the best path to the multicast traffic source. Therefore, the Assert Winner is best positioned to send PIM Join/Prune messages on behalf of all other attached nodes (routers and hosts). The elected DR is redundant when the Assert Winner is active (see discussion in Section 5.9.7).

The downstream routers on the segment also receive the Assert messages and participate in the Assert process, but they are most likely to be losers because they have longer paths to the multicast source (RP or real source). The downstream routers send all their PIM Join/Prune messages to the upstream PIM neighbor, having the best path to the multicast source (RP or real source) as determined by their unicast routing tables (i.e., to the RPF neighbor which in this case is the Assert Winner). Recall from Chapter 3 that a PIM Join/ Prune message contains an Upstream Neighbor Address field that indicates the target of the message; the target is the RPF neighbor to the source (RP or real source). The target of a Join/Prune message is an IP unicast address, not a multicast address.

It is important to note that the election of the IGMPv2/v3 Querier on a multi-access network is based on the router with the lowest IP address (see Chapter 2). This implies that a DR or Assert Winner is unlikely to function also as a Querier, thereby spreading the processing burden across routers on the multiaccess network segment.

5.9.6 PIM AssertCancel Messages

A PIM AssertCancel message is simply an RPT Assert message with an infinite Metric Preference or infinite Route Metric. The Assert Winner sends this message when it deletes the (S, G) or (*, G) multicast forwarding state that had caused the Assert process to occur. Other PIM routers on the multiaccess network segment with forwarding state that notice an Assert message with the infinite metric (i.e., an AssertCancel message) will send their own Assert messages and take over multicast packet forwarding, possibly resulting in duplicate packets on the network segment). This process leads to the establishment of a new Assert Winner (i.e., forwarder) to be reestablished on the network.

The Assert Winner uses an infinite Assert metric for an Assert message that does not match either (S, G) or (*, G) forwarding state because any of these forwarding states have been deleted.

- The Assert Winner with deleted (S, G) forwarding state sends an AssertCancel (S, G) message with an infinite metric, the RPTbit flag is set and the message names S as the multicast source.
- The Assert Winner with deleted (*, G) forwarding state sends an AssertCancel (*, G) message with an infinite metric, the RPT bit is set, and the multicast source in the message is set to zero.

PIM uses AssertCancel messages as an optimization mechanism for the Assert process. The original Assert timeout mechanism (based on the (S, G) or (*, G) Assert Timer) will allow the Assert process on a multiaccess network segment to eventually become consistent, but the AssertCancel mechanism simply causes the process to converge faster. PIM routers require no special processing for an AssertCancel message since it is simply an Assert message sent by the current Assert Winner.

5.9.7 Summary of the PIM Assert Rules

We summarize in this section the key rules that PIM routers use for sending and reacting to Assert messages and the rationale for these rules:

1. **Behavior**: Downstream routers send periodic PIM Join (*, G) and Join (S, G) messages to the appropriate upstream PIM neighbor leading to the multicast traffic source (RP or actual source S), that is, the RPF neighbor as modified by the Assert process. The downstream PIM routers do not always send such messages to the RPF neighbor as indicated by the MRIB. Normal Join message suppression and Prune override rules also apply here.

2. **Rationale**: Sending the periodic and triggered PIM (*, G) and Join (S, G) Join messages to the RPF neighbor as modified by the Assert process instead of to the RPF neighbor indicated in the MRIB, prevents the downstream PIM router from re-triggering the Assert process every time it sends a Join message. Also, sending Join messages to the Assert Winner, prevents multicast traffic from switching back to the "normal" RPF neighbor (as indicated in the MRB) until the Assert times out.

3. **Behavior**: The Assert Winner for (*, G) on a multiaccess network segment such as an Ethernet LAN acts as the local receiver-side DR for (*, G) and is responsible for handling IGMP join and leave of local hosts on the network segment.

4. **Rationale**: This allows a single PIM router to combine the tasks of handling PIM Join/Prunes as well as IGMP joins and leaves on the multiaccess network segment. Without this, the Prune override feature does not work.

5. **Behavior**: The Assert Winner for (S, G) on a multiaccess network segment acts as the local receiver-side DR for (S, G) and is responsible for handling IGMPv3 joins and leaves of local hosts on the network segment.

6. **Rationale**: Same rationale as for Behavior 2.

7. **Behavior**: Downstream PIM routers on a multiaccess network segment send PIM (S, G) and (*, G) Prune override messages to the RPF neighbor as modified by the Assert process and not to the regular RPF neighbor in the MRIB.

8. **Rationale**: Same rationale as for Behavior 1.

9. **Behavior**: A downstream PIM router does not send (at all) an (S, G, rpt) Prune override message if RPF (S, G, rpt) as modified by the Assert process is not equal to (i.e., not the same as) the RPF (*, G) as modified by the Assert process.

10. **Rationale**: With this, the upstream PIM router avoids keeping the (S, G) state alive on the (S, G) SPT when only (*, G) downstream PIM routers and members are left. Also, the downstream router avoids sending (S, G, rpt) Join messages to a router that is not on the RPT (i.e., (*, G) tree).

11. **Behavior**: An Assert Loser that receives a PIM Join (S, G) message containing an IP address in the Upstream Neighbor Address field that is its primary IP address on the receiving interface expires the (S, G) Assert Timer.

12. **Rationale**: This is necessary to allow rapid network convergence if the downstream PIM router that initially sent a PIM Join message to the previous Assert Winner has gone through a network topology change.

13. **Behavior**: An Assert Loser that receives a PIM Join (*, G) message containing an IP address in the Upstream Neighbor Address field, which is its primary IP address on the receiving interface, will expire the (*, G) Assert Timer and all (S, G) Assert Timers that do not have corresponding Prune (S, G, rpt) entries in the compound Join/Prune message.

14. **Rationale**: Same rationale as for Behavior 6.
15. **Behavior**: An Assert Winner for (*, G) or (S, G) state entry sends an AssertCancel (S, G) or (*, G) message when it is about to stop multicast packet forwarding on a (*, G) or an (S, G) state entry. This behavior does not apply to the (S, G, rpt) state.
16. **Rationale**: This allows routers to switch back to the RPT after the last router on the SPT on the multiaccess network segment leaves. Doing this prevents downstream PIM routers on the RPT from keeping the SPT state alive.
17. **Behavior (optional)**: A PIM router resends the PIM (*, G) or (S, G) Assert messages before timing out an (*, G) or (S, G) Assert.
18. **Rationale**: This prevents the periodic forwarding of duplicate multicast packets that would otherwise occur each time that a (*, G) or (S, G) Assert times out and is then reestablished.
19. **Behavior**: When the RPF (S, G, rpt) as modified by the Assert process changes to be the same as the RPF (*, G) as modified by the Assert process, the PIM router needs to trigger sending a Join (S, G, rpt) to the RPF (*, G) as modified by the Assert process.
20. **Rationale**: This allows PIM routers to switch back to the RPT after the last router on the SPT leaves.

5.10   REFRESHING PIM-SM MULTICAST STATE

PIM-SM routers assign a finite lifetime (e.g., 3 minutes, see (*, G) or (S, G) Expiry Timer in the preceding section) to each forwarding state after which the state is deleted. This prevents a forwarding state from being indefinitely maintained in a router even if the information is stale and of no use. For example, if a PIM Prune message is lost and does not reach an upstream router, the associated forwarding state could be retained in the router for a long period of time. A router establishes a lifetime by associating an expiry time for each (*, G) and (S, G) state entry in the MRIB. When the lifetime of a state expires, the router deletes that state. This means that downstream PIM-SM routers must periodically refresh a forwarding state in the upstream router to prevent it from timing out and being deleted.

Thus, to perform state refresh, a PIM-SM router sends a PIM Join/Prune message to the appropriate upstream neighbor once every 60 seconds (see the $t\_periodic$ period discussed earlier). When the upstream router receives a PIM Join/Prune message, it refreshes the associated state by resetting the lifetime. Routers refresh (*, G) state by periodically sending (once every 60 seconds) a PIM (*, G) Join message to the upstream neighbor in the direction of the RP. Routers refresh (S, G) state by periodically sending (once every 60 seconds) a PIM (S, G) Join message to the upstream neighbor in the direction of the multicast source.

Routers periodically send the (*, G) or (S, G) Joins as long as they have non-empty OILs for the (*, G) or (S, G) state or have at least one directly connected receiver for the multicast group G. If routers fail to send these periodic (*, G) or (S, G) Join messages, the associated (*, G) or (S, G) forwarding state entries will eventually time out and be deleted in the MRIB, resulting in branches of the RPT or SPT being torn down.

5.11   ILLUSTRATING PIM-SM SOURCE REGISTRATION PROCESS

Since multicast traffic must first flow from the RP and along the shared tree to receivers, there must be a way in PIM-SM for a source to get multicast traffic to the RP in the first place. This means the RP must first be made aware that a multicast source exists and is currently active, which calls for the *PIM Register messaging mechanism*. The purpose of the *PIM-SM multicast source registration process* is for the FHR or source-side DR to inform the RP about the existence of the multicast source as soon as it starts transmitting multicast data and to deliver the initial multicast packets from the source to the RP to be forwarded on the RPT to receivers. We assume that a BSR has distributed RP information to all routers in the PIM-SM network including the source-side DR. As discussed earlier, an RP performs the following tasks in a PIM-SM network:

- Manage one or several IP multicast groups as determined by the BSR.
- Serve as the root for the shared tree to these multicast groups.
- Accept PIM (*, G) Join messages from receiver-DRs for multicast groups that it manages.
- Accept PIM Register messages from source-side DRs for multicast groups that it manages.
- Announce RP candidacy information to the elected BSR in the PIM-SM domain.

The FHR or source-side DR registers a multicast source with the RP as follows (see Figure 5.14):

- When the multicast source S sends the first multicast packet to multicast group G, its directly connected DR upon receiving the multicast packet, encapsulates it in a PIM Register message and sends it via unicast to the RP for group G.
  - The DR, by checking the source IP of the first multicast packet from the source, will know that it is a directly connected host (i.e., in the same IP subnet) and will proceed to create an (S, G) state entry in the MRIB and register the source with the RP. Note that a source does not need to join a multicast group to send to that group.
- When the RP receives PIM Register messages from the DR and there are active receivers of the group (i.e., Join messages were received for the group and an RPT has already been established), it decapsulates each message and forwards the extracted multicast packet on the RPT to downstream routers and interested receivers of group G. On the other hand, if there are no receivers of the multicast traffic (i.e., no Join messages were received and therefore no active RPT is built for the group), the RP simply discards the received multicast traffic.
- To optimize multicast packet forwarding, the RP sends a PIM (S, G) Join message which travels hop by hop toward the multicast source (actually, the source-side DR).
  - The PIM (S, G) Join message takes the best reverse path from the RP to the source-side DR as determined by the unicast routing table of each router.

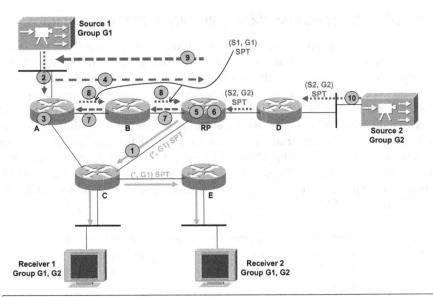

Processing steps:

1. We assume Receivers 1 and 2 have already joined multicast group G1 by sending IGMP Membership Report messages to their respective First-Hop Routers (FHRs), Routers C and E. Also, Routers C and E have successfully joined the shared tree to the RP.
2. Source 1 starts sending multicast traffic to multicast group G1 via its FHR, Router A.
3. Router A being the FHR, responds to the multicast traffic from Source 1 by encapsulating the multicast packets in PIM Register messages.
4. Router A unicasts the PIM Register messages directly to the RP (i.e., the RP is the final destination of the unicast IP packets carrying the PIM Register messages).
5. The RP receives the PIM Register messages, de-encapsulate them, and sees that the encapsulated multicast packets are addressed to multicast group G1.
6. The RP also notices that an active shared tree with a nonempty outgoing interface list (OIL) already exists in its multicast routing table (MRT). The RP, therefore, transmits the de-encapsulated multicast packets on the shared tree toward the members of multicast group G1.
7. Because the RP already has an active shared tree with a nonempty OIL for multicast group G1, it sends an (S1, G1) Join message back to Source 1 to join the SPT, allowing it to pull multicast traffic from Source 1. The Join message travels hop-by-hop (over Router B) back to the FHR of Source 1, Router A.
8. Router A receives the (S1, G1) Join message from the RP and a SPT is created from Router A to the RP. Multicast traffic from Source 1 now begins to flow to the RP via the newly created (S1, G1) SPT.
9. The RP no longer needs to continue receiving the (S1, G1) traffic encapsulated in PIM Register messages, and so, unicasts a PIM Register-Stop message to the FHR, Router A.
10. A new source, Source 2, starts sending multicast traffic to multicast group G2 via its FHR, Router D.
    - The same source registration process takes place and results in the RP joining the (S2, G2) SPT.
    - The RP is now able to pull multicast traffic over the (S2, G2) SPT to be forwarded over the shared tree to members of multicast group G2.

At this point, the RP has joined the (S1, G1) and (S2, G2) SPTs for Source 1 and Source 2, respectively, for multicast groups G1 and G2. Both multicast traffic streams are forwarded on the (*, G1) and (*, G2) shared trees to Receivers 1 and 2.

FIGURE 5.14 PIM-SM source registration process.

- Thus, the routers along the path from the RP to the source-side DR constitute an SPT branch. Each router on this SPT branch creates an (S, G) entry in its MRIB.
- The source-side DR is the root of the SPT, while the RP is a leaf.
- Subsequent multicast data packets from the multicast source travel through the source-side DR along the established SPT to the RP. The RP then forwards these packets along the RPT to the receivers. The purpose of joining the SPT is to allow the RP to "pull" the multicast data directly from the source-DR rather than get it through the more processing intensive PIM registration process.

Note that a multicast source simply sends multicast traffic and has no idea which devices in the network (if any) will receive the traffic. It is the routers in the network that receive the traffic and forward it to whichever end host needs it. The FHR is responsible for making sure that the RP for a given multicast group would receive a copy of that traffic. The FHR, like all routers in the PIM-SM domain, needs to learn the multicast group-to-RP mapping information from a BSR or other RP discovery mechanisms discussed in the subsequent text. With that mapping, the FHR knows the IP address of the RP to which it must forward any given multicast traffic.

Note also that the FHR cannot forward the multicast traffic to the RP by multicast as the routers in between do not know how to forward the traffic; the router does not have the multicast forwarding state information to do so. Instead, the FHR has to encapsulate the multicast packets in IP packets with the unicast IP address of the RP as the destination address and unicast them to the RP. Essentially, the FHR tunnels the multicast packets directly to the RP. This process is known as *Registering* the multicast source and its traffic with the RP. If the RP has any active requests for the multicast traffic from downstream nodes, then it will decapsulate the multicast packets from the PIM Register messages and forward them downstream. If the RP has no currently active requests for the multicast traffic, it simply drops the traffic and signals to the FHR (via a PIM Register-Stop message) to stop sending the PIM Register messages for the traffic.

The RP sends an (S, G) Join message back to the source-side DR to build the SPT to the source, typically, when a data-rate threshold is reached. Once the SPT is established from the source to the RP, the source-side DR starts sending standard multicast packets to the RP as well as multicast packets encapsulated within PIM Register messages. This means that the RP will temporarily receive some duplicate multicast packets from the source through PIM Register messages and via the SPT. Until the SPT is established, the source-side DR will continue to unicast PIM Register messages containing multicast packets to the RP. Once the SPT is built, the source-side DR begins forwarding the same multicast traffic, but this time sent as standard IP multicast packets, down the SPT to the RP. However, as soon as the RP detects standard multicast packets from the source over the SPT, it sends a PIM Register-Stop message to the source-side DR, informing it to stop sending PIM Register messages with multicast packets.

Note that a multicast source does not need to join the group to which it is sending data. The FHR (or DR) can begin receiving multicast traffic from the source without having any (S, G) state for the source; the (S, G) state is created as soon as it receives the first multicast packet from the directly connected source.

5.11.1 SENDING PIM REGISTER-STOP MESSAGES

An RP sends a PIM Register-Stop message via unicast to the source-side DR of a source to instruct it to stop sending (S, G) multicast traffic via PIM Register messages under the following conditions:

- When the RP has joined the SPT rooted at the source and has started receiving (S, G) traffic from the source-side DR over the newly established SPT.
- When the RP has not received PIM Join messages for the multicast group, and therefore, no RPT has been established for the group; the RP does not need the traffic because there are no active receivers.

When the source-side DR receives a PIM Register-Stop message from the RP, it knows that the RP has received its PIM Register messages and one of the above conditions has taken place at the RP. In either case, the DR stops sending PIM Register messages with encapsulated (S, G) multicast packets to the RP.

When the RP begins receiving multicast traffic from the source-side DR both in PIM Register messages and as standard unencapsulated multicast packets, it sends a PIM Register-Stop message to the DR. This is to inform the DR that it is now receiving multicast traffic as standard multicast packets on the SPT.

This means that when the multicast packets arrive at the RP along the SPT, the RP sends a PIM Register-Stop message via unicast to the source-side DR to stop the source registration process. In other words, this process stops the DR from further sending multicast data packets encapsulated in PIM Register messages to it (see Figure 5.15). Once the source-side DR receives this PIM Register-Stop message, it ceases encapsulating multicast packets in PIM Register messages.

Unless the RP initiates an SPT switchover, the source-side DR will continue to encapsulate multicast data packets in PIM Register messages; the registration process will not cease unless the RP has no outgoing interfaces in the (S, G) entry, prompting it to send a PIM Register-Stop message to the source-side DR. This means, another scenario where the RP sends PIM Register-Stop messages to the source-side DR is when it has no receivers belonging to the multicast group.

When a source begins sending multicast traffic to a group but the RP has no interested receivers, the RP discards these packets and sends a PIM Register-Stop message to inform the source-side DR to stop sending PIM Register messages with multicast packets.

5.11.1.1 Understanding the PIM-SM Register Suppression Mechanism

The *Register Suppression mechanism* helps to protect against a source-side DR continuing to send multicast packets to a failed RP. Upon receiving the *first* PIM Register-Stop message, the source-side DR halts the transmission of PIM Register messages encapsulating multicast data and starts the Register-Stop Timer. However, it sets the timer to the *Register_Suppression_Time*, which is the time period during which the DR refrains from sending Register messages to the RP after receiving the Register-Stop message from the RP. When this timer expires, the DR resumes sending its multicast packets to the RP in PIM Register messages.

However, *Register_Probe_Time* seconds (default value is 5 seconds) before the *Register_Suppression_Time* period (the default is 60 seconds) expires, and the source-DR sends a PIM Null-Register message to the RP. A PIM Null-Register

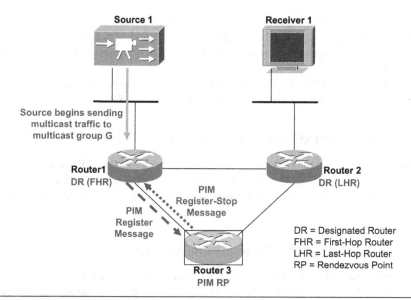

Source 1

Receiver 1

Source begins sending multicast traffic to multicast group G

Router1
DR (FHR)

Router 2
DR (LHR)

PIM Register-Stop Message

PIM Register Message

DR = Designated Router
FHR = First-Hop Router
LHR = Last-Hop Router
RP = Rendezvous Point

Router 3
PIM RP

- In PIM networks (i.e., for all PIM types), the router that is directly connected to a multicast traffic source is called the First-Hop Router (FHR).
  - If the source is connected to a multiaccess network with multiple routers (e.g., an Ethernet network), one of them is selected as the designated router (DR), also called the first-hop DR.
- The router that is directly connected to a receiver is called the Last-Hop Router (LHR).
  - Similarly, if the receiver is connected to a multiaccess network with multiple routers, one of them is selected as the DR, also called the last-hop DR.
- Sometimes the FHR or LHR is simply called the DR (for the source or the receiver).

FIGURE 5.15   PIM-SM source Register-Stop process.

message is a PIM Register message with no encapsulated multicast data packets and with a flag bit, called the Null-Register (or N) bit, set to 1 (see PIM Register message format in Chapter 3). The PIM Null-Register message prompts the RP to determine whether new downstream receivers have joined the multicast group. If this message triggers the RP to send a PIM Register-Stop, the Register-Stop Timer is reset.

The *Register_Probe_Time* of the DR is the period before the Register-Stop Timer expires, when the DR may send a PIM Null-Register to the RP to cause it to resend a PIM Register-Stop message. If no new receivers have joined the multicast group, the RP sends another PIM Register-Stop message to the source-side DR and restarts its Register-Stop Timer (sets it once again to the *Register_Suppression_Time*). Note that PIM timers (like most protocol timers) are normally implemented as countdown timers, so it is easy to determine when the *Register_Probe_Time* starts on this timer.

If a PIM Register-Stop message is received by the source-side DR during the *Register_Probe_Time*, it restarts its Register-Stop Timer, otherwise, it starts sending again PIM Register messages with encapsulating multicast data packets when the *Register_Suppression_Time* expires. After the RP no longer responds with a PIM Register-Stop message to the source-side DR's PIM Null-Register message, the *Register_Suppression_Time* expires and the DR starts sending encapsulated multicast packets to the RP. The RP adopts this method of not responding to PIM Null-Register messages as a way to inform the DR that new members have joined the group on the RPT.

The RP sends a PIM Register-Stop message to the source-side DR immediately after it starts receiving the multicast data packets over the SPT.

5.12   ILLUSTRATING PIM-SM SHARED TREE JOINS

In PIM-SM, the RP is the root node of the shared tree, while the FHR of the multicast source is the root node of the SPT. A receiver-side DR sends Join and Prune messages toward an RP for a multicast group to either join the RPT or remove (prune) a branch from it.

5.12.1   CONTENTS OF THE PIM JOIN/PRUNE MESSAGE

Although, quite often, PIM Joins and Prunes are used or referenced as if they are separate PIM message types, they are in reality, both parts of the same PIM message type, the PIM Join/Prune message with type number 3, as discussed in Chapter 3. A single Join/Prune message contains both a list of sources to join (Join list) and a list of sources to prune (Prune list), either of which may be empty in a given message, depending on the information being communicated to routers on the multicast distribution tree. The ability to carry multiple entries in a Join list and/or Prune list, allows a PIM router to join/prune multiple sources and/or multicast groups using a single PIM Join/Prune message. Sending a single message improves the periodic multicast state refresh on upstream routers on the multicast distribution tree.

The entries of the Join list and Prune list of the PIM Join/Prune message share a common format and contain the following information (among others):

- Multicast Group Address (in Encoded Group Address Format as described in Chapter 3)
- Multicast Source Address (in Encoded Source Address Format as described in Chapter 3) which also includes the setting of the W or WC bit to indicate that the entry is for a shared tree (*, G) Join/Prune, and the setting of the R or RPT bit to indicate that the entry is for a shared (*, G) Join/Prune and should be forwarded up the shared tree.

A Join list includes a set of source addresses that indicate the SPTs or the RPTs that a host wants to join. For example, let us consider a PIM Join/Prune message that has the following information in an entry of the Join list:

- Multicast Source Address, 192.10.10.10; Multicast Group Address, 224.10.10.10, with setting of W and R bits ON (i.e., set to 1).

This information indicates that the entry is a (*, G) Join for the multicast group 224.10.10.10 whose RP is 192.16.20.20.

5.12.2   BUILDING THE PIM-SM SHARED TREE

The receiver-side DR sends Join and Prune messages forwarded hop by hop by each PIM router on the path to the multicast source or the RP. The process of building the PIM-SM shared or RPT is as follows (see Figure 5.16):

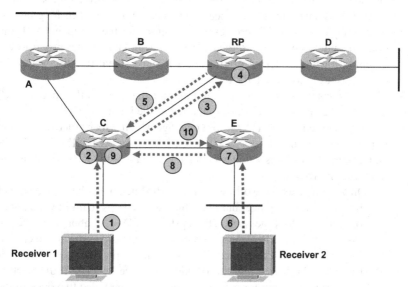

Processing steps:
1. Receiver 1 (the first host) joins the multicast group G by sending an IGMP Membership Report message to Router C.
2. Router C creates a new (*, G) state entry in its multicast routing table (MRT) for group G and also enters the interface leading to Receiver 1 in the outgoing interface lists (OIL) of the (*, G) state entry.
3. After creating the new (*, G) state entry, Router C sends a PIM (*, G) Join message toward the RP to join the shared tree. Note that Router C uses its unicast routing table to determine the interface leading to the RP.
4. The RP receives the (*, G) Join message from Router C, and because it has no previous state for group G, it creates a new (*, G) state entry in its MRT and adds the interface leading to Router C in the OIL of the (*, G) state entry.
5. Now, a shared tree has been constructed from the RP to Router C and Receiver 1, and any multicast traffic for group G that reaches the RP will be forwarded along the shared tree to Receiver 1.
6. Receiver 2 also joins multicast group G by sending an IGMP Membership Report message to Router E.
7. Router E does not have any state information for group G and, therefore, creates a new (*, G) state entry in its MRT and adds the interface leading to Receiver 2 in the OIL of the (*, G) state entry.
8. After creating the new (*, G) state entry, Router E sends a (*, G) Join message toward the RP to join the shared tree for multicast group G.
9. Router C receives the (*, G) Join message and finds that it already has a (*, G) state entry in its MRT for group G. As a result, Router C simply adds the interface leading to Router E in the OIL for the (*, G) state entry.
10. Now, any multicast traffic for group G that reaches the Router C will be forwarded along the shared tree to Router E and Receiver 2.

FIGURE 5.16   PIM-SM shared tree joins.

- A receiver joins a multicast group G by sending an IGMP Membership Report message to its directly connected DR. The DR first checks to see if it has an entry in its multicast forwarding table for group G. If an entry exists for the group, the DR adds the interface on which the IGMP message was received as an outgoing interface for the multicast group. No further PIM protocol action is needed. This means the DR can begin to accept multicast packets for group G.
- If no entry exists, the DR creates a (*, G) entry for the group and adds the outgoing interface. The DR then performs a lookup for the group-to-RP mapping for the requested group. The DR must signal the discovered RP that it wishes to join the RPT for group G.
- The DR consults its unicast routing table for the route to the specified RP and adds the upstream interface to the RP as the incoming (RPF) interface.
- The DR then sends a PIM (*, G) Join message which is forwarded hop by hop via multicast (to the address 224.0.0.13, which is the ALL-PIM-ROUTERS address) until it reaches a router with a (*, G) state or the RP corresponding to multicast group G.
  - On a multiaccess network segment, all PIM neighbors become aware of the (*, G) Join message, but only the indicated upstream PIM neighbor forwards the Join message. This upstream PIM neighbor might be the Assert Winner if a PIM Assert process was invoked as discussed earlier.
- The PIM (*, G) Join/Prune message sent includes the address of the multicast group to be joined and the IP address of the RP. The Prune section of the message is empty for a Join message. There are also two flags in the message that are set by the DR, the Wildcard bit (W or WC bit) and the RPT bit (R or RPT bit), as described in Chapter 3:
  - The WC-bit is set to 1 to indicate that the join address is an RP address rather than a source address.
  - The RPT-bit is set to 1 to indicate that the Join message is propagated along a shared tree to the RP.

5.12.3 PIM (*, G) JOIN MESSAGE PROCESSING AT UPSTREAM ROUTER

Upon receiving a PIM (*, G) Join message from a downstream router, the router checks and performs the following actions:

- **The upstream router is not the RP and is ON the RPT**: The router adds the interface on which the (*, G) Join message was received to the OIL for the group.
  - In this case, a (*, G) state exists for multicast group G in the MFIB. If a (*, G) state already exists, then the (*, G) Join message has reached a node on the RPT, and no more forwarding of the message is done.
- **The upstream router is not the RP and is NOT on the RPT**: The router creates a (*, G) entry in its MFIB and forwards the (*, G) Join message upstream toward the RP.
  - In this case, no state exists, so, the router creates an (*, G) entry, adds the interface in the OIL for this state, and then forwards the (*, G) Join message towards the RP to be part of the RPT.

- **The upstream router is the RP and has an entry for the multicast group**: The router adds the interface on which the (*, G) Join message was received to the OIL for the group.
- **The upstream router is the RP and has no entry for the multicast group**: The router creates a (*, G) entry in its MFIB and adds the receiving interface to the OIL for the group.

Once the (*, G) state is created on all routers from the receiver-side DR to the RP, multicast traffic for G can starts flowing on the RPT to the receivers that joined group G. After the RPT is established, routers along it periodically send PIM Join/Prune messages to upstream neighbors as a "keepalive" or refresh messages. If a PIM router on the tree does not receive a Join/Prune for a known multicast group from a downstream neighbor within the PIM Hold Time (see Join/Prune Message structure in Chapter 3), it prunes the downstream router from the OIL of the group entry.

The PIM-SM routers along the path from the receiver-side DR to the RP form a branch of the shared tree or RPT. Each router on this branch generates a (*, G) entry in its multicast forwarding table. The RP is at the root of the shared tree (RPT), while the receiver-side DRs form the leaves of the RPT. The multicast data packets addressed to multicast group G flow from the source to the RP, along the RPT to the corresponding receiver-side DRs, and finally to the receivers.

5.12.4 Example of PIM-SM Shared Tree Joins

In Figure 5.16, Receiver 1 sends an IGMP Membership Report message to Router C, signaling its desire to join multicast group G. We assume that this is the first receiver attached to Router C that has joined group G, so Router C has no (*, G) state. Router C creates a (*, G) state entry, adds the interface to Receiver 1 to the OIL, and then forwards the PIM (*, G) Join message to its upstream neighbor. Any upstream router that also has no (*, G) state will repeat the process, again forwarding the (*, G) Join message toward the RP. This continues either until the PIM Join message reaches the RP receives, or until an upstream router that already has (*, G) state receives the (*, G) Join message. The result in either case is that routers that receive the (*, G) message will construct an RPT that reaches from the RP to the receiver-DR. Note that, until Receiver 1 sends the IGMP Membership Report message, nothing happens at Router C. Receiver 1 has to initiate the join process for its DR to join the RPT.

When Receiver 2 also joins multicast group G by sending an IGMP Membership Report message to Router E, Router E will create a new (*, G) entry in its MRIB if one does not already exist. Router E creates a (*, G) state entry, adds the interface to Receiver 2 to the OIL, and then forwards the (*, G) Join message to its upstream neighbor, Router C. As a (*, G) state already exists on Router C, the (*, G) Join message has reached a node on the RPT for group G. Router C then enters the interface leading to Router E (i.e., the interface on which the message was received) in the OIL for the (*, G) entry. Multicast traffic then flows on the RPT from Router C to Router E and then to Receiver 2.

Note that receivers can join the RPT for a multicast group even if there are no active sources for that group. When a source becomes active and registers with the RP for the multicast group, the RP can begin forwarding traffic to the receivers, and then join the

SPT rooted at the source to continue more optimally to send traffic to the receivers. Furthermore, sources can register with the RP and send to a multicast group even if no receivers have yet joined the RPT. When receivers eventually join the RPT, the RP can start sending traffic to them and then join the SPT rooted at the source to continue sending traffic to them. This means PIM-SM allows sources and receivers to join the multicast distribution tree at any time they desire without constraints.

5.12.5 SUMMARY OF THE PIM-SM JOIN PROCESS

This section summarizes the join process when receivers are the first to join a multicast group and when a source initially registers with the RP for a multicast group.

5.12.5.1 Receivers Join First the RP for a Multicast Group

This section summarizes the process steps when receivers have already joined a multicast group before a source begins sending traffic to the group:

- Source S starts sending multicast packets to multicast group G.
- Source-side DR receives the multicast packets, encapsulates them in PIM Register messages, and unicasts the messages to the RP. The DR also creates an (S, G) state entry for the source and multicast group because the source is a directly attached host. The DR knows this by examining the source IP address in the received multicast packets and observes that they are both in the same IP subnet.
- RP receives the PIM Register messages, decapsulates them, and sends the multicast packets on the RPT to receivers of multicast group G. RP also creates an (S, G) state entry for the source and multicast group.
- RP sends an (S, G) Join toward the source-side DR to build an SPT for the Source's S traffic.
- RP begins receiving the (S, G) traffic on the SPT from the source-side DR.
- RP sends PIM Register-Stop message to the source-side DR to stop receiving multicast data via PIM Register messages.
- Source-side DR stops sending multicast data via PIM Register messages to the RP.
- (S, G) traffic continues to flow on the SPT from the source-side DR to the RP.

5.12.5.2 A Source Registers First with the RP for a Multicast Group

This section summarizes the process steps when a source initiates sending traffic to the multicast group before receivers have joined the group:

- Source S begins sending multicast packets to multicast group G.
- Source-side DR receives the multicast packets, encapsulates them in PIM Register messages, and unicasts the messages to the RP. The DR also creates an (S, G) state entry for the source and multicast group because the source is a directly attached host.
- RP receives the PIM Register messages but has no receivers for the multicast traffic, and therefore, discards the traffic. *However, the RP still creates an (S, G) state entry for the source and multicast group.*

- RP sends a PIM Register-Stop message to the source-side DR.
- Source-side DR receives the PIM Register-Stop message, stops encapsulating multicast data in PIM Register messages, and discards further multicast packets from the source.
- RP now receives a (*, G) Join from a receiver-side DR for receivers of multicast group G.
- RP sends an (S, G) Join toward the source-side DR to build an SPT for source S.
- RP begins receiving multicast traffic on the SPT from the source-side DR.
- RP forwards the multicast traffic on the RPT to receivers of multicast group G.

5.13   ILLUSTRATING PIM-SM SHARED TREE PRUNES

When a receiver is no longer interested in the multicast data addressed to a multicast group G, it sends an IGMP Leave Group (G) message to its directly connected DR (see Figure 5.17). Upon receiving the IGMP Leave Group message and if the DR has no more receivers of multicast group G on any of its interfaces, it sends a PIM (*, G) Prune message, which travels hop by hop along the RPT until it reaches an appropriate upstream PIM-SM router or the RP for group G. A router on the RPT sends a PIM (*, G) Prune message out the RPF interface to the upstream neighbor when it no longer has any directly connected members or downstream neighbors of multicast group G.

A PIM (*, G) Prune message lists the group and RP address in the Prune section and sets the WC-bit and RPT-bit. Let us consider a PIM Join/Prune message with the following information in the Prune list entry:

- Multicast Source Address, 192.20.20.20; Multicast Group Address, 224.20.20.20, with the setting of both W and R bits OFF (i.e., both set to 0).

This information indicates that the entry is an (S, G) Prune for the multicast group 224.20.20.20 whose source is 192.20.20.20.

Upon receiving the PIM (*, G) Prune message, the upstream node deletes the interface connected to the downstream leaving the receiver from the OIL of the (*, G) state entry and then checks whether it has local receivers for the multicast group G. If no local receivers of group G exist, the upstream PIM-SM node continues to forward the (*, G) Prune message to its upstream router.

When an RP receives a Prune message on an interface, it stops forwarding multicast traffic from the source indicated in the Prune message onto the interface. Only a leaf router (i.e., the router directly attached to the receivers or receiver-side DR) can originate Prune messages. If the last member of a multicast group sends an IGMPv2 Leave Group message to the DR (or, the IGMPv1 state, simply times out), the DR deletes the IGMP state and removes the interface from both the (S, G) and (*, G) OIL for group G. If the DR removes every interface in the OIL of the (*, G) state, meaning it has no receivers on any interface that are members of group G, then it will send a (*, G) Prune message upstream through the RPT to the RP.

If an upstream router also has a null or empty OIL for the (*, G) state, it continues to forward the message toward the RP. If an upstream router still has (*, G) state for receivers on another interface, it will remove only the interface on which the

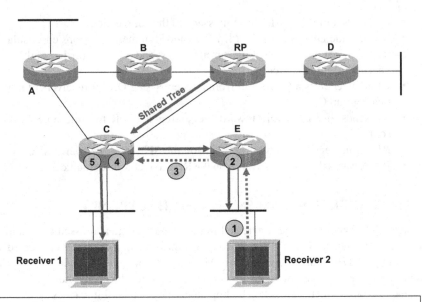

Processing steps:
1. Receiver 2 leaves multicast group G by sending an IGMP Leave message to Router E.
2. Because Receiver 2 is the only host in multicast group G on the outgoing interface of Router E, this interface is removed from the OIL of the (*, G) state entry.
    - The OIL for the (*, G) state entry becomes empty (null), indicating that Router E no longer needs multicast traffic for group G.
3. With an empty OIL for the (*, G) state entry, Router E sends a (*, G) Prune message toward the RP to prune itself from the shared tree.
4. Router C receives the (*, G) Prune message from Router E and removes the interface leading to Router E from the OIL of the (*, G) state entry.
5. However, because Router C still has Receiver 1 as a directly connected host and the OIL for the (*, G) state entry is not empty (null), it remains on the shared tree and continues to forward multicast traffic to Receiver 1.
    - Router C does no send a (*, G) Prune message on the shared tree toward the RP.

FIGURE 5.17   PIM-SM shared tree prunes.

message was received unless the router receives an overriding Join message from a PIM neighbor on the receiving interface. The process of pruning branches on the RPT also applies if the SPT is being used.

In Figure 5.17, Router E, which is the leaf router (i.e., receiver-side DR), receives an IGMP Leave Group message from Receiver 2. Router E processes the Leave Group message and, because there are no other group members left on it, it removes the interface to Receiver 2 from the (*, G) state as well as any interfaces in the (S, G) OIL. The OIL of Router E is now null, so it sends a PIM (*, G) Prune message up the RPT toward the RP.

Router C receives the PIM (*, G) Prune message, which causes the interface leading to Router E to be removed from its OIL of the (*, G) entry in the MRIB. Note that a period normally elapses before the (*, G) Prune message takes effect on Router C. For multiaccess networks, attached routers need to wait a little longer to prune an interface because a PIM neighbor may send an overriding Join message in response to the Prune message. In this case, we assume no such message was received, so the interface to Router E is pruned.

Because the OIL of the (*, G) state on Router C is not null, indicating that Receiver 1 is still a member of group G, Router C does not forward a PIM (*, G) Prune message up the RPT toward the RP. Router C will only prune the interface leading to Router E. If the OIL of the (*, G) state on Router C were null, it will continue forwarding the PIM (*, G) Prune message either until the RP receives the message or until a router on the RPT is reached whose OIL of the (*, G) state is NOT null.

Note that Chapter 4 (on PIM-DM) already discussed the situation where a (*, G) or (S, G) Prune message is sent on a multiaccess network (such as an Ethernet LAN) that has multiple PIM routers attached. PIM-SM employs the same *Prune Override mechanism* described in Chapter 4 for PIM-DM. With this mechanism, any router on the multiaccess network, upon hearing a PIM Prune message, will immediately transmit a Join message to override the Prune message if it is still interested in the multicast traffic.

5.14   ILLUSTRATING PIM-SM SHORTEST-PATH TREE SWITCHOVER

In a PIM-SM domain, each multicast group is associated with one RP and one RPT on it. Before the RP switches over to the SPT, the source-side DR encapsulates all multicast data packets destined to a multicast group in PIM Register messages and sends these messages to the RP. The RP receives these PIM Register messages, extracts the multicast data packets, and forwards them on the RPT to the receiver-side DRs and host receivers. The RP acts as a meeting point for all multicast packets. Sending multicast data through PIM Register messages creates some problems such as the following:

- The source-side DR and the RP need to implement complicated mechanisms for the encapsulation and decapsulation of multicast packets.
- Multicast packets are delivered from the source-side DR along a path that may not be the shortest path to the receivers.
- Increasing the multicast traffic places a bigger burden on the RP, increasing the risk of RP overload or failure.

To solve the cited issues, PIM-SM allows an RP or the receiver-side DR to initiate *an SPT switchover process* (see Figures 5.18 and 5.19):

1. **The RP Initiates an SPT Switchover Process**: Upon receiving the first multicast packets encapsulated in PIM Register messages, the RP sends a PIM (S, G) Join message (via multicast to 224.0.0.13) that travels hop by hop toward the source-side DR to establish an SPT between the DR and the RP. This message contains the IP address of the source, and the WC-bit and RPT-bit are both set to 0 to indicate that the path is a source-based SPT rather than an RPT. Subsequent multicast data packets from the multicast source travel along the established SPT to the RP.
2. **The Receiver-Side DR initiates an SPT Switchover Process**: Upon receiving the first multicast packets from the RP for a multicast group, the

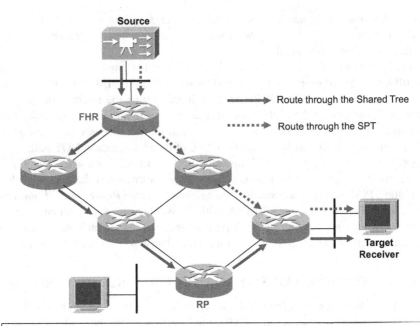

- When a source starts multicasting packets, PIM-SM can switch to a source-rooted tree (SRT), known in PIM-SM as the shortest-path tree (SPT), to improve the network's efficiency.
  - Although a shared tree is able to minimize the network traffic and the costs associated with unnecessary data transmission, the routes in a shared tree might be longer than those in an SPT.
- The First-Hop Router (FHR) on the network determines when the source switches from a shared tree to an SPT. A FHR switches to the SPT when it receives a certain configurable number of packets.
- When all FHRs associated with a specific RP have switched to the SPT, the RP sends a Join/Prune message toward the multicast source.
  - When the multicast source receives this message, it stops sending multicast data through the SPT.

FIGURE 5.18   Shared tree versus shortest-path tree (SPT).

receiver-side DR will see the IP address of the multicast source, so it can send a request directly to the source for the traffic to be sent to it directly rather than through the RP. Using the IP address of the source, the DR initiates an SPT switchover process as follows:

a. The receiver-side DR sends a PIM (S, G) Join message (via multicast to 224.0.0.13) that travels hop by hop toward the source-side DR of the multicast source. As the (S, G) Join message travels to the source-side DR, all the routers on the path install the (S, G) entry in their multicast forwarding table, thus, establishing an SPT branch. The WC-bit and RPT-bit are also both set to 0 in this case.

b. When multicast packets from the source reach a PIM-SM router where the RPT and the SPT diverge, the router drops the multicast packets received from the RPT and sends an *(S, G) RPT-bit Prune message* that

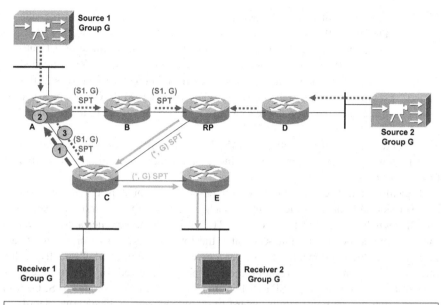

- PIM-SM allows the LHR of a multicast transmission to switch from the shared tree to the SPT for a specific multicast traffic source. Note that the PIM routers and not the receivers initiate the switchover to the SPT of a source.
- The discussion here builds on the previously presented multicast traffic source registration process.

Processing steps:

1. Router C, which is the LHR to Receiver 1, can switch to the SPT for Source 1 and Source 2. For example, for Source 1, Router C sends an (S1, G) Join message toward Source 1.
2. Router A receives the (S1, G) Join message from Router C and adds the interface over which the message was received to the OIL of the (S1, G) state entry in the MRT.
3. By adding the interface to Router C, Router A effectively adds the link to Router C to the (S1, G) SPT.
   - At this point, multicast traffic from Source 1 starts to flow directly to Router C over the (S1, G) SPT.

After creating the (S1, G) SPT from Router A to Router C, there are now two paths over which (S1, G) multicast traffic can flow from Source 1 to Router C, the shared tree and the (S1, G) SPT. This situation results in duplicate multicast traffic being delivered to Router C, creating waste of network bandwidth.

- This means a mechanism (using the (S, G) RPT-bit Prune) must be used to inform the RP to prune the (S1, G) multicast traffic from the shared tree (see discussion on "Pruning a Multicast Traffic Source from the PIM-SM Shared Tree").

FIGURE 5.19 PIM-SM shortest-path tree switchover.

travels hop by hop to the RP. Upon receiving this (S, G) RPT-bit Prune message, the RP prunes off the interface leading to the message sender if it is the only receiver of the (*, G) or RPT traffic on that interface. If no other node needs the (*, G) traffic from the RP, it sends an (S, G) Prune message towards the source-side DR of the multicast source to inform it to stop sending further (S, G) traffic.

c. Finally, multicast data packets are sent directly from the source-side DR along the SPT to the receiver-side DR. Note that the SPT does not include the RP unless the RP itself is located on the shortest path between the multicast source and receiver. Generally, the RP is needed only to start new multicast transfers from sources to receivers. After session initiation, the receiver-side DR sends a PIM (S, G) Join message directly to the source, creating an SPT from the source to the receiver.

Note that the *SPT switchover* allows PIM-SM to build SPTs more economically than PIM-DM which does so through the more bandwidth-consuming and inefficient flood-and-prune mechanism.

Typically, a traffic rate threshold (specified in kilobits) is configured on the receiver-side DR for a multicast group such that, when the threshold is exceeded, the DR switches from the RPT to the SPT. To determine whether a switchover to the SPT should occur, the DR calculates the total aggregate rate of the multicast group traffic flowing down the RPT over a given periodic interval. Typically, if this rate exceeds a configured threshold, the next packet received for that group causes the DR to switch over to the SPT. When this happens, the DR sends an (S, G) Join message that travels hop by hop toward the multicast source. The actual details of how often a router calculates the aggregate traffic rate for the SPT switchover, are implementation-dependent.

As the PIM (S, G) Join messages are received and forwarded by each hop, an SPT is built from the source S to the receiver-side DR. Switching to the SPT allows the shortest path to be used to deliver multicast traffic from the source to the DR. In Figure 5.19, Router C, which is the DR of Receiver 1, initiates a switchover to the SPT for Source 1 by sending a PIM (S1, G) Join toward Source 1. The DR of Source 1, Router A, receives the Join message and adds the interface on which the message was received to the OIL of the (S1, G) state in the MRIB. Multicast traffic then starts flowing on that interface to Router C.

At this point, (S1, G) multicast traffic flows over two paths to Router C, the RPT path via the RP, and the SPT path from Router A to Router C directly. To stop the flow of duplicate (S1, G) traffic to Router C and to prevent the waste of network bandwidth, Router C needs to inform the RP to prune the (S1, G) traffic from the RPT, leaving only the SPT to deliver the traffic to Router C (see discussion in Section 5.14.5).

Depending on the location of the multicast source in relation to the RP, using the SPT can substantially reduce the network delay to the receivers. The drawback is that the routers on the SPT must maintain an increased amount of state as already discussed earlier. Reference [CISCPRWILL03] describes in detail how the maintenance of the (S, G) state leads to relatively higher router memory requirements than the (*, G) state.

5.14.1 Understanding the (S, G) RPT-bit Prune

When the receiver-side DR switches to the SPT rooted at the multicast source, it no longer needs to receive that traffic on the RPT. To stop the flow of this redundant multicast traffic, the receiver-side DR sends an *(S, G) RPT-bit Prune* (which is a special Prune with the RPT-bit set) upstream on the RPT toward the RP. The RPT-bit is set to indicate to the receiving upstream PIM router that the Prune applies to the RPT (and not the SPT). The receiving PIM router interprets the (S, G) RPT-bit Prune as a request to prune the specified (S, G) traffic from the RPT branch on which the message is sent.

Note that, to avoid sending conflicting (S, G) RPT-bit Prune and (*, G) Join on the same router interface, a PIM-SM router will send an (S, G) RPT-bit Prune on the RPT when the RPF neighbor for the (S, G) entry is different from the RPF neighbor of the (*, G) entry [CISCPRWILL03]. This means that the point (node) at which the (S, G) RPT-bit Prune originated is the point at which the RPT and the SPT diverge. In many cases, it is the receiver-side DR that joined the SPT that will originate the (S, G) RPT-bit Prune. However, this is not true when the RPT and the SPT are congruent at the receiver-side DR. If the RPT and SPT are congruent at the DR, then an upstream router will have to originate the (S, G) RPT-bit Prune when it detects it is receiving SPT and RPT traffic from source S but has no need for the RPT traffic. In Figure 5.19, if Router E were to be the receiver-side DR that joined the SPT rooted at Source 1, then Router C is the node that would originate the (S, G) RPT-bit Prune if it has no need for that traffic over the RPT.

When a PIM-SM router receives an (S, G) RPT-bit Prune from a downstream router, it performs the following actions [CISCPRWILL03]:

- Creates an (S, G) entry (if one does not already exist) but sets the RPT-bit for the entry (to 1); that is, creates an (S, G) RPT-bit entry.
- Prunes (i.e., removes) the interface on which the (S, G) RPT-bit Prune was received from the OIL.
- (Re)computes the RPF information (i.e., incoming interface and RPF neighbor) of the (S, G) RPT-bit entry based on the IP address of the RP instead of the IP address of the multicast source.

Note that setting the RPT-bit indicates that the above (S, G) entry applies to the RPT (and not the SPT), and, as a result, the incoming interface of this (special) entry must point up the RPT toward the RP. This means the RPF interface (i.e., the incoming interface) of an (S, G) entry in a PIM-SM router is computed using the IP address of the actual multicast source, *except* when the RPT-bit is set in the entry, in which case the IP address of the RP is used. The (S, G) RPT-bit entry controls the following:

- Setting the RPT-bit of the (S, G) entry allows the receiving router to know which RPF interface to use to forward the (S, G) RPT-bit Prune toward the RP (since this is not a Prune that applies to the SPT rooted at the actual multicast source). The (S, G) RPT-bit entry controls the forwarding of the (S, G) RPT-bit Prune up the RPT toward the RP.
- Setting the RPT-bit of the (S, G) entry also allows the receiving router to know the interface to prune on the RPT for the (S, G) traffic (which is different from an (S, G) traffic prune on the SPT rooted at the source). The (S, G) RPT-bit entry controls the flow of (S, G) traffic down the RPT from the RP (which is different from the flow of (S, G) traffic down the SPT from the source).

5.14.2 FORCING CERTAIN MULTICAST GROUPS TO STAY ON THE SHARED TREE

Although SPTs can reduce network latencies, the decision to allow a receiver-side DR to do an SPT switchover can be made on a multicast group-by-group basis. This is because, in some applications, receivers are better served using the shared tree (or star topology) structure provided by the RP rather than through the SPT after the receiver-side DRs perform SPT switchovers to the multicast source. For example, the network operator may prefer to let the RP handle multicast traffic delivery to receivers for low-rate, one-to-many, or many-to-many applications. Such applications may not warrant the use of the SPT by the receiver-side DR, instead, are best served by the RP through the RPT.

In this case, the network operator can implement mechanisms to force certain multicast groups to stay on the RPT to satisfy application efficiency and network operation requirements. The operator may configure a receiver-side DR to preferably stay on the RPT when attached hosts send requests to join specific groups that are marked as better served via the RPT. Such groups would remain on the RPT as soon as receivers join the groups. The ability to control which groups remain on the RPT also allows the operator to control the amount of multicast state maintained by routers in the PIM-SM domain. This is because the amount of multicast state maintained by routers affects the scalability of a PIM-SM implementation.

5.14.3 ILLUSTRATING PIM-SM SHORTEST-PATH TREE JOINS

Joining the SPT rooted at a multicast source allows multicast traffic to be sent directly to receivers without having to go through the RP, thereby, reducing traffic forwarding delays and the processing load on the RP. Although routers on the SPT would have to maintain (S, G) forwarding state which consumes more router resources as described in [CISCPRWILL03], the join process provides more direct forwarding and RP offloading. Also, the amount of (S, G) state maintained in this case by PIM-SM routers is still much less than what routers would maintain in a PIM-DM network.

It is important to note that the flood-and-prune behavior of PIM-DM requires all routers in the domain to maintain (S, G) state entries in their MRIBs for all active sources even if there are no active receivers for those sources. Allowing LHRs in PIM-SM to join directly the multicast distribution tree of a source allows the creation of optimal trees without incurring the overheads and inefficiencies associated with PIM-DM. Note that PIM-SM cannot do away with the shared tree (mechanism) and rely solely on the use of SPTs because it has no other way of knowing when a source is active and for it to deliver the first stream of multicast packets; a source registration process to an RP is needed so that multicast traffic forwarding can start over the shared tree, after which an SPT can be used. Although this may look convoluted, PIM-SM has better scalability, efficiency, and network resource usage than PIM-DM, making it the preferred protocol for today's multicast networks.

When a host receiver signals for multicast traffic to a group, its LHR sends a PIM (S, G) Join message that is sent hop by hop toward the FHR of the source. As this message is propagated up the SPT, routers along the path set up (S, G) multicast forwarding state so that the requested traffic can be forwarded back down the SPT to the LHR and the receivers.

Figure 5.20 describes an example of how the LHR (Router E) of Receiver 1 joins an (S, G) SPT rooted at a multicast source S. Note that the Router is able know that

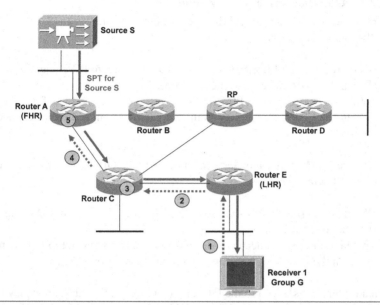

- The PIM router that is directly connected to a source is called the First-Hop Router (FHR), while the one directly connected to a receiver is the Last-Hop Router (LHR).
- In a shared tree, routers (LHRs) with members of multicast group G send (*, G) Join messages toward the RP to join the shared tree and receive multicast traffic for group G.
- Routers can also send (S, G) Join messages toward the multicast traffic source S to join its SPT and directly receive multicast traffic for group G.

Processing steps:
1. Receiver 1 joins the multicast group G by sending an IGMP Membership Report message to Router E.
    - Note that Router E learns that Source S is active because it has received a packet from the source via the RP of the shared tree.
2. Router E joins the SPT for Source S by sending an (S, G) Join message toward the source.
    - Router E uses its unicast routing table to determine the RPF interface to Source S. The Join message is sent over this interface to Source S.
    - In the figure, Router C is the next-hop router to Source S.
3. Router C receives the Join message from Router E and creates an (S, G) state entry in its MRT, and adds the interface on which the Join message was received in the OIL of the (S, G) state entry.
4. After creating the (S, G) state entry, Router C joins the SPT for Source S by sending an (S, G) Join message toward the source.
5. Router A receives the Join message from Router C and adds the interface leading to Router C in the OIL of its existing (S, G) state entry.
    - Note that Router A (which is the FHR of Source S) already created an (S, G) state entry in its MRT as soon as it received the first packet from Source S.

FIGURE 5.20   PIM-SM shortest-path tree joins.

the source S is active because it would have received one or more packets from it via the RPT. After learning about the source via the RPT, the LHR can initiate the creation of the SPT rooted at the source.

5.14.3.1   Observations about PIM Joins

In our observations so far for PIM (S, G) Joins, PIM-SM creates an (S, G) entry under the following conditions:

- Upon receipt of a PIM (S, G) Join from a downstream PIM neighbor.
- When the LHR switches to the SPT rooted at the source.
- When the RP receives a PIM Register message from the FHR for a source.
- When the FHR first receives multicast packets from a directly connected source.

Furthermore, a PIM-SM router adds an interface to the OIL of a (*, G) or (S, G) entry under the following conditions:

- When a (*, G) or (S, G) Join is received from a downstream PIM neighbor via the interface.
- When a directly connected host sends an IGMP Membership Report message on the interface requesting to join multicast group G.

When an interface is added to the OIL of a (*, G) or (S, G) entry, an expiry timer is started and begins counting down to zero. If nothing happens (i.e., no Join or IGMP Membership Report is received) and the timer expires, the interface is removed from the OIL of the state entry. This means the timer is reset any time a PIM Join or IGMP Report message from a directly connected host is received on the interface. Note that PIM-SM routers periodically send (*, G) or (S, G) Join to refresh (*, G) or (S, G) state in upstream PIM routers. Sending such refresh Joins also resets the expiry timers of the upstream interfaces, preventing them from expiring and being removed from the OIL of the (*, G) or (S, G) state.

5.14.4   Illustrating PIM-SM SHORTEST-PATH Tree Prunes

When attached receivers of an LHR no longer need multicast traffic sent to a group, the LHR sends a PIM (S, G) Prune message on the SPT toward the multicast source to prune off that traffic. As the PIM Prune message is propagated hop by hop on the SPT, each router updates its multicast forwarding state, usually by deleting the (S, G) forwarding state.

Figure 5.21 describes an example of how the LHR (Router E) prunes the (S, G) SPT rooted at source S when its only receiver (Receiver 1) leaves multicast group G. Note that the PIM Prune Override mechanism mentioned earlier and described in detail in Chapter 4 for PIM-DM, also applies here when a PIM Prune message is sent on a multiaccess network with several PIM routers attached to it.

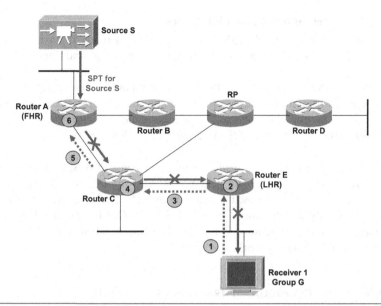

- Branches in a PIM-SM SPT can be pruned using (S, G) Prune messages similar to the prune process using (*, G) Prune messages in PIM-SM shared trees.
  - The PIM-SM Explicit Join/Prune mechanism can be used in SPTs as well as shared trees.
- In the situation where an (S, G) Prune message is sent over a multiaccess network with multiple PIM-SM routers and some of these routers still wish to stay on the SPT, the Prune Override mechanism used in PIM-DM can still be used in PIM-SM to prevent the interested routers on the multiaccess network from being pruned from the SPT.

Processing steps:
1. Receiver 1 leaves multicast group G by sending an IGMP Leave message to Router E.
2. Because Receiver 1 is the only host in multicast group G on the outgoing interface of Router E, this interface is removed from the OIL of the (S, G) state entry.
   - The OIL for the (S, G) state entry becomes empty (null), indicating that Router E no longer needs multicast traffic for group G.
3. With an empty OIL for the (S, G) state entry, Router E sends a (S G) Prune message towards the Source S to prune itself from the SPT.
4. Router C receives the (S, G) Prune message from Router E and removes the interface on which the Prune message was received from the OIL of the (S, G) state entry.
5. Because Router C has no directly connected host and the OIL for the (S, G) state entry is empty (null), it also sends an (S, G) Prune message toward the source.
6. Router A receives the (S, G) Prune message from Router C and removes the interface on which the Prune message was received from the OIL of the (S, G) state entry.
   - However, because Router A is the FHR for Source S and even though the OIL of the (S, G) state entry is empty, it will still keep the (S, G) state entry in its MRT but drop any multicast packets from the source.

FIGURE 5.21   PIM-SM shortest-path tree prunes.

5.14.4.1   Observations about PIM Prunes

In our observations so far for PIM Prunes, a PIM-SM router removes an interface from the OIL of a (*, G) or (S, G) entry under the following conditions:

- When a PIM (*, G) or (S, G) Prune (that is not overridden by a PIM Join) is received from a downstream PIM neighbor on the interface and the interface has no directly connected member(s) of the multicast group.
- When the expiry timer of the interface counts down to zero (i.e., expires).

Note that, unlike a PIM (*, G) Prune, generally, when a PIM-SM router receives an (S, G) Prune from a downstream neighbor, it waits until the (S, G) state times out before it sends the (S, G) Prune upstream on the SPT; the message is not forwarded immediately, only after the state times out [CISCPRWILL03]. In PIM-DM, a pruned interface is typically not removed from the OIL of an (S, G) entry, instead, it is maintained in the OIL but only marked as pruned.

5.14.5   PRUNING A MULTICAST TRAFFIC SOURCE FROM THE PIM-SM SHARED TREE

As shown in Figures 5.19 and 5.22, after a receiver-side DR has established an SPT to a source after receiving initial traffic over the RPT, duplicate traffic flows to the DR over the SPT and RPT paths from the source. PIM-SM allows the receiver-side DR to use a special Prune, the (S, G) RPT-bit Prune, to instruct the RP to prune the source's traffic from the RPT, leaving only the SPT to deliver the traffic to the DR. The (S, G) RPT-bit Prune has the R or RPT bit (also called the RPT-bit), as described in Chapter 3, which indicates that the Prune applies to the RPT and should be forwarded on the RPT toward the RP.

In Figure 5.22, the DR of Receiver 1, Router C, sets the RPT-bit in the (S1, G) Prune and sends it on the RPT and toward the RP to inform routers on the tree path to prune multicast traffic from Source 1 from the RPT. After receiving this Prune, the RP updates its multicast forwarding state and stops forwarding (S1, G) multicast traffic to Router C (since, in this example, there are no other routers on that path that need the (S1, G) traffic).

In this case, the RP in turn sends an (S1, G) Prune toward the source-side DR of Source 1, Router A, to turn off the (S1, G) multicast traffic sent to it (since no other routers downstream of the RP need this traffic in this example). This message travels hop by hop until it reaches the DR of Source 1. The DR receives the Prune, updates its multicast forwarding state, and stops sending (S1, G) multicast traffic to the RP, leaving only the SPT to deliver the traffic to Router C.

Router E continues to receive (S1, G) traffic from the SPT via Router C and is not even aware of the (S1, G) RPT-bit Prune process that just took place upstream. Router E is not even aware that Router C performed a switchover to the SPT for Source 1. Note that in Figure 5.22, multicast traffic from Source 2 still flows through the RP to receivers.

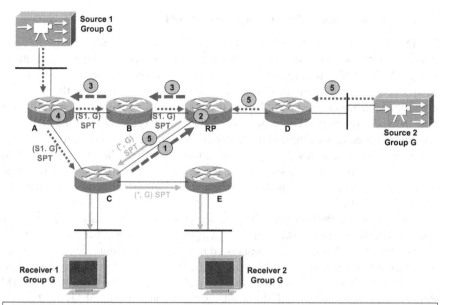

- When (S, G) multicast traffic is delivered via the shared tree and the (S, G) SPT, a special type of PIM Prune message (i.e., the (S, G) RPT-bit Prune)) is used to inform the RP to prune the source from the shared tree.
- This special prune has the RPT flag (or bit) set in the Prune list entry.
- The RPT flag indicates that the Prune message is applicable to the shared tree and should be forwarded along the shared tree toward the RP.

Processing steps:

1. Setting the RPT-bit in an (S1, G) Prune message and sending the message along the shared tree informs the PIM routers along the tree to prune multicast traffic from Source 1 from the shared tree.
   - Router C transmits an (S1, G) RPT-bit Prune message along the shared tree toward the RP to prune multicast traffic from Source 1 from the shared tree.
2. The RP receives the RPT-bit Prune message and updates its MRT to prevent (S1, G) multicast traffic from being forwarded along the link to Router C.
   - Because the link to Router C is the only interface on the shared tree on which (S1, G) traffic can flow from the RP onto the shared tree, we can see that the RP itself no longer has any need for the (S1, G) traffic. Note that our focus here is multicast traffic from Source 1, not Source 2.
3. The RP sends an (S1, G) Prune message toward Source 1 to stop the flow of the unneeded (S1, G) multicast traffic. The Prune message travels hop by hop though Router B until it reaches the FHR of Source 1, Router A.
4. Router A receives the (S1, G) Prune message and prunes the interface leading to the RP (through Router B). Now, (S1, G) traffic is only sent over the link between Router A and Router C.
   - Router E still receives (S1, G) traffic from Router C and is not even aware that its upstream router (Router C) has switched over to the (S1, G) SPT.
5. The second multicast transmission (S2, G) still flows through the RP and along the shared tree to Receivers 1 and 2 because this is the only (S2, G) SPT available.

FIGURE 5.22 Pruning a multicast traffic source from the PIM-SM shared tree.

5.14.6 RECEIVER JOINS ALONG THE PIM-SM SPT

In PIM-SM, as soon as the SPT is constructed between a source and the RP, any intermediate router that lies on the SPT path can use the created (S, G) state to deliver (S, G) traffic from the SPT to any directly attached receivers and to downstream neighbors from whom PIM Join messages were received for the multicast group. Note that, in Figure 5.23, Router B created an (S, G) state only when the RP sent an (S, G) Join to the DR for Source S (i.e., Router A) to construct the SPT. This implies that receivers connected to Router B can join the SPT for Source S without requiring the multicast traffic to pass through the RP. Once the SPT is established between the source and the RP, Router B can promptly transmit (S, G) traffic to interested receivers as soon as they send requests, bypassing the need to route the traffic through the RP.

However, before the SPT is established, the RP receives multicast traffic from the source through unicasted PIM Register messages. Consequently, Router B has no (S, G) state to deliver (S, G) traffic to interested receivers. In this situation, Router B has no choice but to send an (*, G) Join toward the RP to facilitate the reception of the desired traffic. During this process, multicast traffic travels to the RP via unicast PIM Register messages, and the RP decapsulates them and transmits them on the RPT back to Router B even though Router B lies on a potential SPT path to the source. However, once the SPT is established, Router B can simply retrieve the (S, G) traffic from the SPT, eliminating the need to involve the RP.

Even if Router B sends a (*, G) Join message to the RP after the SPT is set up to the source, the RP will realize that the sender is on the incoming interface for the source. Consequently, the RP will refrain from sending the (S, G) traffic back on that interface, allowing Router B to effortlessly retrieve the traffic from the SPT. PIM routers do not forward receive multicast traffic back on the incoming interface (i.e., the incoming interface must not be in the OIL of the (S, G) state), except in the "RP-on-a-stick", also called the "one-leg-RP" configuration described in [CISCPRWILL03].

5.14.7 NOTE ABOUT MAINTAINING PIM-SM (S, G) FORWARDING STATE

The discussion here relates to the (S, G) state entry in the MRIB of an FHR (or source-side DR) and in any intermediate PIM-SM router.

5.14.7.1 PIM-SM (S, G) Forwarding State in a Source-Side DR

When a source has multicast data to send to a particular group, it will start transmitting that data to its FHR or source-side DR, without any form of signaling or solicitation. The multicast data is sent as unsolicited data and the source-side DR takes the necessary steps to get the data to the multicast group members as discussed in various sections above. Note that the DR can tell if a source is directly connected by examining the IP address in the source address field of the multicast packet to see if it is in the same IP subnet. The DR then unicasts the received multicast data encapsulated in PIM Register messages to the RP. The source-side

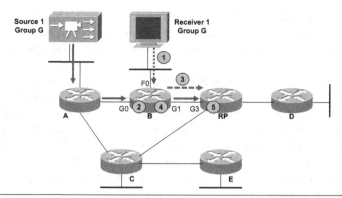

- It is important to note that when a PIM router with a receiver (Router B) is located along the (S, G) SPT between the multicast source and the RP and the RP has already joined the SPT, multicast traffic does not have to first flow to the RP and then be turned around and sent back to Router B.
- We assume that multicast traffic is flowing along the (S, G) SPT from Router A to the RP.
- The (S, G) state entry on the FHR, Router A, is used to forward (S, G) traffic through Router B and along the (S, G) SPT to the RP.

Processing steps:
1. Receiver 1 (the first member) joins multicast group G by sending an IGMP Membership Report message to Router B on Interface F0.
2. Router B receives the IGMP Membership Report message and adds an entry in its IGMP Membership Cache to indicate that Receiver 1 is a member of group G on Interface F0.
   - Router B adds Interface F0 to the OIL of the (*, G) state entry, which causes F0 to be added to all (S, G) entries under the (*, G) state entry.
3. Because Receiver 1 is the first member to join group G, Router B updates its MRT entries for group G and can start forwarding (S, G) traffic to Receiver 1. It does no have to send a (*, G) Join message along the shared tree to the RP, but if it does. Step 5 describes what happens.
4. When Router B receives a multicast packet from the source sent to group G, it performs a lookup in its MRT, finds a matching (S, G) entry, and forwards the packet as follows:
   - Router B performs a RPF check using the (S, G) entry to determine if the packet arrived on the correct incoming interface. In this case, the RPF check succeeds because the packet arrived on the incoming interface, G0.
   - Router B then forwards the packet out all interfaces in the OIL. Because Router B is using the (S, G) entry, the packet is forwarded on Interface F0 to Receiver 1, and on Interface G1 toward the RP.
   - Router B simply grabs any (S, G) traffic as it flows through it to the RP, and forwards it on all interfaces in the OIL of the (S, G) entry. This is because Router B is already on the (S, G) SPT and, therefore, receives multicast traffic from the source via a more direct path (i.e., directly from the FHR, Router A).
5. Although, Router B sent a (*, G) Join message to the RP, this would not cause duplicate (S, G) traffic to flow back on the shared tree from the RP to Router B.
   - Given that the incoming interface (Interface G3) of a multicast packet cannot appear in the OIL of the (S, G) entry, Interface G3 is not maintained in the OIL of the RP's (S, G) entry.
   - This means when the RP receives an (S, G) multicast packet, a search of its MRT will not show Interface G3 in the OIL of the (S, G) entry, and, as a result, that packet will not be forwarded back on Interface G3 toward Router B. A RPF check of the packet shows that the packet arrived on the correct incoming interface (S3). Note that PIM-SM routers always forward on the (S, G) entry if one exists.
   - Using the (S, G) entry, the RP forwards the (S, G) traffic out all the interfaces in the OIL of the (S, G) entry. (S, G) traffic from the source is not forwarded back to Router B.

FIGURE 5.23 Receiver joins along the PIM-SM SPT.

DR at the same time establishes an (S, G) state entry in its MRIB for the source and multicast group. When the RP receives the multicast data encapsulated in PIM Register messages, it also creates (S, G) state entries in its MRIB for the source and multicast group.

To optimize the transfer of multicast data, the RP initiates the creation of an SPT rooted at the source-side DR by sending a PIM (S, G) Join to the DR. All routers on the RPF path to the source-side DR, upon receiving the Join message will create an (S, G) entry in their MRIBs. The SPT is eventually created when the source-side DR receives the (S, G) Join message. The RP switches over to the SPT when it starts receiving multicast data on SPT and sends a PIM Register-Stop message to the source-side DR to stop sending PIM Register messages with encapsulated multicast data.

When the source-side DR starts sending multicast data over the SPT using the (S, G) state in its MRIB, it starts an expiry timer (i.e., the (S, G) Keepalive Timer which is usually a countdown timer) for this entry. This expiry timer is reset every time the source-side DR sends an (S, G) packet over the SPT. If the expiry timer counts down to zero, then the source-side DR assumes that the source has stopped sending data to the multicast group and proceeds to delete the (S, G) state entry in the MRIB.

5.14.7.2 PIM-SM (S, G) Forwarding State in Any Other PIM-SM Router

Note that the same behavior applies when the source-side DR forwards multicast data to an LHR or receiver-side DR that initiated the creation of an SPT. Note that, other than the source-side DR, each router that forwards multicast data using an established (S, G) entry also maintains an associated expiry timer (i.e., (S, G) Keepalive Timer) for each interface in the OIL of the group and deletes the interface's state entry when the timer expires.

As discussed earlier, a PIM-SM router uses the (S, G) Keepalive Timer to keep the interface's (S, G) state alive when no explicit (S, G) Join messages are received on the interface. The timer is reset each time the router receives an (S, G) Join from a downstream PIM neighbor on the interface, and it is also reset when the router has directly attached multicast group members on the interface (indicated by the receipt of IGMP Membership Report messages). Note that resetting the timer every time an (S, G) Join is received implies that there are still (S, G) receivers on the interface and the router is not wasting network bandwidth sending unwanted data. The (S, G) Keepalive Timer is described in various preceding sections.

5.15 ILLUSTRATING PIM-SM DESIGNATED ROUTER ELECTION

As discussed earlier, PIM routers connected to a multiaccess network segment such as an Ethernet LAN use PIM Hello messages to elect one router to act as the DR of the network. In PIM-DM, the DR has meaning only if the network segment uses IGMPv1 because IGMPv1 does not support an IGMP Querier election mechanism. In the absence of such a mechanism, the router that is elected as the DR functions as the IGMP Querier of the network segment. In PIM-SM, the role of the DR is much more elaborate as described here.

5.15.1 Role of the PIM-SM Designated Router

The DR of a multicast source (i.e., source-side DR) is responsible for sending PIM Register messages containing multicast packets from the source to the RP, receiving and acting on PIM Register-Stop messages sent by the RP, and sending PIM Null-Register messages to the RP when appropriate. The DR of a multicast receiver (i.e., the receiver-side DR) is responsible for sending a PIM (*, G) Join message towards the RP of a multicast group when a host sends a request (through an IGMP Membership Report) to join the group, sending a PIM (*, G) Prune message toward the RP when all receivers attached to it leave a multicast group, sending a PIM (S, G) toward the multicast source to establish a more optimal SPT, and sending a PIM (S, G) Prune message when all receivers attached to it leave a multicast group.

5.15.2 PIM-SM Designated Router Election

In Figure 5.24, Router A and Router B are connected to a common multiaccess network segment with IP address 192.16.1.1.1/24 and with one receiver, Receiver 1, of multicast group 225.1.10.10. Because PIM-SM is based on the Explicit Join model, only the DR (Router A, having the higher IP address 192.16.1.250) is permitted to send a (*, G) PIM Join to the RP to construct the RPT for the group. If both Router

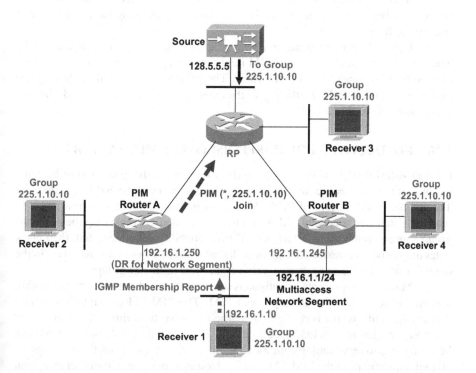

FIGURE 5.24 PIM-SM Designated Router.

A and Router B are allowed to send (*, G) Joins to the RP, parallel paths would be created, resulting in Receiver 1 receiving duplicate multicast traffic from the RP.

By the same token, if Receiver 1 has been a multicast source, and a DR is not present, both routers will send PIM Register messages, resulting in the RP receiving duplicate Register messages and multicast packets. This example shows the importance of electing a DR (Router A) for the network segment to perform the functions described in the preceding text.

5.15.3 PIM-SM DESIGNATED ROUTER FAILOVER

PIM-SM also provides a method to detect the failure of the current DR of a multicast network segment. If for some reason the DR, Router A, fails, Router B will detect the failure when its PIM neighbor adjacency with Router B times out. When this happens, a new DR election will take place, and Router B will become the new DR; the DR election will be more involved if multiple routers are still active on the network segment after the DR failure.

In Figure 5.24, Router B is aware that an active member of the multicast group (Receiver 1) still exits on the network because it continues to see the IGMP Membership Report message from Receiver 1. As a result, Router B already and still has an active IGMP state for the multicast group 225.1.10.10, which will cause Router B to send an (*, 225.1.10.10) Join to the RP as soon as it is elected the new DR. Doing so reestablishes a new branch of the RPT to Router B, allowing multicast traffic to continue to flow to Receiver 1.

Similarly, if Receiver 1 were a multicast source, Router B, upon being elected the new DR, would immediately send PIM Register messages to the RP upon receiving the next multicast packets from this source. The RP, upon receiving the PIM Register messages from Router B, would trigger the creation of an SPT to Router B, the new source-side DR of Receiver 1.

5.16 RENDEZVOUS POINT (RP) DISCOVERY MECHANISMS

For a PIM-SM domain to operate correctly, all routers in the domain must be capable of mapping a specific multicast group address to the same RP in the domain. The RP is a core concept of PIM-SM. For all multicast traffic sent to a group to reach all interested receivers, all routers in the PIM domain must map the multicast group address to the same RP address. If this capability is not provided, then black holes may appear in the forwarding of multicast packets, where some receivers in the domain may not be able to receive traffic from some multicast groups.

A PIM domain represents a contiguous set of routers configured to operate within a common boundary and all implement PIM. The PIM-SM domain must ensure that any RP address that is configured, learned, or advertised through any of the RP discovery mechanisms is reachable from all routers in the PIM domain. An RP can be configured to serve multiple multicast groups (i.e., a range of multicast groups) or all multicast groups in the PIM-SM domain. However, only one RP can serve a given multicast group or range in the PIM-SM domain at any given time.

Note that a PIM domain can further be divided into multiple administrative scope regions, where each region has one or more border routers that have been configured such that, traffic to a range of multicast group addresses will not be forwarded across the border routers. Chapter 1 discusses administratively scoped IP multicast forwarding [RFC2365]. The modified criteria for administratively scoped multicast regions are that the region is convex concerning multicast packet forwarding based on the MRIB, and all PIM routers within the scoped region must be able to map the scoped multicast groups to the same RP within that region. All PIM routers within the same administrative scope region must map a particular administratively scoped multicast group address to the same RP within that region.

Note that a PIM-SM domain does not need to use only a single mechanism to provide the routers within the domain with the information required to perform the group-to-RP mapping. Four group-to-RP mechanisms are discussed in this section; Static RP, Embedded-RP, Auto-RP, and Bootstrap Router (BSR) mechanisms. Each method for RP discovery has its own weaknesses, strengths, and level of complexity. The BSR mechanism is currently the recommended method for RP discovery because it is easy to configure, is well-tested, and is stable.

5.16.1 STATIC RP

A Static RP, which is the simplest solution, is where the network operator configures manually group-to-RP mappings on all routers in a PIM domain. Typically, using Static RP requires configuring all leaf routers (i.e., source-side DRs and receiver-side DRs) with the IP address of an RP for a multicast group or set of groups. Generally, a PIM router is required to support at a minimum the static configuration of group-to-RP mappings. Although such a mechanism provides a basic interoperability mechanism for PIM routers, it is not robust to RP failures.

Static configuration of RPs generally has poor scalability and does not dynamically adapt to router or link failures, except when used in conjunction with the Anycast-RP mechanism (see discussion in the subsequent text). Also, configuring Static RP for a large PIM network can be a tedious task and prone to errors as a result of mistyped information. Configuring Static RPs in a small PIM-SM network is relatively simple, but it can be very difficult in a large, complex PIM-SM network. When there is the need to change the RP address or reassign the RP task to another router in the network, the network administrator has to manually update this information on all routers in the network. During this update process, the RP information may be inconsistent on routers in the network until the update process is complete. This inconsistency in addition to human errors may cause multicast forwarding outages until all routers have the same RP information.

Generally, the network operator configures a Static RP only as a backup for the dynamic RP discovery mechanism to enhance the operation manageability and robustness of a multicast network. For a simple, small-sized network, one RP is most often enough for forwarding multicast traffic throughout the PIM-SM network. The position of this RP can be statically configured on each router in the PIM-SM domain. In most cases, however, a PIM-SM domain spans a wide geographical area and a large amount of multicast traffic needs to be forwarded through multiple routers to widely distributed multicast group members.

To lessen the burden on any particular RP and to optimize the topological structure of the RPT, the network operator would typically configure multiple Candidate-RPs in a PIM-SM domain, among which an RP is dynamically elected for one or more particular multicast groups using dynamic RP discovery mechanisms such as Auto-RP and BSR mechanisms. Each RP elected from the Candidate-RPs serves a different multicast group range; a group or group range cannot be served by more than one RP. For this purpose, an Auto-RP or BSR must be configured in the PIM-SM domain. For example, the BSR normally serves as an administrative mechanism or interface for the PIM-SM domain.

A PIM-SM domain can support only one BSR at any given time but can have multiple Candidate-BSRs ready to be used. Once the active BSR of the domain fails, a new BSR is automatically elected from the Candidate-BSRs to avoid multicast service interruption. Note that a PIM-SM router can serve as a Candidate-RP and a Candidate-BSR at the same time.

5.16.2 EMBEDDED-RP

Reference [RFC3956] defines an address allocation policy called Embedded-RP, essentially a multicast group-to-RP mapping mechanism, where the address of an RP is encoded in the IPv6 multicast group address within a multicast packet. Embedded-RP applies to IPv6 multicasting only and provides a group-to-RP mapping mechanism. In this mechanism, a PIM-SM router derives the address of the RP for a multicast group transparently from the encoded IPv6 multicast address instead of obtaining it from local configuration or RP discovery protocols like the BSR mechanism.

With Embedded-RP, the IPv6 PIM-SM domain does not have to use BSR or other RP configuration mechanisms throughout the domain, as each IPv6 multicast group address in a packet specifies the RP to be employed. This mechanism provides a simple multicast group-to-RP mapping solution for IPv6 interdomain multicasting (MSDP [RFC3618] not needed) as well as IPv6 intra-domain multicasting with scoped multicast addresses (e.g., BSR not needed). The packet with the Embedded-RP as it is propagated, provides a way of communicating the information about (active) multicast sources to routers within a PIM-SM domain and in other multicast domains.

When a receiver wishes to join a multicast group and issues a Multicast Listener Discovery (MLD) Report message, the receiver-side DR will initiate the join process by sending a PIM-SM Join message toward the RP encoded in the IPv6 multicast address, irrespective of whether that RP is located in the local or remote PIM-SM domain. When a source sends traffic to a multicast group, the source-side DR will send the multicast packets encapsulated in PIM Register messages and unicast them to the RP address encoded in the multicast address (in the special case where the source-side DR is also the RP, such forwarding is only conceptual).

Compared to the other multicast group-to-RP mapping mechanisms, which can precompute the mapping for new multicast group requests, a PIM-SM using the

Embedded-RP mapping mechanism must recompute the mapping for every new IPv6 multicast group address in a packet that maps to a different RP. For efficiency, the router may cache the mapping results in an implementation-specific manner to avoid recomputing the mapping for every Embedded-RP packet.

The RP being mapped to, the DR adjacent to the multicast traffic source, and any PIM-SM router on the path from any receiver to the RP must support the Embedded-RP group-to-RP mapping mechanism. PIM-SM routers along the paths for SPT formation as well as those that respond to PIM Register-Stop messages do not need to support this mechanism, as their construction can be accomplished with an (S, G) Join messages.

5.16.3 AUTO-RP

When PIM-SM version 1 (PIM-SMv1) was introduced, network operators were required to manually configure the IP address of the RP on all leaf routers (routers directly connected to sources or receivers); configuration is also known as Static RP. To allow dynamic configuration of RP information, Cisco introduced the Auto-RP mechanism for PIM-SMv1, allowing dynamic distribution of multicast group-to-RP mappings in a PIM-SMv1 network. Auto-RP was developed by Cisco to provide automatic discovery of the RP before the BSR mechanism was specified for PIM-SMv2 [CISCPRWILL03]. Although Auto-RP has been obsoleted by the BSR mechanism, it is still discussed here because of its historical significance and to show the limitations that led to the development of the BSR mechanism.

5.16.3.1 How Auto-RP Works

To implement Auto-RP, the network operator designates certain routers as *Candidate-RPs* in the PIM-SM domain and these routers are identified by unique IP addresses, usually assigned to a loopback interface in the router. The operator also manually designates and configures one or more routers as *Auto-RP Mapping Agents*, unlike in the BSR mechanism where the mapping agents (called BSRs) are elected. These RP Mapping Agents are responsible for mapping multicast groups to particular RPs. Auto-RP uses two reserved IPv4 multicast addresses, *224.0.1.39* and *224.0.1.40*.

An Auto-RP Mapping Agent receives the RP announcement messages from the Candidate-RPs configured in the network and arbitrates conflicts. The RP Mapping Agent then creates consistent multicast group-to-RP mappings and transmits this information to all other routers in a *PIM-DM flooding* fashion as described here. This allows all routers in the multicast domain to automatically discover which RP to use for any given multicast group.

When a router in the PIM-SM domain is configured as a Candidate-RP for one or more multicast groups, it uses *RP-Announce messages* to advertise itself and the multicast groups for which it is a Candidate-RP (see Figure 5.25). A router may be configured to advertise itself as the Candidate-RP, for example, for the multicast group ranges 239.25.0.0 to 239.255.255.255 and 224.0.0.0 to 231.255.255.255. The Candidate-RP multicasts these messages every RP_ANNOUNCE_INTERVAL (default is 60 seconds) to the reserved *Cisco-RP-Announce multicast address*

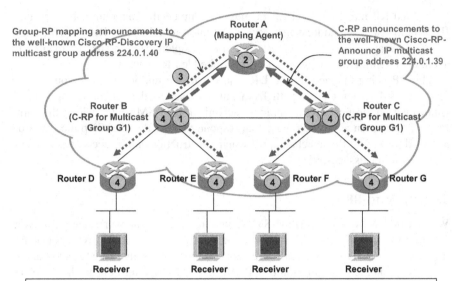

Group-RP mapping announcements to the well-known Cisco-RP-Discovery IP multicast group address 224.0.1.40

Router A (Mapping Agent)

C-RP announcements to the well-known Cisco-RP-Announce IP multicast group address 224.0.1.39

Router B (C-RP for Multicast Group G1)

Router C (C-RP for Multicast Group G1)

Router D   Router E   Router F   Router G

Receiver   Receiver   Receiver   Receiver

- Cisco PIM routers in a PIM-SM network join the well-known Cisco-RP-Discovery IP multicast group address 224.0.1.40 in order to learn/receive active Group-to-RP mapping information that is maintained in a specific Cisco router that is configured as the Mapping Agent. The Mapping Agent itself may also be an RP.
- Mapping Agents also join the well-known Cisco-RP-Announce IP multicast group address 224.0.1.39 in order to learn which PIM routers are possible Candidate-RPs (C-RPs) in the PIM-SM network.

Processing steps:
1. Routers B and C (which are both C-RPs) multicast their RP candidate announcements to the Cisco-RP-Announce multicast group address 224.0.2.39.
2. Router A (which is configured as the Mapping Agent) receives these RP candidate announcements and selects the PIM router (C-RP) with the highest IP address as the active RP.
3. The Mapping Agent then multicasts the selected Group-to-RP mapping information to all PIM routers in the network using the well-known Cisco-RP-Discovery IP multicast group address 224.0.1.40.
4. All the PIM routers in the network (which have already automatically joined the Cisco-RP-Discovery IP multicast group when they started up) receive the Group-to-RP mapping information.

FIGURE 5.25   Auto-RP mechanism.

224.0.1.39 (using UDP port 496). Each RP-Announce message contains a *hold-time* field with a value that indicates to the RP Mapping Agent how long the Candidate-RP announcement is valid. The Candidate-RP sets the *holdtime* field value to 3 times the RP_ANNOUNCE_INTERVAL (default is 180 seconds). The RP Mapping Agents configured for the PIM-SM domain listen for messages on this multicast address.

The RP Mapping Agent (Router A in Figure 5.25) listens to the multicast address 224.0.1.39 for advertised RP-Announce messages, then selects from all of these messages, a single RP for a multicast group based on the numerically highest IP address of all the Candidate-RPs for the group. The information from the received

RP-Announce messages is used to establish entries in the RP Mapping Agent's *Group-to-RP Mapping Cache*. The Mapping Agent creates only one entry in the Mapping Cache for any received group-to-RP range even if multiple Candidate-RPs sent RP announcements for the same multicast group. The Mapping Agent selects the Candidate-RP with the highest IP address and adds this address as an entry in the Group-to-RP Mapping Cache.

A router when configured as an RP Mapping Agent, automatically joins the multicast group 224.0.1.39. The RP Mapping Agent then uses *RP-Discovery messages* to advertise the complete list of multicast group-to-RP mappings in its Group-to-RP Mapping Cache. The Mapping Agents follow a few rules when building their RP-Discovery messages:

- If a Mapping Agent receives two RP-Announce messages with announcements that have the same multicast group range but different RPs, it will select the announcement with the highest RP IP address.
- If the Mapping Agent receives two RP announcements where one multicast group is a subset of another but the RPs are different, it will send both.
- The Mapping Agent will group all other RP announcements without any conflict resolution.

The Mapping Agent multicasts the contents of its Group-to-RP Mapping Cache in RP-Discovery messages every RP_DSICOVERY_INTERNAL (default is 60 seconds) to the reserved *Cisco-RP-Discovery multicast address 224.0.1.40* (using UDP port 496) (see Figure 5.25). All routers in the network at system startup time automatically join the multicast group 224.0.1.40 to be able to receive the multicast group-to-RP mapping information carried in RP-Discovery messages. Each RP-Discovery message also contains a *holdtime* field with a value that indicates to routers in the network how long the advertised group-to-RP mapping information is valid. The Mapping Agent sets the *holdtime* field value to 3 times the RP_DISCOVERY_INTERVAL (default is 180 seconds).

The Mapping Agent stores the RP information for a multicast group obtained from received RP-Discovery messages in the Group-to-RP Mapping Cache and sets an expiry timer for that entry in the cache. This timer is initialized to the *holdtime* value in the received RP-Announce message, which is the period that must expire before the Mapping Agent deletes that group-to-RP mapping entry from the Mapping Cache. When an entry expires, the Mapping Agent selects a new corresponding group-to-RP mapping information and sends that information in RP-Discovery messages to all routers in the PIM-SM domain.

All Cisco routers in the PIM-SM domain listen for RP-Discovery messages sent to this multicast address, enabling them to identify the correct RP for each known multicast group. If the PIM-SM domain has multiple RP Mapping Agents, each agent receives transmissions from all others. Subsequently, all the Mapping Agents, excluding the one with the highest IP address, discontinue transmitting RP-Discovery messages.

All regular routers in the multicast domain listen to the multicast group address 224.0.1.40 for the RP-Discovery messages. Based on the content of RP-Discovery messages, a router populates its Auto-RP Cache when it learns about multicast group-to-RP mappings. The Auto-RP Cache contains both "negative" and "positive" entries.

- When a router looks for an RP for a multicast group, it will first scan through the negative entries in the Auto-RP Cache. If a match is found in this list for a multicast group, it considers that group to be PIM-DM. Note that the router effectively ignores RP information for the negative entries.
- If the router does not find the group in the "negative" list, it looks it up in the "positive" list. Because every multicast group in this list is bound to a particular RP, conflicts may exist when multiple RPs map to overlapping multicast group address ranges. The router then uses the longest prefix match rule to resolve all conflicting mapping: if multiple matches exist, the router selects only the one with the longest prefix length.

Usually, the network operator configures multiple Candidate-RPs on a network for either load balancing or redundancy, or both. For load balancing, the operator configures a *group-mapping access-list* so that each RP services a range of multicast group addresses. For redundancy, the operator would configure both RPs to service the same group address ranges. In such a case, The Mapping Agent selects the RP with the highest IP address, but the other is still available for failover.

The network operator may configure the Auto-RP Mapping Agent to perform filtering of incoming RP announcements sent by Candidate-RPs. With this, the Mapping Agents filter only received Auto-RP announcements by listening to the multicast address 224.0.1.39. A Mapping Agent inspects RP announcements, and if a match is found for a multicast group and the RP IP address, it takes action based on a "permit" or "deny" statement.

An important concern about Auto-RP is how messages sent to the multicast group addresses 224.0.1.39 and 224.0.1.40 are propagated across the multicast domain. Because the domain has no explicit RP information defined for these multicast groups, such messages must use PIM-DM forwarding. This requires the configuration of PIM Sparse-Dense Mode on all router interfaces within the multicast domain, which can be a tedious thing to do in a large-scale network. The *Auto-RP Listener* feature can be used to address this problem.

If a router is not able to receive RP-Discovery messages and its group-to-RP mapping information expires, it switches to a statically configured RP (if one was specified). If no Static RP is configured, then the router switches the multicast group(s) to PIM-DM [CISCPRWILL03], since no RP information is needed in this mode of operation.

5.16.3.2 Configuring Multiple Auto-RP Mapping Agents for Redundancy

A network operator may configure two or more RP Mapping Agent in the PIM-SM domain for redundancy, so that, in the event the primary Mapping Agent fails, the secondary one will continue to operate to provide the required services. However, in practice, when multiple Mapping Agents are used in the same domain, each one works independently, multicasting RP-Discovery messages containing multicast group-to-RP mapping information to all routers in the domain. This means that when two Mapping Agents, Mapping Agent A and Mapping Agent B, are configured in the domain, each will send its own RP-Discovery messages to the routers in the domain, resulting in each router receiving RP-Discovery messages from both Mapping Agents.

Note that both Mapping Agents receive the same RP announcements from the Candidate-RPs in the network and use the same selection algorithm (which is based on the Candidate-RP with the highest IP address) to select the RP for a multicast group. This means all routers in the domain at any given time will create the same multicast group-to-RP mapping information in their Group-to-RP Mapping Cache entries even though they received redundant information from multiple Mapping Agents. The only noticeable difference (which does not affect the functioning of the multicast routers) is that the entries in a router's Group-to-RP Mapping Cache for RP-Discovery messages received from Mapping Agent A and Mapping Agent B may indicate a different source for the group-to-RP mapping information, which in itself has no detrimental effects for multicast forwarding; the group-to-RP mapping information is the same.

The main advantage of configuring multiple Mapping Agents is that they can operate simultaneously and independently and do not need to maintain a master-slave relationship between themselves nor require any complex failover mechanism or protocol in the event of a Mapping Agent failure. With each Mapping Agent operating simultaneously and independently, redundancy is seamlessly provided and each router in the PIM-SM domain is provided with identical group-to-RP mapping information.

Note that RP-Discovery messages are transmitted via UDP and, thus, are transmitted unreliably without the provision to detect missing messages and allow retransmission of messages. Using multiple Mapping Agents in the PIM-SM domain for redundancy, therefore, provides the unintended benefit of increasing the reliability of RP-Discovery message transmission and the delivery of group-to-RP mapping information to routers in the domain, because the Mapping Agents are always transmitting redundant information.

5.16.3.3 Using the Time-to-Live (TTL) and Access List Mechanisms to Constrain Auto-RP Messages and Multicast Traffic

When a Candidate-RP is being configured, the TTL value (i.e., TTL scope in hop count) that is specified in transmitted RP-Announce messages by that device must be carefully chosen to be sufficiently large enough to ensure that the messages reach all RP Mapping Agents in the PIM-SM domain; the messages must be able to reach the far side of the domain. Similarly, the TTL scope of RP-Discovery messages must be sufficiently large enough to allow these messages to reach all routers in the domain so that they can all receive the group-to-RP mapping information.

Desirably, the TTL scope must be configured to cover the maximum diameter of the PIM-SM domain. This configuration ensures that RP-Announce and RP-Discovery messages will be sent with a TTL that is sufficiently large enough to reach all nodes in the domain. The network operator may also configure an access list (i.e., access filters) to set up multicast boundaries to prevent RP-Announce and RP-Discovery messages from traveling beyond those boundaries.

A border router in this case will run the access lists to prevent these messages (sent to multicast addresses 224.0.1.39 and 224.0.1.40) from crossing into or out of the configured boundary. The access lists may also be used to prevent administratively scoped multicast traffic (sent to the address range from 239.0.0.0 to 239.255.255.255) from crossing into or out of the scoped boundary. Configuring a multicast boundary for a sub-domain has the additional benefit of preventing RP-Announce and RP-Discovery messages originated by routers outside the sub-domain from leaking into the sub-domain and creating multicast forwarding problems.

For example, the multicast boundary can filter RP-Announce messages sent by a bogus or rogue Candidate-RP outside the domain. This filtering prevents them from reaching the Mapping Agents within the domain and causing potential issues. Without filtering, the Mapping Agents may select this bogus Candidate-RP if its IP address is higher than the addresses of the valid internal Candidate-RPs. The Mapping Agents in this case would advertise this bogus Candidate-RP to all routers within the domain, causing them to use it when initiating multicast forwarding to a group. Such hijacking of multicast forwarding has serious security implications not to mention the potential disruptions in multicast traffic forwarding and services.

The multicast boundary may also filter external RP-Discovery messages (possibly bogus ones), preventing them from crossing (leaking) into the scoped boundary and causing problems. Providing all routers in the network with correct multicast group-to-RP mapping information is critical to maintaining proper PIM-SM operations.

5.16.3.4   Limitations of Auto-RP: "The Chicken-and-Egg Problem"

Auto-RP introduces a "chicken-and-egg problem"; its primary purpose is to enable routers to automatically discover the RPs for a given multicast group. However, for routers to receive the RP-Announce and RP-Discovery messages through multicast, the PIM-SM routers do not have initial multicast state for these groups nor know an RP to which they would need to send Join messages. This lack of knowledge prevents the routers from knowing how to propagate the RP-Announce and RP-Discovery messages, creating a "chicken-and-egg problem". It is essential to note that PIM-DM and PIM-SM create the initial multicast state for a source as follows:

- In PIM-DM, the routers in the multicast domain do not have an initial multicast state; therefore, PIM-DM floods multicast data from a source, hop by hop to all parts of the domain to allow routers to create a multicast state for the source. Routers can then prune interfaces that do not have receivers interested in the multicast traffic.
- In PIM-SM, routers on the path from a multicast source to the designated RP do not have an initial multicast state for the source; so, PIM-SM allows the source-side DR to register the source with the RP using unicast PIM Register messages. The RP then has the option to send a PIM (S, G) Join message towards the DR, allowing each router that receives the message

to create an (S, G) state, and eventually, an SPT to be created between the source and the RP. Multicast data can then be sent natively along the SPT from the source to the RP since each router on the SPT already has an (S, G) state.

In Figure 5.26, Router A and Router C advertise themselves as Candidate-RPs in the network through RP-Announce messages. These two routers will transmit their RP-Announce messages addressed to 224.0.1.39 on all directly connected interfaces where PIM is enabled. We assume Router B is configured as the Auto-RP Mapping Agent of the network. The Mapping Agent receives the RP-Announce messages from

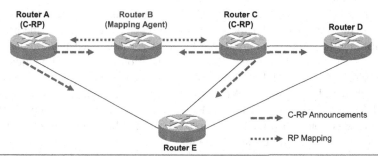

- Each C-RP announces itself for one or more multicast groups by sending RP-Announce messages to the multicast address 224.0.1.39. on all directly connected interfaces where PIM is enabled
- The Auto-RP Mapping Agent gathers information about all C-RPs by listening to the RP-Announce messages.
- The Mapping Agent builds a mapping table that lists the currently best C-RP for each range of multicast groups, with the mapping agent choosing the C-RP with the highest IP address if multiple C-RPs support the same multicast groups.
- The Mapping Agent sends RP-Discover messages to the multicast address 224.0.1.40 advertising the mappings on all directly connected interfaces where PIM is enabled; (i.e., to only directly connected PIM neighbors).
- All PIM routers listen for RP-Discover messages sent to 224.0.1.40 to learn the mapping information and find the correct RP to use for each multicast group.
- Router B, the Mapping Agent, sends RP-Discover (mapping) messages to Router A and Router C and these PIM routers have now learned which RP they can use.
- However, Routers D and E do not receive the RP mapping messages for the following reasons:
    - In PIM-SM, which operates on a "pull" or Explicit Join model, multicast traffic is only forwarded when a downstream PIM router requests it via a PIM (*, G) Join message which is sent to the RP.
    - So, neither Router A nor Router C would forward multicast packets (RP mapping messages) to Routers D and E unless they request it.
    - However, because Routers D and E do not know the address of the RP, they cannot send PIM Join messages to be able to receive multicast traffic including the RP-Discovery messages
    - These routers would need to send a PIM Join toward the RP, which they do not know yet, which is a classical chicken and egg problem.
- Two solutions are available for solving the Auto-RP chicken and egg problem:
    - PIM Sparse-Dense mode
    - PIM Auto-RP Listener

FIGURE 5.26   Limitations of Auto-RP: chicken-and-egg problem.

Router A and Router C, elects Router A as the RP (assuming it has the highest IP address), and then advertises this information to all routers in the network.

The Mapping Agent sends RP-Discovery messages, containing the RP address of Router A and the groups that it will serve. The Mapping Agent sends these messages (addressed to 224.0.1.40) on all directly connected interfaces where PIM is enabled. Router A and Router C, being directly attached routers, receive these messages and learn which RP to use. However, because Router D and Router E are not directly attached to the Mapping Agent, they do not receive the RP-Discovery messages. Also, because Router C (being a PIM-SM router) has not joined an RP for the multicast group 224.0.1.40 and has no initial multicast state for the group, it cannot forward the messages to Router D and Router E.

It is important to note that a PIM-SM has to join an RP for a multicast group to be able to create a state for the group and to receive traffic sent to the group. In PIM-SM, multicast traffic is only forwarded when a router requests it through a PIM (*, G) Join message. For example, Router A is not going to forward multicast messages addressed to 224.0.1.40 to Router E unless Router E requests it. This is a classical chicken-and-egg problem. When Router D/Router E wants to receive traffic for 224.0.1.40, they will have to send a PIM Join to the RP address for group 224.0.1.40. However, these routers (in fact, all routers except the Mapping Agent) have no idea what the RP address is for group 224.0.1.40.

To overcome this "chicken-and-egg problem", Cisco developed a variation of PIM called PIM Sparse-Dense Mode. In PIM Sparse-Dense Mode, a router in the multicast domain uses PIM-DM rules when it does not know the identity of the RP responsible for a group, and PIM-SM rules when it knows the identity of the designated RP. So, when using Auto-RP, the routers in the domain would use PIM Sparse-Dense Mode long enough to learn the group-to-RP mappings advertised by the Auto-RP Mapping Agent, and then switch to PIM-SM. Additionally, if any other multicast traffic is sent by a source before the routers learn the group-to-RP mapping information through Auto-RP, this multicast traffic would still be forwarded using PIM-DM rules.

Cisco proposed two options for solving the Auto-RP problem (see discussion here):

- PIM Sparse-Dense Mode
- PIM Auto-RP Listener

The BSR mechanism, which does not suffer the Auto-RP problems, is now the preferred method for advertising group-to-RP mapping information in PIM-SM and BIDIR-PIM networks.

5.16.3.5 PIM Sparse-Dense Mode

With Auto-RP, the multicast group addresses 224.0.1.39 and 224.0.1.40 play a central role in announcing multicast groups and RP information across the multicast domain. However, as no explicit RP information exists in the domain for these groups, messages addressed to them must use PIM-DM forwarding. Thus, a prerequisite for using the Auto-RP mechanism is that all interfaces in the network must be configured in PIM Sparse-Dense Mode.

An interface configured in PIM Sparse-Dense Mode is treated in either PIM-SM or PIM-DM of operation, depending on the mode the multicast group is operating. If a multicast group is associated with a known RP, the interface operates in the PIM-SM. If a multicast group is not associated with any known RP, the interface operates in the PIM-DM and multicast packets will be flooded over this interface. In Figure 5.26, PIM Sparse-Dense Mode allows messages to 224.0.1.40 to be flooded throughout the network so that Router D and Router E can also identify the correct RP address to use.

In Auto-RP, the PIM-DM multicast group 224.0.1.40 in the multicast domain is used to announce multicast group-to-RP mappings from a central location. This mechanism, which was only intended for use with PIM-SMv1, does not have much use if the PIM-SM domain does not also run PIM-DM in parallel. Auto-RP is not currently standardized or used in practical PIM-SM networks because of its limitations and drawbacks.

5.16.3.6   PIM Auto-RP Listener

The Auto-RP Listener feature is a solution that allows a multicast domain to use Auto-RP without risking any multicast groups falling back to PIM-DM forwarding. This feature works in combination with PIM-SM enabled on all router interfaces (not PIM Sparse-Dense Mode). However, even with this feature, messages sent to the two Auto-RP multicast group addresses, 224.0.1.39 and 224.0.1.40, are flooded in PIM-DM. The routers in the network will use PIM-DM only for the 224.0.1.39 and 224.0.1.40 addresses. With this feature, no other multicast groups are allowed to use PIM-DM, and thus, the undesirable situation of PIM-DM flooding fallback is eliminated.

5.16.3.7   Differences between Auto-RP and the BSR Mechanism

One advantage of Auto-RP is that any required changes to the RP designation in the PIM-SM network need only be configured only on the routers designated as RPs, sparing the need for changes on the leaf routers. Additionally, Auto-RP supports the ability to scope the RP address within the PIM-SM domain. To implement scoping in the PIM-SM domain, the network operator has to define the TTL value allowed for the Auto-RP advertisements.

The BSR mechanism discussed here provides dynamic RP discovery services similar to Auto-RP but defines Candidate-RPs that send RP information to an elected BSR. The BSR then relays the group-to-RP mapping information to all routers in the PIM-SM domain. The BSR distributes RP information using Bootstrap messages carried within PIM messages. PIM messages are defined as link-local multicast messages propagated from PIM router to PIM router. This single-hop method of propagating RP information throughout the domain does not allow TTL scoping to be used with the BSR mechanism. The BSR mechanism effectively provides the same services similar to Auto-RP, except that it does not require the PIM-DM to disseminate RP information, and it does not support TTL scoping within the PIM-SM domain.

The BSR mechanism, rather than using PIM-DM to propagate its RP information, shares the group-to-RP mappings via Bootstrap messages on a hop-by-hop basis; such messages are flooded from one router to another in the domain. The Bootstrap message flooding procedure utilizes RPF: a router, upon receiving a Bootstrap message, applies an RPF check based on the source IP address in the message. If the RPF check succeeds, the router floods the message out of all PIM-enabled interfaces until all routers in the domain learn the mapping information.

Unlike the Auto-RP Mapping Agent, the BSR does not select the best RP for every multicast group address range it learns about but instead builds a set of Candidate-RPs and then shares this information with other PIM routers via Bootstrap messages. It is up to each router to select the best matching RP from the RP-Sets advertised by the BSR. However, all routers must select the same RP for a given multicast group. The RP selection algorithm used (discussed in a section below), however, allows all routers in the domain to select the same RP for any given multicast group.

5.16.4 BOOTSTRAP ROUTER (BSR)

The Bootstrap Router (BSR) mechanism [RFC5059] specifies a method for the automatic election of a special router in the PIM domain called a BSR which allows routers in the multicast domain to learn about RPs for multicast groups (i.e., group-to-RP mappings). Any router in the PIM domain that is configured to be a potential RP (i.e., a Candidate-RP (C-RP)) reports its candidacy via unicast to the BSR. The BSR then uses a domain-wide flooding mechanism to distribute its chosen set of RPs throughout the PIM domain. The BSR mechanism is designed to be dynamic, self-configuring, and robust to PIM router failures. The BSR can be used in PIM-SM and BIDIR-PIM networks.

Similar to other PIM control messages, Bootstrap messages are carried in IP packets with the IP protocol number of 103. Usually, the BSR multicasts Bootstrap messages with the IP TTL of 1 to the ALL-PIM-ROUTERS multicast group address (224.0.0.13 for IPv4 and ff02::d for IPv6), but in some circumstances, the BSR may unicast Bootstrap messages to a specific PIM neighbor. PIM messages sent to the address 224.0.0.13 are forwarded on a hop-by-hop basis to ALL PIM routers in the multicast domain.

The combination of unicasting Candidate-RP-Advertisement messages to the BSR and multicasting Bootstrap messages to the well-known multicast address 224.0.0.13 (which is essentially flooding these messages to all PIM routers in the domain) eliminates the need for PIM-DM for the BSR mechanism to function as seen in Auto-RP. This combination of announcing RP information in unicast and multicast PIM messages in the BSR mechanism eliminates the "chicken-and-egg problem" seen in Auto-RP.

5.16.4.1 BSR Protocol Overview

A PIM router maintains a set of group-to-RP mappings, called the *RP-Set*, which it uses to determine the RP for a given multicast group. The following elements are contained in a group-to-RP mapping:

- Multicast group address range, expressed as an IP multicast address and mask (prefix length)
- RP priority

- RP address
- Hash mask length
- SM/BIDIR flag

In general, these group-to-RP mappings may encompass multicast group address ranges that overlap in arbitrary ways, indicating that a particular multicast group address may be associated with multiple group-to-RP mappings. In such cases, the PIM router employs a deterministic algorithm to select only one of the RPs (see discussion later). This algorithm ensures all routers in the PIM domain to make the same RP selection and uses a hash function (that takes the hash-mask length as one input) in the case where a multicast group address range has multiple RPs with the same priority.

The BSR mechanism allows a BSR to create group-to-RP mappings, which are then quickly distributed to all the PIM routers in the domain. It is adaptive, able to detect when an RP becomes unreachable, and modify the RP-Sets so that the unreachable RP will be no longer used in the domain.

To adopt the BSR mechanism, the network operator configures some of the PIM routers within a PIM domain as potential RPs (i.e., *Candidate-RPs*) for the PIM domain. The actual RPs for the PIM domain (a subset) will eventually be chosen from these Candidate-RPs. In addition, some of the PIM routers in the PIM domain are configured as *Candidate-BSRs* to provide some measure of redundancy in the network in the face of BSR failure. One of these Candidate-BSRs will be elected as the active *BSR* for the PIM domain, and *Bootstrap messages* will be used to announce the result of this election to all the PIM routers in the PIM domain. The Candidate-BSRs will then advertise their candidacy status to the elected BSR. The BSR selects a subset of the Candidate-RPs and uses Bootstrap messages to distribute corresponding group-to-RP mappings to all the PIM routers in the PIM domain (see Figure 5.27).

The BSR mechanism has the following four basic phases (although in practice, all of these phases may be occurring simultaneously):

- **BSR Election**: Each Candidate-BSR originates Bootstrap messages, each message containing a BSR Priority field (see Bootstrap message format in Chapter 3). The PIM routers within the PIM domain receive and flood the Bootstrap messages throughout the PIM domain. A Candidate-BSR that receives a Bootstrap message with a higher-priority Candidate-BSR than itself will suppress sending further its own Bootstrap messages for some time. The single Candidate-BSR remaining from this process becomes the elected BSR, and the Bootstrap messages it sends will inform all the other PIM routers in the domain that it is the elected BSR.
- **Candidate-RP Advertisement**: Each Candidate-RP within the PIM domain transmits (*unicasts*) *Candidate-RP-Advertisement messages* periodically to the elected BSR to enable it to create and distribute the RP-Set information within the PIM-SM domain. A Candidate-RP-Advertisement message includes the IP address of the router (usually the router's

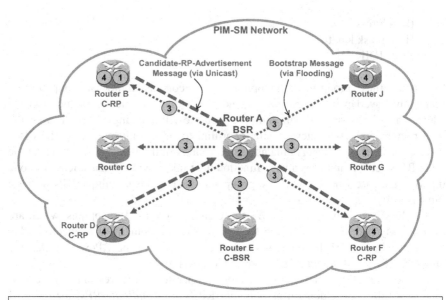

- The BSR floods PIM Bootstrap messages hop-by-hop to distribute all Group-to-RP mapping information to all PIM routers in the network.
  - A PIM-SM router may receive one or more possible Group-Range-to-RP mappings.
  - Each Group-Range-to-RP mapping specifies a range of multicast group addresses (expressed as a multicast group address and mask) and the RP to which such group addresses should be mapped.
  - Each Group-Range-to-RP mapping may also have an RP priority associated with it.
- More than one PIM router can be configured as a C-RP for a multicast group to provide redundancy.
- C-RPs send their C-RP advertisements to the currently elected BSR via unicast.
- Bootstrap messages contain the set of all known Group-to-RP C-RP advertisements (also called the candidate RP-set or RP set) that have been received from the C-RPs in the network.
- Every PIM router in the network receives an identical RP-set and runs the same hashing algorithm on the RP-set to select the currently active identical RP for a given multicast group or group range.

Processing steps:
1. Routers B, D, and F (all C-RPs) send their C-RP advertisements directly to the BSR via unicast.
2. Router A (the currently elected BSR) receives the C-RP advertisements and stores them in its local RP-set cache.
3. The BSR periodically transmits PIM Bootstrap messages (containing the contents of its local RP-set cache) out all of its interfaces.
   - These PIM Bootstrap messages are flooded hop-by-hop throughout the network to all PIM-SM routers.
4. The PIM routers receive the PIM Bootstrap messages and store the RP-set information in their local RP-set caches, and select the current RP(s) by running a common RP hashing algorithm.

FIGURE 5.27 Bootstrap Router (BSR) mechanism.

loopback interface address), priority of the advertising Candidate-RP, a Hold Time (i.e., a timeout value), in addition to a list of multicast group address ranges it supports/serves. This allows the elected BSR to learn about possible RPs that are currently running and reachable. Candidate-RPs send Candidate-RP-Advertisement messages via *unicast* to the BSR. Each Candidate-RP includes a timeout value (Hold Time) in its Candidate-RP-Advertisement message, upon receiving this message, the BSR uses this timeout value to start a Candidate-RP timeout timer. If the BSR fails to receive a subsequent Candidate-RP-Advertisement message from the Candidate-RP when the timer times out, the BSR assumes the Candidate-RP to have expired or become unreachable.

- **RP-Set Formation**: The BSR receives Candidate-RP-Advertisement messages and selects the appropriate Candidate-RP information for each multicast group to form an *RP-Set* (i.e., a subset of the Candidate-RPs forms an RP-Set). An RP-Set is a collection of information representing mappings between multicast groups and RPs. In general, the BSR does this in such a way that the RP-Set is neither too large that it cannot inform all the PIM routers in the domain about the set, nor too small that the multicast traffic load is excessively concentrated on some RPs. The BSR should also attempt to generate an RP-Set that changes less frequently.
- **RP-Set Flooding**: Subsequent Bootstrap messages that the BSR sends include the generated RP-Set information. These Bootstrap messages from the BSR are flooded through the PIM domain, ensuring that the RP-Set quickly reaches all the PIM routers in the domain. Actually, Bootstrap messages are multicast to the ALL-PIM-ROUTERS multicast address 224.0.0.13 and are forwarded on a hop-by-hop basis to all PIM routers in the multicast domain; the flooding process means propagating the messages to all PIM routers in the domain. The BSR periodically (default is every 60 seconds) originates Bootstrap messages encapsulating its own IP address together with the RP-Set information and floods these messages to the entire PIM-SM domain it serves to ensure RP-Set consistency after network failure and restoration.
- Upon receiving a Bootstrap message, a PIM router will add the group-to-RP mappings contained in the message to its local pool of group-to-RP mappings obtained from other RP discovery methods (e.g., Static RP configuration). The PIM router computes the final group-to-RP mappings from this local pool according to the rules of the specific multicast routing protocol (PIM-SM or BIDIR-PIM) and uses that mapping information to construct multicast distribution trees.

In the event a PIM domain becomes partitioned for some reason, each partition that is separated from the old BSR will elect its own BSR. This elected BSR will distribute an RP-Set containing RPs to all PIM routers reachable within that partition. When the PIM domain heals and is no longer partitioned, another BSR election will automatically take place and only one of the BSRs will continue to transmit Bootstrap messages. As is expected at the time the PIM domain is partitioned or healing, some disruption in multicast packet forwarding may occur. The duration of the packet forwarding disruption period will be on the order of the round-trip time of the partitioned region and the *BS_Timeout* value.

5.16.4.2 Administrative Scoping and BSR

This section describes protocol modifications to the BSR mechanism to allow it to be used in a PIM domain divided into *administratively scoped multicast regions* (simply referred to as *admin-scope zone* or *scope zone*). Using administrative scoping, a PIM domain can be divided into multiple admin-scope zones, each scope zone associated with a set of multicast group addresses and comprising a convex connection of a set of PIM routers.

Several *Zone Border Routers* (ZBRs) are configured to act as the boundary of the admin-scope zone. The network operator configures the ZBRs to not forward multicast traffic for any of the admin-scoped IP multicast group addresses into or out of the admin-scoped zone. It is important to note that the creation of a given admin-scope boundary results in at least two scoped zones: one on either side of the admin-scoped boundary.

An administratively scoped IPv4 multicast zone is associated with a set of multicast addresses represented by an IPv4 multicast address and an IPv4 prefix length [RFC2365]. An administratively scoped IPv6 multicast zone is associated with a set of IPv6 multicast addresses represented by a single *Scope ID* value. Reference [RFC4291] defines the set of IPv6 multicast addresses corresponding to a given *IPv6 Scope ID* value. For example, an IPv6 Scope ID of 5 maps to the 16 IPv6 multicast address ranges, that is, ff[0-f]5::/16.

Some topological restrictions apply to admin-scope zones. The boundary of the admin-scope zone must be complete and convex. This means that the boundary must not allow any path to be established from the inside of the scoped zone to the outside that does not pass through a configured ZBR, and that the multicast path between any arbitrary pair of multicast routers in the scope zone must stay always within the scope zone.

The use of administrative scoping with BSR results in some complications because a PIM router within the scoped zone should not use an RP that is located outside the scoped zone. Thus, some modifications to the basic BSR mechanism are required to ensure that a router within the scoped zone does not use an outside RP. This is accomplished by allowing each admin-scope zone of a PIM domain to run its own separate copy of the basic BSR mechanism as described above.

Thus, each admin-scope zone performs its own BSR election, where each Candidate-RP will typically register to the BSR of all admin-scope zones it belongs to, and each PIM router receives Bootstrap messages for all admin-scope zones it belongs to. The Bootstrap messages that a BSR sends for a particular admin-scope zone contain information about the RPs that PIM routers within that admin-scope zone must use for the set of multicast group addresses configured for that scope zone.

The BSR marks Bootstrap messages to indicate which admin-scope zone they belong to. The BSR floods these admin-scoped Bootstrap messages in the normal way as described above, but any ZBR of the admin-scope zone will not forward the messages across that scope zone boundary.

For correct functioning of the BSR mechanism with an admin-scope zone, each admin-scope zone must have at least one Candidate-BSR and must have at least one Candidate-RP that is configured to be a Candidate-RP for the set of multicast group addresses associated with that scoped zone. Even when a PIM domain is using administrative scoping, the PIM domain should still run a copy of the BSR mechanism, known as the *Non-Scoped BSR mechanism*, to allow RP information to be distributed for multicast groups, which are not administratively scoped. A copy of the BSR mechanism that runs in each admin-scope zone is called a *Scoped BSR*.

The network operator needs to configure only the Candidate-BSRs and the ZBRs of the admin-scope zone to know about the existence of the scope zone. Other PIM routers in the scope zone, including the Candidate-RPs, learn of their existence from the Bootstrap messages they receive.

All PIM routers in a PIM domain using the BSR mechanism and admin-scope multicast group address ranges must be capable of receiving Bootstrap messages. They should also store the BSR election winner and the advertised RP-Set for all admin-scope zones applicable to the domain.

5.16.4.3 BSR State and Timers

A PIM router that supports the BSR mechanism maintains the following state.

1. RP-Set
2. State for each configured or learned admin-scope zone Z:
   - State at all PIM routers:
     - Current Bootstrap Router's IP Address
     - Current Bootstrap Router's BSR Priority
     - Last Bootstrap message received from current BSR
     - Bootstrap Timer
     - Per group-to-RP mapping:
       - Group-to-RP Mapping Expiry Timer (GET)
   - State at a Candidate-BSR for admin-scope zone Z:
     - One of the following states: {"Candidate-BSR", "Pending-BSR", "Elected-BSR"}
   - State at a router that is not a Candidate-BSR for admin-scope zone Z:
     - One of the following states: {"Accept Any", "Accept Preferred"}
       - Scope-Zone Expiry Timer
   - At the current BSR for admin-scope zone Z only:
     - Per group-to-C-RP mapping:
       - Group-to-C-RP Mapping Expiry Timer (CGET)
   - At a Candidate-RP only:
     - C-RP Advertisement Timer

5.16.4.4 Bootstrap Router Election

For simplicity, the BSR mechanism uses Bootstrap messages for both the BSR election and the distribution of the RP-Set to PIM routers. Each Bootstrap message that the BSR sends indicates the admin-scope zone to which the message belongs. If the "Z-bit" (i.e., Administrative Scope Zone bit) is set (to 1) in the first Group Address field (in Encoded Group Address format) of the Bootstrap message, then the message is called a *Scoped Bootstrap message*. The "Z-bit" is a 1-bit field in the Encoded

Group Address format (see Chapter 3). If the Z-bit is not set in the first Group Address field of the Bootstrap message, then the message is called a *Non-Scoped Bootstrap message.*

In an IPv4 Scoped Bootstrap message, the scope of the message is indicated in the first Group Address field of the message, which can be any sub-range of the multicast address 224/4. In an IPv6 Scoped Bootstrap message, the scope of the message is indicated by the *Scope ID* of the first Group Address field of the message, which must have a Mask Length of at least 16. For example, an IPv6 multicast group address range of ff05::/16 with the Z-bit set indicates that the Bootstrap message is for the admin-scope zone with Scope ID 5. If the Mask Length field value of the first Group Address field in a scoped IPv6 Bootstrap is less than 16, the receiving PIM router must drop the message and should log a warning.

The state machine on a PIM router for Bootstrap messages depends on whether or not the network operator has configured the router to be a Candidate-BSR for a particular admin-scope zone. Figure 5.28 illustrates the Per-Scope-Zone state machine for a Candidate-BSR, while Figure 5.29 shows the state machine for a PIM router that is not configured to be a Candidate-BSR.

Using techniques similar to the election of the Root Bridge in bridged Ethernet LANs, the current BSR of a PIM-SM domain is elected as part of the normal process of flooding Bootstrap messages to all routers in the domain. The BSR election mechanism associates a weight with each Candidate-BSR. To ensure that certain

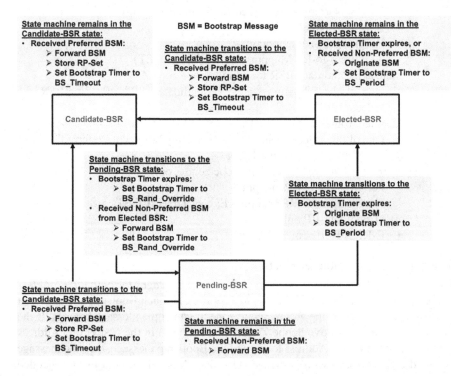

FIGURE 5.28   Per-Scope-Zone Candidate-BSR state machine.

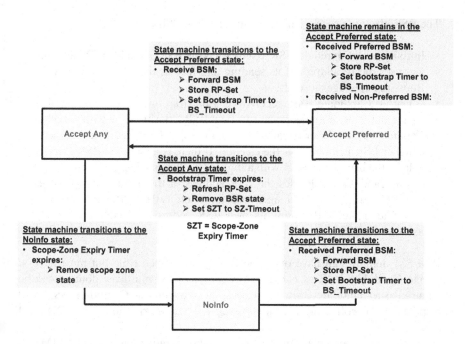

FIGURE 5.29 Per-Scope-Zone state machine for Non-Candidate-BSRs.

Candidate-BSRs are preferred over others during the BSR election process, the network operator may configure some Candidate-BSRs with higher BSR Priority values than others (see Chapter 3). This approach allows the operator to determine which Candidate-BSRs will be primary and backup (secondary) BSRs in the network. The outcome of the hop-by-hop flooding of Bootstrap messages and the simultaneous occurrence of the BSR election process is that all routers in the PIM-SM domain also automatically identify the IP address of the currently elected BSR. This process also enables all Candidate-RPs to learn the identity of the current BSR so that they can unicast Candidate-RP-Advertisement messages to that node.

The network operator typically configures multiple Candidate-BSRs to provide redundancy to the BSR function. Unlike in Auto-RP, only one BSR must be active in the PIM-SM domain at any given time. The BSR election mechanism allows another Candidate-BSR to be elected as the new active BSR from the set of all Candidate-BSRs in the network should the active BSR fail. However, in the event, all configured Candidate-BSRs cease to receive Bootstrap messages (all fail to operate as expected), their group-to-RP mapping information will eventually expire. Generally, in such a case, routers in the PIM-SM domain will switch to use a statically configured RP as discussed earlier. Normally, the network operator also configures a Static RP as a backup for the BSR mechanism to enhance the availability of RP information for the PIM-SM domain.

To define the weight of a Candidate-BSR, the unsigned BSR Priority field value and the IP address of the BSR (in the BSR Address field) from the Bootstrap message (see Chapter 3) are concatenated, with the BSR Priority field value representing the most significant bits and the IP address representing the least-significant bits.

The BSR election process can be summarized as follows:

- Initially, each Candidate-BSR assumes it is the BSR of the PIM-SM domain, and uses the IP address of its sending interface as the BSR address in the Bootstrap messages it sends.
- When a Candidate-BSR receives a Bootstrap message from another Candidate-BSR, it first compares its own BSR Priority value with the other Candidate-BSR's Priority carried in the message. The Candidate-BSR with a higher BSR Priority wins the election. If there is a tie in the BSR Priority values, the Candidate-BSR with a higher IP address wins the election. The losing Candidate-BSR uses the BSR address of the winner to replace its own BSR address and no longer considers itself as the BSR, while the winning Candidate-BSR retains its own BSR address and continues seeing itself as the BSR.

A PIM-SM domain can have only one BSR at any given time but must have at least one Candidate-BSR as backup. Any router in the multicast domain can be configured as a Candidate-BSR. The BSR is elected from the Candidate-BSRs and is responsible for collecting and advertising RP-Set information in the PIM-SM domain.

The BSR, which also plays the role of the administrative interface of a PIM-SM domain, sends the constructed RP-Set information in Bootstrap messages to all routers in the PIM-SM domain. The border of a PIM domain is also a boundary of a Bootstrap message; each BSR and message has its specific service scope. A network operator may partition a PIM-SM domain into several smaller admin-scope zones, and Bootstrap messages cannot cross a scope zone border in either direction.

In each admin-scope zone, a unique BSR is elected from the Candidate-BSRs. The Candidate-RPs in the scope zone send Candidate-RP-Advertisement messages to the zone's BSR. The BSR summarizes the Candidate-RP-Advertisement messages to form an RP-Set and advertises it to all routers in the PIM-SM domain. All the routers in the zone use the same hash algorithm to obtain the RP address corresponding to specific multicast groups.

The BSR periodically floods Bootstrap messages within the scope zone at intervals of *BS_Period*. Upon receiving a Bootstrap message, any Candidate-BSR retains the RP-Set for a length of time equal to the *BS_Timeout*, during which no BSR election occurs. If the BSR state times out and the Candidate-BSRs do not receive a Bootstrap message from the BSR, a new BSR election process is triggered among the Candidate-BSRs.

5.16.4.4.1   *Per-Scope-Zone Candidate-BSR State Machine*

A Candidate-BSR may be in one of three states in the Candidate-BSR state machine for a particular admin-scope zone (Figure 5.28):

- **Candidate-BSR**: In this state, the local router is a BSR candidate for the admin-scope zone, but another PIM router is currently the preferred BSR.

- **Pending-BSR**: In this state, the local router is a BSR candidate for the scope zone. However, currently, no other router is the preferred BSR, and the local router is not yet the elected BSR. This is a temporary state of the per-zone Candidate-BSR state machine that prevents rapid oscillation of the choice of the BSR during the BSR election.
- **Elected-BSR**: In this state, the local router is the elected BSR for the admin-scope zone and is positioned to perform all BSR functions.

In addition to these three states, the PIM router maintains the Bootstrap Timer which it uses to time out old BSR information. During the BSR election process, the Bootstrap Timer also plays a role in terminating the Pending-BSR state. The values of this timer are as follows:

- The *BS_Period* of this timer (with a default value of 60 seconds) is the period the BSR has to wait before originating periodic Bootstrap messages.
- The *BS_Timeout* of this timer (with a default value of 130 seconds) is the time interval after which the elected BSR is timed out if no further Bootstrap messages are received from the BSR. A router must set the *BS_Timeout* to be larger than the *BS_Period*, even if their values differ from the defaults. Reference [RFC5059] recommends setting *BS_Timeout* to $(2 \times BS\_Period + 10$ seconds).
- The *BS_Min_Interval* of this timer (with a default value of 10 seconds) is the minimum time interval after which the BSR may originate Bootstrap messages.
- The *BS_Rand_Override* of this timer is the randomly chosen time interval that routers use to reduce Bootstrap message network overhead during the BSR election. Reference [RFC5059] describes how this parameter is computed.

The initial state for a configured admin-scope zone is "Pending-BSR" in which the PIM router initializes the Bootstrap Timer to *BS_Rand_Override*. This happens if the router is a Candidate-BSR at startup, and if the router is reconfigured to become Candidate-BSR later.

5.16.4.4.2 *Per-Scope-Zone State Machine for Non-Candidate-BSR Routers*

A PIM router that is a Non-Candidate-BSR uses the state machine shown in Figure 5.29 for admin-scope zones discovered from Bootstrap messages. The Non-Candidate-BSR may be in one of three states for a particular admin-scope zone:

- **NoInfo**: In this state, the router has no state information about the admin-scope zone and no timers are running (about this scope zone). Conceptually, the router instantiates the state machine only when it receives a Scoped Bootstrap message for an admin-scope zone for which it has no prior knowledge. However, because the router immediately transitions to the Accept Any state unconditionally, one may consider the NoInfo state as a virtual state in some sense.

- **Accept Any**: In this state, the router is aware of an active BSR, and will accept the first Bootstrap message it receives as providing the identity of the new BSR and the RP-Set.
- **Accept Preferred**: In this state, the router is aware of the identity of the current BSR and uses the RP-Set provided by Bootstrap messages sent by that BSR. The router will accept only Bootstrap messages from that BSR or from a Candidate-BSR with a higher weight than the current BSR.

In addition to these three states, the router maintains two timers, the Bootstrap Timer which it uses to time out old BSR information, and the Scope-Zone Expiry Timer which it uses to time out the admin-scope zone itself if it does not receive further Bootstrap messages specifying the scope zone.

The *SZ_Timeout* of the Scope-Zone Expiry Timer (with a default value of 1,300 seconds) is the time interval following the last Bootstrap message after which the router will time out an admin-scope zone if it has not received a Bootstrap message for that scope zone. The router must set the *SZ_Timeout* larger than *BS_Timeout*, even if their values differ from the default values. Reference [RFC5059] recommends the *SZ_Timeout* be set to ($10 \times BS\_Timeout$).

The NoInfo state is the initial state for a scope zone for which the router does not have knowledge. The state machine that the router uses for admin-scope zones explicitly configured locally on it and for the global scope (which always exists) differs from the Per-Scope-Zone state machine for Non-Candidate-BSRs in Figure 5.29 as follows:

- The state machine has no NoInfo state.
- The state machine does not maintain a Scope-Zone Expiry Timer. Hence, the state machine does not have the event "Scope-Zone Expiry Timer Expires" in Figure 5.29, and the router does not execute any actions with regard to this timer.

The Accept Any state is the initial state for this state machine.

The PIM router only processes a Bootstrap message from a directly connected PIM neighbor for which it has an active Hello state. The BSR sends a Bootstrap message to the ALL-PIM-ROUTERS multicast group address (224.0.0.13), while a PIM router sends a No-Forward BSM toward the BSR that originated the Bootstrap message. The router sends a No-Forward BSM when it has recently restarted and has no BSR state for that admin-scope zone. A Bootstrap message is not forwarded if its N-bit (also called the No-Forward bit) is set (to 1).

Additionally, if a PIM router supports unicast Bootstrap messages, it accepts a unicast Bootstrap message if it is addressed to the router itself. This acceptance occurs because the router has recently restarted and has no BSR state for that admin-scope zone. Furthermore, the Bootstrap message must not have arrived on an interface configured as an admin-scope border for the multicast address contained in the first Group Address field of the Bootstrap message.

5.16.4.5 Sending Candidate-RP-Advertisement Messages

Every Candidate-RP will periodically send a Candidate-RP-Advertisement message via unicast transmission to the BSR, for each admin-scope zone for which it has a state. This is to inform the BSR of the Candidate-RP's readiness to function as an RP for those admin-scope zones. The Candidate-RP sends these messages at intervals of *C_RP_Adv_Period* (of the C-RP Advertisement Timer) except when a new BSR is elected. The default value of *C_RP_Adv_Period* is 60 seconds.

After the election of a new BSR, the Candidate-RP is required to send one to three Candidate-RP-Advertisement messages to that BSR. The Candidate-RP waits for a small randomly selected delay equal to *C_RP_Adv_Backoff* (of the C-RP Advertisement Timer) before sending each subsequent message. Sending preferably three such messages allows the BSR to quickly identify which RPs are active, and because some messages may be lost when a new BSR is elected due to changes in the network. The Candidate-RP implements this by setting the C-RP Advertisement Timer to *C_RP_Adv_Backoff* when the new BSR is elected, as well as setting a counter to 2. Whenever the C-RP Advertisement Timer expires, the Candidate-RP first sends a Candidate-RP-Advertisement message as usual. Next, if the counter is non-zero, the Candidate-RP decrements it and again sets the C-RP Advertisement Timer to *C_RP_Adv_Backoff* instead of *C_RP_Adv_Period*. The default value of *C_RP_Adv_Backoff* is from 0 to 3 seconds.

The BSR uses the Priority field values in Candidate-RP-Advertisement messages to select which Candidate-RPs to include in the RP-Set. The lower the Priority field value, the higher the priority of sending Candidate-RP. A value of zero is the highest possible priority. By default, a Candidate-RP should send Candidate-RP-Advertisement messages with the Priority field set to 192.

When a Candidate-RP is powering down, it should immediately transmit a Candidate-RP-Advertisement message to the BSR for each admin-scope zone for which it is currently serving as an RP. The Hold Time field value in this message should be set to 0. The BSR, upon receiving this message, will immediately time out the Candidate-RP and generate a new Bootstrap message with the Hold Time field of the powering down RP set to 0.

A Candidate-RP-Advertisement message contains a list of Group Address and Group Mask field pairs (in Encoded Group Address format as described in Chapter 3). This enables a Candidate-RP to specify the multicast group address ranges for which it is prepared to be the RP. If the Candidate-RP is selected to be an RP, it may enforce the associated admin-scope zone when receiving PIM Register or Join/Prune messages.

A Candidate-RP is configured with a list of multicast group address ranges for which it should advertise itself as the Candidate-RP. A Candidate-RP uses the following algorithm to determine which multicast group address ranges to report to a given BSR.

- For each multicast group address range R in the list, the Candidate-RP advertises that address range in Candidate-RP-Advertisement messages to the Scoped BSR for the smallest scope that "contains" R.
  - For IPv6, the Candidate-RP determines the scope containing the address range R by matching the Scope ID of the multicast group address range with the scope of the BSR.
  - For IPv4, the Candidate-RP determines the scope containing the address range R as the longest prefix match, among the known admin-scope multicast address ranges.

- • If the Candidate-RP finds no scope that contains the multi-cast group address range R, then it includes the range R in the Candidate-RP-Advertisement message sent to the Non-Scoped BSR.
- • If no Non-Scoped BSR is known, then the Candidate-RP does not include the address range R in any Candidate-RP-Advertisement message.
- • Furthermore, for each IPv4 multicast group address range R in the list and for each Scoped BSR whose scope multicast address range is strictly contained within R, the Candidate-RP should, by default, advertise (via Candidate-RP-Advertisement messages) the multicast scope address range of that BSR to that BSR.
- • For each IPv6 multicast group address range R in the list with prefix length less than 16, the Candidate-RP should, by default, advertise (via Candidate-RP-Advertisement messages) to the Scoped BSR with the corresponding Scope ID, each sub-range of prefix length 16.
  - • For IPv6, the mask length of all multicast group address ranges that the Candidate-RP includes in the Candidate-RP-Advertisement message sent to a Scoped BSR must be greater than or equal to 16.

If the Candidate-RP runs this algorithm and finds that there are no multicast group ranges to advertise to the BSR for a particular admin-scope zone, it must not send a Candidate-RP-Advertisement message to that BSR. A Candidate-RP must not send a Candidate-RP-Advertisement message with no multicast group address ranges in it. If the Candidate-RP is also the BSR for more than one admin-scope zone, then it may combine the Candidate-RP-Advertisement messages for these admin-scope zones into a single message.

If the Candidate-RP is also a ZBR for an admin-scope zone, then it must set the Admin Scope Zone bit (Z-bit) in the Candidate-RP-Advertisement messages it sends for that admin-scope zone, otherwise, it must not set this bit.

5.16.4.6   Creating the RP-Set at the BSR

After receiving a Candidate-RP-Advertisement message, a PIM router proceeds to decide which of the multicast group address ranges contained in the message to accept. The router checks each group address range in the message to examine if it is elected as the BSR for any admin-scope zone containing the group address range, or if it is elected as the Non-Scoped BSR. If any of these options is true, the router accepts the group address range; if not, it ignores the group range.

If the router accepts the group address range, it creates a group-to-Candidate-RP mapping for this group range and takes the RP Address from the Candidate-RP-Advertisement message. If this mapping is not already part of the existing Candidate-RP-Set, the router adds the mapping to the Candidate-RP-Set and initializes the associated Group-to-C-RP Mapping Expiry Timer (CGET) to the Hold Time taken from the Candidate-RP-Advertisement message. The router sets the priority of the included RP (for the corresponding group address range) to the Priority field value in the Candidate-RP-Advertisement message.

If the router finds that the mapping is already part of the Candidate-RP-Set, it updates it with the Priority field value in the Candidate-RP-Advertisement message and resets its associated CGET to the Hold Time taken from the Candidate-RP-Advertisement message. If the Hold Time is zero, the router immediately removes the mapping from the Candidate-RP-Set. The *C_RP_Mapping_Timeout* of the CGET is taken from the Hold Time field of the Candidate-RP-Advertisement message.

5.16.4.6.1 Hash Mask Length Field of a Bootstrap Message

The Hash Mask Length field value in a Bootstrap message (see Chapter 3) is a global property of the BSR and, therefore, applies to all group-to-Candidate-RP mappings managed by the BSR. When the CGET expires, the router removes the corresponding group-to-Candidate-RP mapping from the Candidate-RP-Set.

5.16.4.6.2 Generating and Sending Bootstrap Messages

The BSR generates the RP-Set from the Candidate-RP-Set. The network operator may configure a local policy on the BSR to limit the number of Candidate-RPs included in the RP-Set. The BSR may override the multicast group range indicated in a Candidate-RP-Advertisement message unless the Priority field value in the Candidate-RP-Advertisement message is less than 128.

If the BSR is configured to identify the Candidate-RPs of both BIDIR-PIM and PIM-SM within the same multicast group address range, it must only include RPs for one of the protocols in the Bootstrap messages. The default behavior is for the BSR to give preference to BIDIR-PIM.

To add to a Bootstrap message, the BSR subdivides the RP-Set into sets that include {Group Address range, RP Count, RP addresses} as the key elements (see Bootstrap message format in Chapter 3). For each RP Address, the BSR sets the RP Hold Time field to the Hold Time taken from the Candidate-RP-Set, subject to the constraint that this value must be greater than the *BS_Period* and should be greater than $(2.5 \times BS\_Period)$ in case some Bootstrap messages are lost. If the BSR determines that some Hold Times from the Candidate-RP-Sets do not satisfy this constraint, it must replace those Hold Times with a value satisfying the constraint, except when the Hold Time is zero (which is used to immediately withdraw group-to-Candidate-RP mappings).

The Bootstrap message format allows the BSR to perform "Semantic Fragmentation" if the length of the original Bootstrap message exceeds the maximum IP packet length limit of the sending interface. However, to reduce the need for Semantic Fragmentation, it is more desirable not to configure a large number of routers as Candidate-RPs.

In general, the BSR originates Bootstrap messages at regular intervals with each message sent every *BS_Period*. Reference [RFC5059] recommends that the BSR also originates a Bootstrap message whenever the RP-Set to be announced in the message changes. This usually happens when the BSR receives Candidate-RP-Advertisement messages from a new Candidate-RP, or when a Candidate-RP is shutting down (Candidate-RP-Advertisement message with a Hold Time field value of zero). However, the BSR must send the messages with a minimum of *BS_Min_Interval* spacing between them.

After the election of a new BSR, that BSR will first send one Bootstrap message (which is likely to be empty since it has not yet received any Candidate-RP-Advertisement messages), and then wait at least *BS_Min_Interval* before sending a new Bootstrap message. During that waiting period, the BSR is likely to have received Candidate-RP-Advertisement messages from all usable Candidate-RPs (since it is expected that a Candidate-RP should send one or more Candidate-RP-Advertisement messages with small random delays of *C_RP_Adv_Backoff* when a new BSR is elected). For this case, where the PIM routers may not yet have been provided with a usable RP-Set, the BSR should originate a Bootstrap message as soon as *BS_Min_ Interval* has elapsed. One way of accomplishing this is for the BSR to decrease the Bootstrap Timer to *BS_Min_Interval* whenever the RP-Set changes, while the timer is left alone and not changed if it is less than or equal to *BS_Min_Interval*.

5.16.4.6.3   Sending Scoped Bootstrap Messages

A BSR originates separate Scoped Bootstrap messages for each admin-scope zone for which it is the elected BSR. It also originates Non-Scoped Bootstrap messages if it is the elected Non-Scoped BSR. The BSR adds each group-to-Candidate-RP mapping in precisely one of these Bootstrap messages, that is, the Scoped Bootstrap message for the smallest scope containing the group address range of the group-to-Candidate-RP mapping, if any, or the Non-Scoped Bootstrap message, otherwise.

A Scoped Bootstrap message must contain at least one multicast group address range, and the first group range in a Scoped BSR message must have its Z-bit (i.e., Admin Scope Zone bit in the Encoded Group Address format) set. This multicast group address range identifies the scope of the Bootstrap message. In an IPv4 Scoped Bootstrap message, the first multicast group address range is the group range corresponding to the scope of the Bootstrap message. In an IPv6 Scoped Bootstrap message, the first group address range may be any group address range as long as all the group address ranges in such a Bootstrap message must have a Mask Length field value of at least 16 and its Scope ID must be the same as the scope of the Bootstrap message.

Apart from identifying the multicast scope, the first multicast group address range in a Scoped Bootstrap message is treated like any other group address range concerning group-to-RP mappings. That is, all group-to-RP mappings in the RP-Set that cover this group address range, if any, must be included in this first group address range in the Bootstrap message. After this group address range, other group address ranges in this multicast scope in the Scoped Bootstrap message (for which there are RP mappings) can appear in any order. The Z-bit of all multicast group address ranges other than the first should be set to 0 when the message is sent and must be ignored on receipt.

5.16.4.6.4   When a BSR Is Shutting Down

When an elected BSR is shutting down, it should immediately send a Bootstrap message containing its current RP-Set, but with the Priority field of the message set to the lowest priority value possible. Sending such a message causes a new BSR to be elected more quickly.

5.16.4.7   Forwarding Bootstrap Messages

Generally, a BSR originates a Bootstrap message that is forwarded hop by hop by intermediate routers if it passes the Bootstrap Message Processing Checks. However, a Bootstrap message that has its N-bit (i.e., No-Forward bit) set is not forwarded. Also, a unicast Bootstrap message is usually not forwarded. An implementation of the BSR mechanism may, however, choose to resend a No-Forward or unicast Bootstrap message in a multicast Bootstrap message, in which case the N-bit must be cleared. The N- bit must be cleared since the receiving PIM router does not perform the RPF check when the N-bit is set.

Hop-by-hop forwarding here implies that it is the encapsulated Bootstrap message in the IP packet itself that is forwarded, not the entire IP packet with the message. Each hop receives a Bootstrap message and constructs an IP packet for each of its interfaces on which the message is to be forwarded; each constructed IP packet contains the entire Bootstrap message that was received.

When a hop forwards a Bootstrap message, it forwards it on all multicast-capable interfaces with PIM neighbors (including the interface on which the message was received). However, it is essential to note that the message is not forwarded on an interface if it is an admin-scope boundary interface for the admin-scope zone indicated in the first multicast group address range in the Bootstrap message.

To optimize the forwarding process, a hop may choose not to forward a Bootstrap message on the interface on which the message was received if the interface is a point-to-point interface. On an interface with multiple PIM neighbors (e.g., an interface attached to a multiaccess network segment), the router should forward an accepted Bootstrap message (one that passes the Bootstrap Message Processing Checks) on the interface on which that Bootstrap message was received. However, if numerous PIM neighbors exist on that interface, the router may delay forwarding the Bootstrap message on that interface by spacing them with some additional small random delay to prevent message implosion on that interface. The router may have a configuration option to be used to disable message forwarding on the interface on which the message was received, but the default behavior is to forward on that interface.

The rationale for forwarding a Bootstrap message on the interface on which the message was received (in addition to the other interfaces) is that the routers on a multiaccess network segment (such as an Ethernet LAN) may not have consistent routing information at the time the message is received. If the underlying routing protocol used guarantees that the PIM routers on the multiaccess network segment will have consistent routing information, then the router may safely disable forwarding on the incoming interface.

A ZBR of an admin-scope zone constrains all Bootstrap messages that are of equal or smaller scope than the configured scope zone boundary. That is, the interfaces on which the scope zone boundary is configured will not accept from, originate to, or forward to the outside, Scoped Bootstrap messages. For Ipv4, the ZBR checks the first multicast group address range in the Scoped Bootstrap message to determine if the scope is contained in it or is the same as the group address range of the configured zone boundary. For IPv6, the ZBR compares the scope of the first multicast group address range in the Scoped Bootstrap message and the scope of the configured zone boundary.

5.16.4.8   Bootstrap Messages to New and Rebooting PIM Routers

When PIM routers on a multiaccess network segment receive a PIM Hello message from a new PIM neighbor or one with a new Generation ID from an existing PIM neighbor, one router on that network segment sends a stored copy of the Bootstrap message for each admin-scope zone to the new or rebooting PIM router. Sending the Bootstrap message enables new or rebooting routers on the network to quickly learn the RP-Set.

The Designated Router (DR) on the multiaccess network segment is responsible for sending the copy of the Bootstrap message, but, if the new or rebooting PIM router is the DR, the PIM router that would be elected as the DR (if the new or rebooting PIM router is excluded from the DR election process) will be responsible for sending the message.

Before sending the Bootstrap message copy, the router must wait until it has sent a triggered PIM Hello message on the interface attached to the multiaccess network segment, otherwise, the Bootstrap message will be discarded by the new PIM neighbor.

5.16.4.8.1   No-Forward Bootstrap Messages

As stated above, a No-Forward Bootstrap message has the N-bit (No-Forward bit) set. All PIM routers that use the BSR mechanism should support the sending of No-Forward Bootstrap messages and should also accept such messages. PIM routers must not perform the RPF check during the Bootstrap message processing check for a No-Forward Bootstrap message. A No-Forward message has the same IP source and destination addresses as the usual multicast Bootstrap messages.

5.16.4.8.2   Unicast Bootstrap Messages

For backward compatibility with the older version of the BSR mechanism, implementations of the newer BSR mechanism may support unicast Bootstrap messages. The implementation should be configurable to allow an instantiation of the BSR mechanism to decide whether to send unicast Bootstrap messages instead of or in addition to No-Forward Bootstrap messages and to decide whether to accept such messages. Unicast Bootstrap messages are sent via unicast transmission to the PIM neighbor.

5.16.4.9   Receiving and using the RP-Set

PIM-SM and BIDIR-PIM routers use the RP-Set received from the BSR to select an RP to use as the root of a shared tree. These routers may obtain RP-Sets from other sources as discussed here. Reference [RFC5059] does not specify how PIM routers create the final group-to-RP mappings from these RP-Sets. However, reference [RFC7761] describes one such algorithm as summarized in Figure 5.30 and describes in detail in a section later. In general, the PIM router recalculates the mappings when any of its RP-Sets change.

Some of the multicast group-to-RP mappings in a received RP-Set may indicate group address ranges that apply to PIM-SM only, while others indicate group address ranges to be used by BIDIR-PIM only. A PIM router will only use the

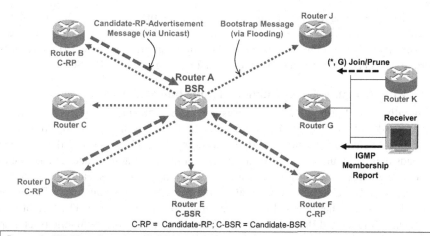

Group-to-RP Mapping at each PIM router:
It is possible for a PIM router to receive multiple mappings from the BSR, all of which might match the same multicast group address. The algorithm for performing the group-to-RP mapping is as follows:
1. The router uses the given multicast group address to perform the longest match on the group address range to obtain a list of C-RPs.
   - If two or more group-range-to-RP mappings match a particular multicast group address, the router selects the one with the longest mask as the mapping to use.
2. If the group-range-to-RP mappings have the same mask length, the router selects from this list of matching C-RPs, the C-RPs with the highest priority.
3. If only one RP remains in the list, the router uses that C-RP.
4. If multiple C-RPs are still in the list, the router uses the PIM hash function to choose one as the C-RP to use.
   - If there is more than one matching entry with the same longest mask, and the C-RP priorities are identical, then the router applies a hash function to choose the RP.
      - That is, if the C-RPs remaining in the list have the same priority, the C-RP with the largest hash value wins.
   - If the C-RPs have the same hash value, then the router selects the C-RP with the highest IP address.
A PIM router invokes this algorithm under the following conditions:
- When a LHR (i.e., receiver-side DR) receives an IGMP Membership Report message for a multicast group for which the router does not know the RP and needs to determine an RP for the group.
- A router has received a PIM (*,G) Join/Prune message.

FIGURE 5.30 Group-to-RP mapping at a PIM-SM router.

mappings that apply to the protocol it supports and will ignore the others. If a router determines that a mapping is not already part of the RP-Set, it will add it to the RP-Set and initialize the associated Group-to-RP mapping Expiry Timer (GET) to the Hold Time indicated in the received Bootstrap message. The router sets the priority of the mapping to the Priority field value in the Bootstrap message. The *C_RP_Mapping_Timeout* of the GET is taken from the Hold Time of the Candidate-RP-Advertisement message.

If the router finds that a mapping is already part of the received RP-Set, it updates it with the Priority field value indicated in the received Bootstrap message and resets its associated GET to the Hold Time in the Bootstrap message. If the Hold Time is zero, the router will immediately remove the mapping from the RP-Set.

5.16.4.10 Semantic Fragmentation of Bootstrap Messages

Generally, a BSR periodically advertises the RP-Set information in Bootstrap messages to all routers in the PIM-SM domain. The BSR may split up a Bootstrap message into "Semantic Fragments" if the resulting IP packet carrying the message exceeds the maximum allowed IP packet size for the sending interface. The BSR can send a single Bootstrap message as multiple Semantic Fragments (each encapsulated in a separate IP packet), as long as all of the Semantic Fragments carry Fragment Tags that indicate that they belong to the same Bootstrap message. The format of a single non-fragmented Bootstrap message is the same as that of a Semantic Bootstrap message Fragment (see Chapter 3).

Each Semantic Fragment has the same format, and all Fragments of a given Bootstrap message have identical values for the following message fields: Type, N-bit (No-Forward bit), Fragment Tag, Hash Mask Length, BSR Priority, and BSR Address. Only the fields associated with the group-to-RP mapping in the Bootstrap Message Fragment may differ between fragments.

Semantic Fragmentation is useful when a Bootstrap message exceeds the MTU of the interface on which the message will be forwarded. Relying solely on IP fragmentation means the entire Bootstrap message is lost if the encapsulating IP packet is lost. However, with Semantic Fragmentation, losing a single IP packet only causes the loss of the Semantic Fragment encapsulated in that IP packet. As described above, a PIM router only needs to receive all the group-to-RP mappings for a specific multicast group address range to update that address range. This means that losing a Semantic Fragment due to the loss of the encapsulating IP packet, only affects the group address ranges for which the lost Semantic Fragment contains RP mapping information.

The BSR should be as much as possible to split the Bootstrap message so that each multicast group address range (and all of its RP information) can fit entirely inside one Bootstrap Message Fragment and IP packet with the required MTU. If such a Fragment is lost, the PIM router will retain the state from the previous Bootstrap Message Fragment for the group address ranges from the missing Semantic Fragment. Each Fragment that the router receives will be used to update the RP information for the group ranges contained in that Fragment, and the router will be able to use immediately the new group-to-RP mappings for those group address ranges. The router obtains the information from the missing Fragment when the next Bootstrap message is transmitted by the BSR.

If the BSR finds that the list of RPs for a single multicast group address range is long, it may split the information across multiple Bootstrap Message Fragments to avoid IP fragmentation. In this case, the PIM router must receive all the Bootstrap Message Fragments comprising the information for that group address range before it can modify the group-to-RP mapping in use. The RP Count field in the Bootstrap message is employed for this purpose. The router receiving Bootstrap Message

Fragments from the same Bootstrap message (i.e., that have the same Fragment Tag) must wait until it has received Bootstrap Message Fragments providing RPs equal to RP Count for that group address range, before using the new group-to-RP mapping for that group address range. If a single Bootstrap Message Fragment from such a large group address range is lost, then the router will have to keep that entire group address range until the next Bootstrap message is sent. Consequently, in this case, the benefit of using Semantic Fragmentation is not that obvious.

Now, we describe how a BSR would remove multicast group address ranges it previously sent. A PIM router that receives a set of Bootstrap Message Fragments cannot determine if a group address range is missing. If the router has received a group address range before, it assumes that, that group address range still exists, and that the Bootstrap Message Fragment describing that group address range has been lost. In this case, the router should retain the missing group address range information for *BS_Timeout*. Thus, when the BSR wants to remove a group address range, it should include that group range in a Bootstrap message, but with an RP Count field set to zero, and it should resend this information in each Bootstrap message after *BS_Timeout*.

When a BSR finds that a Bootstrap message exceeds the MTU, it will split the message into multiple Bootstrap Message Fragments:

- Upon receiving a Bootstrap Message Fragment that contains the RP-Set information of one multicast group range, a non-BSR router will update the corresponding RP-Set information directly.
- If the RP-Set information of one multicast group range is carried in multiple Bootstrap Message Fragments, a non-BSR router will update the corresponding RP-Set information upon receiving all these Bootstrap Message Fragments.

If the BSR were to encapsulate a Bootstrap message in an IP packet and split the packet into IP fragments if the message exceeds the MTU (using IP fragmentation), the loss of a single IP fragment would lead to the unavailability of the entire Bootstrap message. The use of Semantic Fragmentation of Bootstrap messages solves this problem. As the RP-Set information contained in each Semantic Fragment is different, the loss of some IP packets will not result in dropping of the entire Bootstrap message.

5.16.5 ANYCAST-RP THROUGH PIM-SM (PIM ANYCAST-RP)

The PIM-SM specification [RFC7761] allows only a single active RP to be used for a given multicast group in a PIM-SM domain. For this reason, the optimal placement of RPs in a PIM-SM domain can be problematic for the network provider. The *PIM Anycast-RP* concept [RFC4610] allows a network operator to deploy multiple active RPs (i.e., an *Anycast-RP Set*) per multicast group in a single PIM-SM domain to achieve RP load sharing and redundancy. Unlike the Anycast-RP mechanism described in [RFC3446] (and in Chapter 6) that requires the use of MSDP [RFC3618], the PIM Anycast-RP mechanism does not require the use of MSDP. Note that MSDP only applies to IPv4. A PIM-SM domain that supports IPv6 will be able to use the PIM Anycast-RP mechanism for IPv6 addresses; MSDP Anycast-RP (which supports only IPv4) cannot be used in this case.

Using an Anycast-RP Set, source-side DRs in a PIM-SM domain can be configured to register multicast sources statically or dynamically with a member RP using the Anycast-RP Address. Since the RPs in the Anycast-RP Set have the same Anycast IP address, an IGP such as OSPF or IS-IS is required to route packets from a DR to the nearest RP with the best route. If the routers are evenly distributed throughout the PIM-SM domain, the processing loads on the RPs within the domain will be distributed. If the RP with the best route to a DR goes out of service, the IGP of the PIM-SM domain changes the route to the closest operating RP in the Anycast-RP Set that has the same Anycast IP address. All RPs in the Anycast-RP Set are connected by the IGP, consequently, all of them share information about active sources in the domain.

Other than providing load-sharing capabilities, deploying a (PIM or MSDP) Anycast-RP mechanism allows the PIM-SM network to have faster convergence when an RP fails. To allow multicast receivers to use the closest RP, multicast packets from a source need to reach all RPs in the Anycast-RP Set to find joined receivers. Reference [RFC3446] extends the PIM Register mechanism in the PIM-SM specification so that the PIM Anycast-RP functionality can be used without requiring MSDP.

5.16.5.1   PIM Anycast-RP Overview

The main features of the Anycast-RP mechanism are as follows:

- The network operator chooses a unique unicast IP address to be used as the *Anycast-RP Address*. This IP address can be configured statically or distributed using a dynamic routing protocol to all routers in the PIM-SM domain.
- A set of routers in the PIM-SM domain (called an Anycast-RP Set) is selected to act as RPs and are collectively assigned and shared the unique Anycast-RP Address.
- Each RP in the Anycast-RP Set is configured with a local loopback address that is set to the shared Anycast-RP Address. The loopback address must be reachable by all routers in the PIM-SM domain.
- Each RP in the Anycast-RP Set is also configured with its own separate (unique or non-shared) unicast IP address which it uses for communication with the other RPs.
- An IGP injects the Anycast-RP Address (or an IP prefix that covers that Anycast-RP Address) into the PIM-SM domain.
- Each RP in the Anycast-RP Set is configured with the non-shared IP addresses of all other RPs in the Anycast-RP Set. *The network operator must consistently configure this non-shared IP address in all RPs in the Anycast- RP Set.*

Each RP in the Anycast-RP Set is configured with two IP addresses; a shared RP address this set as a loopback address and a separate, unique local IP address. Each RP in the Anycast-RP Set using its configured separate, unique IP address, establishes static peering with other Anycast-RP Set members, allowing it to communicate with those peers.

5.16.5.2 PIM Anycast-RP Mechanism

Figure 5.31 illustrates the operation of the PIM Anycast-RP mechanism in a PIM-SM domain using three RPs where multicast receivers join the closest RP according to the IGP's routing metrics. Note that the Anycast-RP Address in the domain must be different from the IP addresses used by the RPs in the Anycast-RP Set for communicating with each other.

The following procedure is used when the source, as depicted in Figure 5.31, starts sending multicast traffic:

- The source sends multicast packets to its DR.
- The source-side DR sends a PIM Register message carrying the multicast packets and addressed to the Anycast-RP Address (i.e., RPA); the destination address of the Register message is the RPA and the source address is that of the DR's sending interface. The PIM-SM domain's IGP delivers the PIM Register message to the nearest RP, in this case, RP 1.
- RP 1 receives the unicast PIM Register message, decapsulates it, and sends the multicast packets down its RPT to local receivers, if any.
- RP 1 is configured with the non-shared IP address of RP 2 and RP 3. Since the PIM Register message did not originate from any of these RPs in the Anycast-RP Set (i.e., the message's source IP address is not that of an Anycast-RP Set member but from another PIM router in the domain), RP 1 assumes the PIM Register message is originated by a source-side DR. If the PIM Register message is not addressed to the Anycast-RP Address, then an error has occurred and the message should be rate-limited and logged.
- RP 1 then unicasts a copy of the PIM Register message from the source-side DR to both RP 2 and RP 3. RP 1 uses its own non-shared IP address as the source address of the IP packet encapsulating the PIM Register message sent to RP2 and RP 3. The IP packet's destination IP address is the shared Anycast-RP Address. RP1 will unicast the IP packet to all of its Anycast-RP peers, ensuring source state information is distributed to all RPs in the Anycast-RP Set in the multicast domain.
- RP 1 may join the SPT by sending an (S, G) Join message towards the source-side DR. However, RP 1 must create an (S, G) state.
- RP 1 sends a PIM Register-Stop back to the source-side DR. If, for some reason, the PIM Register messages unicasted to RP 2 and RP 3 are lost, then when the DR's Register-Stop Timer expires, it will resend PIM Register messages to RP 1 (the closest RP according to the IGP)) to allow all RPs in the Anycast-RP Set to again obtain the (S, G) state.
- RP 2 receives the unicast Register message from RP 1, decapsulates it, and also sends the multicast packets down its RPT to all local receivers (Receiver 1). RP 2 does not forward the received Register message from RP 1 to RP 3 since the source IP address of the message is the non-shared IP address of an Anycast-RP Set member (RP 1).

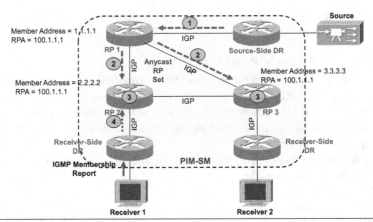

- An Interior Gateway Protocol (IGP) is used between all of the Anycast-RP set members in a "logical" mesh configuration to ensure that multicast source state information is distributed to all Anycast-RP set members in the PIM domain (i.e., to allows all RPs to be in sync regarding the active sources).
- PIM-SM routers are configured to register (statically or dynamically) with the Anycast-RP set using the specified Anycast-RP address (100.1.1.1).
- Because the Anycast-RP set has one specific Anycast Address, IGP such as OSPF is used to route packets from any PIM-SM router to an Anycast-RP member with the best route.
- In the figure, a multicast source within a PIM-SM domain sends multicast traffic to multicast group G, and the receivers joins the multicast group.

Processing steps:
1. RP 1 receives a unicast PIM Register message from the source-side DR connected to the multicast traffic source that is destined to the Anycast-RP address (RPA).
    - A PIM source-side DR will register the source with the closest RP to build an optimal SPT. On the other hand, the receiver-side DR of a receiver joins the closest RP to build an optimal RP tree (RPT) .
2. Because the PIM Register message is not from another Anycast-RP set member (RP 2 or RP 3), RP 1 considers the Register message to be from the source-side DR.
    - RP 1 receives PIM Registration message and creates an (S, G) state entry in its MRT.
    - RP 1 changes the source IP address of the PIM Register message to its own IP address and unicasts the PIM message to each of the Anycast-RP set members (RP 2 and RP 3).
    - A PIM router that acts as both a source-side DR and an RP would create a PIM Register message and then unicast that message to the other Anycast -RP set members.
    - An RP must forward the PIM Register message from the source-side DR to other Anycast-RP set members to allow all RPs to synchronize their multicast source information.
3. RP 2 and RP 3 receive the PIM Register message and find out that the source IP address of the Register message is an Anycast-RP set member address. These RPs stop forwarding the PIM Register message to other router.
    - After obtaining the multicast source information from RP 1, RP 2, and RP each send PIM (S, G) Join messages toward the source to create an SPT.
4. After receiving a IGMP Membership Report message from Receiver 1, the receiver-side DR sends a PIM (*, G) Join message toward the closest RP (RP 2). An RPT rooted at RP 2 is then established.
    - When the multicast traffic reaches RP 2 along the SPT, this RP forwards the traffic along the RPT to Receiver 1.
    - After receiving the multicast traffic, the receiver-side DR determines whether to initiate an RPT-to-SPT switchover process based on its configuration.

FIGURE 5.31   Anycast-RP through PIM-SM (PIM Anycast-RP).

- RP 2 may wait to send a PIM Register-Stop message back to RP 1 if it decides to join the SPT. RP 2 waits until it has received multicast data packets from the source on the SPT before sending the PIM Register-Stop message. If RP 2 decides to wait, it will send the PIM Register-Stop when the next PIM Register message is received. If RP 2 decides not to wait, it will send the PIM Register-Stop immediately.
- RP 2 may join the SPT by sending an (S, G) Join message toward the multicast source. However, RP 2 must create an (S, G) state.
- If an RP receives the PIM Register message from RP 1, but has no receivers for the group, it can discard the message and its multicast packets. In this case, the RP sends a PIM Register-Stop message back to RP 1. However, the RP will create an (S, G) state so that when a receiver joins the group, it can quickly join the SPT for the source and start forwarding traffic to the receiver.
- RP 1 receives and processes the PIM Register-Stop messages from RP 2 and RP 3.

When a source becomes activated in a PIM Anycast-RP domain, its DR will register the source with the closest RP in the set. The RP decapsulates the message and creates the (S, G) state. The RP will re-encapsulate the PIM Register message with the local Anycast IP peering address as the source IP address of the encapsulating IP packet, and unicast it to all Anycast-RP peers. The re-encapsulation of the PIM Register message in IP packets and unicasting it to Anycast-RP peers ensures that the multicast source state is distributed to all RPs in the Anycast-RP Set.

5.16.5.3 Observations and Guidelines for the PIM Anycast-RP Mechanism
Reference [RFC3446] provides the following guidelines for implementing the PIM Anycast-RP mechanism:

- An RP will send a copy of a PIM Register message only if the source IP address of the message Register is NOT the non-shared IP address of an Anycast-RP Set member (i.e., the PIM Register message is originated by a source-side DR and not another Anycast-RP Set member).
- Each source-side DR will send (i.e., unicast) PIM Register messages to the Anycast-RP Address (i.e., to the closest physical RP). Therefore, no changes to the standard DR logic are required.
- Multicast packets flow to all receivers irrespective of which RP they have joined.
- The source-side DR sends PIM Register messages to a single RP (in the Anycast-RP Set). It is the responsibility of the closest RP to the DR that receives the PIM Register messages to send (unicast) copies of the message to all other RPs in the Anycast-RP Set.
- Only the logic in the RPs in the Anycast-RP Set changes. The change pertains to how an RP unicast copies PIM Register messages to other peer RPs. There are no changes in how PIM Register-Stop messages are processed. However, an Anycast-RP implementation may suppress sending PIM Register-Stop messages when a PIM Register message is received from an RP.

- The rate-limiting of PIM Register and Register-Stop messages is performed end-to-end. That is from the source-side DR to RP 1 to {RP 2 or RP 3}. No specific rate-limiting logic is needed between the peer RPs.
- When network topology changes occur in the PIM-SM domain, the existing SPT adjusts itself as in the PIM-SM specification [RFC7761].
- Changes in the configuration of the physical peer RP are as fast as the unicast IGP convergence.
- The network operator may mix an RP that does not support the Anycast-RP mechanism with RPs that do. However, the non-supporting RP should not allow multicast sources (i.e., their DRs) to send PIM Register messages to it, but may have receivers joining it.
- If a source-side DR sends PIM Null-Register messages (which are PIM Register messages with an IP header and no IP payload), these messages must be replicated to all of the Anycast-RP Set members so that the source state remains alive for active multicast sources.
- The network operator should keep the number of RPs in the Anycast-RP Set small so that the amount of non-native replication of traffic is kept to a minimum.

The Anycast-PIM mechanism was developed to remove the dependence on using the MSDP Anycast-RP method, as described in Chapter 6. The PIM Anycast-RP mechanism removes the requirement of MSDP peering between the Anycast-RPs as seen in the MSDP Anycast-RP method. However, to advertise multicast sources within a PIM-SM domain to other PIM-SM domains and to allow external sources from other domains to be discovered, MSDP is still required for this purpose. It is recommended that an implementation of a PIM Anycast-RP Set should not be mixed with MSDP peering among the PIM Anycast-RP Set members in a PIM-SM domain; MSDP is only used for implementing an Anycast-RP Set, as described in Chapter 6.

5.16.6 MULTICAST GROUP-TO-RP MAPPING

A PIM-SM router receives one or more possible multicast group-range-to-RP mappings via one of the mechanisms described earlier, with each mapping specifying a range of multicast group addresses (expressed as a multicast group address and network mask) and the RP to which those groups map to. Each group-range-to-RP mapping may also have a priority associated with it. The router may receive multiple multicast group-range-to-RP mappings, all of which may match the same multicast group address, as common in the case where the BSR mechanism is used. A PIM-SM router (potentially, a source- or receiver-side DR) uses the following algorithm for performing the group-to-RP mapping:

1. The router uses the specified/requested multicast group address to perform the *longest match* on the multicast group address range to obtain a list of RPs.
2. From this list of matching RPs (for the group address), the router selects the RPs with the *highest priority*. The router eliminates any RPs from the list with lower priorities.

3. If only one RP remains in the list after eliminating the lower priority RPs, the router uses that RP.
4. If multiple RPs remain in the list, the router uses the PIM hash function (described in the subsequent text) to select one RP.

The cited rules are further refined by the PIM-SM router as follows during the RP selection process:

a. If the PIM-SM router finds that two or more group-range-to-RP mappings match a particular multicast group address, the router uses the RP from the group-range-to-RP mapping with the longest mask.
b. If the group-range-to-RP mappings have the same mask length, then the router selects the RP with the highest priority.
c. If more than one matching group-range-to-RP mappings is having the same longest mask and priority values, then the router applies a hash function (see below) to choose the RP.

A DR invokes this algorithm when it needs to determine an RP for a given multicast group, for example, when it receives a multicast packet or IGMP Membership Report for a multicast group for which it needs to know the correct RP to use. Furthermore, all PIM-SM routers upon receiving a (*, G) Join/Prune message will invoke the mapping function.

Note that if changes occur in the set of possible group-range-to-RP mappings, each PIM-SM router will need to check whether such changes have affected any existing multicast groups. Such changes, for example, may cause a DR or acting DR to send a PIM Join message to rejoin a multicast group, or cause it to restart sending PIM Register messages encapsulating multicast packets from a source to the new RP.

5.16.7 RP Hash Function

All routers within a PIM-SM domain use the *same* hash function to map a given multicast group address to one of the RPs in the matching set of group-range-to-RP mappings (i.e., the set of group-range-to-RP mappings that all have the same longest mask length and highest priority value). The input to the algorithm is the multicast group address G, the hash-mask M, and the addresses of the Candidate-RPs from the group-range-to-RP mappings, and the output is a single RP address to be used.

The PIM-SM protocol requires that all routers in the PIM-SM domain hash to the same RP (except during network transient periods). Each router must use the following hash function:

1. The router computes a value for the RP addresses in the matching group-range-to-RP mappings as follows:

$$\text{Value } (G, M, C(i)) = \{1103515245 \times [(1103515245 \times (G\&M) + 12345) \text{ XOR} \\ C(i)] + 12345\} \bmod 231$$

where C(i) is the RP address and M is a hash-mask (see also Table 5.2).

If the PIM-SM domain uses the BSR mechanism, the hash-mask that a router uses is carried in the Bootstrap messages it receives. If the domain is not using the BSR, the hash-mask may be provided by an alternative mechanism that also supplies the group-range-to-RP mappings, or else the hash-mask that the router uses defaults to a mask with 1s in the most significant 30 bits for IPv4 and 1s in the most significant 126 bits for IPv6. The hash-mask allows the router to always hash a small number of consecutive multicast group addresses (e.g., 4) to the same RP address.

For address families other than IPv4, the 32-bit digest that the PIM-SM router uses as C(i) and G in the algorithm must first be derived from the actual RP address or multicast group address. It is essential for the PIM-SM domain to consistently use such a digest method throughout. In the case of IPv6 addresses, [RFC7761] recommends using the equivalent IPv4 address for an IPv4-compatible address (i.e., an IPv4-Compatible IPv6 Address). For all other IPv6 addresses, the recommended method involves using the Exclusive-OR of each 32-bit segment of the IPv6 address.

For example, the PIM-SM router computes the digest of the IPv6 address 3ffe:b00:c18:1::10 as follows:

$$0x3ffe0b00 \oplus 0x0c180001 \oplus 0x00000000 \oplus 0x00000010,$$

where the $\oplus$ symbol represents the Exclusive-OR operation.

2. *The PIM-SM chooses the candidate RP address with the highest resulting hash value as the RP for the multicast group G. The router chooses the RP with the highest IP address if more than one RP has the same highest hash value.*

5.16.7.1 Summary of the RP Hash Algorithm

All PIM routers use the same hash algorithm to select an RP for a given multicast group.

TABLE 5.2

Values in the Hash Function

Parameter	Description
Value	Hash value
G	IP address of the multicast group
M	Hash mask length
C(i)	IP address of the C-RP
&	Logical operator of "AND"
XOR	Logical operator of "Exclusive-OR"
mod	Modulo operator, which gives the remainder of an integer division

---

- At each PIM router, the hash algorithm takes as input variables, the Candidate-RP address C(i), group address G, and a hash-mask M, and returns a hash value Value (G, M, C(i)).
- The router runs the hash algorithm on all the Candidate-RP addresses in the RP-Set whose advertised multicast group address range matches the target group G.
- From this set of Candidate-RPs, the router selects the Candidate-RP with the highest hash value as the RP for the target group G.
- If two Candidate-RPs happen to have the same hash value, the one with the highest IP address is selected as the RP for multicast group G; the IP address is used as the tiebreaker.

The hash-mask M is usually taken from the Hash Mask Length field of the received Bootstrap message. By modifying the hash-mask, the network operator can control the number of consecutive multicast group addresses that map to the same Candidate-RP in the RP-Set. For example, if the hash-mask M is a 30-bit hash-mask 0xFF-FF-FF-FC, four consecutive multicast group addresses will hash (i.e., map) to a single Candidate-RP address C(i). The network operator may use this important feature of the hash algorithm, for example, when separate multicast groups are sent related data and the operator wants all of these related groups to share the same RP in the multicast domain.

5.16.7.2 Using the Hash Function

Every multicast router in the PIM-SM domain receives the Bootstrap messages containing group-to-RP mappings and uses that information to populate their RP caches. It is up to each router to select the best matching RP from the RP-Set advertised by the BSR. All routers must select the same RP for the same group. To fully utilize the group-to-RP information, routers should select different RPs for different groups. All routers must yield the same load balancing result on the RPs to maintain synchronous mapping. The RP mapping procedure works as follows.

- Input: Group Address (G), RP-Set {C(1), C(2), ..., C(N)}, Mask (M).
  - This information is used as the input to the hash function.
  - {C(1), C(2)...., C(N)} are the IP addresses of the RPs mapped to the group address G.
  - The Mask (M) is calculated based on the mask length distributed by the BSR.
- For each RP IP address, calculate the hash function value:
  - Value $1 = $ Hash(G & Mask, C(1)),
  - Value $2 = $ Hash(G & Mask, C(2)) ...
  - Value $N = $ Hash(G & Mask, C(N)).

Note that the multicast Group IP address (G) is ANDed with the Mask value (M). Thus, the hash function uses only the first hash-mask-length bits of the multicast group address to calculate the hash value. Using a "pseudo-random" selection procedure, the hash function partitions the whole multicast address space among different RPs in the RP-Set. Each RP will be assigned approximately $2^{[32-hash\_mask\_length]}$ multicast groups, provided there are enough RPs to evenly distribute the multicast traffic load. Note that the default mask length value is 0, indicating that the multicast group address is ignored when computing the hash value and all groups map to the same RP.

5.16.7.3   Observations When Using the Hash Function to Select an RP for a Multicast Group

The inputs to the hash function are G (the multicast group address), M (the hash mask value), and C (the IP address of the RP). The hash mask is a 32-bit value that is advertised by the BSR in the Bootstrap messages. To determine the RP for a multicast group, a PIM router inputs these into the hash function, which in turn returns a hash value. The router selects RP with the highest hash value. The default hash mask value is 0, which means that the hash function calculates the hash value based only on the IP address of the RP. The following can be observed when the hash mask changes:

- The remaining bits in the hash mask that are not covered by the mask determine how many multicast groups will map to an RP.
- The hash mask is a 32-bit value, so, if a 31-bit mask is used (0xFF-FF-FF-FE), only one bit is left that is not covered by the mask. With a single bit, two hash values are created, implying two multicast groups will map to one RP.
- If a 30-bit hash mask is used (0xFF-FF-FF-FC), two bits are left that are not covered by the mask. With two bits, four hash values are created, implying four multicast groups will map to one RP.

The given observations imply that a network operator can use the hash mask length to configure load balancing on the RPs in the PIM-SM domain. The hash mask that is selected and advertised by the BSR in Bootstrap messages decides how many multicast groups ultimately map to one RP.

5.16.7.3.1   Example Use Case 1

As an example, let us consider two Candidate-RPs with the same priority in a PIM-SM domain. We assume both can become the RP for the entire 239.0.0.0/8 multicast range. We also assume multicast hosts in the domain want to receive traffic for the following eight multicast groups: 239.0.0.0, 239.0.0.1, 239.0.0.2, 239.0.0.3, 239.0.0.4, 239.0.0.5, 239.0.0.6, 239.0.0.7.

- When a hash mask of 0 is used (i.e., no hash mask used), all eight multicast groups will be assigned to one RP.
- If a 31-bit hash mask is used (0xFF-FF-FF-FE), two multicast groups are assigned to each RP:
  - RP1: 239.0.0.0, 239.0.0.1 and RP2: 239.0.0.2, 239.0.0.3
  - or RP1: 239.0.0.4, 239.0.0.5 and RP2: 239.0.0.6, 239.0.0.7

- If a 30-bit hash mask is used (0xFF-FF-FF-FC), four multicast groups are assigned to each RP:
  - RP1: 239.0.0.0, 239.0.0.1, 239.0.0.2, 239.0.0.3
  - RP2: 239.0.0.4, 239.0.0.5, 239.0.0.6, 239.0.0.7

5.16.7.3.2   Example Use Case 2

Let us assume there are two Candidate-RPs, Candidate-RP-A and Candidate-RP-B, for multicast group address range 239.0.0.0–239.255.255.255 (which is the entire administratively scoped multicast address group range). We assume that a 30-bit hash-mask M is advertised, 0xFF-FF-FF-FC.

- This hash-mask results in four consecutive multicast groups hashing to the same Candidate-RP.
- Given that there are two Candidate-RPs, Candidate-RP-A and Candidate-RP-B, and that the address in the group address range 239.0.0.0 hashes to Candidate-RP-A, then Candidate-RP-A will also be assigned as the RP for the next three consecutive multicast group addresses, 239.0.0.1, 239.0.0.2, and 239.0.0.3.
- Assuming the output of the hash algorithm is evenly distributed, Candidate-RP-A will be assigned as RP for half of the groups in the 239.0.0.0–239.255.255.255 range and Candidate-RP-B will be assigned as RP for the other half.

5.16.7.4   RP Failover in the PIM-SM Domain

All routers in a PIM-SM domain that uses the BSR mechanism maintain the complete RP-Set of Candidate-RP advertisements in the Group-to-RP Mapping Caches. Additionally, each entry in the Mapping Cache contains a Hold Time that specifies how long the corresponding Candidate-RP advertisement is valid. Each entry has an expiry timer that is initialized to the Hold Time value that was contained in the associated Candidate-RP entry of the received Bootstrap message (see Bootstrap Message format in Chapter 3).

The Hold Time value of the entry is the period that must elapse before the router will delete the Candidate-RP entry in the Group-to-RP Mapping Cache. Deleting the expired entry causes the router to initiate a new computation of the hash algorithm to determine new RPs for any active multicast groups. If the deleted Candidate-RP entry is an active RP for a multicast group, the router will select a new RP for that group and will send a new (*, G) Join toward that new RP.

5.17   MODIFICATIONS TO PIM-SM FOR SOURCE-SPECIFIC MULTICAST AND DESTINATION ADDRESSES

The Source-Specific Multicast (SSM) multicast service model [RFC4607] uses a subset of the PIM-SM protocol mechanisms specified in [RFC7761]. A single router can support both the regular PIM-SM model [RFC7761] and the SSM semantics [RFC4607]; both can coexist on the same platform and be implemented using the PIM-SM protocol [RFC7761]. As discussed later, a range of multicast addresses is reserved for SSM, currently 232.0.0.0/8 for IPv4 and ff3x::/32 for IPv6. The choice of semantics in a router supporting both models is determined by the multicast group address used in both multicast data packets and PIM messages.

5.17.1 PIM-SM Modifications for SSM Destination Addresses

When using SSM with a multicast address G in the SSM range, the following rules override the normal PIM-SM protocol behavior:

1. A PIM router using SSM semantics MUST NOT send a PIM (*, G) Join/Prune message under any circumstance.
2. A PIM router using SSM semantics MUST NOT send a PIM (S, G, rpt) Join/Prune message under any circumstance.
3. A PIM router using SSM semantics MUST NOT send a PIM Register message for any multicast packet that is addressed to an SSM address.
4. A router using SSM semantics MUST NOT forward multicast packets based on (*, G) or (S, G, rpt) state. The (*, G)- and (S, G, rpt)-related state functions for multicast packet forwarding are NULL for any SSM address.
5. A router acting as an RP MUST NOT forward any multicast data packet encapsulated in a PIM Register message and containing an SSM destination address and SHOULD send a PIM Register-Stop message to the source's DR in response to such a PIM Register message.
6. A router MAY omit the creation and maintenance of (S, G, rpt) and (*, G) states for SSM destination addresses as a way of optimization, since such a state is not needed for SSM packets.

The last three rules target SSM-unaware "legacy" routers that may send (PIM *, G) and (S, G, rpt) Join/Prunes messages or PIM Register messages carrying SSM destination addresses.

5.17.2 PIM-SSM-Only Routers

An SSM implementation may choose only the subset of the PIM-SM protocol that provides the SSM forwarding semantics. An SSM-only router MUST implement the following portions of the PIM-SM specification [RFC7761]:

• PIM Hello messages, neighbor discovery, and DR election
• Downstream (S, G) state machine
• Upstream (S, G) state machine
• (S, G) Assert state machine
• Multicast packet forwarding rules

An SSM-only router does not need to support the following PIM-SM protocol elements:

- PIM Register state machine
- Bootstrap Router election
- (*, G) and (S, G, rpt) Downstream state machines
- (*, G) and (S, G, rpt) Upstream state machines
- (*, G) Assert state machine
- Keepalive Timer
- SPTbit

An SSM-only router should treat the Keepalive Timer as always running, and the SPTbit as always being set for a multicast packet with an SSM destination address.

5.18   PIM SOURCE-SPECIFIC MULTICAST (PIM-SSM)

Reference [RFC4607] designates IPv4 address range 232.0.0.0 to 232.255.255.255 (i.e., 232/8) as SSM destination addresses and the IPv6 address prefix FF3x::/32 (where "x" is any valid Scope Identifier) for use by source-specific applications and protocols. This reference defines extensions to IP multicast routing that apply to packets sent to SSM addresses and how IP hosts and routers support these extensions. Further discussions about the use of SSM in networks are provided in [RFC4604] and [RFC3569]. This section focuses only on the use of IGMPv3 in SSM. Readers may refer to [RFC4604] for how IGMPv1/2 and MLDv1/2 messages are handled in SSM.

SSM is a multicast service model in which a receiver requests multicast traffic by specifying both the IP address of the source and the multicast group destination address to receive the traffic. SSM uses only SPTs (no shared trees or RPTs). SSM does not require the RPs and RPTs, thus, there is no need for RP discovery mechanisms like BSR, Auto-RP, and MSDP. The neighbor discovery mechanism of PIM-SSM is the same as in PIM-DM and PIM-SM. PIM-SSM and PIM-SM use the same DR election mechanism, as described in the preceding text.

Multicast group management protocols, such as IGMPv1 [RFC1112], IGMPv2 [RFC2236], and IGMPv3 [RFC3376], allow IPv4 hosts to signal multicast group membership information to neighboring routers. IGMPv3, in particular, and, as discussed in Chapter 2 of this book, provides the ability for a host on a network segment to selectively request or filter traffic (via IGMPv3 Membership Report messages) from individual sources sending traffic to a multicast group. MLDv2 [RFC3810], which is used by IPv6 hosts, offers similar functionality to IGMPv3 (i.e., the source filtering functionality of IGMPv3 but for IPv6). Both IGMPv3 and MLDv2 support source filtering required for SSM.

Reference [RFC4607] defines SSM delivery semantics for a packet sent to an SSM address. In SSM, a host that receives a packet with source IP address S and SSM destination address G delivers it to each upper-layer protocol "socket" having specifically requested to receive packets sent by source S to SSM address G; packets are sent to only those host sockets. A socket is an implementation-specific parameter (e.g., the socket parameter of Unix system calls) that the host uses to distinguish between different service-requesting entities within the host (e.g., processes, programs, or communication endpoints within a process or program). Any source may send a packet to any SSM address, and the network and end-hosts deliver the packet according to this semantics. The term *"channel"* refers to the network service identified by the source-group (S, G) pair, where G is an SSM address and S is the source host address. *SSM channels* can be defined on an individual or multiple-source bases, which enforce the one-to-many concept of SSM applications. Each group in an SSM channel may be associated with multiple sources. When a source (S) transmits packets to an SSM destination address (G), a receiver, by subscribing to the (S, G) channel, can receive these packets.

SSM defines network-layer support for any source to communicate with many receivers (i.e., one-to-many). The benefits of SSM include the following:

- SSM eliminates cross-delivery of traffic when two sources in the multicast routing domain simultaneously send traffic to the same destination address. SSM allows multiple sources (S1, S2, S3) and different applications to simultaneously use the same SSM destination address (G) explicitly, (S1, G), (S2, G), (S3, G), and so on.
- As a consequence, SSM avoids the need for inter-host coordination when choosing multicast destination addresses.
- SSM avoids many of the multicast routing protocols and algorithms needed in the traditional multicast service model, for example, the shared trees and RPs of PIM-SM. The router mechanisms required to support SSM are largely a subset of those used in PIM-SM, for example, the SPT mechanism of PIM-SM can be used in SSM.

SSM uses only a subset of the PIM-SM features such as the SPT, DR, and some PIM protocol messages (Hello, Join, Prune, and Assert). However, some features of SSM are unique to it. Similar to the traditional multicast routing protocols (e.g., PIM-DM, PIM-SM), an SSM source does not need to know the set of receivers interested in the traffic it sends. An SSM source does not know the identity of receivers or the number of receivers in the network.

SSM is ideal for applications such as TV channel distribution and other businesses involving content distribution. Banking and stock trading applications may also use SSM as it provides more control over the hosts that are sending and receiving information over the network. SSM is particularly well-suited to applications that receive disseminated traffic from one or more sources whose identities are known to the applications before they begin. For example, in commercial broadcast TV, the receivers already know the identities of the traffic sources (which can be TV channels coming from the broadcaster). Additionally, a data dissemination application may have primary and secondary sources, with the requirement that receivers use the secondary source in case the primary source fails. This application may implement one channel for each data source and advertise both channels to receivers.

5.18.1 SEMANTICS OF SSM ADDRESSES

SSM extends the interface between the IP module and upper-layer protocols (e.g., TCP, UDP) to allow a socket to "Subscribe" to or "Unsubscribe" from a particular SSM channel (S, G) identified by a source IP address S and an SSM destination address G. In SSM, packets sent to an SSM destination address G, must also specify a corresponding source address S. Multiple applications on different source hosts can send traffic to the same SSM destination address G without conflicts because packets sent by a source Si are delivered only to those sockets that requested packets specifically from Si sent to SSM destination address G.

The key distinguishing property of SSM is that it identifies a channel as the combination of a unicast source IP address S and a multicast destination address G in the SSM address range (see example in Figure 5.32). For example, the channel, (S, G) = (**192.0.20.1**, 232.8.9.10) is different from the channel (S, G) = (**192.0.20.20**, 232.8.9.10), even though both channels have the same SSM destination address. Similarly, for IPv6, the channels (S, G) = (2001:3618::1, FF33::1234) and (S, G) = (2001:3618::2, FF33::1234) represent two different SSM channels.

In PIM-DM and PIM-SM, a multicast service is associated with or identified by a single multicast group address G. In PIM-DM and PIM-SM, any source host can send traffic to a multicast group G. Similarly, in SSM, any source host can send traffic to an SSM destination address G. However, in PIM-DM and PIM-SM, a packet sent by a source host S to a multicast destination address G, is delivered to the multicast group identified by only G. In SSM, a packet sent by source S to an SSM

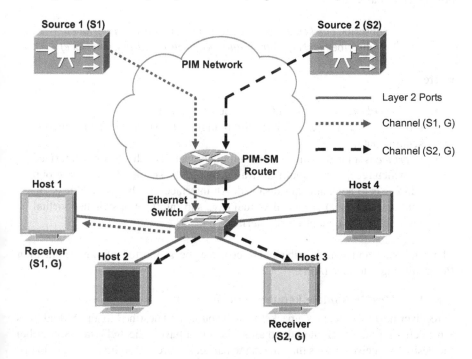

FIGURE 5.32 Example PIM-SSM network.

destination address G is delivered to the channel identified by (S, G). The receiver operations allowed on a multicast group in a PIM-DM or PIM-SM network are colloquially called "Join (G)" and "Leave (G)". The receiver operations allowed on an SSM channel (S, G) are called "Subscribe (S, G)" and "Unsubscribe (S, G)". Note that the techniques and protocols necessary to support SSM are largely a subset of those used to support PIM-DM and PIM-SM.

5.18.2 IP Host Requirements

We discuss in this section the requirements that hosts need to support SSM. Reference [RFC4604] defines the modifications required on the host and router portions of IGMPv3 and MLDv2 to support SSM. This reference describes what an SSM-aware host is the API requirements and the IGMPv3/MLDv2 protocol requirements of an SSM-aware host. SSM can be used by any host that supports IGMPv3/MLDv2 source filtering API. An SSM-aware host recognizes the SSM address range and is capable of applying SSM semantics.

5.18.2.1 Extensions to the IP Module Interface for SSM

To use SSM, the interface between the IP module and upper-layer protocols is extended to allow applications to request reception (Subscribe) or cease reception of (Unsubscribe) all packets sent to a particular SSM channel. The following are abstract interface functionality that can be provided in a host in an implementation-specific manner:

Subscribe *(socket, source_address, group_address, interface)*
Unsubscribe *(socket, source_address, group_address, interface)*

where

- *source_address* is the IP address of the data source
- *group_address* is the multicast group address to which the data source is sending data.
- *interface* is a local parameter that uniquely identifies the network interface on which reception of multicast traffic sent to the specified multicast group address is to be enabled or disabled. An interface may be physical (e.g., an Ethernet interface) or logical/virtual (e.g., sub-interface or switched virtual interface (SVI) on a physical interface).

The Subscribe and Unsubscribe interfaces may be supported via an Application Programming Interface (API).

5.18.2.2 Host IP Module Requirements for SSM

A receiver host that receives a packet from a source and destined to an SSM address must deliver it via the IP module to all sockets that have indicated (via a Subscribe) the desire to receive packets that match the packet's source IP address, destination IP address (which is an SSM address), and the arriving interface. The IP module interface must not deliver the packet to other sockets on the host.

When a socket on host H is the first to subscribe to an SSM channel (S, G) on interface I, the IP module on the host sends a request on interface I to indicate to multicast routers on its network segment that the host wishes to receive traffic sent by source S to SSM destination G. Similarly, when a socket that is the last on a host to unsubscribe from an SSM channel on interface I, the IP module on the host sends a request on interface I to unsubscribe from that channel.

The IP modules send requests using IGMPv3 messages for IPv4 [RFC3376] or MLDv2 messages for IPv6 [RFC3810], as discussed in Chapter 2. To support the SSM service model, an IPv4 host must implement the host portion of IGMPv3 (or MLDv2 for IPv6). The host must also conform to the IGMPv3 and MLDv2 behaviors described in [RFC4604].

5.18.2.2.1 IGMPv3 Host Requirements

An IGMPv3 host may report more than one SSM channel in a single IGMPv3 Membership Report message either by including multiple sources within an IGMPv3 Group Record or by including multiple Group Records (see Chapter 2). A Group Record that a host sends for an SSM destination address may (under normal SSM operation) be any of the following types:

- **Record Type = 1**: MODE_IS_INCLUDE as part of a Current-State Record
- **Record Type = 5**: ALLOW_NEW_SOURCES as part of a State-Change Record
- **Record Type = 6**: BLOCK_OLD_SOURCES as part of a State-Change Record

A host may send a Report message that includes both SSM destination addresses and non-SSM destination addresses, in the same message. Additionally, a host may send a Report message with a CHANGE_TO_INCLUDE_MODE record (Record Type = 3) in some cases, for example, when the host configuration change includes an SSM address range change. A router that receives such a Group Record should process it according to the normal IGMPv3 rules.

An SSM-aware host should not send a Report message with any of the following IGMPv3 Group Record types for an SSM address as explained in [RFC4604]:

- **Record Type = 2**: MODE_IS_EXCLUDE as part of a Current-State Record
- **Record Type = 4**: CHANGE_TO_EXCLUDE_MODE as part of a Filter-Mode-Change Record

5.18.2.2.2 Handling IGMPv3 Group-Specific Query Messages

If an SSM-aware host receives an IGMPv3 Group-Specific Query message for an SSM address, it must respond with an IGMPv3 Report message if the group address contained in it matches the SSM destination address of any of its subscribed SSM channels, as specified in [RFC3376].

5.18.2.2.3   Handling IGMPv3 and MLDv2
Group-and-Source-Specific Query Messages

An IGMPv3 router typically sends an IGMPv3 Group-and-Source-Specific Query message to query an SSM channel that a host on one of its interfaces has requested to leave by transmitting a BLOCK_OLD_SOURCES Group Record. A host must respond to an IGMPv3 Group-and-Source-Specific Query message for which the multicast group and source addresses in the Query message match any SSM channel for which the host has a subscription, as required by [RFC3376]. Furthermore, the host must be able to process a Query message that contains multiple sources listed per multicast group.

5.18.3 ROUTER REQUIREMENTS

An SSM-aware router is aware of the SSM address range used to provide the SSM service model. Such a router recognizes the SSM address range and is capable of applying SSM semantics. A router that receives an IP packet with an SSM destination address from a source must silently drop it unless a host or router on one of its interfaces (i.e., attached network segment) has signaled a desire to receive packets sent from that source and to that SSM destination address.

Multicast routing protocols such as PIM-SM already can communicate source-specific joins from hosts to neighboring routers. PIM-SM, with slight modifications, can be used to provide SSM semantics. A router that supports the SSM service model must implement the multicast router processing portion described in the IGMPv3 specification [RFC3376] for IPv4 (or MLDv2 for IPv6), as well as the PIM-SSM subset of the PIM-SM protocol described in [RFC7761]. A router that supports SSM must also conform to the IGMPv3 (or MLDv2) behavior described in [RFC4604].

In PIM-SSM, the successful establishment of an SPT forwarding path (S, G) from the source S to any receiver in the multicast domain, is done by the PIM-SM routers performing hop-by-hop forwarding of the explicit PIM Join request from the receiver toward the source S. PIM-SM selects the forwarding path for the explicit Join request such that a loop-free SPT path is created. A PIM-SM router that supports PIM-SSM must also ensure that the PIM-SSM implementation (at least) supports the ability to use the PIM-SM unicast routing for this purpose. A multicast network may concurrently support multicast using the multicast address space used by PIM-SM and SSM using addresses in the SSM address range.

5.18.3.1 Handling IGMPv3 Report Messages

A host sends IGMPv3 Report messages to report source-specific subscriptions in the SSM address range. A router should ignore a Report message containing a Group Record of either of the following types if it refers to an SSM destination address:

- MODE_IS_EXCLUDE as part of a Current-State Record
- CHANGE_TO_EXCLUDE_MODE as part of a Filter-Mode-Change Record

The receiving router may choose to log an error in either of the above cases but it must process any other Group Record types contained in the same Report message. The router must process a CHANGE_TO_INCLUDE_MODE Filter-Mode-Change Record as per the normal IGMPv3 rules.

5.18.3.2 Handling IGMPv3 Query Messages

IGMPv3 Query messages are handled as follows:

- **IGMPv3 General Query Messages**: An SSM router sends periodic IGMPv3 General Query messages as per the IGMPv3 specification with no change in behavior.
- **IGMPv3 Group-Specific Query Messages**: IGMPv3 routers that support SSM may send IGMPv3 Group-Specific Query messages for addresses in the SSM address range.
- **IGMPv3 Group-and-Source-Specific Query Messages**: Routers send IGMPv3 Group-and-Source-Specific Query messages when a receiver on a network segment has indicated that it is no longer interested in receiving traffic from a particular (S, G) pair and to determine if there are any remaining hosts on that segment still interested in traffic from that (S, G) pair. A router sends Group-and-Source-Specific Query messages within the SSM address range when it receives a BLOCK_OLD_SOURCES Group Record for one or more source-specific groups.

5.18.4 How PIM-SSM Works

PIM-SSM requires the routers to perform the following actions:

- Support source-specific IGMPv3 Membership Report and Query messages at the leaf or edge routers.
- Receive IGMPv3 Membership Report messages for SSM channels in the SSM address range and, if no entry (S, G) exists in the SSM channel table, create one.
- Send PIM-SSM (S, G) Join messages directly and immediately after receiving an IGMPv3 Membership Report from a host receiver.
- Restrict forwarding data to SPTs within the SSM address range.
- Send periodic PIM (S, G) Join messages to maintain a steady SSM tree state.
- Use standard PIM-SM SPT procedures for unicast routing changes, but ignore PIM-SM rules associated with the SPT for the (S, G) route entry.
- Receive PIM (S, G) Prune messages and use standard PIM-SM procedures to remove interfaces from the SPT.
- Forward multicast data packets to interfaces leading to the downstream neighbors that sent PIM-SSM (S, G) Join messages, or to interfaces with locally attached SSM group members.
- Drop multicast data packets that do not exact-match (S, G) lookup in the (S, G) forwarding table.

The main processes when a host subscribes to an SSM channel are described as follows:

- A host subscribes to an SSM channel by sending an IGMPv3 Membership Report message, signaling the desire to join multicast group G with traffic from source S.
- Upon receiving this Report message, the DR first checks whether the multicast group address in the message falls in the SSM address range. If so, the host's receiver-side DR sends a PIM (S, G) Join message to its RPF neighbor for the source S. SSM uses the PIM-SM functionality to create an SPT between the receiver-side DR and the multicast source S, but this SPT is built without the help of an RP.
  - If the multicast group address of interest G is in the SSM address range (default range is 232.0.0.0/8 for IPv4 and FF3x::/32 for IPv6.), the DR sends a subscribe message (i.e., a PIM Join message) for the SSM channel (S, G) subscription which travels hop by hop toward the source S.
- All routers along the path from the DR to the source that receives the PIM (S, G) Join message will create an (S, G) entry to build the SPT, which is rooted at the source S and has all receivers (subscribers) as its leaves. The constructed SPT represents the SSM (S, G) transmission channel.

The SSM receivers can receive traffic only from the (S, G) channels to which they have subscribed. Figures 5.33–5.35 describe in detail how a receiver subscribes to an SSM (S, G) channel. Figure 5.34 also describes how a receiver unsubscribes from an SSM (S, G) channel.

During the use of SSM, any existing RP in the multicast domain is ignored (not required) for a particular range of the SSM range addresses. No PIM (*, G) Joins/Prunes are sent toward any RP, instead, PIM Joins/Prunes are sent directly toward the source S. SSM receivers use only IGMPv3 "joins" (precisely IGMPv3 Membership Report messages) with the appropriate source INCLUDE filters. In addition to not requiring shared trees (i.e., no need for RPs), SSM does not need source discovery through RP-to-RP communication based on MSDP. Although SSM describes receiver operations as subscribe and unsubscribe, it uses the same PIM-SM Join and Prune messages to join and leave the multicast distribution tree. The terminology change is to distinguish SSM receiver operations from those of PIM-SM even though the messages used by the receiver-side DR are identical.

5.18.5 SSM Session Description and Channel Discovery

To support the SSM service model, receiver applications subscribing to SSM channels must be provided mechanisms for discovering both the SSM destination address G and the unicast source address S before subscribing to channels. An application that wants to subscribe to an SSM channel must first discover the channel addresses (S, G). Channel discovery for SSM applications can be provided in several ways, including via session announcement applications, web pages, etc. (see Figure 5.36).

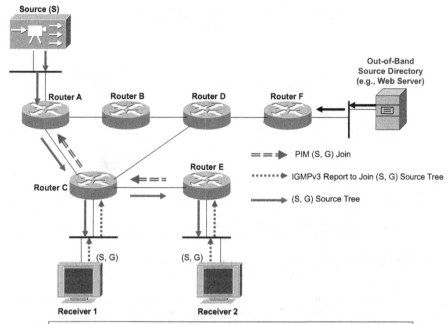

- Receiver learns of multicast traffic source and group/port.
- Receiver sends an IGMPv3 Membership Report to join (S, G) tree.
- Receiver-side DR sends PIM (S, G) Join message directly toward the source.
- The result is the SPT is rooted at the source with no shared tree used.

FIGURE 5.33 Example PIM-SSM and IGMPv3 (S, G) behavior.

After SSM channel discovery, the receiver application can then use the source-filtering capable protocol, IGMPv3 (or MLDv2 for IPv6 systems), to signal to its attached router (i.e., the receiver-end DR) that wants to subscribe to the particular SSM (S, G) channel. IGMPv3 and MLDv2 support the range of capabilities required to realize the SSM service model.

The network operator may construct an SSM channel table on the receiver-side DR with manually configured SSM channel (S, G) entries that map existing multicast groups to their sending multicast source. The operator may apply the following rules to an SSM channel table for an individual receiver-side DR:

- Map one source (S) to multiple multicast groups $(G_1, G_2, ..., G_N)$.
- Map multiple sources $(S_1, S_2, ..., S_N)$ to the same multicast group (G).

Different leaf or edge SSM routers can use different mappings for multicast groups to sources, for example, different SSM channels may map differently even if they are on the same SSM network. A host using IGMPv3 and attached to an SSM edge device can selectively request or filter traffic from sources within a multicast group.

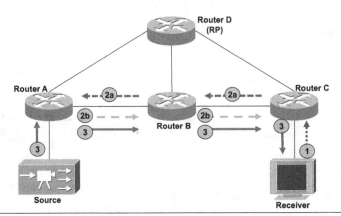

Processing steps:
1. A receiver subscribes to an SSM channel by sending an IGMPv3 Report message to the receiver-side DR (Router C), which announces the receiver's desire to join multicast group G and Source S.
   - Note that the receiver-side DR (which is a directly connected PIM-SM router) does not contact the RP in this process as would be the case in normal PIM-SM operations.
   - PIM-SSM uses the PIM-SM functionality to create an SPT between the receiver and the source but builds the SPT without the help of an RP.
2. The receiver-side DR sends a PIM (S,G) Join message to its RPF neighbor (Router B) leading toward the source.
   a) The PIM (S,G) Join message initiates the source tree (SPT) and then builds the SPT hop-by-hop until it reaches the source-side DR (Router A).
   b) The source tree is built across the network from Router C to Router A. This enables the source-side DR (Router A) to join the source tree (SPT). PIM (S,G) multicast state information is built on the PIM routers on the SPT between the source and the receiver.
3. Using the source tree and the (S, G) state information, multicast traffic is delivered from the source S to the source-side DR (Router A) and then across the network to the receiver - side DR (Router C) and the subscribing receiver.

Unsubscribing from an SSM channel:
- The receiver sends and IGMPv3 Membership Report message with Group Record type BLOCK_OLD_SOURCES to inform the receiver-side DR that it no longer wants to receive the (S, G) multicast traffic; receiver wants to unsubscribe from the (S, G) channel.
- The receiver-side DR then sends an IGMP Group-and-Source-Specific Query message to check if there is any other receiver on the network segment still interested in traffic from the (S, G) channel.
- If the receiver-side DR does not receive any reply, it will send a PIM (S, G) Prune message toward the upstream PIM neighbor.

FIGURE 5.34   How PIM-SSM works: example 1.

The network may apply the following rules to IGMPv3-enabled interfaces on the SSM edge device:

- Send only source-specific IGMPv3 Membership Report messages for addresses in the SSM address range.
- Accept IGMPv3 Membership Report messages.

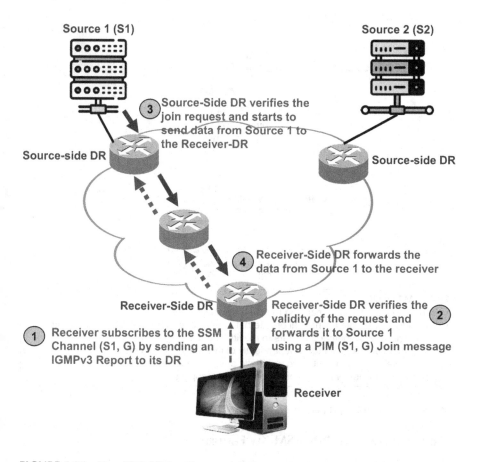

FIGURE 5.35 How PIM-SSM works: example 2.

- Drop IGMPv2 Membership Report messages.
- Discard IGMP messages with a multicast group address outside of the SSM address range.

The SSM edge device may implement IGMPv3 in one of two modes: dynamic and static.

- **Dynamic mode**: In this mode, the SSM edge device learns about new (S, G) pairs from IGMPv3 Membership Report messages sent by hosts and adds them to the SSM channel table.
- **Static mode**: In this mode, the network operator manually configures (S, G) entries in the SSM channel table on the SSM edge device. If an IGMPv3-enabled interface receives a Membership Report message that includes a multicast group not listed in the SSM channel table, it ignores the Report message. The interface also ignores the Report message if the multicast group is in the SSM channel table, but the source address or network mask does not match what is in the channel table.

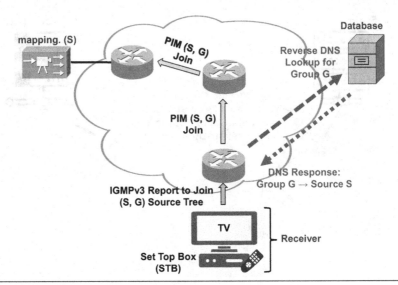

PIM-SSM Mapping:
- Brings Source-to-Group mapping to the receiver-side DR
- The network can use an internal or external database for Source-to-Group mapping:
  - This allows content providers to provide the mapping.
  - It can be implemented independently of the network operator.
  - Database can be set up to use static or DNS-based mapping.

  Note: This provides only one Source per Group mapping.

FIGURE 5.36   PIM-SSM mapping.

5.18.6   SUMMARY OF PIM-SSM KEY FEATURES

- The SSM service model defines a "channel" by an (S, G) pair, where S is a source IP address and G is an SSM destination address. SSM defines channels on a per-source basis, that is, the channel (S1, G) is distinct from the channel (S2, G), where S1 and S2 are different source IP addresses, and G is an SSM destination address.
- Hosts subscribe to SSM channels using group membership management protocols such as IGMPv3 or MLDv2.
- When a host subscribes to an SSM (S, G) channel, it receives data sent only by that source S. In contrast, in PIM-DM or PIM-SM, any host can transmit to a group G. However, when an SSM source selects a channel (S, G) to send traffic to, it is automatically ensured that no other source will be sending traffic on the same channel (except in the case of malicious acts such as address spoofing). This makes it much harder for SSM channel spamming to happen than sources in PIM-SM sending to a multicast group.
- Only source-rooted trees (SRT) or SPT rooted at the data source are needed to implement the SSM model.

- SSM requires the use of SRT or SPT which eliminates the need for the PIM-SM shared tree infrastructure. This means the RP-based shared tree infrastructure of PIM-SM is not required, making the complexity of the SSM multicast routing infrastructure low.

5.19   PIM SNOOPING REVISITED

In a network where a Layer 2 switch (e.g., Ethernet switch) is used to interconnect several IP routers, such as an Internet Exchange Point (IXP), the switch, by default, will flood multicast packets on all multicast router ports, even if those ports do no lead to multicast downstream receivers. When PIM Snooping is enabled on the switch, it limits multicast packets destined for a multicast group to only those multicast router ports that have downstream receivers that have joined the group. With PIM Snooping enabled, the switch learns which of its ports need to receive the multicast traffic within a specific IP subnet or VLAN by listening to the PIM Hello, Join, and Prune messages, and BIDIR-PIM Designated Forwarder (DF) Election messages. Because PIM-DM operates on a flood-and-prune principle, PIM Snooping does not work with PIM-DM; PIM-DM traffic is dropped once PIM Snooping is enabled.

In a BIDIR-PIM network, the PIM Snooping switch snoops on DF Election messages and maintains a list of all DFs for various RPs for the IP subnet or VLAN on which it is located. The PIM Snooping switch sends all traffic to all DFs which ensures that BIDIR-PIM functionality works properly.

To use PIM Snooping, IGMP Snooping must also be enabled on the switch. Figure 5.37 illustrates the case of configuring PIM Snooping on a Layer 2 switch in a network segment that supports PIM-SM routers (including an RP). As discussed in Chapter 2, configuring IGMP Snooping on a Layer 2 switch restricts multicast traffic sent to a multicast group to only switch ports that have host members of that group. Without PIM Snooping enabled in Figure 5.37, the Ethernet Switch E floods the PIM Join message sent by Router D and intended for the RP (Router B) to all connected switches and routers. This is because Ethernet Switch E does not know which port to forward the PIM Join message.

With PIM Snooping enabled in Figure 5.37, the switches, particularly Ethernet Switch E, restrict the PIM Join message from Router D and forward it only to the RP (Router B) that needs to receive it. A PIM Snooping switch typically times out a multicast router port and neighbor router information based on the Hold Time seen in the PIM Hello, Join, and Prune messages.

5.20   PIM-SM ROUTER ARCHITECTURE

Figure 5.38 illustrates a block diagram of the PIM software architecture in a PIM-SM router. The PIM-SM software architecture is split into the following modules, with clearly well-defined interfaces between them.

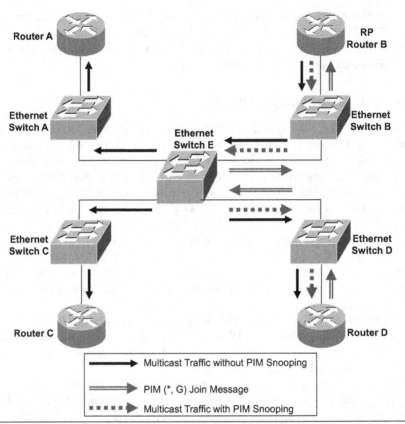

FIGURE 5.37 PIM Snooping.

5.20.1 NEIGHBOR MANAGER

As in many other routing protocols, there are several components of the PIM-SM protocol that deal purely with interactions between neighboring PIM-SM routers.

- PIM Hello messages are sent periodically on each PIM-enabled interface, with a destination address of the ALL-PIM-ROUTERS multicast group. Other PIM messages from a neighbor are not accepted unless a PIM Hello message has previously been received, although this can be disabled by user configuration. Some old PIM-SM implementations do not send PIM Hello messages on point-to-point networks.
- On a multiaccess network interface, a single DR is responsible for advertising PIM Join messages to upstream PIM neighbors, and the group membership status of that interface. The PIM Hello message includes information

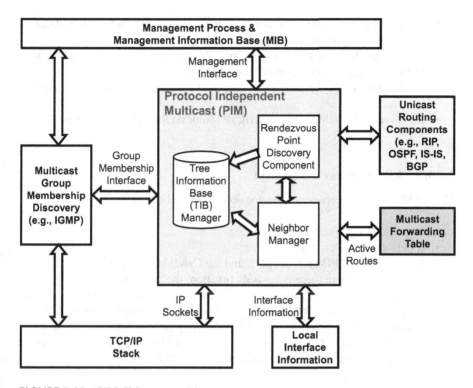

FIGURE 5.38 PIM-SM router architecture.

that allows the election of the DR. The DR is also the router that is responsible for encapsulating a source's multicast data in PIM Register messages and sending them to the RP on the interface.

The Neighbor Manager subcomponent of this architecture performs the cited functions, as well as the following:

- Parses and syntax checks all received PIM messages.
- Maintains the PIM Neighbor MIB (Management Information Base).

5.20.2 Tree Information Base (TIB) Manager

The Tree Information Base (TIB) Manager subcomponent performs the bulk of the protocol processing required by PIM. It is responsible for the following:

- It stores multicast state for the PIM TIB.
- It uses this state to program the router's multicast forwarding table.
- It processes PIM Join/Prune messages and runs the PIM Join/Prune Finite State Machines.

- It tracks the multicast group membership needs of locally attached hosts, as advertised to it over the interface.
- It performs Reverse Path Forwarding (RPF) lookups to route PIM Join/Prune messages to upstream PIM routers.
- It takes part in PIM Assert processing and tracks the Assert state of each interface.
- It maintains the PIM Interface MIB, IP Multicast Route MIB, and Next-Hop MIB.

5.20.3   RP Discovery Component

The RP Discovery Component is responsible for the following:

- It performs Candidate-RP processing.
- It performs BSR processing.
- It maintains the PIM RP-Set MIB and the Candidate-RP MIB.
- In networks where there is no BSR function, the network operator configures the RP for each group on each PIM router (i.e., Static RP method). To facilitate this, the RP Discovery component may maintain an MIB that allows the RP to be configured for each group address (or range thereof). The configured RPs are advertised to the TIB Manager over the internal interface exactly as described above for elected RPs.

REVIEW QUESTIONS

1. Why is PIM-SM referred to as a protocol that uses a pull or Explicit Join model?
2. Explain briefly the main differences between PIM-DM and PIM-SM.
3. What PIM functions are common to both PIM-DM and PIM-SM?
4. What PIM messages are common to both PIM-DM and PIM-SM?
5. What PIM messages are specific to PIM-SM and PIM-DM?
6. What is the role of the Rendezvous Point (RP) in PIM-SM? Include in your answer its main tasks in the PIM-SM domain.
7. What are the two types of RPF Neighbors in PIM-SM?
8. What is the difference between an SPT and an RPT?
9. What is the difference between a PIM (S, G) Join/Prune and a PIM (*, G) Join/Prune message?
10. What is the role of the Designated Router (DR) in PIM-SM? How is this role different from that in PIM-DM? Include in your answer the different types of DRs.
11. What PIM message is used for the DR election? What are the main criteria for electing the DR?
12. What is the purpose of the PIM Register message? Include in your answer the purpose of the PIM-SM multicast source registration process.
13. What is the purpose of the PIM Register-Stop message? Include in your answer the conditions under which this message is sent.

14. What is a PIM Null-Register message and what is its purpose?
15. What are the benefits of RPT to SPT switchover in a PIM-SM domain? Include in your answer the two types of RPT to SPT switchover.
16. What is an (S, G) RPT-bit Prune?
17. What is the purpose of the PIM Assert mechanism?
18. Explain briefly how the PIM Assert Winner is elected.
19. What functions does the PIM Assert Winner perform?
20. What is a PIM AssertCancel message and what is it used for?
21. What is the purpose of refreshing the PIM-SM multicast state in PIM-SM routers?
22. What is the purpose of an RP discovery mechanism in a PIM-SM?
23. What is Static RP? Include in your answer its disadvantages.
24. What is Embedded-RP?
25. What are the roles of the Candidate-RP and RP Mapping Agent in a PIM-SM network using the Auto-RP mechanism? Include in your answer the types of messages they use and how they are sent.
26. What are the drawbacks of the Auto-RP mechanism?
27. Explain briefly why the Bootstrap Router (BSR) mechanism is preferred over the Auto-RP mechanism for PIM-SM networks.
28. What are the roles of the Candidate-RP and BSR in a PIM-SM network? Include in your answer the types of messages they use and how they are sent.
29. What is the purpose of Semantic Fragmentation of Bootstrap messages?
30. What is an Anycast-RP and what are its benefits in a PIM-SM network?
31. Explain briefly how the PIM Anycast-RP mechanism is different from the MSDP Anycast-RP mechanism.
32. What is the purpose of the RP Hash Function?
33. Explain briefly how PIM-SM is different from PIM-SSM.
34. What is PIM Snooping and what are its main benefits?

REFERENCES

[CISCPRWILL03]. B. Williamson, *Developing IP Multicast Networks*, Vol. 1, Cisco Press, 2003.
[RFC2236]. W. Fenner, "Internet Group Management Protocol, Version 2", *IETF RFC 2236*, November 1997.
[RFC2365]. D. Meyer, "Administratively Scoped IP Multicast", *IETF RFC 2365*, July 1998.
[RFC3376]. B. Cain, S. Deering, I. Kouvelas, B. Fenner, and A. Thyagarajan, "Internet Group Management Protocol, Version 3", *IETF RFC 3376*, October 2002.
[RFC3569]. S. Bhattacharyya, Ed., "An Overview of Source-Specific Multicast (SSM)", *IETF RFC 3569*, July 2003.
[RFC3618]. B. Fenner, Ed. and D. Meyer, Ed., "Multicast Source Discovery Protocol (MSDP)", *IETF RFC 3618*, October 2003.
[RFC3810]. R. Vida and L. Costa, "Multicast Listener Discovery Version 2 (MLDv2) for IPv6", *IETF RFC 3810*, June 2004.
[RFC3956]. P. Savola and B. Haberman, "Embedding the Rendezvous Point (RP) Address in an IPv6 Multicast Address" *IETF RFC 3956*, November 2004.

[RFC4291]. R. Hinden and S. Deering, "IP Version 6 Addressing Architecture", IETF RFC 4291, February 2006.

[RFC4604]. H. Holbrook, B. Cain, and B. Haberman, "Using Internet Group Management Protocol Version 3 (IGMPv3) and Multicast Listener Discovery Protocol Version 2 (MLDv2) for Source-Specific Multicast", *IETF RFC 4604*, August 2006.

[RFC4607]. H. Holbrook and B. Cain, "Source-Specific Multicast for IP", *IETF RFC 4607*, August 2006

[RFC4610]. D. Farinacci and Y. Cai, "Anycast-RP Using Protocol Independent Multicast (PIM)", *IETF RFC 4610*, August 2006.

[RFC4760]. T. Bates, R. Chandra, D. Katz, and Y. Rekhter, "Multiprotocol Extensions for BGP-4", *IETF RFC 4760*, January 2007.

[RFC5059]. N. Bhaskar, A. Gall, J. Lingard, and S. Venaas, "Bootstrap Router (BSR) Mechanism for Protocol Independent Multicast (PIM)", *IETF RFC 5059*, January 2008.

[RFC7761]. B. Fenner, M. Handley, H. Holbrook, I. Kouvelas, R. Parekh, Z. Zhang, and L. Zheng, "Protocol Independent Multicast - Sparse Mode (PIM-SM): Protocol Specification (Revised)", *IETF RFC 7761*, March 2016.

6 Multicast Source Discovery Protocol (MSDP)

6.1 INTRODUCTION

PIM-SM [RFC7761] was developed to be used in only one PIM-SM domain. However, in the case where multiple PIM-SM domains are interconnected, the Multicast Source Discovery Protocol (MSDP) allows the distribution of information about active multicast sources in one PIM-SM domain to other PIM-SM domains [RFC3618] [RFC4611]. Generally, routers within a single PIM-SM domain rely on a Rendezvous Point (RP) discovery mechanism, such as the Bootstrap Router mechanism, to learn multicast group-to-RP mappings within the domain, as discussed in Chapter 5. This allows a PIM-SM router to know the RP to use when a host requests traffic from a multicast group (i.e., from a multicast source within the domain).

Note that, other than being assisted through other means, routers in a PIM-SM domain have no way of knowing the active multicast sources in other PIM-SM domains. In the basic application of PIM-SM, multicast sources register (via their Designated Routers (DRs)) only with the Rendezvous-Points (RPs) in the local PIM-SM domain, and the multicast source information of the local domain is not passed on to other PIM-SM domains. As a result, the RPs in the local PIM-SM domain are only aware of the multicast source information within the local domain. Those RPs build multicast distribution trees only within the local domain to deliver multicast data packets from the registered local multicast sources to local receivers. If a mechanism is available that allows RPs of different PIM-SM domains to exchange their multicast source information, local RPs in one domain will be able to join multicast distribution trees in other domains and deliver multicast data to receivers in the local domain.

MSDP provides a mechanism that allows RPs in different PIM-SM domains to share information about active sources. When a PIM-SM domain learns about the active sources in other domains, it can pass that information to its local receivers. Multicast data packets can then be forwarded between the different PIM-SM domains. MSDP was developed to enable Internet Service Providers (ISPs) to peer and exchange multicast source information, thereby allowing the exchange of multicast data packets between them. Generally, an ISP would not want to rely on the RPs maintained by competing ISPs to provide multicast service to their customers. MSDP allows each ISP to maintain its own local RPs and still be able to exchange multicast traffic with other ISPs.

Using MSDP with PIM-SM allows network operators to significantly reduce the complexity of interconnecting multiple PIM-SM domains. Additionally, by breaking

DOI: 10.1201/9781032701967-6

a multicast infrastructure into multiple PIM-SM domains, MSDP enables network operators to establish policies on the multicast groups and active sources that are visible between domains.

This chapter discusses MSDP as a mechanism for interconnecting multiple independent PIM-SM domains. Each PIM-SM domain supports its own local RPs and does not depend on RPs located in other domains. The two primary uses of MSDP are between PIM-SM domains and between Anycast-RPs within a single PIM-SM domain. In the former case, MSDP is used between PIM-SM domains, allowing information about active multicast sources in one domain to be learned by other domains. In the latter, MSDP is used between RPs configured as Anycast-RPs [RFC3446] within a *single* PIM-SM domain, allowing the peer member RPs to synchronize information about the active sources learned by each Anycast-RP peer. MSDP peering used in an Anycast-RP deployment is based on configuring the member RPs as MSDP mesh-groups (fully meshed RPs). The discussion includes how to create MSDP peers, MSDP mesh-groups, and default MSDP peers, and how filters can be used to control and scope MSDP messages and activities. Note that an MSDP peer is a PIM-SM router configured to run MSDP.

6.2 MSDP OVERVIEW

MSDP is an effective mechanism for interconnecting multiple PIM-SM domains, enabling routers in one domain to discover multicast sources in other PIM-SM domains. MSDP allows RPs, and consequently, routers in a PIM-SM domain, to dynamically discover active sources outside of their domain. MSDP allows network operators to reduce the complexity of interconnecting multiple PIM-SM domains. By using MSDP, PIM-SM domains can employ an inter-domain multicast source-based tree instead of a common shared tree for all the domains. RPs in one PIM-SM domain use MSDP to exchange source information with RPs in other domains. MSDP provides a more manageable approach for constructing multicast distribution trees between multiple PIM-SM domains.

An RP in one PIM-SM domain can join the inter-domain source-based distribution tree for active multicast sources in other domains that are sending packets to multicast groups for which the RP has receivers. This is only possible if routers in other multicast domains learn the IP address of the multicast source via Border Gateway Protocol (BGP) or some other inter-domain routing information exchange protocol, such as Multiprotocol BGP (MBGP) [RFC4760]. The RP can join the inter-domain source-based tree because it is the root of the shared tree within its domain, and this shared tree has branches to all nodes in the local domain where there are active receivers. When a Last-Hop Router (LHR), also called the receiver-side Designated Router (DR), learns of a new multicast source outside its PIM-SM domain, it can then send a PIM Join message toward the source to join the inter-domain source-based tree. If an RP in one PIM-SM domain either does not have a shared tree for a particular multicast group, or the outgoing interface list (OIL) of the shared tree is null, it does not send a PIM Join to the multicast source in another PIM-SM domain.

To enable MSDP communication between PIM-SM domains, there is the need to establish an MSDP peering relationship between MSDP-capable routers in one PIM-SM domain and MSDP peers in another domain. The peering relationship is established over a TCP connection, through which the MSDP peers exchange control information. An RP in one PIM-SM domain initiates TCP connections to support MSDP peering sessions with RPs in other PIM-SM domains or with border routers connected to those domains. To establish an MSDP peering relationship over TCP, one MSDP peer (the passive side) listens on the well-known TCP port 639 for new TCP connections. The MSDP peer on the other side initiates an active TCP connect to this well-known port. The MSDP peer with the higher IP address will listen on this port.

The algorithm for connection establishment is designated to prevent call collisions, eliminating the necessity for a call collision procedure. However, the primary drawback of this algorithm is that the connection startup time depends entirely on the active side and the configuration of its *ConnectRetry Timer* (refer to the discussions on MSDP timers in the subsequent section). The passive side can only listen and cannot initiate connection establishment. The state machine governing how MSDP peers establish peering sessions is described in [RFC3618].

Each PIM-SM domain may have one or more peering TCP connections, creating a virtual topology. The purpose of this virtual topology of TCP connections is to enable each PIM-SM domain to discover active multicast sources in other domains. If a domain has receivers that have signaled interest in multicast sources in other domains, the normal source-tree distribution mechanism used in PIM-SM can be employed to transfer multicast data over an inter-domain multicast distribution tree.

When an RP in one PIM-SM domain first learns, through PIM Register messages (see Chapter 3), of a new local active multicast source, it construct an MSDP Source-Active message and sends it to its MSDP peers (refer to MSDP message types in the subsequent section). All RPs in any one domain that intend to originate or receive Source-Active messages (see Figure 6.1 and Figure 6.2) must first establish

0	7	15	23	31
Type (1 Byte)		Length (2 Bytes)	Value	
........(variable length)				

- **Type (8 Bits)**: This describes the format of the Value field.

  The following TLV Types have been defined in RFC 3618:

Code	Type
1	IPv4 Source-Active
2	IPv4 Source-Active Request
3	IPv4 Source-Active Response
4	KeepAlive
5	Reserved (Previously: Notification)

- **Length (16 Bits)**: This is the length of the Type, Length, and Value fields in bytes. The minimum length required is 4 bytes, except for Keepalive messages. The maximum TLV length is 9192 bytes.

- **Value**: This is a variable length field and its format is based on the Type value. The length of the Value field is Length field minus 3. All reserved fields in the Value field MUST be transmitted as zeros and ignored on receipt.

FIGURE 6.1 MSDP TLV format.

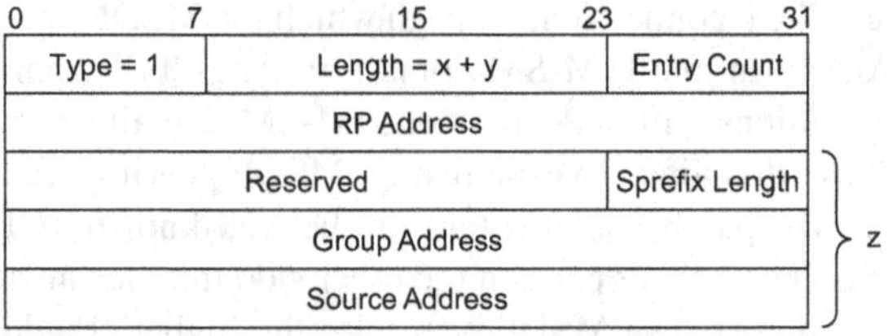

0 7	15	23	31
Type = 1	Length = x + y		Entry Count
RP Address			
Reserved			Sprefix Length
Group Address			
Source Address			

- **Type (8 Bits)**: IPv4 Source-Active TLV is type 1.

- **Length x**: This is the length of the control information in the message. x is 8 bytes (for the first two 32-bit quantities) plus 12 times Entry Count bytes.

- **Length y**: If 0, then there is no data encapsulated. Otherwise, an IPv4 packet follows and y is the value of the Total Length field in the header of the encapsulated IP packet. If there are multiple (S,G) entries in a Source-Active message, only the last entry may have encapsulated data and it must reflect the source and destination addresses in the header of the encapsulated IP packet.

- **Entry Count (8 Bits)**: This is the count of z entries (see diagram), which follow the RP address field. This is to enable multiple (S,G)s from the same domain to be encoded efficiently for the same RP address. A Source-Active message containing encapsulated data typically has an Entry Count of 1 (i.e., only contains a single entry, for the (S,G) representing the encapsulated packet).

- **RP Address (32 Bits)**: This is the address of the RP in the domain the source has become active in.

- **Reserved (24 Bits)**: This field MUST be transmitted as zeros and MUST be ignored by a receiver.

- **Sprefix Length (8 Bits)**: This is the route prefix length associated with source address. This field MUST be transmitted as 32 (/32).

- **Group Address (32 Bits)**: This is the multicast group address the active source has sent data to.

- **Source Address (32 Bits)**: This is the IP address of the active multicast source.

FIGURE 6.2   IPv4 Source-Active TLV format.

MSDP peering with other RPs in other domains. The peering can be done either directly or via an intermediate MSDP peer.

6.3   MSDP MESSAGE TYPES

MSDP has four basic message types, each encoded in the Type-Length-Value (TLV) data format (see Figure 6.1): Source-Active message, Source-Active Request message, Source-Active Response message, and KeepAlive message.

6.3.1   Source-Active Message

MSDP uses Source-Active messages to advertise active sources discovered in a PIM-SM domain. A Source-Active message, structured as shown in Figure 6.2, contains the following main fields:

- IP address of the originating RP (in the RP Address field).
- Group address to which the multicast source is sending data (in the Group Address field).
- Source address of the multicast source (in the Source Address field).

The maximum size of a Source-Active message that can be sent is 9192 bytes, and this size does not include the TCP, IP, and Layer 2 headers.

6.3.2 SOURCE-ACTIVE REQUEST MESSAGE

MSDP uses Source-Active Request messages to seek a list of active sources for a specific multicast group. An MSDP peer maintains a catalog of active (S, G) pairs in its Source-Active Cache, which it references when receiving these messages. Employing Source-Active Request messages to inquire about the list of active sources for a group can reduce join latencies. This approach is favored over waiting for all active sources in the multicast group to be readvertised by RPs through Source-Active messages, which may take up to 60 seconds.

6.3.3 SOURCE-ACTIVE RESPONSE MESSAGE

An MSDP peer sends Source-Active Response messages in response to a Source-Active Request message. A Source-Active Response message contains the IP address of the RP originating the message and one or more (S, G) pairs of the active sources in the domain of the originating RP that are stored in the Source-Active Cache.

6.3.4 KEEPALIVE MESSAGE

An MSDP peer sends KeepAlive messages every 60 seconds to maintain the MSDP session with another peer. If a peer does not receive KeepAlive messages or Source-Active messages for 75 seconds, the MSDP session is reset.

Figure 6.3 illustrates the format of the KeepAlive TLV used by MSDP. An MSDP peer sends a KeepAlive TLV to a peer if and only if it has no MSDP messages to be sent to the peer within the *KeepAlive-Period* in seconds (see discussion on MSDP timers). The peer sends KeepAlive messages to keep the MSDP connection alive. The length of the KeepAlive message is 3 bytes, which comprises the one-byte Type field and the two-byte Length field.

6.3.5 ORIGINATING SOURCE-ACTIVE MESSAGES

This section describes how Source-Active messages are originated. An RP MSDP peer starts sending Source-Active messages when a new source goes active within its local PIM-SM domain. A local multicast source is a source that is directly connected to the RP or a source that is registered by the source's First-Hop Router (FHR). Thus, an RP originates Source-Active messages only for local sources in its PIM-SM domain (i.e., for local sources that register with it). Typically, the RP denotes a local

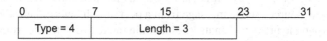

FIGURE 6.3   KeepAlive TLV format.

source by setting a flag bit in the (S, G) entry of its Multicast Routing Information Base (MRIB). This flag indicates that the source qualifies as a candidate to be advertised by the RP to other MSDP peers.

Note that an RP that is not the active Designated Router (DR) on a shared network should not originate Source-Active messages for directly connected sources on that shared network. This RP should only originate Source-Active messages in response to receiving PIM Register messages from the DR.

When the RP detects a source in its local PIM-SM domain, it creates an (S, G) state in the MRIB. The RP detects new sources either by the receipt of a PIM Register message or by the receipt of the first (S, G) packet from a directly attached multicast source.

6.3.6 RECEIVING AND PROCESSING SOURCE-ACTIVE MESSAGES

An MSDP peer only accepts Source-Active messages from the MSDP RPF peer, that is, the MSDP peer on the best path back toward the message's originator. A peer must ignore the same Source-Active message arriving from other MSDP peers, otherwise Source-Active forwarding loops can occur. To allow a peer to deterministically select the MSDP RPF peer for an arriving Source-Active message, knowledge of the MSDP topology is required. However, unlike unicast routing protocols, MSDP does not send routing updates to distribute topology information. MSDP needs the MSDP topology for the Source-Active Reverse Path Forwarding (RPF) check mechanism (see discussion in the subsequent section).

MSDP infers the MSDP topology information by using the BGP or MBGP [RFC4760] routing information as the best approximation of the MSDP topology. This information is used for the Source-Active RPF check mechanism. Hence, an MSDP topology must follow the BGP peer topology. Apart from a few exceptions (such as the use of default MSDP peers and the MSDP peers that form an MSDP mesh-group), MSDP peers should, in general, also be (M)BGP peers (i.e., the peer router must support both MSDP and (M)BGP). We use BGP and MBGP interchangeably in our discussion.

Each MSDP peer that receives a Source-Active message, forwards it away from the originating RP address in a peer-RPF flooding fashion. An MSDP peer examines its RPF MRIB (i.e., the MRIB it uses for RPF) to determine which peer, leading toward the originating RP of the Source-Active message, is the best peer to accept its message; the best peer lies on the least-cost route to the originating RP. This best peer, which provides the least-cost path to the originating RP, is called an *RPF peer*. If the MSDP peer receives the Source-Active message from a non-RPF peer that leads toward the originating RP, it will reject the message. Otherwise, the MSDP peer will forward the message to all its MSDP peers (except the one from which the Source-Active message is received).

When an MSDP peer, which is also acting as RP for its own PIM-SM domain, receives a new Source-Active message from a peer, it will determine if there are any multicast group members within its local domain interested in traffic from any group described by an (S, G) entry within the Source-Active message. The RP will check for a (*, G) state entry in its MRIB with a non-empty outgoing interface list (OIL); a non-empty state entry implies that some nodes/hosts in the domain are interested in the multicast group G.

If the RP finds a non-empty (*, G) state entry, it triggers a PIM (S, G) Join event toward the remote multicast source as if a PIM Join/Prune message was received that is addressed to the RP itself. Triggering a PIM (S, G) Join event sets up a branch of the source tree to the RP's local domain. Subsequent multicast packets from the data source arrive at the RP via this source-tree branch and are forwarded along the RP's shared tree inside the local domain. In the event leaf, PIM routers with the local domain want to join the source tree rooted at the remote source, they have the option of doing so using the existing PIM-SM procedures. Finally, if an RP in a PIM-SM domain receives a PIM Join message for a new multicast group G, it should trigger a PIM (S, G) Join event for each active (S, G) entry for that group in its local Source-Active Cache.

The process of sending and receiving Source-Active messages among RPs in the different PIM-SM domains is sometimes called "flood-and-join" because, if any RP in a domain is not interested in the sent multicast group, it can ignore the Source-Active message. Otherwise, it can join the inter-domain multicast distribution tree for the source.

6.3.6.1 Processing Source-Active Messages

An MSDP peer performs the following actions whenever it receives a Source-Active message:

1. Using the address G in the Group Address field of the (S, G) Source-Active message, the MSDP peer locates the associated (*, G) entry in its MRIB. If the peer finds the (*, G) entry and its OIL is not null, then there are active receivers in the local PIM-SM domain interested in multicast traffic from the source S advertised in the Source-Active message.
2. The MSDP peer then creates an (S, G) entry in the MRIB for the source S advertised in the Source-Active message.
3. If the MRIB did not already contain the (S, G) entry, the MSDP peer immediately sends a PIM (S, G) Join message toward the remote source S to join its source-based tree (i.e., SPT).
4. The MSDP peer then floods the Source-Active message to all other MSDP peers except the following:
   a. The MSDP peer from which the Source-Active message was received.
   b. Any MSDP peers that are members of the same MSDP mesh-group as this MSDP peer (if this peer is configured as a member of an MSDP mesh-group).

Note that Source-Active messages are stored locally in the MSDP peer's Source-Active Cache.

6.4   USING MSDP TO INTERCONNECT
MULTIPLE PIM-SM DOMAINS

When MSDP is deployed in an internetwork of PIM-SM domains, an RP in one domain maintains MSDP peering relationships with MSDP-enabled routers in other domains (see Figures 6.4 and 6.5). This MSDP peering relationship is done over a TCP connection, through which the MSDP peer exchanges information about multicast sources sent to multicast groups. As discussed earlier, MSDP peers use TCP port 639 for their peering connections. Similar to BGP, which uses TCP for BGP peering, using point-to-point TCP connections for MSDP peering means each MSDP peer must be explicitly configured. The TCP connections between MSDP RP peers are realized through the underlying unicast routing protocols.

The MSDP peer with the lower IP address assumes the active role and initiates the opening of the TCP connection. The peer with the higher IP address waits in the LISTEN state for the active side to make the TCP connection. MSDP peers transmit MSDP KeepAlive messages on their interfaces every 60 seconds. The arrival of multicast data packets at an MSDP peer performs the same function as the receipt of an MSDP KeepAlive message and keeps the MSDP TCP session from timing out. If an MSDP peer does not receive KeepAlive messages or multicast data packets for 75 seconds, the TCP connection is reset.

An RP that receives multicast source information from other PIM-SM, allows local PIM-SM routers (LHRs or receiver-side DRs) to use that information to establish a source-based tree path to a particular source in another domain. If the local domain has receivers that are interested in traffic from a multicast source in another domain, multicast packets are delivered using the normal, source-based distribution tree-building mechanism defined for PIM-SM [RFC7761]. MSDP is used to advertise to all interconnected PIM-SM domains, the sources sending to a particular multicast group. These advertisements must originate at an RP in the source's domain.

Figure 6.4 explains the type of peering that can occur when using MSDP. An MSDP peer can be an RP or a non-RP. The network operator can create an MSDP peer on any PIM-SM router in the network; the MSDP peers that assume different roles in the PIM-SM network will function differently.

The MSDP peers that can be configured on PIM-SM routers include the following types (Figure 6.4):

1. MSDP peers configured on RPs:
    a. **Source-side MSDP peer**: This is the MSDP peer that is closest to the multicast source, typically the RP the source registers with (i.e., the source-side RP), like RP A in PIM-SM domain A in Figure 6.4. The source-side RP generates Source-Active messages and sends them to its remote MSDP peer to supply it with the locally registered multicast source information. A source-side MSDP peer must be configured on the source-side RP, otherwise, it would not be able to advertise the registered multicast source information to other PIM-SM domains through Source-Active messages.

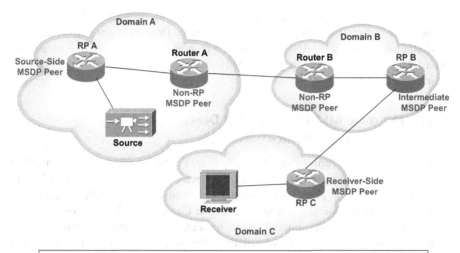

- MSDP peering is usually configured between RP devices, but any other router can also be a MSDP peer.
- Once multicast source are discovered, PIM-SM and MSDP mechanisms allow multicast receivers in one domain to receive multicast data from sources located in remote domains.

FIGURE 6.4   MSDP peering.

     b. **Intermediate MSDP peer**: This is an MSDP peer that also leads to remote MSDP peers, like RP B in PIM-SM domain B. An intermediate MSDP peer receives Source-Active messages from one remote MSDP peer, and forwards them to other remote MSDP peers, functioning as a relay of multicast source information.

     c. **Receiver-side MSDP peer**: This is the MSDP peer closest to the multicast receivers, typically the RP to which PIM (*, G) Join messages are sent when hosts join a multicast group G (i.e., receiver-side RP), like RP C in PIM-SM domain C. After receiving a Source-Active message from an MSDP peer, the receiver-side MSDP peer extracts the multicast source information carried in the message and joins the multi-domain source-rooted tree rooted at the source in the remote PIM-SM domain. When the receiver-side MSDP peer receives multicast data from the multicast source, it forwards the data to the local receivers along its shared tree or RP tree (RPT).

2. MSDP peers configured on common PIM-SM routers that are not RPs: Router A and Router B, which are common PIM-SM routers, are configured as MSDP peers. Such MSDP peers just receive and forward Source-Active messages.

The peering between RPs can be done either directly between RPs that are MSDP speakers, or via an intermediate non-RP MSDP peer. An intermediate MSDP router does not originate periodic Source-Active messages on behalf of active multicast sources in other domains. In general, an RP must only originate a Source-Active message for a directly connected source or a source that has registered with it (via PIM Register messages). Also, only RPs may originate Source-Active messages. Intermediate MSDP routers may forward Source-Active messages that they receive from other PIM-SM domains.

6.4.1 Deploying MSDP in a PIM-SM Domain Running the BSR Mechanism

In a PIM-SM domain running the Bootstrap Router (BSR) mechanism, the active RP for a range of multicast groups is dynamically elected from several Candidate-RPs as discussed in Chapter 5. Thus, to enhance network robustness when RPs are deployed, a PIM-SM domain typically has more than one Candidate-RP. However, since the RP election process result is unpredictable, it is desirable for MSDP peering relationships to be built among all Candidate-RPs in the PIM-SM domain. This allows the Candidate-RP that gets elected the active RP (the winner Candidate-RP), to be always ready to participate in MSDP peering relationships, while the loser Candidate-RPs will play the role of common PIM-SM routers in the PIM-SM domain with the configured MSDP peers.

6.4.2 MSDP and MBGP

Before MSDP is configured, the IP addresses of all MSDP peers (preferably their loopback addresses) must be known in BGP [RFC4271] as shown in Figure 6.5. The use of BGP here implies the use of Multiprotocol Extensions for BGP, also known as Multiprotocol BGP (MBGP or MP-BGP) [RFC4760]. MBGP is an extension to BGP that allows different address families (i.e., different types of addresses) to be advertised simultaneously. BGP as standardized in [RFC4271], supports only IPv4 unicast addresses, while MBGP supports both IPv4 and IPv6 addresses as well as unicast and multicast variants of these address families.

MBGP is designed to allow information about the topology of IPv4 multicast-capable routers in an internetwork to be advertised separately from the topology of normal IPv4 unicast routers. Thus, MBGP provides a way of building a multicast routing topology that is different from the unicast routing topology in an internetwork. Although MBGP enables the advertisement of inter-domain multicast routing information, a multicast routing protocol such as the PIM is needed to build the multicast distribution trees and to forward multicast traffic.

MBGP provides the following routing information capabilities:

- Typically, an MBGP router maintains and stores unicast and multicast routing information in different routing tables, ensuring their separation.
- An MBGP router supports unicast and multicast routing information and constructs different network topologies for each.
- An MBGP router can be configured to maintain unicast and multicast routes based on routing policies provided by the network operator.

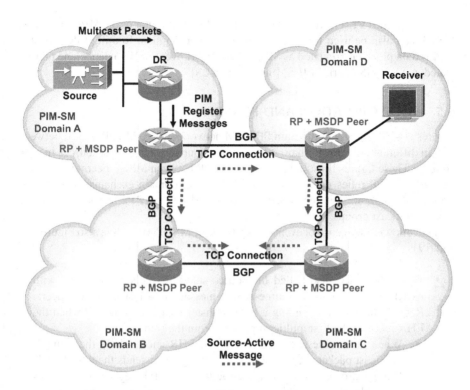

FIGURE 6.5   Running MSDP between RP peers.

MBGP plays an important role when deploying MSDP between multiple PIM-SM domains. MBGP is commonly used to exchange routes for multicast traffic distribution between two different administrative domains, for example, between different autonomous systems. The different PIM-SM domains must exchange information about routes to the multicast sources in each domain, allowing routers in each domain to perform RPF checks correctly. PIM routers use the unicast routing table to perform these RPF checks, and these routes are learned via an IGP like IS-IS or OSPF. However, (M)BGP is most commonly used to exchange routing information between different PIM domains.

The network operator can apply different policies to multicast routes exchanged through MBGP. Multicast has its own address family in MBGP, making it easy to understand the separation of policies. The prefixes learned under the MBGP multicast address family are interpreted the same way as static multicast routes (see Chapter 1) and used for RPF checks on the router that receives such routes. These multicast routes are propagated by MBGP to every neighbor configured for the multicast address family.

MBGP is also commonly used in MPLS Layer 3 VPN deployments, to advertise VPN labels associated with VPN routes coming from customer sites over the MPLS network. The VPN routes and their labels are used to distinguish between different customer traffic (VPN traffic) at the Provider Edge (PE) router of the MPLS network. MBGP can also be used for VPN deployment over Segment Routing (SR) over the MPLS data plane (abbreviated as SR-MPLS), or SR over the IPv6 data plane (abbreviated as SRv6) [SRPart1CFILS] [SRPart2CFILS].

6.5   MSDP OPERATION AND PEER-RPF

Figures 6.4–6.7 show inter-domain PIM-SM networks where MSDP is used between RPs in different domains to share information about active multicast sources in each domain. These figures illustrate the use of MSDP between MSDP peers in the internetwork. MSDP relies on BGP or MBGP for inter-domain exchange of multicast source information. It is recommended to run MSDP on RPs that send traffic to global multicast groups.

The following sequence of events describes how MSDP works (see also Figures 6.6 and 6.7):

- When the FHR, also called the source-side DR, registers a source with its RP, that RP sends a Source-Active message to all of its MSDP peers. Register here means sending a PIM Register message to the RP when the FHR receives the first multicast packets from the source.
  - When the source first goes active, the FHR encapsulates the source's multicast packets in PIM Register messages and sends them to the RP. If the source times out and goes active again, this registration process takes place again. This is different from the periodic Source-Active messages sent by the RP that contain all multicast sources that are registered to it. Those Source-Active messages are MSDP control packets sent to MSDP peers and do not contain encapsulated multicast packets from active sources.
- The Source-Active message sent identifies the IP address of the multicast source, the multicast group that the source is sending traffic to, and the IP address of the RP originating the message (see message format Figure 6.2).
- Each MSDP peer that receives the Source-Active message floods it to all of its downstream peers away from the message's originator. In some cases, an RP MSDP peer may receive a copy of a Source-Active message from more than one MSDP peer. To prevent looping of Source-Active messages, the RP MSDP peer consults its BGP routing table (i.e., next-hop database) to determine the correct next-hop toward the originator of the Source-Active message. If the MSDP peer is configured with both MBGP and unicast BGP tables, it will check the MBGP table first, and then the unicast BGP table. The next-hop neighbor found is the RPF peer for the originator of the message. An MSDP peer drops Source-Active messages that are received from the originator on any interface other than the interface leading to the RPF peer. The process of flooding Source-Active messages is referred to as *peer-RPF flooding*. The use of the peer-RPF flooding mechanism requires BGP or MBGP to be running in conjunction with MSDP.

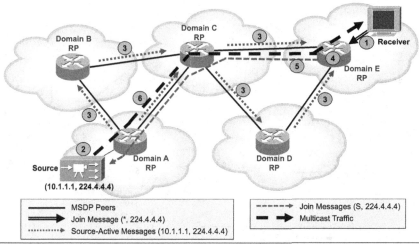

- Each PIM-SM domain has an independent RP that is peered via MSDP to other RPs in other domains. Each RP knows about all active multicast traffic sources in its domain.

Processing steps:

1. Let us assume that a receiver in PIM-SM Domain E has joined multicast group 224.4.4.4 when its LHR sent a PIM (*, 224.4.4.4) Join message to the local RP.
2. We assume also that a multicast traffic source 10.1.1.1 in Domain A has started sending multicast traffic to group 244.4.4.4 via its FHR.
3. Domain A's RP learns of the local source (10.1.1.1) through the normal PIM Registration mechanism, and starts to periodically send Source-Active messages containing the source IP address (10.1.1.1), the multicast group address (224.4.4.4), and the IP address of the originating RP to its MSDP peers.
   - All the MSDP nodes Reverse Path flood the Source-Active messages in the network away from the originating RP to avoid looping of Source-Active messages.
   - An MSDP peer performs Reverse Path Flooding using the originator's RP address in the Source-Active message to determine whether an incoming Source-Active message was received on the correct interface leading back to the originator. If the message arrived on the correct interface, it is flooded downstream to the other MSDP peers.
4. When the RP of Domain E receives the Source-Active message, it checks in its multicast routing table (MRT) and finds that it has an active receiver for multicast group 224.4.4.4.
5. Upon detecting an active receiver, the RP of Domain E sends a PIM (S, G) Join message toward the multicast traffic source 10.1.1.1.
6. The FHR of the source in Domain A receives the (S, G) Join message. Note that, as the Join message travels to the FHR, a branch of the (S, G) source tree is constructed from the RP of Domain E to the source.
   - Multicast traffic from the source now flows across the (S, G) source tree to Domain E's RP and then along the local shared tree to the receiver.

Each RP in a domain that receives a Source-Active message examines whether any receivers for the multicast group exist in the domain.

- If a receiver exists in the domain, an RPT for the multicast group G is maintained between the domain's RP and the receivers. The RP creates an (S, G) entry and sends an (S, G) Join message which travels hop-by-hop toward the multicast source, and the SPT is established across the PIM-SM domains.
- Subsequently, multicast traffic flows to the domain's RP along the SPT, and from the RP to the receiver-side DR along the RPT. After receiving the multicast traffic, the receiver-side DR determines whether to initiate an RPT-to-SPT switchover process based on its configuration.
- If no receivers exist in the domain, the domain's RP neither creates an (S, G) state entry in its MRT nor sends a PIM (S, G) Join message toward the multicast source.

Once a domain's RP receives information about a multicast source in another domain, it no longer relies on RPs in other PIM-SM domains. The receivers in the domain can override the RPs in other domains and directly join the multicast SPT rooted at the source.

- The source-side DR sends multicast data packets directly to the remote domain's RP.

FIGURE 6.6   Using MSDP to share source information between RPs in each domain.

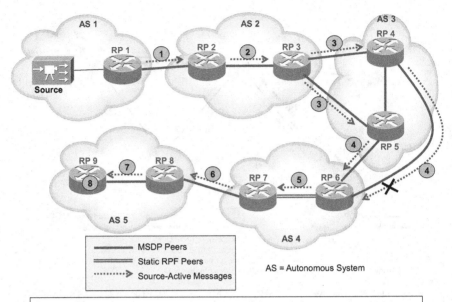

Assumptions:
- IP address of RP 5 is higher than that of RP 4.
- RP 6 and RP 7 are static RPF peers.

Processing steps:
1. RP 1 generates a Source-Active message and forwards it to its MSDP peer RP 2.
2. RP 2 checks the RP address in the Source-Active message and sees that it is the same as that of RP 1, meaning, RP 1 is the originator of the Source-Active message.
    - RP 2 then accepts and forwards the Source-Active message.
3. RP 3 accepts and forwards the Source-Active message, because RP 2 and RP 3 are located in the same AS, and RP 2 is the next-hop of RP 3 leading to RP 1.
4. RP 4 and RP 5 accept the Source-Active message, because RP 3 is in the same MSDP mesh-group with RP4 and RP 5.
    - RP 4 and RP 5 then forward the Source-Active message to their MSDP peer RP 6, rather than to other members of the MSDP mesh-group.
5. RP 4 and RP 5 are located in the closest AS (AS 3) on the route to RP 1.
    - However, RP 6 accepts and forwards only the Source-Active message from RP 5 because the IP address of RP 5 is higher than that of RP 4.
6. RP 7 accepts and forwards the Source-Active message because RP 6 is its static RPF peer.
7. RP 8 accepts and forwards the Source-Active message because RP 7 is the exterior BGP (eBGP) or Multiprotocol BGP (MBGP) next-hop of the peer-RPF route to RP 1.
8. RP 9 accepts the Source-Active message because it is the only RP closest to RP 8.

FIGURE 6.7   MSDP peer-RPF (Reverse Path Forwarding).

- Each Source-Active message received by an MSDP peer is subjected to a peer-RPF check and multicast policy–based filtering, so that only Source-Active messages that have arrived along the correct path from the originating RP, and passed the filtering are accepted and forwarded. This peer-RPF check is to avoid looping of Source-Active messages. In addition, the network operator may configure several MSDP peers

into an MSDP mesh-group, to avoid flooding of Source-Active messages between peers of the MSDP mesh-group.
- A peer-RPF check involves comparing the RP address in the Source-Active message against the MSDP peer that sent the message. Each MSDP peer receives and forwards the Source-Active message away from the originating RP address in a peer-RPF flooding fashion. The peer forwards the message to its MSDP peers except the peer from which the Source-Active message is received.
- Note that (M)BGP is not required in MSDP mesh-group scenarios nor scenarios with a default MSDP peer (see default MSDP peer).
- Source-Active messages are forwarded from one MSDP peer to another in the internetwork, allowing the multicast source information to traverse all PIM-SM domains and reach all RPs.
- When an RP MSDP peer receives a Source-Active message, it checks to see whether there are any multicast members of the advertised groups in its local domain. The RP does this by checking whether it has interfaces on the (*, G) OIL that have group members (directly attached members or those signaled via PIM (*, G) Join messages).
  - If the RP determines that there are no local group members, it does nothing.
  - If it determines that there are group members, it sends an (S, G) Join message toward the multicast source in the remote domain.
  - To trigger an (S, G) Join, the RP searches its route table to determine the interface that has the best path to the source.
  - The RP sends the (S, G) Join message out of this interface to inform the next upstream router that it wants to receive multicast packets for group G from source S.
  - Upon receiving the (S, G) Join message, the upstream router adds the interface on which the message was received to the OIL for the group and forwards the (S, G) Join similarly to its upstream router.
  - Doing so results in a branch of the inter-domain source-based tree being constructed across autonomous system boundaries to the local RP.
  - After the (S, G) Join message reaches the DR of the multicast source, a branch of the SPT is built from the source to the RP in the remote domain. Multicast traffic then flows from the source across the inter-domain SPT to the remote RP, and then down the RPT of the remote domain to the local receivers.
  - As the RP receives multicast packets from the source via the inter-domain source-based tree, it will then forward them down its own shared tree (RPT) to the multicast group members in the (local) domain.
  - The DRs of the local multicast group members then have the option of joining the source-based tree (SPT) rooted at the remote source using standard PIM-SM procedures. Upon receiving the multicast traffic from the local RP, the receiver-side DR can initiate an RPT-to-SPT switchover process if configured to do so.

- The RP that originated the Source-Active message continues to send periodic Source-Active messages for the (S, G) state every 60 seconds and for as long as the source is sending packets to the multicast group.
    - When an RP MSDP receives a Source-Active message, it caches that message. Let us assume, for example, that an RP MSDP peer receives a Source-Active message for (10.1.1.1, 224.4.4.4) from the originating RP 10.5.5.5.
  - The RP MSDP consults its MRIB and finds that there are no active members for group 224.4.4.4, so it forwards the Source-Active message to its MSDP peers downstream of RP 10.5.5.5. If a host in the local domain, then sends a join to the RP for multicast group 224.4.4.4, the RP adds the interface to the host to the OIL of its (*, 224.4.4.4) entry.
  - Since the RP MSDP caches Source-Active messages, it will have an entry for (10.1.1.1, 224.4.4.4), and can join the multi-domain source-based tree as soon as a host sends a request to join the group. Most RP MSDP implementations support the caching of Source-Active messages.

6.6   MSDP PEER-RPF RULES

MSDP-aware routers use MSDP peer-RPF rules for forwarding Source-Active messages to all parts of an internetwork of MSDP-enabled PIM-SM domains. In the traditional RPF checks used by multicast routers when forwarding multicast packets, a packet's source IP address is compared against the interface on which the packet was received (see Chapter 1). In this case, if the arriving interface does not hold the best (lowest-cost) path back to the multicast traffic source (i.e., the path the receiving router would normally use to reach the source), the packet is dropped.

However, in an MSDP Peer-RPF check, the RP address carried in the Source-Active message is compared against the MSDP peer from which the message was received. Except in the case of MSDP mesh-groups, a Source-Active message sent by an RP address is accepted from only one MSDP peer to avoid Source-Active messages from looping in the network.

6.6.1   BASIC MSDP PEER-RPF CHECKS

The basic MSDP peer-RPF rules are described in Figure 6.8. Being also PIM routers, MSDP routers also maintain for their peer-RPF checks, an MRIB which is the multicast topology table. The MRIB is typically derived from the unicast routing table, or other routing protocols such as MBGP [RFC4760]. A peer-RPF route is a route in the MRIB that the router chooses for a given IP address. An MSDP router that receives a Source-Active message from an MSDP peer uses the peer-RPF route for the message's originating RP, to determine if it should accept the Source-Active message.

It should be noted that MSDP peers, that are NOT in the ESTABLISHED state of the MSDP Connection state machine (i.e., MSDP peers that are down), are not eligible for consideration in the peer-RPF checks.

- MP(N, R) is an MSDP peering between N and R.
- MPP(T, N) is an MSDP peering path (with zero or more MSDP peers) between T and N, e.g., MPP(T, N) = MP(T, A) + MP(A, B) + MP(B, N).
- SA(S,G,T) is a Source-Active message for source S on multicast group G originated by an RP T.

An Source-Active message originated by T and received by R from N is accepted if N is the MSDP peer-RPF neighbor for R, and is discarded otherwise. The peer-RPF neighbor N is chosen deterministically using the first of the following rules that matches. N is the RPF neighbor of R with respect to T for the following conditions:

1. If N originated the Source-Active message (i.e., Router N is Router T), then N is also the peer-RPF neighbor, and its Source-Active messages are accepted by R.
2. If N is a member of R's mesh-group, or is the configured peer, then N is the peer-RPF neighbor, and its Source-Active messages are accepted by R period.
3. If N is the BGP next-hop of the active multicast RPF route toward T (i.e., N is the eBGP NEXT_HOP of the peer-RPF route for T), then N is the peer-RPF neighbor, and its Source-Active messages are accepted by R.
4. If N is an eBGP or iBGP peer of R, and the last autonomous system (AS) number (ASN) in the BGP AS-Path attribute to T is the same as N's ASN, or if N is the IGP next-hop for T and the route for T is learned via an IGP (e.g., OSPF, IS-IS), then N is the peer-RPF neighbor, and its Source-Active messages are accepted by R. The following scenarios exist here:
   a. Sending MSDP peer N is an iBGP peer.
   b. Sending MSDP peer N is an eBGP peer.
   c. Sending MSDP peer N is NOT a BGP peer.
   d. Sending MSDP peer N is an IGP next-hop of T.
5. If N uses the same next-hop as the next-hop to T, then N is the peer-RPF neighbor, and its Source-Active messages are accepted by R.
6. If N resides in the closest AS in on best path towards T, and If multiple MSDP peers reside in the closest AS, then the peer with the highest IP address is the peer-RPF neighbor.
7. If N is configured as the static RPF-peer for T, then N is the peer-RPF neighbor, and its Source-Active messages are accepted by R.

The peer-RPF check is not performed in the following cases:
- The MSDP peer is the originating RP of the MSDP Source-Active message.
- The MSDP peer is a mesh-group peer. In this case, the receiving node does not forward the MSDP Source-Active message to any other mesh-group member.
- The MSDP peer is configured as the default MSDP peer.
- The MSDP peer is the one and only MSDP peer configured.

FIGURE 6.8   MSDP peer-RPF forwarding rules.

6.6.1.1   Preference Order of Routing Information for MSDP Peer-RPF Checks

For the peer-RPF checks, an MSDP peer gives preference to the different routing tables in the following order:

- Static multicast route
- MBGP routes
- Unicast routes

Note that as discussed in Chapter 1, static multicast routes are only used in RPF checks and not for multicast data forwarding, unlike unicast routes which can be used for both. Any configured static multicast route for a source overrides the

RPF interface information indicated in the unicast routing table. The MSDP peer always checks the MRIB before the unicast RIB (URIB). If there is no route in any of these tables to the MSDP peer, then the peer-RPF check will fail, and the MSDP Source-Active message will be discarded.

6.6.1.2 Static RPF Peers

Note that configuring static RPF peers avoids peer-RPF checks of Source-Actives messages (see Rule 7 in Figure 6.8). An MSDP peer can accept Source-Active messages from its static RPF peers that pass the local filtering policy without peer-RPF checks.

An internetwork of PIM-SM domains may be configured to allow the sharing of multicast source information among the domains without changing the unicast topology structure [H3CMULTGUID]. To do this, the network operator needs to configure MSDP peering relationships for the RPs of the various PIM-SM domains in the internetwork, and then configure static RPF-peering relationships for the MSDP peers to allow the sharing of multicast source information among the PIM-SM domains without the need for peer-RPF checks. *Note that there is no need to run (M)BGP between static RPF peers; an MSDP peer only needs to know its configured static RPF peer to accept Source-Active messages from it.*

6.6.1.3 Using Specific MSDP Peer-RPF Forwarding Rules

In this section, we focus, particularly, on the sub-rules under Rule 4 in Figure 6.8. These particular rules for peer-RPF checks for Source-Active messages are dependent on the BGP peerings between the MSDP peers:

- **Peer-RPF Check Rule 4a**: Sending MSDP peer is also an interior (M)BGP peer.
- **Peer-RPF Check Rule 4b**: Sending MSDP peer is also an exterior (M) BGP peer.
- **Peer-RPF Check Rule 4c**: Sending MSDP peer is NOT an (M)BGP peer.
- **Peer-RPF Check Rule 4d**: Sending MSDP Peer is an Interior Gateway Protocol (IGP) peer.

These specific peer-RPF check rules are discussed in greater detail in various subsequent sections.

An MSDP peer does not perform peer-RPF checks in the following cases:

- If the MSDP peer that sent the Source-Active message is the only MSDP peer, which is the case if only a default MSDP peer or a single MSDP peer is configured.
- If the MSDP peer that sent the Source-Active message is a member of an MSDP mesh-group.
- If the IP address of the MSDP peer that sent the Source-Active message is the RP address contained in the Source-Active message.

6.6.1.4   Implications and Benefits of the MSDP Peer-RPF Forwarding Rules

The use of the aforementioned MSDP peer-RPF check rules can provide the following benefits to the network operator:

- The network operator can use BGP Route Reflectors (RRs) for iBGP peering without having run MSDP on them. The operator can use this capability to reduce the load on RRs.
- The network operator can use an IGP like OSPF or IS-IS for the RPF checks, and thereby create MSDP peerings without running (M)BGP. This capability is particularly useful in a customer's enterprise network that does not run (M)BGP and requires a larger MSDP topology than MSDP mesh-groups can provide.
  - Note that an IGP peering must always be between directly connected MSDP peers, otherwise the RPF checks will fail.
- The network operator can implement MSDP peerings between multicast routers that are located in autonomous systems that are not directly connected (i.e., with one or more autonomous systems between them). The operator can use this capability in BGP Confederation configurations and for redundancy.

6.6.2   How an MSDP Peer Determines Which Rule to Apply to Peer-RPF Checks

An MSDP peer uses the following logic to determine which peer-RPF check rule to apply when a Source-Active message is received:

- Look for the (M)BGP neighbor that has the same IP address as the MSDP peer that sent the message.
  - If the (M)BGP neighbor that has the matching IP address is an internal (M)BGP (i(M)BGP) peer, apply Rule 4a.
  - If the (M)BGP neighbor that has a matching IP address is an external (M)BGP (e(M)BGP) peer, apply Rule 4b.
  - If no matching (M)BGP neighbor is found, apply Rule 4c.

The aforementioned peer-RPF check rule selection implies that *the IP address configured for the MSDP peer in a given router must match the IP address configured for the (M)BGP peer on the same router; both MSDP and (M)BGP must use the same IP address, usually a loopback address on the node.* Note that apart from default MSDP peers and MSDP peers that form an MSDP mesh-group, MSDP peers must always also be (M)BGP peers.

6.6.3   What is a Default MSDP Peer?

In most use cases, an MSDP peer is also configured as a BGP peer. Also, in most cases, there is little or no benefit in running BGP from a transit autonomous system to a stub autonomous system or a non-transit autonomous system, particularly if the stub or non-transit autonomous system is not multihomed. In such cases, BGP is typically not run between the stub autonomous system and its transit autonomous system, but this can cause some problems when deploying MSDP. Generally, in normal use cases, it is sufficient to configure a static default route between the stub autonomous system and its transit autonomous system. This static route points to the stub IP prefixes at the transit autonomous system.

Now let us consider the scenario where a stub autonomous system is also a multicast domain, and its RP must peer with an RP in the multicast domain in the transit autonomous system. Note that an MSDP peer normally depends on the BGP next-hop database for its peer-RPF checks. However, a network operator can disable MSDP's dependency on BGP (for peer-RPF checks) by defining default MSDP peers in the stub and transit autonomous systems from which to accept all Source-Active messages without performing the peer-RPF checks (Figure 6.9). Disabling peer-RPF checks in this scenario is current industry practice as described in the subsequent section. Because the stub autonomous system peers with the transit autonomous system over a single path, peer-RPF checks are not necessary; there is only one path linking the two systems and therefore no possibility of routing loops.

An operator may also configure a stub autonomous system to have MSDP peerings with two or more RPs in the transit autonomous(s) system for the sake of redundancy. However, an MSDP peer in the stub autonomous system cannot simply accept Source-Active messages from multiple default MSDP peers in the transit autonomous system(s), because there is no peer-RPF check mechanism used in this case (as stated earlier). Instead, the MSDP peer in the stub autonomous system would have to accept Source-Active messages from only one MSDP peer in the transit autonomous system,

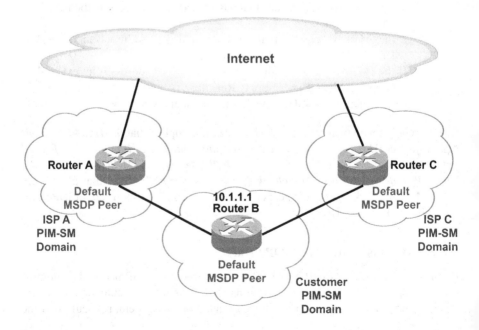

FIGURE 6.9   Default MSDP peer scenario.

and if that peer fails, it would then accept Source-Active messages from the other peer in that system. Of course, the underlying assumption here is that both default MSDP peers in the transit autonomous system(s) are sending the same Source-Active messages to the stub's MSDP peer.

Figure 6.9 shows a scenario where a network operator may use default MSDP peers [CISCMSDP2016]. A default MSDP peer can be configured when the router in the stub autonomous system is not in a BGP peering relationship with an MSDP peer in the transit autonomous system. If a default MSDP peer is configured in the transit autonomous system, the router (in the stub autonomous system) accepts all Source-Active messages from that default MSDP peer. In this figure, Router B in a customer network (which is a stub autonomous system) is connected to the Internet through two Internet service providers (ISPs), one having Router A and the other Router C. We assume that BGP or MBGP is not running between these routers. ISP A and ISP C are both transit autonomous systems.

For hosts in the customer network to learn about multicast sources in the ISP domain or other domains, Router B is configured to identify Router A as its default MSDP peer. Default MSDP Router B advertises Source-Active messages to both default MSDP peer Router A and default MSDP peer Router C, but accepts Source-Active messages from one default MSDP peer, either from Router A only or Router C only. If Router A is configured as the first (primary) default MSDP peer, it will be the peer used by Router B if it is up and running. Only when Router A is not available will Router B accept Source-Active messages from Router C. This is the behavior when Router B does not have an IP Prefix List (see [AWEYFDVR21]) for filtering Source-Active messages.

If Router B is configured with an IP Prefix List, an MSDP peer will be accepted as a default MSDP peer only for the IP prefixes in the IP Prefix List. An IP Prefix List (which implements a policy filtering mechanism for IP prefixes) when configured on a router, allows the router to either permit or deny configured IP prefixes based on certain matching conditions. Multiple active default MSDP peers can be configured when an IP Prefix List is associated with each. But if no IP Prefix Lists are configured on Router B, multiple default MSDP peers can still be configured, but only the primary peer will be the active default MSDP peer as long as Router B has connectivity to this peer and the peer is alive. If the primary configured MSDP peer goes down or the connectivity to it goes down, the second (secondary) configured default MSDP peer becomes the active default MSDP peer.

6.6.4 MSDP MESH-GROUP SEMANTICS

Configuring some subset of MSDP speakers in a PIM-SM domain in a full mesh configuration result in an MSDP mesh-group. An MSDP mesh-group is created by configuring a group of MSDP routers in a fully meshed configuration with each router using MSDP to connect to all other routers in the group. Each of the MSDP peers in the group has an MSDP connection or MSDP peering relationship with every other MSDP peer in the group.

Network operators use MSDP mesh-groups to reduce the flooding of Source-Active messages, typically in intra-domain multicast deployments. Figure 6.10 shows an MSDP mesh-group example network and the semantics for forwarding Source-Active messages.

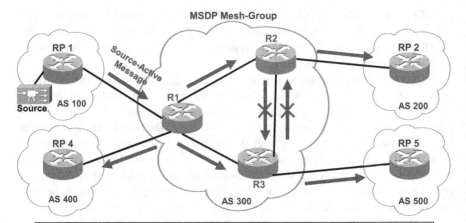

Routers R1, R2, and R3 are members of the same MSDP mesh-group. The
semantics of the mesh-group are as follows:
1. If a member of a particular mesh-group (e.g., R1) receives an Source-Active
   message from an MSDP peer that is not a member of the mesh-group (RP 1), and
   the Source-Active message passes the peer-RPF check, then R1 forwards the
   Source-Active message to all members of mesh-group (R2 and R3) and to any
   other MSDP peers (RP 4).
2. If a member of a mesh-group (e.g., R3) receives a Source-Active message from
   an MSDP peer that is also a member of the same mesh-group (R1), R3 accepts
   the Source-Active message and forwards it to all of its peers that are not part of
   mesh-group (RP 5). R3 MUST NOT forward the Source-Active message to other
   members of that mesh-group (R1 and R2).

FIGURE 6.10   MSDP mesh-group semantics.

It is important to note that, the creation of a mesh-group (just like iBGP full
mesh [AWEYLSPV21]) assumes that any member of the group will not forward
Source-Active messages to other members of the group because the message originator is required to forward it to all other group members. To allow the message originator (each group member is a potential originator) to forward received Source-Active
messages to all other group members, the mesh-group must be created as a full mesh
with MSDP peering between all members.

When an MSDP peer in an MSDP mesh-group receives a Source-Active message from
another MSDP peer in the group, it assumes that this Source-Active message is already
sent to all the other MSDP peers in the group. As a result, the receiving MSDP peer is
not required to flood the Source-Active message to the other MSDP peers in the group.

An MSDP peer member of an MSDP mesh-group would forward Source-Active
messages received from outside the mesh-group and pass the peer-RPF check, to
other members in the mesh-group. An MSDP mesh-group member would accept
a Source-Active message from inside the group without performing a peer-RPF
check, but would not forward that message to any other mesh-group member.
This mechanism not only avoids the flooding of Source-Active messages but also
simplifies the peer-RPF check mechanism because MBGP does not need to be run
between the MSDP mesh-group members.

The benefits of MSDP mesh-groups are summarized as follows:

- **Optimizes flooding of Source-Active messages**: MSDP mesh-groups are particularly useful for optimizing Source-Active message flooding when two or more peers are in an MSDP mesh-group.
- **Reduces the amount of Source-Active message traffic across the internetwork**: The use of MSDP mesh-groups means Source-Active messages would not be flooded to other peers in the mesh-group.
- **Eliminates MSDP peer-RPF checks for internally forwarded Source-Active messages**: Configuring an MSDP mesh-group means Source-Active messages will always be accepted from mesh-group peers without requiring peer-RPF checks.

6.7   SOURCE-ACTIVE MESSAGE CACHING

As required by [RFC3618], an MSDP router MUST cache Source-Active messages. Caching allows the MSDP router to pace or throttle the forwarding of MSDP messages. Caching also allows the router to reduce PIM Join latency for new receivers of a multicast group G at an originating RP because the router has an existing MSDP (S, G) state. In addition, caching greatly aids the network operator in performing diagnosis and debugging of various network problems.

An MSDP router must provide a mechanism like Source-Active message caching to reduce the forwarding of new Source-Active messages. The router uses the Source-Active Cache to reduce message forwarding storms and does this by not forwarding Source-Active messages unless they are in the Source-Active Cache, or are new Source-Active messages that the MSDP router will cache for the first time. The router also uses the Source-Active Cache to reduce message forwarding storms by advertising them from the cache at a slower pace. The router advertises messages at a period of no more than two times the SA-Advertisement Timer interval and not less than once in an SA-Advertisement Period.

6.7.1   CONFIGURING THE SOURCE-ACTIVE CACHE MECHANISM

To reduce the time spent for MSDP peers in the internetwork of PIM-SM domains to obtain the multicast source information, the network operator can use the Source-Active Cache mechanism to cache (S, G) entries contained in Source-Active messages locally on each MSDP peer. However, the more (S, G) entries that are cached by the peer, the larger the memory space it needs.

After the Source-Active Cache mechanism is enabled, when the MSDP peer receives a new (*, G) Join message, it would search its Source-Active Cache first [H3CMULTGUID]:

- If the peer does not find a corresponding (S, G) entry in the cache, it will wait for the next Source-Active message from any of its MSDP peers.
- If a peer finds the corresponding (S, G) entry in the cache, it will join the corresponding SPT rooted at the remote source.

To protect the MSDP peer against denial of service (DoS) attacks, the operator can set a limit on the number of (S, G) entries the peer can cache.

6.8 CONFIGURING MSDP MESSAGES

This section discusses additional ways MSDP messages are created and used by MSDP peers [H3CMULTGUID].

6.8.1 CONFIGURING SOURCE-ACTIVE MESSAGES TO CARRY MULTICAST DATA PACKETS

Sometimes a multicast source may send multicast data to its source-side DR at an interval larger than the aging time of the (S, G) entry at the DR. When the (S, G) expires, the source-side DR has to restart encapsulating multicast data packets in PIM Register messages and sending them to the source-side RP. The source-side RP would then transmit the (S, G) information to the RPs in remote PIM-SM domains through Source-Active messages. A remote RP would then send an (S, G) Join message to the source-side DR to build an SPT. However, if the (S, G) entry has timed out at the source-side DR, receivers in other remote domains can never receive the multicast data from the multicast source.

To address this problem, if the source-side RP is configured to encapsulate PIM Register messages in Source-Active messages, then if it has a multicast packet to deliver, it can simply encapsulate a PIM Register message containing that multicast packet in a Source-Active message, and send it out to other remote RPs. After receiving such a Source-Active message, the remote RPs would decapsulate the Source-Active message and then forward the multicast data packet contained in the PIM Register message to the local receivers along the local RPT.

6.8.2 CONFIGURING SOURCE-ACTIVE REQUEST MESSAGES

By default, when an RP MSDP peer receives a new PIM Join message, it does not send a Source-Active Request message to any MSDP peer, instead, it would wait for the next Source-Active message from its MSDP peers. However, doing this will cause a delay in the time the receiving MSDP will take to obtain remote multicast source information. Thus, to enable a new MSDP peer to receive active multicast source information as early as possible, the MSDP peer can be configured to send Source-Active Request messages to the designated MSDP peers upon receiving a PIM Join message for a new local receiver.

When an MSDP peer is enabled to send Source-Active Request messages, upon receiving a PIM Join message from a new multicast receiver, the peer will send a Source-Active Request message to the remote MSDP peer, and the remote peer will respond by sending multicast source information from its Source-Active Cache. Sending a Source-Active Request message allows the MSDP peer to quickly receive the information about all active multicast sources.

6.8.3 Configuring Source-Active Message Filtering Rules

A network operator can configure Source-Active message creation rules to enable an MSDP peer to filter the (S, G) entries to be advertised when creating a Source-Active message. This is to allow the propagation of multicast source information to be controlled. The operator can also configure a filtering rule for receiving or forwarding Source-Active messages. This is to enable an MSDP to filter the (S, G) forwarding entries to be announced when receiving or forwarding a Source-Active message, allowing the propagation of multicast source information to be controlled at the reception or forwarding of a Source-Active message.

The operator may configure a time-to-live (TTL) threshold for multicast data packets that are encapsulated in a Source-Active message to limit the propagation range of such Source-Active messages:

- Before the MSDP peer creates a Source-Active message with an encapsulated multicast data packet, it will check the TTL value of the multicast data packet. If the TTL value is less than the MSDP peer's TTL threshold, it does not create the Source-Active message. If the TTL value is greater than or equal to the peer's TTL threshold, it will encapsulate the multicast data packet in a Source-Active message and forward the message to remote MSDP peers.
- When an MSDP peer receives a Source-Active message with encapsulated multicast data packets, it will decrement the TTL value of the multicast packet by 1 and then checks the TTL value. If the TTL value is less than the MSDP peer's TTL threshold, it does not forward the Source-Active message to the designated MSDP peer. If the TTL value is greater than or equal to the TTL threshold, it will re-encapsulate the multicast data packet in a Source-Active message and forward the message to other MSDP peers.

6.9 MSDP TIMERS

The main timers used by MSDP are as follows: *SA-Advertisement Timer, SA Cache Entry Timer, Peer Hold Timer, KeepAlive Timer,* and *ConnectRetry Timer.*

6.9.1 SA-Advertisement Timer

An RP that originates Source-Active messages will do so periodically as long as the multicast source sends data. The RP has one *SA-Advertisement Timer* that covers the sources that the RP may advertise. The *SA-Advertisement-Period* MUST be set to 60 seconds [RFC3618]. Within each *SA-Advertisement* interval, an RP MUST not send more than one periodic Source-Active message for a given (S, G) pair. RPs originate periodic Source-Active messages to keep active source announcements alive in remote Source-Active Caches.

Furthermore, an originating RP is required to trigger the transmission of a Source-Active message as soon as it receives data from a local multicast source for the first time. The RP may send this initial Source-Active message in addition to the periodic Source-Active message forwarded in that first 60 seconds for that (S, G) pair.

6.9.2 SA-ADVERTISEMENT TIMER PROCESSING

An RP that originates periodic Source-Active messages (i.e., messages advertising the local active multicast sources for which it is the registering RP) MUST spread their generation over the *SA-Advertisement-Period* (which is its message reporting interval). Also, as soon as the MSDP process is configured, the RP starts the *SA-Advertisement Timer*. The RP resets the *SA-Advertisement Timer* to *SA-Advertisement-Period* seconds when it expires and starts the advertisement of its local active multicast data sources.

The RP advertises its active sources as follows: It assembles its active sources into a Source-Active message until the largest MSDP message that can be sent is created, or no more active sources are available to pack and then sends the message. The RP repeats this process periodically within the *SA-Advertisement Period* to the extent that all its active sources are advertised. Given that MSDP is a periodic protocol, RPs send all cached Source-Active messages when a peering TCP connection is established. The RP deletes the *SA-Advertisement Timer* when the MSDP process is de-configured.

6.9.3 SA CACHE TIMEOUT (SA-STATE TIMER)

Each entry in the local Source-Active Cache of an MSDP peer has an associated *SA-State Timer*. An MSDP peer starts an *(S, G) SA-State-Timer* when it initially receives an (S, G) Source-Active message. The peer resets this timer to *SG-State-Period* if another (S, G) Source-Active message is received before the *(S, G) SA-State Timer* expires. The setting of the *SG-State-Period* MUST NOT be less than *SA-Advertisement-Period + SA-Hold-Down-Period*.

6.9.4 PEER HOLD TIMER

An MSDP peer initializes the *Peer Hold Timer* to *HoldTime-Period* when its peering TCP connection is established, and resets the timer to *HoldTime-Period* when it receives any MSDP message. Finally, the peer deletes the timer when its peering TCP connection is closed. The setting of the *HoldTime-Period* MUST be at least 3 seconds. Reference [RFC3618] recommends 75 seconds for the *HoldTime-Period*.

6.9.5 KEEPALIVE TIMER

Once any two MSDP routers have established an MSDP TCP connection, each side of the TCP connection will send an MSDP KeepAlive message and also set a *KeepAlive Timer*. If one router detects that the *KeepAlive Timer* has expired, it will send a KeepAlive message, and restart its *KeepAlive Timer* to an interval referred to as the *KeepAlive-Period*.

The peer router sets the *KeepAlive Timer* to *KeepAlive-Period* when it is powered up. The router resets the timer to *KeepAlive-Period* each time it sends an MSDP message to the peer, and resets the timer when it expires. Finally, the router deletes the *KeepAlive Timer* when it closes the peer's TCP connection. The setting of the *KeepAlive-Period* MUST be less than *HoldTime-Period* and MUST be at least 1 second. Reference [RFC3618] recommends 60 seconds for the *KeepAlive-Period*.

6.9.6 CONNECTRETRY TIMER

The parameter *ConnectRetry-Period* is the time interval an MSDP peer will have to wait after an MSDP peering session is reset before attempting to reestablish the peering session. The MSDP peer with the lower IP address uses the *ConnectRetry Timer* to transition from an INACTIVE to a CONNECTING state. The peer maintains one *ConnectRetry Timer* per peer, and the setting of the *ConnectRetry-Period* SHOULD be 30 seconds. By default, an MSDP peer must wait 30 seconds after an MSDP session is reset before attempting to reestablish the session with the other peer.

The MSDP peer initializes the *ConnectRetry Timer* to *ConnectRetry-Period* when it attempts to actively open a TCP connection to its peer. The peer retries establishing the connection when the *ConnectRetry Timer* expires and resets it to *ConnectRetry-Period*. The peer deletes the timer if either the connection transitions into an ESTABLISHED state or the peer is de-configured.

6.10 MSDP DEPLOYMENT SCENARIOS

MSDP is used primarily in two main scenarios [RFC3618] [RFC4611], inter-domain (between PIM-SM domains) and intra-domain (within a single PIM-SM domain). Reference [RFC4611] describes current best practices for deploying intra-domain and inter-domain MSDP with PIM-SM. The typical MSDP deployment utilizes PIM-SM and MBGP which are defined by the IETP as Multiprotocol Extensions for BGP-4 [RFC4760]. Reference [RFC4611] describes how PIM-SM and MBGP work together to provide intra-domain and inter-domain multicast service. In the discussion here, references to BGP implies MBGP, which is a BGP extension that supports IPv4 and IPv6 as well as unicast and multicast variants of these address families (all instances of internal BGP (iBGP) and external BGP (eBGP) refer to iMBGP and eMBGP, respectively).

Transit service providers typically deploy MSDP to allow their networks to be part of the global multicast infrastructure. This is done by using MSDP to connect the upstream and downstream end-points of the transit network to the peer multicast networks, providing transit multicast services.

Typically, edge multicast networks use one of two options to be part of the global multicast infrastructure: use the RPs in the service provider networks, or implement their own RPs and connect these to the service provider networks using MSDP. One advantage of deploying a local RP in the edge multicast network and using MSDP for connectivity to the service provider network is that the edge network can configure internal multicast groups that are not visible to the service provider's RP. This allows internal multicast in the edge network to be able to keep working if there are connectivity problems to the provider network, or that the provider's RP and MSDP are experiencing problems and cannot provide satisfactory service. In the simplest scenario, the edge network does not have internal multicast groups, thereby making MSDP deployment unnecessary.

6.10.1 DEPLOYING MSDP BETWEEN PIM-SM DOMAINS IN DIFFERENT AUTONOMOUS SYSTEMS

MSDP can be used between PIM-SM [RFC7761] domains, to communicate information about active multicast traffic sources in other domains. The information provided by MSDP allows hosts in different domains to learn about active multicast traffic sources in other PIM-SM domains. Figure 6.11 shows an example of an inter-domain

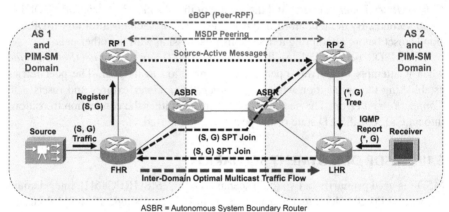

ASBR = Autonomous System Boundary Router

- The two PIM-SM domains in two different autonomous systems.
- MSDP uses TCP port 639 for its peering connections.
- The LHR may decide to join the (S, G) SPT, resulting in inter-domain optimal multicast traffic flow.
- Note that the eBGP peering requirements is met using MBGP. MBGP is an extension to BGP that allows different types of address families to be distributed in parallel. MBGP supports IPv4 and IPv6 addresses as well as unicast and multicast variants of each.
- MSDP was designed to work with IPv4 and not IPv6.

Main processing steps:
1. Receiver joins the (*, G) tree by sending an IGMP Membership Report message to the receiver-side DR.
2. MSDP peering is configured, with MBGP used in parallel to ensure that the peer-RPF checks PASS.
3. The multicast traffic source sends traffic and the source-side DR registers the source with its local RP.
4. MSDP shares information about sources with peers via MSDP Source-Active messages.
5. The remote RP joins the source (S,G) tree and starts delivering multicast traffic via its shared tree to interested receivers.
6. The receiver-side DR may decide to join the (S, G) tree if the SPT switchover is enabled, resulting in inter-domain optimal multicast traffic flow.

FIGURE 6.11 MSDP use case 1: inter-domain multicast with MSDP peering between RPs in different PIM-SM domains (or autonomous systems).

scenario with MSDP peering between RPs located in different PIM-SM domains (or autonomous systems).

Generally, a one-to-one MSDP peering is used between the PIM-SM domains, and the MSDP peers utilize peer-RPF rules that are deterministic as described later in the subsequent section (i.e., except forwarding between peers that belong to the same MSDP mesh-group). MSDP peerings can be aggregated on a single MSDP peer in a domain, with the peer typically supporting from one to hundreds of MSDP peerings (similar in scale to BGP peerings).

6.10.2 Deploying MSDP between PIM-SM Domains in the Same Autonomous Systems

Figure 6.12 shows an example of an inter-domain scenario with MSDP peering between RPs in different PIM-SM domains *in the same autonomous system*. MSDP can also be used between a group of RPs that have been assigned a common IP Anycast Address (i.e., Anycast-RPs) within a PIM-SM domain [RFC3446]. Creating Anycast-RPs in a PIM-SM domain allows the member RPs to synchronize information about the active multicast sources being served by each Anycast-RP peer (through the Interior Gateway Protocol (IGP) reachability information exchanged in the autonomous system). Chapter 5 describes the implementation of Anycast-RPs in a PIM-SM domain without the use of MSDP [RFC4610] (MSDP is not required in this case).

The MSDP peering used in the Anycast-RP scenario is typically based on the implementation of MSDP mesh-groups, where each mesh-group comprises multiple Anycast-RP peers. In this case, a mesh-group can consist of two to tens of Anycast-RP peers, although using more than ten RPs is not typical. In addition, a deployment may configure one or more of these mesh-group peers to have one-to-one

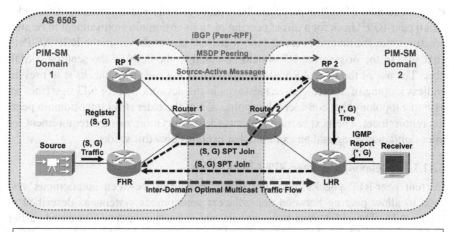

- The two administratively isolated PIM-SM domains are within the same autonomous system.

FIGURE 6.12 MSDP use case 2: inter-domain multicast with MSDP peering between RPs in different PIM-SM domains in the same autonomous system.

MSDP peerings with other MSDP peers outside the local PIM-SM domain, allowing for the discovery of external multicast traffic sources. It is also common to use MSDP for Anycast-RP deployment without necessarily having external MSDP peering; MSDP is simply used for peering the Anycast-RPs.

6.11   INTER-DOMAIN MSDP PEERING

This section describes the most common methods used for inter-domain MSDP peering and some deployment examples.

6.11.1   Peering between PIM-SM Border Routers

We consider a network environment where MSDP peers within a bounded PIM-SM domain are provided their own RP within that domain. Furthermore, we assume that the PIM-SM domain has its own Autonomous System Number (ASN) and one or more MBGP routers. The PIM-SM domain may also have multiple MSDP-capable routers. We also assume that each of the border routers of the PIM-SM domain has an external MSDP and MBGP peering with its peer routers.

When deploying these external MSDP peering, the network operator typically configures both the MSDP peering and MBGP peering using the same IP address. Typical examples of this type of MSDP deployment are as follows:

- When service providers have direct peerings with other providers
- When service providers peer at an Internet Exchange
- When service providers use their edge router to implement MSDP/MBGP peering with customers.

Prior to current MSDP deployment best practices, the requirement for the (older strict) peer-RPF check for a direct peering in an inter-domain environment to be successful is that the first ASN carried in the MBGP best path (i.e., in the BGP AS-Path attribute) to the originating RP should be equal to the ASN of the sending MSDP peer. The use of the BGP AS-Path information in the peer-RPF checks is to prevent endless looping of Source-Active messages in the network. Figure 6.13 describes an example topology that considers the application of the older strict inter-domain peering requirement. The next section presents the (newer) more relaxed requirement for inter-domain peering and an example that explains how this works.

6.11.1.1   Relaxing the Peer-RPF Check Rules

Current peer-RPF checks relax the rules for peering between autonomous systems to allow peering between non-adjacent autonomous systems as described in Figure 6.14. The older strict inter-domain peering requirements (described earlier and in Figure 6.13) would have failed in this environment, but the (newer) modified relaxed rules succeed and also provide more inter-domain peering flexibility.

Using the newer modified peer-RPF rules, RP 4 in AS 400 will choose the MSDP peer in the closest autonomous system that lies along the best BGP path to the

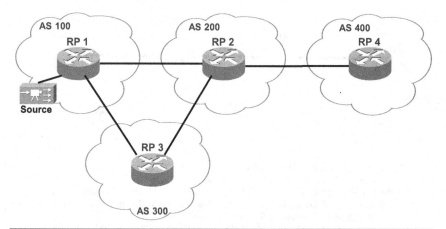

- In older MSDP implementations, for a direct peering in an inter-domain environment to be successful, the first autonomous system number (ASN) in the MBGP best path to the originating RP (RP 1) should be the same as the ASN of the MSDP peer.
- RP 4 receives a Source Active message, originated by RP 1, from RP 2.
- RP 2 also has an MBGP peering with RP 4.
- The MBGP first hop autonomous system from RP 4, in the best path to the originating RP, is AS 200.
- The ASN of the sending MSDP peer is also AS 200.
- In this case, the peer-RPF check succeeds, and RP 4 accepts the Source-Active message.

- The peer-RPF in this topology will fail when the MBGP first hop autonomous system, in the best path to the originating RP, is AS 200, and the origin autonomous system of the sending MSDP peer is AS 300.

- The use of the BGP AS Path information prevents endless looping of Source-Active messages.

FIGURE 6.13   Peering between PIM-SM border routers.

originating RP; RP 4 will then accept Source-Active messages coming from AS 200 even though it is not the first autonomous system leading back to RP 1. If the closest autonomous system has multiple MSDP peers to routers within it, the MSDP peer with the highest IP address is selected as the RPF peer.

6.11.1.2   Inter-Domain Peering Examples and How Peer-RPF Check Rules Are Applied to Source-Active Messages

This section uses examples of MSDP and (M)BGP topologies to explain how Rules 4b and 4c are used for MSDP peer-RPF checks.

6.11.1.2.1   Peer-RPF Check Rule 4b: Sending MSDP Peer Is Also an Exterior (M)BGP Peer

This peer-RPF check rule is applied when the MSDP peer that sent the Source-Active message is also an e(M)BGP peer (see Figure 6.15). The RPF check proceeds as follows when this rule is applied:

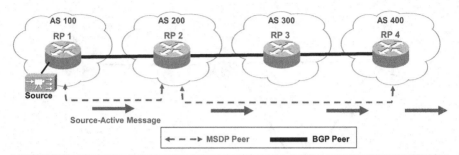

- Source-Active message receiver = RP 4
- In the previous and the older peer-RPF check rule:
  - If the first autonomous system number (ASN) in the BGP AS-Path attribute to the originating RP is NOT equal to the ASN of the sending MSDP peer, then the peer-RPF check FAILs and RP 4 rejects Source-Active message.
  - This means, RP 4 in AS 400 cannot MSDP peer with RP 2 in AS 200, since AS 300 is the first ASN in the MBGP best path to AS 100 and RP 1.
- In the relaxed (modified) peer-RPF check rule in RFC 4611:
  - Choose the MSDP peer in the CLOSEST autonomous system along the best path to the originating RP.
  - In this case, RP 4 will choose the peer in the closest autonomous system along the best MBGP autonomous system path to the originator RP 1. RP 4 will then accept Source-Active messages coming from AS 200.
  - If there are multiple MSDP peers to routers within the same autonomous systems (i.e., AS 200), the peer with the highest IP address is chosen as the RPF peer.

FIGURE 6.14   Relaxing the peer-RPF check rules to allow acceptance of Source-Active messages along the RPF path.

1. The receiving MSDP peer searches its BGP MRIB for the best path that leads back to the RP that originated the Source-Active message. If the peer does not find a path in the MRIB, it then searches its unicast RIB (URIB) for a path to the originating RP. If still the peer does not find a path, the peer-RPF check fails.
2. If any of the abovementioned searches succeed (i.e., the best path to the originating RP is found), the peer then examines the properties of the BGP AS-Path attribute of this best path. If the peer finds that the first autonomous system listed in the BGP AS-Path attribute of this best path to the RP is the same as the autonomous system of the e(M)BGP peer (which is also the MSDP peer that sent the Source-Active message), then the peer-RPF check succeeds, otherwise it fails.

6.11.1.2.1.1   Implications of This RPF Check Rule on MSDP   For this rule (and MSDP peer-RPF checks) to work, the network operator must ensure that the MSDP topology follows or mirrors the (M)BGP topology. In general, wherever an e(M)BGP peer connection is configured between two routers, an MSDP peer connection should also be created. However, the IP address of the remote MSDP peer connection does not have to be the same as that of the remote e(M)BGP peer connection. These IP addresses do not have to be identical because the BGP topology between two e(M) BGP peers is not described by the BGP AS-Path attribute.

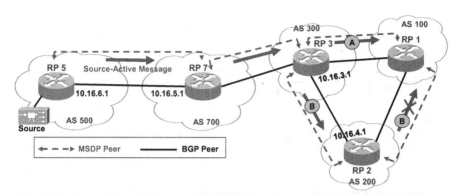

When the sending MSDP peer is an eBGP peer:
1. Find the BGP best path to the originating RP.
   - Search the different routing tables in the following preference order: first the static multicast route (mroute), MBGP or multicast routing table (MRT), and then the unicast routing table (URT).
   - If no path to the originating RP is found, then the RPF check fails.
2. Apply the peer-RPF test condition:
   - Is the first autonomous system number (ASN) in the BGP AS-Path attribute to the originating RP = the ASN of the sending MSDP peer?
   - If yes, then peer-RPF check succeeds.

Path A in figure:
- Source-Active message receiver = RP 1
- First ASN in the BGP best path to originating RP = 300
- ASN of sending MSDP peer = 300
- First ASN in the BGP best path to originating RP = ASN of sending MSDP peer, therefore, peer-RPF check succeeds and RP 1 accepts Source-Active message.

Path B in figure:
- Source-Active message receiver = RP 1
- First ASN in the BGP best path to originating RP = 300
- ASN of sending MSDP peer = 200
- First ASN in the BGP best path to originating RP != ASN of sending MSDP peer, therefore, peer-RPF check fails, and RP 1 rejects Source-Active message.

FIGURE 6.15   Sending MSDP peer is an eBGP peer.

6.11.1.2.2   Peer-RPF Check Rule 4c: Sending MSDP Peer Is NOT an (M)BGP Peer

This peer-RPF check rule is applied when the MSDP peer that sent the Source-Active message is NOT a (M)BGP peer at all (see Figures 6.16 and 6.17). The peer-RPF check proceeds as follows when this rule is applied:

1. The receiving MSDP peer searches its BGP MRIB for the best path to the RP that originated the Source-Active message. If the peer does not find a path in the MRIB, it then searches the URIB for a path to the originating RP. If still the peer does not find a path, the peer-RPF check fails.
2. If any of the mentioned searches succeed (i.e., the best path to the RP that originated the Source-Active message is found), the peer then searches the BGP MRIB for the best path to the MSDP peer that sent the Source-Active message.

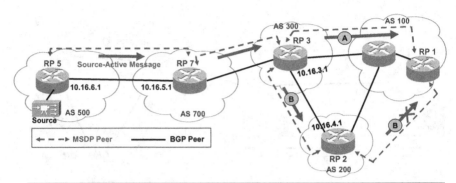

When the sending MSDP peer is NOT an eBGP peer:
1. Find the best path to the originating RP.
   - Search the different routing tables in the following preference order: first the static multicast route (mroute), MBGP or multicast routing table (MRT), and then the unicast routing table (URT).
   - If no path to the originating RP is found, then the RPF check fails.
2. Find the BGP best path to the sending MSDP peer.
   - Search the different routing tables in the following preference order: first the static multicast route (mroute), MBGP or multicast routing table (MRT), and then the unicast routing table (URT).
   - If no path to the originating RP is found, then the RPF check fails.
3. Note the ASN of the sending MSDP peer.
   - That is the origin ASN (i.e., last ASN) in the BGP AS-Path to the sending MSDP peer.
4. Apply the peer-RPF test condition:
   - Is the first ASN in the BGP AS-Path attribute to the originating RP = the ASN of the sending MSDP peer?
   - If yes, then peer-RPF check succeeds.

Path A in figure:
- Source-Active message receiver = RP 1
- First ASN in the BGP best path to originating RP = 300
- ASN of sending MSDP peer = 300
- First ASN in the BGP best path to originating RP = ASN of sending MSDP peer, therefore, peer-RPF check succeeds and RP 1 accepts Source-Active message.

Path B in figure:
- Source-Active message receiver = RP 1
- First ASN in the BGP best path to originating RP = 300
- ASN of sending MSDP peer = 200
- First ASN in the BGP best path to originating RP != ASN of sending MSDP peer, therefore, peer-RPF check fails and RP 1 rejects Source-Active message.

FIGURE 6.16 Sending MSDP peer is NOT a BGP peer: example 1.

If the peer does not find a path in the MRIB, it then searches its URIB. If still it does not find a path, the RPF check fails.

  a. The autonomous system of the MSDP peer that sent the Source-Active message to the current peer is the origin autonomous system, which is the last autonomous system listed in the BGP AS-Path attribute received by the current MSDP peer.

3. If the first autonomous system listed in the BGP AS-Path attribute for the best path to the RP is the same as the autonomous system of the MSDP peer that sent the Source-Active message, then the peer-RPF check succeeds, otherwise it fails.

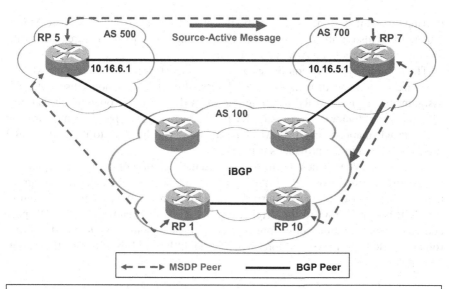

- Source-Active message receiver = RP 10
- First ASN in the BGP best path to originating RP = 700
- ASN of sending MSDP peer = 700
- First ASN in the BGP best path to originating RP = ASN of sending MSDP peer, therefore, peer-RPF check succeeds and RP 1 accepts Source-Active message.

This example shows that there is more flexibility in MSDP peer placement.

FIGURE 6.17   Sending MSDP peer is NOT a BGP peer: example 2.

6.11.2 PEERING BETWEEN NON-BORDER ROUTERS

When MSDP peering is implemented between the border routers of any two PIM-SM domains, this can restrict the scalability of intra-domain MSDP because there is the need to also maintain MBGP and MSDP peerings internally toward these border routers. Within any of these domains (i.e., intra-domain), the border router acts as the announcer of the next-hop toward the originating RP. For this to work, the network operator must ensure that all intra-domain MSDP peerings match or mirror the MBGP path back toward the domain's border router. As discussed earlier, external MSDP (eMSDP) peerings rely on BGP AS-Path information for peer-RPF checks. On the other hand, internal MSDP (iMSDP) peerings rely on the announcer or advertiser of the next-hop for peer-RPF checks.

6.11.2.1 Multi-Hop Peering Scenario

While typically eMBGP peering is implemented directly between the border routers of two PIM-SM domains, it is common for the eMSDP peer to be located well inside the transit provider's autonomous system (multi-hop peering). Providers who require more flexibility in the placement of MSDP peering, commonly select a few dedicated MSDP routers located within their core networks to implement inter-domain MSDP peerings to their customers. Typically, the provider implements these core MSDP routers to be also in the intra-domain MSDP mesh-group and configures them with an Anycast address as an Anycast-RP group.

The provider typically configures all multicast routers in the autonomous system to statically point to the Anycast-RP address. Providers commonly use static RP assignment for group-to-RP mapping due to its deterministic operational features. The Bootstrap Router (BSR) or Auto-RP mechanisms (see Chapter 5), which provide dynamic RP mapping in PIM-SM domains, may also be used to disseminate RP information within the provider's network.

For a Source-Active message to be accepted in the multi-hop peering environment (see Figure 6.18a), the peer-RPF check relies on the next (for the older strict requirement) or closest (for the newer/current relaxed requirement) autonomous system in the BGP best path toward the originating RP. This also requires the MSDP peer address to be in the same autonomous system as the autonomous system of the border router's MBGP peer. Furthermore, MBGP should be used to advertise the MSDP peer address.

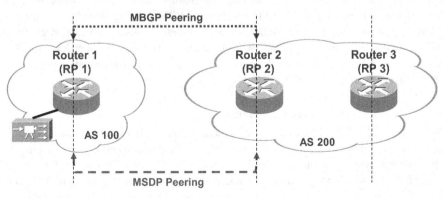

FIGURE 6.18   Peering between non-border routers.

In the multi-hop peering example in Figure 6.18a, customer Router R1 is MBGP peering with Router R2 and, R1 is MSDP peering with Router R3. In this case, R2 and R3 must be in the same autonomous system or, must appear to AS 100 to be from the same autonomous system if private ASNs are used. If there are multiple MSDP peers to routers within the same autonomous system (i.e., AS 200), the MSDP peer that has the highest IP address will be selected as the MSDP RPF peer. Router R1 must also have in its MBGP table the MSDP peer address of R3.

From Router R3's perspective, AS 100 (i.e., Router R1) is the MBGP next ASN in the BGP best path toward the originating RP. Thus, as long as AS 100 is the next (or closest) autonomous system in the BGP best path toward the originating RP (Router R1), peer-RPF checks will succeed on Source-Active messages arriving from R1.

6.11.2.2   Single-Hop Peering Scenario

In the single-hop scenario (Figure 6.18b), Router R2 at the border (instead of R3) MSDP peers with R1. In this case, the MBGP address of R2 becomes the announcer/ advertiser of the next-hop for R3, toward the originating RP (Router R1). Additionally, R3 must peer with that R2 MBGP address. Furthermore, all AS 200 intra-domain MSDP peers need to follow/mirror iMBGP (or an IGP) peerings toward R2 since iMSDP relies on peering with the address of the MBGP (or an IGP) advertiser of the next-hop toward the originating RP.

6.11.3   MSDP Peering without BGP

In this MSDP use case, an organization deploys its own RP and has an MSDP peering with its service provider but does not support BGP peering with the provider. As mentioned earlier, MSDP relies on BGP AS-Path information to learn the MSDP topology required for peer-RPF checks and Source-Active message forwarding. However, there are several network scenarios where MSDP can be deployed without BGP. This means there are some special deployment scenarios where performing a peer-RPF check on the BGP AS-Path information is not required. These scenarios include:

- Only one MSDP peer connection is used.
- There is a direct connection to the originating RP (i.e., directly connected originating RP).
- An MSDP mesh-group is used.
- A default MSDP peer (i.e., default MSDP route) is configured.
- The deployment allows for MSDP peer-RPF checks to be performed using an IGP next-hop or IGP advertiser to the originating RP (see Section 6.12.2).

Typically, an organization will configure a unicast default route from the border router of its network to the border router of the service provider's network, and then implement MSDP peering with the provider's MSDP router. If the organization's network also supports internal MSDP peerings, then the organization will need to configure an MSDP default peer on its border router that points to the service provider network. This allows the organization to learn all external multicast sources, and also advertise internal multicast sources. In the case where only a single MSDP peering is used toward the service provider (i.e., no internal MSDP peerings in the organization's network), then the organization's network (which becomes a stub site), will only have an MSDP default peering toward the service provider and will not require the peer-RPF checks.

6.11.4 MSDP PEERING AT A MULTICAST EXCHANGE

A Multicast Internet Exchange (MIX) allows different multicast service providers to peer with each other over a common IP subnet (or by using point-to-point VLANs). This enables them to share MSDP Source-Active messages about active multicast sources in their respective networks (see Figure 6.19). In the MIX, each service provider will implement MSDP and MBGP peering with each other provider's directly connected MIX IP address. Each provider's MIX router will send/receive Source-Active messages to/from its MSDP peers. This allows each MIX router to forward Source-Active messages throughout its domain and to the provider's customers and any direct peerings of the provider.

6.12 INTRA-DOMAIN MSDP PEERING

This section describes the different methods used for intra-domain MSDP peering and some deployment examples.

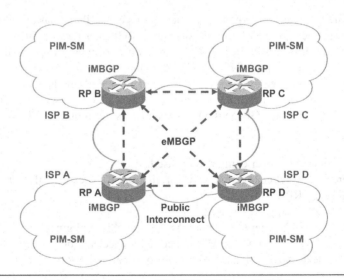

- The peering solution at the MIX use PIM-SM MSDP, and MBGP.
- The ISPs run MSDP and iMBGP internally.
- The ISPs perform multicast peering at a public interconnect using eMBGP.
  - The border routers run eMBGP.
- The MSDP peering amongst the RPs is fully meshed.
- All MSDP peers set a common metric distance for eMBGP.

FIGURE 6.19 ISP requirements at the Multicast Internet Exchange (MIX).

6.12.1 PEERING BETWEEN MSDP- AND MBGP-CONFIGURED ROUTERS

For intra-domain peering, the next-hop IP address of the iBGP peer, or the IGP next-hop information is typically used for the MSDP peer-RPF checks. From the earlier discussion, inter-domain BGP and MSDP peering relies on the BGP AS-Path information for the peer-RPF checks. For this reason, a successful peer-RPF check for intra-domain peering requires that the IP address of the MSDP peer be the same as the internal MBGP (iMBGP) peer, whether or not the MSDP and MBGP peers are directly connected as explained in Figure 6.20.

In Figure 6.20, RP 1 MSDP and MBGP peers with Router 1 (using IP address 10.16.3.1), and with Router 2 (using IP address 10.16.4.1). When the MSDP Source-Active message arrives at RP 1 from Router 1, the MSDP peer-RPF check for 10.16.6.1 (i.e., RP 5) passes because RP 1 receives the Source-Active message from MSDP peer 10.16.3.1, which is also the correct MBGP next-hop for 10.16.6.1 (RP 5). When RP 1 receives the same Source-Active message from MSDP peer 10.16.4.1 (Router 2), the MBGP lookup for 10.16.6.1 (RP 5) shows a next-hop of 10.16.3.1, not 10.16.4.1, so the peer-RPF check correctly fails, preventing a forwarding loop.

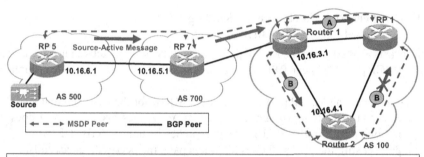

When the sending MSDP peer is an iBGP peer:
1. Find the best path to the originating RP in the BGP tables. This means, find the BGP peer that advertised the path (i.e., the IP address of the BGP peer that sent this path). Note that this path is not the same as the BGP next-hop of the path.
   - Search the different routing tables in the following preference order: first the static multicast route (mroute), MBGP or multicast routing table (MRT), and then the unicast routing table (URT).
   - If no path to the originating RP is found, then the peer-RPF check fails.
2. Apply the peer-RPF test condition:
   - Is sending MSDP peer = BGP peer address?
   - If yes, then peer-RPF check succeeds.

Path A in figure:
- Source-Active message receiver = RP 1
- iBGP peer address (advertising best path to originating RP 5) = 10.16.3.1
- Sending MSDP peer address = 10.16.3.1
- Sending MSDP peer address = iBGP peer address, therefore, peer-RPF check succeeds, and RP 1 accepts Source-Active message.

Path B in figure:
- Source-Active message receiver = RP 1
- iBGP peer address (advertising best path to originating RP 5) = 10.16.3.1
- Sending MSDP peer address = 10.16.4.1
- Sending MSDP peer address != iBGP peer address, therefore, peer-RPF check fails, and RP 1 rejects Source-Active message.

FIGURE 6.20 RPF check Rule: sending MSDP peer is also an iBGP peer.

This deployment would also fail when a Source-Active message from Router 1 is sent to RP 1 if RP 1 was MBGP peering with an IP address other than the address 10.16.3.1 of Router 1. This means network operators deploying intra-domain peering must ensure that the MSDP and MBGP (or other IGP) peering IP addresses must match unless the deployment supports a scenario where the peer-RPF check can be skipped as discussed in the subsequent section.

Although the requirements for peer-RPF checks to be successful in intra-domain peering are straightforward, some common network topology configuration mistakes can make the peer-RPF checks fail as explained in Figures 6.21 and 6.22.

- Figure 6.21 explains the common mistake of not using the same IP address for the MSDP and iMBGP peers
- Figure 6.22 explains the common mistake when using BGP Route Reflectors which does not follow normal iBGP full mesh forwarding rules.

An intra-domain peering must ensure that such mistakes are avoided to ensure the successful operation of the MSDP deployment.

6.12.1.1 Peer-RPF Check Rule 4a: Sending MSDP Peer Is Also an i(M)BGP Peer

This rule is applied when the MSDP peer that sent the Source-Active message is also an i(M)BGP peer. The peer-RPF check proceeds as follows when this rule is applied:

1. The receiving MSDP peer searches BGP MRIB for the best path that leads back to the RP that originated the Source-Active message. If the peer does not find a path in the MRIB, it then searches its unicast RIB (URIB) for a path. If still, the peer still does not find a path, the peer-RPF check fails.

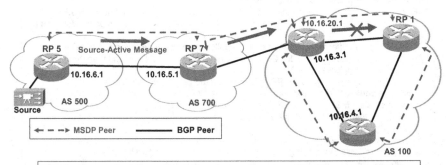

This happens when there is a failure to use the same IP addresses for MSDP peers as iBGP peers:
- Source-Active message receiver = RP 1
- iBGP peer address (advertising best path to originating RP 5) = 10.16.3.1
- Sending MSDP peer address = 10.16.20.1
- Sending MSDP peer address != iBGP peer address, therefore, peer-RPF check fails, and RP 1 rejects Source-Active message.

FIGURE 6.21 Sending MSDP peer is an iBGP peer: common network topology mistakes that can cause the RPF checks to fail.

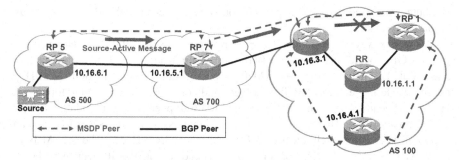

This happens when a BGP Route Reflector (RR) is used which does not follow
normal iBGP full mesh forwarding rules:
• Source-Active message receiver = RP 1
• iBGP peer address (advertising best path to originating RP 5) = 10.16.1.1.
    ▪ This is the IP address of the RR, which is not an MSDP peer of RP 1.
• Sending MSDP peer address = 10.16.3.1
• Sending MSDP peer address != iBGP peer address, therefore, peer-RPF check fails,
  and RP 1 rejects Source-Active message.

FIGURE 6.22   Sending MSDP peer is an iBGP peer: common network topology mistakes that can cause the RPF checks to fail.

2. If any of the abovementioned searches succeed (that is, the best path to the originating RP is found), the peer then determines the IP address of the BGP neighbor that lies on this best path. This IP address is then the IP address of the BGP neighbor that sent the BGP Update messages containing the BGP path to the peer.

   a. The IP address of the BGP neighbor is not the same as the BGP Next-Hop address indicated for the path in the BGP Update message. This is because i(M)BGP peers do not update the BGP Next-Hop attribute of an advertised BGP path [AWEYLSPV21]. The BGP Next-Hop address is usually not the same as the IP address of the BGP peer that sent a BGP path.

   b. The IP address of the BGP neighbor is not necessarily the same as the BGP Router ID of the BGP peer that sent the BGP path.

3. If the receiving MSDP peer determines that the IP address of the MSDP peer that sent the Source-Active message is the same as the IP address of the BGP neighbor (i.e., the IP address of the BGP peer that sent the BGP path to the peer), then the peer-RPF check succeeds, otherwise it fails.

6.12.1.1.1   Implications of This Peer-RPF Check Rule on MSDP

For this rule (hence MSDP peer-RPF checks) to work, the MSDP topology must follow or mirror the (M)BGP topology. In general, wherever an i(M)BGP peer connection is created between two i(M)BGP routers, an MSDP peer connection should be created between the same two routers. More specifically, the IP address of the remote MSDP peer connection must be the same as that of the remote i(M)BGP peer connection. These IP addresses must be the same because the BGP AS-Path attribute is not used to describe the BGP topology between i(M)BGP peers within an autonomous system.

If it were always the case that i(M)BGP peers updated the BGP Next-Hop address in the BGP Update message for a BGP path when sending the Update message to another i(M)BGP peer, then the i(M)BGP peer could rely on the BGP Next-Hop address to describe the i(M)BGP topology (and consequently, the MSDP topology). However, because the default behavior for i(M)BGP peers is not to update the BGP Next-Hop address in BGP Update messages when passing the messages to peers, an i(M)BGP peer cannot rely on the BGP Next-Hop address to describe the (M)BGP topology (as well as the MSDP topology). Instead, the i(M)BGP peer uses the IP address of the i(M)BGP peer that sent the BGP Update message for the BGP path to describe the i(M)BGP topology (and the MSDP topology) within the autonomous system.

The network operator must exercise extreme care when configuring the IP addresses of the MSDP peer to ensure that the same IP address is used as both i(M)BGP and MSDP peer IP addresses.

6.12.2   MSDP Peer is Not a BGP Peer (or No BGP Peer is Present)

It is common in MSDP intra-domain deployments to have only a few routers running MBGP or the domain is not running MBGP at all. The problem this scenario presents is that the requirement of having the MSDP peer IP address being the same as the MBGP peer IP address cannot be met. To get around this requirement, the following topologies can be used, as they relax the intra-domain MSDP peer-RPF check rules:

- Deploy the MSDP peer to be the only MSDP peer.
- Configure the MSDP peer as a mesh-group peer.
- Implement peering with the originating RP.
- Configure a default MSDP peer.
- Rely on an IGP for MSDP peer-RPF checks as explained in Figure 6.23.

A common approach used by network operators to get around the intra-domain BGP peering requirement when more than one MSDP peer is configured in the domain is to implement MSDP mesh-groups. When an MSDP mesh-group is configured, then no peer-RPF checks on arriving Source-Active messages are required when those messages are received from an MSDP mesh-group peer. In this case, Source-Active messages are always accepted from MSDP mesh-group peers. As discussed earlier, the concept of MSDP mesh-groups is to reduce the amount of Source-Active message traffic in the network since these messages, when received from a mesh-group peer, are not flooded to peers within that same mesh-group. MSDP mesh-groups must be configured to be fully meshed.

6.12.2.1   RPF Check Rule 4d: Sending MSDP Peer Is an IGP Peer

Another option that can be used to work around the problem of not running BGP to MSDP RPF peers, is to perform peer-RPF checks using an IGP like OSPF, or IS-IS.

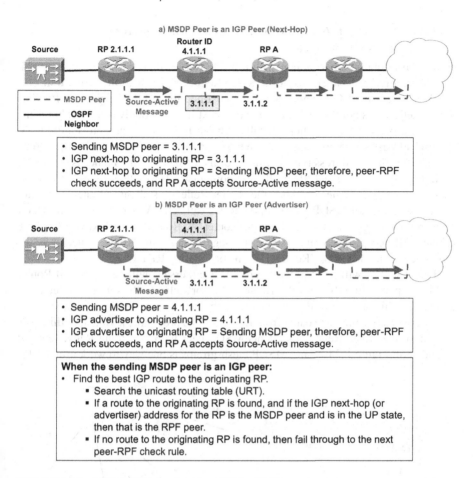

FIGURE 6.23   MSDP RPF checks using IGP (no BGP).

This option allows for customers of an enterprise, who are not running BGP and who do not want to deploy MSDP mesh-groups, to use their existing IGP to perform the MSDP peer-RPF checks (as shown in Figure 6.23).

6.12.3   USING MSDP AND BGP ROUTE REFLECTORS

In normal BGP usage where iBGP routers that are not BGP Confederation members, or BGP Route Reflector clients are deployed, all these iBGP routers must be fully meshed to prevent routing loops. This section examines the deployment of MSDP in intra-domain environments with BGP Router Reflectors [AWEYLSPV21] [RFC4611]. A BGP Route Reflector is a router BGP router in an autonomous system that is designated to reflect/pass BGP routes learned from an iBGP peer to other iBGP peers and eBGP peers, and routes learned from eBGP peers to all iBGP peers. Unlike in the fully meshed iBGP configuration, all iBGP routers that form an iBGP peering relationship only peer with the Route Reflector [AWEYLSPV21].

6.12.3.1 Scenario 1: Accepting Source-Active Message from the Route Reflector

In the intra-domain environment with a Route Reflector, as shown in Figure 6.24, MSDP requires that the clients of the Route Reflector peer with the Route Reflector itself since it is the BGP announcer of the next-hop toward the originating RP. The Route Reflector is not the BGP next-hop (the next-hop is actually Router 1) but is the announcer of the BGP next-hop. Recall from our previous discussion (Figure 6.23) that the address of the announcer of the next hop (which in Figure 6.24 is the Route Reflector) is the IP address typically used for the MSDP peer-RPF checks.

In Figure 6.24, Router 1 (the BGP next-hop) forwards MSDP Source-Active messages to the Route Reflector. Also, the Router Reflector's clients, Router A, Router B, and Router C, all MSDP peer with the Route Reflector. When the Route Reflector forwards the Source-Active message to Router A, Router B, and Router C, these clients will accept the Source-Active message because the Route Reflector is the announcer of the next-hop (Router 1) to the originating RP address.

The peer-RPF will fail and the Source-Active message will be rejected if Router 1, MSDP peers directly with the Route Reflector's clients Router A, Router B, or Router C. This is because the announcer of the next-hop is the Route Reflector but the Source-Active message came from Router 1. The proper deployment, in this case, is to have the Route Reflector's clients MSDP peer with the Route Reflector itself as shown in Figure 6.24. Using MSDP mesh-groups is one way to work around this

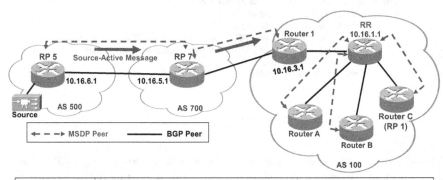

- In this Route Reflector (RR) topology, MSDP requires that the clients of the RR (i.e., Routers A, B, and C) peer with it since the RR is the BGP announcer (advertiser) of the next hop toward the originating RP (i.e., Router 1 is the next-hop).
  - The RR is not the BGP next hop but is the announcer of the BGP next hop.
  - The announcer of the next hop is the address typically used for MSDP peer-RPF checks.
- Routers A, B, and C also MSDP peer with RR.
- Router 1 forwards MSDP Source-Active messages to the RR.
- When the RR forwards the Source-Active message to its clients Routers A, B, and C, these clients will accept the Source-Active message because the RR is the announcer of the next hop to the originating RP address.

- The peer-RPF will fail if Router 1 MSDP peers directly with Routers A, B, or C, because the announcer of the next hop is the RR but the Source-Active message came from Router 1. Proper MSDP deployment is to have the RR clients MSDP peer with the RR as in the figure.

FIGURE 6.24   iBGP topology with Route Reflector example 1: accepting Source-Active message from the Route Reflector.

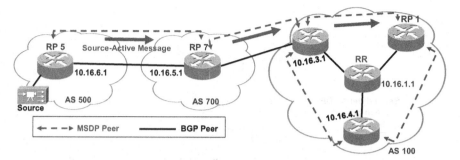

- Source-Active message receiver = RP 1
- iBGP peer address (advertiser of next-hop to originating RP 5) = 10.16.1.1, the Route Reflector (RR)
- Sending MSDP peer address = 10.16.3.1
- But BGP next-hop = 10.16.3.1
- Sending MSDP peer address = BGP next-hop address, therefore, peer-RPF check succeeds, and RP 1 accepts Source-Active message.

FIGURE 6.25 iBGP topology with Route Reflector example 2: accepting Source-Active message from BGP next-hop.

requirement. Also, using external MSDP peerings will not work in this environment (Figure 6.24) since the peer-RPF checks in this case compare the next ASN between MBGP and MSDP peerings, instead of the IP address of the announcer of the next-hop.

6.12.3.2 Scenario 2: Accepting Source-Active Message from BGP Next-Hop

Figure 6.25 describes how the MSDP peering requirement can be relaxed by avoiding the MSDP peering of Router A, Router B, and Router C with the advertiser of the next hop (i.e., the Route Reflector). This new relaxed rule allows the Route Reflector's clients to MSDP peer with the next-hop (Router 1), in addition to iBGP peer with the advertiser of the next hop (the Route Reflector). In Figure 6.25, Router 1 is the next-hop, and Router A, Router B, and Router C, MSDP peer with it, allowing the peer-RPF checks to succeed and Source-Active messages received from Router 1 to be accepted.

6.12.4 Using Hierarchical MSDP Mesh-Groups

In intra-domain multicast environments with a large number of MSDP peers, it is not uncommon to see the deployment of hierarchical mesh-groups as shown in Figure 6.26. Such a deployment allows the different mesh-groups to forward messages to one another, thereby, reducing the number of MSDP peerings per router (due to the requirement of configuring a full mesh among the MSDP peers) and, consequently, reducing router load. Implementing a good hierarchical mesh-group (i.e., one that prevents message looping) requires configuring a core mesh-group in the backbone, and having the core routers of the core mesh-group serve as aggregation routers for the leaf (or second-tier) mesh-groups.

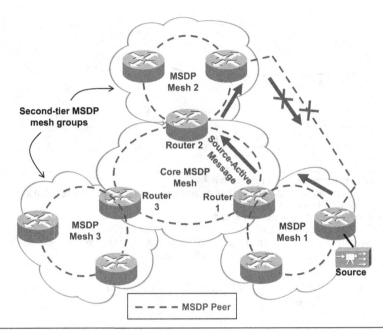

- A network can use hierarchical MSDP mesh-groups to help reduce MSDP peering.
- To present Source-Active message forwarding loops, second-tier MSDP mesh groups must NOT peer directly with each other.

FIGURE 6.26   Hierarchical MSDP mesh-groups to reduce MSDP peering.

In Figure 6.26, Router 1, Router 2, and Router 3 are configured as a core MSDP mesh-group, and each router serves as an MSDP aggregation router for its leaf (or second-tier) mesh-group. Since a peer that receives a Source-Active message from a mesh-group peer is not allowed to forward that message to any other peers within that same mesh-group, Source-Active messages will not loop. This means network operators must avoid creating topologies that connect mesh-groups in a loop. For example, in Figure 6.26, the network operator must create a topology such that the second-tier mesh-groups 1, 2, and 3, do not directly exchange Source-Active messages with each other, otherwise, endless looping of Source-Active messages will occur.

Also, creating redundancy between mesh-groups can cause Source-Active message loops, and should be avoided when implementing hierarchical mesh-groups. For instance, if Router 3 is replaced by two routers that connect the leaf mesh-group 3 with the core mesh-group, a Source-Active message loop would be created between mesh-group 3 and the core mesh-group, because each leaf mesh-group (Router 1 and Router 2) must be fully meshed with the two peer routers replacing Router 3.

6.13   ANYCAST-RP THROUGH MSDP (MSDP ANYCAST-RP)

MSDP was originally developed for inter-domain multicast source discovery, but MSDP can be used for implementing an Anycast-RP in an intra-domain environment to provide redundancy and load-sharing capabilities. Enterprise and service provider networks typically use Anycast-RP in a network to meet fault tolerance requirements within a single PIM-SM domain. The Anycast-RP is a useful application of MSDP within PIM-SM networks.

To achieve RP load sharing and redundancy, a network operator can use an Anycast-RP mechanism together with MSDP mesh-groups within a multicast domain with multiple RPs [RFC3446] as shown in Figure 6.27. This mechanism allows an arbitrary number of RPs to be configured as an MSDP mesh-group in a single shared-tree PIM-SM domain. One or more of the Anycast-RPs forming the mesh-group, may also have additional one-to-one MSDP peering with MSDP peers outside that PIM-SM domain, allowing the discovery of active external multicast sources. Note that the use of MSDP for Anycast-RP without external MSDP peering is common. It should be noted that the Anycast-RP mechanism can also be implemented without using MSDP as described in Chapter 5.

6.13.1 RATIONALE FOR THE ANYCAST-RP MECHANISM

PIM-SM as defined in RFC 7761 and described in Chapter 5, allows only a single active RP to be used for a given multicast group. For this reason, the optimal placement of RPs in a PIM-SM network (e.g., multi-regional PIM-SM network) can be problematic for the service provider.

The Anycast-RP mechanism relaxes PIM-SM's constraint that requires that only one multicast group-to-RP mapping can be active at any given time. The single

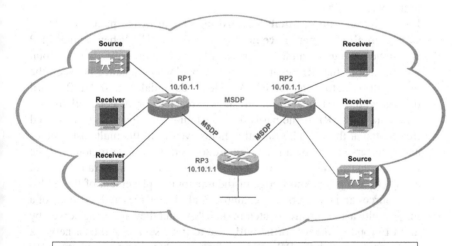

• The Anycast RP mechanism can be implemented using MSDP and PIM-SM.
• Multiple RPs can be deployed in a PIM domain with the same IP addresses. Each RP is assigned the same IP address (Anycast address).
• Multicast traffic sources and receivers use the closest RP (according the IGP routing metric).
• Intra-domain Anycast RPs are used to provide redundancy and load sharing.
• Sources registered with one RP are made known to other RPs using MSDP.
• When an RP goes down, sources and receivers are taken to a new RP via (fast converging) unicast routing.

FIGURE 6.27 Anycast-RP.

group-to-RP mapping requirement has several network design and operational implications and challenges, which include the following:

- **The need to understand multicast traffic distribution and concentration, which in turn affects optimal RP placement**: Given the varying user
  types and requirements, traffic mix, and dynamics, it is almost impossible
  for the network operator to fully capture the multicast traffic distribution
  and concentration. The dynamic nature of multicast group membership,
  means the network operators may not have a priori knowledge of the topological distribution of the group members. This makes optimal single RP
  placement in the PIM-SM domain a very difficult task.
- **Does not provide scalable PIM Register message decapsulation from
  multicast source (when using the shared tree)**: The original PIM-SM
  standard [RFC7761] was not defined to support multiple active RPs per
  multicast group. This makes it difficult to scale the RP processing capacity
  per group (or shared tree) using multiple RPs as sources and group members
  increase.
- **Leads to slow network convergence when an active RP fails**: The original PIM-SM standard does not define capabilities for failover to backup RPs
  (which slows network convergence time). It also does not allow the sharing
  of PIM Register message decapsulation load among multiple active RPs per
  group in a domain. Furthermore, even if multiple RPs are configured with
  some serving as backup, it can take considerable convergence time to switch
  to the backup RPs.
- **Possibility of sub-optimal forwarding of multicast packets due to
  sub-optimal/improper placement of the single RP**: When a single RP
  is assigned to a given multicast group, all PIM Join messages to that group
  will be sent to that RP regardless of the topological distance between the
  message originators and the RP. A node sends initial data to that RP until
  the configured SPT switchover threshold is reached, or the node will always
  send data to the RP if the network is configured to always use the shared
  tree rooted at the RP. This situation holds even if all the multicast sources
  and receivers served by a given RP are located in a single region, and the
  RP is topologically distant from them. Note that a network operator may not
  always have a priori knowledge of the topological placement of the multicast sources and receivers. For example, if all the sources and receivers of a
  given multicast group are located in the USA, and they are being served by
  an in Europe, multicast traffic will have to traverse a long transit network
  twice, once to reach the RP, and back from the shared tree rooted at the RP
  again, creating inefficient use of network resources.
- **Multicast sources and receivers may have to depend on a distant RP**:
  Using a single active RP per multicast group may result in local multicast
  traffic sources and receivers becoming dependent on an RP that is topologically distant from them.

These observations about using a single active RP per group in a PIM-SM network
have been seen in large-scale multicast deployments. As a result, network operators

have understood that a mechanism that allows multiple active RPs per multicast group to be configured in a single PIM-SM domain is needed. Further, such a mechanism should also address the network design and operational issues highlighted earlier.

The Anycast-RP mechanism was developed to address the need for better RP failover times (consequently, network convergence time), and sharing of the PIM Register message decapsulation load among two or more RPs in a PIM-SM domain. This mechanism is primarily intended for applications in networks using MSDP, MBGP, and PIM-SM for native multicast services, although it is not limited to these protocols. Particularly, any PIM-SM network that also supports MSDP can use the Anycast-RP mechanism.

Note that MSDP is designed to allow the various RPs in the PIM-SM domain to maintain a consistent view of active multicast traffic sources. It should be noted, however, that a PIM-SM domain that deploys the Anycast-RP mechanism is not required to run MBGP. *A key requirement of the Anycast-RP mechanism is that the single Anycast IP address used by the multiple RPs MUST NOT be used as the RP Address in MSDP Source-Active messages sent by the RPs.*

6.13.2 THE ANYCAST-RP MECHANISM

Enterprises and service providers commonly deploy this mechanism within a multicast domain that has two or more RPs within the domain. The multiple RPs are assigned the same IP address (i.e., an Anycast address) which is typically configured on a loopback interface on each RP (i.e., a loopback IP address). The RPs are configured to form MSDP peers with each other using their individual loopback addresses and to form a fully meshed MSDP mesh-group. The RPs are configured as a fully mesh-group to keep all the RPs in sync regarding the active multicast sources in the domain. Typically, the loopback address used for MSDP peering is also the IP address used for the MBGP peering. MSDP is configured between all the RPs in the Anycast-RP set, ensuring that all of the RPs share information about active multicast sources in the domain.

All routers within the multicast domain learn the Anycast-RP address through mechanisms such as static RP assignment, BSR, or Auto-RP (see Chapter 5). The PIM-SM routers in the domain are configured to register multicast source (statically or dynamically) with the closest Anycast-RP member using the same Anycast-RP address. Since all the RPs in the Anycast-RP set have the same Anycast address, an IGP such as OSPF routes the PIM Register messages from source-side DRs to the RP with the best route. By distributing the RPs evenly throughout the multicast domain, their processing loads will be distributed. If the RP with the best route to a DR becomes unavailable, the IGP of the multicast domain changes the route to the closest operating RP that has the same Anycast-RP address.

Each Designated Router (DR) in the multicast domain will send PIM Register messages and multicast group joins (i.e., IGMP Membership Report messages) to the Anycast-RP address. Multicast routers then use unicast routing to direct the PIM Register messages and joins to the nearest Anycast-RP. In the event a particular Anycast-RP fails, the domain uses unicast routing to direct subsequent PIM Register messages and joins to the next nearest Anycast-RP. The nearest RP will then forward an MSDP update to all MSDP peers that make up the Anycast MSDP mesh-group.

6.13.3 WORKINGS OF THE ANYCAST-RP MECHANISM

The Anycast-RP mechanism allows a network operator to configure multiple RPs per multicast group, and distribute the RPs in a PIM-SM domain, allowing topologically closeness to the multicast sources and receivers. Figure 6.28 describes in detail the inner workings of the Anycast-RP mechanism.

The steps for configuring an Anycast-RP mechanism in a PIM-SM domain are as follows:

1. **Create the set of multicast group-to-Anycast-RP address mappings:**
   As the first step, the network operator creates the set of multicast group-to-Anycast-RP address mappings to be used in the PIM-SM domain. Each member RP of the Anycast-RP set must be configured with the same set of group-to-Anycast-RP address mappings. This mapping is used by the non-RP routers in the PIM-SM domain.

2. **Configure each RP that is to be a member of the Anycast-RP for the multicast address group range with an Anycast IP address:**
   In this step, the operator configures each member RP for the multicast address group range with the same Anycast IP address. If a dynamic mechanism is used to advertise multicast group-to-RP mappings (e.g., BSR or Auto-RP mechanism), the single Anycast IP address should be used for the RP address.

   Each member RP is configured with the same Anycast IP address using a numbered 32-bit interface address on the RP (typically, using a logical interface address). Member RPs then advertise multicast group-to-RP mappings using this unicast 32-bit interface address (which functions as the Anycast address). This causes multicast group members (receivers to send PIM Join messages and source to send PIM Register messages) toward the topologically closest RP.

   The member RPs implement MSDP peering with each other using an IP address that is unique to each RP (not the Anycast address). Since an Anycast address is not a unique address (and is shared by multiple nodes in the network), a router MUST NOT use the Anycast address as its Router ID, because doing so can prevent adjacencies and/or peerings from being established.

3. **Configure MSDP peerings between each of the Anycast-RPs in the set:**
   Unlike the multicast group-to-RP mapping advertisements which use the single Anycast IP address, MSDP peerings between the members of the Anycast-RP set must use a unique unicast IP address for each endpoint (rather than the Anycast address). These unique unicast IP addresses can be chosen similarly to addressing of BGP peerings, for example, the use of loopback addresses for iBGP peering, or the of physical interface IP addresses for eBGP peering. It should be noted that the member RPs MUST NOT use the Anycast IP address as the RP address in MSDP Source-Active messages (as this would cause the peer-RPF check to fail).

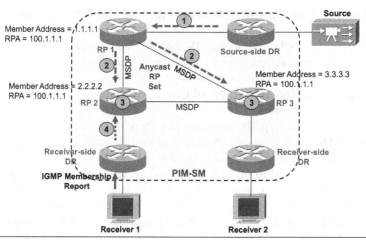

FIGURE 6.28   Anycast-RP through MSDP (MSDP Anycast-RP).

- Multiple RPs with the same IP address are configured for one multicast group and MSDP peering relationships is configured between the RPs.
- MSDP is used between all of the Anycast RP members in a mesh configuration to ensure that multicast source state information is distributed to all Anycast RP members in the PIM domain (i.e., to allow all RPs to be in sync regarding the active sources).
- PIM-SM routers are configured to register (statically or dynamically) with the Anycast RP set using the specified Anycast RP address (100.1.1.1).
- Because the Anycast RP set has one specific anycast address, an Interior Gateway Protocol (IGP) such as OSPF is used to route packets from any PIM-SM router to an Anycast RP member with the best route.
- In the figure, a multicast source within a PIM-SM domain sends multicast traffic to multicast group G, and the receivers joins the multicast group.

Processing steps:

1. RP 1 receives a unicast PIM Register message from the source-side DR connected to the multicast traffic source that is destined to the Anycast RP address (RPA).
   - A PIM source-side DR will register the source with the closest RP while the receiver-side of a receiver joins the closest RP to build an optimal RP tree (RPT).
2. Because the PIM Register message is not from another Anycast RP member (RP 2 or RP 3), RP 1 considers the Register message to be from the source-side DR.
   - RP 1 receives PIM Registration message and creates an (S, G) state entry in its MRT.
   - RP 1 learns of the source and starts to periodically send Source-Active messages containing the source IP address, the multicast group address, and the IP address of the originating RP (i.e., RP 1) to its MSDP peers (i.e., RP2 and RP 3).
3. RP 2 and RP 3 receive the Source-Active message and find out that the source IP address of the message is an Anycast RP member address.
   - The Anycast RPs share the registered multicast source information through the exchange of Source-Active messages.
   - After obtaining the multicast source information from RP 1, RP 2, and RP, each send PIM (S, G) Join messages toward the source to create an SPT.
4. After receiving a IGMP Membership Report message from Receiver 1, the receiver-side DR sends a PIM (*, G) Join message toward the closest RP (RP 2). An RPT rooted at RP 2 is then established.
   - When the multicast traffic reaches RP 2 along the SPT, this RP forwards the traffic along the RPT to Receiver 1.
   - After receiving the multicast traffic, the receiver-side DR determines whether to initiate an RPT-to-SPT switchover process based on its configuration.

4. **Configure the non-RP routers with the multicast group-to-Anycast-RP-address mappings:**

    Each non-RP router in the PIM-SM domain must learn the set of multicast group-to-RP mappings, which can be done through static configuration, BSR, or Auto-RP mechanism.

5. **Ensure that the Anycast IP address is reachable by all routers in the PIM-SM domain:**

    As the final step, the network operator must ensure that all routers in the PIM-SM domain can reach the Anycast IP address. Typically, this is accomplished by causing each member RP of the Anycast-RP set to use the domain's IGP to inject the /32 Anycast IP address into the domain. All the downstream routers in the PIM-SM domain must be configured to "know" that the Anycast address (which is bound to the loopback interface of an RP in the RP Set) is the IP address of their local RP. The IGP will automatically route and select the topologically closest RP for each source and receiver.

Each MSDP peer in the PIM-SM domain will receive and forward Source-Active messages away from the RP address using peer-RPF flooding. The MSDP peers examine their BGP routing tables to determine which MSDP peer is the next-hop toward the RP originating the Source-Active message. It should be noted that using MSDP in this way, forces the nodes along the path from the message receiver to the source to create a PIM (S, G) state. Some nodes may not contain the (S, G) state if a single RP was used in the domain and receivers were forced to stay on the shared tree.

6.13.4 BENEFITS OF DEPLOYING ANYCAST-RPs

The benefits of Anycast-RP are as follows:

- **Optimal RP path**: A multicast source registers with the closest RP so that it can build an SPT with the optimal path to the source-side DR. A receiver joins the closest RP so that an RPT with the optimal path can be built to the receiver-side DR.
- **Load balancing between RPs**: Each RP just needs to maintain a subset of the overall source/group information within the PIM-SM domain, and is responsible for forwarding only a part of the overall multicast data requested by receivers, thus, providing load balancing between different RPs.
- **Redundancy backup between RPs**: When an RP in the Anycast-RP Set fails, the multicast sources that previously registered with it, or the receivers that previously joined it, can register with or join any other available closest RP in the Anycast-RP Set, thus providing redundancy and backup between RPs.

6.14   FILTERING SOURCE-ACTIVE MESSAGES

As the number of PIM (S, G) state information increases in internetworks such as the Internet, it becomes beneficial for RPs to filter which multicast sources they describe in Source-Active messages. A network operator may implement filtering as part of network policy and also as a way to reduce (S, G) state information in multicast routers. Generally, MSDP peers in transit domains do not filter Source-Active messages because doing so will prevent the flood-and-join multicast model from guaranteeing the learning of multicast sources throughout the Internet (i.e., Source-Active message filtering by transit domains may prevent multicast receivers from connecting to active sources).

In general, network operators express policies using MBGP [RFC4760]. Allowing transit domains to pass Source-Active messages unfiltered causes MSDP messages to flow in the desired direction and the peer-RPF mechanism to fail when the messages flow in the wrong direction. An exception is when an administrative scope boundary is used [RFC2365]. Particularly, MSDP peers must not send Source-Active messages for a PIM (S, G) state to peers that are on the other side of an administrative scope boundary for a multicast group G.

Generally, it is beneficial to filter the process of originating Source-Active messages to ensure that only intended local multicast sources can originate such messages. In addition, the network operator may configure MSDP speakers to filter which Source-Active messages can be received and forwarded.

Typically, a PIM-SM domain contains a significant amount of (S, G) state that is local to the domain. However, in the absence of proper filtering, Source-Active messages carrying these local (S, G) announcements may be advertised beyond the multicast domain to the global MSDP infrastructure. One example is when domain-local applications use global IP multicast addresses and multicast sources use private IP source addresses as described in [RFC1918]. To avoid making domain-local (S, G) information globally visible and to improve the scalability of MSDP, the network operator may beneficially implement an external Source-Active message filter list to prevent the unnecessary creation, forwarding, and caching of (S, G) state of domain-local multicast sources.

By implementing proper filtering on the origination, receipt, and forwarding of Source-Active messages, the multicast network can significantly reduce the possibility of unexpected and unintended growth in the MSDP state. However, the network operator can configure a Source-Active-cache state limit as a final safeguard against MSDP state spikes. Desirably, the network operator may also configure a rate limiter for the creation of new Source-Active state entries when an MSDP peering has reached a stable state (i.e., when any two MSDP peers have established the peering and the initial Source-Active state has been transferred).

To mitigate multicast state explosion in routers during malicious attacks such as denial of service attacks, network operators use Source-Active message filters and rate limits to limit the sources and multicast groups that will be exchanged between RPs. The operator may configure filtering and limiting functions such as access lists of source or multicast group addresses, that are not allowed to be propagated to other domains using MSDP. The operator may also limit the absolute maximum acceptable number of Source-Active state entries, or impose a rate limit on the creation of new Source-Active state entries after the connection has been established.

6.14.1 SOURCE-ACTIVE MESSAGE ORIGINATION FILTERS

By default, an RP that runs MSDP will originate Source-Active messages for all local multicast sources that have registered with it (via PIM Register messages sent by their source-side DRs). An RP will (by default) advertise all local sources that have registered with it in Source-Active messages, which in some cases is not desirable to the network operator. For example, if multicast sources inside a PIM-SM domain use private IP addresses (for example, network 10.0.0.0/8) as their source IP addresses, it is desirable for the network operator to configure a Source-Active origination filter to restrict those private IP addresses from being advertised to other MSDP peers in the Internet.

To control which multicast sources are advertised in Source-Active messages, the network operator may configure Source-Active message origination filters on an RP. Using Source-Active message origination filters, the sources advertised in Source-Active messages can be controlled as follows [CISCMSDP2016]:

- The operator can configure an RP to prevent it from advertising local multicast sources in Source-Active messages. The RP will still forward Source-Active messages received from other MSDP peers in the normal manner, just that, it will not originate any Source-Active messages for those local sources.
- The operator can configure an RP to only originate Source-Active messages for local multicast sources sending traffic to specific multicast groups that match (S, G) pairs defined in the Extended Access List (see [AWEYFDVR21]). The RP will not advertise all other local sources in Source-Active messages.
- The operator can configure an RP to only originate Source-Active messages for local multicast sources sending traffic to specific multicast groups that match BGP autonomous system paths defined in a BGP AS-Path Access List (see [AWEYLSPV21]). The RP will not advertise all other local sources in Source-Active messages.
- The operator can configure an RP to only originate Source-Active messages for local multicast sources that match the criteria defined in a Route Map (see [AWEYFDVR21]). The RP will not advertise all other local sources in Source-Active messages.
- The operator can configure on an RP, a Source-Active message origination filter that includes an Extended Access List, BGP AS-Path Access List, Route Map, or a combination of these. An RP that is configured with such an origination filter, will advertise any local sources in Source-Active messages only when all conditions are true.

6.14.2   USING OUTGOING FILTER LISTS IN MSDP

An MSDP peer (by default) would forward all Source-Active messages it receives to all of its MSDP peers. However, a network operator may create outgoing filter lists to prevent Source-Active messages from being forwarded to MSDP peers. As discussed in [CISCMSDP2016], outgoing filter lists apply to all outgoing Source-Active messages, whether originated locally by the RP or received from other MSDP peers. However, Source-Active message origination filters apply only to Source-Active messages locally originated by the RP.

Using an outgoing filter list, the network operator can control the Source-Active messages that an RP can forward to an MSDP peer as follows [CISCMSDP2016]:

- The operator can filter all outgoing Source-Active messages an RP forwards to a specified MSDP peer, by configuring it to completely stop forwarding its Source-Active messages to that MSDP peer.
- The operator can filter a subset of the outgoing Source-Active messages an RP forwards to a particular MSDP peer based on (S, G) pairs defined in an Extended Access List. This is done by configuring the RP to only forward Source-Active messages to the MSDP peer that match the (S, G) pairs permitted in the Extended Access List. The RP will stop forwarding all other Source-Active messages to the MSDP peer.
- The operator can filter a subset of outgoing Source-Active messages an RP forwards to a particular MSDP peer based on match criteria defined in a Route Map. The operator can do this by configuring the RP to only forward Source-Active messages that match the criteria defined in the Route Map. The RP will stop forwarding all other Source-Active messages to the MSDP peer.
- The operator can filter a subset of outgoing Source-Active messages an RP has received from a particular MSDP peer based on the advertising RP address contained in the Source-Active message. This is done by configuring the RP to filter outgoing Source-Active messages based on the originating RP, even after a Source-Active message has been transmitted across one or more MSDP peers. The RP will stop forwarding all other Source-Active messages to the MSDP peer.
- The operator can configure an outgoing filter list on an RP for limiting Source-Active messages that include an Extended Access List, Route Map, and either an RP Access List (for limiting messages to certain RPs) or an RP Route Map. An RP configured as such will forward an outgoing Source-Active message when all conditions are true.

The network operator must be careful not to arbitrarily filter Source-Active messages since that can result in downstream MSDP peers being starved of Source-Active messages for legitimate active multicast sources. Normally, the operator will use outgoing filter lists only to reject undesirable multicast sources, such as sources using source addresses that are private IP addresses.

6.14.3 USING INCOMING FILTER LISTS IN MSDP

An MSDP peer (by default) will receive all Source-Active messages sent from its MSDP peers. However, the network operator may create incoming filter lists to control the source information that an RP receives from its MSDP peers.

Using incoming filter lists, the operator can control the incoming Source-Active messages that an RP receives from its MSDP peers as follows [CISCMSDP2016]:

- The operator can filter all Source-Active messages arriving at an RP from a particular MSDP peer by configuring the RP to ignore all Source-Active messages sent from that MSDP peer.
- The operator can filter a subset of incoming Source-Active messages from a particular MSDP peer based on (S, G) pairs defined in an Extended Access List. The operator does this by configuring the RP to only receive Source-Active messages from the MSDP peer that match the (S, G) pairs defined in the Extended Access List. The RP will ignore all other incoming Source-Active messages from that MSDP peer.
- The operator can filter a subset of Source-Active Request messages arriving from a particular MSDP peer based on match criteria defined in a Route Map. This can be done by configuring the RP to only receive Source-Active messages that match the criteria defined in the Route Map. The RP will ignore all other incoming Source-Active messages from that MSDP peer.
- The operator can filter a subset of Source-Active messages arriving from a particular MSDP peer based on both (S, G) pairs defined in an Extended Access List and on match criteria defined in a Route Map. The operator does this by configuring the RP to only receive Source-Active messages that both match the (S, G) pairs defined in the Extended Access List and match the criteria defined in the Route Map. The RP will ignore all other incoming Source-Active messages from that MSDP peer.
- The operator can filter a subset of Source-Active messages arriving from a particular MSDP peer based on the advertising RP address contained in the Source-Active message. This is done by configuring the RP to filter arriving SA messages based on their originating MSDP peer, even after the Source-Active message may have already been transmitted across one or more MSDP peers.
- The operator can configure an incoming filter list on an RP that includes an Extended Access List, Route Map, and either an RP Access List (for limiting messages from certain RPs) or an RP Route Map. An RP configured as such will receive an incoming Source-Active message only when all conditions are true.

Note also that, care must be exercised not to arbitrarily filter Source-Active messages since this can result in downstream MSDP peers being starved of Source-Active messages for legitimate active multicast sources. Normally, the operator will use incoming filter lists only to reject undesirable multicast sources, such as sources whose source addresses are private IP addresses.

6.14.4 USING SOURCE-ACTIVE REQUEST MESSAGES

A network operator may configure a noncaching MSDP peer to send *Source-Active Request messages* to one or more specified MSDP peers [CISCMSDP2016]. If a non-caching RP MSDP peer is connected to an MSDP peer that is caching Source-Active messages, the operator can reduce host join latencies for the noncaching MSDP peer by enabling it to send Source-Active Request messages to a caching MSDP peer. When a host sends a request to join a particular multicast group, the noncaching RP will send a Source-Active Request message to its caching MSDP peers.

If the caching MSDP peer has source information for the requested multicast group, it will send that information to the requesting RP in a *Source-Active Response message*. The requesting RP uses the information contained in the Source-Active Response message but does not forward that message to any other MSDP peers. If a noncaching RP receives a Source-Active Request message, it will send an error message back to the requestor. Most MSDP implementations support caching of MSDP Source-Active messages.

6.14.5 SOURCE-ACTIVE REQUEST MESSAGE FILTERS

An MSDP peer (by default) honors all Source-Active Request messages received from its MSDP peers. The receiving peer sends cached source information to the requesting MSDP peers in Source-Active Response messages. However, a network operator may create a Source-Active Request filter on an MSDP peer to control the arrival and reception of Source-Active Request messages that it will honor from specified MSDP peers.

An MSDP peer with a Source-Active Request filter controls the incoming Source-Active Request messages it will honor from MSDP peers as follows [CISCMSDP2016]:

- The operator can filter all Source-Active Request messages arriving at an MSDP peer from a particular MSDP peer by configuring the peer to ignore all Source-Active Request messages from that MSDP peer.
- The operator can filter a subset of Source-Active Request messages from a particular MSDP peer based on the multicast groups defined in a Standard Access List. This is done by configuring the MSDP peer to honor only Source-Active Request messages that match the multicast groups defined in a Standard Access List. The receiving MSDP peer will ignore Source-Active Request messages from that particular peer for other multicast groups.

6.15 MSDP MD5 PASSWORD AUTHENTICATION

An MSDP session can use authentication mechanisms to protect itself against the injection of spoofed TCP segments into the MSDP connection [CISCMSDP2016]. An MSDP implementation may use the TCP MD5 Signature Option [RFC2385] as an authentication mechanism. The Message Digest 5 (MD5) Signature Option may be used to protect a TCP connection between two MSDP peers. Using this feature protects against the threat of spoofed TCP segments being introduced into the MSDP TCP connection. The TCP MD5 Signature Option is described in detail in [AWEYLSPV21] for BGP but equally applies to MSDP.

When MSDP MD5 password authentication is used, each TCP segment sent on the TCP connection between MSDP peers is verified. Both MSDP peers of the TCP session must be configured with the same secret key or password. Each peer verifies the MD5 digest of every TCP segment sent on the MSDP TCP connection before accepting it (see detail in [AWEYLSPV21]).

REVIEW QUESTIONS

1. Explain what MSDP is used for and why it cannot be used with PIM-DM.
2. What is the purpose of the MSDP Source-Active message?
3. What is the purpose of the MSDP Source-Request message?
4. What is the purpose of the MSDP Source-Response message?
5. What is the purpose of the MSDP KeepAlive message?
6. What is the purpose of the MSDP peer-RPF checks?
7. What is peer-RPF flooding of Source-Active messages?
8. What is a static RPF peer?
9. Explain briefly what a default MSDP peer is.
10. What is an MSDP mesh-group and what are its benefits?
11. What is the purpose of an MSDP Source-Active Cache? Include how this cache is used.
12. What is a Multicast Internet Exchange (MIX)?
13. What is an Anycast-RP through MSDP (or MSDP Anycast-RP)? What are its benefits?
14. Give two examples of why a network operator may want to filter Source-Active messages.

REFERENCES

[AWEYFDVR21]. James Aweya, *IP Routing Protocols: Fundamentals and Distance-Vector Routing Protocols*, CRC Press, Taylor & Francis Group, ISBN 9780367710415, May 2021.

[AWEYLSPV21]. James Aweya, *IP Routing Protocols: Link-State and Path-Vector Routing Protocols*, CRC Press, Taylor & Francis Group, ISBN 9780367710361, May 2021.

[CISCMSDP2016]. Cisco System, IP Multicast: PIM Configuration Guide, Chapter: Using MSDP to Interconnect Multiple PIM-SM Domains, March 17, 2016.

[H3CMULTGUID]. H3C, *IP Multicast Configuration Guide, Chapter 8, MSDP Configuration*, H3C SR8800 Documentation Set.

[RFC1918]. Y. Rekhter, B. Moskowitz, D. Karrenberg, G. J. de Groot, and E. Lear, "Address Allocation for Private Internets", *IETF RFC 1918*, February 1996.

[RFC2365]. D. Meyer, "Administratively Scoped IP Multicast", *IETF RFC 2365*, July 1998.

[RFC2385]. A. Heffernan, "Protection of BGP Sessions via the TCP MD5 Signature Option", *IETF RFC 2385*, August 1998.

[RFC3446]. D. Kim, D. Meyer, H. Kilmer, and D. Farinacci, "Anycast Rendevous Point (RP) mechanism using Protocol Independent Multicast (PIM) and Multicast Source Discovery Protocol (MSDP)", *IETF RFC 3446*, January 2003.

[RFC3618]. B. Fenner, and D. Meyer (Eds.), "Multicast Source Discovery Protocol (MSDP)", *IETF RFC 3618*, October 2003.

[RFC4271]. Y. Rekhter, T. Li, and S. Hares (Eds.), "A Border Gateway Protocol 4 (BGP-4)", *IETF RFC 4271*, January 2006.

[RFC4610]. D. Farinacci and Y. Cai, "Anycast-RP Using Protocol Independent Multicast (PIM)", *IETF RFC 4610*, August 2006.

[RFC4611]. M. McBride, J. Meylor, and D. Meyer, "Multicast Source Discovery Protocol (MSDP) Deployment Scenarios", *IETF RFC 4611*, August 2006.

[RFC4760]. T. Bates, R. Chandra, D. Katz, and Y. Rekhter, "Multiprotocol Extensions for BGP-4", *IETF RFC 4760*, January 2007.

[RFC7761]. B. Fenner, M. Handley, H. Holbrook, I. Kouvelas, R. Parekh, Z. Zhang, and L. Zheng, "Protocol Independent Multicast - Sparse Mode (PIM-SM): Protocol Specification (Revised)", *IETF RFC 7761*, March 2016.

[SRPart1CFILS]. Clarence Filsfils, Kris Michielsen, and Ketan Talaulikar, *Segment Routing Part I*, January 17, 2017.

[SRPart2CFILS]. Clarence Filsfils, Kris Michielsen, Francois Clad, and Daniel Voyer, *Segment Routing Part II: Traffic Engineering*, May 17, 2019.

7 Bidirectional PIM (BIDIR-PIM)

7.1 INTRODUCTION

This chapter describes a variant of PIM-SM [RFC7761] called Bidirectional PIM (BIDIR-PIM) [RFC5015], which constructs bidirectional shared distribution trees connecting multicast traffic sources and receivers. Using a Designated Forwarder (DF) election mechanism operating on each link of the multicast network, BIDIR-PIM builds bidirectional trees that connect the sources and receivers. Many-to-many communication, such as multi-side, multi-participant video conferencing, may involve multiple parties interested in information from multiple multicast sources simultaneously. Those parties may also be interested in sending information to other parties at the same time. BIDIR-PIM was developed to address this kind of many-to-many communication problem.

In a PIM-DM or PIM-SM domain, each router along the source-rooted tree (SRT), also known as the shortest-path tree (SPT), must create source-specific state, i.e., an (S, G) entry for each multicast source, leading to significant consumption of system resources. Reference [CISCPRWILL03] details how maintaining (S, G) state instead of (*, G) state results in relatively higher router memory requirements. BIDIR-PIM is derived from PIM-SM, but unlike PIM-SM, it builds and maintains bidirectional shared trees (or RPTs), each rooted at an RP Address (associated with an RP Link in the BIDIR-PIM domain) and connecting multiple multicast sources with multiple receivers. Multicast sources send traffic forwarded through the RP Address to receivers along the bidirectional RPT. Each BIDIR-PIM router does not maintain any source-specific (S, G) state but only a (*, G) multicast routing entry, providing significant savings in system resources compared to PIM-SM and PIM-DM.

The elected DFs on the network links offer a mechanism for natively forwarding multicast packets from sources to the RP Address of the network. Subsequently, the packets follow the shared distribution tree to receivers without necessitating PIM routers along the multicast paths to maintain source-specific state (i.e., (S, G) state). The DFs are elected during RP Address discovery, and the collectively elected DFs on the links establish multicast traffic paths to the RP Address, thereby eliminating the need for data-driven protocol events observed in PIM-SM.

7.2 BIDIR-PIM PROTOCOL OVERVIEW

As discussed in Chapter 5, PIM-SM constructs unidirectional shared distribution trees enabling the forwarding of multicast traffic from a data source to receivers of a particular multicast group. Unlike PIM-SM, which permits the creation of source-routed trees (i.e., source-specific trees), BIDIR-PIM does not support this

DOI: 10.1201/9781032701967-7

capability and only facilitates bidirectional trees. In BIDIR-PIM, the RP Address acts as the root of the bidirectional shared tree for each multicast group, and distinct multicast groups can utilize separate RP Addresses within a PIM domain.

PIM-SM [RFC7761], which employs unidirectional shared trees, supports two methods for distributing multicast packets on the shared tree. These methods differ in the way multicast packets sent by a source are forwarded to the RP:

- Initially, when a multicast source begins transmitting packets to a multicast group, its First-Hop Router (FHR), also known as the source-side Designated Router (DR), encapsulates multicast data packets in special control messages called Register messages and sends these messages via unicast transmission toward the RP. The RP receives the PIM Register messages, decapsulates them to obtain the original multicast packets, and then distributes them on the shared tree to the receivers of the group.
- A transition from the shared multicast distribution mode using PIM Register messages is made at a later stage. PIM-SM achieves this by establishing source-specific state on all PIM routers along the multicast traffic path between the source and the RP. PIM-SM uses this source-specific state to natively forward multicast packets from that source to the receivers of the multicast group.

These two mechanisms have some significant drawbacks for multicast traffic forwarding. Encapsulating multicast packets from a source in PIM Register messages results in significant processing delays and bandwidth overhead. Also, forwarding multicast packets from a source using the source-specific state (in the PIM-SM routers) creates additional protocol and memory requirements, as explained in [CISCPRWILL03].

BIDIR-PIM eliminates both multicast packet encapsulation in PIM Register messages and source-specific state by allowing multicast packets to be natively forwarded from a source to the RP using only shared tree state, that is, (*, G) state (see Figure 7.1). Unlike PIM-SM, this mode of forwarding multicast packets from a source to a multicast group does not require any data-driven protocol events. BIDIR- PIM scales well because it does not maintain any source-specific (S, G) state. BIDIR-PIM is most suitable for multicast networks with dense dispersed sources and dense dispersed receivers.

7.3   TERMINOLOGY AND BIDIR-PIM PROTOCOL STATE

This section discusses the terminology related to BIDIR-PIM and the protocol state maintained by BIDIR-PIM routers.

7.3.1   TERMINOLOGY

We define the following terms, which should be considered in addition to those defined in Chapters 4 and 5. These terms have special significance for understanding the roles of routers participating in BIDIR-PIM:

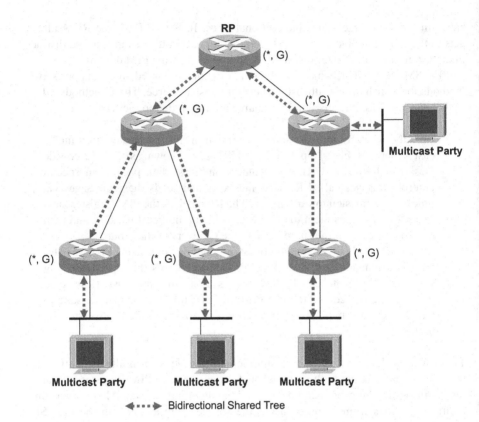

FIGURE 7.1 Bidirectional shared tree example.

- **Multicast Routing Information Base (MRIB)**: This database contains multicast topology information, typically derived from the existing unicast routing table (e.g., constructed by OSPF, IS-IS), or a routing protocol such as Multiprotocol BGP (MBGP) [RFC4760] that is capable of carrying multicast-specific topology information.
  - PIM routers use the MRIB for establishing the Reverse Path Forwarding (RPF) interface toward the multicast traffic source (actual source or RP). This applies to all PIM protocol types: PIM-DM [RFC3973], PIM-SM [RFC7761], and BIDIR-PIM [RFC5015].
  - PIM-SM routers use the MRIB to decide where to forward PIM Join/Prune messages.
  - BIDIR-PIM routers use the MRIB as the database for obtaining the routing metrics used in the DF election process.
- **Rendezvous Point Address (RPA)**: BIDIR-PIM uses the RPA as the root of the bidirectional multicast distribution tree for a range of multicast groups. The RPA is an address that must be routable from all BIDIR-PIM routers in the PIM domain. The RPA does not have to be the IP address of a physical interface on a real router in the domain, unlike PIM-SM, which requires an actual router

in the PIM domain to be configured as the RP. When receivers send IGMP Membership Report messages [RFC2236] [RFC3376] requesting to join a multicast group, BIDIR-PIM routers send Join messages that propagate hop by hop toward the RPA.

- **Rendezvous Point Link (RPL)**: The RPL for a particular RPA is the physical network link in the BIDIR-PIM domain to which the RPA belongs. In BIDIR-PIM, all multicast packets sent to multicast groups that map to a specific RPA are forwarded toward the RPL of that RPA. A distinguishing feature of BIDIR-PIM is that the RPL is the only link in the BIDIR-PIM domain on which a DF election does not take place.

- **Upstream**: This means toward the root (RPA) of the BIDIR-PIM multicast distribution tree. This is the direction multicast packets from sources would travel toward the RPL.

- **Downstream**: This means away from the root of the BIDIR-PIM multicast distribution tree. This is the direction multicast packets coming from the RPL to receivers would travel.

- **Designated Forwarder (DF)**: The concept of a DF is at the core of BIDIR-PIM. A single DF is elected on every link for each RPA in a BIDIR-PIM domain (this includes both multiaccess network segments such as those based on Ethernet and point-to-point links). The only exception is that no DF exists on the RPL. *The router on a link with the best route to the RPA (as determined by metrics in the MRIB) becomes the DF of the link.* The DF for a given RPA is responsible for forwarding downstream heading multicast packets (i.e., from the RPL) onto its link and forwarding upstream heading multicast packets from its link toward the RPL. The DF performs these tasks for all the bidirectional multicast groups that map to the given RPA. The DF on a link is also responsible for receiving PIM Join messages from downstream BIDIR-PIM routers on the link and propagating them toward the RPA, as well as ensuring that multicast packets sent to a group are forwarded to local receivers (discovered through IGMP Membership Report messages [RFC2236] [RFC3376]).

- **RPF Interface**: This is the router interface that has the best route to a particular IP address (as indicated in the MRIB). If multiple least-cost paths exist to that IP address, then the interface with the highest IP address is usually used as the RPF interface. A BIDIR-PIM router uses the MRIB to determine the RPF interface of the RPA for a multicast group. The RPF interface is the interface that the router would use to send multicast packets toward the RPL for a given multicast group. The router recomputes the RPF interface to the IP address periodically to account for network topology changes that may cause it to change. Periodic recomputation of the RPF interface also allows the multicast routing to converge faster after a network topology change.

- **RPF Neighbor**: This is the PIM neighbor of a router that holds the best route to a particular IP address (as indicated in the MRIB). In BIDIR-PIM, the RPF neighbor for a multicast group is not necessarily the router on the RPF interface that the local router would use to send PIM Join messages for that multicast group; the router sends PIM Join messages to the DF on the RPF interface for the multicast group.

- **Tree Information Base (TIB)**: This database holds the collection of proto-col state at a PIM router. A BIDIR-PIM router creates this database when it receives PIM Join/Prune messages, PIM DF Election messages, and IGMP information from local hosts. Essentially, the TIB stores the protocol state of all multicast distribution trees at the router.

A bidirectional (*, G) multicast distribution tree carries traffic both upstream from sources toward the RPA and downstream from the RPA to receivers. As a result, the strict RPF-based rules used in PIM-DM and PIM-SM do not apply to BIDIR-PIM. This is because BIDIR-PIM routers can accept multicast traffic on many potential incoming interfaces.

7.3.2   BIDIR-PIM PROTOCOL STATE

This section describes the protocol state that BIDIR-PIM routers should maintain for BIDIR-PIM to function correctly. This state is preserved in the TIB, as it holds the pro-tocol state of all the multicast distribution trees at a router. However, most PIM routers will use the state in the TIB to build a Multicast Forwarding Information Base (MFIB), also called a multicast forwarding table, which the router updates when the relevant state in the TIB changes. The protocol state described below is only an abstract state definition required to specify a BIDIR-PIM router's behavior. A BIDIR-PIM imple-mentation can maintain whatever internal state it requires, as long as it provides the same externally visible protocol behavior to other BIDIR-PIM routers.

The TIB state in a BIDIR-PIM router can be divided into two sections:

- **RPA state**: This state maintains information for the DF election process for each RPA.
- **Group state**: This state maintains a group-specific distribution tree for multicast groups that map to a given RPA.

The state that a BIDIR-PIM router should maintain is described below. Note that a BIDIR-PIM implementation only maintains a state when that state is relevant for multicast packet forwarding operations. For example, the "NoInfo" state may be assumed when the router lacks other state information, rather than being a state that is explicitly held.

7.3.2.1   General Purpose State

A BIDIR-PIM router maintains the following state that is not specific to an RPA or multicast group:

- **Neighbor State (for each neighbor):**
  - Neighbor's Generation ID (see Chapter 3)
  - Neighbor Liveness Timer
  - Other information taken from the neighbor's Hello messages

7.3.2.2 Rendezvous Point Address (RPA) State

A BIDIR-PIM router maintains multicast group-to-RPA mapping information, which is created through various means such as static configuration or an automatic RP discovery mechanism like the Bootstrap Router (BSR) mechanism [RFC5059] (see Chapter 5). The router maintains the following state for each RPA:

- **RPA**: This is the actual RPA used
- **Designated Forwarder (DF) State (for each router interface)**:
  - Acting DF information:
    - DF IP Address
    - DF-metric
  - Election information:
    - Election State
    - DF Election Timer (DFT)
    - Message Count (MC)
  - Current best offer:
    - IP address of best offering router
    - Best offering router metric

7.3.2.3 Multicast Group State

A BIDIR-PIM router maintains the following state for each multicast group G:

- **Group state (for each interface)**:
  - **Local Membership state**: One of the following is stored: {"NoInfo", "Include"}. The router creates the local membership state through the local multicast group membership mechanism (IGMP) running on the interface.
  - **PIM Join/Prune state**: The router creates a Join/Prune state when it receives PIM (*, G) Join/Prune messages on the interface. The router uses this for calculating the outgoing interface list (OIL) and for deciding whether it should send a Join (*, G) message upstream. The olist (G) (i.e., OIL for multicast group G) is the list of interfaces on which the router must forward packets to group G.
    - One of the following states is stored: {"NoInfo", "Join", "PrunePending"}
    - **Prune-Pending Timer**: See discussion below.
    - **Join/Prune Expiry Timer**: See discussion below.
  - **Non-interface-specific state:**
    - **Upstream Join/Prune Timer**: The router uses this timer to send out periodic Join (*, G) messages and to send Join (*, G) messages to override Prune (*, G) messages from peers on an upstream LAN interface.
    - **Last RPA Used**: The router stores the last RPA used because if the multicast group-to-RPA mapping changes, then it must tear down and rebuild the state for multicast groups associated with the changed RPA.

In our discussion, RPF_interface(RPA) represents the interface in the MRIB that has the best route for routing packets to the RPA. RPF_DF(RPA) represents the PIM neighbor to which PIM Join messages must be sent to build the bidirectional shared tree (for a multicast group) rooted at the RPL for a particular RPA. This PIM neighbor is the DF on the RPF_interface(RPA).

All BIDIR-PIM timers are countdown timers, where a timer is set to a value and count down to zero, triggering an action at that point. The timers can also be implemented as count-up timers, where the timer compares an absolute stored expiry time against a real-time clock. Typically, when a timer is started or restarted, it is set to the default value discussed below.

7.4   PIM NEIGHBOR DISCOVERY

PIM routers send Hello messages on their interfaces to discover neighboring PIM routers. The routers use the information contained in the received PIM Hello messages to update their Neighbor State. The neighbor discovery mechanism used by BIDIR-PIM is the same as that of PIM-SM and PIM-DM. Chapters 3–5 describe the procedures for generating and processing PIM Hello messages, as well as for maintaining Neighbor State.

BIDIR-PIM capable routers are required to include the Bidirectional Capable PIM Hello Option in all Hello messages they send (see Chapter 3). A BIDIR-PIM router uses the Bidirectional Capable Option to advertise its ability to participate in the BIDIR-PIM protocol. Chapter 3 describes the format of the Bidirectional Capable Option carried in PIM Hello messages. If a BIDIR-PIM router receives a Hello message from one of its neighbors that does not contain the Bidirectional Capable Option, it must log the error to the router administrator in a rate-limited manner.

7.5   RPA DISCOVERY

Routers in a BIDIR-PIM domain discover the range of multicast group addresses operating in bidirectional mode and the RPA serving the group range, using the same RP discovery methods used by PIM-SM (see the discussion in Chapter 5). In PIM-SM, an RP serving a multicast group must be configured with a real IP address. However, in BIDIR-PIM, a multicast group is associated with a virtual RP Address or RPA (which is associated with an RPL). The link corresponding to the IP subnet of the RPA is the RPL.

In BIDIR-PIM, an RPF interface is the interface that points to an RPA, and an RPF neighbor is the address of the next-hop to the RP.

BIDIR-PIM domain can use either static RP configuration or an automatic RP discovery mechanism, such as the PIM BSR mechanism [RFC5059] for RPA discovery. The BSR mechanism is designed to work with both PIM-SM and BIDIR-PIM. Both PIM-SM and BIDIR-PIM use the same algorithm for multicast group-to-RP mapping, as discussed in Chapter 5.

The network operator can configure routers in a BIDIR-PIM domain as Candidate-RPs (precisely "Candidate-RPAs"). The BSR receives Candidate-RP-Advertisement messages containing Candidate-RP information from the Candidate-RPs and organizes the information into an RP-Set, which is then flooded throughout the entire BIDIR-PIM domain. Subsequently, other routers in the BIDIR-PIM domain calculate mappings between specific group ranges and the corresponding RPAs based on the received RP-Set. Candidate-RPs periodically send Candidate-RP-Advertisement messages to the BSR, enabling it to learn the most recent RP-Set information from the received messages.

The BSR includes its own sending interface IP address together with the RP-Set information in its Bootstrap messages and then floods these messages to all routers in the BIDIR-PIM domain. Each Candidate-RP includes a timeout value (i.e., Hold Time) in its Candidate-RP-Advertisement messages. Upon receiving a Candidate-RP-Advertisement message, the BSR extracts this timeout value and starts a Candidate-RP timeout timer. If the BSR fails to receive a subsequent Candidate-RP-Advertisement message from the Candidate-RP within the timeout interval, it assumes the Candidate-RP to have expired or become unreachable.

Only one active BSR can exist in a BIDIR-PIM domain at any given time, but the domain can have at least one Candidate-BSR. The network operator can configure any router as a Candidate-BSR, and one of them is elected as the BSR to collect and advertise RPA information in the BIDIR-PIM domain. The BSR election process is similar to that for PIM-SM (as described in Chapter 5).

The BSR functions as the administrative interface of the BIDIR-PIM domain and sends the constructed RP-Set information in Bootstrap messages to all routers in the BIDIR-PIM domain. Each BSR has its specific service scope, and the border of a BIDIR-PIM admin-scope zone is also the boundary of Bootstrap messages. The network operator may partition a BIDIR-PIM domain into several smaller different admin-scope zones, and Bootstrap messages sent by a BSR in a scope zone cannot cross the border of the zone in either direction.

A unique BSR is elected from the Candidate-BSRs in each BIDIR-PIM domain or admin-scope zone. The Candidate-RPs in each admin-scope zone send Candidate-RP-Advertisement messages to their local BSR. The BSR organizes the content of these advertisement messages to form an RP-Set and advertises it to all routers in the admin-scope zone. All routers in a BIDIR-PIM domain or admin-scope zone use the same hash algorithm to generate the RP Address corresponding to specific multicast groups. Each admin-scope zone will have its own BSR, which serves a specific multicast group range, while the global scope zone also supports its own BSR, which serves all the rest of the multicast groups. Zone border routers (ZBRs) form the boundary of each admin-scope zone, and multicast protocol messages (such as PIM Assert messages and Bootstrap messages) that belong to the multicast address range of an admin-scope zone cannot cross the zone boundary.

The winner of the BSR election multicasts its IP address and RP-Set information through Bootstrap messages to all routers within the zone it serves. The BSR floods Bootstrap messages throughout the admin-scope at intervals of *BS_Period*. Any Candidate-BSR that receives a Bootstrap message retains the RP-Set information for a length of time equal to *BS_Timeout*, during which no BSR election takes place. If the BSR state times out and the Candidate-BSRs do not receive a Bootstrap message from the BSR, the Candidate-BSRs will initiate a new BSR election process among themselves.

Similar to PIM-SM, the BSR of a BIDIR-PIM network may perform "semantic fragmentation" of a Bootstrap message if its length exceeds the maximum IP packet length limit of the sending interface (see details in Chapter 5). In this case, because the RP-Set information contained in each semantic fragment is different, the loss of some IP packets will not result in the dropping of the entire Bootstrap message.

7.6   DATA PACKET FORWARDING RULES

The DF for multicast groups mapping to a given RPA on each link has the following unique responsibilities:

- The DF is the only BIDIR-PIM router responsible for forwarding multicast packets traveling downstream from the RPL onto the link.
- The DF is the sole BIDIR-PIM router responsible for forwarding multicast packets traveling upstream from the link toward the RPL.
- The DF is the exclusive BIDIR-PIM router that should receive all PIM Join requests from the routers on that link for forwarding toward the RPL.

BIDIR-PIM routers that are non-DF on a link and where the link also serves as their RPF interface toward the RPA are allowed to perform the following multicast packet forwarding actions for BIDIR-PIM multicast groups:

- They may forward multicast packets traveling away from the RPL onto the link toward downstream receivers.
- They may forward multicast packets traveling from downstream multicast sources onto the link toward the RPL (provided they are the elected DF for the downstream link from which the packets were received).

During multicast packet forwarding, the BIDIR-PIM router will first check to see whether it should accept the packet based on the TIB state and the interface on which the packet arrived. The router accepts the packet if it arrives on the RPF interface used to reach the RPA (i.e., the packet is traveling downstream from the RPL) or will accept the packet if it is the elected DF on the interface on which the packet arrived (i.e., the packet is traveling upstream toward the RPL). Routers forward multicast traffic naturally from the beginning; there is no need to tunnel multicast data to an RP, as done in PIM-SM.

If the router determines that the multicast packet should be forwarded, it will build an OIL for the packet. Finally, the router removes the incoming interface from the OIL it has created, and if the resulting OIL is not empty, it will forward the packet out of those interfaces.

7.6.1   Upstream Forwarding at RP

The network operator can use one of the following options to configure the RPA of the BIDIR-PIM domain:

- **RPA as a routable IP address**: When configuring a BIDIR-PIM domain, the network operator may choose to assign the RPA to an IP address that does not belong to a physical router but instead should be simply a routable address. BIDIR-PIM routers that have interfaces on the RPL to which the RPA belongs will forward multicast traffic upstream onto the link. PIM Join messages sent by the Last-Hop Router (LHRs) of receivers in the BIDIR-PIM domain will be propagated hop by hop until they reach one of the BIDIR-PIM routers connected to the RPL, where they will terminate (since no DF is elected on the RPL).

- **RPA as the IP address of a physical router interface**: The network operator may instead choose to configure the RPA to be the IP address of a physical interface of a specific BIDIR-PIM router in the domain. That BIDIR-PIM router must still forward multicast packets upstream onto the RPL, and its behavior will be no different from any other BIDIR-PIM router with an interface on the RPL.
- **RPA as the IP loopback address of a router**: The operator may configure the BIDIR-PIM domain to operate similar to a PIM-SM domain where a single router (the RP) is configured as the root of the shared distribution tree. In this case, the RPA can be configured to be the IP loopback address of a BIDIR-PIM router.

7.6.2 Source-Only Branches

A source-only branch of the BIDIR-PIM distribution tree for a multicast group address G does not lead to any receivers but is used for forwarding multicast packets traveling upstream from a source toward the RPL. BIDIR-PIM routers that are along a source-only branch of the bidirectional shared tree only have the RPF interface to the RPA in their OIL for multicast group G, and consequently, do not need to maintain any group-specific state.

In this case, a BIDIR-PIM router performs upstream forwarding of multicast traffic using only an RPA-specific state. A BIDIR-PIM implementation may choose to maintain a multicast group state for source-only branches for accounting or performance measurement. However, doing so requires the BIDIR-PIM implementation to depend on data-driven events (to discover the multicast groups that have active sources), thus forgoing one of the main benefits of BIDIR-PIM.

7.6.3 Directly Connected Sources

Unlike PIM-SM, the main advantage of using a DF in BIDIR-PIM is that the BIDIR-PIM domain is no longer required to provide special treatment for sources that are directly connected to a router. The BIDIR-PIM domain does not need to differentiate such sources from other multicast traffic because they will be automatically picked up by the DF and forwarded upstream toward the RPA. This removes the requirement for BIDIR-PIM routers to perform directly connected source checks for multicast traffic sent to groups that do not have existing state, as in PIM-SM.

7.7 PIM JOIN/PRUNE MESSAGES

BIDIR-PIM routers send PIM Join/Prune messages to construct group-specific distribution trees that connect receivers to the RPL. Last-Hop Router (LHRs) that are elected as the DF on an interface with directly connected receivers of a group send PIM Join messages. The BIDIR-PIM routers propagate the PIM Join messages hop by hop toward the RPA of the multicast group until they reach a BIDIR-PIM router connected to the RPL.

The contents of a PIM Join/Prune message include a list of joined and pruned groups. A BIDIR-PIM router processing a received PIM Join/Prune message effectively considers each joined or pruned group as individual sets by applying the state machines described in this section. When a BIDIR-PIM router is processing a Join/Prune message whose Upstream Neighbor Address field contains the router's own IP address, the (*, G) Join and Prune messages can affect the router's Downstream state machine. When processing a Join/Prune message whose Upstream Neighbor Address field contains the IP address of another router, most of the join or prune entries in the message could affect the router's Upstream state machine.

7.7.1 RECEIVING (*, G) JOIN/PRUNE MESSAGES

Upon receiving a PIM Join (*, G) or Prune (*, G) message, the BIDIR-PIM router must first check whether the RP Address in the message matches the RPA of group G (i.e., RPA(G), which is the router's view of what the RPA is). The router must silently discard the PIM Join or Prune message if the RP Address in the message does not match RPA(G). Note that the RP Address is contained in the Encoded Source Address Format when the W and R bits are set to 1; that is, the corresponding Joined or Pruned Source field of the message contains an RP Address and not the address of the actual multicast source (see Chapter 3).

If a router has not yet been provided with the RPA information for a multicast group (e.g., a BSR message has not been recently received), then it may choose to accept a PIM Join (*, G) or Prune (*, G) message sent to it and treat the RP Address in the message (in Encoded Source Address Format) as the RPA of group G (i.e., RPA(G)). If the router finds that the newly discovered RPA obtained from the message did not previously exist for any other multicast group, then it has to initiate a DF election process.

Note that a BIDIR router will process a PIM Join (*, G) message addressed to it even if it is not the elected DF for the RPA of group G on the interface on which the message was received. This provides an optimization in BIDIR-PIM to remove the Join delay, which is equal to one Join period (i.e., $t\_periodic$), in the situation where a new DF receives Pass and Join messages and processes them in the reverse order. The BIDIR-PIM forwarding logic ensures that the router will not forward multicast packets that it has received on such an interface while it is not the elected DF on the interface (unless the interface is the router's RPF interface toward the RPA).

A BIDIR-PIM router maintains the Downstream Group Per-Interface state machine shown in Figure 7.2 for receiving and processing PIM (*, G) Join/Prune messages from downstream routers. This state machine has the following three states:

- **NoInfo**: This state indicates that the interface has no (*, G) Join state and no related timers are running.
- **Join**: This state indicates that the interface has (*, G) Join state. If the router is the elected DF on the interface, then having this (*, G) Join state will

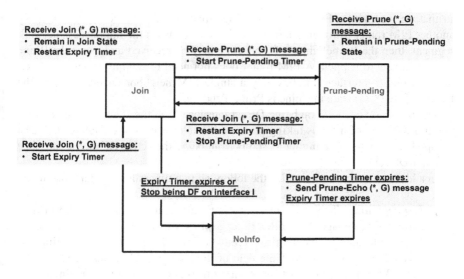

FIGURE 7.2   Downstream Group Per-Interface state machine.

cause the router to forward multicast packets addressed to group G on the interface.

- **PrunePending**: This state indicates that a Prune (*, G) message has been received on the interface from a downstream BIDIR-PIM neighbor, and the router is waiting to see whether another downstream router will send a (*. G) Join message to override the Prune message. In regards to multicast packet forwarding, this state functions exactly like the Join state.

In the state machine in Figure 7.2, the transition events "Receive Join (*, G) message" and "Receive Prune (*, G) message" imply that Join and Prune (*, G) messages are received on an interface with the Upstream Neighbor Address fields of the messages set to the router's primary IP address on the interface. If the Upstream Neighbor Address field contains an incorrect address, then the state transitions associated with receiving these messages in this state machine must not occur, although receiving such messages may cause state transitions in other state machines in the router.

For an unnumbered IP interface on a point-to-point link, the router's IP address should match the source IP address used by the router in the source address field of PIM Hello messages sent over that unnumbered interface. However, it is recommended that the PIM router also accept PIM Join/Prune messages with an Upstream Neighbor Address field of all zeros on point-to-point links.

The "Send PruneEcho (*, G)" action in the state machine in Figure 7.2 is triggered when the PIM router ceases multicast data packet forwarding on an interface due to receiving a Prune (*, G) message on that interface. A PruneEcho (*, G) represents a Prune (*, G) message that an upstream PIM router sends on a multiaccess network segment (LAN) with its IP address in the message's Upstream Neighbor Address field. The purpose of a PruneEcho (*, G) message is to provide additional reliability so that, in the event a Prune (*, G) message that should have been overridden by another PIM router (through a Join (*, G)) is lost locally on the multiaccess network segment, then the PruneEcho (*, G) message may be received and cause the Prune (*, G) override to happen. A PIM router does not need to send a PruneEcho (*, G) message on an interface that has only a single PIM neighbor during the time the Per-Interface (*, G) state machine is Prune-Pending.

The transition event "Stop being DF on interface I" in the state machine implies that a re-election of a DF is taking place on the interface for the RPA of multicast group G. The router is changing its status from being the active DF on the interface to a non-DF router.

In addition, the router maintains the following two timers for the state machine:

- **Expiry Timer**: The router restarts this timer when it receives a valid PIM Join (*, G) message. When this timer expires, the interface state reverts to the NoInfo state for the multicast group G. The *J/P_HoldTime* of this timer is derived from the Hold Time field of the received PIM Join/Prune message. When the router starts or restarts this timer, it configures the timer to the Hold Time field value in the PIM Join/Prune message that triggered the timer.
- **Prune-Pending Timer**: The router initiates this timer upon receipt of a valid PIM Prune (*, G) message. Upon expiration of this timer, the interface state reverts to the NoInfo state for the multicast group G. The *J/P_Override_Interval* of this timer (with a default value of 3 seconds) is the short period during which the router must wait after receiving a PIM Prune message to allow other routers on the network segment to send a Join message and override the Prune message. When the router initializes this timer, it sets it to the *J/P_Override_Interval* if the router has more than one BIDIR-PIM neighbor on that interface, otherwise, the router sets it to zero, causing it to expire immediately. As discussed in Chapter 5, the value of the *J/P_Override_Interval* used by the router is interface-specific and depends on both the *Propagation_Delay* and the *Override_Interval* values extracted from the LAN Prune Delay Option in received PIM Hello messages. These two values may change when Hello messages are received.

7.7.2 Sending Join/Prune Messages

A BIDIR-PIM router uses the Downstream Group Per-Interface state machine described above to maintain (*, G) Join state when receiving Join/Prune messages from downstream BIDIR-PIM routers. The router uses this state to determine whether to propagate a PIM Join (*, G) upstream toward the RPA. The router transmits these Join (*, G) messages in the upstream direction, specifically on the RPF interface toward the RPA, and these messages are targeted at the DF on that interface.

If a PIM Join (*, G) message is intended to be propagated upstream, the router must also be attentive to messages on its upstream interface from other BIDI-PIM routers on that network segment, as these messages may modify its behavior.

- If the router detects a PIM Join (*, G) message sent to the correct upstream BIDIR-PIM neighbor, it should refrain from sending its own Join (*, G) message.
- If the router observes a PIM Prune (*, G) message sent to the correct upstream BIDIR-PIM neighbor, it should be ready to promptly send a Join (*, G) message to override that Prune (*, G) message.
- Finally, if the router notices that the Generation ID of the correct upstream BIDIR-PIM neighbor has changed, it can infer that the upstream neighbor has lost state, and it should be ready to promptly send a PIM Join (*, G) message to refresh the state.

Furthermore, when the next-hop toward the RPA changes, it prompts the router to switch from the old next-hop and to send a Join message toward the new next-hop. Any of the following two events can cause such a change:

- The router's MRIB shows that the RPF Interface toward the RPA has changed. In this scenario, the router uses the DF on the new RPF interface as the new RPF Neighbor.
- There is a re-election of a DF on the RPF interface, and a new router becomes the DF.

The Upstream (*, G) state machine maintained by a BIDIR-PIM router has only the following two states (see Figure 7.3):

- **Not Joined**: This state indicates that the router does not need to send a (*, G) Join message to join the RPA's shared distribution tree for multicast group G.
- **Joined**: This state indicates that the router has joined the RPA's shared distribution tree for multicast group G.

Additionally, the router maintains a timer called the Upstream Join Timer, which is used to trigger the sending of a PIM Join (*, G) message to the upstream BIDIR-PIM neighbor toward the RPA. It is sent toward the DF on the RPF interface for the RPA of multicast group G. The $t\_periodic$ of this timer (with a default value of 60 seconds) is the period (spacing) between Join/Prune messages.

The $t\_suppressed$ of this timer is the suppression period during which the router must wait to see if another router on the network segment will send a PIM Join message, thus avoiding the need to do so itself. The default value of $t\_suppressed$ is a random value between 1.1 times $t\_periodic$ and 1.4 times $t\_periodic$ when suppression is enabled on the interface, otherwise, the value is 0.

The $t\_override$ of the Upstream Join Timer is the random delay a BIDIR-PIM router must wait before sending a PIM Join message. This helps prevent response implosion when multiple routers on the multiaccess network segment send Join messages to override a Prune. The default value of this parameter is a random value between 0 and 0.9 times $J/P\_Override\_Interval$.

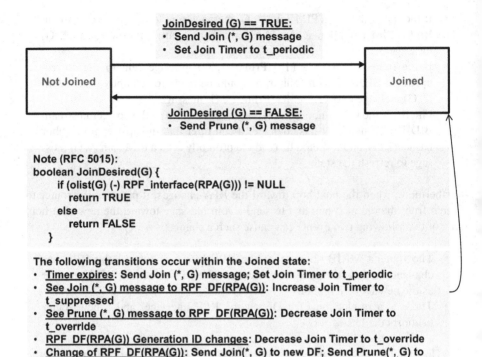

```
boolean JoinDesired(G) {
    if (olist(G) (-) RPF_interface(RPA(G))) != NULL
        return TRUE
    else
        return FALSE
}
```

The following transitions occur within the Joined state:
- **Timer expires**: Send Join (*, G) message; Set Join Timer to t_periodic
- **See Join (*, G) message to RPF_DF(RPA(G))**: Increase Join Timer to t_suppressed
- **See Prune (*, G) message to RPF_DF(RPA(G))**: Decrease Join Timer to t_override
- **RPF_DF(RPA(G)) Generation ID changes**: Decrease Join Timer to t_override
- **Change of RPF_DF(RPA(G))**: Send Join(*, G) to new DF; Send Prune(*, G) to old DF; set Timer to t_periodic

FIGURE 7.3   Upstream Group state machine.

7.8   DESIGNATED FORWARDER (DF) ELECTION

A network segment with multiple multicast routers attached to it may forward the same multicast packets to the RPA repeatedly. To address this problem, BIDIR-PIM uses a DF election mechanism to elect a unique forwarder (i.e., DF) for every network segment for each RPA within the BIDIR-PIM domain and allows only the DF to forward multicast data to the RPA.

This section describes the BIDIR-PIM DF election mechanism (designed to be fail-safe). This mechanism is used to elect a DF for each RPA on each link in a BIDIR-PIM domain. Note that the DF election is not performed on the RPL for an RPA; the DF election is not necessary for an RPL.

7.8.1   DF ELECTION REQUIREMENTS

During the DF election process, the router on a link with the best route to the RPA is chosen as the DF. This elected DF is responsible for forwarding multicast traffic between the RPL and the link for the range of multicast groups served by the RPA. Different multicast groups that have traffic passing through a router connecting to the link and share a common RPA, also share the same upstream direction.

Consequently, the upstream forwarder (DF) elected on each link does not have to be done on a multicast group-specific basis but instead can be done on an RPA-specific basis. Since the number of RPAs is typically small in the BIDIR-PIM domain, the number of DF elections that have to be performed is significantly lower.

To optimize the creation of the RPA's shared distribution tree, the router that wins the DF election process should have the best route to the RPA, according to the unicast routing metrics reported by the MRIB. BIDIR-PIM routers participating in the DF election process use the same comparison rules as the PIM-SM Assert process when comparing metrics from different unicast routing protocols (see Chapter 5).

BIDIR-PIM routers on a link perform the DF election process when information on a new RPA first becomes available. The routers can reuse the result as new BIDIR-PIM multicast groups that map to the same RPA are encountered. However, there are some conditions under which the routers reperform the DF election:

- Any of the routers on the link experiences a change in the unicast routing metric to reach the RPA.
- The interface (RPF Interface) on which the RPA is reachable has changed to an interface on which the router was previously the elected DF.
- A new BIDIR-PIM neighbor that must participate in the DF election process starts up on a link and needs to know the results of the current election.
- The elected DF becomes unavailable or fails. This could be detected through PIM Neighbor state timeout or RPF change at a downstream router, as indicated by the MRIB.

The DF election process is designed to be robust enough to ensure that all BIDIR-PIM routers on the link have a consistent view of which router is the currently elected DF.

7.8.2   DF Election Process

This section describes the main elements of the DF election process. To elect the DF for a particular RPA on a link, the BIDIR-PIM routers on the link exchange their unicast routing metrics to reach the RPA. The routers use Offer, Winner, Backoff, and Pass messages to advertise their metrics to the RPA.

7.8.2.1   DF Election Messages

This section describes the PIM control messages used in the DF election process. The DF Election message formats are described in Chapter 3.

- **Offer (Contains {*OfferingID, Metric*})**: This message is sent by a BIDIR-PIM router wishing to announce on the link that it has a better metric to the RPA than the one reported so far.
- **Winner (Contains {*DF-ID, DF-Metric*})**: This message is sent by a BIDIR-PIM router when assuming the role of the DF on the link or when reasserting its role as the DF in response to worse Offers from other routers.
- **Backoff (Contains {*DF-ID, DF-Metric, OfferingID, OfferMetric, BackoffInterval*})**: The DF sends this message to acknowledge better

Offers from other routers on the link. This message instructs other routers on the link with equal or worse Offers to wait until the DF passes the DF role to the router that sent the best Offer.

- **Pass (Contains {*Old-DF-ID, Old-DF-Metric, New-DF-ID, New-DF-Metric*}):** This message is used by the old DF to inform the router that previously sent the best Offer to assume DF responsibilities. The *Old-DF-Metric* represents the current metric of the old DF at the time the Pass message is sent.

A router uses the RPF Interface and metrics to reach the RPA, as indicated in the MRIB, to advertise metrics for the DF election:

- When a router is participating in the election of a DF for an RPA on the interface that serves as the RPF Interface used to reach that RPA (as indicated in its MRIB), it must always advertise an infinite metric in the election messages it sends.
- When a router is participating in the election of a DF for an RPA on an interface that is not the RPF Interface (as indicated in the MRIB), it must advertise the metrics as provided by the MRIB in the election messages it sends.

In the DR election protocol described below, participating routers repeatedly exchange messages *Election_Robustness* times to enhance the reliability of the protocol. In all those cases, the routers retransmit the message spaced in time by a small random interval. The parameter *Election_Robustness* (which is a constant with a default value of 3) represents the minimum number of election messages that must be lost for the BIDIR-PIM DF election process to fail.

Figure 7.4 summarizes the main steps in the DF election process on a link for a particular RPA. Without the DF election mechanism, both Router B and Router E can receive multicast packets from the source via Router A and forward them to the RPA. Both routers may also forward multicast packets to downstream nodes on the local network segment. As a result, the RPA (configured on Router C) may receive duplicate multicast packets from Router B and Router E. With the DF election mechanism, once Router B and Router E receive the RPA information, they will initiate a DF election process for the RPA:

1. Router B and Router E send DF Election messages via multicast to the All-PIM-ROUTERS multicast address (224.0.0.13). The election messages carry the RPA, the Sender's Metric Preference, and the Sender's Route Metric of the unicast route, multicast static route, or MBGP route to the RPA.
2. The router with a route with the highest Metric Preference becomes the DF.
3. In the case of a tie in the Metric Preference values, the router with the route having the lowest Route Metric wins the DF election.
4. In the case of a tie in the Route Metric, the router with the highest IP address (as indicated in the source IP address field of the IP packet containing the election message) wins the DF election.

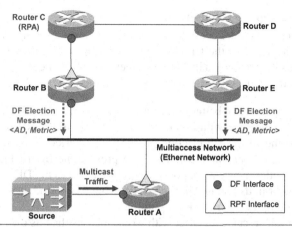

FIGURE 7.4   Designated Forwarder (DF) election.

- The RP Address (RPA) does not necessarily belong to a physical router but is simply a routable ("virtual") IP address.
  - In our discussion, we assume that a single physical router (the RP) acts as the root of the bidirectional distribution tree, and the RPA is configured to be the loopback interface of this router.
- The figure shows a multiaccess network (subnet) with multiple multicast routers, where duplicate multicast packets can be forwarded to the RPA. To address this problem, BIDIR-PIM employs a Designated Forwarder (DF) election mechanism to elect a DF on the multiaccess network for each RPA serving a range of multicast groups.
  - Only the DFs can forward multicast packets toward the RPA.
  - DF election is not necessary for an RP Link (RPL).
- Without the DF election mechanism, both Router B and Router E can receive multicast packets from Router A. As a result, the RPA (Router C) will receive duplicate multicast packets. Also, Routers B and E can forward duplicate packets to downstream routers on the local subnet.
- With the DF election mechanism, once Router B and Router E receive the RPA information, they each multicast a DF Election message to the ALL-PIM ROUTERS multicast address (224.0.0.13) to initiate a DF election process. The DF Election message carries the RPA, Sender's Metric Preference and Sender's Metric of the unicast route, or static multicast route to the RPA.
- A DF is elected as follows:
  1. The router with the best Metric Preference becomes the DF.
     - The Metric Preference is conceptually similar to the Administrative Distance (AD), also called the Route Preference, used in unicast route selection (which indicates the trustworthiness of the routing information source when multiple routing sources provide routes to the same destination). The routing information source with the lowest AD is preferred.
  2. If the routers have the same Metric Preference, the router with the lowest Sender Metric becomes the DF.
  3. If the routers have the same Sender Metric, the router with the highest IP address becomes the DF.

Note that the Metric Preference is sometimes referred to as the Administrative Distance or Route Preference of a route to a given IP address [AWEYFDVR21] [AWEYFCDM22]. It is an integer value that represents the trustworthiness of the routing information source that provided the route to the given IP address.

7.8.2.2 Bootstrap DF Election

Initially, when a DF has not been elected on a link, routers learning about a new RPA will start participating in the DF election process by transmitting Offer messages. A router sends Offer messages including its metric to reach the RPA. Also, the router periodically retransmits Offer messages with a period of *Offer_Interval*.

- If a router receives a better Offer than its own from a BIDIR-PIM neighbor (i.e., Offer message with a better routing metric to the RPA), it will stop participating in the DF election process for a period equal to (*Election_Robustness* × *Offer_Interval*). This will provide the BIDIR-PIM neighbor with the better metric an opportunity to be elected as the DF.
- If the router finds that no DF is elected during this period, it will restart the DF election process from the beginning.
- A router may receive an Offer with worse metrics than its own at any point during the initial DF election process. In such cases, it will restart the DF election process from the beginning.

The above ensures that all BIDIR-PIM routers, except the best candidate router on the link, will stop advertising their own Offers.

If, after advertising its metrics for *Election_Robustness* number of times on the link for the RPA without receiving any Offer from any other BIDIR-PIM router on the link, a router will assume the role of the DF on the link. At that point, the router will transmit a Winner message (see Chapter 3) on the link, declaring itself as the winner to every other BIDIR-PIM router on the link and proving the metrics it is using.

Routers on the link, upon receiving a Winner message, will cease participating in the DF election process and record the identity of the winner along with the metrics it is using. If a router, after receiving the message, determines that its own metrics are better than those reported by the winner, it will record the identity of the winner, but reinitiate the DF election process in an attempt to take over as the DF, while accepting the winner only as the acting DF for the link.

7.8.2.3 Loser Metric Changes

Whenever a non-DF router detects that its unicast routing metric to an RPA has improved compared to the value previously advertised by the acting DF, it should take action eventually to elect the DF for the link. When the non-DF router detects that it now has a better metric to the RPA, it will restart the DF election process by transmitting Offer messages with this new, improved metric. It is important to note that if at any point during the DF election process, a router does not receive a response after *Election_Robustness* retransmissions of an Offer, it will take up the role of the DF on the link and announce to the other routers that it is the winner as described above.

- If the DF receives an Offer that is worse than its current metric, it will respond with a Winner message, declaring its status and indicating its better metric. The originator of the Offer, upon receiving the Winner message, will record the identity of the DF and then abort the DF election process.

- If the DF receives an Offer that is better than its current metric, it will record the identity and metrics of the router that sent the Offer. Subsequently, the DF will respond with a Backoff message (see Chapter 3). This message instructs the router that sent the Offer to postpone DF election actions for a short period to allow the network and the unicast routing protocol to stabilize. It also provides other routers on the link the opportunity to send in their own Offers. The Backoff message includes the new metric and address of the router sending the Offer. All routers on the link that receive the Backoff message and have pending Offers with worse metrics than those in the message (including the router that originated the Offer) will hold on to any further Offers they have for a period defined in the Interval field of the Backoff message (see Chapter 3).
- If the DF receives a better Offer from a third router during the *Backoff_ Period*, it will send a Backoff message for the new Offer and restart the *Backoff_Period*.

Before the *Backoff_Period* expires, the DF (playing the role of acting DF), will use a Pass message (see Chapter 3) to nominate the router that sent the best Offer as the new DF. The Pass message includes the IP addresses and metrics of both the old DF (i.e., sender) and new DF (i.e., nominated). As soon as the old DF transmits the Pass message, it will cease performing further DF tasks. The new DF receives the Pass message and immediately assumes the role of the DF on the link. All other BIDIR-PIM routers on the link will record the identity of the new DF and its metric. Note that the described event constitutes an RPF Neighbor change, which may cause BIDIR-PIM routers on the link to send PIM Join messages to the new DF.

7.8.2.4 Winner Metric Changes

If the DF detects that its routing metric to the RPA has changed to a value worse than the previous value, it will transmit a set of Winner messages advertising the new metric on the link randomly spaced apart by *Election_Robustness*. Any router on the link that receives these messages but has a better metric to the RPA may respond with an Offer message that triggers the same handoff procedure described earlier. Until all routers on a link receive a Pass or Winner message indicating the DF has changed, they will assume the DF has not changed.

The BIDIR-PIM routers on the link are under no pressure to make this handoff quickly as long as the acting DF still has a path to the RPL. The old path to the RPL may now be suboptimal, but it can still be used for BIDIR-PIM forwarding while the DF re-election is in progress.

7.8.2.5 Winner Loses Path

If a BIDIR-PIM router detects that the RPF Interface to the RPA changes to be on a link on which it is the acting DF, then it is no longer in the position to perform packet forwarding on that link. The router, therefore, immediately ceases to be the DF on the link and restarts the DF election process. Since its path to the RPA is through that link, the router includes an infinite metric in the Offer messages it sends.

7.8.2.6 Late Router Starting Up

A BIDIR-PIM router that starts up on a link just after the DF election process has completed for that link will not immediately know the results of the DF election. As a result, this late-starting router will begin advertising its metric in Offer messages on the link. When this happens, the router currently elected DF on the link will respond by transmitting a Winner message on the link if its metric is better than the metric in the received Offer message or by transmitting a Backoff message if its metric is worse than the metric in the Offer message.

7.8.2.7 Winner Dies

Whenever the elected DF on a link fails, the other routers on the link have to elect a new DF. The speed at which the routers can achieve this depends on whether the link has any downstream routers on it.

- If downstream routers exist on the link, typically, their advertised next-hop (as indicated in the MRIB) before the DF fails will be the DF itself. The downstream routers will, therefore, notice either a change in the metric for the route leading to the RPA or a change in next-hop away from the DF and can transmit Offer messages to restart the DF election process.
- If a router detects (according to its MRIB) that the RPA is now reachable through the same link via another upstream BIDIR-PIM router, it will send an Offer message with an infinite metric.
- If the link has no downstream routers, the only way other upstream BIDIR-PIM routers can detect a DF failure is through the timeout of the PIM Neighbor state information, which can take a significantly longer time to happen.

7.8.3 DESIGNATED FORWARDER ELECTION PROTOCOL

This section describes the DF election process in BIDIR-PIM. A BIDIR-PIM router maintains a per-RPA DF election state for each multicast-enabled interface, as shown in Figure 7.5.

7.8.3.1 DF Election State Machine

The following four states are maintained for this state machine:

- **Offer**: This is the initial state in the DF election process, where the router believes it can eventually become the winner (elected DF) and periodically send Offer messages.
- **Lose**: In this state, the router knows that either a different router on the link has become the election winner, or that no router on the link has a path to the RPA.
- **Win**: In this state, the router is the acting DF without any other router on the link contesting.
- **Backoff**: In this state, the router is the acting DF, but another router on the link has sent an Offer to take over as DF.

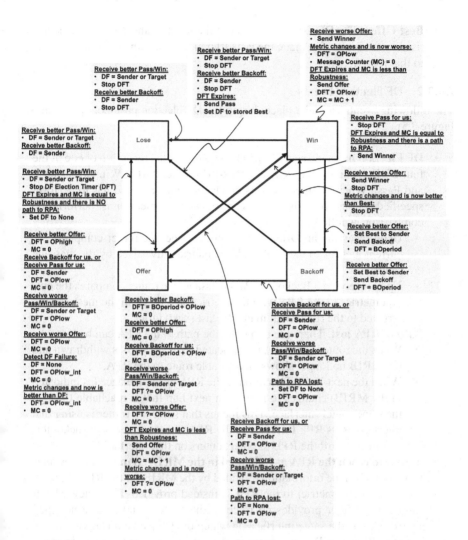

FIGURE 7.5 Designated Forwarder Election state machine.

The state machine considers a router to be an acting DF if it is in the Win or Backoff states.

The variables and timers described below are used in the operation of the DF election protocol:

- **Acting DF Information**: A router uses this to store the identity and the metrics advertised by the DF election winner, that is, the currently acting DF.
- **DF Election Timer**: The router uses this to schedule the transmission of Offer, Winner, and Pass messages.
- **Message Count**: The router uses this to maintain the number of times it has transmitted an Offer or Winner message.

- **Best Offer**: The DF uses this to record the identity and the metrics advertised by the router that made the last Offer and for sending the Pass message to that router.

7.8.3.2 DF Election Events

The following events can take place during the DF election protocol operation (see Figure 7.5):

- **DF Election message reception**: This represents the reception of one of the four DF Election messages by a BIDIR-PIM router (Offer, Winner, Backoff, and Pass). When a router receives an election message and has to perform specified actions when the metrics are better or worse, it must perform the comparison as follows:
  - Upon receiving an Offer or Winner message, the router compares the current metrics to the RPA with the metrics advertised by the message sender.
  - Upon receiving a Backoff or Pass message, the router compares the current metrics to the RPA with the metrics advertised in the message and targeted to the router that made the last (best) Offer.
- **Path to RPA lost**: There are two ways the path to the RPA can be lost.
  - When the route to the RPA (as indicated in the MRIB) is withdrawn and the MRIB no longer shows an available route to the RPA.
  - When the next-hop information to the RPA on an interface (as indicated in the MRIB) changes to indicate a next-hop that is reachable through the same router interface. This means that since the router is using that interface as its RPF Interface to the RPA, it cannot perform packet forwarding toward the RPL to other routers on that interface.
- **Metric to reach the RPA as indicated in the MRIB changes**: This event is triggered when the information provided by the MRIB for the RPA changes, and a new path (metric) to the RPA is instead provided. If the new MRIB information either provides no route to the RPA or indicates a next-hop interface to be the same interface on which the DF election is taking place, then the "Path to RPA lost" event, as described above, is triggered instead.
- **DF Election Timer (DFT) expiration**: Expiration of the DFT can trigger message transmission and state machine transitions.
- **Detection of DF failure**: DF failure can be detected through the timeout of the PIM Neighbor state.

7.8.3.3 DF Election Actions

The following notation is used in the DF Election state machine action descriptions (see Figure 7.5):

- This denotes the operation in which the router lowers a timer to a new value. If the timer is not running, then the router will start using the new value. If the router finds that the timer is running with an expiry value that is lower than the new value, then the router will not alter the timer.

When the state machine encounters the action "set DF to Sender or Target" during receipt of a Winner, Pass, or Backoff message, this means the following:

- Upon receiving a Winner message, the router sets the DF to be the router that originated the message and records its metrics.
- Upon receiving a Pass message, the router sets the DF to be the target of the message (i.e., the new Winner) and records its metrics.
- Upon receiving a Backoff message, the router sets the DF to be the router that originated the message and records its metrics.

When a DF election process is initiated, the state machine starts in the Offer state, sets the Message Counter (MC) to zero, and the DFT to *OPlow*.

The DFT has the following parameters (see Figure 7.5):

- The *Offer_Period* (or *OPeriod*) of this timer (with a default value of 100 ms) is the time interval that the router has to wait to repeat sending Offer and Winner messages.
- The *Backoff_Period* (or *BOPeriod*) of this timer (with a default value of 1 second) is the period that the acting DF of the link has to wait after receiving a better Offer and sending the Pass message, before transferring the DF responsibility to the new Winner.
- The *OPlow* of this timer is the actual randomly chosen delay value used between repeated message transmissions. This is a random value between 0.5 and *Offer_Period*.
- The *OPhigh* of this timer is the time interval that the router has to wait to allow a router with a better Offer to become the DF. The default value is *Election_Robustness* × *Offer_Period*.

7.8.4 ENHANCEMENTS FOR DF ELECTION RELIABILITY

The BIDIR-PIM specification introduces two features to enhance the reliability of the DF election process. It is very important to avoid situations where two routers assume the role of the DF on the same link for BIDIR-PIM to operate correctly. While these enhancements are not necessary for proper BIDIR-PIM operation, they can be useful in diagnosing and correcting anomalies.

7.8.4.1 Missing Pass Messages

After a DF has been elected on a link, any router on the link whose metrics have changed to become better than the metrics of the running DF will attempt to assume DF responsibilities. If during the re-election of the DF, the acting DF or the network experiences conditions that cause the loss of all the election messages (like a CPU overload or network malfunction), the new Winner will transmit three Offer messages on the link and assume the role of the DF, resulting in two DFs on the link. This situation is highly undesirable and should be corrected by fixing the overloaded or multifunctioning router. Ideally, such a situation should be detected by the network operator.

When a router assumes the DF role on a link and has not received a Pass message from the known old DF, it can mark the PIM neighbor information for the old DF accordingly. As soon as the router (new Winner) receives the next PIM Hello message from the old DF, it can retransmit Winner messages for all the RPAs for which it is serving as the DF. The router may also log the anomaly in a rate-limited manner to alert the network operator.

7.8.4.2 Periodic Winner Announcement

The BIDIR-PIM specification adds one safety feature by allowing the DF on a link for each RPA to periodically send a Winner message announcing its status. The router can restrict the transmission of the periodic Winner message to occur only for RPAs that have active multicast groups, thus, avoiding the transmission of such periodic BIDIR-PIM control messages in areas of the network without sources or receivers for a particular RPA.

7.9 ILLUSTRATING HOW BIDIR-PIM WORKS

A bidirectional RPT in a BIDIR-PIM domain consists of two parts: a source-side RPT and a receiver-side RPT (see Figures 7.6–7.8). The source-side RPT is rooted at the RPA, and the routers that directly connect to the sources are considered as leaves of the RPT. The receiver-side RPT is also rooted at the RPA, and the routers that directly connect to the receivers are considered as leaves of the RPT. The section describes the processes for building these two BIDIR-PIM RPT parts.

7.9.1 BUILDING THE RECEIVER-SIDE RPT

The process for building a receiver-side RPT in a BIDIR-PIM domain is similar to that for building a PIM-SM shared tree or RPT (Figure 7.6):

1. Assume that Receiver B joins a multicast group G by sending an IGMP Membership Report message to inform its directly connected router, Router 9. Router 9 is the DF on the network segment (and also is the Designated Router (DR) in the PIM-SM sense) for Receiver B.
2. Upon receiving this message from Receiver B, Router 9 generates a PIM (*, G) Join message, performs an RPF check for the correct interface leading to the RPA, and sends the message toward the RPA on its upstream interface, where Router 7 is the RPF neighbor. The PIM (*, G) Join message is forwarded hop by hop on the RPF interfaces of each hop until it reaches the RPA of multicast group G.
3. The routers along the path from the directly connected router of the receiver to the RPA form a branch of the RPT for group G, and each router on this branch creates a (*, G) entry in its multicast forwarding table.
4. Router 7 receives the PIM (*, G) Join message from Router 9, and if multicast traffic for group G is already being sent out by Router 3 to the RPL of the RPA, Router 7 can then start forwarding that traffic to Router 9, which then sends it to Receiver B. Recall that there is no DF elected on the RPL.

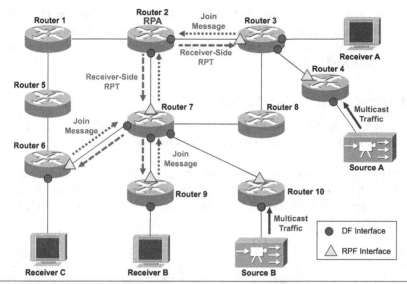

- A bidirectional RPT is made of a source-side RPT and a receiver-side RPT.
- The receiver-side RPT is rooted at the RP, and the BIDIR-PIM routers that directly connect to the receivers act as leaves.
- The source-side RPT is also rooted at the RP, and the BIDIR-PIM routers that directly connect to the sources act as leaves. Different processes are used for building these two RPTs.

Building the RP Tree (RPT) at the receiver side:
- The process for building a BIDIR-PIM receiver-side RPT is the same as the process for building an RPT in PIM-SM:
    1. When a receiver signals the desire to join the multicast group G, it sends an IGMP Membership Report message to inform the directly connected router.
    2. After receiving the IGMP Membership Report message, the directly connected router transmits a PIM (*, G) Join message, which is forwarded hop-by-hop to the RP for the multicast group.
    3. The BIDIR-PIM routers along the path from the receiver's directly connected router to the RP form an RPT branch.
        - Each router on this branch adds a (*, G) state entry to its multicast forwarding table.

Leaving the multicast group G:
- After a multicast receiver leaves the multicast group G (by sending an IGMP Leave message), the directly connected router multicasts a PIM (*, G) Prune message to all PIM routers on the subnet.
- The PIM (*, G) Prune message travels hop-by-hop along the reverse direction of the RPT to the RP.
- After receiving the PIM (*, G) Prune message, an upstream node removes the interface that connects to the downstream node from the outgoing interface list (OIL) of the (*, G) state entry.
- At the same time, the upstream router checks if there are any other receivers for that multicast group. If no receivers for the multicast group exist, the router continues to forward the PIM (*, G) Prune message to its upstream router.

FIGURE 7.6   Building the RP tree (RPT) at the receiver side.

When Receiver B in the BIDIR-PIM domain is no longer interested in the multi-cast data sent to multicast group G, its directly connected router, Router 9 sends a (*, G) Prune message, which travels hop by hop along the reverse direction of the RPT to the RPA. Each upstream node, upon receiving this (*, G) Prune message, deletes the interface connected with the downstream node from the OIL of the (*, G) entry and checks whether it has receivers for that multicast group. If no receivers exist, the router continues to forward the (*, G) Prune message to its upstream BIDIR-PIM router.

7.9.2 BUILDING THE SOURCE-SIDE RPT

Compared to the receiver-side RPT, the process of building the source-side RPT in the BIDIR-PIM domain is relatively simple, as shown in Figure 7.7:

1. When a multicast source, for example, Source A, transmits multicast packets addressed to multicast group G, its DF on its sending interface, Router 4, performs an RPF check for the correct interface leading to the RPA for

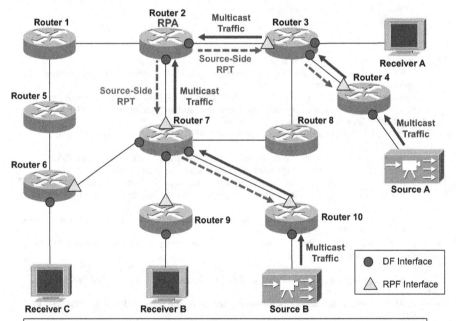

• The process for building a BIDIR-PIM source-side RPT is relatively simple compared to the receiver-side RPT:
   1. When a multicast source sends multicast packets to the multicast group G, the DF in each network segment (subnet) unconditionally forwards the packets to the RPA.
   2. The BIDIR-PIM routers along the path from the directly connected router of the source to the RPA constitute an RPT branch.
      • Each BIDIR-PIM router on this branch adds a PIM (*, G) state entry to its multicast forwarding table.
• After a bidirectional RPT is created, the multicast sources send multicast traffic to the RPA along the source-side RPT. The RP then forwards the traffic to the receivers along the receiver-side RPT.

FIGURE 7.7   Building the RP tree (RPT) at the source side.

multicast group G. Router 4 finds the upstream interface and starts forwarding the multicast traffic toward the RPA, where Router 3 is the RPF neighbor and the next router on the path toward the RPA.

2. All routers (DFs) on each network segment that receive the multicast traffic perform an RPF check for the interface leading to the RPA for multicast group G and unconditionally forward the traffic to the RPA.
3. The routers (DFs) along the path from the directly connected router of the multicast source (Router 4) to the RPA form a branch of the RPT. Each router on this branch creates a (*, G) entry to its multicast forwarding table.

After a bidirectional RPT is created in the BIDIR-PIM domain for a multicast group G, multicast traffic is forwarded from the sources along the source-side RPT to the RPA and along the receiver-side RPT from the RPA to the receivers.

If a multicast source and a receiver are located on the same side of the RPA for a multicast group G, the source-side RPT and the receiver-side RPT for that RPA and group may converge at a BIDIR-PIM router in the domain before reaching the RPA (see Figure 7.8). In this case, multicast packets are directly forwarded to the receiver by the BIDIR-PIM router (Router 3) at which the two RPTs meet, instead of by the RPA.

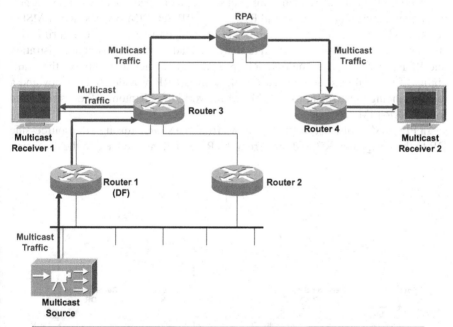

- If a multicast source and a receiver are on the same side of the RPA, the source-side RPT and the receiver-side RPT might meet at a node (Router 3) before reaching the RPA.
- In this case, the multicast packets from the multicast source to the receiver are directly forwarded by the node (Router 3), instead of by the RPA.

FIGURE 7.8 Example BIDIR-PIM RP-based distribution.

7.10   RP REDUNDANCY WITH BIDIR-PIM: PHANTOM-RP

The RP and its variant, the RPA, are fundamental components in PIM-SM and BIDIR-PIM, making high availability of the RP or RPA an important concern when designing a PIM-SM or BIDIR-PIM network (see Figure 7.9). In a PIM-SM (or BIDIR-PIM) domain, the selection of the active RP (RPA) for each multicast group should be consistent among all routers in the domain to ensure that there is only one active RP (RPA) for a group at any given time. The active RP (or RPA) can be elected using an automatic discovery mechanism, like the BSR (discussed in Chapter 5), or configured manually on every router in the domain (Static RP). Static RP does not provide RP redundancy and failover capabilities, making the BSR mechanism more preferable.

The PIM Anycast-RP (see Chapter 5) and the MSDP Anycast-RP (see Chapter 6) are the two RP redundancy mechanisms used in PIM-SM networks (see Figure 7.10). The Phantom-RP is the equivalent RP redundancy mechanism used in BIDIR-PIM networks (see Figure 7.11). These RP (or RPA) redundancy mechanisms provide RP (or RPA) failover capabilities, something that cannot be provided using Static RP configuration.

For example, there is a need for RP redundancy in a large PIM-SM network where multicast groups can have a high number of sources and receivers. In this case, the network operator can configure several RPs into an RP-Set (PIM Anycast-RP or MSDP Anycast-RP) to provide high availability to the multicast network. Configuring load sharing among the RPs allows them to share the load of multicast source registration and RPT processing. The multiple RPs provide redundancy and improve the availability of the multicast domain. Just as the Anycast-RP provides redundancy and a load-balancing mechanism for a PIM-SM network, the Phantom-RP does the same for a BIDIR-PIM network.

In PIM-SM, multicast traffic first flows from the source through the source-side DR to the designated RP, and then from the RP and along the RPT to the receivers.

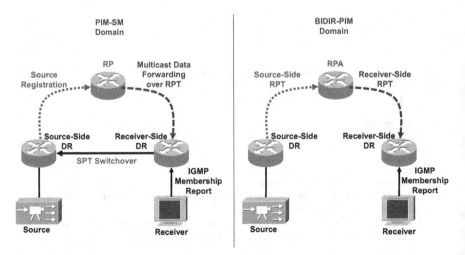

FIGURE 7.9   RP in PIM-SM versus RPA in BIDIR-PIM.

If SPT switchover is enabled on the receiver-side DR, the multicast data would flow directly from the source to the receivers via the SPT, bypassing the RPT. RP failure in PIM-SM affects multicast source registration directly and RPT joins from receiver-side DRs for new receivers. Configuring two or more RPs as an Anycast-RP allows them to share the source registration load and act as hot back-ups for each other.

The RPs in the Anycast-RP set provide failover and redundancy within the PIM-SM domain. For PIM source registration, the source-side DR sends PIM Register mes-sages to the closest RP (load balancing for source registering). For PIM Joins/Prunes, the receiver-side DR sends these messages to the closest RP as determined by the unicast routing table (traffic load balancing if SPT switchover is not turned on). If one of the RPs in the Anycast-RP set goes down, unicast routing ensures that these messages will be sent in the direction of the next closest RP. This functionality can be implemented using the PIM Anycast-RP or MSDP Anycast-RP mechanism (see Figure 7.10). Note that MSDP supports only IPv4, meaning MSDP Anycast-RP can only be used in a PIM-SM that supports IPv4. In either of the two implementations, the RP handling the multicast source registration for the PIM-SM domain will share the source information with any of the members of the Anycast-RP set. In case of RP failure, the RP convergence time depends on the convergence time of the IGP used in the PIM-SM domain.

BIDIR-PIM uses only bidirectional shared trees, and all multicast packets flow up and down the shared tree in a bidirectional manner. The RPA, which is simply a virtual IP address, does not represent a physical node as the RP in PIM-SM; it does not act as a meeting point for source registration nor as a physical node for shared traffic. The RPA, as discussed earlier, is only a reference point or virtual RP on the network. The RPA can be viewed as a routing vector that points to a place in the

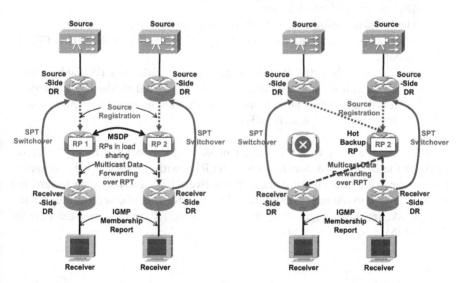

FIGURE 7.10   MSDP Anycast-RP for PIM-SM.

BIDIR-PIM domain where all the multicast traffic converges. The RPA for a group is just a reference to the root of the bidirectional shared tree for that group. RPA failure for a multicast group in this case has a direct effect on all sources and receivers sharing the same RPA.

7.10.1 CONFIGURING A PHANTOM-RP

The Phantom-RP Address (which provides a backup mechanism for the BIDIR- PIM domain) just like the RPA, can be configured as an IP address that is not assigned to any particular device. This RPA does not need to reside on any physical router interface. To use this backup mechanism, the RPA can be configured as an IP address in an IP subnet that will be advertised with two different network mask lengths by the routers in the BIDIR-PIM network via the IGP. As discussed for PIM-SM, the network operator typically uses several RPs for different multicast group address ranges. For a given multicast group in a BIDIR-PIM domain, the operator will define only one active RPA at any given time, with one or several backup RPAs (also not defined on any particular router).

The operator would typically use the following approach to configure a Phantom-RP for a BIDIR-PIM domain:

- Define all Candidate-RPAs as a loopback interface address that belongs to a particular IP subnet (address) in the BIDIR-PIM domain (this includes the one that will be the active RPA).
  - This loopback address is in reality one of the other IP addresses in an IP subnet but is defined on the loopback interface of a device.
- Each Candidate-RPA uses the same loopback interface address but with a different network mask length.
- The IP subnet address (associated with the loopback interface) and network mask of each Candidate-RPA are advertised by the IGP of the BIDIR-PIM domain.
  - This way, the active RPA for a group is the Candidate-RPA that has the route with the longest subnet mask as advertised by the IGP (regardless of the routing metric); the next RPA with the more precise network mask becomes the active RPA.

In this case, the RPA with the longest mask length is configured as the active RPA for the BIDIR-PIM domain, while the RPA with the shorter mask length is the backup RPA (see Figure 7.11). If the active RPA fails, the route toward the RPA falls back to the next Candidate-RPA that advertises the second-longest network mask, and so on. Figure 7.12 shows a Phantom-RP configuration example for BIDIR-PIM.

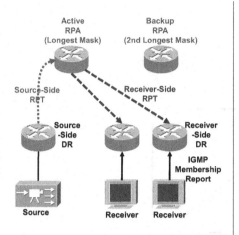
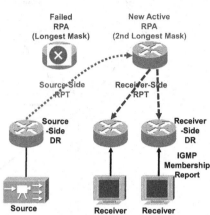

Convergence time to use the Backup RPA depends on how fast the IGP of the BIDIR-PIM domain converges and the delay in the election of the DFs on the links in the domain

FIGURE 7.11 Phantom-RP for BIDIR-PIM.

In case of an active RPA failure, the RPA convergence time depends on the convergence time of the IGP used in the BIDI-PIM domain plus the delay in electing the DFs in the domain (RPA convergence = IGP convergence time + potential DF election delay).

REVIEW QUESTIONS

1. What are the main differences between PIM-SM and BIDIR-PIM?
2. What is a Rendezvous Point Address (RPA) in BIDIR-PIM?
3. What is a Rendezvous Point Link (RPL) in BIDIR-PIM?
4. What is the role of the Designated Forwarder (DF) in BIDIR-PIM?
5. What is the RPF interface in BIDIR-PIM?
6. What is the RPF Neighbor in BIDIR-PIM?
7. Describe briefly how the DF is elected in BIDIR-PIM.
8. Explain the purpose of the BIDIR-PIM Offer, Winner, Backoff, and Pass messages.
9. What is the Phantom-RP in BIDIR-PIM? Describe briefly how it is configured.
10. In the event of an active RPA failure when a Phantom-RP is used in a BIDIR-PIM domain, what factors influence the RPA convergence time?

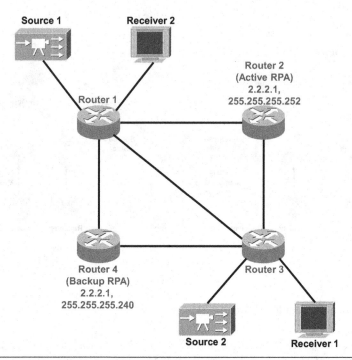

- The IP address 2.2.2.1 with network mask 255.255.255.252, is configured on the loopback interface of Router 2 as the active RPA.
- The loopback interface of Router 4 is configured as the backup RPA; IP address 2.2.2.1 with mask 255.255.255.240.
- The loopback address (with mask) of Router 2 and Router 4 are advertised by the IGP throughout the BIDIR-PIM domain.
- If the active RPA (on Router 2) goes down for some reason, the backup RPA (on Router 4) takes over as the active RPA since it has the next longest mask. All routers will point to the new active RPA 2.2.2.2 with mask 255.255.255.240 based on their IGP table.

FIGURE 7.12   Phantom-RP example.

REFERENCES

[AWEYFDVR21]. James Aweya, *IP Routing Protocols: Fundamentals and Distance-Vector Routing Protocols*, CRC Press, Taylor & Francis Group, ISBN 9780367710415, May 2021.

[AWEYFCDM22]. James Aweya, *Designing Switch/Routers: Fundamental Concepts and Design Methods*, CRC Press, Taylor & Francis Group, ISBN 9781032317694, October 2022.

[CISCPRWILL03]. B. Williamson, *Developing IP Multicast Networks*, Vol. 1, Cisco Press, 2003.

[RFC2236]. W. Fenner, "Internet Group Management Protocol, Version 2", *IETF RFC 2236*, November 1997.

[RFC3376]. B. Cain, S. Deering, I. Kouvelas, B. Fenner, and A. Thyagarajan, "Internet Group Management Protocol, Version 3", *IETF RFC 3376*, October 2002.

[RFC3973]. A. Adams, J. Nicholas, and W. Siadak, "Protocol Independent Multicast - Dense Mode (PIM-DM): Protocol Specification (Revised)", *IETF RFC 3973*, January 2005.

[RFC4760]. T. Bates, R. Chandra, D. Katz, and Y. Rekhter, "Multiprotocol Extensions for BGP-4", *IETF RFC 4760*, January 2007.

[RFC5015]. M. Handley, I. Kouvelas, T. Speakman, and L. Vicisano, "Bidirectional Protocol Independent Multicast (BIDIR-PIM)", *IETF RFC 5015*, October 2007.

[RFC5059]. N. Bhaskar, A. Gall, J. Lingard, and S. Venaas, "Bootstrap Router (BSR) Mechanism for Protocol Independent Multicast (PIM)", *IETF RFC 5059*, January 2008.

[RFC7761]. B. Fenner, M. Handley, H. Holbrook, I. Kouvelas, R. Parekh, Z. Zhang, and L. Zheng, "Protocol Independent Multicast - Sparse Mode (PIM-SM): Protocol Specification (Revised)", *IETF RFC 7761*, March 2016.

Index

Printed in the United States
by Baker & Taylor Publisher Services

Printed in the United States
by Baker & Taylor Publisher Services